WORLD GEOGRAPHY
Eastern Hemisphere

my**World**
INTERACTIVE

 **Pearson**

Boston, Massachusetts   Chandler, Arizona
Glenview, Illinois   New York, New York

To start, download the free Pearson BouncePages app on your smartphone or tablet. Simply search for the Pearson BouncePages app in your mobile app store. The app is available for Android and IOS (iPhone®/iPad®).

Activate your digital course videos directly from the page.

To launch the videos look for this icon.

1. **AIM** the camera so that the page is easily viewable on your screen.
2. **TAP** the screen to scan the page.
3. **BOUNCE** the page to life by clicking the Bounce icon.

ISBN-13: 978-0-32-896492-5
ISBN-10: 0-32-896492-1

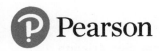

AUTHORS

Program Authors

Gregory H. Chu

was professor and chair of geography at the University of Wisconsin-LaCrosse and editor of *FOCUS on Geography*, a journal published by the American Geographical Society. A native of Hong Kong, he earned his Ph.D. in geography from the University of Hawaii and has served as Program Director of Geography and Regional Science (currently Geography and Spatial Science) at the National Science Foundation, on the Editorial Board of *Cartographic Perspectives*, and on the Board of Directors of the North American Cartographic Information Society. He is working with Korea's National Geographic Information Institute, an equivalent of the US Geological Survey, on the publication of *The National Atlas of Korea, volumes I, II, III*, and is co-authoring volume IV.

Don Holtgrieve

received his Ph.D. in geography from the University of Oregon and was professor of geography and environmental studies in the California State University System for 30 years. He now teaches geography and environmental planning at the University of Oregon. His attraction to geography was the interdisciplinary nature of the field and the opportunity to do research out-of-doors. Dr. Holtgrieve enjoys bringing his "real-world" experiences as a high school teacher, community planner, park ranger, and consultant to government agencies into his writing and teaching.

In Memoriam: Susan Hardwick

passed away before work began on *myWorld Geography Interactive*. A geography professor at the University of Oregon, an expert on the human geography of North America, past president of the National Council for Geographic Education, co-host of the public television series, *The Power of Place*, and recipient of many geography education awards, she was a co-author of the first edition of *myWorld Geography*.

TEACHER REVIEWERS

Colleen Eccles
Instructional Coach and PDLT
Samuel Ogle Middle School
Bowie, Maryland

Dana L. Roberts, Ed. S
Academic Coach and Gifted Lead Coordinator
Lindley Middle School
Mableton, Georgia

Piper Hudmon
Content Specialist/Secondary Social Studies
Muscogee County School District
Columbus, Georgia

PROGRAM CONSULTANTS

ELL Consultant
Jim Cummins Ph.D.
Professor Emeritus, Department of Curriculum,
   Teaching, and Learning
University of Toronto
Toronto, Canada

Differentiated Instruction Consultant
Marianne Sender
In-Class Resource Teacher
Renaissance @ Rand Middle School
Montclair, New Jersey

Reading Consultant
Elfrieda H. Hiebert Ph.D.
Founder, President, and CEO of TextProject, Inc.
University of California, Santa Cruz

Inquiry and C3 Consultant
Dr. Kathy Swan
Professor of Curriculum and Instruction
University of Kentucky
Lexington, Kentucky

PROGRAM PARTNERS

 NBC Learn, the educational arm of NBC News, develops original stories for use in the classroom and makes archival NBC news stories, images, and primary source documents available on demand to teachers, students, and parents. NBC Learn partnered with Pearson to produce the topic opening videos that support this program.

 Campaign for the Civic Mission of Schools is a coalition of over 70 national civic learning, education, civic engagement, and business groups committed to improving the quality and quantity of civic learning in American schools.

 Constitutional Rights Foundation is a nonprofit, nonpartisan, community-based organization focused on educating students about the importance of civic participation in a democratic society. The Constitutional Rights Foundation is the lead contributor to the development of the Civic Discussion Quests for this program.

CONTENTS

TOPIC 1
Introduction to Geography

TOPIC 2
Europe Through Time

CONTENTS

TOPIC 3
Europe Today

TOPIC 4
Northern Eurasia

CONTENTS

TOPIC 5
Africa

TOPIC 6
Southwest Asia Through Time

CONTENTS

TOPIC 7
Southwest Asia Today

TOPIC 8
South Asia

TOPIC 9
East Asia

CONTENTS

TOPIC 10
Southeast Asia

TOPIC 11
Australia and the Pacific

DIGITAL RESOURCES

Core Concepts

These digital lessons introduce key concepts for all of the social sciences and personal finance.

Culture
Economics

Geography
Government and Civics

History
Personal Finance

Topic Videos

Begin each topic with a front seat view of its people.

TOPIC 1
Above the Forest Canopy

TOPIC 2
Good Queen Bess

TOPIC 3
Europe at Her Doorstep

TOPIC 4
Expanding His Horizons

TOPIC 5
A String of Dreams

TOPIC 6
The Code of Hammurabi

TOPIC 7
Maayan and Muhammad

TOPIC 8
Nancy's Fruitful Loan

TOPIC 9
Xiao's Lake

TOPIC 10
A Minangkabau Wedding

TOPIC 11
Jack Connects to His Culture

Lesson Videos

Preview key ideas from the lesson in these videos.

TOPIC 2
Lesson 1 The Agricultural Revolution
Lesson 2 Impact of Geography on Early Greece
Lesson 3 Rome's Cultural Gifts
Lesson 4 The Byzantine Empire's Place in History
Lesson 5 The Growth of Medieval Towns
Lesson 8 The Modern History of Europe

TOPIC 3
Lesson 1 History's Impact on Southern Europe
Lesson 2 Introducing the European Union
Lesson 3 Governments and Economies of Scandinavia
Lesson 4 Challenges Facing Eastern Europe

TOPIC 4
Lesson 3 The Geography of Russia
Lesson 4 Russia's Modern Economy

TOPIC 5
Lesson 2 Pharaohs of Ancient Egypt
Lesson 3 The Influence of Islam in West Africa
Lesson 4 The Modern History of West and
  Central Africa

Lesson 5 Where People Live and Work in West and
  Central Africa
Lesson 6 The Economies of Southern and Eastern Africa

TOPIC 6
Lesson 1 Adapting to Life in Mesopotamia
Lesson 2 The Assyrian and Persian Empires
Lesson 3 The Central Beliefs of Judaism
Lesson 4 The New Testament
Lesson 5 The Five Pillars of Islam
Lesson 6 The Rise and Fall of the Abbasid Dynasty

TOPIC 7
Lesson 2 Where People Live in Southwest Asia
Lesson 3 The Modern History of Turkey and Iran
Lesson 4 Introducing Israel and Its Neighbors

TOPIC 8
Lesson 1 Features of the Indus Valley Civilization
Lesson 2 Hindu Traditions and Practices
Lesson 3 Teaching and Spread of Buddhism
Lesson 4 Rise of the Mughal Empire
Lesson 5 The Geography of South Asia

Interactive Primary Sources

Go to the original sources to hear voices from the time.

Interactive Biographies

21st Century Skills Tutorials

Learn, practice, and apply important skills using these online tutorials.

Analyze Cause and Effect
Analyze Data and Models
Analyze Images
Analyze Media Content
Analyze Political Cartoons
Analyze Primary and Secondary
  Sources
Ask Questions
Avoid Plagiarism
Being an Informed Citizen
Categorize
Compare and Contrast
Compare Viewpoints
Compromise
Consider and Counter Opposing
  Arguments
Create a Research Hypothesis
Create Charts and Maps
Create Databases
Develop a Clear Thesis
Develop Cultural Awareness
Distinguish Between Fact and
  Opinion

Draw Conclusions
Draw Inferences
Evaluate Existing Arguments
Evaluate Web Sites
Generalize
Generate New Ideas
Give an Effective Presentation
Identify Bias
Identify Evidence
Identify Main Ideas and Details
Identify Trends
Innovate
Interpret Sources
Make a Difference
Make Decisions
Make Predictions
Organize Your Ideas
Participate in a Discussion or
  Debate
Paying Taxes
Political Participation
Publish Your Work
Read Charts, Graphs, and Tables

Read Physical Maps
Read Political Maps
Read Special-Purpose Maps
Search for Information on the
  Internet
Sequence
Serving on a Jury
Set a Purpose for Reading
Share Responsibility
Solve Problems
Summarize
Support Ideas With Evidence
Synthesize
Take Effective Notes
Use Content Clues
Use Parts of a Map
Voting
Work in Teams
Write a Journal Entry
Write an Essay

Interactivities

Explore maps one layer at a time to see how events unfolded over time, go on a gallery walk to examine artifacts and primary sources, analyze data, and explore key historical sites and objects in 3D!

INTERACTIVE MAPS
Earth's Continents Topic 1
Make a Map Interactivity Topic 1 Lesson 1
Forms of Government Among Countries of the World
  Topic 1 Lesson 8
Europe Through History Topic 2
Growth of the Roman Republic, 500 BCE to 44 BCE
  Topic 2 Lesson 3
Spread of Christianity in Europe Topic 2 Lesson 5
The Black Death, 1347–1351 Topic 2 Lesson 5
Renaissance Italy's City-States Topic 2 Lesson 6
Major European Religions, About 1600 Topic 2
  Lesson 6
Napoleon's Europe (1804–1815) Topic 2 Lesson 7
European Union, 2014 Topic 2 Lesson 8
Effects of World War I on European Boundaries
  Topic 2 Lesson 8
European Union, 2014 Topic 5 Lesson 8
Europe's Cultural Diversity Topic 3

Southern European Culture Topic 6 Lesson 1
Northwestern Europe's Economies Topic 6 Lesson 2
The Three Regions of Northern Eurasia Topic 4
Growth of Russia 1300–1584 Topic 4 Lesson 1
From Russian Empire to Soviet Union, 1914–1923
  Topic 4 Lesson 2
The Fall of the Soviet Union Topic 4 Lesson 2
Russian Energy Production Topic 4 Lesson 4
African Climates Topic 5
European Imperialism in Africa Topic 5 Lesson 4
Colonial Rule and Independence Topic 5 Lesson 4
Southwest Asia: Empires and Countries Topic 6
Mesopotamian Empires Topic 6 Lesson 2
The Spread of Christianity Topic 6 Lesson 4
Religious Diversity in the Middle East Topic 6 Lesson 7
Conflicts in Southwest Asia Topic 7
Regional Conflicts Topic 7 Lesson 4
Geographic Features of South Asia Topic 8
Maurya and Gupta Empires Topic 8 Lesson 1

Atlas Maps

SPECIAL FEATURES

Quest

Ask questions, explore sources, and cite evidence to support your view!

Geographic Sources

Excerpts from original sources allow you to witness history.

Primary Source Quotations

Quotations in the text bring history to life.

Analysis Skills

Practice key skills.

SPECIAL FEATURES

All of these resources are found right here in your student textbook.

Biographies

Read about the people who made history.

Charts, Graphs, Tables, and Infographics

Find these charts, graphs, and tables in your text. It's all about the data!

SPECIAL FEATURES

All of these resources are found right here in your student textbook.

Timelines

Maps

Where is it found? Find out with these maps.

ENGLISH-LANGUAGE ARTS HANDBOOK

As you explore world geography in this course, you will read informational texts and primary sources. For this course and in other courses and beyond, you will need to think critically about the texts you read to absorb information and be able to express your thoughts about world events, past and present. You will need to communicate your ideas through writing (summaries, arguments, informative essays, and narratives), speaking (debates and one-on-one and small group discussions), and by giving presentations.

This Handbook will give you some tools for reading critically and expressing your ideas. The Quests and other activities in this program give you opportunities to write and speak about your ideas and create projects that will help you practice these skills.

▶ INTERACTIVE

The 21st Century Skills Tutorials, found on Realize, support many of the skills discussed here. Go online to find a Quick Reference, video of the skill being modeled, and more.

READING

Analyze Informational Text

Reading nonfiction texts, like a magazine article or your textbook, is not the same as reading a fictional story or novel. The purpose of reading nonfiction is to acquire new information. It's something that you, and the adults around you, do all the time.

Process What You Read When you read informational text, it helps to know what to look for and what questions to ask yourself as you read. Use the chart below as a guide when you read.

	Look for	Questions to Ask	For More Help
Central Ideas and Details	• Central ideas or claims • Supporting details or evidence	• What is the subject or main point of this text? • What details support the main point? • What inferences do you need to make? • How does the author develop a few central ideas throughout a text?	▶ **Skills Tutorial** • Identify Main Ideas and Details • Draw Inferences • Summarize
Word Choice	• Unfamiliar words and phrases • Words and phrases that produce a certain effect on a reader	• What inferences about word meaning can you make from the context? • What tone and mood are created by word choice? • What alternate word choices might the author have made?	▶ **Skills Tutorial** • Draw Inferences
Text Structure	• Ways the author has organized the text • Ways sentences and paragraphs work together to build ideas • Clue words signaling a particular structure	• Does the text have a specific structure? • For instance, is it structured by sequence or chronology? By comparisons and contrasts? By causes and effects?	▶ **Skills Tutorial** • Identify Evidence • Analyze Cause and Effect • Sequence • Compare and Contrast

Evaluate Arguments

One important reason to read and understand informational text is so you can recognize and evaluate written arguments. An argument is a logical way of presenting a belief, conclusion, or stance. A good argument is supported with reasoning and evidence and will often address opposing claims. Study the model below to see how the writer developed an argument about the impact of writing on the world.

Here the writer clearly states the claim.

The writer uses this example to support one of the claims.

The claim is supported by an example from Babylonian civilization.

The writer finishes by summarizing the impact of writing on our lives today.

Writing Has Changed the World

At one time, knowledge was shared by word of mouth. By 3000 BCE, however, ancient peoples had created systems of writing. Over time, writing has grown in importance.

At first, writing was a practical way to record information. The Sumerians began writing to keep track of grain production. In time, people found additional uses for writing. Scholars began to write about mathematics and science. They created calendars and wrote about their history. Much of what we know about the Sumerians, Egyptians, and the Maya comes from their writings.

Perhaps most importantly, writing has been used to unite people. For example, Hammurabi had his law code written in stone. It was displayed throughout the Babylonian empire. All the people knew the laws. For the first time, an entire empire was united by the written word.

People today find it hard to imagine a world without writing. Print and online sources provide a steady stream of written words. It began as a way to count bushels of grain, but now it's our greatest source of knowledge.

▶ INTERACTIVE

Go online for these interactive skills tutorials:
- Evaluate Arguments
- Consider and Counter Opposing Arguments
- Support Ideas with Evidence

Analyze Visuals

Another key component of understanding informational texts is being able to understand any visuals that go with written text, like the maps, graphs, charts, and photos. Study the chart and the example to help you analyze some common types of visuals in your social studies text.

	Look for	For More Help
Maps	• Read the title. • Read the key. • Study the locator globe, scale bar, and compass rose. • Apply the key and labels to the map.	▶ **Skills Tutorial** • Use Parts of a Map • Read Physical Maps • Read Political Maps • Read Special-Purpose Maps
Graphs and Tables	• Read the title. • Use labels and key. • Look for patterns or changes over time.	▶ **Skills Tutorial** • Read Charts, Graphs, and Tables • Create Charts and Maps
Photographs	• Identify the content. • Note emotions. • Read captions or credits. • Study the image's purpose. • Consider context. • Respond.	▶ **Skills Tutorial** • Analyze Images • Analyze Political Cartoons

World Population by Income

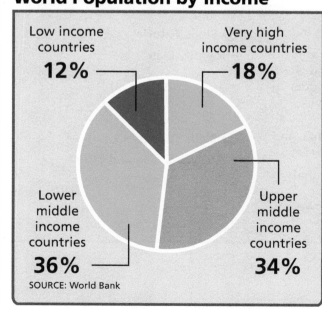

Low income countries **12%**

Very high income countries **18%**

Lower middle income countries **36%**

Upper middle income countries **34%**

SOURCE: World Bank

❶ What is the title of the circle graph?

❷ Read the labels. What does each segment of the graph show?

❸ How does the size of the four different income groups compare?

❹ What conclusion can you draw from this data?

Analyze Primary and Secondary Sources

A primary source is information from someone who saw or was part of what is being described. A secondary source is information recorded later by someone who was not part of the event. You will encounter many primary and secondary sources throughout your textbook and in Quests and other activities. Study these questions and the model primary sources that follows to help you unlock the meaning of these sources.

	Questions to Ask	For More Help
Determine the Author's Purpose	• Is the source written mainly to convey information, like a textbook? • Or, is its purpose to persuade you to think a certain way, like an opinion piece in a newspaper?	▶ **Skills Tutorial** • Analyze Primary and Secondary Sources • Analyze Media Content • Draw Inferences
Determine the Author's Point of View	• What is the author's point of view? • Is the author's point of view shaped by subjective influences such as feelings, prejudices, experiences? • Is the author's point of view shaped by his or her field of study?	▶ **Skills Tutorial** • Analyze Primary and Secondary Sources • Compare Viewpoints
Compare Viewpoints	• How is the author's point of view different from that of other authors' writing on the same subject? • Does the author avoid including certain facts that would change his or her point of view?	▶ **Skills Tutorial** • Compare Viewpoints
Analyze Word Choice	• Does the author use words in a neutral, factual way? • Does the author use loaded words that try to persuade the reader to think a certain way?	▶ **Skills Tutorial** • Identify Bias
Analyze Interactions	• How have individuals, events, and ideas influenced each other? • What connecting words signal these interactions (*next, for example, consequently, however,* etc.)?	▶ **Skills Tutorial** • Analyze Cause and Effect

Primary Sources Model Shi Huangdi founded the Qin dynasty. His rule was marked by great accomplishments as well as strict and sometimes cruel actions. This excerpt describes Shi Huangdi's rule. Study the excerpt and call-outs to help you better understand the author's purpose, word choices, and point of view.

Shi Huangdi Memorial Inscription

The adjectives are all positive and suggest that Emperor Shi Huangdi was a good emperor.

A new age is inaugurated by the Emperor;
Rules and measures are rectified, . . .
Human affairs are made clear
And there is harmony between fathers and sons.
The Emperor in his [wise ways], [kindness], and justice
Has made all laws and principles [understandable].

This inscription was ordered by Shi Huangdi, so the writer probably needed to make the descriptions positive.

He set forth to pacify the east,
To inspect officers and men;
This great task accomplished
He visited the coast.
Great are the Emperor's achievements,
Men attend diligently to basic tasks,
Farming is encouraged, . . .

The author only refers to Shi Huangdi's positive actions and not his more controversial ones.

All the common people prosper;
All men under the sky
Toil with a single purpose;
Tools and measures are made uniform,
The written script is standardized,
Wherever the sun and moon shine. . . .

—*The Records of the Grand Historian*, Sima Qian.

Sima Qian lived about 100 years after the life of Shi Huangdi. He is quoting from a marker put up during Shi Huangdi's time.

Support Your Analyses With Evidence

Historians and other writers make assertions, or claims, about events. Before accepting a claim as fact, however, look carefully at the evidence the author provides. Study the chart and the model secondary source to learn more about how to use evidence to support your ideas.

	Look for	Questions to Ask	For More Help
Support Your Analyses With Evidence	• The subject of the passage • Any assertion or claim that something is true • Appropriate evidence to support the claim • How well the evidence supports the claim, either explicitly or by inference	• What is the passage about? • Are there claims that something is true? • If so, what language supports the claim? • Does the evidence support the claim? • Did the author convince you that the claim was correct?	▶ **Skills Tutorial** • Identify Evidence • Support Ideas with Evidence

Model Secondary Source Look for evidence in this model passage. Do you think the main point is supported by the evidence?

The subject of a passage is usually stated toward the beginning of the passage. This passage's subject is how technology can improve people's standard of living.

This sentence explains how technology was introduced to the Maasai.

This sentence shows how the Maasai's standard of living improved because of technology.

Advances in technology can change people's lives and raise their standard of living. Standard of living is the level of comfort enjoyed by a person or a society. For example, the Maasai people of eastern Africa are cattle herders. They often must kill lions who threaten their cattle, but lions are endangered. So people who want to protect the lions have brought new GPS and computer technology to the Maasai. Some Maasai now use these devices to track the movement of lions, enabling them to move their herds away from the lions. As a result, they kill fewer lions. They also have more money because they don't lose cattle.

WRITING

Use the Writing Process

Writing is one of the most powerful communication tools you will use for the rest of your life. Follow these steps to strengthen your writing.

Prewriting: Plan Your Essay

1. **Choose a topic.** Often your teacher will provide you with a topic. Sometimes, you will be able to choose your own. In that case, select a topic that you care about and that you think will interest others.

2. **Narrow your focus.** Most writers begin with too broad a topic and need to narrow their focus. For example, you might decide to write about the Renaissance. You will need to narrow your focus to a single artist or discovery in order to write a meaningful essay.

3. **Gather information.** Collect facts and details you'll need to write your essay. Research any points that you are unsure about.

4. **Organize your ideas.** Writers often find it useful to create an outline to help them plan their essay. You need not create a formal outline, but you'll at least want to jot down your main ideas, the details that support them, and the order in which you will present your ideas. A graphic organizer can help you organize your ideas. Here is a graphic organizer for a paper on the Italian artist and scientist Leonardo da Vinci:

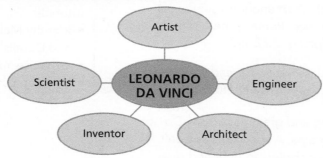

The Renaissance Man

Artist · Scientist · **LEONARDO DA VINCI** · Engineer · Inventor · Architect

5. **Write a thesis statement.** A thesis statement focuses your ideas into a single sentence or two and tells readers what the essay is about.

Drafting

1. **Maintain a clear focus.** If you find that your writing is starting to get off track, go back to your thesis statement.

2. **Elaborate for interest and emphasis.** Give details and specific examples about each point in your essay.

3. **Provide evidence.** Evidence is key to convincing an audience. Provide factual, concrete evidence to back up your ideas and assertions.

Revising, Editing, and Rewriting

1. **Add transition words.** Make cause-and-effect relationships clear with words such as *because, as a result,* and so on. To compare or contrast ideas, use linking words, such as *similarly, both,* and *equally* or *in contrast, instead,* and *yet.* Use words such as *first, second, next,* and *finally* to help readers follow steps in a sequence. Look at the following examples. In the revised version, a reader knows the correct order in which to perform the steps.

First Draft	Revision
Geographers form an educated guess called a hypothesis. They test that hypothesis with further research.	<u>Next</u>, geographers form an educated guess called a hypothesis. <u>Then</u>, they test that hypothesis with further research.

2. **Focus on how well you have addressed your purpose.** Be sure that your essay addresses your purpose for writing. For a problem-solution essay, that means anticipating opposing arguments and responding to them. For a cause-and-effect essay, stress the way one event leads to the next.

3. **Focus on your audience.** Check that you have not left out any steps in your essay and that your audience can follow your thinking. Make sure that your writing will hold your audience's interest.

4. **Review organization.** Confirm that your ideas flow in a logical order. Write your main points on sticky notes. Reorganize these until you are satisfied that the order best strengthens your essay.

5. **Revise sentences and words.** Use both short and long sentences. Scan for vague words, such as *good* or *nice.* Replace them with specific and vibrant words, such as *helpful* or *friendly.*

6. **Peer review.** Ask a peer—a friend or classmate—to read your draft. Is it clear? Can your reader follow your ideas? Revise confusing sections.

> ▶ **INTERACTIVE**
>
> Go online for these interactive skills tutorials:
> - Identify Main Ideas and Details
> - Organize Your Ideas
> - Write an Essay

Proofread Always proofread for spelling and grammar errors. Do not simply rely on spellchecking apps or programs. A spellchecker won't catch the difference between *see* and *sea* or between *deer* and *dear.*

Use Technology

Here are a few ideas:

- ☑ Use a word processing program to plan and write your essay.
- ☑ Use the Internet for research (see guidelines later in this Handbook).
- ☑ Use email and other online tools to collaborate with classmates.
- ☑ Create informative charts, graphs, and diagrams for presentations.
- ☑ Share your writing with others through a blog or website.

Write an Argument

In addition to evaluating other writers' arguments, you also need to be able to express arguments of your own, in writing and speaking. An argumentative, or persuasive, essay sets forth a belief or stand on an issue. A well-written argument may convince the reader, change the reader's mind, or motivate the reader to take a certain action.

In this program, you'll practice writing arguments in some Document-Based Inquiry Quests and Writing Workshops, with support in your ▤ **Active Journal**. Use the checklist to help you write a convincing argument.

An Effective Argument Includes

☑ a precise claim

☑ consideration of alternate claims, or opposing positions, and a discussion of their strengths and weaknesses

☑ logical organization that makes clear connections among claim, reasons, and evidence

☑ valid reasoning and evidence, using credible sources and accurate data

☑ a concluding statement or section that follows from and supports the argument

☑ formal and objective language and tone

☑ error-free grammar, including accurate use of transitions

▶ **INTERACTIVE**

For more help, go online for these interactive skills tutorials:
- Evaluate Arguments
- Consider and Counter Opposing Arguments
- Support Ideas with Evidence

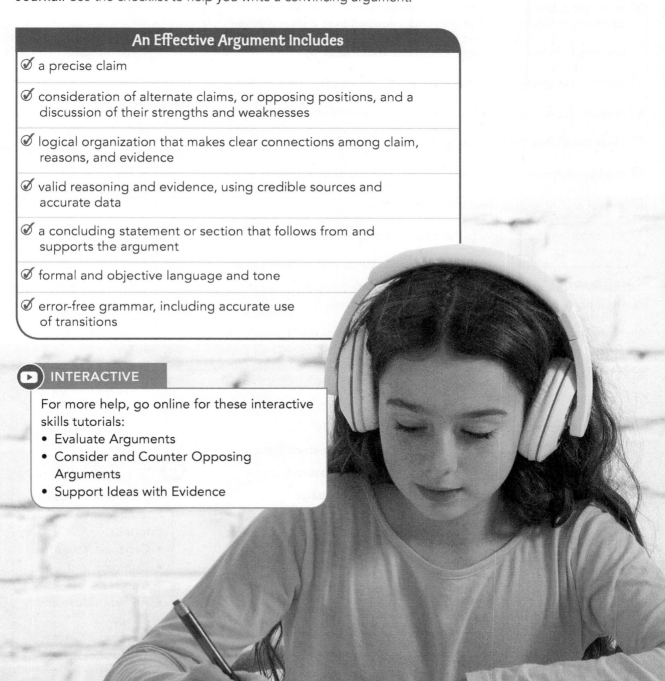

Write Informative or Explanatory Essays

Informative or explanatory texts present facts, data, and other evidence to give information about a topic. Readers turn to informational and explanatory texts when they wish to learn about a specific idea, concept, or subject area, or if they want to learn how to do something.

An Effective Informative/Explanatory Essay Includes
✓ a thesis statement that introduces the concept or subject
✓ an organization (such as definition, classification, comparison/contrast, cause/effect) that presents information in a clear manner
✓ headings (if desired) to separate sections of the essay
✓ definitions, quotations, and/or graphics that support the thesis
✓ relevant facts, examples, and details that expand upon a topic
✓ clear transitions that link sections of the essay
✓ precise words and technical vocabulary where appropriate
✓ formal and objective language and tone
✓ a conclusion that supports the information given and provides fresh insights

Suppose you are writing an essay comparing and contrasting life in different parts of Europe.

Your thesis statement might be "Life varies in different parts of Europe. The languages that people speak, the religions they practice, and the goods they produced can differ in many ways."

Your organization might be:

I **Western Europe**
   A. Family
   B. Language
   C. Religion
   D. Economy

II **Eastern Europe**
   A. Family
   B. Language
   C. Religion
   D. Economy

OR

I **Family**
   A. Western Europe
   B. Eastern Europe

II **Language**
   A. Western Europe
   B. Eastern Europe

III **Religion**
   A. Western Europe
   B. Eastern Europe

IV **Economy**
   A. Western Europe
   B. Eastern Europe

> ▶ INTERACTIVE
>
> Go online for these interactive skills tutorials:
> - Organize Your Ideas
> - Compare and Contrast
> - Analyze Cause and Effect
> - Develop a Clear Thesis

Write Narrative Essays

A narrative is any type of writing that tells a story. Narrative writing conveys an experience, either real or imaginary, and uses time order to provide structure. Usually its purpose is to entertain, but it can also instruct, persuade, or inform.

An Effective Narrative Includes
✓ an engaging beginning in which characters and setting are established
✓ a well-structured, logical sequence of events
✓ narrative techniques, such as dialogue and description
✓ a variety of transition words and phrases to convey sequence and signal shifts from one time frame or setting to another
✓ precise words and phrases, relevant descriptive details, and sensory language that brings the characters and setting to life
✓ a conclusion that follows naturally from the story's experiences or events

Model Narrative This passage is a fictional letter from a young woman in Rome to her aunt. Notice how it begins by establishing the setting as Rome at the time of the invasion of Vandals, one of the Germanic peoples. Note that the writer also offers details on how the invasion of the Vandals is affecting her life.

Dear Aunt Lavinia,

Everyone is telling me not to be afraid, but I think they are foolish. The Vandals are at the gates of Rome, threatening to enter at any minute. We hear stories of death and destruction wherever the invading armies go. They have already sacked many villages. Food is becoming more scarce because they have ripped up the fields. There remains only the grain stored in our warehouse. Mother and Father are not sure that the Emperor's armies can protect us. They have packed a box with our most precious things so we can move quickly. Please be ready to receive us, if we can get away from here with our lives.

Your loving niece, Portia

▶ **INTERACTIVE**

For more help, go online for these interactive skills tutorials:
- Sequence
- Draw Conclusions
- Write an Essay
- Write a Journal Entry

Find and Use Credible Sources

You will often need to conduct research using library and media sources to gain more knowledge about a topic. Not all of the information that you find, however, will be useful—or reliable. Strong research skills will help you find accurate information about your topic.

Using Print and Digital Sources An effective research project combines information from multiple sources. Plan to include a variety of these resources:

- ☑ **Primary and Secondary Sources:** Use both primary sources (such as interviews or newspaper articles) and secondary sources (such as encyclopedia entries or historians' accounts).

- ☑ **Print and Digital Resources:** The Internet allows fast access to data, but print resources are often edited more carefully. Plan to include both print and digital resources in order to guarantee that your work is accurate.

- ☑ **Media Resources:** You can find valuable information in media resources such as documentaries, television programs, podcasts, and museum exhibitions.

- ☑ **Original Research:** Depending on your topic, you may wish to conduct original research, such as interviews or surveys of people in your community.

Evaluating Sources It is important to evaluate the credibility and accuracy of any information you find. Ask yourself questions such as these to evaluate sources:

- ☑ **Authority:** Is the author well known? What are the author's credentials? Does the source include references to other reliable sources? Does the author's tone win your confidence? Why or why not?

- ☑ **Bias:** Does the author have any obvious biases? What is the author's purpose for writing? Who is the target audience?

- ☑ **Currency:** When was the work created? Has it been revised? Is there more current information available?

Using Search Terms Finding information on the Internet is easy, but it can be a challenge to find facts that are useful and trustworthy. If you type a word or phrase into a search engine, you will probably get hundreds of results.

Did you know?

Beware of some online encyclopedias. They can be a good starting place for information, but their contributors are not required to fact-check their submissions.

However, those results are not guaranteed to be relevant or accurate. These strategies can help:

- ✓ Create a list of keywords before you begin using a search engine.

- ✓ Enter six to eight keywords.

- ✓ Choose unique nouns. Most search engines ignore articles and prepositions.

- ✓ Use adjectives to specify a category. For example, you might enter "ancient Rome" instead of "Rome."

- ✓ Use quotation marks to focus a search. Place a phrase in quotation marks to find pages that include exactly that phrase.

- ✓ Spell carefully. Many search engines correct spelling automatically, but they cannot catch every spelling error.

- ✓ Scan search results before you click them. The first result isn't always the most useful. Read the text before you make a choice

Avoiding Plagiarism Whenever you conduct research, you must be careful to give credit for any ideas or opinions that are not your own. Presenting someone else's ideas, research, or opinion as your own—even if you have phrased it in different words—is plagiarism. Plagiarism is the equivalent of stealing. Be sure to record your sources accurately so you can identify them later. When photocopying from a source, include the copyright information. Include the web addresses from online sources.

Quoting and Paraphrasing When including ideas from research into your writing, you will need to decide whether to quote directly or paraphrase. You must cite your sources for both quotations and paraphrases. **A direct quotation** uses the author's exact words when they are particularly well-chosen. Include complete quotations, without deleting or changing words. Enclose direct quotations in quotation marks. **A paraphrase** restates an author's ideas in your own words. Be careful to paraphrase accurately. A good paraphrase does more than simply rearrange an author's phrases, or replace a few words with synonyms.

Formats for Citing Sources When you cite a source, you acknowledge where you found your information and give readers the details necessary for locating the source. Always prepare a reference list, called a bibliography, at the end of a research paper to provide full information on your sources.

INTERACTIVE

Go online for these interactive skills tutorials:
- Search for Information on the Internet
- Evaluate Web Sites
- Take Effective Notes
- Avoid Plagiarism

Did you know?

A citation for a book should look like this: Pyles, Thomas. *The Origins and Development of the English Language*. 2nd ed. New York: Harcourt, 1971. Print. A citation for a website should include this information: Romey, Kristin. "Face of 9,500-Year-Old Man Revealed for First Time." *National Geographic*, Jan. 2017. *news. nationalgeographic.com* Web. 20 Jan. 2017.

Write Research Papers

You will often need to conduct research in the library or on the Internet for a project or essay. In this program, you will conduct research for Quest projects and some Writing Workshop assignments. Before you begin, review the information in Use the Writing Process as well as in Find and Use Credible Sources in this Handbook. Then follow these additional tips to help you make the most of your research.

1. Narrow or Broaden Your Topic
Choose a topic that is narrow enough to cover completely. If you can name your topic in just one or two words, it is probably too broad. For example, a topic such as South American history would be too broad. When you begin to research, pay attention to the amount of information available. If there is way too much information when you begin your research on your topic, narrow your focus.

On the other hand, you might need to broaden a topic if there is not enough information available. A topic is too narrow when it can be thoroughly presented in less space than the required size of your assignment. It might also be too narrow if you can find little or no information in library and media sources. Broaden your topic by including other related ideas.

2. Generate Research Questions
Use research questions to focus your inquiry. For example, instead of simply hunting for information about economic development, you might ask, "How does economic development help the people of a country?" or "How can countries successfully promoted economic development?" As you research your topic, continue to ask yourself questions. Follow your new questions in order to explore your topic further. Refocus your research questions as you learn more about your topic.

3. Synthesize Your Sources
Effective research writing is more than just a list of facts and details. Good research synthesizes—gathers, orders, and interprets—those elements. These strategies will help you synthesize effectively:

☑ Review your notes. Look for connections and patterns among the details you have collected.

☑ Organize notes or notecards to help you plan how you will combine details.

☑ Pay close attention to details that emphasize the same main idea.

☑ Also look for details that challenge each other. For many topics, there is no single correct opinion. You might decide to conduct additional research to help you decide which side of the issue has more support.

▶ INTERACTIVE

For more help, go online for these interactive skills tutorials:
- Ask Questions
- Create a Research Hypothesis
- Synthesize

SPEAKING AND LISTENING

Discuss Your Ideas

A group discussion is an informal meeting of people that is used to openly discuss ideas, readings, and issues. You can express your views and hear those of others. In this program, you'll participate in Discussion Inquiry Quests and many one-to-one, group, and teacher-led discussions. You'll work with different partners on many topics and issues. Use the Keys to Effective Discussions to help you be an active participant in lively discussions.

Keys to Effective Discussions
✓ Come to discussions prepared, having studied the required material and/or read relevant background information.
✓ Build on others' ideas and express your own ideas clearly.
✓ Be sure that your comments directly contribute to the topic, text, or issue under discussion.
✓ Give specific evidence for the points you wish to make.
✓ Follow rules for civic discussions, including letting everyone have a chance to speak and listening carefully to others' points of view.
✓ Pose and respond to specific questions and issues with elaboration and details.
✓ Be prepared to demonstrate your understanding of the different perspectives people have put forth during the discussion.
✓ Acknowledge the views of others respectfully, but ask questions that challenge the accuracy, logic, or relevance of those views.

▶ INTERACTIVE

Go online for these interactive skills tutorials:
• Participate in a Discussion or Debate
• Support Ideas With Evidence
• Work in Teams

Give an Effective Presentation

Many of the Quests in this program will require you to give a presentation to your teacher and classmates, and sometimes even to a wider audience. These presentations will be good practice for the presentations you will need to give in school and in professional settings. You can speak confidently if you prepare carefully and follow this checklist.

Keys to Effective Presentations

☑ Prepare your presentation in advance and practice it in order to gain comfort and confidence.

☑ Present your claims and findings in a logical sequence so that your audience can easily follow your train of thought.

☑ Use relevant descriptions, facts, and specific details.

☑ Consider using nonverbal elements like hand gestures and pauses to emphasize main ideas or themes.

☑ Use appropriate eye contact, adequate volume, and clear pronunciation.

☑ Use appropriate transitions (*for example, first, second, third*) to clarify relationships.

☑ Use precise language and vocabulary that is specific to your topic.

☑ Provide a strong conclusion.

☑ Adapt your wording to your purpose and audience. Use formal English for most presentations, but try to sound natural and relaxed.

☑ Include multimedia components such as you see in the chart to clarify information.

Maps	Graphs/Charts/Diagrams	Illustrations/Photos	Audio/Video
Clarify historical or geographical information	Show complex information and data in an easy-to-understand format	Illustrate objects, scenes, or other details	Bring the subject to life and engage audiences

▶ INTERACTIVE

Go online for these interactive skills tutorials:
- Give an Effective Presentation
- Create Charts and Maps
- Support Ideas With Evidence

Effective Listening

Active listening is a key component of the communication process. Like all communication, it requires your engaged participation. Follow the Keys to Effective Listening to get the most out of discussions, presentations by others, lectures by your teacher, and any time you engage in listening.

Keys to Effective Listening

☑ Look at and listen to the speaker. Think about what you hear and see. Which ideas are emphasized or repeated? What gestures or expressions suggest strong feelings?

☑ Listen carefully to information presented in different media and formats—including videos, lectures, speeches, and discussions—so you can explain how the information you learn contributes to the topic or issue you are studying.

☑ Listen for the speaker's argument and specific claims so that you can distinguish claims that are supported by reasons and evidence from claims that are not.

☑ Listen to fit the situation. Active listening involves matching your listening to the situation. Listen critically to a speech given by a candidate for office. Listen with kindness to the feelings of a friend. Listen appreciatively to a musical performance.

▶ INTERACTIVE

For more help, go online for these interactive skills tutorials:
- Identify Bias
- Identify Evidence
- Distinguish Between Fact and Opinion
- Evaluate Existing Arguments

TOPIC 1 Introduction to Geography

GO ONLINE to access your digital course

- VIDEO
- AUDIO
- ETEXT
- INTERACTIVE
- WRITING
- GAMES
- WORKSHEET
- ASSESSMENT

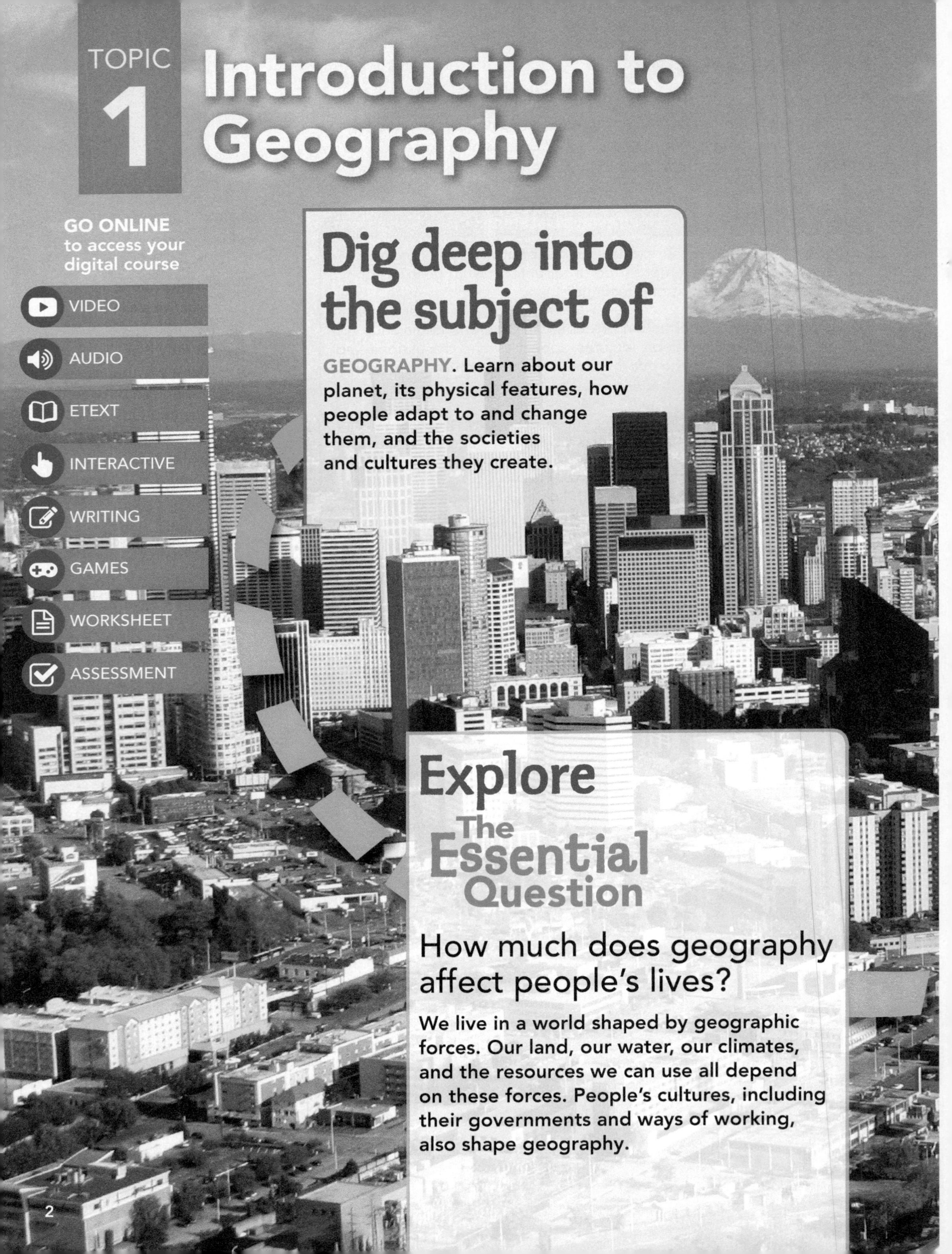

Dig deep into the subject of

GEOGRAPHY. Learn about our planet, its physical features, how people adapt to and change them, and the societies and cultures they create.

Explore The Essential Question

How much does geography affect people's lives?

We live in a world shaped by geographic forces. Our land, our water, our climates, and the resources we can use all depend on these forces. People's cultures, including their governments and ways of working, also shape geography.

Seattle, Washington, with Mount Rainier in the background

Watch

NBC LEARN

BOUNCE TO ACTIVATE ▶ VIDEO

Above the Forest Canopy

Meet Elizabeth Burakowski, a geographer investigating the impact of forest growth on climate.

Read

about the physical and human geography of our world.

Regional Atlas

World: Physical

CONTINENTS AND OCEANS

Earth's seven large land areas are called continents. They are separated by vast bodies of water—the five oceans that cover most of Earth's surface.

Learn more about the world's major physical features by making your own map in your Active Journal.

INTERACTIVE

Topic Map

The American Cordillera

Notice the long line of mountains running down the western sides of North and South America. This chain of mountains, including the Rocky Mountains, shown in the photograph, and the Andes, is called the American Cordillera. Rivers flow west from these mountains to the Pacific Ocean, or east to the Atlantic Ocean, Gulf of Mexico, or Caribbean Sea.

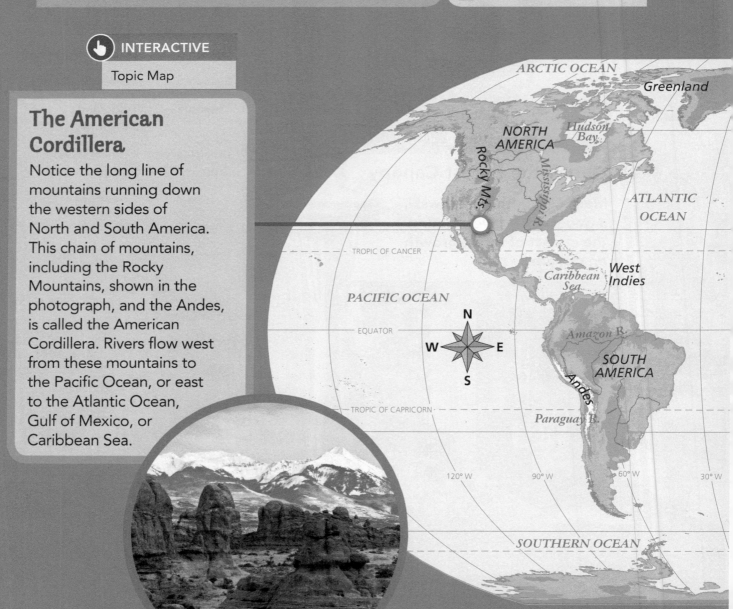

Two Continents in One

No body of water separates Europe from Asia. The traditional boundaries between them are the Ural Mountains, shown in this photograph; the Caucasus Mountains; and the Caspian, Black, and Aegean seas. The landmass Europe and Asia share is known as Eurasia.

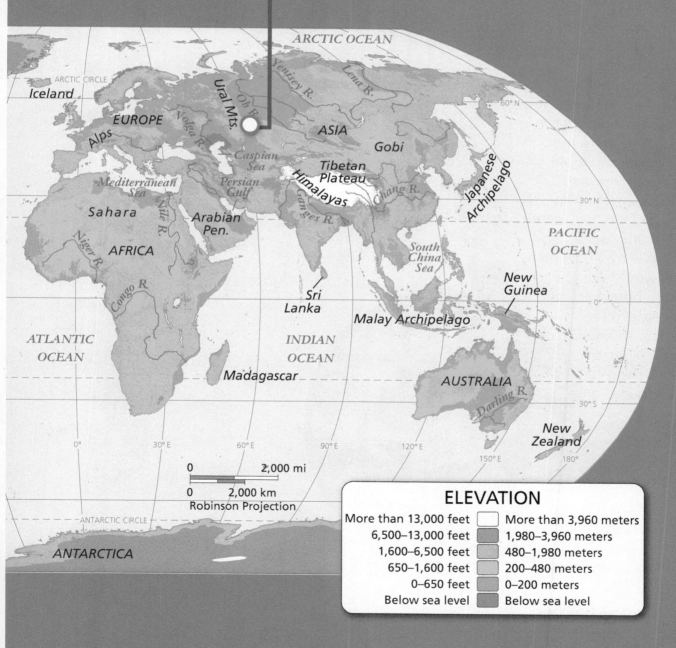

ARCTIC OCEAN

ARCTIC CIRCLE

Iceland

EUROPE

Alps

Ural Mts.

Volga R.

Ob R.

Yenisey R.

Lena R.

ASIA

60° N

Gobi

Caspian Sea

Tibetan Plateau

Himalayas

Chang R.

Japanese Archipelago

30° N

Mediterranean Sea

Persian Gulf

Sahara

Nile R.

Ganges R.

Arabian Pen.

PACIFIC OCEAN

Niger R.

AFRICA

Congo R.

South China Sea

New Guinea

Sri Lanka

Malay Archipelago

0°

ATLANTIC OCEAN

INDIAN OCEAN

Madagascar

AUSTRALIA

Darling R.

30° S

New Zealand

0°   30° E   60° E   90° E   120° E   150° E   180°

0   2,000 mi
0   2,000 km
Robinson Projection

ANTARCTIC CIRCLE

ANTARCTICA

ELEVATION

More than 13,000 feet	More than 3,960 meters
6,500–13,000 feet	1,980–3,960 meters
1,600–6,500 feet	480–1,980 meters
650–1,600 feet	200–480 meters
0–650 feet	0–200 meters
Below sea level	Below sea level

1 Regional Atlas

World: Regions

REGIONS OF THE WORLD

In this course, you will explore the world by region. The course divides the world into the 11 regions shown on this map.

Learn more about world regions by making your own map in your Active Journal.

Many People, Many Groups

One of the hardest things to understand about the world is that there are nearly 8 billion people living here. This map divides the world into the regions you will learn about in this course. This map also shows how many people would live in each region if there were only 100 people in the entire world. These people belong to many different ethnic groups.

United States and Canada
5 people

Middle America
3 people

South America
6 people

Most Populous Continent

Notice how many of the world's people live in Asia. Leaving out Northern Eurasia, 58 out of 100 people in the world—more than half— live in Asia, many in cities like Mumbai, India, shown in the photograph.

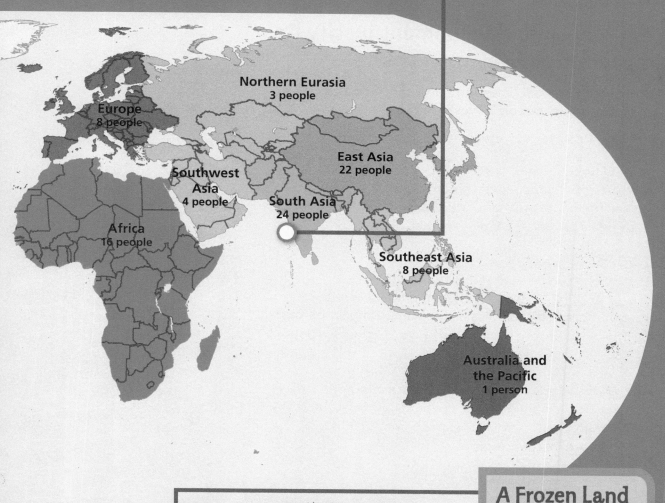

Northern Eurasia
3 people

Europe
8 people

East Asia
22 people

Southwest
Asia
4 people

South Asia
24 people

Africa
16 people

Southeast Asia
8 people

Australia and
the Pacific
1 person

A Frozen Land

Antarctica is the only continent where no people have settled.

Quest
Project-Based Learning Inquiry

Balancing Development and the Environment

Quest KICK OFF

Governments promote economic development projects hoping to create jobs for their people. If they succeed, people will be better off. But economic development can harm the environment. Which is more important?

Can economic development justify its impact on the environment?

Explore the Essential Question "How much does geography affect people's lives?" in this Quest.

▼ A building under construction

1 Ask Questions
Why are both economic development and preserving the environment important? Write your questions about these goals in your 📕 Active Journal.

2 Investigate
As you read the lessons in this topic, look for **Quest CONNECTIONS** about choices made to boost development and examples of the human impact on the environment. Record information in your 📕 Active Journal.

3 Conduct Research
Find valid and relevant sources of information on economic development plans in your city or state and their possible environmental impact. Record what you find in your 📕 Active Journal.

Quest FINDINGS

4 Write a Blog Post
Are the benefits of the development worth the costs to the environment? Write a blog post that expresses your views on the issue.

LESSON 1
Geography Basics

GET READY TO READ

START UP
Study the photo of an area in China. What does it suggest about the ways geographic features can shape life on Earth?

GUIDING QUESTIONS
- How can we locate points on Earth's surface?
- How can we use the five themes of geography?
- What are the best ways to show Earth's surface?
- How can we understand what maps show?
- What are the different kinds of maps?

TAKE NOTES

Literacy Skills: Summarize
Use the graphic organizer in your 📖 Active Journal to take notes as you read the lesson.

PRACTICE VOCABULARY
Use the vocabulary activity in your 📖 Active Journal to practice the vocabulary words.

Vocabulary

geography	longitude
cardinal direction	scale
intermediate direction	distortion
latitude	projection

Academic Vocabulary

interaction
pattern

Geography is the study of the human and nonhuman features of Earth, our home planet. Geographers try to answer two basic questions: Where are things located? Why are they there? To answer these questions, geographers study oceans, plant life, landforms, countries, and cities. Geographers also study how Earth and its people affect each other.

Describing Locations
When someone asks you what happened yesterday, you respond easily by retelling the day's events. You don't stop to consider that the idea of yesterday is a human invention, one of the ideas that we use to measure when events take place. Geographers use human inventions to discuss where things are located on Earth. One of those inventions is the concept of direction. Another is the imaginary lines geographers draw on Earth to locate objects precisely.

Directions In order to study Earth, geographers need to measure it and locate points on its surface. One way to do this is with directions.

The Global Grid

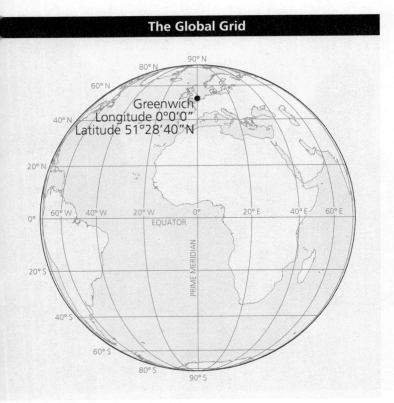

Greenwich
Longitude 0°0'0"
Latitude 51°28'40"N

PRIME MERIDIAN

EQUATOR

Analyze Diagrams
Latitude and longitude form a global grid that can be used to precisely locate places on Earth. **Use Evidence** How does the distance between two lines of longitude differ along their length?

Geographers use both cardinal and intermediate directions. The **cardinal directions** are north, east, south, and west. **Intermediate directions** lie between the cardinal directions. For example, northwest is halfway between north and west.

Latitude Earth is an almost perfect sphere, or round-shaped body. Geographers have drawn imaginary lines around Earth to help locate places on its surface. One of these is the Equator, a line drawn around Earth halfway between the North and South Poles. The Equator marks zero degrees (0°) of latitude. **Latitude** is the position north or south of the Equator. It is measured in degrees. Degrees are units that measure angles. Lines of latitude are divided into 180 degrees, 90 north of the Equator and 90 south of it. Each degree can be further divided into 60 minutes (60') and each minute can be divided into 60 seconds (60").

Lines of latitude form east-west circles around the globe. Lines of latitude are also called parallels, because they are parallel to one another. That means they never cross.

The Equator divides Earth in half. Each half of Earth is called a hemisphere. The half of Earth north of the Equator is known as the Northern Hemisphere. The half of Earth south of the Equator is the Southern Hemisphere.

Longitude Geographers have also drawn imaginary north-south lines that run between the North Pole and the South Pole on Earth's surface. One of these lines is the Prime Meridian, which passes through Greenwich, England. The Prime Meridian and the other north-south lines measure **longitude**, or the position in degrees east or west of the Prime Meridian. Lines of longitude are also called meridians.

The half of Earth east of the Prime Meridian is known as the Eastern Hemisphere. The half of Earth west of the Prime Meridian is the Western Hemisphere. There are 360 degrees of longitude, which are divided into 0° to 180° east and 0° to 180° west.

Global Grid Latitude and longitude form a global grid. You can describe the location of any point on Earth's surface using degrees of longitude and latitude. For example, Greenwich, England, is located at 0° longitude and about 51°29' north latitude.

✓ READING CHECK **Summarize** Why are latitude and longitude useful to geographers?

Geography's Five Themes

Geographers use five different themes, or ways of thinking. These themes are location, place, region, movement, and human-environment **interaction**. The themes can help answer a geographer's two basic questions: Where are things located? Why are they there?

Location Geographers begin to study a place by finding where it is, or its location. There are two ways to talk about location. Absolute location describes a place's exact position on Earth in terms of its longitude and latitude. Relative location, or the location of a place relative to another place, is another way to describe location. For example, you can say that Washington, D.C., is about 200 miles southwest of New York City.

Place Geographers also study place. Place refers to the mix of human and nonhuman features at a given location. For example, you might talk about how many people live in a particular place and the kinds of work they do. You might mention that a place is hilly or that it is flat. Another way to define a place is by its climate, or long-term weather patterns. You might say a place has a humid climate with cool winters and hot summers.

Region Geographers use the theme of region to group places that have something in common. A region is an area with at least one unifying physical or human feature such as climate, landforms, culture, or history. Cities are often part of a larger metropolitan area that includes surrounding suburbs. Together that city and those suburbs form a region. A region may share a job market or a road and rail network. New technology, such as high-speed railroads, may give places new unifying features and connections. This can create new regions.

Analyze Diagrams
The U.S. Capitol has a relative location of about seven blocks east of the Washington Monument. **Synthesize Visual Information** What is the absolute location of the Capitol in Washington, D.C.?

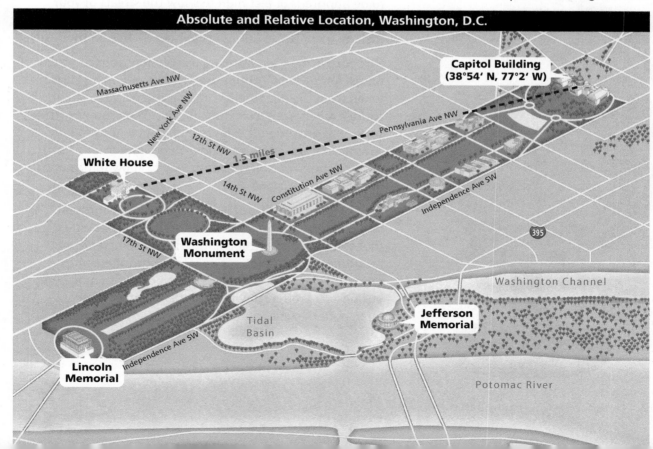

Absolute and Relative Location, Washington, D.C.

Capitol Building (38°54' N, 77°2' W)

Massachusetts Ave NW

New York Ave NW

12th St NW

Pennsylvania Ave NW

White House

14th St NW   Constitution Ave NW

Independence Ave SW

17th St NW

1.5 miles

Washington Monument

395

Washington Channel

Independence Ave SW

Tidal Basin

Jefferson Memorial

Lincoln Memorial

Potomac River

Movement The theme of movement explores how and why people, goods, and ideas move from one place to another. A daily movement of trucks and trains supplies a city with food, fuel, and other basic goods.

Human-Environment Interaction The theme of human-environment interaction considers how people affect their environment, or their natural surroundings, and how their environment affects them. The creation of a dam in a river is an example of human-environment interaction.

Other examples of human-environment interactions include human settlement **patterns**. People tend to settle in areas that have favorable geographic features, such as bodies of water, flat land with fertile soil, and moderate temperatures. Today, more than 50 percent of the world's population is located on or near seacoasts, and eight of the world's ten most populous cities are directly on the coast.

Academic Vocabulary
pattern • *n.*, arrangement, structure, or trend

☑ **READING CHECK** **Classify and Categorize** Which theme or themes of geography does the Mississippi River Valley represent?

How Do Geographers Show Earth's Surface?

Geographers use a number of different models to represent Earth's surface. Each model has its own strengths and weaknesses.

Globes A globe is a model of Earth with the same round shape as Earth itself. With a globe, geographers can show the continents and oceans of Earth much as they really are. The only difference is the **scale**, or the area a given space on the map or globe corresponds to in the real world. For example, one inch on a globe might correspond to 600 miles on Earth's surface.

Analyze Images Globes show Earth's shape accurately. **Identify Main Ideas** What is the main weakness of globes?

Globes are not always practical to use. A globe would have to be hundreds of feet high to show the streets of your town. Such a globe would be impossible to carry around. Instead, people use flat maps to help them find their way.

Photographs Geographers use photographs as well as maps. Aerial photographs are pictures of Earth's surface taken from the air. Satellite images are pictures of Earth's surface taken from a satellite in orbit. They show Earth's surface in great detail. However, it can be hard to find specific features, such as roads, on a photograph. For this reason, maps are still the main way to show information about Earth's surface.

Geographic Information Systems A geographic information system (GIS) is a computer-based system that stores and uses information linked to geographic locations. GIS is useful not only to geographers and mapmakers, but also to government agencies and businesses. It offers a way to connect a great deal of information to the same place.

Analyze Images This aerial photograph shows a view of the Jordan River, which is located in Southwest Asia. **Synthesize Visual Information** What can you learn from this photograph about this part of Earth's surface?

Global Positioning System The Global Positioning System (GPS) is a network of 24 satellites used to pinpoint locations on Earth with great accuracy. The satellites orbit Earth twice a day. They are arranged in a pattern that provides coverage of nearly all the planet. The system works by allowing users to send and receive signals from the satellites. Technology aboard the satellites calculates and sends back the user's exact location on Earth.

GPS was originally designed for the military. Geographers use the technology to study features and events on Earth's surface, such as storm systems. People use GPS to navigate ships and planes. Hikers use it to find their way in the wilderness.

Digital Maps For hundreds of years, maps were drawn or printed on paper. Maps can now appear at the touch of a phone or computer screen. Digital maps are maps that are stored in a computer or other electronic equipment. They have an advantage over printed maps in that they can be easily updated to show changes on Earth's surface. In addition, the scale of the map can be manipulated at the touch of a mouse or screen. A viewer can zoom in to locate a house on a street or zoom out to view an entire city.

The viewer of a digital map can select the type of map shown for a given area. For example, options allow the viewer to choose an aerial view or a road map view of the same area. The viewer picks the type of map that best serves the purpose he or she has in mind. Geographers use digital maps for different types of studies, such as classifying soil types in an area or identifying features on the ocean floor. The public uses digital maps too, particularly for finding directions.

Did you know?

The world's oldest known map dates to 2500 BCE and is a clay tablet.

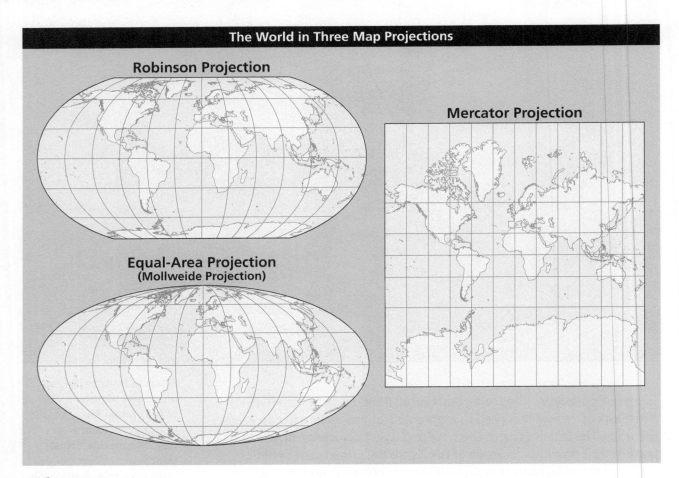

The World in Three Map Projections

Robinson Projection

Mercator Projection

Equal-Area Projection
(Mollweide Projection)

Analyze Diagrams
A Robinson projection and an equal-area projection show the true sizes of landmasses, but they differ in the accuracy of their shapes. A Mercator projection shows true shapes and directions but not distances or sizes. **Synthesize Visual Information** When might you want to use a Robinson projection instead of a Mercator projection?

Map Projections Flat maps and photos have one major problem. Earth is round, but a map or photo is flat. Can you flatten an orange peel without stretching or tearing it? There will be sections that are stretched or bent out of shape.

Showing Earth on the flat surface of a map always brings some **distortion**, or loss of accuracy in the size or position of objects. Something is going to look too large, too small, or out of place. To show a flat image of Earth's round surface, mapmakers have come up with different **projections**, or ways to show Earth on a flat surface. Each projection has some kind of distortion.

Examples of projections include equal-area, Mercator, and Robinson. An equal-area projection (also called a Mollweide projection) shows the correct size of landmasses, but their shapes are distorted. The Mercator (mur KAYT ur) projection shows correct shapes and directions, but not true distances or sizes. Mercator maps make areas near the poles look bigger than they are. The Robinson projection shows nearly the correct size and shape of most land areas. However, even the Robinson projection has distortions, especially in areas around the edges of the map.

✓ READING CHECK Identify Implied Main Ideas How are maps different from globes?

Understanding Maps

Maps are used for different purposes. However, they all share certain features, such as a map title, map key, locator map, scale bar, and compass rose. Each of these features helps you read and understand the information on the map.

Reading a Map The title tells you the subject of the map. A map's key explains the symbols and colors on the map. A locator map shows where the area on the map is located within a larger area. A map's scale bar shows how much space on the map represents a given distance on Earth. Maps may use a grid showing lines of longitude and latitude that can help you find locations. A compass rose is a diagram of a compass showing directions. Some maps have insets. These are smaller maps on the same page as the main map that may show areas outside the main map's borders or a close-up of an area on the main map.

Types of Maps The map projections, or ways to represent Earth's surface, that you have studied can be used to show different things about the area they cover. For example, they might represent the physical landscape, political boundaries, ecosystem zones, or almost any other feature of an area. People use different kinds of maps in different situations.

Political maps show political units, such as countries or states. They may also show capitals of countries, or the centers of their government, and other major cities. They may use colors to distinguish the various countries or states, helping the user identify them easily.

INTERACTIVE

Make a Map

GEOGRAPHY SKILLS

This map shows the various parts of a map: ❶ is the map title; ❷ is the key; ❸ is a locator map; ❹ is the scale bar; ❺ shows part of the map's grid; ❻ is the compass rose; and ❼ indicates two inset maps.

1. **Movement** Using the scale bar, estimate how many miles you would travel if you went from New Jersey to California.

2. **Use Evidence** What does the key to this map show?

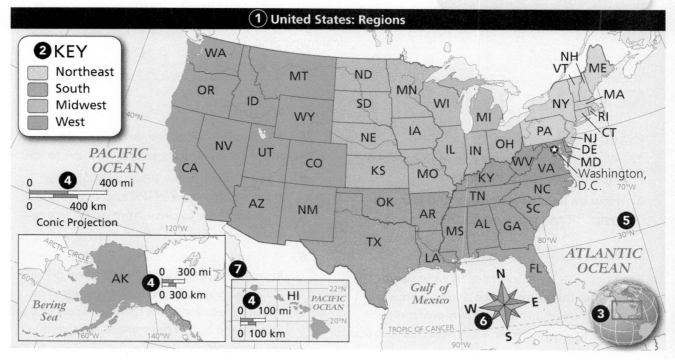

❶ United States: Regions

❷ KEY
- Northeast
- South
- Midwest
- West

PACIFIC OCEAN

0 — 400 mi

0 — 400 km

Conic Projection

AK — Bering Sea — ARCTIC CIRCLE

0 — 300 mi

0 — 300 km

HI — PACIFIC OCEAN

0 — 100 mi

0 — 100 km

Gulf of Mexico

TROPIC OF CANCER

ATLANTIC OCEAN

N
W — E
S

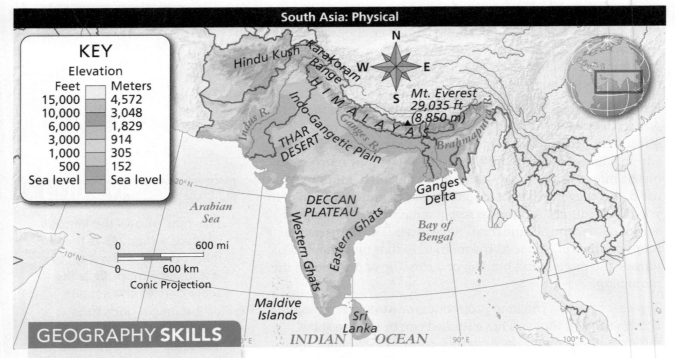

South Asia: Physical

KEY

Elevation

Feet	Meters
15,000	4,572
10,000	3,048
6,000	1,829
3,000	914
1,000	305
500	152
Sea level	Sea level

Hindu Kush
Karakoram Range
HIMALAYAS
Mt. Everest
29,035 ft
(8,850 m)
Indus R.
Indo-Gangetic Plain
Ganges R.
Brahmaputra
THAR DESERT
Arabian Sea
DECCAN PLATEAU
Ganges Delta
Western Ghats
Eastern Ghats
Bay of Bengal
Maldive Islands
Sri Lanka
INDIAN OCEAN

0   600 mi
0   600 km
Conic Projection

20°N
10°N

90° E   100° E

GEOGRAPHY SKILLS

Physical maps use colors to represent elevation.

1. **Place** Are the areas of highest elevation in the northern or southern half of South Asia?

2. **Use Evidence** Based on the map, what are the major rivers of South Asia?

A physical map shows the physical, or natural, features of a place. One feature that physical maps often include is elevation, or height above sea level. Physical maps usually use different colors to indicate different elevations.

Special-purpose maps show the location or distribution of specific human or physical features. One might show the distribution of natural resources in a country. A highway map is another kind of special-purpose map.

☑ READING CHECK **Compare and Contrast** How do political and physical maps differ?

☑ Lesson Check

Practice Vocabulary

1. What is the difference between **cardinal** and **intermediate directions**?

2. How do lines of **longitude** and **latitude** pinpoint any place on Earth?

Critical Thinking and Writing

3. **Compare and Contrast** In what ways do the themes of place and region work with movement and human-environment interaction to create a portrait of a location on Earth?

4. **Summarize** What are the basic parts of a map and what does each part show readers?

5. **Draw Conclusions** What type of map does a cell phone's GPS app use to show a person how to drive from one place to another?

6. **Writing Workshop: Gather Evidence** In your ▱ Active Journal, write three or more ways geography has affected your life. You will use these ideas in a narrative essay you will write at the end of the topic about the effects of geography on daily life.

Create a Mental Map

Follow these steps and use the example in the source to create a mental map.

INTERACTIVE

Create Charts and Maps

1 **Define Boundaries of Your Mental Map.** A mental map is a map drawn from your memory to show someone what an area looks like. You can also use it to show what you know about an area. The first step is to figure out how big a mental map you need.

   a. If you were making a mental map of what you see in your neighborhood on an average day, how much of it would you include?

   b. What would be the borders of the mental map?

2 **Determine the Key Features of Your Mental Map.** You would need to start with a diagram of streets if you are in the city, or nearby roads and highways if you are in the country. Think about the buildings or places where you go that you would need to include. What other landmarks or places in your neighborhood should appear?

   a. What buildings would you want to show on your mental map? Consider the places where you spend most of your time.

   b. Why would the street or road names help someone to understand your mental map?

3 **Create a Key for Your Mental Map.** Remember that a key explains the meaning of any symbols on the map. Anyone reading the map can refer to the key to see what a map symbol means and use the compass rose to find directions.

   a. If someone followed the sample mental map, in which direction would they go to get from school to the home of the student who made it?

   b. Which location shown on the map could the mental map maker not easily use a bus to reach?

Primary Source

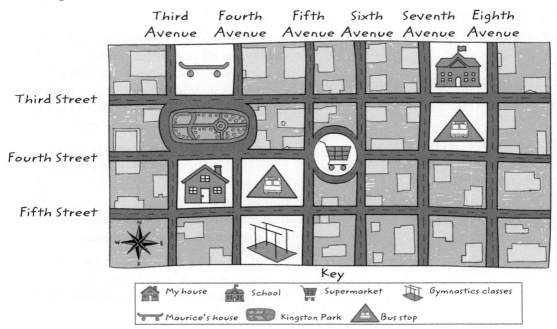

Our Planet, Earth

GET READY TO READ

START UP
Study the photograph of an area in Peru. What aspects of geography can you identify in this picture?

GUIDING QUESTIONS
- How does Earth's movement explain the days and seasons?
- What is Earth's internal structure?
- What forces shape Earth's surface?

TAKE NOTES
Literacy Skills: Interpret Visual Information
Use the graphic organizer in your 🗐 Active Journal to take notes as you read the lesson.

PRACTICE VOCABULARY
Use the vocabulary activity in your 🗐 Active Journal to practice the vocabulary words.

Vocabulary

equinox	deposition
solstice	plate
weathering	tectonics
erosion	fault
	magma

Academic Vocabulary

portion
sustain

Why do we have seasons? Why do some days have more light than others? How did the land where we live take the form that it did? These are all questions that can be answered by Earth's position and movements in space and by forces both inside and on the surface of Earth.

Earth in Space

Earth, the sun, the planets, and the stars in the sky are all part of our galaxy, or cluster of stars. We call our galaxy the Milky Way because its stars look like a trail of spilled milk across a night sky far from city lights. Our sun is one of its billions of stars.

Even though the sun is about 93 million miles (150 million km) away, it provides Earth with heat and light. To understand how far Earth is from the sun, consider that this distance is nearly 4,000 times the distance around Earth at the Equator.

Rotation of Earth As Earth revolves around the sun, it is also rotating, or spinning, in space. Earth rotates around its axis.

Each complete turn, or rotation, takes about 24 hours. At any one time, it is night on the side of Earth facing away from the sun. As Earth rotates, that side of Earth turns to face the sun, and the sun appears to rise. The sun's light shines on that side of Earth. It is daytime. Then, as that side of Earth turns away from the sun, the sun appears to set. No sunlight reaches that side of Earth. It is nighttime.

Time Zones Because Earth rotates toward the east, the day starts earlier in the east than it does farther west. Over short distances, the time difference is small. For example, the sun rises about four minutes earlier in Beaumont, Texas, than it does in Houston, 70 miles to the west. But if every town had its own local time, people would have a hard time keeping track. So governments have agreed to divide the world into standard time zones, or areas sharing the same time. Times in neighboring zones are one hour apart.

The Prime Meridian The Prime Meridian, in Greenwich, England, is at the center of one of these zones. The standard time in that zone is sometimes known as Greenwich Mean Time (GMT), or Universal Time (UT). Other time zones are sometimes described in terms of how many hours they are behind or ahead of UT. For example, Central Standard Time in the United States is UT–6, which means six hours behind UT.

☑ READING CHECK **Identify Main Ideas** What causes daytime to turn to nighttime?

Analyze Images Earth rotates toward the east, causing the day-night cycle. **Draw Conclusions** Which part of the United States will see daylight first?

👆 INTERACTIVE

How Does Earth Move?

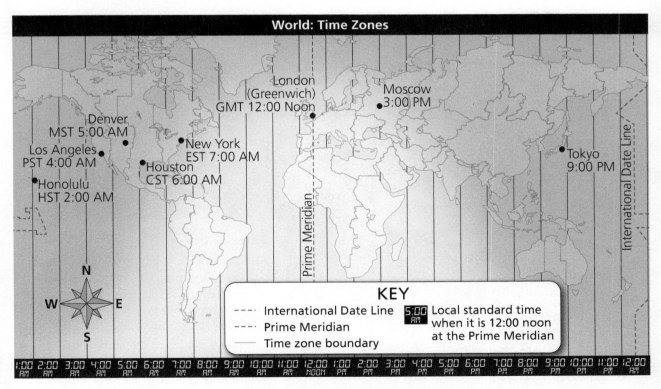

Analyze Diagrams Earth is divided into time zones. Most neighboring zones are one hour apart. **Infer** If it is 8 P.M. in New York, what time is it in Los Angeles?

Why Are There Seasons?

Earth travels around the sun in an oval-shaped orbit. An orbit is the path one object makes as it revolves around another. Earth takes 365 1/4 days, or one year, to make one complete journey around the sun, called a revolution.

Earth's axis, an imaginary line between the North and South poles, is tilted relative to its orbit. Therefore, as Earth makes a revolution, direct sunlight moves north and south of the Equator as the year progresses. That is why seasons occur.

March Equinox

About March 21, the sun is directly overhead at noon on the Equator. At this point in Earth's orbit, its axis is tilted neither toward nor away from the sun. An **equinox** (EE kwih nahks) is a point at which, everywhere on Earth, days and nights are nearly equal in length. March brings the spring equinox in the Northern Hemisphere and the fall equinox in the Southern Hemisphere.

June Solstice

About June 21, the North Pole is tilted closest to the sun. This brings the heat of summer to the Northern Hemisphere. This is the summer solstice in the Northern Hemisphere and the winter solstice in the Southern Hemisphere. A **solstice** (SOHL stis) is a point at which days are longest in one hemisphere and shortest in the other.

Earth's orbit around the sun affects the length of daylight as well as the seasons. An **equinox** (EE kwih nahks) is a point at which, everywhere on Earth, days and nights are nearly equal in length. A **solstice** (SOHL stis) is a point at which days are longest in one hemisphere and shortest in the other. The winter solstice has the shortest length of daylight, and the summer solstice the longest.

☑ READING CHECK **Draw Conclusions** How can days be short and cold in one hemisphere when they are long and hot in another?

Analyze Diagrams
Seasons are caused by the tilt of Earth's axis as it revolves around the sun. **Synthesize Visual Information** Which hemisphere gets the most daylight at the December solstice?

December Solstice
About December 21, the South Pole is tilted closest to the sun. This is the winter solstice in the Northern Hemisphere and the summer solstice in the Southern Hemisphere. The lack of sunlight in the Northern Hemisphere brings the cold of winter.

September Equinox
About September 23, the sun is again directly overhead at noon on the Equator, and all of Earth has days and nights of equal length. This is the fall equinox in the Northern Hemisphere and the spring equinox in the Southern Hemisphere. Less direct sunlight in the Northern Hemisphere brings the chill of fall there.

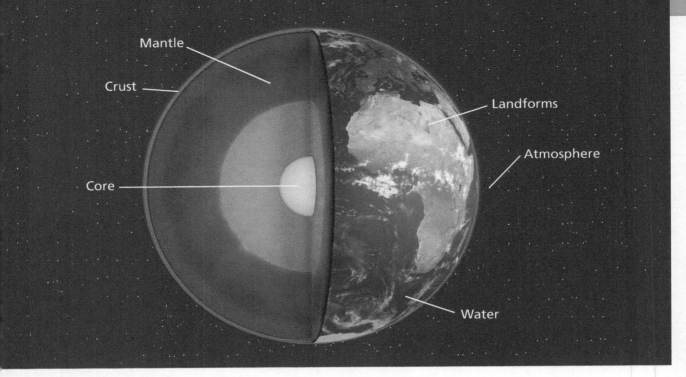

Mantle

Crust

Core

Landforms

Atmosphere

Water

Analyze Diagrams
Above Earth's surface is the atmosphere, a thick layer of gases or air that includes life-giving oxygen. Earth's atmosphere acts like a blanket, holding in heat from the sun, which makes life possible. **Draw Conclusions** On which part of the Earth's structure do people live?

Earth's Structure

Understanding Earth's inner and outer structure will help you to understand the forces that shape the world we live in. Earth's inner layers include the core and mantle. Its outer layers are the crust, including landforms, the water found at its surface, and the atmosphere.

Inside Earth A sphere of very hot metal at the center of Earth is called the **core**. Despite temperatures greater than 5,000°F (3,000°C), the inner core is solid because of the great pressure of the layers above it. The outer core is hot liquid metal.

The **mantle** is a thick, rocky layer around the core. The mantle is also hot, with temperatures greater than 3,300°F (1,800°C). The mantle is solid, but its temperature makes it fluid, or able to flow.

Land and Water The layer of rocks and minerals that surrounds the mantle is called the **crust**. The crust is thinnest beneath the ocean floor and thickest beneath high mountains.

The surface of the crust includes the land areas where people live as well as the ocean floor. Only about 29 percent of Earth's surface is land. There are many different landforms, or shapes and types of land. Water covers about 71 percent of Earth's surface. The oceans hold about 97 percent of Earth's water. This water is salty. Most fresh water, or water without salt, is frozen in ice sheets around the North and South Poles. Only a tiny **portion** of Earth's water is unfrozen fresh water. Fresh water comes from lakes, rivers, and ground water, which are fed by rain and snow.

Academic Vocabulary
portion • *n.,* part of a whole

☑ READING CHECK **Identify Main Ideas** What two layers lie below Earth's surface, and what layer is found atop them?

What Forces on Earth's Surface Shape the Land?

Two kinds of processes shape the landforms on Earth's surface: processes on Earth's surface that wear Earth's crust down, and processes beneath its surface that push the crust up. Forces on Earth's surface wear down and reshape the land.

Weathering **Weathering** is a process that breaks rocks down into tiny pieces. There are two kinds of weathering: chemical weathering and mechanical weathering. In chemical weathering, rainwater or acids carried by rainwater dissolve rocks. In mechanical weathering, moving water, ice, or sometimes wind breaks rocks into little pieces. Mechanical weathering can happen after chemical weathering has weakened rocks.

Weathering helps create soil. Tiny pieces of rock combine with decayed animal and plant material to form soil. Soil and pieces of rock may undergo **erosion,** a process in which water, ice, or wind remove small pieces of rock and move them somewhere else.

Soil is required to **sustain** plant and animal life and for agriculture. Because of this, weathering is very important to human settlement patterns. As you read earlier, people tend to settle in areas that have fertile soil and ample water. This makes it easier to grow the crops needed to feed a community.

Weathering can be a constructive force that helps form soil. Erosion can be a destructive force that carries fertile topsoil away and leaves land unsuitable for farming. In the 1930s, a combination of drought, unwise farming practices, and strong winds led to the Dust Bowl in the central United States. For nearly a decade, dust storms stripped the land of soil. Many farmers were forced to abandon their land and move west to find jobs.

Shaping Landforms Weathering and erosion have shaped many of Earth's landforms. These landforms include mountains and hills. Mountains are wide at the bottom and rise steeply to a narrow peak or ridge. Hills are lower than mountains and often have rounded tops. While forces within Earth create mountains, forces on Earth's surface wear them down.

The parts of mountains and hills that are left standing are the rocks that are hardest to wear away. Millions of years ago, the Appalachian Mountains in the eastern United States were as high as the Rocky Mountains of the western United States. Rain, snow, and wind wore the Appalachians down into much lower peaks.

Rebuilding Earth's Surface When water, ice, and wind remove material, they deposit it farther downstream or downwind to create new landforms. **Deposition** is the process of depositing, or dropping, eroded material. Plains, or large areas of flat or gently rolling land, are often formed by the deposition of material carried downstream by rivers. Deltas are flat, fan-shaped plains built in the seabed where a river fans out and deposits material over many years.

Academic Vocabulary
sustain • *v.*, to provide something necessary; to maintain

Analyze Images
The power of the wind to shape landforms is clear in these structures from Arches National Park in Utah. **Classify and Categorize** What process shaped these rocks?

A plateau is a large, mostly flat area that rises above the surrounding land. Plateaus often have at least one side that is a steep slope. At the top of this slope is usually a layer of rock that is hard to wear down. Valleys are stretches of low land between mountains or hills. Rivers often form valleys where there are rocks that are easy to wear away.

READING CHECK Compare and Contrast How is erosion different from weathering?

What Forces Inside Earth Shape the Land?

Forces deep inside Earth are constantly reshaping its surface. **Plate tectonics** is a process involving huge blocks of Earth's crust and upper mantle that are called tectonic plates. Tectonic plates include continents or parts of continents, along with parts of the ocean floor.

Earth's tectonic plates lie upon a layer of hot mantle rock, which flows like melted plastic. Plates may move atop the mantle an inch or two (a few centimeters) a year.

Over time, the movement of tectonic plates creates mountains. When two plates of crust push against each other, the pressure makes the crust bend to form steep mountains.

Earthquakes When plates slide against each other, earthquakes occur. They often occur at seams in Earth's crust called **faults,** often near the boundaries between plates. Earthquakes cause the ground to shake. Some earthquakes are too small

GEOGRAPHY **SKILLS**

The map shows Earth's major tectonic plates and the directions in which they are moving. Earthquakes and volcanoes occur along plate edges.

1. **Movement** In what direction is the Pacific Plate moving in relation to the Eurasian Plate?

2. **Infer** Why is the Ring of Fire sometimes called the Pacific Ring of Fire?

World: Tectonic Plates

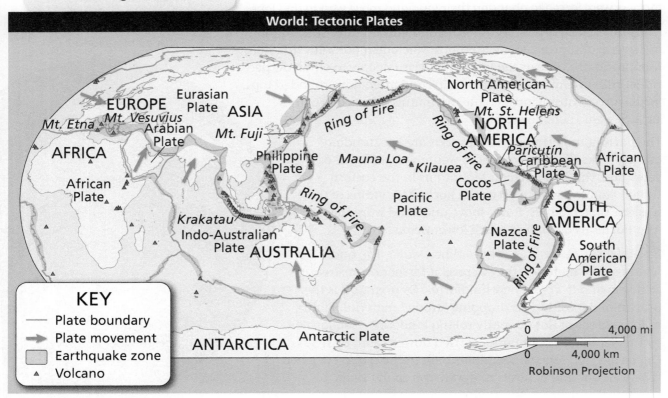

KEY
— Plate boundary
→ Plate movement
▢ Earthquake zone
▲ Volcano

for people to feel. But others can destroy buildings and cause great harm. For example, the 1906 San Francisco earthquake killed more than 3,000 people.

Volcanoes When plate movement forces oceanic crust beneath continental crust, steam and heat are released, melting the rocks above. This causes the rock to melt and rise, forming volcanoes. The Pacific Ring of Fire describes the chain of volcanoes forming a semicircle around the eastern, northern, and western edges of the Pacific Ocean. Here, oceanic plates are forced beneath continental plates. This movement creates dynamic belts of earthquakes and volcanoes.

Volcanoes spew **magma,** or molten rock, from inside Earth to the surface. When magma erupts out of a volcano and flows onto Earth's surface, it is called lava. Volcanic eruptions can be very dangerous for people, but volcanoes also serve an important purpose. When lava cools, new land forms. Undersea volcanoes can even grow into islands after thousands of years of eruptions.

Natural Hazards Volcanoes and earthquakes are examples of natural hazards, or dangers. Other natural hazards include hurricanes, tornadoes, landslides, and floods.

These events threaten lives and property. But people can take steps to prepare for natural disasters, so that damage will not be as severe when a disaster strikes. For example, architects can design buildings that will not collapse when the ground shakes. Local governments can set routes for people to leave affected areas during a hurricane. Citizens can practice what to do during an earthquake and keep emergency supplies at home.

✓ READING CHECK Identify Supporting Details What are some ways people prepare for natural hazards?

Analyze Images
Volcanoes pour out hot lava, ash, rocks, and poisonous gases, making them dangerous. **Identify Cause and Effect** What causes volcanoes to erupt?

✓ Lesson Check

Practice Vocabulary

1. What is the difference between an **equinox** and a **solstice**?

2. How are **faults** related to **plate tectonics**?

Critical Thinking and Writing

3. **Draw Conclusions** How might our lives change if Earth's atmosphere were damaged? Explain.

4. **Draw Conclusions** To choose a safe location for a new town, what questions about processes inside Earth and on its surface would you ask? Explain.

5. **Classify and Categorize** Consider three different landforms. For each, list the main processes that form it. Are the processes inside Earth or on its surface? How are the different processes related?

6. **Writing Workshop: Gather Evidence** In your ▤ Active Journal, describe an experience you have had with the seasons, extreme weather, or a natural disaster like an earthquake or flood.

Identify Cause and Effect

Follow these steps and use the source to identify cause and effect.

INTERACTIVE

Analyze Cause and Effect

1 **Identify the key event.** Choose one event or condition that you want to explain. Once you have chosen an event, you can look for possible causes and effects of that event. If you're reading a piece of text, you might identify the most important event.

   a. What is the most important event?

   b. What happened in this event?

2 **Study earlier events or conditions as possible causes of the key event.** A cause of the key event must happen before the key event. Look for earlier events or conditions by asking, "Why did the key event happen?" or "What led to the key event?"

   a. What condition precedes the key event?

   b. How is that condition related to the key event?

3 **Study later events or conditions as possible effects of the event.** Events often have their own effects. They may include short-term effects or longer lasting ones. To find later events, ask "What did the key event lead to?" or "What was a result of the key event?"

   a. What happened next after the event?

   b. What happened after that?

   c. What happens at the December solstice?

   d. How is the movement of Earth around the sun connected to that?

Secondary Source

The Cycle of the Seasons

Earth is tilted on its axis. As a result, the amount of heat from the sun that reaches the Northern and Southern Hemispheres changes during the year. At the March equinox, the sun is directly over the Equator and heats both hemispheres equally. This is the beginning of spring in the Northern Hemisphere and of autumn in the Southern.

As Earth moves around the sun, its tilt angles the Northern Hemisphere toward the sun. At the June solstice, the Northern Hemisphere receives more heat than the Southern Hemisphere. It is summer north of the Equator and winter south of it.

Earth continues to revolve around the sun. At the September equinox, the sun is over the Equator again, and the two hemispheres receive equal amounts of heat again. This signals the beginning of autumn north of the Equator and of spring to the south.

Over the next months, the Southern Hemisphere is tilted more and more toward the sun and the Northern Hemisphere more and more away from it. Because of this, southern areas receive more heat and at the December solstice, summer begins there. The Northern Hemisphere receives less heat. Winter begins.

Climates and Ecosystems

GET READY TO READ

START UP
Study the photograph of a tropical rain forest. How does it show a relationship between a climate and communities of plants and animals?

GUIDING QUESTIONS
- How is climate different from weather?
- Why do temperatures, precipitation, and air movements vary over time and space?
- What are Earth's main climate regions?
- How do climates affect Earth's ecosystems?

TAKE NOTES
Literacy Skills: Determine Central Ideas
Use the graphic organizer in your 📕 Active Journal to take notes as you read the lesson.

PRACTICE VOCABULARY
Use the vocabulary activity in your 📕 Active Journal to practice the vocabulary words.

Vocabulary		Academic Vocabulary
weather	prevailing winds	reverse
climate	tropical cyclone	moderate
tropics	biome	
temperate zone	ecosystem	
water cycle		

Some areas of Earth are hot and dry, and some are cooler and often wet. Some areas have similar temperatures throughout the year, and others have wide swings from one season to another. Earth has many different types of climate, and those differences shape life on Earth.

Climate and Weather
You have learned about the powerful forces that affect Earth, including movements of Earth in space, water, and sunlight. These forces also shape Earth's weather patterns. Weather patterns can vary widely from one region to another.

Weather or Climate? Do you look outside before you choose your clothing in the morning? If so, you are checking the weather. **Weather** is the condition of the air and sky at a certain time and place. Or do you choose your clothing based on the normal weather for the time of year in the place where you live? If so, you dress according to your local climate. **Climate** is the average weather of a place over many years.

Academic Vocabulary
reverse • v., to turn around;
to turn into the opposite

How you feel about today's weather may depend on your local climate. If you live in a place with a wet climate, you may be unhappy to see rainy weather, because your climate means that you get rain frequently. On the other hand, if you live in a dry climate where water is scarce, you might be very happy to see rainy weather. Earth's climates cause humans to respond to the various elements in a variety of ways.

Rain is a form of precipitation, which is water that falls to the ground as rain, snow, sleet, or hail. Temperature is a measure of how hot or cold the air is. Precipitation and temperature are the main ways to describe both daily weather and long-term climate.

Comparing Climates Climate graphs show the average climate for a place for each month of a year. A climate graph has a curved line that shows average temperatures for each month. It has bars that show average monthly precipitation.

☑ READING CHECK **Compare and Contrast** How is climate different from weather?

Why Do Temperatures Differ?

Energy from the sun heats Earth. Because Earth's surface is curved, different areas of the planet receive different amounts of direct sunlight. As a result, some regions are warmer than others.

In addition, temperature patterns change from season to season. In January, it is winter in the Northern Hemisphere and summer in the Southern Hemisphere. In July, the seasons are **reversed**.

Latitude Differences The polar zones, or high latitudes, are the areas north of the Arctic Circle and south of the Antarctic Circle. In the polar zones, the sun is near or below the horizon all year. Temperatures stay cool to bitterly cold.

Analyze Graphs This climate graph shows that Chicago has cold winters, hot summers, and moderate precipitation year-round. **Use Visual Information** Which season is rainiest in Chicago?

Climate of Chicago, Illinois

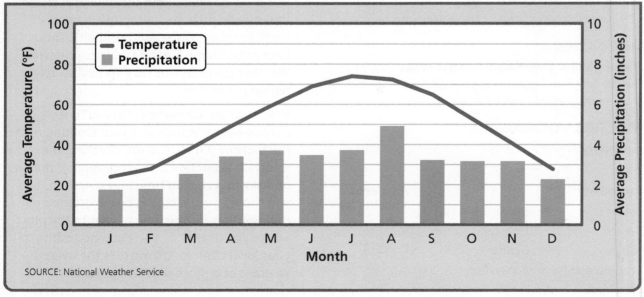

SOURCE: National Weather Service

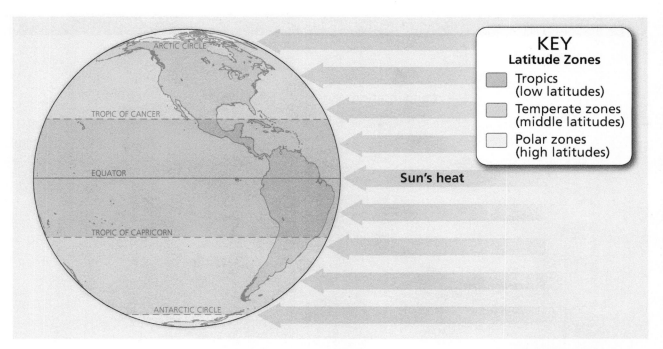

KEY
Latitude Zones

☐ Tropics
(low latitudes)

☐ Temperate zones
(middle latitudes)

☐ Polar zones
(high latitudes)

Sun's heat

The **tropics**, or the low latitudes, are the areas between the Tropic of Cancer and the Tropic of Capricorn. In the tropics, the sun is overhead or nearly overhead all year long. In this region, it is usually hot.

The **temperate zones**, or the middle latitudes, are between the high and low latitudes. They have a hot summer, a cold winter, and a **moderate** spring and fall.

Altitude Differences Temperatures are cooler in areas with high altitude. Altitude is height above sea level. As altitude increases, temperature drops. That is true everywhere on Earth, even in the tropics.

☑ READING CHECK **Identify Supporting Details** How does the curvature of Earth explain differences in temperature at different distances from the Equator?

How Does Water Affect Climate?

Water also shapes climates. The amount of precipitation an area receives is a factor in climate. Water affects temperature as well.

Oceans and Climate Global temperature differences and wind patterns create ocean currents, which act like large rivers within the oceans. These currents move across great distances. They move warm water from the tropics toward the poles and cool water from the poles toward the tropics. The water's temperature affects air temperature near it. Warm water warms the air; cool water chills it.

Bodies of water affect climate in other ways, too. Water takes longer to heat or cool than land. As air and land heat up in summer, water remains cooler. Wind blowing over the cool water helps cool land nearby. So in summer, areas near an ocean or lake will be cooler than inland areas at the same latitude and altitude.

Analyze Diagrams The sun heats Earth unevenly, causing climate to vary in different zones of latitude. **Use Visual Information** Which zones cover the smallest areas of Earth's surface?

Academic Vocabulary
moderate • *adj.*, not extreme; mild

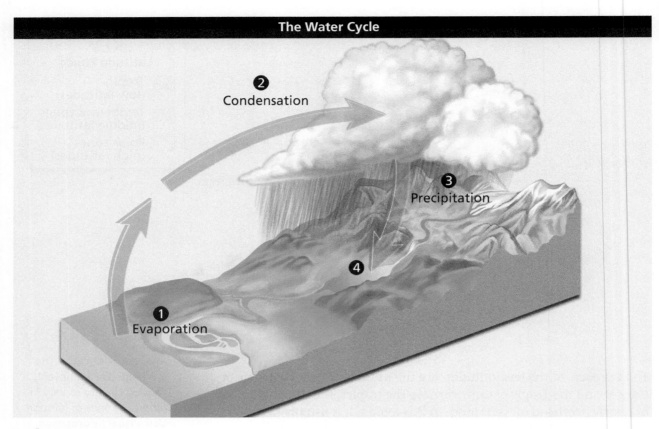

② Condensation

③ Precipitation

④

① Evaporation

Analyze Diagrams
In Step ❶ of the water cycle, water changes from liquid to a gas. In Step ❷, it returns to liquid form. In Step ❸, the water falls to earth, where it remains (Step ❹) until it evaporates.

Use Visual Information
What part of the water cycle returns water to Earth's surface?

In the winter, on the other hand, water remains warmer than land. So in winter, areas near oceans or lakes are warmer than inland areas. For example, the Gulf Stream, a warm current in the Atlantic Ocean, travels northeast from the tropics. It carries warm water all the way to western Europe. That warm water helps give western Europe a much milder climate than other regions at the same latitude.

The Water Cycle Earth's water is always moving in a process called the water cycle. The **water cycle** is the movement of water from Earth's surface into the atmosphere and back again. It follows four steps. In the first step, the sun's energy makes water from oceans, lakes, and rivers evaporate, or change from a liquid to a gas called water vapor. The water vapor rises into the atmosphere and cools.

As it cools, the water vapor condenses, or changes back into a liquid, and millions of tiny drops of water form into clouds. Sometimes the water droplets freeze into ice crystals. In step 3, ice crystals or larger droplets of water fall to the ground as rain, snow, sleet, or hail, which are all forms of precipitation. This can happen when air moves up over a hill or mountain or when air rises in a storm system.

In step 4, precipitation can seep into the ground or fall into a body of water. Eventually, the water evaporates again, continuing the water cycle.

✓ READING CHECK **Sequence** How does Earth's water move in the water cycle?

Air Circulation and Precipitation

Belts of rising and sinking air form a pattern around Earth. Hot air rises near the Equator. It cools and sinks at the edge of the tropics, rises in the temperate zones, and sinks over the poles.

Patterns of Winds Global air patterns form as heated air rises and cooled air falls. At the same time, air at the surface is also blowing toward the east or west. The result is **prevailing winds**, which are the winds that most frequently blow across a region.

Precipitation Patterns Precipitation is heaviest near the Equator, where moist air is heated and rises. It is also heavy along coastlines, where moist air blows onshore and is forced to rise. Precipitation is lightest where cool air sinks near the poles and at the edges of the tropics, where deserts are normally found.

Most storms occur when two air masses of different temperatures or moisture contents come together. Some storms bring small amounts of rain or snow, while others bring heavy wind and rain and cause damage.

A **tropical cyclone** is an intense rainstorm with strong winds that forms over oceans in the tropics. A tornado is a swirling funnel of wind that can reach 300 miles (500 km) per hour.

✓READING CHECK Draw Conclusions How do air circulation and precipitation affect people?

Did you know?

What's the rainiest place on Earth? A small settlement named Mawsynram in India receives more than 460 inches of rain (more than 11,680 mm) a year. That's nearly 40 feet (12 m) of rain!

Analyze Diagrams
Rising and sinking air form global wind patterns. **Use Visual Information** In what pattern do air cells circulate in the atmosphere?

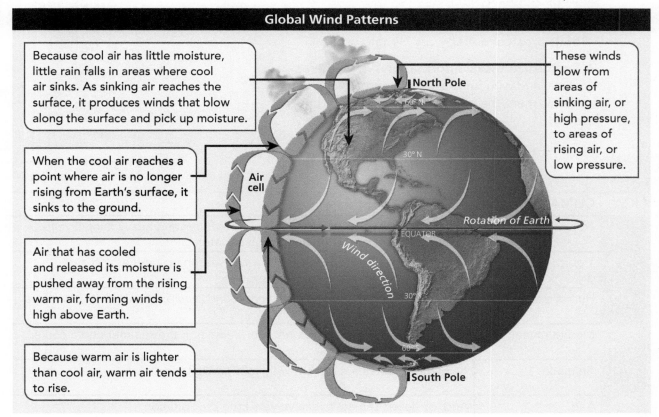

Global Wind Patterns

Because cool air has little moisture, little rain falls in areas where cool air sinks. As sinking air reaches the surface, it produces winds that blow along the surface and pick up moisture.

When the cool air reaches a point where air is no longer rising from Earth's surface, it sinks to the ground.

Air that has cooled and released its moisture is pushed away from the rising warm air, forming winds high above Earth.

Because warm air is lighter than cool air, warm air tends to rise.

These winds blow from areas of sinking air, or high pressure, to areas of rising air, or low pressure.

North Pole

60° N

30° N

Air cell

Wind direction

Rotation of Earth

EQUATOR

30°

60°

South Pole

Types of Climate

As you have learned, temperatures are warmest in the tropics and are coolest close to the poles. Precipitation is greatest near the Equator. These patterns of temperature and precipitation create world climate regions. Climate regions are areas that share a similar climate. There are three major groups of climate regions. Warm climates include

▲ Continental climates in North America can bring heavy snow in winter.

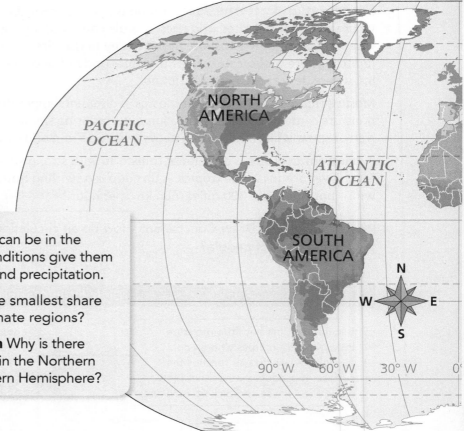

GEOGRAPHY SKILLS

Even areas separated by oceans can be in the same climate region because conditions give them similar patterns of temperature and precipitation.

1. **Place** Which continent has the smallest share of its area covered by dry climate regions?

2. **Synthesize Visual Information** Why is there more land with tundra climate in the Northern Hemisphere than in the Southern Hemisphere?

KEY	CLIMATE TYPE	DESCRIPTION
	Tropical wet	Tropical wet climates combine hot temperatures and heavy rainfall year-round. They are clustered around the Equator.
	Tropical wet and dry	Tropical wet and dry climates have a wet season in summer and a dry season in winter but are warm year-round.
	Humid subtropical	Humid subtropical climates have year-round precipitation with mild winters and hot summers.
	Mediterranean	Mediterranean climates have hot, dry weather in the summer and a cooler rainy season in the winter.
	Semiarid	Semiarid climates are dry but with light precipitation.
	Arid	Arid, or desert climates, receive very little precipitation.

tropical wet, tropical dry, and humid subtropical climates. Temperate climates include maritime, continental warm summer and continental cool summer, and Mediterranean. Dry and cold climates include the arid, semiarid, subarctic, tundra, and ice-cap climates.

READING CHECK **Draw Conclusions** In the winter, what kind of weather would you expect in a continental warm summer climate?

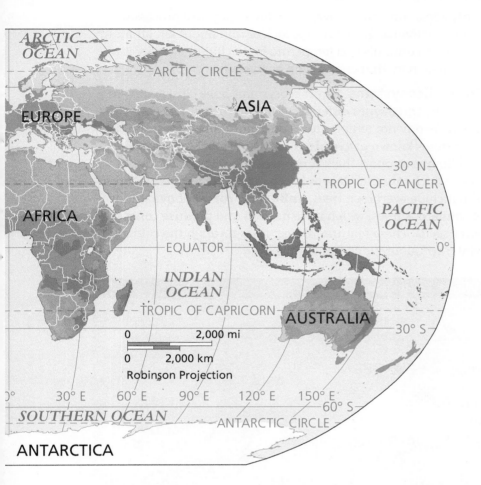

▼ Much of Australia is covered by arid or semiarid climates.

KEY	CLIMATE TYPE	DESCRIPTION
	Maritime	Maritime climates are wet year-round, with mild winters and cool summers. They exist where moist winds blow onshore.
	Continental warm summer	Continental warm summer climates have year-round precipitation; warm summers; and cold, snowy winters.
	Continental cool summer	Continental cool summer climates also have year-round precipitation, but they have generally lower temperatures.
	Subarctic	Subarctic climates have limited precipitation, cool summers, and very cold winters.
	Tundra	Tundra climates have cool summers and bitterly cold, dry winters.
	Ice cap	Ice-cap climates near the poles are bitterly cold and dry year-round.

Biomes and Ecosystems

Regions on Earth that are made up of similar communities of plants and animals are called **biomes**. An **ecosystem** is a group of plants and animals that depend on one another and their environment for survival. Biomes may contain a variety of ecosystems. However, biomes are also sometimes called ecosystems. There are three types of ecosystems: forest, grassland, and cold climate types.

Ecosystems can change over time due to physical processes or human activities. For example, lack of rain might kill off many plants and animals in a temperate forest. Building a city is a human activity that changes an ecosystem.

Forest Ecosystems Forest ecosystems have closely growing trees. The three types differ according to the climate zone they are in. Steady hot temperatures and moist air support the rich ecosystems known as **tropical rain forests**. Moist temperate climates support thick **temperate forests** of deciduous tress, which lose their leaves in the fall. Some temperate forests also include evergreen trees. **Subarctic forests** have stands of coniferous trees, which have needles and produce cones to carry seeds. These features protect trees through the cold, dry winters of subarctic climates.

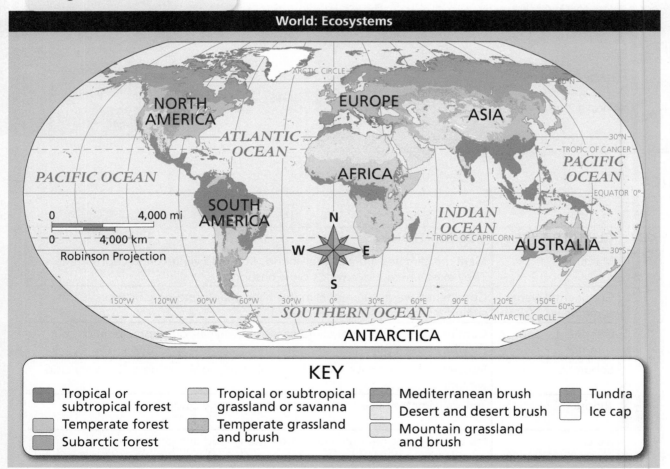

World: Ecosystems

KEY

- Tropical or subtropical forest
- Temperate forest
- Subarctic forest
- Tropical or subtropical grassland or savanna
- Temperate grassland and brush
- Mediterranean brush
- Desert and desert brush
- Mountain grassland and brush
- Tundra
- Ice cap

Grassland Ecosystems Five ecosystems have mainly grasslands and brush. Grasslands are large areas covered by grasses. Brush includes bushes, shrubs, and low-lying plants. As with the forests, these types of ecosystems depend on their climate.

Tropical or subtropical grassland or savanna is found in tropical areas with dry seasons. A savanna is a park-like landscape of grasslands with scattered trees that can survive dry spells. **Temperate grassland and brush** is an ecosystem of vast grasslands that cover regions that get more rain than deserts but too little to support forests. The **Mediterranean brush** ecosystem is found in Mediterranean climates. They have low bushes that have to hold water from winter rains to survive hot, dry summers. The **desert and desert brush** ecosystem is found in dry semiarid areas and deserts with some rain. These ecosystems support low-lying desert plants that need little water and can live in extreme temperatures. The driest desert areas have little or no plant life. In **mountain grassland and brush** regions, vegetation depends on elevation, since temperatures drop as altitude increases.

Cold Climate Ecosystems The third group of ecosystems is based on the cold climates at and near the poles. Cold ecosystems include the tundra and areas around the poles. These polar regions are marked by ice caps.

The **tundra** is an area of cold climate and low-lying plants. Here, grasses grow and low shrubs bloom during brief, cool summers. Animals of the tundra can survive the cold temperatures and scarce food. The **ice cap** ecosystem is found around the poles, where extreme cold makes life impossible for plants and most animals.

☑ READING CHECK **Identify Implied Main Ideas** How do climate differences affect plant and animal life?

Quick Activity

What's the correct ecosystem for different plants and animals? Go to your ▱ Active Journal for an activity that leads to placing them correctly.

☑ Lesson Check

Practice Vocabulary

1. **Summarize** What are the three most important factors that influence **climate**?

2. **Compare and Contrast** How do temperatures in the **tropics** differ from temperatures in the **temperate zones**?

Critical Thinking and Writing

3. **Sequence** Rank these ecosystems from most to least precipitation: temperate forest, tropical grassland, and Mediterranean brush.

4. **Classify and Categorize** How is today's weather related to your region's climate?

5. **Draw Inferences** Considering the amount of moisture in cool air, predict the level of precipitation in a tundra climate.

6. **Draw Conclusions** How does altitude affect temperature in different latitudes?

7. **Writing Workshop: Gather Evidence** Write notes in your ▱ Active Journal describing an experience with the climate or ecosystem where you live and how it affected you.

People and the Environment

GET READY TO READ

START UP
Study the photograph. How have people interacted with the environment in the place shown here?

GUIDING QUESTIONS
- How do people depend on the environment and either harm or protect it?
- What are the causes and effects of population growth, movement by people, and urbanization?

TAKE NOTES
Literacy Skills: Draw Conclusions
Use the graphic organizer in your 📙 Active Journal to take notes as you read the lesson.

PRACTICE VOCABULARY
Use the vocabulary activity in your 📙 Active Journal to practice the vocabulary words.

Vocabulary

natural resource   emigrate
fossil fuel   push factor
industrialization   pull factor
deforestation   urbanization
biodiversity

Academic Vocabulary

impact
lifestyle

The climate where you live affects your life. Your environment affects you in other ways, too. This works in both directions. The actions that people take have an effect on the environment as well.

Environment and Resources
People depend on their natural environment to survive. We need the environment to provide energy, water, food, and other materials. In prehistoric times, people lived in areas where they could hunt, gather food, and find fresh water. Later, people settled where they found pasture for their livestock or fertile soils and sufficient water for farming. Today, rapid transportation and other technologies allow people to be less dependent on their immediate environment. However, people still need access to resources.

Renewable and Nonrenewable Resources
Water is one example of a **natural resource,** or a useful material found in the environment. People depend on many kinds of natural resources. These resources can be divided into two types: renewable and nonrenewable resources.

A renewable resource is a resource that natural forces or people can replace in a relatively short time. Examples of renewable resources include water, plants, and animals. All of these resources can be replaced over time if they are used wisely. For example, if you cut down a tree, you can plant another in its place.

A nonrenewable resource is a resource that cannot be replaced, or can be replaced only over millions of years. Nonrenewable resources include non-living things such as minerals, metal ores, and fossil fuels. **Fossil fuels** are formed over millions of years from the remains of plants and animals. Coal, natural gas, and petroleum are fossil fuels. When nonrenewable resources such as fossil fuels are used up, they are gone.

Energy Resources Some sources of energy, such as wind and sunlight, are renewable. Today, we mostly rely on nonrenewable energy resources such as coal and petroleum. Because these sources are nonrenewable, Earth will eventually run out of them.

> ☑ READING CHECK Identify Main Ideas How are renewable and nonrenewable resources formed?

Land Use

The ways people use land depend on both culture and the natural environment. In many regions, land use has changed over time.

Reasons for Land Use How people use land depends partly on the features of the land itself. For example, people living in temperate climates with fertile soil may use the land mainly for farming. People in arctic areas may use land mainly for hunting.

INTERACTIVE

Oil: Long to Form, Quick to Use

Analyze Charts
This chart compares renewable and nonrenewable resources. **Classify and Categorize** Which of the resources listed here cannot be replaced?

Major Natural Resources

RESOURCE	TYPE	FORMATION	MAJOR USES
Soil	Renewable	Formed slowly from rocks and organic material through natural processes	Agriculture
Water	Renewable	Renewed through the water cycle	Drinking, agriculture, washing, transportation
Plants	Renewable	Usually grow from seeds; require water and sunlight	Food, lumber, clothing, paper
Animals	Renewable	Formed through natural reproduction; require water and food	Food, agricultural labor, transportation, clothing
Fossil fuels	Nonrenewable	Formed over millions of years from plant and animal material	Energy, plastics, chemicals
Minerals	Nonrenewable	Formed over millions of years through natural geologic processes	Automobile parts, electronics, and many other human-made products

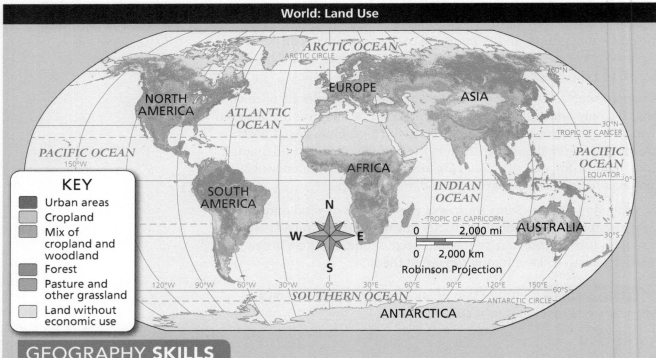

World: Land Use

KEY
- Urban areas
- Cropland
- Mix of cropland and woodland
- Forest
- Pasture and other grassland
- Land without economic use

0 — 2,000 mi
0 — 2,000 km
Robinson Projection

GEOGRAPHY SKILLS

This map shows how people use land in different regions.

1. **Region** Which areas on this map are all but unused?

2. **Infer** In which category of land use would you expect cattle ranches?

Quest CONNECTIONS

How does the way people use land affect the environment? Record your ideas in your ⬛ Active Journal.

Even in similar environments, however, people may use land differently because they have different customs and ways of life. For example, a wetland in a developing country might be converted to farmland. A wetland in a developed country might be filled in to create a shopping mall.

Changes in Land Use Land use can change over time. For example, colonization has led to many changes in land use. Colonization is the movement of new settlers to an area. When settlers bring a different culture to a region, they may change its landscape. For example, many European colonists settled in the Americas. Clearing land for their farms led to dramatic changes in land use.

Since the 1800s, industrialization has changed landscapes in many countries. **Industrialization** is the development of machine-powered production and manufacturing. When industrialization took place, large cities grew up around factories. Technology, such as machines for clearing land and building roads, has made it easier for people to change their environment. This change has allowed the growth of suburbs. A suburb is a residential area on the edge of a city or large town.

In the United States and some other countries, most people live in cities or suburban areas. Although cities and suburbs cover a relatively small area, they are an important use of land. Land uses covering large areas include cropland, forests, and grassland.

☑ **READING CHECK** **Draw Conclusions** How have people adapted to and changed the environment?

What Impact Do People Have on the Environment?

All people need food, water, clothing, and shelter. To meet these needs, people have to use materials from their environment. By using resources, people have **impacts** on the environment in their daily lives.

Extracting Resources People extract, or remove, many kinds of natural resources from the environment. For example, to get wood for building houses, people cut down trees.

Extracting resources can harm ecosystems and the environment. For example, cutting down too many trees can cause deforestation. **Deforestation** is the loss of forest cover in a region. Animals that live in the forest may suffer as a result. Drilling oil wells and transporting oil can lead to oil spills, which harm the land and water. Deforestation and producing oil can also reduce biodiversity. **Biodiversity** is the number of types of living things in a region or ecosystem.

Other Impacts People also affect the environment by growing food or producing goods and services. For example, when land is plowed, soil is loosened and can easily wash away when rain falls.

People's activities can also produce pollution, or waste that makes the air, soil, or water less clean. For example, many farmers use chemicals called fertilizers and pesticides to help plants grow and to kill pests. These chemicals can help farmers produce more food. They can also harm the environment by causing pollution.

Pollution is a spillover. A spillover is an effect on someone or something not involved in an activity that brought about that effect. For example, air pollution affects everyone who breathes the polluted air, even people who did not cause the pollution. Some types of air pollution are produced locally and are spread by winds to other parts of the world. When air pollution crosses state or national borders, governments must work together to try to reach a solution.

Finding the Best Solution People try to increase the positive and decrease the negative effects of using resources. For example, using a resource might lead to economic growth but also create dangerous pollution. Working together, people, governments, and businesses can try to use resources wisely.

Advances in technology can also help protect resources and the environment. One way of protecting the environment is for people to use public transportation instead of private cars. Buses and trains burn less fuel and create less air pollution per passenger than do cars. People can also use clean energy sources, such as solar power and wind power. They are considered clean energy sources because they do not pollute the air.

✓**READING CHECK** **Draw Conclusions** How might future uses of technology affect Earth?

Academic Vocabulary
impact • *n.*, an effect

Analyze Images
Deforestation occurs when large tracts of forest are cut down. **Draw Conclusions** Why does deforestation reduce biodiversity?

Population

Today, the world's population is more than 7 billion. When people first began farming around 12,000 years ago, it was fewer than 10 million. Earth's population grew slowly, eventually reaching 1 billion, or 1,000 million, by 1800. Since then, better food production, healthier **lifestyles**, and better healthcare have caused a population boom.

Measuring Growth Demographers are scientists who study human populations. They measure the rate at which a population is growing. To do this, demographers compare birth rates and death rates. The birth rate is the number of live births per 1,000 people in a year. The death rate is the number of deaths per 1,000 people in a year. When the birth rate is higher than the death rate, a population tends to grow. Population can also change when people move into or out of a region.

Causes of Growth Until about two hundred years ago, the global birth rate was only slightly higher than the death rate. As a result, the population grew slowly. Then came the Industrial Revolution, which brought many changes.

Improvements in food production increased the food supply and made food healthier. Living conditions improved. Better medical care saved many lives. These and other changes led to a much lower death rate in most regions. By 1950, the world's population had begun to soar.

Analyze Graphs Human population has increased dramatically in the past 200 years and is expected to continue to grow. **Use Visual Information** How many people are there expected to be in 2100?

Effects of Growth Population growth can have positive effects. For example, a growing population can produce and consume more goods and services. This can improve a country's standard of living. However, rapid population growth can also cause problems. The population can grow faster than the supply of food, water, medicine, and other resources, putting a strain on those resources.

World Population, 1–2100

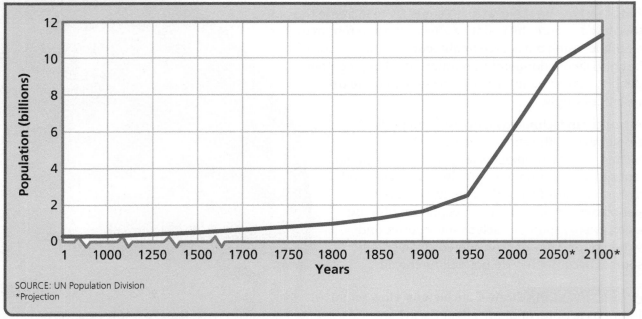

SOURCE: UN Population Division
*Projection

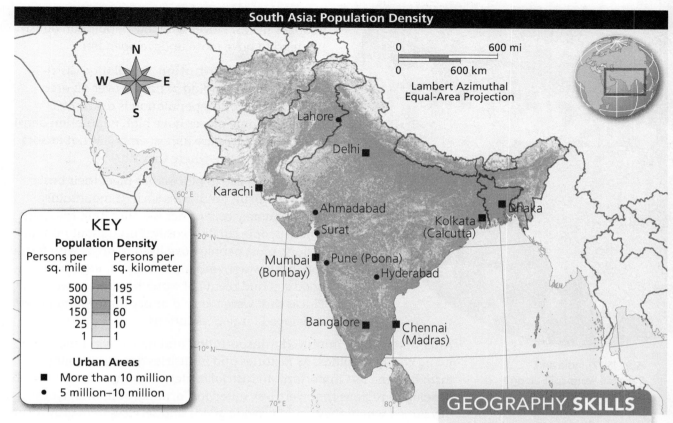

South Asia: Population Density

KEY

Population Density

Persons per sq. mile	Persons per sq. kilometer
500	195
300	115
150	60
25	10
1	1

Urban Areas

■ More than 10 million

● 5 million–10 million

Lambert Azimuthal Equal-Area Projection

The problems caused by rapid population growth are greatest in poor developing countries. A lack of clean food and water can lead to widespread starvation and disease. In these places, the infant mortality rate—the number of infant deaths per 1,000 births—is high.

The environment often suffers from rapid population growth as well, as people use up resources to survive. With more people, pollution increases. People cut down forests for firewood or to clear land for farming. This can lead to desertification, or the spread of dry desert-like conditions, making it harder to grow enough food.

Population Density A country's population is the total number of people living within its borders. Geographers study a country's population to learn more about life in that country.

Population density is the number of people per unit of land area. It is expressed as the number of people per square mile or square kilometer. Population density gives us a way to describe how thickly settled an area is. It also lets us compare places of different sizes and populations. The density figure for any country is an average. Population density can vary greatly from one part of a country to another. Some areas may be less suitable for large populations.

The more people there are per square mile, the more crowded a place is. Cities with high population densities tend to have crowded housing.

GEOGRAPHY SKILLS

A population density map shows where people are concentrated by representing the number of people living in a unit of area.

1. **Place** Which areas on the map have the highest population density?

2. **Synthesize Visual Information** Compare this map to the climate map in Lesson 3. Why is population density lower in the western part of this region?

▲ In 1947, India and Pakistan were split along religious lines. Many people moved to live in the country where most people followed the same religion.

These places require many resources to meet people's needs. Places with low population densities tend to have more undeveloped land.

Population Distribution Population distribution is the spreading of people over an area of land. The world's population is distributed unevenly. Some places have high population densities. Other places are almost empty. What factors lead people to live where they do?

People try to live in places that meet their basic needs. Difficult landforms such as mountains, and extremely cold or hot weather limit the areas where people can live easily. Throughout human history, most people have lived in areas with fertile soil, fresh water, and mild climates. Regions with good soil and plenty of water became crowded. Places that were too cold or dry for farming never developed large populations.

After about 1800, improved transportation and new ways of making a living changed things. As factories and industries grew, the ability to farm became less important. Industrial centers and large cities could develop in regions that were less suited for farming. Still, most cities developed where they could provide goods and services to nearby farming populations. Today, population tends to be highest in areas that were centers of early farming, industry, or trade.

✓ READING CHECK **Compare and Contrast** What are some good and bad effects of increasing population in an area?

Why Do People Move?

For thousands of years, people have migrated to new places. Migrating is moving as a group from one place to another. Scientists believe that more than 50,000 years ago, modern humans migrated for the first time from Africa to Asia. Over thousands of years, their descendants spread slowly across Asia and Europe. Some crossed from Asia to Australia and the Americas.

Forms of Migration People often migrate within a country. In modern times, this internal migration has largely been movement to cities and suburbs from the countryside. People generally migrate to cities to cities and suburbs so they can find jobs.

People also move from one country to another. When people leave their home country, they **emigrate,** which means to migrate out of a place. To enter a new country is to immigrate. Moving to another country can lead to big changes in a person's life. For example, people moving to a new country may have to learn a new language and new customs. Mass migration can greatly change a region's culture and society. Migration can also affect a region's government, economy, and environment.

Reasons for Migration People who migrate are often looking for a better life. They may move to escape poverty or mistreatment for their religion, ethnicity or sexual orientation. War or other conflict often forces people to migrate. These reasons for migration are called push factors. **Push factors** are reasons that push people to leave their home country. People forced to leave their homes are known as refugees.

Other reasons for migration are known as pull factors. **Pull factors** pull, or attract, people to new countries. One example of a pull factor is a supply of good jobs in a country that people migrate to.

People generally migrate because they choose to do so. For example, millions of Europeans chose to migrate to the United States during the 1800s and early 1900s. Some of these people were Irish, fleeing a shortage of food. Others were Jews escaping persecution, or mistreatment. Millions more have come from Asia and Latin America since then.

History is also full of involuntary migrations. For the most part, these involved the forced movement of enslaved people. In the late 1400s, European slave traders began buying and selling captured Africans. They shipped most of these enslaved people to the Americas. As many as 10 million enslaved Africans were forced to migrate to the Americas.

☑ READING CHECK **Identify Supporting Details** What are some of the reasons that cause people to migrate from one place to another?

Urbanization

In many parts of the world, people are migrating to urban areas from rural areas. Urban areas are cities. Rural areas are settlements in the country. For example, many people living in rural China have moved to cities in search of jobs in recent years. The movement of people from rural areas to urban areas is called **urbanization**.

Analyze Graphs World urbanization has increased over time. **Synthesize Visual Information** How do the urban and rural populations expected in 2050 compare to those in 1950?

World Urbanization

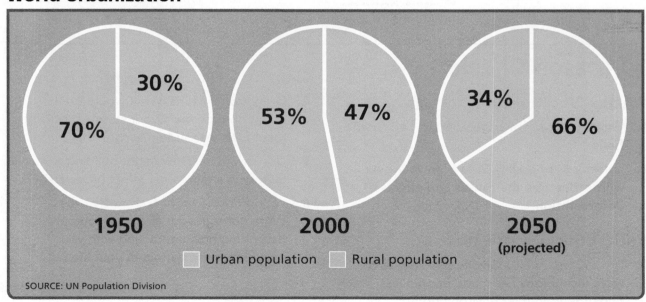

1950: 70% / 30%
2000: 53% / 47%
2050 (projected): 34% / 66%

☐ Urban population   ☐ Rural population

SOURCE: UN Population Division

The Shift From Rural to Urban

Over the last two hundred years or so, billions of people around the world have moved from rural areas to cities. Today, for the first time in history, more than half of the world's population live in cities and towns.

In Europe and North America, urbanization began around 1800 as modern industry developed. As a result, people moved to cities to fill new jobs. Today, urbanization is happening most quickly in Asia and Africa, where people are moving to cities for similar reasons.

Analyze Images Mexico's capital, Mexico City, has overcrowding that contributes to pollution. **Infer** Why might having a dense population lead to pollution?

Challenges of Urbanization Rapid urbanization has created challenges, especially in poor countries. In some cases, cities simply have more people than they can handle. These cities cannot provide the housing, jobs, schools, hospitals, and other services that people need. One result is the spread of slums, or poor, overcrowded urban neighborhoods. Most people in slums are unable to meet their basic needs, such as safe housing and clean water.

Urbanization can also create challenges in wealthy countries. Today, most large urban areas have a central core city. The core city has stores, office buildings, government buildings, and some housing. In the United States, most people live in the suburbs surrounding core cities. As U.S. urban areas grow, so does suburban sprawl. Suburban sprawl is the spread of suburbs away from the core city.

Because most people in suburbs use cars for transportation, suburban sprawl can increase pollution and energy use. Today, many towns and cities are working to limit sprawl.

✓ READING CHECK **Identify Main Ideas** What are some causes of urbanization?

☑ Lesson Check

Practice Vocabulary

1. **Identify Supporting Details** List two **fossil fuels**.

2. **Identify Supporting Details** In your own words, describe the causes and effects of **deforestation**.

Critical Thinking and Writing

3. **Draw Conclusions** Give two examples of ways technology has made people less dependent on their environment.

4. **Draw Conclusions** What would be the effect on daily life if your state's supply of fossil fuels was suddenly cut in half?

5. **Use Evidence** How might building a factory in a rain forest affect biodiversity?

6. **Writing Workshop: Gather Evidence** Write notes in your ▰ Active Journal describing how interacting with your environment has affected your life.

Culture and Society

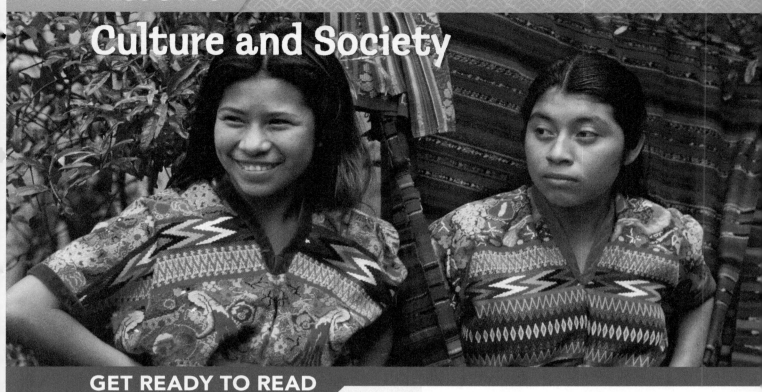

GET READY TO READ

START UP

Study the photograph of these Guatemalan women wearing the traditional clothing of their Mayan culture. How does clothing reflect culture?

GUIDING QUESTIONS

- How are societies structured?
- How do languages, religion, and the arts express culture?
- How do cultures change?

TAKE NOTES

Literacy Skills: Use Evidence

Use the graphic organizer in your ▣ Active Journal to take notes as you read the lesson.

PRACTICE VOCABULARY

Use the vocabulary activity in your ▣ Active Journal to practice the vocabulary words.

Vocabulary	Academic Vocabulary
culture	unify
society	negative
social structure	
social class	
cultural diffusion	
standard of living	

People live in groups, and those groups have a deep and lasting influence on members' lives. That influence comes from the language, religion, and customs of the group. It also comes from the way relationships within the group are organized.

What Is Culture?

All people have the same basic needs and wants, such as food, clothing, and shelter. But different cultures respond to those needs and wants in different ways. A **culture** is the beliefs, customs, practices, and behaviors of a particular nation or group of people.

Features of Culture Features that make up a culture are known as cultural traits. Cultural traits include language, laws, religion, values, food, clothing, and many other customs. Children learn cultural traits from their parents and other adults. People also learn cultural traits from the mass media and from organizations they belong to. Common cultural traits are called norms, which are behaviors that are considered normal in a particular society.

Analyze Images This man is tending rice in Bali, Indonesia. Rice is a common food in Balinese culture. **Use Visual Information** What other features of Balinese culture can you see in the photograph?

Some cultural traits remain constant over many years. But culture can change over time as people adopt new cultural traits. For example, Americans dress differently today than they did 100 years ago.

Culture and Geography People can shape their environment by meeting their basic needs for food, clothing, and shelter. People of different cultures use the land in different ways. They build houses differently. They plant different crops and build settlements differently.

The environment can also shape culture. When people move from one place to another, their culture can change in response to new climates and land forms.

A single culture can dominate a region. A culture region is an area in which a single culture or cultural trait is dominant. Earth has thousands of different culture regions. Common traits that **unify** a culture region include shared religion or language. Culture regions are often different from political units. Occasionally, a culture region may cover an entire country. In Japan, for example, nearly everyone speaks the same language, eats the same foods, and follows the same customs. A country often includes more than one culture region.

Culture regions can also include several countries. For example, the Arab world forms a culture region in Southwest Asia and North Africa. Arab Muslims are the majority in many countries in these regions. They share the religion of Islam, the Arabic language, and other traits.

✅ READING CHECK **Draw Conclusions** Does every country form a single culture region? Explain.

Families and Societies

Culture, society, and family are all related. A **society** is a group of people with a shared culture who have organized themselves to meet their basic needs. Societies can be large or small. A group of a few dozen hunter-gatherers may be a society. So may a country of more than a billion people, such as India or China.

Kinds of Families The most basic unit of any society is the family. Family structures vary in different cultures. Two common family units are the nuclear family and the extended family. A nuclear family is a family that consists of parents and their children. An extended family includes parents, children, and other family members, such as grandparents, aunts, uncles, and cousins. In developing countries, it can be common for extended families to work or live together.

Academic Vocabulary
unify • *v.*, to bring together into one unit or group

Kinds of Societies Every society has a social structure. A **social structure** is a pattern of organized relationships among groups of people within a society. People interact with one another, with groups, and with institutions. For example, you probably attend a school. The teachers and other students are part of your social structure. You may also take part in a sports team or some other group. They would be part of your social structure as well. Workplaces are part of an adult's social structure.

People belong to different social groups. Sometimes they form social groups on purpose. For example, immigrants to a new city might form their own church, synagogue, or temple. This would allow them to carry on their religious traditions. But the religious center would likely become a social center as well. It would become a place where people of a certain culture could come together, meet others of their group, and share activities.

A group might not begin as a social group. Think of what happens when students join a team sport at school. At first, the students are a diverse collection of individuals. Over time, though, relationships develop among the players. As that takes place, the team becomes a social group and not just a collection of individuals.

Societies often organize members according to their social class. A **social class** is a group of people living in similar economic conditions. In modern societies, the main groupings are upper class, middle class, and lower class. A wealthy, highly educated investor would be part of the upper class. A poor, uneducated farm worker would be part of the lower class. In developed countries, such as the United States, most people are in the middle class.

☑ READING CHECK **Compare and Contrast** What is the difference between social structure and social class?

Analyze Images Many Americans are part of large, extended families. **Use Visual Information** What characteristics of this family make it an extended family?

Language

Cultures could not exist without language. The set of spoken sounds, written symbols, or hand gestures that is language makes it possible for people to communicate. Without language, people would not be able to share information or ideas. They could not pass on cultural traits to their children.

Languages often vary from one culture to another. Within a country, differences in language can keep people from distinct cultures apart and make it harder to unify the country. Language differences can also keep the people in different countries apart by preventing communication.

▼ American Indian languages are in the "Other" languages group on the map.

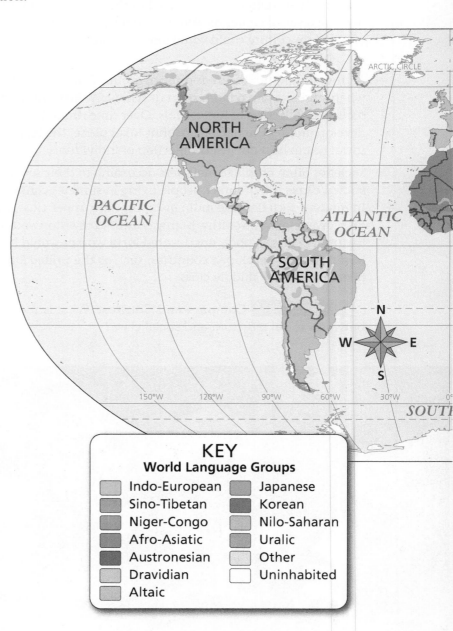

▲ These teens from Argentina in South America speak Spanish, which belongs to the Indo-European language group.

KEY
World Language Groups

- Indo-European
- Sino-Tibetan
- Niger-Congo
- Afro-Asiatic
- Austronesian
- Dravidian
- Altaic
- Japanese
- Korean
- Nilo-Saharan
- Uralic
- Other
- Uninhabited

People who speak different languages sometimes turn to a third language in order to communicate with each other. In modern times, English has often served as a common language for people around the world.

Languages that are similar form language groups, such as those shown on the map. The languages in a language group share a common ancestor. This ancestor was a language spoken so long ago that it gradually developed to become several related languages.

☑ READING CHECK **Identify Main Ideas** How are language and culture related?

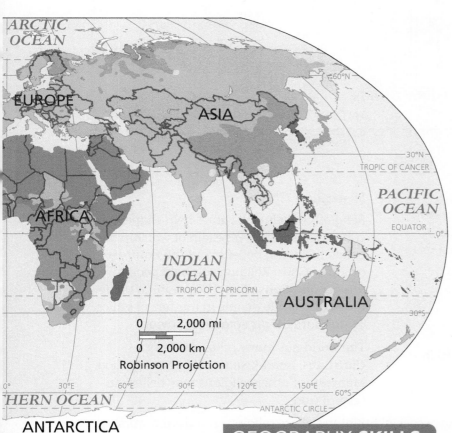

▲ These teens in China speak Mandarin, part of the Sino-Tibetan language group found in Asia.

GEOGRAPHY **SKILLS**

This map shows the distribution of the major language groups spoken around the world.

1. **Place** What language group dominates most of North and South America?

2. **Synthesize Visual Information** Which language group appears to have spread across the Indian Ocean?

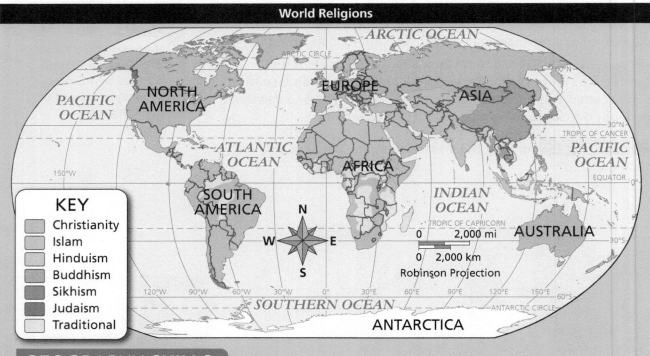

World Religions

KEY
- Christianity
- Islam
- Hinduism
- Buddhism
- Sikhism
- Judaism
- Traditional

GEOGRAPHY SKILLS

The map shows the most widely followed religions around the world. While the map shows the religions with the largest number of followers in each region, many regions have important religious minorities, and every major religion has followers worldwide.

1. **Region** Where is Islam the dominant religion?

2. **Draw Conclusions** Why do you think traditional religions are generally found in small areas?

Religion

Religious beliefs and values help shape cultures. Religion is a system of worship and belief, including belief about the nature of a God or Gods. Religion can help people answer questions about the meaning of life. It can also guide people in matters of ethics, or standards of acceptable behavior.

The world has many religions. Jews, Christians, and Muslims believe in one God. Members of other religions may believe in several Gods.

All religions have special buildings where religious rituals and worship take place. For Christianity, it is a church. In Judaism, that place is a synagogue. In Islam, it is a mosque. In Hinduism and Buddhism, it is a temple. Most religions have an institutional clergy, the body of people trained to carry out religious duties and lead ritual worship. Each religion also has its own prayers and rituals. Followers also observe special religious holidays.

Judaism Judaism is based on a belief in one God, whose spiritual and ethical teachings are recorded in the Hebrew Bible. It began in the Middle East around 2000 BCE. By 100 CE, Jews lived in Europe, Southwest Asia, and North Africa. The Jewish State of Israel was established in 1948. There are about 14 million Jews worldwide.

Christianity Christianity is based on the teachings of Jesus, who Christians believe was the son of God. The Christian Bible is their sacred text. Christianity began in Southwest Asia around 30 CE and spread first to Europe and Africa and later to the rest of the world. There are more than 2 billion Christians.

Islam Islam is based on the Quran, a sacred text. The Quran contains what Muslims believe is the word of God as revealed to Muhammad beginning in 610 CE. Islam spread across Southwest Asia and North Africa, then to the rest of the world. There are almost 2 billion Muslims.

Hinduism Hinduism evolved gradually over thousands of years in South Asia. It has several sacred texts. Hindus believe that everyone in the universe is part of a continuing cycle of birth, death, and rebirth. There are more than 1 billion Hindus.

Buddhism Buddhism is based on the teachings of Siddhartha Gautama, known as the Buddha, who was born in India in the 500s BCE. The Buddha's teachings include the search for enlightenment, or a true understanding of the nature of reality. There are somewhat less than 500 million Buddhists.

Sikhism Sikhism is based on the writings of several gurus, or prophets. Guru Nanak founded Sikhism about 1500 CE in South Asia. Sikhism's teachings include the cycle of rebirth and the search for enlightenment. There are about 24 million Sikhs.

Traditional Religions Traditional religions include thousands of distinct religions. These religions tend to be passed down by word of mouth instead of through sacred texts. Each has its own set of beliefs, some having to do with gods or spirits. Examples include many traditional African religions.

☑ READING CHECK **Identify Supporting Details** How does religion help shape a culture?

The Arts

The arts are an important aspect of culture. Works of art deal with topics or issues that are important to a society. Art can even change society. For example, books that describe poverty or environmental problems can lead to public support for solving those problems.

Art can also deal with universal themes, which are subjects or ideas that relate to people all over the world. For example, the paintings of Pablo Picasso, the songs of the Beatles, and the plays of William Shakespeare deal with the universal themes of love, death, justice, peace, and war. Artists convey their ideas through visual arts, architecture, works of literature, and music.

▼ A scene from a performance of a Chinese opera, an art form that includes music and drama

Visual Arts Art forms meant to be seen, such as painting, sculpture, and photography, are known as the visual arts. The visual arts can express emotions and spiritual ideas. They can also show us what life is like in other cultures and how people lived in the past. For example, a mosaic can show us how people lived during the Byzantine empire.

Architecture Architecture is the design and construction of buildings. A person who designs buildings is an architect. Architectural works can be important cultural symbols. Architecture can show us what a society values and how it uses its resources.

Literature Literature is written work such as fiction, poetry, or drama. These works convey universal themes by telling a story. Works of literature set in the past give us a look at how people lived in another time. For example, in *A Passage to India*, E.M. Forster takes the reader on a trip to India during the time of British rule in the early 1900s. In *Main Street*, Sinclair Lewis gives readers a glimpse of life in small-town America 100 years ago.

Literature can also tell us what ideas a society considers important. There are many examples of literature that have transcended the boundaries of societies to convey universal themes about justice. For instance, John Steinbeck described the unjust treatment of poor farm workers in California in the 1930s in *The Grapes of Wrath*.

Analyze Images Street musicians, like this group from Trinidad, Cuba, perform in cities and towns around the world. **Use Visual Information** Which instruments in this photo are familiar to you? Which instruments are not familiar?

Music Music is an art form that uses sound, usually produced by instruments or voices. Music varies widely in different societies and cultures. It also changes over time as tastes change. What one person considers beautiful music might be unpleasant noise to someone from a different place or time period. The music of the Beatles or the Rolling Stones may not be your taste. But listening to it tells you about people's tastes in the 1960s, when it was popular.

Music often conveys universal themes such as love or justice. The song "We Shall Overcome" was an important part of the American civil rights movement. Groups in many cultures have used the song in their own struggles for social justice.

Music also conveys religious themes. Most religions have sacred music that is sung to praise God. Many pieces of sacred music have crossed cultural boundaries and are cherished in many parts of the world.

☑ **READING CHECK** Summarize What are two ways in which the arts are related to society?

EXAMPLES OF CULTURAL DIFFUSION

FOOD

Tomatoes native to **South America**

Returned to **Americas** in dishes brought by European settlers

Reached **Europe** by cultural diffusion

LANGUAGE

Citrus Fruit was called a naramgi in Kannada, in **South Asia**

and finally an orange in English in **Europe**

then a naranj in Arabic in **Southwest Asia**

RELIGION

Buddhism formed in **India**

Brought from **East Asia** and **Southeast Asia** to the **United States**

Brought to **Tibet, China, Myanmar, Thailand, Cambodia**

Brought from **China** to **Japan, Korea, Vietnam**

Cultural Diffusion and Change

All cultures change over time. That is, their cultural traits change. Traits from one culture can spread to nearby cultures and influence them. The spread of cultural traits from one culture to another is called **cultural diffusion.** It can involve the spread of material culture, or objects. It can also mean the spread of ideas and values. Cultural traits often have spread through trade, migration, and war.

As traders move among different cultures, they carry with them features of their own culture, such as food or religious beliefs. Traders expose people to these new traits. In a similar way, migrants bring cultural traditions with them to their new homelands. For example, immigrants to the United States have brought with them foods, languages, music, ideas, and other cultural traits. Some of these traits have become part of American culture. War spreads culture traits as well. Just like traders, soldiers take their culture with them to new lands.

There are many positive effects of cultural diffusion. Useful ideas, products, or ways of doing things can move from one culture to another. The changes can improve people's lives. Exposure to ideas of equality and the chance to see women in nontraditional roles in entertainment media, for example, have helped improve the lives of women in some societies.

Yet there may also be **negative** effects of cultural diffusion. If customs change too quickly, people may feel that their culture is threatened. Some people today worry that rapid communication is creating a new global culture that threatens diversity. These people fear that the things that make people and cultures unique and interesting might disappear.

READING CHECK Identify Main Ideas Why do cultures change?

Analyze Diagrams The movements of foods, words, and religions are all examples of cultural diffusion. **Apply Concepts** What other example of cultural diffusion can you think of?

Academic Vocabulary
negative • *adj.,* unwanted; harmful

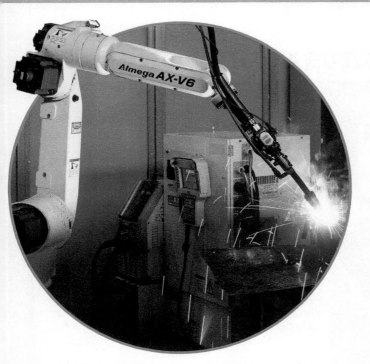

Science and Technology

Science and technology are important parts of culture. Science is the process of acquiring knowledge of the natural world through experiments. Technology is the way in which people use tools and machines. New technologies may rely on knowledge gained from science.

Technology can help spread culture, and improved communication has sped cultural change. The Internet, for example, has made instant communication common. Today, Americans can find out instantly what people in places such as Peru, India, or Japan are wearing, eating, or creating. If we like some of these traits, we may borrow them and make them a part of our culture. Traits of American culture have spread to other lands through American movies and television shows.

Analyze Images Robots like this one are now used in manufacturing. **Draw Conclusions** How might these machines affect standards of living?

Many advances in science and technology have transformed people's lives and raised their standard of living. **Standard of living** is the level of comfort enjoyed by a person or a society. Modern technology allows people to make more goods with less effort. Modern medicine can treat and prevent illnesses that were fatal in the past. More children attend school than in the past, and fewer people go hungry. Our homes are full of gadgets that make life easier. Our workplaces are safer. People live better and longer lives now than 100 years ago.

☑ READING CHECK **Draw Conclusions** How do you think technology might change culture in the future?

☑ Lesson Check

Practice Vocabulary

1. How does migration result in **cultural diffusion**?

2. What is the relationship between technology and **standard of living**?

Critical Thinking and Writing

3. **Draw Conclusions** As technology makes it easier for people to travel to different countries, how might world culture regions change?

4. **Infer** What other aspects of culture might link people in a country who speak different languages?

5. **Use Evidence** Give two examples of ways in which today's cultures are influenced by past cultures.

6. **Writing Workshop: Gather Evidence** Think about your culture and the culture of the people around you. Write ideas about your culture and other cultures with which you are familiar in your ▱ Active Journal.

LESSON 6
Economics Basics

GET READY TO READ

START UP

How does this image of a farmers' market show how our society meets its members' wants and needs?

GUIDING QUESTIONS

* What is economics?
* What are the effects of economic activity?
* How do economic systems differ?
* How can people make the most of their money?

TAKE NOTES

Literacy Skills: Compare and Contrast
Use the graphic organizer in your 📓 Active Journal to take notes as you read the lesson.

PRACTICE VOCABULARY

Use the vocabulary activity in your 📓 Active Journal to practice the vocabulary words.

Vocabulary		**Academic Vocabulary**
economics	producer	minimum
opportunity cost	consumer	principle
demand		
supply		

You are engaged in economic activity every day. When you put on clothes, you are wearing goods that someone made and that you or your family purchased. When you eat a meal, you are eating the food that someone produced. That food was sold to a string of businesses until it was sold to someone in your family. How these activities fit together is the subject of economics.

Economic Concepts

Economics is the study of how people meet their wants and needs. Societies must answer three basic economic questions:

* What goods and services should be produced?
* How should goods and services be produced?
* Who uses or consumes those goods and services?

Goods are physical products such as food, shirts, and cell phones. Services are helpful or valuable actions—often involving skill—offered by businesses such as hotels, restaurants, hospitals, and banks.

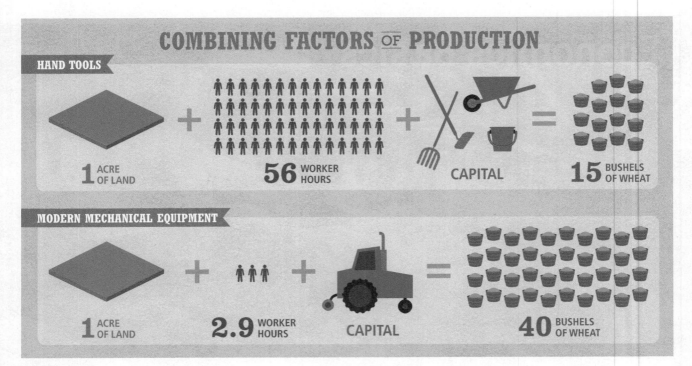

COMBINING FACTORS OF PRODUCTION

HAND TOOLS

1 ACRE OF LAND + 56 WORKER HOURS + CAPITAL = 15 BUSHELS OF WHEAT

MODERN MECHANICAL EQUIPMENT

1 ACRE OF LAND + 2.9 WORKER HOURS + CAPITAL = 40 BUSHELS OF WHEAT

Analyze Diagrams Factors of production can be combined in different ways. **Infer** Based on this diagram, how does using more capital change the amount produced and the need for labor?

People must use resources to make goods and services. Those resources are called factors of production. The three factors of production are land, labor, and capital. Land includes natural resources. Labor is work that people do. Capital includes money and human-made goods such as machinery and buildings.

There are many ways to combine factors of production to produce goods and services. Generally, though, increasing capital makes it possible to make more goods and services with the same amount of labor.

Making Choices There is no limit to the things that people want, but there are limits to what can be produced. The difference between wants and reality creates scarcity, which is having a limited quantity of resources to meet unlimited wants. Since people have limited money and time, they have to choose what they most want to use them on. The money or the time you spend on one thing cannot be spent on something else. Making a choice involves an **opportunity cost**, or the cost of what you have to give up.

Economics also involves demand and supply. **Demand** is the desire for a certain good or service. **Supply** is the ability and willingness to produce a good or service. Demand and supply are connected to price. If the demand for a product increases, its price will tend to rise. Suppliers may respond to the increased price by producing more. If its supply increases, the price will tend to fall.

The opposite is also true. If demand for a product falls, its price also falls. Suppliers may respond to the lower price by producing less. If supply falls, assuming demand remains the same, the price will rise.

INTERACTIVE

Answering the Three Basic Economic Questions

Making Goods and Services Economies bring together producers and consumers. **Producers** are people or businesses that make and sell goods or services. **Consumers** are people or businesses that buy, or consume, goods or services.

Producers try to win consumers' business by offering better products or services for lower prices than other producers in their industry. If they can sell more products or services, they usually increase production or expand their services. But producers will not make more products if the sale price is less than the marginal cost. Marginal cost is the cost of making one more unit of the product. Therefore, the marginal cost for the producer sets a **minimum** price for the product.

Businesses make products because of economic incentives. An incentive is something that encourages people to act in a certain way. The desire to earn money gives most producers an incentive to make and sell products or services. The incentive to save money leads most consumers to look for lower prices.

☑ READING CHECK **Infer** How might a change in the price of one good or service lead to changes in prices of other goods or services?

Economic Process

The economic process is complicated, but its basic idea is simple: Producers and consumers exchange goods and services in a market. A market is an organized social institution allowing producers and consumers to trade goods and services.

Throughout history, people have often engaged in barter, the trading of goods and services for other goods and services. Today, the means of exchange in a market is usually money. Modern governments issue money in the form of currency—either cash (paper bills and metal coins) or electronic units deposited in bank accounts.

Academic Vocabulary
minimum • *adj.,* lowest acceptable level

Analyze Graphs As the supply of apples increases, the price decreases. The opposite is true when the supply of apples decreases—the price increases. **Draw Conclusions** Given the demand and supply shown here, what price will match both supply and demand for apples?

Supply and Demand for Apples

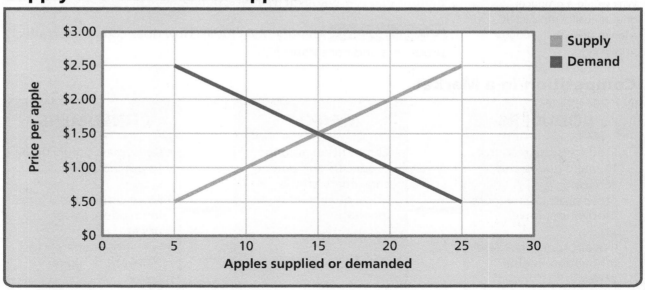

Types of Businesses Businesses can be grouped in different ways. One grouping is by industry. A farmer is in the agricultural industry. Companies that make cars, televisions, or cell phones are in the manufacturing industry. Warehouses may be part of the wholesale industry. Stores are part of the retail industry.

Businesses and the Economic Process Businesses want to make a profit. Profit is the money a company has left after subtracting its costs from the money it has received from its sales. To make a profit, companies try to reduce expenses and increase revenue. Revenue is the money earned by selling goods and services. The price of resources used to produce goods and services affects profit. If resources become more expensive, the cost of making goods with them will also increase. Businesses' profits will drop unless they can raise prices.

Companies can increase profit and revenue through specialization, the act of concentrating on a limited number of goods or activities. Specialization allows companies to use resources more efficiently and to increase production.

Companies' profits are affected by competition, which is the struggle among producers for consumers' money. If one company raises the price of its products, another company may sell similar goods for a lower price to win more business. Companies also use advertising to help increase demand for their products and to compete with other companies.

An economy grows when businesses produce and sell more goods and services. In a growing economy, prices may increase over time. This general increase in prices is called inflation. Prices may also fall. A general decline in prices is called deflation.

Economies do not keep growing forever. Eventually, economic activity falls for a time as production slows and consumers buy fewer goods and services. This lack of demand for goods and services can lead to increased unemployment. A decline in production over six or more months in a row is known as a recession.

☑ READING CHECK **Identify Main Ideas** How does competition affect producers and consumers?

Analyze Diagrams
Competition shapes interaction among producers, buyers, and sellers. **Draw Conclusions** Why would a producer offer a quality product at a lower price than another producer?

Competition in a Market

PRODUCERS	MARKET	CONSUMERS
• Producers use resources to make goods and services. • More producers = more innovation, lower prices. • Fewer producers = less innovation, higher prices.	• Competition among producers and among consumers affects price, quality, and innovation.	• Consumers use income to purchase goods and services. • More consumers = more innovation, lower prices. • Fewer consumers = less innovation, higher prices.

Economic Systems

Each society's economic system determines how people make and distribute goods and services. There are four types of economic systems: traditional, market, command, and mixed. The roles of individuals, businesses, and government vary in each system. Economic goals and incentives can also vary.

Traditional Economy A traditional economy is an economy in which people make economic decisions based on their group's customs and values. They usually satisfy their needs and wants through hunting or farming, as their ancestors did. People in traditional economies usually do not want to change their basic way of life.

This static nature of the economy is one disadvantage of traditional economies. People do not usually have a high standard of living. Advantages include the lack of waste associated with this economy and the knowledge of what one's role is within the society. Today, traditional economies are not common.

Market Economy A market economy is an economy in which individual consumers and producers make economic decisions. This type of economy is also called capitalism. Market economies are based on the **principles** of freedom, competition, and profit. Market economies encourage people to establish new businesses by giving them economic freedom. They are free to do what they want, within the law, and to earn as much profit as they can.

Market economies have many benefits. Because people own their own businesses, they have a stake in the businesses' success. That stake makes them highly motivated to find new, better, or faster ways of doing things. In this way, market economies encourage technological innovation and efficiency. Producers focus on making the products that consumers want as inexpensively as possible. They offer those products at prices that consumers are willing to pay.

However, like all economic systems, the market economy does have downsides. It can encourage the growth of huge companies that have little competition and can therefore dictate high prices for their products. It also may result in an unequal distribution of income, leaving some people very rich and some very poor. In addition, some services, such as national defense or police protection, may not function well under private ownership. That is because it would be difficult for businesses to get all members of society to share in the cost of these services.

Command Economy A command economy is an economy in which the central government makes all economic decisions. This kind of system is also called a centrally planned economy. In a command economy, individual consumers and producers do not make basic economic decisions.

Analyze Images Market economies encourage people to start new businesses. **Identify Main Ideas** What incentive drives people to start a new business?

Academic Vocabulary
principle • *n.*, basic value

 INTERACTIVE

Examining Different Economic Systems

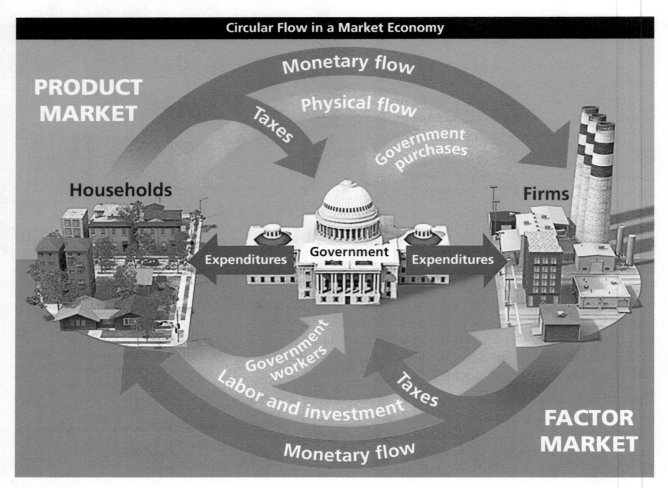

Circular Flow in a Market Economy

PRODUCT MARKET

Monetary flow

Physical flow

Taxes

Government purchases

Households

Expenditures

Government

Expenditures

Firms

Government workers

Labor and investment

Taxes

Monetary flow

FACTOR MARKET

Analyze Diagrams This diagram shows the circular flows of economic activity in a mixed economy. **Infer** What are examples of the flow of money from households to firms and the physical flow from firms to households?

This lack of economic freedom is one disadvantage of command economies. Another disadvantage is lack of competition and lack of incentives motivating workers and managers. Why should they work hard when they do not own the business and have little stake in its success?

A command economy does have some advantages. There is little unemployment because the government makes sure everyone has a job. Also, the social welfare of the public may be valued more than profit. Income tends to be more evenly shared.

Mixed Economy In reality, pure market and pure command economies do not exist. Most societies have mixed economies, with varying degrees of government control. A mixed economy combines elements of traditional, market, and command economic systems.

An example of a mixed economy is socialism. In socialism, some businesses are controlled by the state or worker cooperatives. However, some goods and services are distributed through individual decisions in a market. A socialist government aims to level the extremes of wealth between the rich and poor. It provides many welfare benefits, ensuring that the poor and disabled are cared for. One disadvantage of socialism is the need for higher taxes to pay for these services. Business owners do not gain the full reward of their hard work because of these taxes.

Countries such as North Korea and Cuba have mixed economies that are close to pure command economies. In these countries, government owns and controls most businesses and makes most economic decisions.

Countries such as the United States and Australia have mixed economies that are closer to pure market economies. In these countries, most economic decisions are made by individuals and businesses. The government makes some economic decisions, however. For example, government passes laws to protect consumers' rights. Government spending and taxation provide jobs and services and influence economic growth.

✓ READING CHECK Identify Main Ideas What are the differences among traditional, command, and market economies?

Personal Finance

Income is the money that people receive from the work they do or the money they save or invest. It is the main resource that people use to meet their needs and wants. Like all resources, income is limited. But people's needs and wants are unlimited. For that reason, people need to make choices as they manage their income.

Budgeting and Saving A key tool in money management is a budget. A budget is a plan that shows income and expenses over a period of time.

▼ A teen earns some money babysitting to have resources to meet her wants.

Analyze Images People put money in bank accounts because they are safe and so they can easily use the money to make purchases. **Identify Main Ideas** What incentive may banks offer to persuade people to deposit their money?

In a budget, income should be equal to or greater than expenses. A budget should also include money reserved for saving. Saving is the act of setting aside money for future use. Many people save by putting their money in a bank. A bank is a business that keeps money, makes loans, and offers other financial services.

Many people who save money in banks do so using checking or savings accounts. Banks may pay interest on money deposited in these accounts. Interest is the price paid for using someone else's money. The interest that banks pay is an incentive for people to save money.

Credit Banks use deposits to make loans to people and businesses. These loans help people buy houses or make other large purchases. They help businesses get started or grow. As a result, banks are a big part of economic growth.

Loans are a form of credit. Credit is an arrangement in which a buyer can borrow to purchase something and pay for it later, such as by using a credit card. Credit helps consumers and business buy goods and services that they could not buy otherwise. Credit has a cost, however. Banks charge interest on the money they lend to people and businesses. As a result, it costs more for a consumer to purchase a good using credit than to pay cash for the good at the time of purchase. The availability of loans and credit depends on supply and demand.

READING CHECK Identify Supporting Details What is the cost of credit, and what impact does it have on a consumer's spending?

☑ Lesson Check

Practice Vocabulary

1. **Compare and Contrast** How do changes in **supply** and **demand** affect a price differently?

2. **Identify Supporting Details** What is **opportunity cost**?

Critical Thinking and Writing

3. **Identify Main Ideas** What are the three basic economic questions that all societies must answer?

4. **Compare and Contrast** What are the differences between a command economy and a market economy?

5. **Summarize** How do government policies affect free market economies such as the U.S. economy?

6. **Draw Conclusions** How does a budget help people set aside money for saving?

7. **Writing Workshop: Gather Evidence** In your ▱ Active Journal, write notes that describe experiences you have had with your local economy as a worker or consumer.

LESSON 7
Trade and Development

START UP

What does this photograph of the port of Los Angeles suggest about the importance of trade?

GUIDING QUESTIONS

- How and why does trade take place?
- Why are barriers sometimes placed on trade?
- How and why do countries seek economic development and higher productivity?

TAKE NOTES

Literacy Skills: Identify Cause and Effect

Use the graphic organizer in your 📓 Active Journal to take notes as you read the lesson.

PRACTICE VOCABULARY

Use the vocabulary activity in your 📓 Active Journal to practice the vocabulary words.

Vocabulary

trade
comparative advantage
trade barrier
tariff
free trade
development

developed country
developing country
gross domestic product (GDP)
productivity

Academic Vocabulary

domestic
foreign

No country can make everything it needs. In order to obtain the goods it cannot produce, it engages in trade. **Trade** is the exchange of goods and services. Countries try to promote trade so that their economies can grow and their people can live better lives.

Trade Basics

In the past, most people grew or hunted much of their own food. They made their own clothing. They built their own homes. Today, however, most people depend on others to supply goods and services. Our world is interdependent. That is, people and countries depend on one another for goods and services. No country has all the factors of production needed to supply its needs.

Resources are not distributed evenly. A country may be rich in some resources but lack others it needs. Different regions in the same country may also have different resources. The uneven distribution of resources promotes economic interdependence. People and countries depend on others to meet their needs. Scarcity of resources leads countries to trade.

Analyze Images Parts of the United States have fertile soil and climates suited to growing wheat. **Draw Conclusions** How can other countries benefit from the comparative advantage of the United States in wheat production?

⬤ **INTERACTIVE**

Identifying Resources and Specialization

Deciding What to Produce How does a society decide which products it should make and sell to other societies and which products it should buy through trade? A society must consider its comparative advantage. **Comparative advantage** is what a country is good at producing, or its ability to produce a product more efficiently than other products. Let's say a country can produce 10,000 cell phones or 100 televisions using the same resources. That country is better off concentrating on producing the cell phones because it can earn more by producing them. Another country can produce 2,000 televisions using the same resources it would need to make 1,000 cell phones. That second country has a comparative advantage in producing televisions.

In general, the economy of a society works best when the society specializes in producing the goods or services for which it has a comparative advantage. It uses the money it earns from selling the products it makes efficiently to buy products it cannot make in an efficient manner. This specialization makes trade possible.

Trade and Geography To get the products we need and want, we engage in trade. When individuals engage in trade, they do so because they gain from that trade. Trade benefits both the buyer and the seller.

Geographic location can give a country or region advantages in trade. For example, a region that is close to an ocean can more easily ship goods overseas. On the other hand, a manufacturing plant located far away from a market will need to add transportation costs to its products, making them higher in price. Countries that are near each other can trade at lower cost than those that are more distant. It costs less to move goods by truck between the United States and Canada than it does by truck, ship, and another truck between the United States and India.

Geography can affect trade in another way. When it is summer in the Northern Hemisphere, farms and orchards in the United States produce the fruit that Americans buy in stores. Those farms and orchards cannot grow these products in the winter, however. Winter in the Northern Hemisphere is summer in the Southern Hemisphere. Producers in Chile grow blueberries, grapes, and other fruit and ship them to the United States for sale. As a result, Americans can eat fresh fruit all year.

Types of Trade All of the buying and selling that takes place within a country is known as **domestic** trade. Domestic trade involves producers and consumers located inside the same country. When you go to the store to buy apples grown on a nearby farm, that is domestic trade.

Domestic producers and consumers can also engage in international trade, or trade with **foreign** producers and consumers. International trade involves exports and imports. Exports are goods and services produced within a country and sold outside its borders. Imports are goods and services sold in one country but produced in another.

International trade requires a system for exchanging different currencies. Consumers in a country use their country's currency to buy imported goods. The company that made those goods wants to be paid in the currency of its own country. A system must exist for exchanging these two currencies. This system is the international currency market. This market sets prices for each currency in terms of other currencies. Using the currency market, companies in the United States can trade with companies in other countries.

✅ **READING CHECK** **Identify Main Ideas** What are two ways in which geography affects the location of economic activities?

Academic Vocabulary
domestic • adj., taking place within a country
foreign • adj., coming from outside a country

Analyze Diagrams China and the United States trade with each other. **Use Evidence** How can you tell that trade between these two countries is not equal?

TRADE BETWEEN THE UNITED STATES AND CHINA

U.S. exports to China
$116 billion
China's rank among U.S. export destinations
3rd

U.S. imports from China
$482 billion
China's rank among U.S. import sources
1st

Sources: CIA World Factbook; U.S. Census Bureau

U.S. exports to China
Billions of U.S. dollars

Food (esp. soybeans)	$16.9 billion
Aircraft and parts	$15.4 billion
Machinery and equipment	$14.8 billion
Automobiles	$9.1 billion
Semiconductors	$6.0 billion

Chinese exports to the United States
Billions of U.S. dollars

Cell phones	$64.6 billion
Clothing	$45.9 billion
Computers	$43.8 billion
Computer equipment	$30.4 billion
Toys and games	$27.6 billion

Quest CONNECTIONS

What is the environmental impact of expanding trade? Record your findings in your Active Journal.

Trade Barriers and Free Trade

If imported goods are cheaper than domestic goods, consumers will usually buy more of them. These lower prices can harm domestic producers by reducing their sales. Governments sometimes try to protect domestic producers by enacting a trade barrier. A **trade barrier** is a government policy or restriction that limits international trade. The three types of trade barriers are tariffs, quotas, and embargoes. A **tariff** is a tax on imports or exports. A quota is a set limit on the number of units of a good that can be imported. An embargo is a ban on all trade with a country and thus differs from tariffs and quotas, which allow some trading to occur.

A tariff was one of the contributing causes of the Great Depression. The Great Depression was a severe economic downturn that affected countries around the world. It was a time of hardship, with many businesses closing and many workers losing their jobs. Aiming to protect U.S. workers from overseas competition, the federal government passed the Smoot-Hawley Tariff Act in 1930. The act was originally intended to protect farmers, but it was expanded to protect workers in a wide variety of industries. Tariff rates on imports reached historic highs. The problem was that these high U.S. tariffs angered the governments of other countries. They responded with similar high tariffs against U.S. exports. As a result, international trade decreased by 66 percent between 1929 and 1934. At a time when nations needed trade to boost their economies, the tariff wars encouraged ill will and likely lengthened the economic downturn.

As a result, many countries, including the United States, began working toward **free trade**, or the removal of trade barriers. In 1947, for example, the United States signed the General Agreement on Tariffs and Trade (GATT). The mission of GATT is to reduce tariffs and other trade barriers among its 153 member nations. The agreement underscores the dynamic relationship between U.S. trade policies and its free enterprise system—free trade gives consumers lower prices and more choices. It also helps U.S. producers sell products in other countries.

There are drawbacks to free trade, however. Domestic producers can suffer if consumers prefer cheaper imported goods. As a result, some U.S. workers may lose their jobs.

READING CHECK Identify Implied Main Ideas How do consumers benefit from free trade?

Analyze Graphs This graph shows the percentage of the world's population that lives in countries with different levels of income. **Infer** Which category includes the countries that have benefited least from trade?

World Population by Income

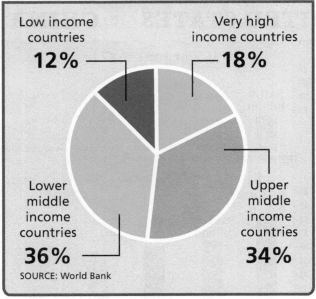

Low income countries **12%**

Very high income countries **18%**

Lower middle income countries **36%**

Upper middle income countries **34%**

SOURCE: World Bank

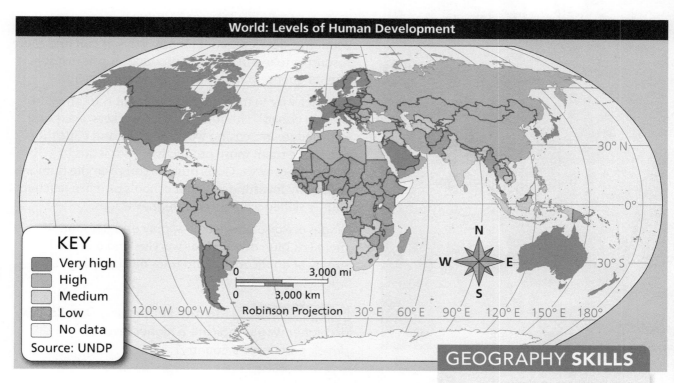

World: Levels of Human Development

KEY
- Very high
- High
- Medium
- Low
- No data

Source: UNDP

0   3,000 mi
0   3,000 km
Robinson Projection

Economic Development

Economists use the concept of development to talk about a country's economic well-being. **Development** is economic growth or an increase in living standards.

Measuring Economic Development When they study development, economists look at factors like people's education, literacy, and life expectancy. They also examine people's purchasing power, or their ability to buy goods and services. This gives clues to the general standard of living that the people of a country have. In high-income countries, workers earn relatively high pay for their work. As a result, they have high purchasing power and enjoy a high standard of living. In low-income countries, wages are poor. These workers have low purchasing power and a low standard of living.

A **developed country** is a country with a strong economy and a high standard of living, such as the United States or Japan. Only a small percentage of the world's countries are highly developed. Most nations are classified as **developing countries**. Developing countries, such as Haiti or Ethiopia, have less productive economies and lower standards of living.

Economists use gross domestic product to measure a country's economy. **Gross domestic product (GDP)** is the total value of all goods and services produced in a country in a year.

GEOGRAPHY SKILLS

Countries can be compared in development, which is measured in terms of their health, education, and standard of living.

1. **Region** On which continent is the level of development the lowest?

2. **Synthesize Visual Information** How is the information in this map related to the information in the chart World Population by Income?

 **INTERACTIVE**

Identifying Patterns of Development

Increasing Development A country can increase economic development in many ways. It can find more resources to use in creating products. It can invest in capital goods such as factories and equipment.

Another way to increase development is to invest in human capital. Human capital is workers' skills and knowledge. Increasing workers' skills and education can make them more productive. That leads to economic growth. Governments can promote human capital by investing in better schools or more teachers. Highly skilled workers earn higher wages.

Wages are also affected by supply and demand. If there is a high demand for workers and a limited supply of applicants, companies must pay higher wages to attract workers.

☑ READING CHECK **Identify Supporting Details** Why do higher wages indicate a higher level of development for a country?

Analyze Images When people like these students in India take classes to gain new skills, they are investing in their human capital. **Infer** What benefit do these students hope to gain?

Productivity and Growth

A country can develop by increasing **productivity**. Productivity is the amount of goods and services produced given the amount of resources used. A business that increases productivity can produce goods and services more efficiently.

Improved technology can boost productivity and lead to economic growth. For example, many workers now use computers to do tasks more quickly. However, it can be difficult for poor countries to afford new technology.

☑ READING CHECK **Identify Supporting Details** Why does higher productivity help countries develop?

☑ Lesson Check

Practice Vocabulary

1. What are **tariffs**, and why do governments sometimes use them?

2. How is **comparative advantage** related to trade?

3. Why do economists use **gross domestic product** to measure a country's economy?

Critical Thinking and Writing

4. **Identify Main Ideas** How does specialization encourage international trade and make countries interdependent?

5. **Draw Conclusions** Why do countries need a system for exchanging currencies?

6. **Identify Supporting Details** How can a society increase its level of development?

7. **Writing Workshop: Gather Evidence** Write ideas in your 📓 Active Journal about your experiences buying or using items made in another country.

Economic Data Sources

Data about the economies of different countries can help to explain how one country's economic system differs from others. Burundi, Kenya, Rwanda, Tanzania, and Uganda are neighbors in eastern Africa and in some ways are quite similar. Yet there are important differences between their economies, as shown in the chart and on the map.

▶ Coffee fields in Kenya

East African Economies

Country	GDP growth rate	Workforce in farming	Economic system
Burundi	2.95%	93.6%	Largely traditional
Kenya	5.47%	75%	Mixed; mainly market
Rwanda	7.04%	90%	Mixed; mainly market
Tanzania	6.84%	80%	Mixed; large government role
Uganda	5.0%	40%	Mixed; mainly market

SOURCE: CIA World Factbook

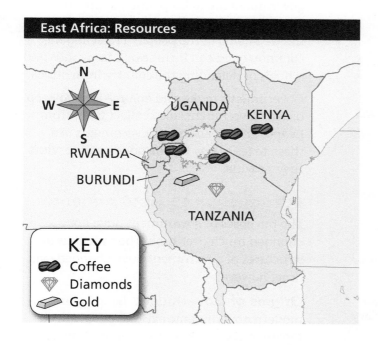

East Africa: Resources

KEY
- Coffee
- Diamonds
- Gold

Analyzing Geographic Sources

Cite specific evidence from either the map or the chart to support your answers.

1. **Use Visual Information** Based on the map, which country is likely to have the strongest economy? Why?

2. **Analyze Charts** Based on the chart, which country most likely has the weakest economy? Why?

LESSON 8
Government

IN GOD WE TRUST

GET READY TO READ

STARTUP
Look at the photo of a President speaking to the U.S. Congress. Write down three things that you want to learn about government.

GUIDING QUESTIONS
- What are the purposes of government?
- How do types of government differ?
- How are governments organized?
- Why do conflict and cooperation occur between countries?

TAKE NOTES
Literacy Skills: Classify and Categorize
Use the graphic organizer in your 📓 Active Journal to take notes as you read the lesson.

PRACTICE VOCABULARY
Use the vocabulary activity in your 📓 Active Journal to practice the vocabulary words.

Vocabulary

government	monarchy
constitution	unitary system
democracy	federal system
authoritarian government	

Academic Vocabulary

effective

inherit

A **government** is a group of people who have the power to make and enforce laws for a country or area. The basic purposes of government are to keep order, to provide services, and to protect the common good, or the well-being of the people. Protecting the common good can include building roads and schools or defending the country from attack.

Governments make and enforce laws to keep order. Governments also collect taxes from people and businesses. Governments use these taxes to pay for the goods and services they provide.

Introduction to Government
The purposes of government have not changed much over time. The functions and structures of government have changed over time, however.

Origins of Government Long before modern governments existed, people lived together in groups. These groups often had leaders who kept order and made decisions for the group. This arrangement was a simple form of government.

More complex governments first appeared in Southwest Asia more than 5,000 years ago. By that time, groups of people had settled down to farm land. Villages had grown into cities. People found that they needed an organized way to resolve problems and oversee tasks such as repairing irrigation canals and distributing food. They formed governments to manage those tasks.

Different types of government developed over time. In ancient Greece, for example, states centered on cities developed. In Athens, Greece, they progressed from rule by kings to a form of direct rule by the people. Later, the Romans created the republic, in which the people chose representatives to govern them. Like the Romans, the people who created the U.S. government made it a republic.

Powers of Government Today, most governments are based on a constitution. A **constitution** is a set of basic rules and principles for organizing and running a government. A constitution also identifies the powers of a government. Those powers are either limited or unlimited.

Limited government means that government actions are limited, or restricted, by law. Limited governments work to protect the common good and provide for people's needs. In 1689, the king and queen of England accepted limits to their power in the English Bill of Rights. It listed several rights that all England's people had and the government could not take away. In the United States, government actions are limited by the U.S. Constitution in order to protect people's individual freedoms.

Many of these freedoms are spelled out in the first ten amendments to the Constitution. These amendments are called the Bill of Rights. Generally, people in a limited government may gather freely, express their opinions, and work to change government policies.

Quest CONNECTIONS

What power does a government have to protect the environment? What are the limits on those powers? Explore your ideas in your 📓 Active Journal.

Analyze Images The senate of ancient Rome was part of the government of the first republic. **Compare and Contrast** How does a republic differ from rule by a king?

Unlimited government means that there are no **effective** limits on government actions. In an unlimited government, such as China's, a ruler or a small ruling group has the power to make all decisions for a country or society. Unlimited power can lead to tyranny, or the unjust use of power. Unlimited governments often do not protect citizens' basic rights. For example, they may censor, or restrict, citizens' access to the Internet and their ability to write or speak freely.

☑ **READING CHECK Compare and Contrast** How do limited and unlimited governments differ?

Forms of Government

Governments can control different kinds of areas. A state is a region that shares a common government. The first real states—called city-states—developed in Southwest Asia more than 5,000 years ago. A city-state is an independent state consisting of a city and the territory it controls. Later, some military leaders conquered large areas and ruled them as empires, which are states containing several countries.

Today, the world is divided into nation-states. These are states that are independent of other states. All nation-states have some common features. They have a specific territory with clearly defined borders. They have governments, laws, and authority over citizens.

Each nation-state has a government, but there are many different kinds of government. Each one has its own systems and functions. Throughout history, most nation-states were one of two types, autocracies or oligarchies. Autocracies are ruled by one person, typically a king or queen in the past. Oligarchies are governments in the hands of a small group of people. Today, however, many nation-states have some form of democracy, in which citizens hold political power.

▼ This election rally in France shows that citizens have a voice in a democracy.

Democracy **Democracy** is a form of government in which citizens hold political power. Citizens are the ultimate source of government power and authority in a democracy. In a direct democracy, citizens come together to pass laws and select leaders. In a representative democracy, citizens elect representatives to make government decisions. The powers of a democratic government are usually limited. The United States is an example of a representative democracy.

Authoritarian Government An **authoritarian government** is one in which all power is held by a single person or a small group. Autocracies and oligarchies in the past were often authoritarian. Government may control all aspects of life. Another form of authoritarian government is communism, a political and economic system in which government owns all property and makes all economic decisions. Cuba and North Korea have communist systems. The powers of an authoritarian government are unlimited. Authoritarian governments that are not led by a royal family are called dictatorships.

Monarchy A **monarchy** is a form of government in which the state is headed by a monarch. A monarch is typically a king or queen. The position is **inherited** by family members. Monarchies may be authoritarian or democratic. The powers of a monarchy can be limited or unlimited. Absolute monarchs rule with unlimited power over authoritarian governments. Monarchs in constitutional monarchies have powers that are limited by a constitution. Constitutional monarchies are often democracies. Saudi Arabia is an example of an authoritarian absolute monarchy. The United Kingdom is an example of a constitutional monarchy. It is also a democracy in which the monarch has very little power.

READING CHECK **Classify and Categorize** Which form of government relies most on its citizens?

Academic Vocabulary
inherit • *v.*, to receive something passed down from a family member

 **INTERACTIVE**

Forms of Government Among Countries of the World

THE THREE BRANCHES OF THE U.S. GOVERNMENT

Legislative Branch

- Passes laws
- Imposes taxes and decides how they will be used
- Has power to declare war
- Representatives (435) and senators (100) elected by state voters

Executive Branch

- Enforces laws
- Conducts foreign policy
- Commands armed forces
- President and Vice President chosen by Electoral College based on votes in each state

Judicial Branch

- Decides whether laws have been broken
- Judges whether laws or executive actions follow the Constitution
- U.S. Supreme Court (nine justices) named by President with Senate's approval

Analyze Charts The three branches of the U.S. government have distinct powers. **Identify Supporting Details** Which branch controls spending?

Government Structures

Countries distribute power between the central government and governments of smaller areas. We can learn more about a government by examining its structure and principles.

Systems of Government Governments can distribute power in three basic ways: the unitary system, the federal system, and the confederal system. In a **unitary system**, a central government makes all laws for the entire country. In a **federal system**, power is divided among central, regional, and local governments. Central governments are responsible for national affairs. Regional governments include state or provincial governments. Local governments include county, city, and town governments. In a confederal system, a group of independent states join together and give limited powers to a common government.

Most countries have a unitary system. The United States and some other countries have a federal system. The confederal system—also called a confederation—is rare.

Branches of Government Under the U.S. Constitution, power is divided among three branches of government: the legislative, executive, and judicial branches. This division is called separation of powers. The Constitution also establishes a system of checks and balances that limits each branch's power. Each branch has some power to check, or limit, the actions of the other branches.

Other countries may organize their branches in different ways. For example, the head of the U.S. executive branch is the President. In many countries with a parliament, the head of the executive branch is the prime minister. In this system, citizens do not choose the prime minister directly. Instead, the political party that has the most seats in the parliament chooses its leader as the prime minister.

Principles of Government Every government has basic principles that affect the way it serves its people. You can evaluate different government systems and functions by how well they work for the common good. Authoritarian governments may seek to control all aspects of society, even people's actions and beliefs. They often disregard individual rights. Most democratic governments act to protect individual rights and the common good.

In the United States, government follows basic democratic principles. For example, government follows the rule of law. That is, government powers are defined by laws that limit its actions. Also, government decides issues by majority rule. A law cannot pass unless the majority—most—of the representatives vote for it. At the same time, the majority may not take away the basic rights and freedoms of minority groups or individuals. In other words, government must balance majority rule with minority rights.

☑ READING CHECK Identify Supporting Details What are three key democratic principles?

Conflict and Cooperation

Every country has clearly defined territory and sovereignty over that territory. Sovereignty means supreme authority, or power. Every country also has a central government. The central government takes care of matters that affect the whole country. This includes dealing with other countries' governments.

▼ Two governments cooperate to achieve common goals. Individuals can also cooperate to achieve goals, like these volunteers working together to build a house.

Most countries have a set of goals for relations with other countries. Those goals are the country's foreign policy. A country's foreign policy reflects its values and interests. Interactions between governments can take the form of conflict or cooperation.

Conflict and War A country's foreign policy can lead to conflict with other countries. This conflict can come in the form of taking different sides on international issues or joining with other nations to try to block actions by another country's government. Conflict can also take the form of war, or the use of military force. Wars begin for many reasons. Some wars begin as conflicts over control of land or resources. Others result from religious disagreements, political revolutions, or conflict between ethnic or religious groups. Wars can lead to widespread death and destruction.

Cooperation Many people view the world as a global community in which people should cooperate to avoid conflict and help others. This cooperation may take the form of a treaty, a formal agreement between two or more countries. Some treaties are agreements to help defend other countries. Other treaties are agreements to limit the harmful effects of war. For example, the Geneva Conventions list rules for the proper treatment of wounded soldiers, prisoners, and civilians.

Countries also join together in various organizations. The United Nations (UN) is the largest international organization that works for peace. Nearly every country in the world belongs to the UN. Governments send representatives to the UN to engage in diplomacy. Diplomacy is managing relationships among countries through negotiation.

GEOGRAPHY SKILLS

The European Union is an organization of nearly 30 countries that cooperate in many ways, including a currency shared by most of them.

1. **Place** What is different about the United Kingdom?

2. **Classify and Categorize** Which member countries do not use the euro?

The European Union, 2017

KEY
Member
€ Uses common EU currency (euro)
*Member in 2017 but planned to leave EU

0   400 mi
0   400 km
Lambert Azimuthal Equal-Area projection

Governments work with one another to improve their countries' economies through trade agreements as well. International trade can provide new goods and markets. Trade agreements involving multiple countries have become common in recent years. For example, the European Union (EU) includes many nations of Europe and provides for free trade among those nations.

Governments also cooperate for reasons other than avoiding conflict. For example, governments often work with one another to improve public health and give humanitarian aid. The International Federation of Red Cross and Red Crescent Societies provides medical aid, food, and other relief services to victims of war or natural disasters. The World Health Organization fights disease, especially among the world's poor, by providing health information, medical training, and medicine. CARE International seeks to end world poverty through development and self-help.

Some global organizations cooperate to boost the economies of developing nations. The World Bank provides loans for projects aimed at promoting economic development. The International Monetary Fund (IMF) seeks to prevent and resolve financial crises by offering advice, information, and loans.

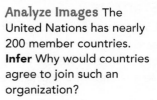

Analyze Images The United Nations has nearly 200 member countries. **Infer** Why would countries agree to join such an organization?

☑ READING CHECK **Summarize** How do governments resolve conflict and cooperate?

☑ Lesson Check

Practice Vocabulary

1. How are the **unitary system** and the **federal system** similar and different?

2. How does a **constitution** help promote limited government?

Critical Thinking and Writing

3. **Compare and Contrast** Who do you think is more likely to speak out against the government: a citizen in a limited government or a citizen in an unlimited government? Explain.

4. **Identify Implied Main Ideas** How might access to information about the government on the Internet differ between a democracy and a country with an authoritarian government?

5. **Classify and Categorize** What are the local, state, and national governments that have control over the community in which you live?

6. **Writing Workshop: Gather Evidence** Write ideas in your 📓 Active Journal about an interaction you have had with someone who works in your local government or a government agency. Think about the services that the worker provided.

Citizenship

GET READY TO READ

START UP

Look at the photograph of a naturalization ceremony in which people are becoming citizens of the United States. What do you think it means to be a citizen of the United States? Explain.

GUIDING QUESTIONS

- What are the rights and responsibilities of citizens?
- How has citizenship varied among nations and over time?

TAKE NOTES

Reading Skills: Identify Main Ideas
Use the graphic organizer in your 📗 Active Journal to take notes as you read the lesson.

PRACTICE VOCABULARY

Use the vocabulary activity in your 📗 Active Journal to practice the vocabulary words.

Vocabulary	Academic Vocabulary
citizen	ceremony
naturalization	significance
civic life	
democratization	

The United States is a representative democracy. In a democracy, all political power comes from citizens. A **citizen** is a legal member of a country. Being a citizen grants a person certain rights within that country. He or she also has certain responsibilities.

Citizenship in the United States

In the United States, most people become citizens by being born on U.S. territory. Immigrants to the United States can become citizens through a legal process known as **naturalization**.

Becoming a U.S. Citizen The requirements for becoming a naturalized citizen of the United States are fairly simple. In general, one must be at least 18 years old and must have been a legal permanent resident of the United States for at least five years. The rules also state that an applicant must be of "good moral character." For instance, he or she should not have a record of criminal activity. The applicant also must know how to read, write, and speak English. This requirement is relaxed in some cases, such as when an applicant is a citizen's elderly family member.

Someone hoping to be naturalized must also answer questions in an interview. Some of those questions test the person's knowledge of civics, which is the study of rights and duties of citizens.

The process for becoming a naturalized citizen includes a naturalization **ceremony**. At this ceremony, the applicant swears an oath of allegiance to the United States. He or she promises to support the Constitution and to serve in the U.S. armed forces if called upon to do so.

Academic Vocabulary

ceremony • *n.,* formal, structured event with legal or religious significance

Citizens' Rights and Responsibilities Americans have important rights and responsibilities that are essential elements of citizenship. Our basic rights are protected by the Bill of Rights, the first ten amendments to the U.S. Constitution. The Bill of Rights and other laws protect rights such as freedom of speech, freedom of religion, and freedom of the press. If the government violates these rights, citizens can fight the injustice in court. Many of these rights are guaranteed to noncitizens as well.

Americans also have responsibilities. For example, we have the right to speak freely, but we also have the responsibility to allow others to say things we may not agree with. Citizens have responsibilities to stay informed, to vote, to pay taxes, and to obey the law, among others. As Americans we take pride in our democracy and our rights, freedoms, and responsibilities as citizens. We see ourselves as people who value freedom as our most precious right.

Our responsibilities include civic engagement. Civic engagement is participation in government and **civic life**, or activities having to do with one's society and community.

Unifying Principles Participating in the democratic process—by voting and engaging in these civic activities—expresses patriotism and support for our country's ideals. It reflects our individual contributions to building "a more perfect union." That phrase, from the opening of the U.S. Constitution, states what the people who wrote the Constitution saw as a goal of that document.

Analyze Diagrams There are many ways for citizens to get involved with their community and to participate in government. **Classify and Categorize** Which methods involve joining with other citizens?

CITIZEN RIGHTS AND RESPONSIBILITIES

Rights

- Freedom of speech, religion, press, assembly
- Right to vote
- Right to a fair and speedy trial
- Right to have a lawyer
- Right to equal treatment
- Right to bring lawsuit if suffering damage

Responsibilities

- Allow others to exercise their freedoms
- Register to vote
- Be informed about issues
- Serve on a jury and as a witness in a trial if called
- Pay taxes
- Obey laws
- Participate in civic life

Popular phrases connected with a nation often express its principles. If you look at the back of any U.S. coin, you see the words *E PLURIBUS UNUM.* The phrase has great meaning and historical **significance**.

It is a Latin phrase that means "out of many, one." The Continental Congress chose the phrase in 1782 for the Great Seal of the United States. It originally applied to the 13 colonies that rebelled against Britain—13 separate colonies forming one union. Today, it signifies the unity of a diverse nation.

Civic Participation Voting is both a right and a responsibility for U.S. citizens. But there are other types of civic engagement that are important for citizens. Perhaps the most important is to be informed. Citizens also have a responsibility to make their voices heard so that elected officials know what people want them to do.

Academic Vocabulary
significance • *n.,*
importance

☑ READING CHECK **Identify Main Ideas** What is the main protection for American citizens' basic rights?

Differences in Citizenship

Ideas about rights and responsibilities can change over time. The idea of citizenship has changed over time in other ways as well. **Democratization** is an increase in democracy. This process has expanded full citizenship rights to different groups over time. This process can also be seen in the large number of countries that have adopted democratic forms of government over the past 200 years.

CIVIC PARTICIPATION

KEEP INFORMED

VOTE

CONTACT OFFICIALS

SPEAK AT TOWN MEETING

SIGN A PETITION

CITIZEN ACTION

JOIN A POLITICAL PARTY

JOIN AN INTEREST GROUP

RUN FOR OFFICE

Analyze Charts Being informed is basic to other kinds of civic participation, because citizens need to understand the issues that affect the common good.
Infer Why is joining a political party an important part of civic participation?

Democracies, like the United States, rely on the consent of the governed. That is, citizens get to choose the government officials who represent them and who make and enforce laws. These governments are also limited governments that protect basic human rights of their people such as freedom of speech and freedom from unfair imprisonment. Before democratization, countries often did not protect these rights or did not protect these rights for all people.

The members of the United Nations recognize certain rights as universal, or belonging to all people. The UN Declaration of Human Rights lists the rights that all people should have, including life, liberty, and security. The UN works to protect these rights around the world.

Despite this work, some people do not enjoy these rights. Some countries have nondemocratic governments. Citizens who live in countries with authoritarian governments, such as dictatorships, usually cannot take part in government or express their views openly. These governments do not protect human rights. They often punish people who speak out against leaders or their policies. They may arrest them and send them to prison. Some dictators even have political opponents killed.

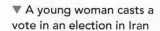
▼ A young woman casts a vote in an election in Iran

Today, international trade, transportation, and communication link the world's people. As a result, some people think that we should see ourselves as citizens of a global community. They believe that we are responsible for supporting human rights and equality for all people around the world.

☑ READING CHECK **Compare and Contrast** How do the basic rights of citizens vary between democratic and nondemocratic countries?

☑ Lesson Check

Practice Vocabulary

1. Name two ways American **citizens** can participate in the political process.

2. Give at least three examples of ways students can participate in **civic life**.

Critical Thinking and Writing

3. Identify Supporting Details Identify at least one right of U.S. citizens. Describe a responsibility that comes with that right.

4. Draw Conclusions How do the rights of U.S. citizens reflect our national identity?

5. Explain an Argument Do you think people who live in a democracy should be required to fulfill their civic responsibilities?

6. Writing Workshop: Use Descriptive Details In your ▤ Active Journal, write ideas about how you have experienced your rights or responsibilities as a citizen.

History Basics

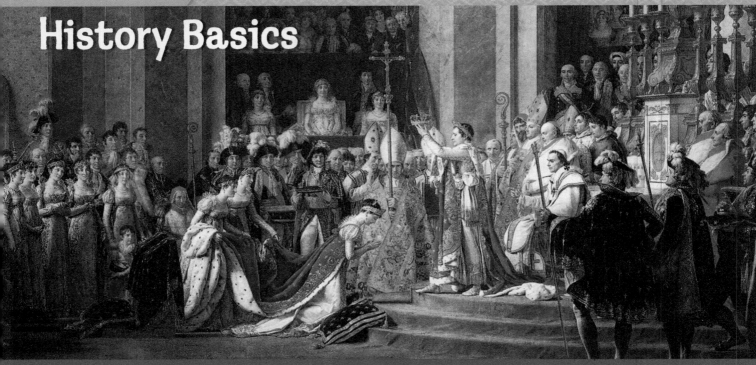

GET READY TO READ

START UP

Look at the image of Napoleon crowning himself emperor of France. What are two things historians could learn from a historic painting like this one?

GUIDING QUESTIONS

- How have people measured time?
- How do historians use historical sources?
- How do historians use archaeology and other sources?

TAKE NOTES

Literacy Skills: Identify Main Ideas
Use the graphic organizer in your 📓 Active Journal to take notes as you read the lesson.

Practice Vocabulary

Use the vocabulary activity in your 📓 Active Journal to practice the vocabulary words.

Vocabulary

		Academic Vocabulary
timeline	artifact	continuity
chronology	secondary source	point of view
period	archaeology	
prehistory	anthropology	
primary source		

History might seem a straightforward field of study. After all, historians study the past. Whatever happened has already happened—that can't be changed. There are records of what happened, and those records should contain the true story of events as they unfolded.

In fact, though, the historian's job is very difficult. Past events might be done, but there are not always records of those events. Even when there are records, they are not always complete or trustworthy. Sometimes records have conflicting information. How does a historian decide which account to believe? In some ways, studying history is like solving a mystery. Historians have to look for clues that would provide a logical explanation for what happened and why.

Measuring Time

Just as geographers work to locate places in space, historians work to locate events in time. To understand history, we need to know the order in which events took place and their relation in time to other events.

Using a Timeline Historians use timelines as a tool. A **timeline** is a line marked off with a series of events and dates. Historians use timelines to put events in a **chronology**, a list of events in the order in which they occurred. Timelines help historians identify and make sense of patterns of change. Historians also are able to analyze **continuity** across time and space by studying timelines.

A timeline is flexible. It can be made to cover a day, a year, a decade (ten years), a century (one hundred years), a millennium (one thousand years), or any other timespan in history.

A **period** is a length of time singled out because of a specific set of events or developments that happened during that time. A period is also sometimes called an era.

Historians use periods and eras to organize and describe human activities. For example, the Second Industrial Revolution was an era in the United States that spanned the late nineteenth century (1800s) into the early twentieth century (1900s). This era was marked by inventions that had dramatic impacts on agriculture, communications, transportation, and ways of life.

Organizing Time The past is often split into two parts, prehistory and history. **Prehistory** is the time before people invented writing and could begin to record events. *History* refers to written history, which began about 5,200 years ago. Some places, such as the United States, had no written records before about 500 years ago. In these places, history began much later.

Today, much of the world dates events using the labels BCE, for "before the common era," and CE, for "common era." In this system, dates that are BCE are counted backward. That is, 1,000 BCE occurred 999 years before 1 BCE. There is no year 0, so 1 BCE is followed by 1 CE, and dates are then counted moving forward. Another way to describe these dates is to use the terms BC, for "before Christ," and AD, meaning *anno Domini,* Latin for "in the year of the Lord."

Academic Vocabulary
continuity • *n.,* connection of events or developments in an unbroken stream

Analyze Charts The timeline shows major laws affecting American Indians from the 1820s to the 1970s. **Sequence** How many years passed between the Indian Reorganization Act and the law that promoted self-determination?

Key Legislation Affecting American Indians, 1800–2000

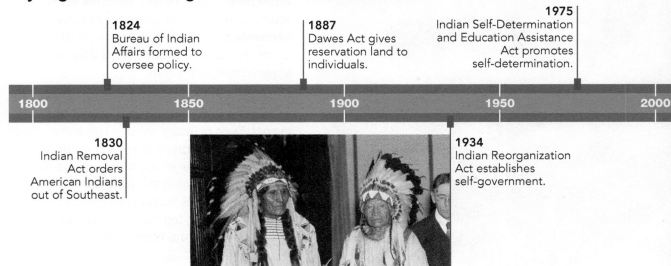

1824 Bureau of Indian Affairs formed to oversee policy.

1887 Dawes Act gives reservation land to individuals.

1975 Indian Self-Determination and Education Assistance Act promotes self-determination.

1800   1850   1900   1950   2000

1830 Indian Removal Act orders American Indians out of Southeast.

1934 Indian Reorganization Act establishes self-government.

The abbreviations BC and AD are based on the traditional belief that Jesus—called "Christ" by Christians—was born in the year AD 1. Dates AD are the same as dates CE, so AD 1 is 1 CE. Dates BC are the same as dates BCE.

Some groups of people have distinct calendars and organize time differently. The Jewish religious calendar counts the years since the creation of the world, according to Jewish tradition. The Islamic calendar begins the year when the prophet Muhammad moved to the city of Medina.

Today much of the world uses the Gregorian calendar, which has a 365- or 366-day year. It is based on the movement of Earth around the sun. The Jewish year, based on both the sun and the moon, varies from 353 to 385 days to adjust to the solar year. The Islamic year is based on the cycles of the moon and lasts about 354 days.

✓ READING CHECK **Summarize** How is a timeline a flexible tool?

Historical Sources

Historians try to understand and describe the past accurately. To understand past events, historians identify and collect historical sources. They consider information from each source in relation to its historical context, or events that happened in the time and place of the source.

Primary and Secondary Sources A **primary source** is information that comes directly from a person who experienced an event. A primary source consists of what the person writes, says, or creates about the event. Primary sources include letters, diaries, and photographs.

Artifacts are also primary sources. An **artifact** is an object made by a human being, such as a tool or a weapon.

Analyze Images Artifacts such as these ancient tools are primary sources that hold important clues to the past. **Identify Main Ideas** What makes these objects artifacts?

Historians use primary sources to understand events from the points of view of people who lived at the time an event occurred. They construct a thesis about the event that is supported by evidence in primary sources.

Books, articles, movies, news services, and other media sources that describe or make sense of the past are secondary sources. A **secondary source** is information about an event that does not come from a person who experienced that event.

Evaluating Historical Sources Historical sources do not always give a true account of events. Even primary sources can be wrong or misleading. A writer's personal opinions may influence what he or she writes. Sometimes the person recording the event may not present all details accurately. Historians must evaluate sources, looking at them in light of what is known from other sources.

JOIN, or DIE.

A historian must also be cautious when using secondary sources. Not all secondary sources are equally valid or reliable. For example, the Internet includes millions of well-researched articles, books, and other reliable secondary sources. However, any Internet search will also find many inaccurate websites.

Historians and students of history—like you—must evaluate a source to determine if it is reliable. When you examine primary and secondary sources, ask yourself questions like these:

- Who created the source material? A witness to an event may be more trustworthy than someone looking back at the event from a later time. However, a scholar or publication with a good reputation is also a reliable source. For example, a college professor who specializes in a period of Chinese history would be a reliable source on that period in China.

- Is the information fact or opinion? A fact is something that can be proved true or false. An opinion is a personal belief. Opinions are valuable not as a source of facts but as a clue to the author's judgments or feelings.

- Does the material seem to have a bias? It is possible for bias to affect visual sources, such as cartoons and photos, as well as verbal sources, such as speeches and written material. Biased material often leaves out facts that do not support the author's point of view, or it stresses facts that do support the author's point of view but presents those facts in a misleading way. As part of their examination of sources, historians analyze the **point of view** of the individuals or groups that created them when interpreting an historical event.

READING CHECK Identify Main Ideas What is a primary source?

Analyze Political Cartoons Benjamin Franklin drew this famous cartoon in 1754. It urged American colonists to unite to protect themselves during the French and Indian War. It was later reused during the American Revolution. **Draw Conclusions** Does this political cartoon convey facts or opinions?

Academic Vocabulary
point of view • *n.,* the way a person sees a matter

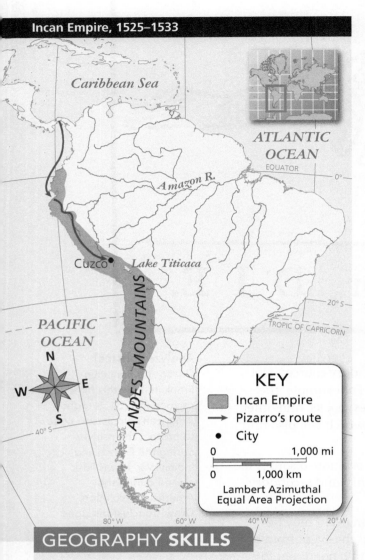

Incan Empire, 1525–1533

Caribbean Sea

ATLANTIC OCEAN

EQUATOR

Amazon R.

0°

Cuzco • Lake Titicaca

20° S

TROPIC OF CAPRICORN

PACIFIC OCEAN

ANDES MOUNTAINS

N W E S

40° S

KEY

◻ Incan Empire
→ Pizarro's route
• City

0   1,000 mi
0   1,000 km

Lambert Azimuthal
Equal Area Projection

80° W   60° W   40° W   20° W

GEOGRAPHY SKILLS

This historical map shows the size of the Incan empire.

1. **Region** Where was the Incan empire found?

2. **Infer** Why do you think the map shows the city of Cuzco and no others?

👆 **INTERACTIVE**

Piecing the Past Together

Historical Maps

When you read about a historical event such as an important battle, it can be hard to get a clear picture of what really happened. You may have to understand how landforms such as rivers and hills affected the battle. Perhaps you will need to know the location of a nearby town, railroad, or road that influenced the fighting. Sometimes the best way to learn about a historical event or period is by examining a historical map.

A historical map is a special-purpose map that provides information about a place or certain time in history. Historical maps can show information such as migration, trade patterns, or other facts.

Historical maps have certain features. Most have a title and a key. Most use colors and symbols to show resources, movement, locations of people, or other features.

Use the following four steps to become familiar with historical maps.

- Read the title. Note the date, the time span, and other information about the subject of the map. If the map includes a locator map, examine it to see what region is shown.

- Study the map quickly to get a general idea of what is shown. Read any place names and other labels. Note any landforms.

- Examine the map's key. Pick out the first symbol or other entry, read what it stands for, and find an example on the map. Repeat this process for the remaining key entries until you understand them all. The keys of historical maps may show more than one color, each one representing a different territory. Use the colors to understand how space was divided in the past.

- Study the map more thoroughly. Make sure you have a clear understanding of the map. If you need help, reread the related section of your textbook or examine the map again.

☑ **READING CHECK** **Identify Main Ideas** What is a historical map?

Archaeology and Other Sources

Over time, much of the ancient world has disappeared. Large cities have collapsed into ruins. Buildings and artifacts are now buried under layers of soil and sand or covered by thick forests. Meanwhile, if there are no written records from a past period, historians cannot rely on written records. The science of archaeology aims to uncover this hidden past. **Archaeology** is the scientific study of past cultures through the examination of artifacts and other evidence.

Archaeologists are part treasure hunters and part detectives. They explore the places where people once lived and worked, searching for artifacts such as tools, weapons, and pottery. They study the objects they find to learn more about the past. Artifacts can help us identify the resources available to ancient people. Archaeologists use artifacts to understand how these people used technology and how they adapted to their environment.

Anthropology also helps historians understand the past. **Anthropology** is the study of humankind in all aspects, especially development and culture. Anthropologists also seek to understand the origins of humans and the ways humans developed physically.

Anthropology sometimes involves studying fossils—bones and other remains that have been preserved in rock. It also involves a great deal of research of scholarly articles, researching other discoveries, and networking with scholars and museums worldwide to gain an understanding of new findings and bring new interpretations to old findings.

▲ Archaeologists and anthropologists search for remains of the past at digs such as this one.

☑ **READING CHECK** **Classify and Categorize** How do archaeology and anthropology help us understand the past?

☑ Lesson Check

Practice Vocabulary

1. How do **timelines** show historical events or **periods**?

2. Is an account of an event written by someone who was not at the event a **primary source** or a **secondary source**?

Critical Thinking and Writing

3. Identify Supporting Details What questions should be asked to evaluate a source?

4. Use Evidence What are three things you might put in the key to a historical map of ancient trade routes?

5. Draw Conclusions How does the work of archaeologists and anthropologists help historians understand the past?

6. Writing Workshop: Add Details Add descriptive details to some of your notes in your 📗 Active Journal to make the narrative you will write more complete and interesting to read.

☑ Review and Assessment

VISUAL REVIEW

Geography: Causes and Effects

Causes	Effects
Earth's tilt, revolution; rotation	Seasons; days and nights
Movement of tectonic plates	Positions of continents, mountain ranges; volcanoes, earthquakes
Weathering, erosion, deposition	Shapes of landforms
Latitude, temperature, precipitation, wind, altitude	Climate of a region
Climate, landforms, resources, economic activity	Human settlement patterns, population density

Key Concepts of Economics

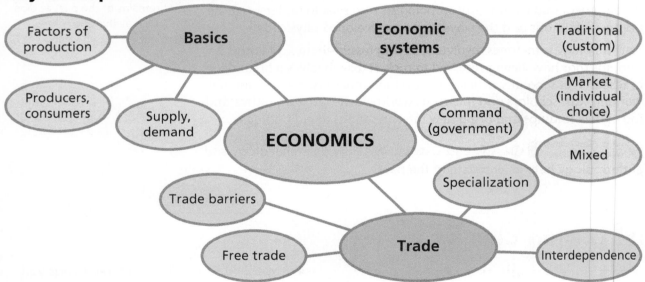

READING REVIEW

Use the Take Notes and Practice Vocabulary activities in your
📙 Active Journal to review the topic.

 INTERACTIVE

Practice vocabulary using
the Topic Mini-Games.

Quest FINDINGS

Write a Blog Post

Get help for writing
your blog in your
📙 Active Journal.

ASSESSMENT

Vocabulary and Key Ideas

1. How are **latitude** and **longitude** related to **absolute location**?

2. What is the difference between a region's **weather** and its **climate**?

3. What is the difference between **push factors** and **pull factors**?

4. Explain the relationship between **development** and a **standard of living**.

5. How are **equinox** and **solstice** related to the hemispheres?

6. How do **supply** and **demand** interact to set prices?

7. How are **primary sources** and **secondary sources** alike? How are they different?

Critical Thinking and Writing

8. **Identify Main Ideas** What are the three basic economic questions that all societies must answer?

9. **Infer** Explain what the following statement means: While trees are a renewable resource, it often takes human effort to make them renewable.

10. **Synthesize** How do language, religion, and customs combine to help define a culture region?

11. **Draw Conclusions** Suppose that a country borders three other countries. How do you think its geography might affect its trade and foreign policy?

12. **Revisit the Essential Question** How much does geography affect people's lives?

13. **Writing Workshop: Write a Narrative** Look back at the ideas you wrote in your 📃 Active Journal. Use them to write a narrative essay that explores your experiences with geography.

Analyze Primary Sources

14. Which option below best describes the purpose of this passage?
    A. declaring the unlimited power of the government
    B. establishing the government as a democracy
    C. defining both federal and state rights
    D. establishing which previous laws it is based upon

"We the People of the United States, in Order to form a more perfect Union, establish Justice, insure domestic Tranquility, provide for the common defence, promote the general Welfare, and secure the Blessings of Liberty to ourselves and our Posterity, do ordain and establish this Constitution for the United States of America."

—*Preamble, U.S. Constitution*

Analyze Maps

Use the map at right to answer the following questions.

15. Which coast of the United States is most likely to have earthquakes?

16. The mountains shown on the west coast of North America are volcanoes. Why are they located where they are?

17. What forces inside Earth cause earthquakes along the Ring of Fire?

▼ **Pacific Ring of Fire**

Europe Through Time

GO ONLINE
to access your
digital course

▶ VIDEO

◀)) AUDIO

📖 ETEXT

👆 INTERACTIVE

✏️ WRITING

🎮 GAMES

📄 WORKSHEET

☑️ ASSESSMENT

From ancient through modern times,

EUROPE has been a center of civilization and a source of ideas and practices that have shaped the rest of the world.

Explore The Essential Question

How should we handle conflict?

Europe has faced many conflicts since ancient times. Many conflicts were wars, but some were about ideas or beliefs. What caused these conflicts, and how have countries in Europe solved them?

▲ The Colosseum, an amphitheater built for sports and other entertainment almost 2,000 years ago, still stands in Rome, Italy.

Watch

BOUNCE TO ACTIVATE • ▶ VIDEO

Good Queen Bess

Meet Elizabeth I and see her response to the Spanish Armada.

Read

about a region that gave birth to ancient civilizations, empires, and ideas that shaped the world we live in.

Europe: Physical

A CONNECTED CONTINENT

Europe is usually considered a continent, but it is connected to Asia to make a larger landmass called Eurasia.

Learn more about Europe by making your own map in your Active Journal.

INTERACTIVE

Topic Map

Peninsulas and Islands

Europe is a region of many peninsulas, seas, and islands. Its largest island is Great Britain, made up of mountains and plains in England, Wales, and Scotland.

A Fertile Plain

The North European Plain, stretching from France to Poland, was covered with forests long ago. Now it contains fertile farmland and big cities.

Where Land Meets Sea

The southern end of the Balkan Peninsula is made up of smaller, narrow peninsulas facing islands in the Aegean Sea. This land of seacoasts was home to ancient Greek civilization.

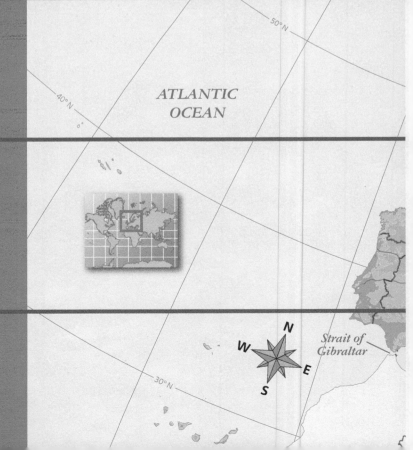

ELEVATION

More than 13,000 feet		More than 3,960 meters
6,500–13,000 feet		1,980–3,960 meters
1,600–6,500 feet		480–1,980 meters
650–1,600 feet		200–480 meters
0–650 feet		0–200 meters
Below sea level		Below sea level

— Country border
▲ Highest point in the region

0 ———— 600 mi
0 ———— 600 km

Azimuthal Equidistant Projection

ATLANTIC OCEAN

Strait of Gibraltar

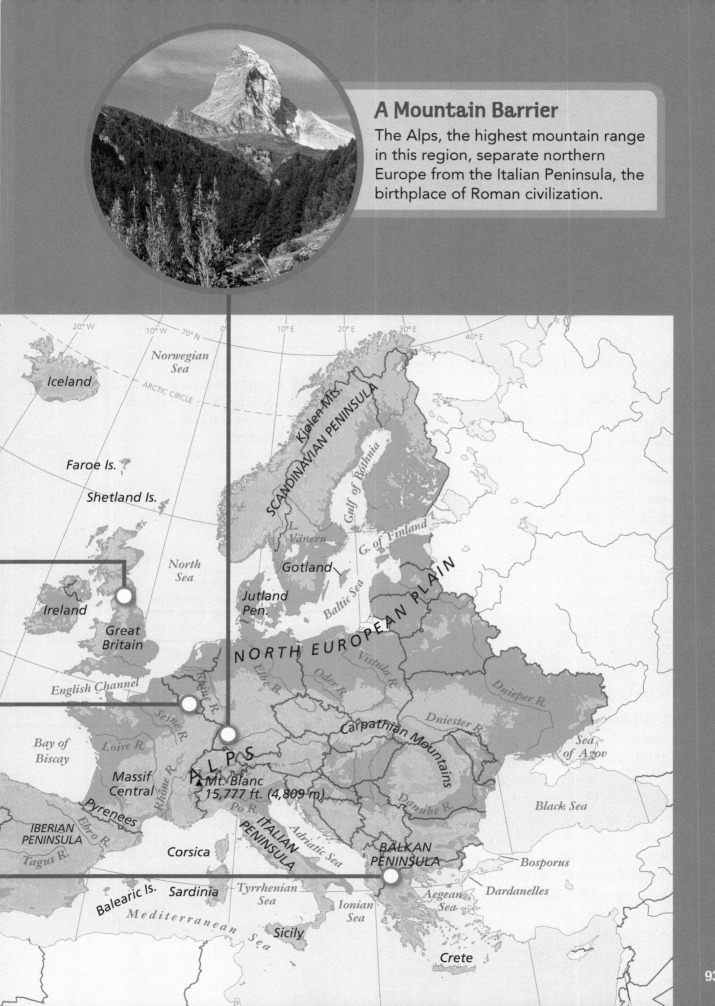

A Mountain Barrier

The Alps, the highest mountain range in this region, separate northern Europe from the Italian Peninsula, the birthplace of Roman civilization.

2 Regional Atlas

Europe: Climate

A REGION OF CONTRASTS

Most parts of Europe have temperate climates, though temperatures and climate vary widely. Northern areas have cold subarctic and tundra climates.

Mild West

Western Europe has a warmer climate than other regions this far north because of the warm North Atlantic current. London averages 24 inches (621 mm) of precipitation a year. Its average monthly temperature ranges from 40° F (5° C) in January to 66° F (19° C) in July.

Hotter South

Southern Europe has a warm, dry climate. Most of its rain falls in winter. Athens, Greece, averages 16 inches (397 mm) of rain in a year, most of it falling from October through January. Average temperatures range from 49° F (10° C) in January to 82° F (28° C) in July and August.

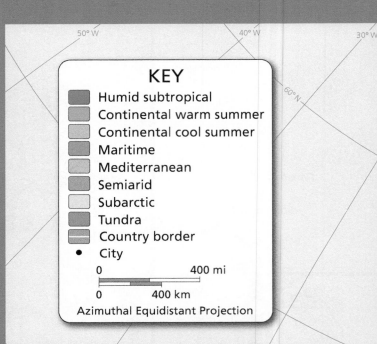

KEY
- Humid subtropical
- Continental warm summer
- Continental cool summer
- Maritime
- Mediterranean
- Semiarid
- Subarctic
- Tundra
- Country border
- • City

| 0 | 400 mi |
| 0 | 400 km |

Azimuthal Equidistant Projection

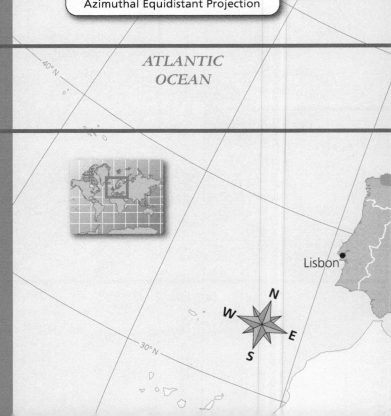

ATLANTIC OCEAN

Lisbon

The Cold North

Oulu in northern Finland has a cold, dry subarctic climate. Its average January temperature is just 13° F (−11° C), and its average July temperature is 60° F (16° C). Just 18 inches (456 mm) of precipitation fall in an average year.

Reykjavík

Norwegian Sea

ARCTIC CIRCLE

Oulu

North Sea

Baltic Sea

London

Berlin

Kiev

Paris

Innsbruck

Budapest

Bucharest

Black Sea

Rome

Valencia

Mediterranean Sea

Athens

Quest

Document-Based Writing Inquiry

Planning a New Government

Quest KICK OFF

A country in Europe has declared independence and a new government needs to be formed. It is your job as an advisor to suggest the best form of government for this newly formed country to minimize conflict.

How should governments be formed?

What forms of government did you learn about in this topic? Explore the Essential Question "How should we handle conflict?" in this Quest.

1 Ask Questions

As a government advisor, you are the expert! Get started by making a list of questions that will guide your research. Write the questions in your 📓 Active Journal.

2 Investigate

As you read the lessons in the topic, look for **Quest** CONNECTIONS that provide information on what makes an ideal government. Capture notes in your 📓 Active Journal.

▲ Federal judges in Germany wear red robes for certain occasions. Germans vote for their government representatives, who have the responsibility to appoint these judges.

3 Examine Primary Sources

Next, explore a set of primary sources from European thinkers about government. Capture notes in your 📓 Active Journal.

Quest FINDINGS

4 Write Your Official Report

At the end of the topic, you will write an official report to recommend the best form of government to a country that has declared independence and needs a new government. Get help for writing your report in your 📓 Active Journal.

Early European Cultures

BOUNCE TO ACTIVATE ▶ VIDEO

GET READY TO READ

START UP

Examine the image of the cave painting found in Lascaux, France. Think about what the images reveal regarding daily life in prehistoric times. What was most important to these early peoples?

GUIDING QUESTIONS

- How did people first come to Europe?
- What changes did farming bring to Europe?
- What changes did the Bronze Age bring?

TAKE NOTES

Literacy Skills: Main Idea and Detail
Use the graphic organizer in your 📓 Active Journal to take notes as you read the lesson.

PRACTICE VOCABULARY

Use the vocabulary activity in your 📓 Active Journal to practice the vocabulary words.

Vocabulary	Academic Vocabulary
Neanderthal	sophisticated
Homo sapiens	permanent
Bronze Age	

Modern humans migrated to Europe thousands of years ago. They relied on hunting and gathering to survive. As they began to farm, populations grew and societies became more complex.

Europe's First People

The first people to arrive in Europe migrated from Africa about 1 million years ago. They most likely traveled on foot. The migration was slow. Many probably came seeking animals to hunt. The first people were not modern humans. They were an earlier species that had smaller brains and looked different from modern humans. Over thousands of years, scientists think, they gradually developed into a type of early humans known as **Neanderthals**.

Modern Humans About 45,000 years ago, most scientists believe that modern humans, or ***Homo sapiens***, migrated from Africa into Asia, and from there to Europe and other parts of the world. *Homo sapiens* means "wise person." These early humans gradually replaced the Neanderthals across Europe.

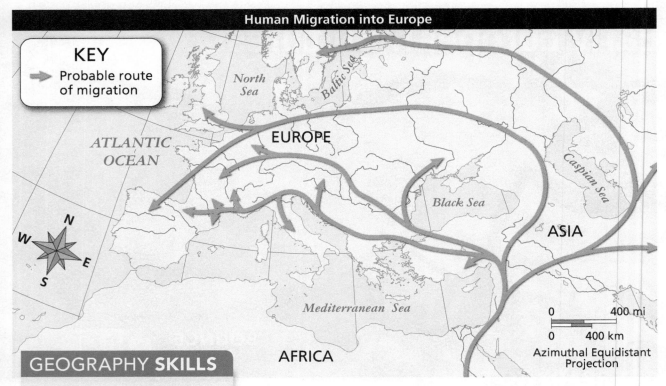

KEY
➡ Probable route of migration

North Sea

Baltic Sea

EUROPE

ATLANTIC OCEAN

Caspian Sea

Black Sea

ASIA

Mediterranean Sea

AFRICA

N W E S

0   400 mi
0   400 km
Azimuthal Equidistant Projection

GEOGRAPHY **SKILLS**

Modern humans migrated into Europe about 45,000 years ago.

1. **Movement** Describe the migration routes that brought modern humans into Europe.

2. **Infer** What factors might have led early humans to migrate into Europe?

Academic Vocabulary
sophisticated • *adj.,* highly developed, complex

Finding animals to hunt and berries, seeds, and nuts to gather was essential. Over time, early humans learned how to use fire, which enabled them to keep warm, cook meat, and keep safe by frightening animals away. These modern humans had much larger brains than Neanderthals and were able to develop more **sophisticated** societies.

Cave Paintings These first modern humans left behind evidence of how they lived. Cave paintings in Europe show animals in what appear to be hunting scenes. It is possible that they also reveal details about religious beliefs.

In 1940, hundreds of cave paintings were uncovered in Lascaux (lahsKOH), France. The paintings mostly show animals, including deer, bison (buffalo), and horses. Archaeologists believe that the paintings were made between about 17,000 and 15,000 BCE, during the Paleolithic Age, or Old Stone Age, which lasted from 2.5 million years ago to about 9,600 BCE. Similar cave art from about the same time period has been discovered in Altamira, Spain.

✓READING CHECK Draw Conclusions Why did early people migrate to Europe?

How Did Farming Change Europe?

The Ice Age, which had kept much of northern Europe too cold and icy to sustain life, ended between 15,000 and 9,000 years ago. As a result, the climate warmed and people slowly migrated north.

Warming Leads to Population Growth People began to migrate into northern Europe. A warmer climate enabled plants and animals to thrive throughout Europe. As more food became available for people to hunt or gather, their population grew. More people were available to help hunt and gather plants, seeds, and nuts.

Agriculture Begins and Spreads Early humans in Southwest Asia discovered that some seeds they had gathered and dropped onto the earth later grew into plants. Soon, they began planting seeds to grow food.

Agriculture, or the raising of plants for human use, caused more population growth. People continued hunt and gather, but they relied more and more on agriculture for food. Farming encouraged people to form **permanent** settlements, or villages, instead of wandering from place to place in search of food.

Farmers and agriculture spread from Southwest Asia into southeastern Europe and Italy in the late 6000s and 5000s BCE. By about 1,000 years later, agriculture had spread across central and northwestern Europe.

Food Surplus and Complex Societies Over time, people were able to grow more food than they needed. This extra food is called a food surplus. With a food surplus, people could trade food for other needs. Some people could specialize in trades or skills other than farming, building a more complex society. A farmer might use extra food to pay someone to make tools that they needed. They could also give leaders their food surplus in exchange for protection. People started to fill different roles in societies.

✓ READING CHECK **Understand Effects** How did farming change Europe?

Analyze Diagrams
Domestication started with dogs. Other animals and fruits, vegetables, and grains followed. **Sequence** How many years passed after the domestication of dogs until horses and cats were domesticated?

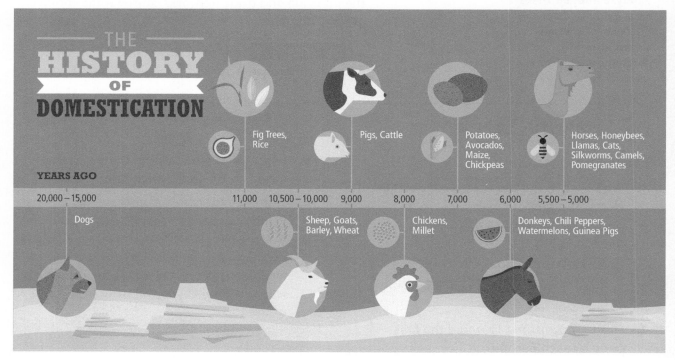

THE
HISTORY
OF
DOMESTICATION

Fig Trees, Rice — Pigs, Cattle — Potatoes, Avocados, Maize, Chickpeas — Horses, Honeybees, Llamas, Cats, Silkworms, Camels, Pomegranates

YEARS AGO

| 20,000–15,000 | 11,000 | 10,500–10,000 | 9,000 | 8,000 | 7,000 | 6,000 | 5,500–5,000 |

Dogs — Sheep, Goats, Barley, Wheat — Chickens, Millet — Donkeys, Chili Peppers, Watermelons, Guinea Pigs

The Bronze Age

During the 3000s BCE, people in Europe began to develop new technologies. These technologies produced better and stronger tools.

Making Stronger Tools People continued to use stone to make most of their tools. However, in some parts of Europe, people began to use copper to make axes and other tools. They dug copper ore, or rocks containing metal, from the ground, heated it until the metal melted—a process called smelting—and collected and later shaped the molten metal. Copper was already being used during the 4000s BCE to make tools and weapons such as spearheads.

By about 3200 BCE, Europeans learned to mix copper with tin, another metal smelted from ore. Together, these metals could be made into bronze, a much stronger metal than copper. The **Bronze Age** describes the period of human history during which people used bronze to make tools and weapons.

How Did Bronze Affect Trade? Bronze tools and other objects made from bronze were stronger and lasted longer. Yet tin ore was needed to make bronze, and it was not widely available in Europe. Thus, the need for tin ore encouraged the development of trade.

As the production of bronze and trade grew, powerful kingdoms emerged. Some of the earliest of these kingdoms in Europe arose in the islands of Greece. Control of the tin trade and trade networks caused some conflicts among kingdoms.

READING CHECK Identify Cause and Effect What caused the Bronze Age, and how did it affect Europe?

Analyze Images These tools were used around 2000 BCE. **Use Visual Information** What do you think these tools were used for?

☑ Lesson Check

Practice Vocabulary

1. Who lived in Europe first, **Neanderthals** or *Homo sapiens*?

2. What was the **Bronze Age**?

Critical Thinking and Writing

3. **Sequence** Which came first, sophisticated societies or farming?

4. **Draw Conclusions** How did the first people reach Europe?

5. **Infer** What effect would the Bronze Age have had on early agriculture?

6. **Writing Workshop: Generate Questions** Write questions in your 📓 Active Journal about what causes war and conflict. These questions will help focus your thinking for an explanatory essay about the causes of war and conflict you will write at the end of the topic.

Ancient Greece

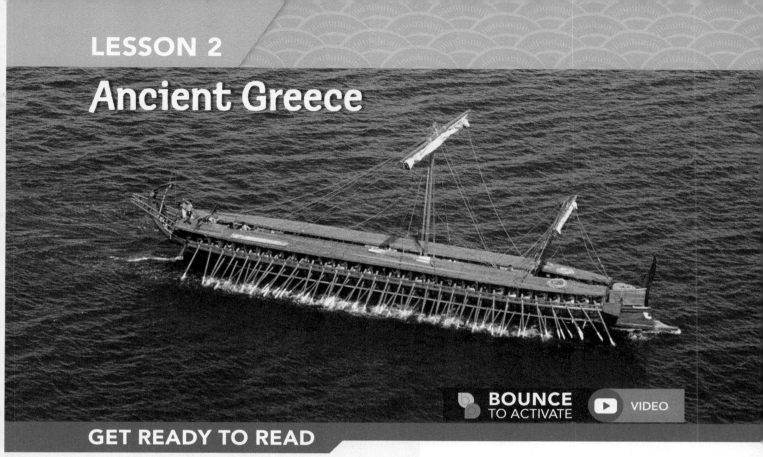

BOUNCE TO ACTIVATE   ▶ VIDEO

GET READY TO READ

START UP

Examine the photo of a reconstructed ancient Greek ship. How might ships like this have been a response to Greece's geography?

GUIDING QUESTIONS

- How did ancient Greek culture respond to Greece's geography?
- How did democracy emerge in ancient Greece?
- What were the most important achievements of the ancient Greeks?

TAKE NOTES

Literacy Skills: Determine Central Ideas
Use the graphic organizer in your 📓 Active Journal to take notes as you read the lesson.

PRACTICE VOCABULARY

Use the vocabulary activity in your 📓 Active Journal to practice the vocabulary words.

Vocabulary

city-state   mythology
citizenship   Socratic
aristocracy   method
democracy
polytheism

Academic Vocabulary

exclude
maintain

Ancient Greece was the birthplace of many of the ideas and values that we share today. Possibly the most important of these ideas was that people should be free to rule themselves, an idea that developed into the form of government called democracy.

The Geography of the Greek World

In ancient times, Greek speakers were scattered across the islands and coast lines of the Mediterranean Sea. Travelers from Europe, Asia, and Africa passed through these lands to exchange goods, ideas, and customs.

A Rugged Land Modern Greece occupies a peninsula, with several small peninsulas branching out into the Mediterranean Sea. The largest of Greece's peninsulas is the Peloponnese (pel uh puh NEEz).

About 2000 BCE, Greek-speaking peoples entered these lands from the north. They settled in mainland Greece and on the islands of the Aegean (ee JEE un) Sea.

Mainland Greece is divided by mountain ranges with narrow valleys and small plains between them. People settled in isolated farming communities in those flatter areas.

A Land Tied to the Sea Divided by mountains, the ancient Greeks looked to the sea. Their fishing and trading ships crisscrossed the waters of the surrounding seas. This led to contact with the older, more complex cultures of North Africa and Southwest Asia.

A Mediterranean Climate Greece has a Mediterranean climate, with mild, wet winters and hot, dry summers. The lack of rain made it difficult to grow shallow-rooted crops such as wheat. On the other hand, this climate was ideal for growing deep-rooted plants such as olive trees and grape vines. The Greeks produced olive oil and wine for trade.

✓READING CHECK Identify Main Ideas How did ancient Greek culture respond to Greece's geography?

Early Greek History

The Greeks were influenced by an early civilization—the Minoans. Minoan culture developed during the 2000s BCE on Crete, an island south of mainland Greece.

Minoan Civilization Minoan civilization was highly advanced. The Minoans had a writing system and built huge stone palaces with running water, like the one at Knossos (NAH sus). Around 1450 BCE, Minoan palaces and towns were mysteriously destroyed. Most historians believe that mainland Greeks were responsible.

The Mycenaeans The Minoans influenced a Greek-speaking civilization that arose on mainland Greece. This civilization, known as Mycenaean (my suh NEE un), developed around 1600 BCE.

The Mycenaeans made fine bronze weapons and pottery. They traded these goods for copper, tin, ivory, and luxury goods from other lands.

Soon, the Mycenaean kingdoms grew weak. Around 1100 BCE, this civilization was destroyed by newcomers from the north who spoke a different form of Greek.

The Dark Age With the fall of the Mycenaeans, Greek culture declined. The following period, which lasted roughly from 1100 to 750 BCE, has been called a dark age. During these centuries, many mainland Greeks migrated across the Aegean, settling the west coast of present-day Turkey, an area that became known as Ionia (eye OH nee uh).

During the Dark Age, Greeks learned to smelt iron from iron ore. Iron was an even stronger metal than bronze and made even more effective weapons and tools. This was the beginning of the Iron Age in Europe.

✅ **READING CHECK** **Understand Effects** What effect did the Dark Age have on ancient Greece?

City-States Emerge

By the 700s BCE, each Greek community had begun to organize itself into a city-state. A **city-state** was an independent state consisting of a city and its surrounding territory. The city-state became one of the most important features of Greek culture.

The City-State Each Greek city-state usually had a marketplace and government center. Here members of the city-state who had legal rights—those who were the citizens—would meet to discuss issues for the entire community.

The idea of citizenship set the Greeks apart. **Citizenship** is membership in a community that gives a person civil and political rights and obligations. Elsewhere in the ancient world, people lived as subjects of a ruler whom they were expected to obey without question. In contrast, ordinary Greeks could have a voice in government decisions.

Greek Society In early times, city-states were governed by an **aristocracy**, a hereditary class of rulers. Aristocracy meant "rule by the best people." These nobles were landowners who owned large areas of land. They enjoyed a relatively high status, or rank in society. Because they did not work the land themselves, they had free time for politics and leisure activities.

These aristocrats made up only a minority of citizens. Many more citizens were small farmers.

Merchants and artisans were often resident aliens. They might be a Greek from another city-state or someone who was not Greek. Although they were free, they were not citizens and had fewer rights than the native-born men of the city-states.

Even though self-government was a feature of most city-states, not everyone could participate in making decisions. Women, enslaved people, and foreigners were all **excluded** from the process.

Academic Vocabulary
exclude • *v.*, to prevent from entering a place or participating in an activity

Analyze Images The ruins of the Parthenon, an ancient temple, sit on the acropolis of Athens, high above the modern city. **Use Visual Information** How does this view of Athens help you understand the idea of an acropolis?

ANCIENT GREEK SOCIETY

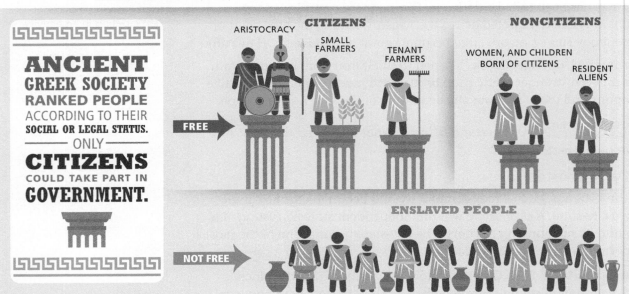

ANCIENT GREEK SOCIETY **RANKED PEOPLE** ACCORDING TO THEIR **SOCIAL OR LEGAL STATUS.** — ONLY — **CITIZENS** COULD TAKE PART IN **GOVERNMENT.**

FREE

NOT FREE

CITIZENS
ARISTOCRACY
SMALL FARMERS
TENANT FARMERS

NONCITIZENS
WOMEN, AND CHILDREN BORN OF CITIZENS
RESIDENT ALIENS

ENSLAVED PEOPLE

Analyze Diagrams
Greek society was divided between citizens and non-citizens and between those who were free and not free. **Synthesize Visual Information** How does the diagram support the information that you read in the text about social divisions in ancient Greece?

Enslaved People The lowest class in Greek society was made up of people living in slavery. Slavery is the ownership and control of other people as property.

Most enslaved people were prisoners of war. Others were bought from slave traders or sold into slavery by their families. Some enslaved people were Greeks but many came from other lands. By the 500s BCE, slavery was widespread in Greece. In some city-states, one-third of the population lived in slavery.

☑ READING CHECK **Identify Supporting Details** How did the ancient Greeks use marketplaces other than for buying and selling?

How Did Democracy Develop in Greece?

Most early city-states had governments based on tyranny or oligarchy. Tyrannies were governments run by a strong ruler. Oligarchies were governments run by a small group of aristocrats. During the 600s BCE, though, the armies of the city-states came to rely on ordinary citizens. In the city of Athens, these ordinary citizens began to resist the domination of aristocrats.

Beginnings of Athenian Democracy In the year 594 BCE, the aristocrats of Athens chose Solon to lead the city-state. Solon reformed the courts. He ended the practice of selling into slavery poor people who could not pay their debts. He also gave some non-aristocratic men the right to vote for officials. These measures set Athens on the path to **democracy**, or a system of rule by the people.

Later Reforms In 508 BCE, Cleisthenes gained power in Athens. His reforms reduced the power of the rich by increasing the number of citizens, including those from lower classes, who could vote. He also

 INTERACTIVE

Athenian Democracy

increased the power of the assembly of all male citizens, which made decisions for the city-state.

The Age of Pericles More reforms followed in the 450s BCE under Pericles. His first major change was to pay citizens for participating in different civic duties. These payments helped poor people to take part in government. Taken together, these reforms created the world's first democracy.

Oligarchy in Sparta Not all Greek city-states were democracies. The powerful city-state of Sparta was an oligarchy. The government was led by two kings, advised by a 28-member Council of Elders.

Sparta's oligarchy was focused on military conquest and control of the large enslaved population, which outnumbered Spartan citizens. Citizens focused on military training, in part so that they could control the enslaved majority.

☑ READING CHECK **Compare and Contrast** How was democracy in Athens different from other forms of government?

The History of Ancient Greece

In mountainous Greece, the area available for farming is limited. As populations grew, there was a serious shortage of land. Beginning in the 700s BCE, Greeks began sailing overseas to found colonies where farmland was available. They settled along the shores of the Mediterranean and Black Seas. Greek colonies covered parts of southern Italy.

The Greek Economy Greeks also produced goods that they could trade for food. The city of Athens grew rich as a center of trade. Its artisans produced pottery, jewelry, and other trade goods, and its merchants grew rich trading these goods for lumber, food, and luxury items.

During the 500s BCE, the Persian empire, centered in Southwest Asia, conquered Greek city-states on the eastern shore of the Aegean Sea. In the early 400s BCE, the Persian empire repeatedly invaded Greece itself. The Greek city-states, led by Athens and Sparta, united to defeat the Persians.

Golden Age and War After the defeat of the Persians, Athens enjoyed a golden age of peace and prosperity. It dominated much of Greece.

Soon, many Greek city-states resented the dominance of Athens. They formed an alliance with Sparta. In the late 400s BCE, the alliances of Athens and Sparta fought a 27-year-long war known as the Peloponnesian (pel uh puh NEE zhun) War. In the end, Athens was defeated. The war devastated much of the Greek world.

Did you know?

Pericles bust with helmet Pericles' head was an unusual shape, so he often wore a helmet that was pushed back to cover it.

Analyze Images This ancient Greek shield shows a scene from Greek mythology, with Dionysus sailing in a boat. **Infer** What do the images on this shield illustrate about the resources that were important to the ancient Greeks?

105

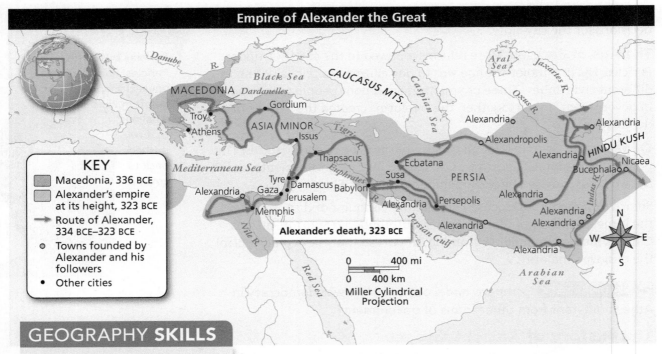

Empire of Alexander the Great

KEY
- Macedonia, 336 BCE
- Alexander's empire at its height, 323 BCE
- Route of Alexander, 334 BCE–323 BCE
- Towns founded by Alexander and his followers
- Other cities

Alexander's death, 323 BCE

0   400 mi
0   400 km
Miller Cylindrical Projection

GEOGRAPHY SKILLS

Alexander built a vast empire in only 13 years.

1. **Location** How far south did Alexander's empire extend?

2. **Identify Cause and Effect** Across which three continents did Alexander's empire stretch? What effect did this conquest have on these lands?

The Empire of Alexander the Great During the 300s BCE, Macedonia conquered land just north of Greece and defeated Greek city-states. Athens and other Greek city-states were forced to become Macedonian allies.

A Macedonian prince named Alexander became king at the age of 20. Within 13 years, Alexander conquered nearly all of Southwest Asia, Egypt, and parts of South Asia. He died at the age of 33. Today he is known as Alexander the Great.

Alexander did not have a child who was old enough to take over the empire, so his generals divided it up. Their heirs ruled Egypt and much of Southwest Asia for 200 years.

Hellenistic Culture Spreads The kingdoms and cities that Alexander conquered exchanged ideas. Greek culture blended with other cultures. The culture of the Mediterranean region came to be called Hellenistic. *Hellenic* is another word for Greek. *Hellenistic* means Greek-derived.

✓ READING CHECK **Draw Conclusions** What impact did Alexander's empire have on the Mediterranean world?

Greek Culture and Achievements

Greek achievements in the arts and sciences transformed the ancient world and have helped shape the modern world.

Greek Mythology The ancient Greeks practiced **polytheism**, the worship of many gods. The Greeks believed that their gods and goddesses existed in human-like form.

Greeks expressed their religious beliefs in their mythology. **Mythology** is a collection of myths or stories about gods and heroes.

Some myths explained the changing of the seasons. Others revealed why so much suffering exists in the world. Many myths explained human behavior or taught moral lessons. Some told the stories of heroes who had amazing strength.

Greek myths and stories are still read and retold today. The myths reveal important truths about human nature.

Greek Religion and Life The Greeks honored their gods with public and private religious rituals. Public meetings began with prayers and animal sacrifices. Women played important roles in some of these public ceremonies. In private homes, families **maintained** household shrines, honoring their favorite gods or goddesses.

Some religious festivals included athletic contests. Athletes displayed their skill and strength to honor the gods. The most famous sports event was the Olympic games. These ancient games took place every four years. They inspired the modern Olympic Games.

Greek Philosophy Several important philosophers lived in Athens, including Socrates, Plato, and Aristotle. They used reason, or logic, to try to understand reality and to discover eternal truths. They also wanted to find natural laws to explain actions in the world.

Socrates asked people question after question to force them to think more clearly. Today, this question-and-answer method of teaching is called the **Socratic method** and is used to educate students in a variety of subjects.

Greek writers also discussed politics and government. For example, Plato wrote a book called *The Republic*, which presented his views about the ideal government. Plato did not approve of the way democracy functioned in Athens. He thought that the ideal city-state would be led by philosopher-kings, who would have the wisdom to make the right decisions.

Quest CONNECTIONS

What was Plato's opinion about the qualities of a good leader? Do you think these qualities are important in government? Record your findings in your 📓 Active Journal.

Academic Vocabulary
maintain • *v.*, to keep in working order

BIOGRAPHY
5 Things to Know About

SOCRATES
Greek philosopher (about 470–399 BCE)

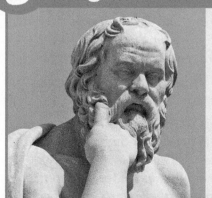

- Socrates challenged accepted beliefs.
- He was accused of not believing in the gods that the city recognized.
- The leaders of Athens charged him with corrupting the young.
- He defended himself by saying, "I have never set up as any man's teacher. But if anyone, young or old, is eager to hear me . . . I never grudge [deny] him the opportunity."
- Socrates was found guilty and sentenced to death in 399 BCE.

Critical Thinking Why do you think Socrates used questions to get people to think for themselves?

▲ This ancient sculpture shows a Greek doctor treating a patient.

The philosopher Aristotle also wrote a book about government, called *Politics*. He argued that the best government would be a balanced one that avoided extremes. Aristotle also believed that citizens must participate in politics in order to be happy.

Greek Writing During the Greek Dark Age, Phoenician sailors and merchants from Southwest Asia dominated the Mediterranean Sea. The Phoenicians used a writing system that had symbols only for consonants. The Greeks used versions of these symbols and added letters to represent vowels, inventing the world's first true alphabet.

Many ancient Greek writers and their works are still famous today. Among them is Homer, whose epic poems the *Iliad* and the *Odyssey*, reflect the Greeks' belief that the gods controlled human lives.

The Greek writer Herodotus is often called "the father of history" because he asked why past certain events had happened, such as the causes of the conflict between the Greeks and the Persians.

Greek Science and Technology Most ancient peoples associated everyday occurrences, like the rising of the sun or common illnesses, with the activities of various gods or spirits. While most Greeks shared these beliefs, some began to look for natural causes of such events. The ancient Greeks observed nature and used reason to try to understand it. Their approach formed the basis for modern science.

They also made many mathematical discoveries, especially in geometry. These mathematical principles played a role in the building and design techniques that allowed the Greeks to build beautiful temples.

The Greeks tried to understand the causes of medical problems. Hippocrates, a Greek doctor, wrote many medical books and ran a school that trained new doctors. He had his students swear an oath, promising to use their knowledge only to help patients.

☑ **READING CHECK** **Use Evidence** What do you think was the Greeks' most important achievement? Support your opinion with evidence.

☑ Lesson Check

Practice Vocabulary

1. How are **democracy** and oligarchy different?

2. How were **polytheism** and **mythology** related in ancient Greece?

Critical Thinking and Writing

3. **Synthesize** How did Greece's geography shape its social, cultural, and political development?

4. **Compare and Contrast** How was Hellenistic culture different from earlier Greek culture, and how did it flourish?

5. **Summarize** Why did the Peloponnesian War devastate ancient Greece?

6. **Writing Workshop: Draft a Thesis Statement** In your 📓 Active Journal, write a thesis statement summarizing what you see as the main causes of war and conflict. Revise you thesis statement as you read the lessons in this topic.

Draw Sound Conclusions and Make Generalizations

INTERACTIVE

Draw Conclusions

Follow these steps and use the chart to learn how to draw sound conclusions and make generalizations from sources.

1 **Study the facts and main ideas in a source.** Identify the facts and information in the text.

2 **Formulate questions about the source.** Ask, "What point is this source trying to make about the government and structure of society in Athens and Sparta?"

3 **Draw conclusions from the source.** Ask, "What conclusions does the source suggest about Athens and Sparta?"

4 **Test any conclusions for soundness.** Ask, "Do the facts in the source support the conclusion?"

5 **Make a generalization about the information in the source.** Ask, "What generalizations can be made about why Athens and Sparta developed different forms of government?"

Athens	Sparta
• **Government:** Direct democracy—assembly of citizens makes some decisions and chooses the Council of 500 to make others.	• **Government:** Oligarchy—two kings and a 28-person Council of Elders (chosen by an unelected assembly) make decisions.
• **Economy:** Based on trade	• **Economy:** Based on farming
• **Values and Education:** Valued art and culture; citizens expected to have healthy body and mind; women had no civil rights.	• **Values and Education:** Valued strength and simplicity; citizens spend years in military training; women had property rights.
• **Location:** Close to the sea; open to travel, trade, and new ideas	• **Location:** Surrounded by mountains on a plain with fertile soil for farming
• **Military:** Powerful navy	• **Military:** Strong army

Ancient Rome

BOUNCE TO ACTIVATE · ▶ VIDEO

GET READY TO READ

START UP
Examine the artwork from ancient Rome. What does the subject matter suggest about what was important to the Romans?

GUIDING QUESTIONS
- How did geography shape ancient Italy and its peoples?
- How did a republic emerge in ancient Rome?
- What were some strengths and weaknesses of the Roman empire?
- What were the key achievements of ancient Rome?

TAKE NOTES
Literacy Skill: Summarize
Use the graphic organizer in your 📙 Active Journal to take notes as you read the lesson.

PRACTICE VOCABULARY
Use the vocabulary activity in your 📙 Active Journal to practice the vocabulary words.

Vocabulary	Academic Vocabulary
republic	consent
constitution	isolated
empire	

Like Greece, the Italian peninsula became a center of power and influence in the ancient world. The Romans borrowed from Greek culture. Ancient Rome made its own contributions to law, language, architecture, and culture.

The Geography and People of Ancient Italy

Around 800 BCE a small settlement called Rome was built along the Tiber River in present-day Italy. In time, this settlement became the center of a mighty empire.

The Italic Peoples Most of the people of Italy belonged to ethnic groups that spoke related Italic languages. These groups included the Latins. At first, they controlled just a small region around Rome. Most of the rest of Italy belonged to other Italic groups.

Many Greeks settled in southern Italy starting around the 700s BCE. They brought their culture with them. Rome was in contact with these cities. The Romans adopted Greek legends and heroes as their own.

The Etruscans The Etruscans were the most powerful people in central Italy when Rome was founded. They lived in Etruria, a region just north of Rome.

The Etruscans had an advanced culture. They borrowed ideas from both the Greeks and the Phoenicians and were skilled artists and builders. The Romans learned construction and engineering skills from the Etruscans.

READING CHECK **Summarize** How did ancient Greeks and Etruscans influence Roman culture?

From Monarchy to Republic

Like Athens and Sparta, Rome began as an independent city-state. Its first form of government was a monarchy.

The Roman Kings In Rome's earliest days, kings ruled the city. They served as head of the army, chief priest, and supreme judge. The Roman kings had the first buildings in the Forum built and led the Romans in wars against neighboring villages.

The kings ruled with the **consent** of Rome's wealthy aristocrats. Older male aristocrats advised the king on important matters.

The Founding of the Republic Over time, Roman aristocrats grew tired of kings. In 509 BCE, leading Romans overthrew the king and formed a **republic**. A republic is a government in which citizens have the right to vote and elect officials to represent them.

The word *republic* comes from the Latin term *res publica,* which means "public thing" or "public business." In the Roman republic, all free adult male citizens could play a role in the city-state's government.

READING CHECK **Identify Main Ideas** Why did Rome form a republic?

Academic Vocabulary
consent • *n.,* approval; permission

Analyze Images The columns are part of the ruins of the Roman Forum, standing in front of a more recent building. **Use Visual Information** How do you think Greek culture influenced the design of the Forum?

INTERACTIVE

Growth of the Roman Republic

▼ Roman senators served in the Senate as an advisory council and later as a governing council.

How Was the Republic Governed?

Rome's system combined three forms of government—monarchy, aristocracy, and democracy. Strong leaders, wealthy aristocrats, and average citizens all played a role.

Rome's Constitution Roman government was structured by a **constitution**, a system of basic rules and principles by which a government is organized. Unlike the U.S. Constitution, the Roman constitution was unwritten. It was based on tradition and custom.

Principles of Republican Government The main idea in Rome's system of government was the separation of powers. This means that power was shared among different people with set roles. Power was also divided among the three branches of government. They were the assemblies, the senate, and the magistrates, or elected officials who enforce the law.

Each branch of government had its own set of powers. They were balanced against the powers of the other branches. One branch could check, or stop, another branch from misusing its power. The Romans also limited officials' power by splitting some offices between two or more men. For example, two leaders called consuls held equal powers. Each could veto—stop or cancel—the action of the other. Roman ideas about separation of powers and limits on power later influenced the U.S. Constitution.

The Romans also limited the power of officials by requiring them to leave office after one year. Even a powerful official could not do too much harm in that short time.

Another important principle in Roman government was the rule of law. This means that the law applied to everyone. Even elected officials could be tried for violating the law after their term of office was over.

Citizens and Officials All free Roman men were citizens. Women and enslaved people had no political rights. Citizens were divided into two groups: plebeians and patricians. Plebeians were ordinary Romans. Patricians were members of high-ranking, mainly wealthy families.

Different Roman assemblies had different powers and different make-ups. In the later republic, an assembly of all ordinary citizens of Rome had the power to make laws. The senate, made up of wealthy Romans who were often former magistrates, had some control over elected officials.

✓ READING CHECK Summarize How did Rome's systems of checks and balances work?

Growth of Roman Power to 44 BCE

KEY
- 500 BCE
- to 264 BCE
- to 146 BCE
- to 44 BCE
- Territory gained from Carthage

BRITAIN · ATLANTIC OCEAN · GAUL · ALPS · Rhine R. · Danube R. · Black Sea · PYRENEES MTS. · SPAIN · CORSICA · Rome · MACEDONIA · Byzantium · ASIA MINOR · New Carthage · SARDINIA · SICILY · Athens · Antioch · SYRIA · CRETE · CYPRUS · Damascus · NUMIDIA · Carthage · Mediterranean Sea · Cyrene · Alexandria · Nile R. · EGYPT · AFRICA

0   400 mi
0   400 km
Lambert Conformal Conic Projection

How Did Rome Expand?

The Romans were feared conquerors. They also made skillful use of diplomacy, or managing relationships with other countries and governments.

Road to Expansion Rome's location on hills made it easy to defend from attackers, while its location along a river leading to a nearby port helped it to grow rich from trade.

Rome's well-organized army helped the republic to expand. Rome began to expand beyond the territory of the Latin people in the 300s BCE. It had conquered all of Italy by 200 BCE.

Rome's main rival for control of the lands around the western Mediterranean was the city-state of Carthage in North Africa. The Romans fought a series of wars with Carthage, ending with a Roman victory and the destruction of Carthage in 146 BCE.

Several Greek city-states in southern Italy and western Greece had been allies of Carthage. During the late 200s, Roman forces began fighting in western Greece. In the end, the Romans conquered Greece. Next the Romans conquered the Hellenistic kingdoms of the eastern Mediterranean. Meanwhile, Rome expanded south into North Africa and west into what are now France, Spain, and Portugal.

Civil Wars Rival military leaders fought a series of civil wars beginning in the 80s BCE. These wars broke out when military commanders refused to obey Rome's republican government, or when the republican government was divided.

A leader named Julius Caesar won one of these civil wars and ruled the republic as a dictator by intimidating the senate and the assemblies.

GEOGRAPHY SKILLS

Rome expanded south, east, and west, and by 44 BCE, Rome controlled land on three continents.

1. **Region** After Rome gained control of Italy, what physical feature influenced where it expanded?

2. **Location** How do you think the expansion of Rome affected trade?

▼ A statue of Caesar Augustus

After Caesar's death, civil wars resumed. It was clear that Rome's republican government could not control Rome's vast armies and territories.

Caesar's adopted nephew, Octavian, won the last civil war. In 27 BCE, Rome's senate named him emperor and gave him the title *Augustus* (meaning "majestic" or "honored"). From then on, he was known as Caesar Augustus, and the Roman republic became an empire. An **empire** is a state containing several countries.

☑ READING CHECK **Summarize** How did Rome expand?

The Empire and the Roman Peace

When Octavian took control of the Roman world, he became Augustus, the first Roman emperor.

Augustus and the Pax Romana After Augustus ended the civil wars that had torn apart the Roman republic, he brought peace to the Roman world. He held nearly total power over the empire, although Rome still had a senate.

Augustus made the empire more stable. He shrank the size of the army and raised soldiers' pay. By bringing peace, Augustus gave the economy a boost, improving life for ordinary people. He also fought corruption. After his death he was made a god, as many emperors who followed were, too.

Augustus's rule began a long period of peace and prosperity known as the *Pax Romana*, or the "Roman Peace." It lasted from 30 BCE to around 180 CE. It was a golden age for the Roman empire. During the *Pax Romana*, no major wars threatened the people of the empire.

Other Emperors When Augustus died, his stepson Tiberius became emperor. Rome was now clearly a monarchy with an emperor who had nearly total power. Though this transfer of leadership within the family seemed to signal that Rome had become a monarchy, there was no formal or set way to choose new emperors. Members of the imperial family and other powerful Romans schemed and even killed to become emperor. Sometimes the Roman army made the final decision.

Some of the emperors after Augustus were successful. Trajan conquered new territory for Rome. Hadrian built walls that protected Roman lands. Marcus Aurelius wrote a famous book of philosophy. Many emperors built aqueducts, public baths, temples, stadiums, and other large buildings in Rome and across the empire.

Other emperors were failures. Some are still known for their cruelty. For example, Nero was accused of killing Roman citizens without cause. He was also the first emperor to persecute people who were Christians.

☑ READING CHECK **Identify Cause and Effect** How did the *Pax Romana* affect the Roman empire?

What Did Rome Achieve?

Roman engineering and other cultural achievements had a profound influence on later cultures, including our own. For centuries, European thinkers and builders relied on Roman examples, which laid a foundation for modern achievements in science and engineering.

INTERACTIVE

3-D Model: The Pantheon

Roman Law Romans created a system of written laws. Roman law forms the basis for systems of law today in much of Europe, Latin America, and other parts of the world.

Latin's Legacy The language of the Romans is called Latin. The Roman empire spread Latin across much of southern and western Europe. Many European languages, including Spanish, Portuguese, French, and Italian, are derived from Latin. Many Latin-based words became part of the English language.

Roman Engineering Roman engineering was the most advanced of its time. The Roman road system stretched for thousands of miles to every corner of the empire. The Romans built strong bridges for their roads. Some of these roads and bridges are still used today.

The city of Rome reached a population of more than 1 million during the early Roman empire and was the largest city in the world at the time. The city required a lot of water. To provide it, the Romans built a system of aqueducts—large pipes or channels, sometimes built on high bridges—to carry water over long distances. The Romans built aqueducts to supply Roman cities in other parts of the empire as well. A few of these are still in use today.

The Romans were the first to build massive, self-supporting domes. They also perfected the use of arches.

✓ **READING CHECK** How did Rome influence the modern world?

Analyze Images Most of Rome's aqueducts were underground or on ground level, unlike this one in Pont du Gard, France. **Infer** Why do you think the Romans did not build as many above-ground aqueducts?

A New Religion and the Fall of an Empire

In 63 BCE, the Romans took control of the Jewish kingdom of Judea, centered in Jerusalem. Soon, a new religion would appear in the region.

Christianity Spreads to Rome Between about 30 and 50 CE, a new religion called Christianity emerged in Southwest Asia. This religion was based on the teachings of Jesus. Jesus was a Jew, or a follower of Judaism. Christianity maintained a number of Jewish beliefs, including monotheism, or belief in one god. Most early Christians were Jews who later adopted Christian beliefs.

Around 50 CE, a Christian named Paul began traveling around the Roman empire converting people who were not Jews to Christianity. Christian communities grew in many parts of the empire. Because Christians would not accept the official Roman religion, Christians faced violence and sometimes death for their beliefs.

Christianity was not the only religion to spread around the Roman empire. Many Jews also left Judea and settled in different parts of the empire, including Europe. Smaller groups of Jews withdrew from society and lived in **isolated** communities in the desert.

Rome Becomes Christian By the early 300s CE though, Christianity had gained many followers and was the leading religion in some Roman cities. In 312, the Roman emperor Constantine had a vision that led him to adopt Christianity.

Christianity gradually became the empire's dominant religion. In 380, Emperor Theodosius declared that Christianity was the official religion of the Roman empire. By this time, Christianity was practiced across the empire.

GEOGRAPHY SKILLS

Christianity spread throughout most of the Roman empire.

1. **Region** Where did most of Paul's journeys take place?

2. **Infer** Why do you think Christianity spread first to Asia Minor instead of to Britain?

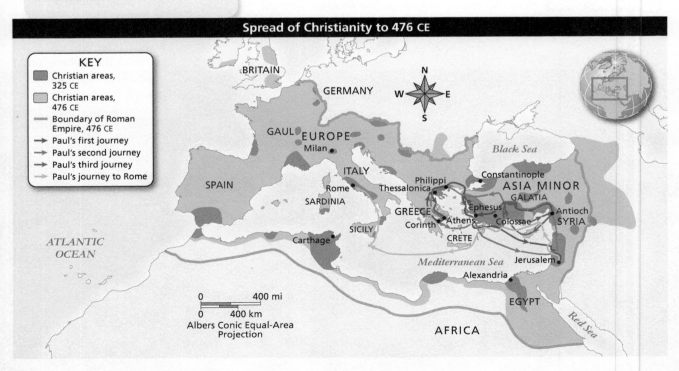

Spread of Christianity to 476 CE

KEY
- Christian areas, 325 CE
- Christian areas, 476 CE
- Boundary of Roman Empire, 476 CE
- Paul's first journey
- Paul's second journey
- Paul's third journey
- Paul's journey to Rome

BRITAIN
GERMANY
GAUL
EUROPE
Milan
ITALY
Rome
SARDINIA
SPAIN
GREECE
Athens
Corinth
SICILY
CRETE
Carthage
ATLANTIC OCEAN
Black Sea
Philippi
Thessalonica
Constantinople
ASIA MINOR
GALATIA
Ephesus
Colossae
Antioch
SYRIA
Mediterranean Sea
Jerusalem
Alexandria
EGYPT
Red Sea
AFRICA

0   400 mi
0   400 km
Albers Conic Equal-Area Projection

As the official religion of the empire, the Christian Church developed a governing structure modeled after the empire's. Bishops were in charge of provinces known as dioceses. Bishops followed five leaders known as patriarchs. One of them, in Rome, was the head of the Church in the western part of the empire.

How Was the Empire Divided? In the late 200s, the Roman emperors divided the empire into two major sections, one in the west and one in the east. Each section had its own emperor. They hoped the empire would be easier to rule in this new form. In 324, Constantine began building a new capital in the east. It came to be called Constantinople; today it is Istanbul, in Turkey. In 395, the empire was permanently divided into an eastern Roman empire, with a capital at Constantinople, and a western Roman empire, with a capital at Ravenna in northern Italy.

Germanic Armies Invade and Rome Falls Tribal peoples lived beyond the Roman empire's northern borders. Many spoke Germanic languages, including languages that later developed into German and English. Peoples along Rome's borders were tempted by its wealth. In the late 300s, Germanic peoples began to invade the empire.

The Romans held off most of these invasions during the 300s, but in the 400s, invaders from Asia drove some Germanic peoples from their homelands. These peoples began seizing Roman territory. Finally, in 476, a Germanic ruler named Odoacer removed the last western Roman emperor from power. The western Roman empire was now divided between several different Germanic peoples. The eastern empire remained intact, though.

☑ READING CHECK **Summarize** Why did the Western Roman Empire fall?

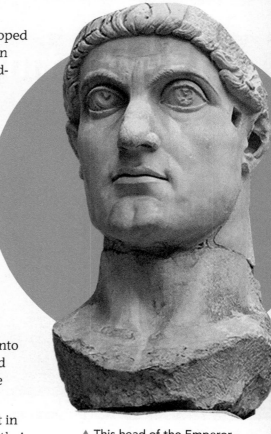

▲ This head of the Emperor Constantine was originally part of a statue that was about 40 feet high.

☑ Lesson Check

Practice Vocabulary

1. How did the Romans build an **empire**?

2. How did the Roman **republic** change after Rome expanded?

Critical Thinking and Writing

3. **Compare and Contrast** How is the United States government similar to and different from Rome's republic?

4. **Use Evidence** Which event happened first, the empire's division into two sections, or Constantine's conversion to Christianity? Did these events occur before, during, or after the *Pax Romana*?

5. **Hypothesize** Why do you think Germanic peoples began to invade Rome in the 300s?

6. **Writing Workshop: Cite Evidence** In your 📓 Active Journal, cite evidence from the lesson that supports your thesis statement about what causes war and conflict. Revise your thesis statement if needed based on new evidence from the lesson.

The Byzantine Empire

GET READY TO READ

START UP

Examine the photograph of the religious painting showing two emperors honoring Jesus and his mother. Work with a partner to write three ideas about Byzantine culture that this image suggests.

GUIDING QUESTIONS

- How did the Byzantine empire rise and fall?
- Why did the Christian Church split into two branches?
- What lasting impact did Byzantine culture have?

TAKE NOTES

Literacy Skills: Draw Conclusions
Use the graphic organizer in your 📓 Active Journal to take notes as you read the lesson.

PRACTICE VOCABULARY

Use the vocabulary activity in your 📓 Active Journal to practice the vocabulary words.

Vocabulary	Academic Vocabulary
icon	authority
Great Schism	core
Justinian's Code	
missionary	

The western Roman empire fell in 476. The eastern Roman empire lasted almost one thousand years more, however.

The New Rome

Emperor Constantine had built Constantinople as a new capital for the Roman empire on the Bosporus, a narrow body of water. It connects the Mediterranean and Black seas and separates Europe from Asia. Constantinople stood at a crossroad of land and sea trade routes. Today, the city still exists and is known as Istanbul, Turkey.

The empire is called "Byzantine" (BIZ un teen) because Constantinople was built on the site of an older city called Byzantium. The people of the empire thought of themselves as Romans. Justinian, who ruled for nearly 40 years, tried to restore Rome's lost empire. His armies won back lands in Italy, Spain, and North Africa. For a time, the Byzantine empire was Europe's greatest power.

☑ **READING CHECK** Identify Main Ideas Why did Justinian want to expand his empire?

How Did the Christian Church Divide?

At first, Christians in Western Europe and the Byzantine empire saw themselves as part of the same church, or Christian religious group. Over time differences between the western and eastern churches grew, and two separate churches developed.

Disagreements Several differences separated the two churches. The western church used Latin, while the eastern church used Greek. The two branches disagreed about the meanings of some prayers.

At first, both churches decorated church buildings with images of Jesus and the saints. These images are called **icons**. During the 700s and 800s, though, eastern church leaders banned the use of icons, since Christian holy writings forbid the worship of images. Western church leaders strongly disagreed. This disagreement drove the western and eastern churches apart.

Also, the patriarch of Rome, called the pope, claimed that he had **authority** over the entire Christian world. Church leaders in the east disagreed.

The Split Finally, in 1054, the pope excommunicated the patriarch of Constantinople, the leader of the eastern church. Excommunicating means declaring that someone is not a member of the church. The patriarch of Constantinople responded by excommunicating the pope.

These acts resulted in a permanent split between the two churches, called the **Great Schism** (SKIZ uhm). After this, the western church was known as the Catholic Church, or Roman Catholic Church. The eastern church was known as the Eastern Orthodox Church.

Academic Vocabulary
authority • *n.*, power to rule or command

Quick Activity

Prepare a brief statement in your 📓 Active Journal to explain the causes and effects of one event from history.

GEOGRAPHY SKILLS

During Justinian's reign, the Byzantine empire reached its greatest size.

1. **Place** What part of the empire was farthest west?

2. **Sequence** When did the Byzantine empire lose control of Egypt?

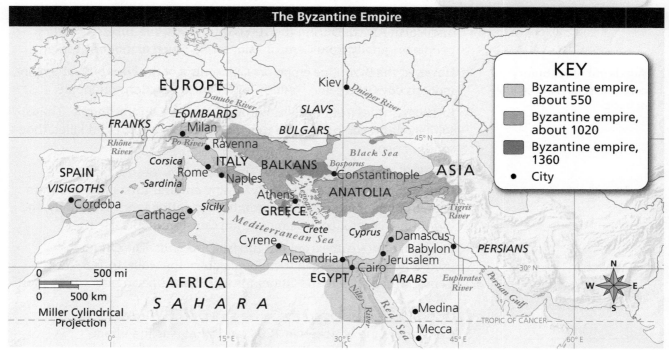

The Byzantine Empire

KEY
- Byzantine empire, about 550
- Byzantine empire, about 1020
- Byzantine empire, 1360
- City

0   500 mi
0   500 km
Miller Cylindrical Projection

Analyze Images This mosaic portrays the Empress Theodora, wife of Justinian. She was one of his most trusted advisers and one of the most powerful women in the ancient world. **Use Visual Information** How does this image help you to understand the importance of the arts in the Byzantine empire?

Academic Vocabulary

core • *n.,* something central or basic

The eastern church was closely connected to the government of the Byzantine empire. Eastern Christianity was the official religion of the empire. The emperor, as the church's political leader, influenced who was named patriarch of Constantinople.

☑ READING CHECK **Draw Conclusions** What was the most important issue in the Great Schism?

The Shrinking Empire

After the death of Justinian, the Byzantine empire slowly shrank. It fell 800 years later.

Foreign Invaders Many outside groups took parts of the empire. Germanic rulers took lands in the west, and Slavic peoples took some in the north. Arab Muslim invaders conquered most of Southwest Asia and North Africa. During the 1000s and 1100s, the Turks, a Muslim people originally from Central Asia, seized much of modern Turkey.

However, the Byzantine emperors kept control of the **core** of their empire, modern-day Greece and western Turkey, including Constantinople.

In 1204, armies from western Europe attacked Constantinople. These soldiers destroyed and looted much of the city's wealth and killed thousands of people.

The Fall of Constantinople The westerners' destruction of Constantinople weakened the Byzantine empire. Turkish armies were able to conquer most of the remaining Byzantine land. Eventually, the Byzantines controlled little more than Constantinople itself.

The final attack came from the Turkish Ottomans. The Ottomans used cannons that helped them break down the walls. In 1453, Constantinople fell to the Ottomans. The Byzantine empire was no more.

☑ READING CHECK **Identify Cause and Effect** Why was Constantinople attacked in 1204, and what was the effect?

INTERACTIVE

Hagia Sophia

The Byzantine Culture and Legacy

The people of the Byzantine empire maintained some Greco-Roman traditions, but their society was also strongly shaped by Eastern Orthodox Christianity. The result was a cultural blend that was unique.

Preserving Roman Law and Culture   Under Justinian, Roman law was collected and organized into a few texts known as **Justinian's Code**, which was published in 529. It gave great power to the emperor. Copies of these texts were preserved in church libraries. Later, these copies became available to rulers in Europe. This development allowed for the revival of Roman law in much of Western Europe and in other parts of the world.

Besides Roman law, the Byzantines preserved many works of Greek and Roman literature that had been destroyed in Western Europe by Germanic rulers. Hundreds of years later, this learning made its way back to Western Europe.

Spreading the Faith   Byzantine **missionaries**, or people who try to convert others to a particular religion, spread the Eastern Orthodox form of Christianity north into eastern Europe. Eastern Orthodox Christianity is still the main religion of most of southeastern Europe, Ukraine, Belarus, and Russia.

☑ READING CHECK   Summarize What are the main connections between the Byzantine empire and the modern world?

▼ Saints Cyril and Methodius, two missionaries who helped spread Christianity to Eastern Europe

☑ Lesson Check

Practice Vocabulary

1. What were **icons**, and why are they important to the history of the Christian Church?

2. What two groups did the **Great Schism** divide?

Critical Thinking and Writing

3. **Identify Supporting Details** Why was Constantinople an ideal location, and how did its location help to spread Byzantine culture?

4. **Compare and Contrast** What do you think was the most important difference between Roman Catholics and Eastern Orthodox Christians that led to the split in the Christian Church?

5. **Sequence** Did Justinian establish his code of laws before or after he expanded the empire? Explain why he created the code at that time.

6. **Writing Workshop: Cite Evidence** In your 📓 Active Journal, cite evidence from the lesson that supports your thesis statement about what causes war and conflict. Revise your thesis statement if needed based on new evidence from the lesson.

The Middle Ages in Europe

BOUNCE TO ACTIVATE ▶ VIDEO

GET READY TO READ

START UP

Examine the image of the stained glass window. What does the image suggest about life in medieval Europe?

GUIDING QUESTIONS

- How was society organized in medieval Europe?
- What role did the Christian Church play in medieval Europe?
- How did the Crusades affect Europe?

TAKE NOTES

Literacy Skill: Identify Cause and Effect
Use the graphic organizer in your 📓 Active Journal to take notes as you read the lesson.

PRACTICE VOCABULARY

Use the vocabulary activity in your 📓 Active Journal to practice the vocabulary words.

Vocabulary

		Academic Vocabulary
feudalism	Crusades	
lord	Black Death	devout
vassal		establish
manor		
serf		

After the collapse of the western Roman empire, military leaders ruled territories across Western Europe. They created a system of government called **feudalism**, which was also a system of land ownership.

Feudal Society

The period from the fall of Rome in 476 to about 1500 is called the Middle Ages. The period came between ancient and modern times. In the early Middle Ages, kings and emperors were too weak to protect their people from invasions. Instead, powerful local military leaders called lords took over this responsibility.

Lords and Vassals Ordinary villagers had to accept the control and protection of these lords in a time of violence and widespread warfare. This was the basis of a system called feudalism, which lasted in much of Europe right through the Middle Ages. European feudalism was a system of rule in which powerful **lords** divided their lands among lesser lords, or **vassals**. In exchange for the land, a vassal pledged his service and loyalty.

The land given the vassal included any towns or buildings on the land, as well as peasants required to farm it. The lord also promised to protect the vassal. In return, the vassal provided military support and money or food for the lord.

Knights and Warfare For lords and vassals, warfare was a way of life. As a result, many boys from noble families trained to become knights, or warriors mounted on horseback. Knights were expected to live by a code of conduct called chivalry, which required them to be brave, loyal, fair in battle, and generous.

During war, knights usually fought on horseback. They used swords, axes, and lances, or long spears. They wore armor to protect themselves from enemies' weapons.

The Medieval Manor The heart of the medieval economy was the **manor**, or the agricultural estate of a lord or vassal. Manors were centered around the land owner's house or castle. In addition, a manor usually included one or more villages and the surrounding fields and forests.

Most medieval Europeans were peasants, or people who worked on farms. Most of these peasants were **serfs**, or people who were legally required to live and work on a specific manor. Serfs were not slaves who could be bought and sold, but they were not free to move or change jobs.

Life on the Manor The peasants on a manor worked together to plant, care for, and harvest crops and raise livestock on the lord's lands. Serfs and other peasants were required to give their lord a large part of the crops and livestock they raised. They also grew crops and raised livestock for themselves and their families.

☑ READING CHECK **Draw Conclusions** In feudalism, who held the most power, and why?

Analyze Images This artwork shows a scene from a feudal manor. **Draw Conclusions** What position do you think the three people in the front of the picture held in society?

Academic Vocabulary
devout • adj., completely committed to religious beliefs

Kingdoms and Conquests

After the fall of Rome, Europe was divided into a patchwork of small, warring kingdoms.

The Age of Charlemagne The leaders of the Germanic tribes that conquered declared themselves kings of the lands they had conquered. Few of them were very strong, though.

One exception to this pattern was Charlemagne, whose leadership allowed him to defeat many feudal lords. He conquered a vast empire in the late 700s and early 800s.

Charlemagne was a **devout** Christian. His military victories reunited much of the original western Roman empire. From the 600s to the 1100s, Christianity gradually spread to Britain and into northern and eastern Europe. Charlemagne's conquests helped spread the Christian faith.

Did you know?

Charlemagne was never really able to read and write very well. He kept a writing tablet under his pillow so that he could practice his writing.

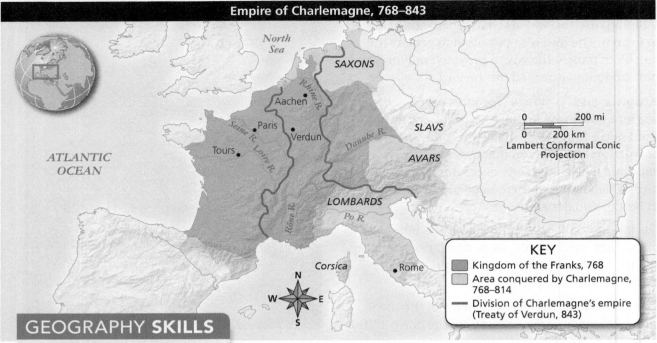

Empire of Charlemagne, 768–843

North Sea

SAXONS

Aachen

Rhine R.

SLAVS

Paris

Seine R.

Verdun

Danube R.

AVARS

Tours

Loire R.

ATLANTIC OCEAN

LOMBARDS

Po R.

Rhône R.

Corsica

Rome

KEY
Kingdom of the Franks, 768
Area conquered by Charlemagne, 768–814
Division of Charlemagne's empire (Treaty of Verdun, 843)

0   200 mi
0   200 km
Lambert Conformal Conic Projection

GEOGRAPHY SKILLS

By 800, Charlemagne had built an empire that stretched across most of Western Europe.

1. **Region** What does the map show about the expansion of Charlemagne's empire?

2. **Compare** Look at the political map of Europe at the beginning of the next topic. Which modern countries lay at least partly within Charlemagne's empire?

A Violent Time Western Europe faced serious challenges from the 700s to the mid-900s. Muslims from North Africa conquered most of present-day Spain and Portugal and parts of Italy. Vikings from Scandinavia conquered parts of Britain, Ireland, and France. Magyars conquered Hungary and threatened Germany. By the late 1000s, though, the Magyars and Scandinavians had accepted Christianity.

The Normans, who were French-speaking descendants of Vikings, conquered England in 1066.

Reviving the Empire After Charlemagne's empire collapsed, the eastern, German part of the kingdom was divided among a number of dukes. A German king known as Otto the Great increased his power by making alliances with other German nobles. In 962, he persuaded the pope to crown him emperor. By adopting this title, Otto was claiming to be the successor of Charlemagne.

Like Charlemagne, Otto worked closely with the Church. After his death, Otto's empire continued to be ruled by his descendants. The empire itself came to be called the Holy Roman Empire. The name of the empire showed that the German kings wanted to create a Christian, or holy, version of the Roman empire.

☑ READING CHECK **Identify Cause and Effect** Why did Christianity spread under Charlemagne's rule?

The Church in Medieval Europe

As Christianity spread, Church leaders influenced not only spiritual life, but also many aspects of nonreligious life. Medieval Europeans believed that the Church was the highest authority over both Church and worldly leaders.

The Church also controlled some land and wealth directly. The pope controlled much of central Italy. Some Church leaders even had their own territories and armies.

The Church sometimes came into conflict with kings and other rulers who wanted a share of the Church's income or control over the naming of bishops. The Church usually won these conflicts.

During this time few people other than priests knew how to read or write. As a result, priests played a valuable role as record-keepers and people who could read and write letters and legal documents.

With so much power, the Christian Church often came into conflict with other religious groups. For example, Europe's Jewish minorities suffered repeated and sometimes violent persecution. Christians also fought wars against Muslims.

✓ **READING CHECK** Identify Main Ideas Why did the Catholic Church have so much power in medieval Europe?

The Crusades and Their Aftermath

Between the 900s and 1200, political power lay with noble lords. Then, in England and France, power began to shift into the hands of kings. These shifts in power came at a time of large-scale military conflicts.

Call for a Crusade In the mid-1000s, Turkish invaders threatened Christians in Southwest Asia, including in the Christian Holy Land, the region where Jesus had lived. In 1095, Pope Urban called for knights of Europe to free the Holy Land from Muslim rule. Christian Europeans saw conquest of the Holy Land as a religious calling. This call launched the **Crusades**, a series of military campaigns to establish Christian control over the Holy Land.

INTERACTIVE

Spread of Christianity in Europe

Analyze Images Gothic cathedrals, like this one in Milan, Italy, featured breathtaking design. Many also had grotesque carved stone creatures known as gargoyles. **Infer** What might a medieval peasant have felt seeing a Gothic cathedral for the first time?

Key Dates in the Crusades

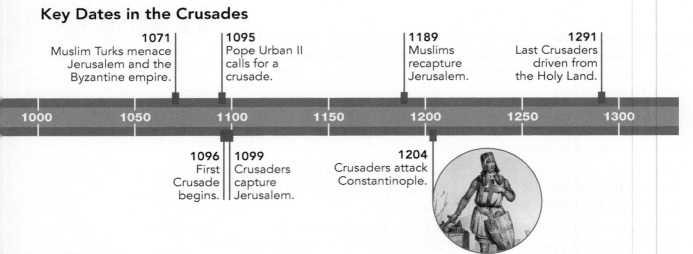

1071
Muslim Turks menace Jerusalem and the Byzantine empire.

1095
Pope Urban II calls for a crusade.

1189
Muslims recapture Jerusalem.

1291
Last Crusaders driven from the Holy Land.

1000 | 1050 | 1100 | 1150 | 1200 | 1250 | 1300

1096
First Crusade begins.

1099
Crusaders capture Jerusalem.

1204
Crusaders attack Constantinople.

Analyze Timeline The Crusades spanned almost two centuries. **Infer** What event probably sparked the First Crusade?

The First Crusade was a success for the Europeans. They won control of Jerusalem by 1099 and **established** Catholic kingdoms in the region. There were later crusades, but none as successful as this first one. Then, in 1189, Jerusalem returned to Muslim rule, and Europeans were largely driven out of Southwest Asia by the late 1200s.

At the same time that Europeans were fighting Muslims in the Holy Land, Christian Spaniards and Portuguese were fighting the Muslims who ruled much of the Iberian Peninsula. The Christian struggle to regain control of the peninsula finally succeeded in the 1400s.

Effects of the Crusades The Crusades created connections between Europe, especially Italian ports such as Venice, and the Muslim world in Southwest Asia and Egypt. Trade across the Mediterranean became a new source of riches for Europeans.

Academic Vocabulary

establish • *v.,* to set up or found

Wealth from trade and from a growing population strengthened the kingdoms of Europe. By taxing trade, kings were able to gain power over their feudal vassals.

With increased trade also came the growth of cities across Europe. Within cities, people exchanged ideas and cultivated learning. Learning from ancient Greece, Rome, and the civilizations of Asia had been preserved and developed by the Byzantines and the Muslim Arabs. The Crusades brought Europeans into contact with these ideas and revolutionized European thought.

☑ READING CHECK **Identify Cause and Effect** How did the Crusades affect Europe?

The End of an Era

Starvation and warfare weakened medieval society in the 1300s. In addition, a terrible illness devastated Europe.

Famine and War In the early 1300s, Europe's steady growth ended. A shift in the climate to cooler, wetter weather caused crop failures. As a result, many Europeans died.

INTERACTIVE

The Black Death, 1347–1351

Meanwhile, war broke out between England and France, two of Europe's strongest kingdoms. The Hundred Years' War would last from 1337 to 1453. Many soldiers seized or damaged crops, which led to starvation in peasant communities. War weakened both countries and damaged their economies.

The Black Death In 1347, a terrible disease reached Europe along trade routes from Asia. The disease struck first in a port on the Black Sea. From there it spread along trade routes to Italy. Within three years, it had ravaged most of Europe, especially in the west. The disease was bubonic plague, carried by fleas on rats. Weakened by hunger, one in three Europeans may have died from the plague. This horrible epidemic, known as the **Black Death**, terrified Europeans.

Effects of the Black Death The Black Death shook the medieval world. Towns and villages lost vast numbers of people from every social rank. People developed a gloomy outlook on life.

Searching for scapegoats, some Europeans falsely blamed Jews for the disease. In Strasbourg, the city council ordered the city's Jews to convert to Christianity or be burned to death. Many Jews across Europe were killed or forced to flee.

With so many people dead, much farmland went unused. Lords found themselves short of people to work their land. Serfs demanded to be paid for their work. Many began to defy their lords and won new rights. In some areas, peasants and townspeople revolted. The Black Death weakened feudalism in Europe.

Analyze Images A monk falls ill during a procession to pray for the end of the plague. **Infer** Why did the Black Death leave Europeans feeling helpless?

☑READING CHECK **Identify Cause and Effect** How did the Black Death affect feudalism and peasants?

☑ Lesson Check

Practice Vocabulary

1. What purpose did the **manor** serve in feudalism?

2. How did the **Black Death** affect **serfs** in western Europe?

Critical Thinking and Writing

3. **Analyze Information** Why did the Crusades begin?

4. **Infer** What purpose did the name "Holy Roman Empire" have?

5. **Understand Effects** How were the rise and growth of towns and trade connected to the Crusades?

6. **Writing Workshop: Cite Evidence** In your ▣ Active Journal, cite evidence in the text that supports your thesis statement about what causes war and conflict. Revise your thesis statement if needed based on new evidence from the lesson.

The Renaissance and Rival Kingdoms in Europe

GET READY TO READ

START UP
Examine the image of the Hall of Mirrors at the Palace of Versailles in France. Write two or three ideas that the size and appearance of this building suggest about the monarchies of Europe at the time that it was built?

GUIDING QUESTIONS
- What were the causes and effects of the Renaissance?
- How did the Reformation affect Europe?
- How did powerful kingdoms develop in Europe?

TAKE NOTES
Literacy Skill: Use Evidence
Use the graphic organizer in your 📓 Active Journal to take notes as you read the lesson.

PRACTICE VOCABULARY
Use the vocabulary activity in your 📓 Active Journal to practice the vocabulary words.

Vocabulary

Renaissance
humanism
Reformation
Counter-
 Reformation
absolute
 monarchy

Academic Vocabulary

prestige
doctrine

During the Middle Ages, life for most Europeans revolved around the manor and the Church. However, change was in the air.

The Birth of the Renaissance
As trade and industry grew, feudalism and manorialism weakened. Cities began to build great wealth in Europe, especially in Italy.

Urban Growth, Learning, and Culture Converge Northern and central Italy began to move away from the feudal system early. City-states such as Venice and Florence dominated this region. Built near the Mediterranean Sea, these city-states served as a natural crossroad between Europe, Southwest Asia, and North Africa.

Through trade, new ideas came to these city-states, and Italians rediscovered the learning of the ancient Greeks and Romans that had been preserved by the Byzantines and Muslims. These new and rediscovered ideas led to the **Renaissance**, a cultural movement that swept through Europe from the 1300s through the 1500s. *Renaissance* is French for "rebirth."

A Shift in Ideas The Renaissance included a shift among thinkers and artists away from religious themes toward the use of reason to understand the human and natural worlds. This new focus, called **humanism**, was a cultural movement of the Renaissance based on the study of ancient Greek and Roman works. Humanists sought a better life here on Earth and not just salvation after death.

At the same time, there was a new emphasis on realistic portrayals of human beings in art. Artists such as Michelangelo and Leonardo da Vinci, who was also a scientist, embraced these trends. Michelangelo's famous works include his statue of David and the paintings on the ceiling of the Sistine Chapel. As an architect, he designed the dome of St. Peter's Basilica in Rome. Da Vinci's most famous painting is *Mona Lisa*.

Also breaking with religious tradition were scientists like Galileo, who found proof that Earth revolved around the sun, rather than the other way around. This idea violated Church doctrine, and he was forced to withdraw his scientific statement.

Supporting the Arts In the Italian city-states, the newly rich gained status by becoming patrons of art and learning. A patron is someone who gives money or other support to a person or group. One of the most powerful banking families in Florence was the Medici (MED ee chee) family. Generations of Medicis were also patrons of the arts. Their support brought **prestige** to both the artists and their patrons.

The Northern Renaissance During the late 1400s and 1500s, Renaissance ideas and styles of art spread from Italy to other countries.

INTERACTIVE

Renaissance Italy's City-States

Academic Vocabulary
prestige • *n.,* having high status in others' eyes

Analyze Images In this painting, Lorenzo de Medici is surrounded by other artists as they study a sculpture by Michelangelo, titled *Faun*. **Synthesize Visual Information** Based on what you have read about Michelangelo, what type of art is reflected in his sculpture?

English writer William Shakespeare was influenced by these ideas. Shakespeare wrote 37 plays—such as *Romeo and Juliet* and *Hamlet*—as well as poems. His work had a profound impact on the development of the English language.

Northern European scientists such as Johannes Kepler and Nicholas Copernicus made new discoveries about the universe. Copernicus published his heliocentric theory in 1543 that described how Earth revolved around the sun rather than vice versa.

The emphasis on reason and inquiry led to critical thinking about the role of the Church by writers such as Dutchman Desiderius Erasmus. Erasmus used satire to criticize Church leaders. Erasmus helped spread humanism and ideas that challenged Church power.

☑ READING CHECK **Recognize Multiple Causes** What causes brought about the Renaissance in Italy?

GEOGRAPHY **SKILLS**

During the Age of Exploration, many explorers followed the routes of earlier explorers.

1. **Movement** Which explorers followed the coast of Africa to Asia?

2. **Use Visual Information** Which explorer's expedition sailed around the world?

What Was the Age of Discovery?

Europeans had traded with Asia since ancient times through Asian merchants. During the Crusades, Europeans brought back silks, jewels, and spices from Asia. By the 1400s, European traders wanted direct access to the riches of South, Southeast, and East Asia.

Why Did Countries Want to Explore? Existing trade routes to South and East Asia were controlled by Venice and Muslim intermediaries. The possibility of direct trade encouraged exploration to find new routes to Asia. New technologies had made longer sea journeys possible. During the 1400s, Portugal, led by Prince Henry the Navigator, explored the seas.

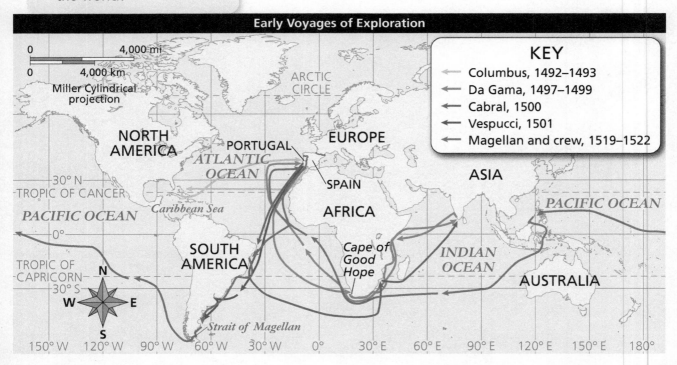

Early Voyages of Exploration

KEY
← Columbus, 1492–1493
← Da Gama, 1497–1499
← Cabral, 1500
← Vespucci, 1501
← Magellan and crew, 1519–1522

Portuguese explorers discovered a direct route around Africa to South and East Asia, allowing them to gain wealth by selling goods such as spices and silk at prices lower than those charged by Venice.

Building Empires Meanwhile, Spain sent Italian explorer Christopher Columbus to find a route to Asia by sailing west across the Atlantic Ocean. Columbus landed on an island in the Caribbean Sea. He thought he was near India so he named the region the Indies. Spain eventually conquered territories in the Americas and set up colonies that brought it great riches. European weapons and diseases killed millions of American Indians.

In time, other European nations followed the Portuguese and Spanish examples. England, France, and the Netherlands built colonial empires in the Americas, Africa, and Asia.

☑ READING CHECK **Identify Cause and Effect** What were the causes and effects of Prince Henry sending out the first wave of explorers?

What Was the Reformation?

The northern European humanists laid the foundation for the **Reformation**, a religious movement that gained momentum in the 1500s, aiming at first to reform the Catholic Church. Reformation thinkers changed European society in ways that are still felt today.

Luther's Challenge An important leader of the Reformation was Martin Luther, a German monk. In 1510, Luther's visit to Rome shocked him. There was corruption among Roman Church leaders, and many priests were poorly trained. Church leaders rose to power through wealth or political influence. The Catholic Church also imposed taxes on its members and raised money by selling indulgences, which cancelled punishment for misdeeds or violations of Church teachings.

In 1517, Luther posted the 95 Theses, criticisms of the Catholic Church, on the door of the main church in Wittenberg, Germany. He challenged the Church's authority and stressed the spiritual, inward character of the Christian faith. Luther was put on trial and ordered to take back his harsh words against the Church. He refused. In 1521, the pope excommunicated, or expelled, Luther from the Church, but his approach to Christianity, called Lutheranism, spread.

Analyze Images Martin Luther was questioned by a German parliament, the diet, a few years after he posted the 95 Theses, but he was not charged and let go. **Infer** How did the way Luther issued his challenge to Church leaders increase the impact of that challenge?

Key Events of the Reformation

1534
King Henry VIII forms a separate Church of England.

1517
Martin Luther posts 95 Theses.

1545
Council of Trent launches the Counter-Reformation.

1618
Thirty Years' War begins.

1500 — 1550 — 1600 — 1650

1541
John Calvin's strict Protestantism prevails in Geneva, Switzerland.

1547–1555
Religious war leaves Germany divided; each ruler decides his territory's religion.

1648
Peace of Westphalia ends Thirty Years' War; Catholics and Protestants accept one another's right to rule.

Analyze Graphs Martin Luther's protest in 1517 launched a long period of religious change in Europe. **Sequence** How many years passed between Luther's action and the beginning of the Catholic Counter-Reformation?

Academic Vocabulary
doctrine • *n.*, article or principle of faith

Protestantism Spreads Lutheranism and other forms of Protestantism spread across northern Europe. French scholar John Calvin became another leader of the Protestant Reformation. He supported the concept of predestination, the idea that God had long ago determined who would gain salvation. At that time, the Catholic Church and some other Protestant churches taught that people had free will to choose or reject the path to salvation.

Calvin taught that salvation was not a human choice, but a decision made by God from the beginning of time. Since no one could know who God has chosen for salvation, all people should lead God-fearing, religious lives. Calvin called this the "**doctrine** of the elect."

In 1529 Henry VIII of England came into conflict with the pope. He decided to take control of the English church away from the pope and form the independent Church of England, or the Anglican Church, which he would lead.

In the Middle Ages, the Bible was available only in Latin, a language ordinary Europeans no longer spoke. By the early 1500s, the Bible's New Testament had appeared in French, Spanish, Italian, and Dutch. Luther's German translation appeared in 1534. Henry VIII soon authorized an English translation. It was now easier for most Europeans to read the Bible and think about its meaning.

The Counter-Reformation As Protestantism spread, Catholics responded in what became known as the **Counter-Reformation**. During the Counter-Reformation, also known as the Catholic Reformation, reformers founded new religious orders, or groups of priests or monks with their own particular structure and purpose. They founded new missionary orders to promote Catholicism. For example, Ignatius of Loyola started the Society of Jesus, or the Jesuits, an influential new missionary order.

In 1545, Pope Paul III began a series of meetings known as the Council of Trent in order to revive the moral authority of the Catholic Church.

They also hoped to stop the spread of Protestantism. The Church enforced the Council's decisions through a system called the Inquisition. Under the Inquisition, people suffered cruel punishments and lost their religious freedoms.

✅ READING CHECK **Summarize** How did the Reformation affect Europe?

Religious Conflict

Conflicts soon broke out between those kings and princes who embraced Protestantism and those who remained committed to the Catholic Church.

War in Germany In 1547, the Holy Roman emperor began a crackdown against Protestants in Germany that resulted in religious war. The war ended in 1555 with the Peace of Augsburg. This treaty allowed each German ruler to decide which religion his realm would follow—Catholic or Protestant. Instead of a unified Catholic empire, Germany was now a group of independent regions with different religious traditions. Northern Germany was mostly Protestant, while most of southern Germany was Catholic.

More Religious Wars In 1579, the Netherlands rebelled against Spanish rule. The mainly Protestant Netherlands gained independence from Catholic Spain and became a major economic and military power.

Henry VIII's daughter, Queen Elizabeth I, sent troops to aid the Dutch rebels in 1588. In retaliation, King Philip II of Spain sent a fleet of ships to attack England. The English navy fought back and won. This fight ended Spain's domination of the seas.

Spain later became involved in the Thirty Years' War, a war largely between Protestants and Catholics. Fought from 1618 to 1649, this war involved most major European countries. It resulted in the deaths of as many as one of every three Germans.

✅ READING CHECK **Identify Supporting Details** What conflicts broke out in Europe in the 1500s and 1600s, and why?

Powerful Kingdoms

The wars of religion increased the authority of monarchs. Monarchs also gained wealth from cities and trade. Leaders needed new forms of government to exercise their growing power.

Strong Rulers in Western Europe Spain became one of the strongest monarchies. It had driven out the last Muslims in the late 1400s, and the wealth it gained from its colonies in the Americas allowed it to pay for strong armies.

👆 INTERACTIVE

Major European Religions, About 1600

Analyze Images Queen Elizabeth I of England sent assistance to the Dutch when they rebelled against Spain. **Draw Conclusions** How did the official religion of England factor into this alliance?

Quest CONNECTIONS

Compare the rule of England to the governments of the rest of Europe at the time. What would be the advantages and disadvantages of ruling England? Record your findings in your Active Journal.

The kings of France used their army to force French nobles to give up power. French King Louis XIV, who was known as the Sun King, embraced the idea of **absolute monarchy**—the idea that because God had made him king, he had an unlimited right to rule. This idea of God-given rule was also called "divine right." Absolute monarchy appealed to monarchs across Europe.

Strong Rulers in Central Europe The Habsburg empire, centered in present-day Austria, gained power by conquering land in central and southeastern Europe during the 1600s and 1700s. The Habsburg emperors ruled as absolute monarchs and also gained control of some areas in Western Europe.

In the late 1700s, the Habsburgs conquered and divided the kingdom of Poland-Lithuania with Russia and the German kingdom of Prussia. As a result, millions of Eastern Europeans lived in empires ruled by foreign monarchs.

Changes in England England, by contrast, had a tradition stretching back to the Middle Ages that kings, in order to raise taxes, had to win approval from Parliament, an assembly of nobles and elected representatives.

King Charles I of England came to the throne in 1625 seeking to rule as an absolute monarch. A civil war broke out in 1642 between parliamentary forces and forces loyal to the king. The king was executed in 1649. Parliamentary forces declared a republic. This republic became a dictatorship, and in 1660 Parliament restored Charles II, the son of Charles I, to the English throne.

Analyze Images
Schönbrunn Palace in Vienna, Austria, was a summer home for the Habsburg rulers.
Compare and Contrast Compare the exterior of this palace with the image of the Palace of Versailles at the beginning of this lesson. What do both buildings have in common?

▲ The Battle of Marston Moor, which took place in 1644 during the English Civil War

After the Catholic James II took the throne in 1685, he clashed with Parliament. As a result, Parliament removed him from the throne and replaced him with a Protestant Dutch prince, William, who had to agree to the English Bill of Rights. This document guaranteed civil rights in England and gave Parliament powers over the king. As a result, while other European powers became absolute monarchies, England became a limited, constitutional monarchy. When Scotland joined with England in 1707 to form the United Kingdom of Great Britain, the kingdom remained a constitutional monarchy.

☑ READING CHECK Use Evidence Why did powerful kingdoms develop in Europe? Use evidence from the text in your response.

☑ Lesson Check

Practice Vocabulary

1. How was the **Renaissance** a rebirth?

2. How was the **Reformation** different from the **Counter-Reformation**?

Critical Thinking and Writing

3. Summarize How did the ideas of the Renaissance spread to northern Europe?

4. Compare and Contrast How were the reasons for Portuguese and Spanish exploration similar?

5. Use Evidence Use this quote from the text to explain the idea behind absolute monarchy: "This idea of God-given rule was also called 'divine right.'"

6. Writing Workshop: Cite Evidence In your 🗐 Active Journal, cite evidence in the text that supports your thesis statement about what causes war and conflict. Revise your thesis statement if needed based on new evidence from the lesson.

The Enlightenment and Revolutions in Europe

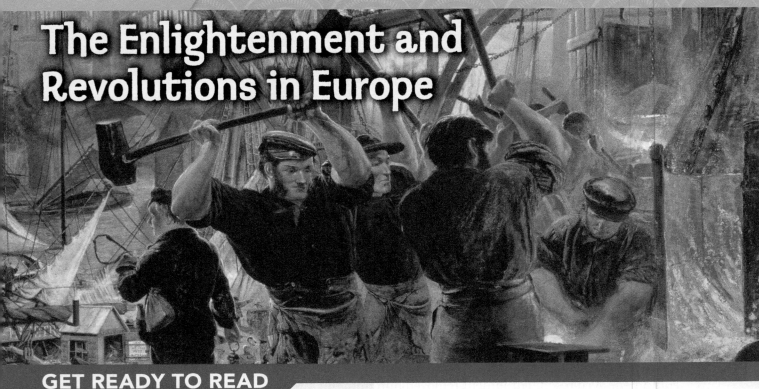

GET READY TO READ

START UP

Scottish artist William Bell Scott created this painting, *Iron and Coal*, in 1861, to show the growth of industry in Britain. Based on the details in the painting, what major changes had taken place in Britain since the early 1700s?

GUIDING QUESTIONS

- What was the Enlightenment?
- What changes did the Industrial Revolution bring?
- How did nationalism and imperialism affect Europe?

TAKE NOTES

Literacy Skill: Classify and Categorize
Use the graphic organizer in your 🗐 Active Journal to take notes as you read the lesson.

PRACTICE VOCABULARY

Use the vocabulary activity in your 🗐 Active Journal to practice the vocabulary words.

Vocabulary

Enlightenment	nationalism	**Academic Vocabulary**
French Revolution	imperialism	radical
Industrial Revolution		access

During the 1600s and 1700s, Europeans began to use the scientific method and reason to solve scientific and social problems. In the late 1700s, new industries began to transform Europe's economies, while political revolution boosted democracy. During the 1800s, new nation-states formed in Europe.

Science and the Enlightenment

In the 1600s and 1700s, European thinkers drew on ancient Greek thought and the Renaissance. These European thinkers stressed the use of reason and logic to solve practical problems.

The Scientific Revolution In the 1600s, Europeans began to think in new ways about the natural world. Isaac Newton used the scientific method, which uses practical tests, logic, and reason to determine the truth. Using this method, Newton discovered gravity. He found that more massive objects pull with greater gravitational force than less massive ones.

There were many contributors to this revolution besides Newton. Among them were Galileo Galilei (gal uh LAY oh gal uh LAY ee), Johannes (yoh HAHN us) Kepler, and René Descartes (ruh NAY day CART).

The Enlightenment In the 1700s, successes in science led European thinkers to use reason and logic to think about society and government. This new way of thinking about the human world is the movement known as the **Enlightenment**.

John Locke of England, and the Baron de Montesquieu (MAHN tuh skyoo) and Jean-Jacques Rousseau (zhawn zhahk roo SOH) of France all contributed ideas about political life that would help shape the United States and European democracies. Key ideas of theirs include natural rights (human rights that belong to all people from birth) and the separation of powers in government. They also discussed the social contract, an unwritten agreement between people and their government.

The French writer Voltaire promoted tolerance, such as religious tolerance. Women's rights also became a key idea during the Enlightenment. Mary Wollstonecraft of England wrote the first major work of feminism, or women's rights.

☑ READING CHECK **Identify Cause and Effect** How did the Scientific Revolution influence the Enlightenment, and what were the roots of both?

The French Revolution and Napoleonic Wars

Enlightenment ideas caused people to begin to question the social, economic, and political order. These ideas helped inspire colonists in North America to rebel against Britain. The success of the American Revolution triggered reactions in France and elsewhere.

The French Revolution In the late 1700s, France faced an economic crisis caused by costly wars its monarchs had waged. Many people were hungry and without jobs. Society was divided into three groups: the clergy, nobles, and common people. The first two groups were wealthy and powerful. The common people outnumbered them but had few rights and paid higher taxes. When the government tried to raise taxes further, French people rebelled in 1789. This rebellion of the common people was the start of the **French Revolution**, a political movement that removed the French king from power and formed a republic.

Quest CONNECTIONS

How did Enlightenment thinkers change how people viewed government's role? Record your findings in your 📓 Active Journal.

▼ This political cartoon shows a member of the common people supporting the clergy and nobles of France.

INTERACTIVE

Napoleon's Europe
(1804–1815)

Academic Vocabulary

radical • *n.*, someone with
extreme views

French revolutionaries forced the French king, Louis XVI, to give up absolute power and acknowledge the basic rights of all citizens. They formed the National Assembly and wrote a document called the Declaration of the Rights of Man and the Citizen. This document was influenced by Enlightenment ideas and the U.S. Declaration of Independence.

Other European powers declared war on France to try to restore the French king's absolute power. **Radicals** known as the Jacobins then took control of the French government. They killed the king, many French nobles, and anyone who opposed them.

Soon, the radicals lost support, but the government that replaced them could not restore order. Wars between France and other European powers were raging. Many French wanted strong leadership.

Napoleon Takes Power A general named Napoleon took power in 1799 and declared himself emperor of France in 1804. Many people in France supported him because he won victories across Europe against France's enemies. Napoleon's ambitions, however, brought more war.

Napoleon built an empire that covered most of Western Europe. In 1812, he invaded Russia. There, his army faced defeat in battle and were caught in the bitterly cold Russian winter without proper clothing or supplies. Most of his soldiers died from the effects of cold and disease. In 1815, he suffered a final defeat by troops from Britain and the German kingdom of Prussia.

Analyze Images French artist Jacques-Louis David painted *Napoleon Crossing the Alps* between 1801 and 1805. **Use Visual Information** What traits did David try to attribute to Napoleon through the style of this painting?

Effects of the Napoleonic Wars Napoleon's defeat prompted European leaders to try to balance nations' powers. They did not want to see another country dominate the region as France had done.

These leaders tried to restore the old order of monarchy across Europe. They placed a king back on the throne of France.

While the French Revolution had failed to end the monarchy, it had strengthened civil rights and the ideal of democracy. Leaders across Europe gave up some of their powers, and absolute monarchy gave way to greater democracy.

✓ READING CHECK **Summarize** How did the French Revolution and the Napoleonic Wars affect Europe?

Analyze Images Women work in a cotton spinning mill in England in 1851. **Draw Conclusions** How would machines that spun thread quickly change the clothing industry?

What Was the Industrial Revolution?

Another type of revolution was occurring in the 1700s. In Britain, new inventions and energy sources triggered the rise of industrialism. As a result, people began to move from farm work to jobs in urban factories.

New Production Methods In the early 1700s, more efficient ways of farming increased the food supply. The population grew at the same time as fewer farmworkers were needed.

By the mid-1700s, British inventors and entrepreneurs developed new technologies that used water power to run machines that made textiles and other goods. This shift from human labor to machine labor is known as the **Industrial Revolution**. While machines replaced human labor, they created jobs for people operating the machines.

New technology soon made the process of production even faster. Steam could power machines anywhere, not just where falling water was found. Steam-powered industries spread across Western Europe. By the mid-1800s, steam-powered railroads were also spreading across the continent. They linked factories to markets and increased the amount of goods that could be made and sold. New technologies in the late 1800s gave rise to industries and products such as cameras, electric motors, and the first automobiles.

Effects of the Industrial Revolution The Industrial Revolution had both positive and negative effects. It greatly increased Europe's wealth and income. It also created thousands of factory jobs in cities and led to the rapid growth of cities.

However, many workers faced brutal conditions and had to work long hours for low pay. Many children also worked long hours and in dangerous conditions. Labor unions organized to fight for better conditions for workers.

The growth of cities brought new problems as well. City life was dirty, dangerous, and unsanitary for most working people.

A group of radical thinkers known as socialists or communists called for workers to join together and seize control of workplaces and government. The best known of these thinkers was the German Karl Marx. Marx believed that rich investors tended to take advantage of working people. He said that the working class needed to overthrow capitalism, which is an economy based on the private ownership of property.

✓ READING CHECK **Identify Main Ideas** What changes did the Industrial Revolution bring?

Nationalism

Napoleon's conquests in the early 1800s prompted many European peoples to seek national unity and independence from foreign rule. As a result, many nationalist revolts broke out around Europe. **Nationalism** is the belief that a person's nation deserves greater loyalty than other groups a person belongs to. Nationalism also involves pride in a person's nation.

Forming New Countries In 1821, Greece declared its independence from the Ottoman empire. Belgium declared independence in 1830. In 1848 revolts in France, Austria, Germany, and Italy jolted Europe.

Italy had long been split into many separate territories, some ruled by foreign powers such as Austria. Nationalists there mounted a successful movement for independence and unification, and the country was finally united in the mid-1800s.

GEOGRAPHY **SKILLS**

Bismarck used three wars to unify Germany.

1. **Location** What was the largest state in Germany before unification?

2. **Draw Conclusions** Northern Germany is largely Protestant and southern Germany largely Catholic. How does the map reflect those differences?

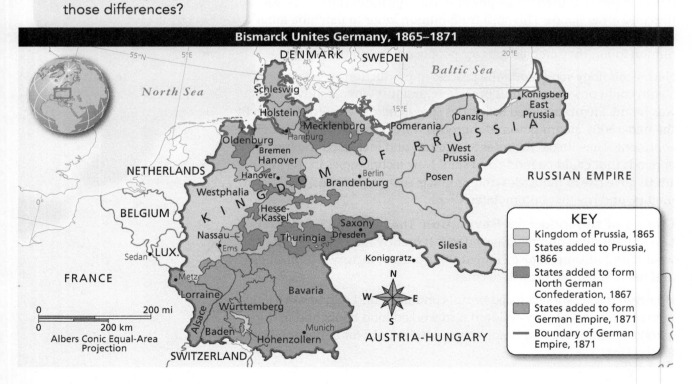

Bismarck Unites Germany, 1865–1871

KEY
- Kingdom of Prussia, 1865
- States added to Prussia, 1866
- States added to form North German Confederation, 1867
- States added to form German Empire, 1871
- Boundary of German Empire, 1871

Meanwhile, Prussia's prime minister, Otto von Bismarck, worked to unify Germany under Prussian leadership through diplomacy and war. In 1871, King William I of Prussia became emperor of a united Germany.

The independence of Greece and the unification of Germany and Italy inspired nationalists across central and Eastern Europe. They hoped to gain independence for their countries from the Habsburg, Russian, and Ottoman empires.

READING CHECK How did nationalism take hold in Europe in the 1800s?

Democratization

The spirit of the French Revolution lived on in Europe during the 1800s. In western and northern Europe, a growing number of countries gained elected legislatures. At first, only affluent men were allowed to vote, and elected legislators were often less powerful than monarchs. But by the late 1800s, the vote had been expanded in many countries, and legislatures gained power.

▲ Scene from a British election in the 1800s

By the late 1800s, many countries of northern and Western Europe were true democracies. Many were constitutional monarchies, while France was a republic, with no king.

Britain saw an increase in democracy, too. A series of reforms during the 1800s made Parliament more representative of the whole country and increased the powers of the elected House of Commons relative to the House of Lords, representing unelected bishops and aristocrats. These reforms also expanded the vote to more of the male population.

READING CHECK Summarize How did Europe become more democratic?

Imperialism

Growing industries needed **access** to resources and markets for their goods. Nations sought new colonies to satisfy those needs. Nationalism fueled competition for foreign lands and resources. By the late 1800s, European nations controlled much of the world.

Causes of Imperialism European **imperialism** was a policy of building an empire through conquest. Europeans believed that they were superior to other peoples and claimed that spreading European culture would "civilize" other peoples.

Academic Vocabulary

access • *n.*, ability to go somewhere or obtain something

Analyze Images The photograph shows the harbor of Hamburg, Germany, in the late 1800s. **Draw Conclusions** Why was the shipping industry important for the policy of imperialism?

Africa, Asia, and Latin America were rich in resources and had millions of potential customers for European businesses resources. Advanced technology and weapons allowed Europeans to conquer those regions.

Carving up the World Britain built an empire in India and planted colonies in Africa, Australia, and Southeast Asia and the Pacific. France conquered areas of Africa and Southeast Asia as well. Portugal, Spain, Belgium, the Netherlands, Germany, and Italy all seized lands outside Europe in the push for colonies.

✓ READING CHECK **Identify Supporting Details** Why did European nations compete for areas of Africa and Asia in the 1800s?

☑ Lesson Check

Practice Vocabulary

1. How was the Scientific Revolution important to the **Enlightenment**?

2. What were some reasons for European **imperialism** in Asia and Africa?

Critical Thinking and Writing

3. **Identify Cause and Effect** What ideas from the American Revolution inspired leaders of the French Revolution?

4. **Understand Effects** How did the Industrial Revolution affect society?

5. **Identify Implied Main Ideas** Why do you think ideas such as socialism and communism developed?

6. **Writing Workshop: Compare and Contrast** List three wars or conflicts described in this topic in your 📓 Active Journal. Compare and contrast the causes of these wars or conflicts.

📖 Geographic Sources

Gouverneur Morris's French Revolution Letter

Gouverneur Morris was an American lawyer, a leader during the American Revolution, and one of the founders of the United States. In 1792, he traveled as an ambassador to France, where he witnessed many of the events of the French Revolution. At the time, Thomas Jefferson was U.S. Secretary of State, supervising ambassadors like Morris. In this excerpt from a letter to Jefferson, Morris describes the trial of French King Louis XVI.

▶ French King Louis XVI faces execution after his trial.

"I now come to the trial of the King and the circumstances connected with it. ... It ... seem[s] strange that the mildest monarch who ever filled the French throne, one who is precipitated from it precisely because he would not adopt the harsh measures of his predecessors ①, a man whom none could charge with a criminal act, should be prosecuted as one of the most nefarious tyrants that ever disgraced the annals of human nature ②. .. Yet such is the fact. I think it highly probable that he may suffer, and that for the following causes: The majority of the Assembly found it necessary to raise against this unhappy prince the national odium ③, in order to justify the dethroning him ... and to induce the ready adoption of a republican form of government. Being in possession of his papers, and those of his servants ... it was *very* easy to create such opinions as they might think proper. ④ The rage which has been excited was terrible; and ... the Convention are still in great straits—fearing to acquit, fearing to condemn, and yet urged to destroy their captive monarch. ⑤"

—letter to Thomas Jefferson from Gouverneur Morris, December 21, 1792

Analyzing Geographic Sources

Use the text to answer the questions below.

1. **Identify Bias** How might Morris's past have affected his point of view toward the French Revolution?

2. **Distinguish Between Fact and Opinion** What does Morris say that reflects his opinions?

3. **Analyze Style and Rhetoric** What language does Morris use when describing the evidence against Louis that helps readers understand his opinion of it?

4. **Determine Author's Point of View** What is surprising about Morris's point of view for someone of his background?

Reading and Vocabulary Support

① Morris is expressing his opinion that Louis XVI has lost the throne because he was not as harsh as kings before him.

② *Nefarious* means "evil," and by "the annals of human nature," Morris means "all of human history."

③ *Odium* means "hatred or disgust."

④ According to Morris, what evidence against the king do his accusers have?

⑤ To be "in great straits" means to be in a difficult position. What difficult decision did the leaders of France face?

Hot and Cold War in Europe

GET READY TO READ

START UP

In this photograph, people celebrate in 1989 when East Germany's government allowed citizens to cross the Berlin Wall, which had separated the people of West and East Germany for decades. Write a few sentences about how you would feel if your country or city were divided.

GUIDING QUESTIONS

- How did two world wars and economic crises affect Europe?
- What was the Cold War, and how did it affect Europe?
- What role has the European Union played in recent European history?

TAKE NOTES

Literacy Skills: Analyze Text Structure
Use the graphic organizer in your 📓 Active Journal to take notes as you read the lesson.

PRACTICE VOCABULARY

Use the vocabulary activity in your 📓 Active Journal to practice the vocabulary words.

Vocabulary
hyperinflation   Cold War
Holocaust   European Union

Academic Vocabulary
recovery
hostility

In the 1900s, two world wars ravaged Europe. After 1945, the Cold War threatened Europe, but it ended in the late 1900s. European countries faced challenges as they aimed for closer cooperation.

Why Were There Two World Wars?

By the early 1900s, a few large empires controlled most of Eastern and central Europe. Meanwhile, European powers formed competing alliances. Nationalism and competition for power led to a long and bitter war.

World War I In 1914, World War I broke out in southeastern Europe and soon involved most countries on the continent. Germany, Austria–Hungary, Bulgaria, and the Ottoman empire formed an alliance that fought the Allied Powers of France, Britain, and Russia.

World War I, as the conflict is now known, dragged on for four long years and resulted in the deaths of millions. The United States entered the war in 1917 and helped the Allied Powers win.

The war finally ended on November 11, 1918. The Allies forced Germany to sign the Treaty of Versailles. Many Germans felt humiliated by the terms of the treaty.

The treaties that ended the war imposed a heavy burden of payments, known as reparations, from Germany, Austria, and Hungary to the victorious Allies. The treaties also took territory from the defeated powers to create new countries in central and Eastern Europe.

Inflation and Depression War reparations strained the finances of Germany, Austria, and Hungary. Partly as a result, in the early 1920s, all three countries experienced serious **hyperinflation**, an economic crisis in which prices skyrocket and currency becomes worthless. People's savings were destroyed.

In 1929, the U.S. stock market crashed. U.S. banks that had lent money to European banks demanded repayment. Those European banks were forced to stop making loans and demanded repayment of loans they had made to European businesses. These demands drove many companies into bankruptcy and threw millions of Europeans out of work.

INTERACTIVE

Effects of World War I on European Boundaries

Analyze Images
German soldiers fight in trenches, dugouts in the ground, during World War I. The use of trenches was widespread during the war. **Draw Conclusions** What would be some advantages and disadvantages of fighting from trenches?

Totalitarian Governments Economic crisis made many countries ripe for leaders responding to people's anger and fears. One new idea was fascism, a political system that stresses national strength, military power, and the belief that the state is more important than the individual. Fascist dictators took power in Spain, Austria, and Italy.

In 1933, Adolf Hitler came to power in Germany as the head of the fascist Nazi Party. The Nazis promised a return to German greatness. Hitler and the Nazis also used posters, pamphlets, speeches, and movies to claim that Germans were superior to all other peoples, especially Jewish people. The Nazis blamed Germany's problems, without justification, on Jews, who already faced prejudice in much of Europe.

Ruthless and ambitious, Hitler set up a totalitarian state in Germany. Totalitarianism is a form of government in which the state has total power over all aspects of life.

World War II In 1939, Germany invaded Poland. This attack began a war with Poland's allies, Britain and France. Germany quickly defeated France and occupied much of Europe.

In 1941, Germany invaded the Soviet Union. In December of that year, the United States joined World War II on the side of the Allies, including Britain and the Soviet Union. Fighting occurred across Europe and around the world. Eventually, the Allies were able to push the Germans out of the countries they had conquered. By 1945, the American-led forces in Western Europe and the Soviet troops in the east were pushing into Germany.

Analyze Images Adolf Hitler was a fiery speaker who was able to shape and control the German people's views through the use of speeches and propaganda. **Recognize Multiple Causes** Using this image as a source, what do you think caused many German people to be easily influenced by Hitler and the Nazis?

- To escape persecution of Jews, Frank hid for two years with her family in a secret portion of a building in the Netherlands.

- She wrote about her activities, fears, and hopes while in hiding.

- Frank and her family members were discovered by the Nazis on August 4, 1944.

- She and her sister were sent to a concentration camp at Bergen-Belsen in October 1944, where they died.

- Frank's diary was later found by family friends. Her father, the only survivor from the family, had it published in 1947.

Critical Thinking Why do you think Frank's father had her diary published?

Effects of World War II In 1945, the Allies defeated Germany, but at great cost. Some 17 million European soldiers died during the war. Millions of civilians died as well. Many civilian deaths occurred as part of the **Holocaust**, the mass murder of Jews by the Nazis during World War II, a result of the Nazis' hatred toward Jewish people. The Nazis murdered 6 million Jews and 5 million people from other groups, mainly in concentration camps.

Fighting and bombing during the war left many European cities in ruins. Poverty and hunger were widespread. Governments that came to power after the war faced severe challenges.

READING CHECK Identify Cause and Effect How did the two world wars affect Europe?

The Cold War in Europe

When Germany was defeated in 1945, U.S. and British forces faced Soviet forces along a line stretching across Germany and Central Europe. The result was the **Cold War**, a period of confrontation between the democratic United States and its allies in Western Europe and the communist Soviet Union and its allies in Eastern Europe.

The West Embraces Democracy To help Europeans rebuild after the war, encourage democracy, and oppose communism, the United States started the Marshall Plan. This **recovery** plan offered American money to help European countries rebuild their economies. The Soviet Union pressured countries under its control to reject this aid.

Helped by U.S. aid, Western Europe's economy recovered quickly. By 1951, factories were producing more than ever. Western European nations formed democratic governments.

Academic Vocabulary
recovery • *n.*, process of rebuilding an economy

NATO and Warsaw Pact, 1977

KEY
- NATO
- Warsaw Pact
- Neutral

ICELAND

NORWAY

FINLAND

SWEDEN

North Sea

IRELAND

UNITED KINGDOM

DENMARK

Baltic Sea

SOVIET UNION

ATLANTIC OCEAN

NETH
BELG
EAST GERMANY
WEST GERMANY
LUXEMBOURG
POLAND
CZECHOSLOVAKIA

FRANCE
AUSTRIA
HUNGARY
SWITZERLAND
ROMANIA

PORTUGAL
SPAIN
ITALY
YUGOSLAVIA
BULGARIA
Black Sea

ALBANIA
GREECE
TURKEY

Mediterranean Sea

0 300 600 mi
0 300 600 km
Lambert Conformal Conic Projection

GEOGRAPHY SKILLS

NATO and the Warsaw Pact were opposing alliances during the Cold War.

1. **Location** Which neutral countries do you think faced the biggest challenges? Explain.

2. **Compare and Contrast** How were the members of NATO and the Warsaw Pact different in location?

In 1949, the United States and Western European countries formed a military alliance called the North Atlantic Treaty Organization (NATO). The group was formed to protect Western Europe from attack by the Soviet Union and its communist allies.

Communists Control the East In response, the Soviet Union and its allies formed a military alliance called the Warsaw Pact in 1955.

The Soviets used force to control Eastern Europe. In 1956, Soviet forces invaded Hungary and blocked democratic change. In 1968, Soviet troops crushed reform efforts in Czechoslovakia.

The Berlin Wall Goes Up The dividing line between the democratic West and communist East ran right through the center of Germany. The Soviets occupied East Germany, which became communist. West Germany, occupied by the Western Allies, became a democracy. The Soviets and Western Allies also divided Germany's capital, Berlin, surrounded by East Germany. East Berlin became the capital of communist East Germany, while West Berlin was democratic.

Over the years, about 2.5 million East Germans fled to the West by crossing into West Berlin. In 1961, East Germany built a wall around West Berlin to prevent escapes. The Berlin Wall symbolized Cold War divisions.

READING CHECK **Connect** How did World War II lead to the political divisions of the Cold War?

Communism Collapses in Europe

By the 1980s, people in Eastern Europe were frustrated. Communist Eastern European economies could not compete with Western market economies. Many people in Soviet-controlled communist nations began to demand democratic reforms.

Communism Fails In communist states, government officials planned what farms should grow and what factories should produce. Officials made decisions based on the state's wishes rather than on people's needs. People had no motive to work hard because the government limited their pay. These problems often led to shortages of food and consumer goods.

In 1985, Mikhail Gorbachev became the new leader of the Soviet Union. Gorbachev was more open to change than previous Soviet leaders. He supported greater democracy and gave Eastern European countries more freedom to choose their own way.

In 1980, a Polish shipyard workers' union called Solidarity had gone on strike. The Polish government granted some union demands, and the union head, Lech Walesa (lek vah WEN suh), became a hero. Solidarity went on strike again in 1988. This time, the government agreed to hold free elections.

Revolution Spreads Poland's example inspired other countries. In Czechoslovakia, thousands of people protested the communist government in 1989. In response, the government agreed to give up power. In free elections later that year, Czechoslovakians elected writer Vaclav Havel (VAHTS lahf HAH vul) as president.

Romania overthrew its communist government in 1989. Hungary's Communist Party collapsed, and in 1990, the country elected a non-communist government. Bulgaria also held its first free elections in 1990.

Analyze Images Lech Walesa addresses a crowd of Solidarity members. **Describe** What are some qualities that an effective leader needs to have?

INTERACTIVE

European Union, 2014

Germany Reunifies The revolutions of 1989 also inspired East Germans to push for democratic change. East Germany's communist government at first refused to make changes. The government then began to respond to some of the protestors' demands.

Finally, on November 9, 1989, East German border guards opened the gates of the Berlin Wall. East and West Germans rushed to greet one another. Demands for reform led to free elections, which replaced the communist government with a democratic government pledged to reunify Germany. A year later, on October 3, 1990, the two halves of Germany reunited.

Academic Vocabulary

hostility • *n.*, strong negative feeling toward someone

The Soviet Union Breaks Up Nationalism and the desire for reform also rocked the Soviet Union. In 1990, the Soviet republic of Lithuania demanded independence. The Soviet army invaded Lithuania.

Soviet citizens took to the streets to protest the invasion. The army refused to fight the people. In 1991, the Soviet Union broke apart into 15 new nations, including Moldova, Ukraine, Belarus, Lithuania, Latvia, and Estonia in Eastern Europe. The largest post-Soviet nation was Russia, in Northern Eurasia.

☑ **READING CHECK** **Explain** Explain how communism failed in Eastern Europe.

Analyze Diagrams The European Union developed slowly over many years. **Draw Conclusions** Which event changed the fundamental nature of the union from an economic one to something else?

The European Union

Past conflicts shaped how Europeans decided to run their countries after World War II. Long-standing **hostility** between Germany and France played a role in fueling Europe's wars. After World War II, West German and French leaders searched for a way to help their societies exist in peace.

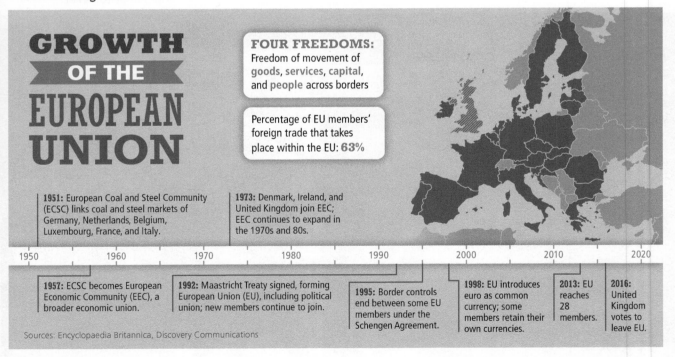

GROWTH OF THE EUROPEAN UNION

FOUR FREEDOMS: Freedom of movement of goods, services, capital, and people across borders

Percentage of EU members' foreign trade that takes place within the EU: **63%**

1951: European Coal and Steel Community (ECSC) links coal and steel markets of Germany, Netherlands, Belgium, Luxembourg, France, and Italy.

1973: Denmark, Ireland, and United Kingdom join EEC; EEC continues to expand in the 1970s and 80s.

1950   1960   1970   1980   1990   2000   2010   2020

1957: ECSC becomes European Economic Community (EEC), a broader economic union.

1992: Maastricht Treaty signed, forming European Union (EU), including political union; new members continue to join.

1995: Border controls end between some EU members under the Schengen Agreement.

1998: EU introduces euro as common currency; some members retain their own currencies.

2013: EU reaches 28 members.

2016: United Kingdom votes to leave EU.

Sources: Encyclopaedia Britannica, Discovery Communications

The European Union In 1951, France and West Germany agreed to coordinate their coal and steel production. This would tie the countries economically and help to prevent future wars. Italy, Belgium, Luxembourg, and the Netherlands also signed the agreement. In 1957, those six countries formed the European Economic Community, or Common Market. This was a free trade zone. It let manufactured goods and services move freely among the countries.

Six more countries had joined the Common Market by 1986. The Common Market nations signed a treaty in 1992 that formed the **European Union (EU)**. The EU is an economic and political partnership among member nations.

In 2002, most EU nations adopted a single currency, or unit of money, called the euro. Sharing a common currency made trade easier. By 2013, the EU had grown to include 28 nations.

Integrating the East The end of communism in Eastern Europe brought new challenges. People in Eastern Europe had operated under state control for so long that many did not know how to start and run private businesses or deal with international markets. Market-based economics required them to learn new ways of doing business. Many factories were outdated and had to close because they could not compete. That cost many people their jobs.

Europeans worked to rebuild ties between east and west. The EU opened membership to Eastern European nations that had democratic governments and strong market economies. Most Eastern nations had to make reforms before joining the EU.

Communist rule had not prepared Eastern European people for democracy either. Many people in formerly communist lands did not trust their leaders. Government corruption had been widespread under communist rule and remained a problem in some countries.

welkom in Nederland

welcome willkommen bienvenue

N 211

Keep right Rechts aanhouden

Analyze Images A sign in the Netherlands welcomes people in Dutch, English, German, and French. **Make Connections** How does this sign reflect life in the European Union?

☑ **READING CHECK** **Draw Conclusions** How did the European Union change Europe?

☑ Lesson Check

Practice Vocabulary

1. Which countries experienced **hyperinflation** after World War I?

2. What was the **Holocaust**?

Critical Thinking and Writing

3. **Summarize** How did the Nazis use propaganda?

4. **Infer** How did the Treaty of Versailles contribute to the rise of Nazism?

5. **Compare and Contrast** How did Eastern and Western Europe differ during the Cold War?

6. **Infer** How did the the growth of the EU promote peace in Europe?

7. **Writing Workshop: Write an Introduction** Write a paragraph in your 📓 Active Journal that introduces your explanatory essay and includes your thesis statement.

☑ Review and Assessment

VISUAL REVIEW

Achievements of Ancient to Early Modern Europe

Ancient Europe	Medieval and Early Modern Europe
• **Greece:** City-states, democracy; trade networks and colonies; spread of Hellenistic culture; philosophy, literature, architecture, science, technology, mathematics, medicine • **Rome:** Republican government, constitution, empire, citizenship; architecture and engineering; Roman law; Latin language; Christianity	• **Byzantine empire:** Spread of Christianity to eastern Europe; Justinian's Code; preservation of ancient culture • **Medieval Europe:** Opening of trade routes through Crusades; growth of strong kingdoms • **Renaissance:** Humanism; art, literature; scientific study • **Reformation:** New approaches to Christianity; voyages of exploration; powerful kingdoms

Achievements of Modern Europe

1600s–1700s
- Scientific Revolution: Use of reason, scientific method; new discoveries
- Enlightenment: Use of reason to study society; ideas of natural rights, freedoms, tolerance

1700s–1800s
- French Revolution: Democratic ideals
- Industrial Revolution: Greater productivity, urbanization, rising living standards
- Nationalism: New states
- Imperialism: Global empires

1900s–2000s
- New technologies
- Peace after two world wars
- Rise and expansion of European Union
- End of Cold War and spread of democracy to Eastern Europe

READING REVIEW

Use the Take Notes and Practice Vocabulary activities in your 📕 Active Journal to help you to review the topic.

👆 INTERACTIVE

Practice vocabulary using the Topic Mini-Games.

Quest FINDINGS

Write Your Official Report

Get help for writing your report in your 📕 Active Journal.

ASSESSMENT

Vocabulary and Key Ideas

1. **Describe** What was the **Hellenistic** period?

2. **Explain** What is a **republic**, and which ancient civilization formed one?

3. **Categorize** Which two groups were divided by the **Great Schism**?

4. **Discuss** How did **patrons** help encourage artistic achievement during the Renaissance?

5. **Recall** What did **absolute monarchs** believe about their powers?

6. **Summarize** What were the main economic reasons for the growth of **imperialism**?

7. **Recall** What two groups of countries, including countries in Europe, opposed each other in the **Cold War**?

Critical Thinking and Writing

8. **Draw Conclusions** What was the connection between trade and the Black Death?

9. **Draw Inferences** How would humanism affect the way people of the Renaissance viewed the authority of the Catholic Church? Explain.

10. **Compare and Contrast** How were the Protestant Reformation and Counter-Reformation similar and different?

11. **Synthesize** How did John Locke and the Baron de Montesquieu help to shape the United States and revolutionary French governments?

12. **Revisit the Essential Question** Throughout European history, what factors generally led to major conflict?

13. **Writing Workshop: Write an Explanatory Essay** Using the evidence, ideas, and notes you wrote in your 📘 Active Journal, synthesize the information to write an explanation to answer this question: "What causes war and conflict?" Use examples of conflicts from at least two lessons to support your explanation.

Analyze Geographic Sources

14. What bias is expressed in this "Address to the German Nobility?" Identify who delivered this address.
    A. Support for Christianity; Otto von Bismarck
    B. Support for Christianity; Adolf Hitler
    C. Criticism of the Catholic Church; Martin Luther
    D. Support for the Catholic Church; Charlemagne

"It has been devised [made up] that the Pope, bishops, priests, and monks are called the spiritual estate; princes, lords, artificers [skilled workers], and peasants, are the temporal estate. This is an artful lie and hypocritical [dishonest] device, but let no one be made afraid by it, and that for this reason: that all Christians are truly of the spiritual estate, and there is no difference among them, save of office [job or position] alone."

Analyze Maps

Use the map at right to answer the following questions.

15. How was Rome's location related to its power?

16. Which area would Roman troops have to cross the Alps to conquer?

17. Which continental area would Romans need to cross a sea to conquer?

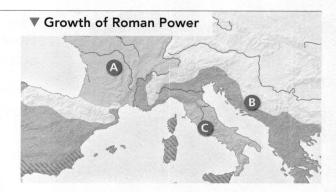

▼ Growth of Roman Power

GO ONLINE
to access your
digital course

▶ VIDEO

🔊 AUDIO

📖 ETEXT

👆 INTERACTIVE

✏️ WRITING

🎮 GAMES

📄 WORKSHEET

☑️ ASSESSMENT

Let's travel

from the Europe of the past to **EUROPE TODAY**. It is easy to move around this continent of many small countries because of high-speed railroads and cooperation within the European Union. You will see the opportunities and challenges Europeans face due to migration and Europe's linked economies. As you visit different European countries, you will see that most Europeans live in its network of cities, with a rich diversity of cultures.

Explore
The Essential Question

What makes a culture unique?

Europe's many countries share a history of cultural change and diversity. Each ethnic group has its own ways of living, its culture. How are the people already living in a place affected by a new culture? How are newcomers changed by the culture they encounter?

Unlock the Essential Question in your 📓 Active Journal.

Read

about a continent shaped by centuries of migration that produced a vibrant region of diverse languages, religions, and cultures in its many countries.

Watch

BOUNCE TO ACTIVATE ▶ VIDEO

Europe at Her Doorstep

Meet Yasmin, a girl from Spain who moved with her family to Sweden. She loves to dance and speaks Spanish, Swedish, French, and English.

◀ Gare de Lyon railway station in Paris, France, is one of the busiest in Europe.

TOPIC 3 Regional Atlas

Europe: Political

A REGION OF MANY COUNTRIES

Though Europe is the world's second smallest continent in area, it has dozens of countries.

Learn more about Europe by making your own map in your Active Journal.

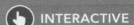

INTERACTIVE

Topic Map

Small Countries

Southeastern and east central Europe contain many small countries. These are the remnants of empires and larger countries that split apart along ethnic lines at the end of World War I and the Cold War.

Newly Free Countries

A string of countries in eastern Europe, from Estonia to Ukraine and Moldova, used to be part of the Soviet Union and gained independence at the end of the Cold War.

50° W
40° W
30° W
COUNTRY (Capital)
1 LUXEMBOURG (Luxembourg)
2 ANDORRA (Andorra la Vella)
3 MONACO (Monaco-Ville)
4 LIECHTENSTEIN (Vaduz)
5 SAN MARINO (San Marino)
6 VATICAN CITY
7 SLOVAKIA (Bratislava)
8 SLOVENIA (Ljubljana)
9 BOSNIA AND HERZEGOVINA (Sarajevo)
10 KOSOVO (Pristina)
11 MONTENEGRO (Podgorica)
12 MACEDONIA (Skopje)
N
E
S
W
40° N
KEY
Country border
Capital city
Other major city
0 400 mi
0 400 km
Azimuthal Equidistant Projection
ATLANTIC OCEAN
PORTUGAL
Lisbon
Gibraltar (U.K.)
30° N

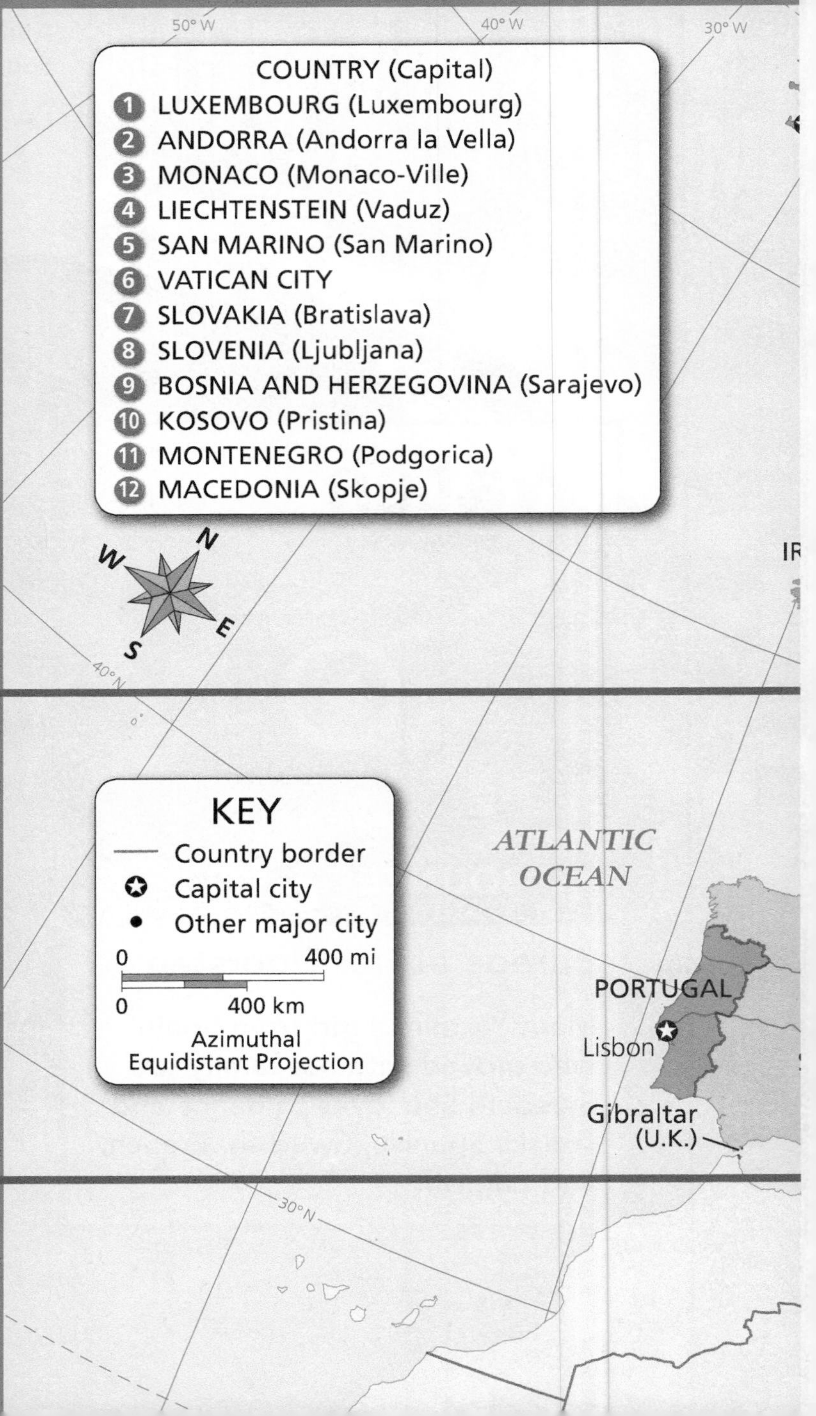

Democracies

The European countries along the Atlantic Ocean and North Sea, from Iceland and Norway to Spain and Portugal, are all strong democracies. Several are nation-states that formed hundreds of years ago, such as France and the United Kingdom, whose Parliament building is shown here.

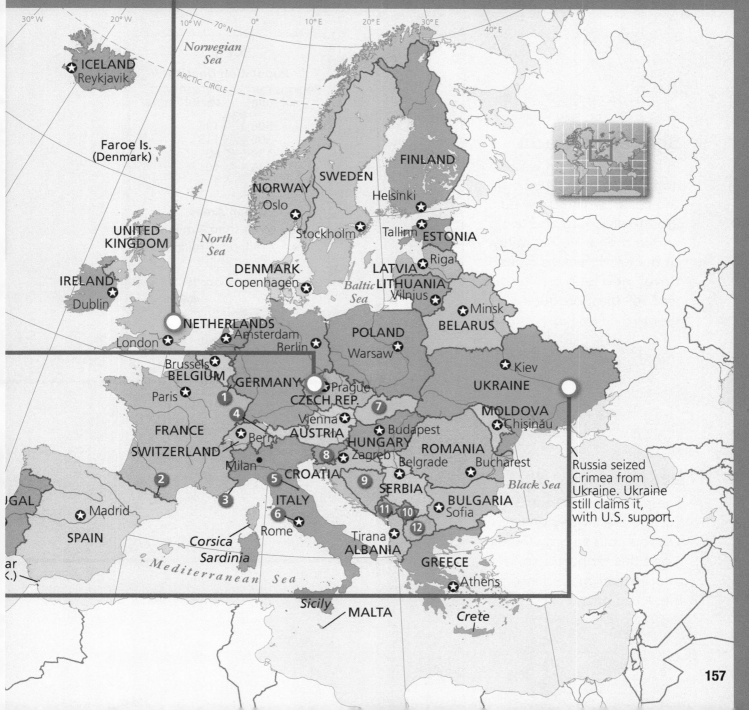

30° W   20° W   10° W   70° N   0°   10° E   20° E   30° E   40° E

Norwegian Sea

ARCTIC CIRCLE

ICELAND
Reykjavik

Faroe Is.
(Denmark)

North Sea

UNITED KINGDOM

IRELAND
Dublin

London

NETHERLANDS
Amsterdam

Brussels
BELGIUM

Paris

FRANCE

SWITZERLAND
Bern

NORWAY
Oslo

SWEDEN
Stockholm

DENMARK
Copenhagen

Berlin

GERMANY

Prague
CZECH REP.

Vienna
AUSTRIA

Milan

FINLAND
Helsinki

Tallinn
ESTONIA

Riga
LATVIA

Baltic Sea

LITHUANIA
Vilnius

Minsk

BELARUS

POLAND
Warsaw

Kiev

UKRAINE

MOLDOVA
Chișinău

Budapest
HUNGARY
Zagreb

CROATIA

Belgrade
SERBIA

ROMANIA
Bucharest

Black Sea

BULGARIA
Sofia

Tirana
ALBANIA

GREECE
Athens

Madrid

SPAIN

Corsica
Sardinia

Rome

ITALY

Mediterranean Sea

Sicily

MALTA

Crete

Russia seized Crimea from Ukraine. Ukraine still claims it, with U.S. support.

1   4   7   2   5   3   8   9   6   11   10   12

157

3 Regional Atlas

Europe: Population Density

A REGION OF CITIES

Much of Europe has a high population density. Over centuries of settlement and economic growth, Europe built up a large population concentrated in its cities.

Shaped by Trade

In Italy, population is concentrated in cities on the coast, which grew up around shipping and trade, and in the fertile Po Valley of the north, where cities developed long ago to buy and sell farm produce.

Nearly Empty North

The northernmost parts of Europe are largely empty. It is too cold to grow many crops this far north, so few people ever moved into these regions.

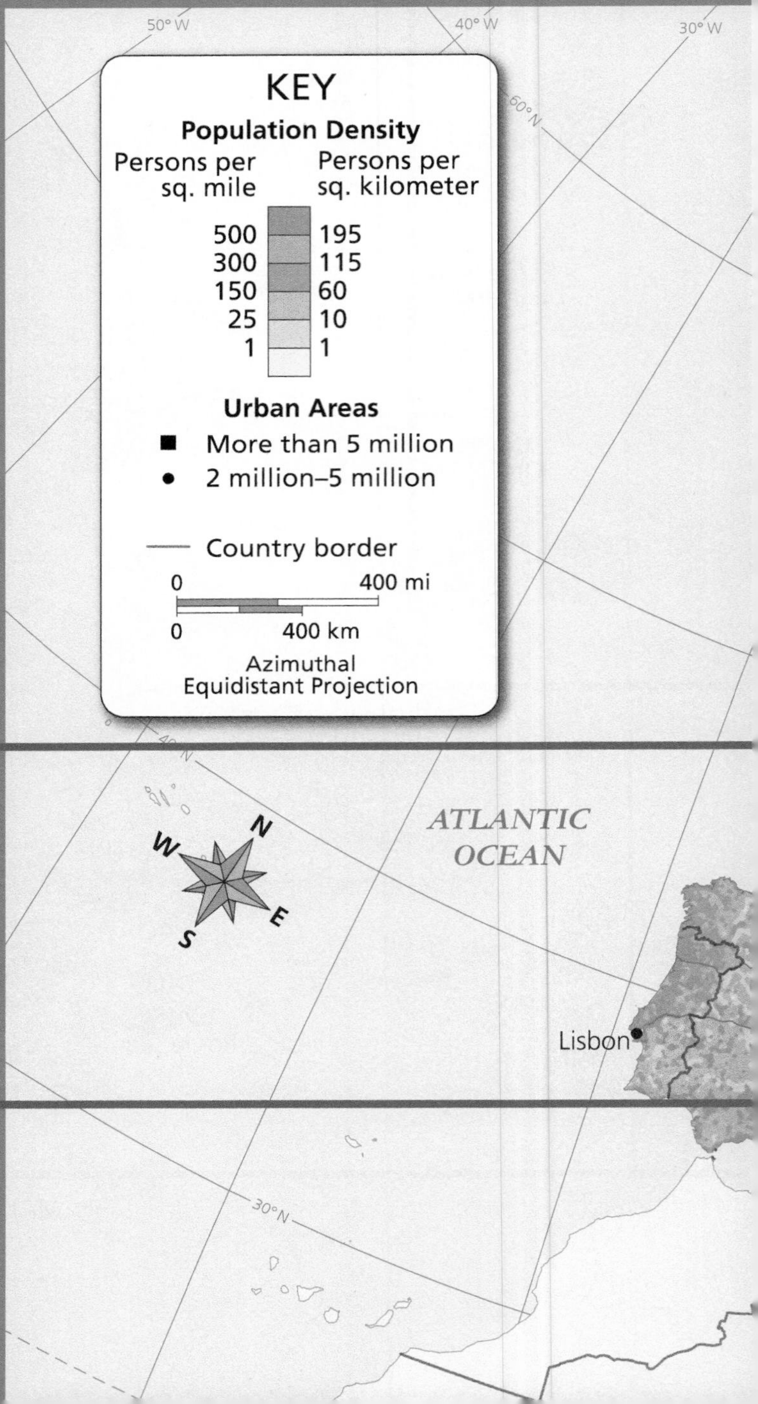

KEY

Population Density

Persons per sq. mile	Persons per sq. kilometer
500	195
300	115
150	60
25	10
1	1

Urban Areas

■ More than 5 million

• 2 million–5 million

— Country border

0 — 400 mi

0 — 400 km

Azimuthal Equidistant Projection

50° W

40° W

30° W

60° N

40° N

30° N

ATLANTIC OCEAN

N W E S

Lisbon

Crowded Western Europe

Many people live in the Netherlands and neighboring areas of Britain and western Europe. This region was the birthplace of the Industrial Revolution, and a dense network of cities has developed here.

Europe: Economic Activity

A REGION OF MODERN ECONOMIES

Many of Europe's countries have modern economies, with highly productive up-to-date factories and transportation and communication systems.

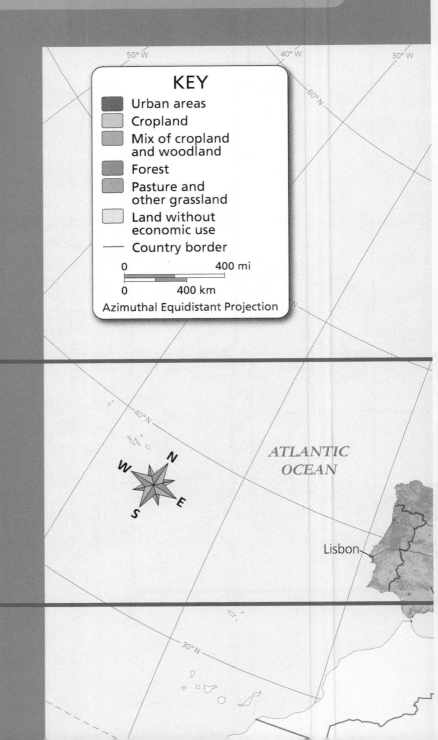

KEY

- Urban areas
- Cropland
- Mix of cropland and woodland
- Forest
- Pasture and other grassland
- Land without economic use
- Country border

0 — 400 mi

0 — 400 km

Azimuthal Equidistant Projection

ATLANTIC OCEAN

Lisbon

Bustling Cities

Most of Europe's people are concentrated in the urban areas dotted across this map. They live in these cities because cities are where the jobs are. They are home to factories, offices, and other workplaces.

A Harsh Climate

In Europe's far north are lands where it is too cold even for forests to grow. These lands have few economic uses.

Farms and Herds

Much of Europe is divided between cropland, forest, and pasture. Flat and fertile plains tend to be used as cropland such as this lavender field in France, while forests and pastures cover hills and mountains.

20° W   10° W   70° N   0°   10° E   20° E   30° E   40° E

Norwegian Sea

ARCTIC CIRCLE

Helsinki

Stockholm

North Sea

Riga

Baltic Sea

Minsk

Manchester

Hamburg

London

Brussels   Berlin   Warsaw

Lille   Rhine-Ruhr   Prague   Katowice   Kiev

Paris   Stuttgart

Frankfurt   Vienna

Munich   Budapest

Milan

Madrid   *Black Sea*

Barcelona   Rome   Sofia

Valencia   Naples

Mediterranean Sea   Athens

Quest
Project-Based Learning Inquiry

Create a Museum Exhibit

Quest KICK OFF

You have been asked by a museum curator to create an exhibit on European cultures. Create an exhibit that shows Europe's cultural diversity today. Include visuals and text to reflect cultures of ethnic groups, historic regions, and recent immigrants.

What distinguishes one culture from another?

Explore the Essential Question "What makes a culture unique?" in this Quest.

1 Ask Questions

What is *culture*? What aspects of a culture distinguish one culture from other cultures? Write your own questions in your 📙 Active Journal.

2 Investigate

As you read the lessons in this topic, look for **Quest CONNECTIONS** that investigate cultural diversity in Europe. Respond to the Connections in your 📙 Active Journal.

▲ A man makes baskets, showing his craft at a German museum.

3 Conduct Research

Find valid sources on Europe's cultural diversity. Possible sources include biographies, interviews, news articles, books, images, and artifacts. Record your findings in your 📙 Active Journal.

Quest FINDINGS

4 Create and Present Your Exhibit

What visuals and written wall panels will you include? Will you include music? Think about how museum exhibits include visuals, text, and layouts. Create a diagram of how you want your exhibit to look and build a model of it. Present your exhibit. Write conclusions about your research and exhibit in your 📙 Active Journal.

Europe's Cultural Diversity

BOUNCE TO ACTIVATE ▶ VIDEO

GET READY TO READ

START UP

Look at the photo of university graduates in Germany. Europe is a multicultural continent of many languages, religions, and other ways of life. How might cultural diversity affect the everyday life of Europe's people?

GUIDING QUESTIONS

- How is Europe's cultural diversity connected to its long history?
- Why are so many different religions found within Europe?
- How has recent history added to Europe's cultural diversity?

TAKE NOTES

Literacy Skills: Identify Cause and Effect
Use the graphic organizer in your 📓 Active Journal to take notes as you read the lesson.

PRACTICE VOCABULARY

Use the vocabulary activity in your 📓 Active Journal to practice the vocabulary words.

Vocabulary
dialect
bilingual

Academic Vocabulary
controversy
belief system

Europe's long and stormy history created a complex mix of languages, religions, and traditions. This cultural diversity is both a strength and a challenge for the region.

Why Does Europe Have So Many Languages?

Languages change over time and are a part of culture. One language may develop into several new languages. Language can also unite people from different cultures and become an important common element.

Indo-European Languages Over thousands of years, invaders brought new languages into Europe. Around 5,000 years ago, invaders from the east introduced a language called Proto-Indo-European to Central Europe. **Dialects**, or language varieties, of Proto-Indo-European spread across the continent. These dialects gradually grew apart into individual languages, known as the Indo-European languages. Most European languages—including English, Irish, Spanish, Greek, and Albanian—are in the Indo-European language group.

Quest CONNECTIONS

New modes of transportation and communication have connected formerly isolated regions. Research how this has affected the diversity of languages and dialects in Europe. Record your findings in your 📓 Active Journal.

👆 INTERACTIVE

Southern European Culture

Analyze Images For centuries, mountain ranges prevented the spread of languages. **Draw Conclusions** How do you think technology like this rail line in Spain have changed this?

The Basque (bask) language survived the spread of the Indo-European languages. Basque endured because it was the language of an isolated part of Europe—the mountains of southern France and northern Spain. Basque is still the language of almost one million people in that region. Most Basques are **bilingual**, which means they speak two languages.

Influence of the Roman Empire As the Roman empire conquered much of Europe around 2,000 years ago, Latin—another Indo-European language—spread across the empire. Modern-day French, Italian, Portuguese, Spanish, and Romanian are all descendants of Latin. They are often called "Romance languages" because of this connection to the Roman empire.

When the Roman empire collapsed about 500 years later, the languages of the conquering Germanic peoples spread to western Europe. The invaders spoke Germanic languages, which were also Indo-European. We know some descendants of these languages today as English, Dutch, German, Danish, Swedish, Norwegian, and Icelandic.

As Slavic peoples moved into Europe, the Indo-European Slavic languages spread across eastern Europe. These include languages spoken in eastern Europe today, including Czech, Serbian, Polish, and Ukrainian. Separate migrations brought the non-Indo-European languages of Finnish and Hungarian to the continent.

Impact of Geography Physical geography has been a major influence on the development of Europe's distinct cultures—including its languages. In the past, mountains, forests, and other physical barriers separated speakers of different dialects. These dialects eventually grew less alike until they became entirely separate languages.

✓ **READING CHECK** **Sequence** How did the Romance languages come to exist in Europe?

Europe: Leading Religion by Country

KEY
- Protestant
- Catholic
- Catholic or Protestant
- Orthodox
- Muslim
- None

Source: CIA World Factbook

ATLANTIC OCEAN

0   500 mi
0   500 km
Lambert Aziumuthal
Equal-Area projection

What Religions Do Europeans Follow?

Europe is a region of many different religions, including Judaism, Christianity, and Islam. For more than 1,000 years, most Europeans have been Christian, though divisions within Christianity have developed over time.

Judaism and Christianity Under the Roman empire, two major religions spread within the empire from Southwest Asia to Europe. Followers of Judaism, or Jews, migrated throughout the empire, bringing their religion with them. Similarly, Christianity spread and eventually became the leading religion.

Christianity became the official religion of the Roman empire in the 300s. By the year 800, most Europeans were Christians.

After Christianity became Europe's dominant religion, Jews faced discrimination and occasional violence. There was also **controversy** within Christianity itself as early as the 800s. Christians in western Europe and eastern Europe began to disagree about religious practices, including details of worship and whether church leaders could marry. Eastern Europeans also rejected the leadership of the Pope, the head of the western church.

These disagreements eventually led to a schism, or split, in Christianity. In northern, western, and central Europe, Christians now belonged to the Roman Catholic Church. Most eastern Europeans became followers of the Eastern Orthodox Church.

Islam and Protestantism During the 1400s, the powerful Ottoman empire spread from Southwest Asia into southeastern Europe. The Ottomans brought Islam, their religion, with them.

GEOGRAPHY SKILLS

This map shows which group or groups form a majority in each European country.

1. **Place** Where are people without any religion the largest group?

2. **Synthesize Visual Information** Which countries show the influence of the Muslim Ottoman empire?

Academic Vocabulary
controversy • *n.*, public disagreement over an issue

Analyze Images Nazi Germany sent millions to death camps during the Holocaust. **Identify Cause and Effect** What effect did this have on the Jewish population in Europe?

Academic Vocabulary
belief system • *n.*, set of ideas about spiritual life and morality

Even after the final fall of the Ottoman empire in 1918, many Muslims, or followers of Islam, remained in southeastern Europe.

During the 1500s, some western European Christians began to break away from the Roman Catholic Church. They protested against the behavior of some Catholic leaders and against some Catholic teachings. These protesters formed new Protestant churches, with beliefs and practices that differed from the Catholics. Protestantism became the dominant form of Christianity in northern Europe, while Catholicism endured in the rest of western Europe.

Twentieth-Century Changes During the 1900s, the religious make-up of Europe began to change. Some European Christians lost interest in organized religion. These Europeans either rejected religion altogether or followed their own private spiritual and **belief system**. In 1910, 95 percent of Europeans were Christian. In 2010, only about 70 percent of Europeans considered themselves Christian.

In the 1950s, people from North Africa, Southwest Asia, and other regions began migrating to Europe. These immigrants altered the continent's religious makeup. Many of these immigrants were Muslim. Today, more than 43 million Europeans practice Islam. Immigrants also brought to Europe other religions, such as Sikhism, Hinduism, and Buddhism.

Europe's Jewish population suffered greatly during the Holocaust. In 1939, most of the world's Jews lived in Europe. But the murder of six million Jews by the Nazis during World War II devastated Europe's Jewish population, which was reduced by two-thirds. Many survivors migrated to Israel or the United States. Despite this tragic loss, Jewish communities remain in many European countries today.

☑ READING CHECK **Identify Supporting Details** Name two divisions that developed within Christianity in Europe.

Recent Migrations in Europe

Migrations have reshaped regions throughout history. Recent migrations to Europe also have brought change to this region as well.

Changing Societies The cultural landscape of Europe changed greatly during the 1900s. Millions of immigrants arriving from both European and non-European countries altered the make-up of European societies. Before these waves of migration, cultural diversity existed mainly among individual European countries and regions. After the immigrants arrived, there was suddenly a lot of cultural diversity *within* the countries themselves.

The years following World War II saw large migrations to and within Europe. Millions of Europeans were displaced, or forced to leave their homes, after the war because of war damage and shifting national boundaries. Immigrants moved to northern Europe from southern Europe, northern Africa, and Southwest Asia as European governments and businesses hired workers to help rebuild the cities and economies of their war-damaged countries.

At the same time, many European colonies in Africa and Asia became independent nations. Some people who had been living in these colonies chose to move to Europe for new opportunities. As the European Union expanded into eastern Europe in the 1990s and 2000s, millions of eastern Europeans moved west.

Immigration mainly affected wealthy western European countries, where immigrants hoped to find employment and a higher standard of living. Often, immigrants from the same homeland lived in the same neighborhoods, providing comfort and familiarity. But this also isolated the immigrants from other people in their new country.

BIOGRAPHY
5 Things to Know About

HARLEM DÉSIR
French politician (1959–)

- Désir was born to a white mother from France and a black father from Guadeloupe, a French territory in the Caribbean.

- His first name is a tribute to the black liberation movements that took place in Harlem in New York City.

- While still in his twenties, he helped found and lead SOS-Racisme, a French group opposed to racism.

- He became the First Secretary of the Socialist Party in 2012, and also France's first black party leader.

- In April 2014, he was named Minister of State for European Affairs.

Critical Thinking How does Désir represent the diversity of Europe today?

Analyze Images Anti-immigration feelings, as seen in this British demonstration, continue to run strong in some regions of Europe. **Infer** What challenges do you think immigrants must overcome when moving to a new country?

Acceptance and Discrimination Europeans used to living in countries with one dominant culture were challenged by the arrival of people with different languages and religions. Many Europeans welcomed the new immigrants and the diversity they brought. But others disliked the changes and responded with rejection and discrimination.

Over the past century, immigrants have made the European workforce larger and younger, which has strengthened Europe's economy. Yet immigrants often have less education and income than other Europeans. Their housing and health care needs have increased the cost of government benefits in their new countries.

Modern Controversy In recent years, a few European Muslims from immigrant families have joined Islamist terrorist groups. A small number have even carried out terrorist acts in cities in France, Belgium, Spain, and Britain.

While the vast majority of European Muslim immigrants are peaceful, some Europeans have grown fearful of Muslim immigrant communities. They are afraid that accepting refugees from war-ravaged Muslim countries such as Syria and Iraq will increase terrorist attacks.

Because Europeans disagree over whether immigrants from outside Europe are an advantage to their societies, immigration has been a source of political controversy in Europe.

✔ READING CHECK **Summarize** Name two reasons some Europeans might find immigration to be an advantage. Then name two reasons some might find it to be a disadvantage.

✔ Lesson Check

Practice Vocabulary

1. How do **dialects** form?

2. Why would Europeans find it an advantage to be **bilingual**?

Critical Thinking and Writing

3. **Compare and Contrast** How do the origins of the Romance languages and Germanic languages differ?

4. **Recognize Multiple Causes** Name two reasons why the Jewish population has fallen in Europe.

5. **Identify Cause and Effect** How did World War II affect migration patterns to and within Europe?

6. **Writing Workshop: Develop a Clear Thesis** Write a sentence in your 🗐 Active Journal making a statement about the impact of cultural diversity in Europe. This sentence will be the thesis statement, or main idea, for the explanatory essay you will write at the end of the topic.

Living and Working in Europe

BOUNCE TO ACTIVATE · ▶ VIDEO

GET READY TO READ

START UP

Look at the photo of Barcelona, Spain. In Europe, steep mountains often rise along sea coasts, influencing settlement patterns and population density. How else might geographic features affect how people live and work in Europe?

GUIDING QUESTIONS

- How do geographic features affect where people live in Europe?
- How have European economies succeeded?
- How does the European Union promote trade?
- What explains the economic success of Germany and Britain?

TAKE NOTES

Literacy Skills: Analyze Text Structure

Use the graphic organizer in your 📓 Active Journal to take notes as you read the lesson.

PRACTICE VOCABULARY

Use the vocabulary activity in your 📓 Active Journal to practice the vocabulary words.

Vocabulary

service sector
human capital
entrepreneurship

Academic Vocabulary

network
relatively

There are many countries in Europe, each with a unique pattern of settlement and unique economic strengths. People tend to settle where there are economic opportunities, which depend on the location of each country's assets, including natural and human resources.

How Geographic Features Affect Where People Live

People choose to live where there are opportunities to work and live well. Over time, advances in industry and technology have changed where Europeans settle.

Settlement Patterns Hundreds of years ago, when most Europeans were farmers, people lived where the soil and climate were good for farming. Today, much of Europe's population is still concentrated in regions where flat or gently rolling land, high quality soil, and mild climate produced rich yields for farmers.

In western Europe, most people live within 100 miles of the coast and its trade and transportation opportunities.

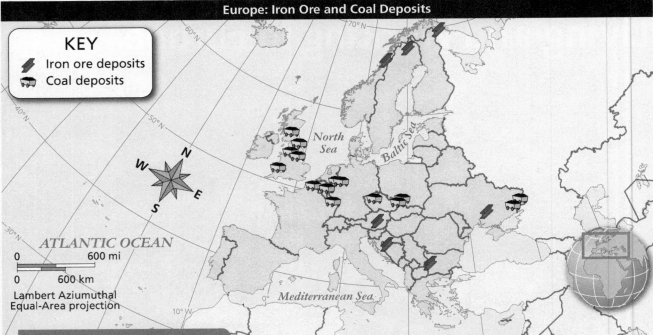

Europe: Iron Ore and Coal Deposits

KEY
- Iron ore deposits
- Coal deposits

ATLANTIC OCEAN

North Sea

Baltic Sea

Mediterranean Sea

0 — 600 mi
0 — 600 km
Lambert Aziumuthal Equal-Area projection

GEOGRAPHY SKILLS

This map shows locations in Europe with sizable deposits of iron ore and coal, needed to make steel.

1. **Interaction** What other factors led to the growth of cities near these resources?

2. **Identify Cause and Effect** How did the presence of these resources affect the distribution of Europe's population?

Academic Vocabulary
network • *n.*, a group of interconnected people or things

In northern Europe, people also live near the coast, where there is milder weather than in the interior, even in the far north. In inland regions, people are concentrated where good soils support farming or industry provides jobs.

Natural Resources and Cities The continent's industrial areas fostered the growth of many major cities. Industries developed near the natural resources on which they depended, such as the coal and iron ore used to make steel. The Rhine–Ruhr region, with nearly 7 million inhabitants, grew up in northwestern Germany around iron and coal deposits.

Cities grew in these industrial regions and along river and coastal water routes that were needed to transport natural resources and finished products. Europe's population began to crowd into these cities and industrial areas in the 1800s.

Today, not nearly as many Europeans work in industries that depend on natural resources—but they do still live in cities. Europe has been called the "urban continent" because so many people live in urban areas. In Britain, Belgium, and Iceland, for example, almost nine out of ten people live in cities. A dense **network** of urban areas spreads across northwestern and central Europe.

Service sector jobs—those that produce services instead of goods—now dominate many European countries' economies. Yet natural resources remain important to the economies of some European countries. For example, oil from the North Sea is essential to Norway. In Poland, coal mines still play a major economic role.

Economies and Migration Europe's economies help to shape the flow of migration within, into, and from the continent. Within Europe, people migrate from places with weak economies to places with stronger economies and lots of jobs. The same is true of immigrants and refugees fleeing political, social, and economic problems in other parts of the world. They tend to settle in Europe's wealthiest cities, particularly in France, Germany, and Britain.

Immigrants, like longtime residents of Europe, avoid settling in parts of Europe that are farthest north. Population increases as you travel south, where there are cities such as Stockholm. When you get as far south as England, in Britain, population is much more dense.

✅ **READING CHECK** **Identify Cause and Effect** How did the growth of European industry lead to the growth of European cities?

Europe's Economies

Europe's economies are market-based but include a substantial role for government. Their success depends on a strong educational system, entrepreneurship, and trade.

A Continent of Mixed Economies As you have learned, there are three basic types of economic systems: traditional economies, market economies, and command economies. All of Europe's economies today are mixed economies. They are part market economy, in that consumers and privately owned businesses usually determine economic activity and prices. European economies also have features of a command economy, such as government involvement in health care, education, and transportation.

The combination of market and command economy is not always balanced. For example, the eastern European country of Belarus leans more toward a command economy. Government-owned businesses outweigh privately owned businesses. In Sweden, the government takes an active economic role in a different way. While the country has a thriving free-market economy, its people pay the government high taxes in exchange for free university education and for child care and healthcare provided by the government.

Education and Entrepreneurship European governments that invest in education are also investing in **human capital**, or employees' knowledge and skills. Europe is home to some of the best-educated workforces in the world, as well as some of the highest literacy rates.

Quick Activity

Follow the instructions in your 📓 Active Journal to create a live population density map of Europe. Discuss the results with classmates.

Analyze Images France has highly skilled workers, like this woman in a bio-tech lab. **Infer** How does this lab show the importance of investing in human capital?

COMPARISON OF LITERACY RATES & GDP PER CAPITA

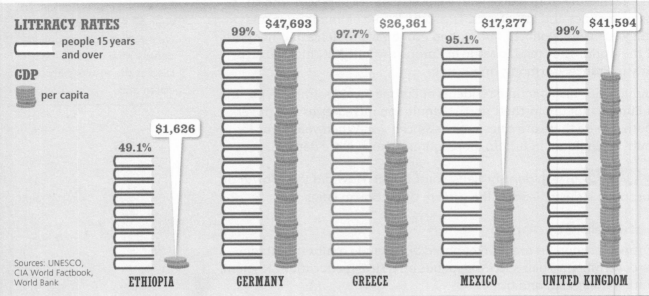

LITERACY RATES

people 15 years and over

GDP

per capita

ETHIOPIA 49.1% $1,626

GERMANY 99% $47,693

GREECE 97.7% $26,361

MEXICO 95.1% $17,277

UNITED KINGDOM 99% $41,594

Sources: UNESCO, CIA World Factbook, World Bank

Analyze Graphs

Literacy is one factor that contributes to higher GDP per capita. **Synthesize Visual Information** Which country shows the closest relationship between these two measures?

The more knowledge a worker has to do his or her job, the better the job will be done. Many European countries invest in human capital by providing free courses and on-the-job training, both of which boost productivity. More high-quality goods are produced at a faster pace. This leads to a higher standard of living for Europeans.

Entrepreneurship, or the ability to start and grow new businesses, is also critical to economic growth in Europe. Some economists have argued that Europe's strong regulation of businesses has limited how many new businesses can develop. But rates of entrepreneurship vary by country. Small businesses—those having fewer than 50 employees— still make up the vast majority of businesses in Europe. In Greece, almost all businesses are small businesses.

Specialization and Trade Countries in Europe have different economic strengths, depending on their natural resources, their types of industries, and the skills of their workers. Different regions of Europe produce the goods and services that their strengths make them best at producing. This is called specialization. For example, the Netherlands is a specialized provider of natural gas within Europe. Romania is a large exporter of automotive parts.

Specialization boosts countries' productivity and standard of living. Each country relies on others to meet its needs for other goods and services through trade. Trade barriers such as tariffs, as well as the process of exchanging currencies, can slow down the flow of goods. Trade agreements can ease these obstacles.

INTERACTIVE

GDP of Southern European Countries

READING CHECK Draw Conclusions What are some advantages and disadvantages of Sweden's mixed economy?

The European Union

The European Union was begun as a way to eliminate restrictions on trade among European countries. One of the main purposes of the European Union, or EU, is to make trade within Europe as easy and inexpensive as possible through a common market. Member countries can trade freely with one another without export limits, trade barriers, or taxes owed at country borders. Citizens can also move freely among countries to work and study.

European countries are **relatively** small, with short distances between one another. This makes specialization and trade that much easier.

In 22 EU member countries and three European countries that are not in the EU, people can also travel freely, without any border checkpoints. These countries make up what is known as the Schengen Area. Many EU countries have also adopted a common currency, called the euro, that eliminates the problem of exchanging different currencies in order to trade.

The EU has grown to include 28 countries. Of the countries that have not joined, many have trade agreements with the EU through another organization called the European Free Trade Association. One exception is Belarus, which belongs to the Eurasian Economic Union, a rival free-trade group made up of countries in Northern Eurasia.

☑ READING CHECK **Identify Main Ideas** Explain how adopting a common currency can help trade.

GEOGRAPHY **SKILLS**

Countries in Europe can join the EU or not, adopt the euro or not, and be in the Schengen area or not.

1. **Place** Which country chose to leave the EU?

2. **Compare and Contrast** How do different regions of Europe compare in terms of accepting these agreements?

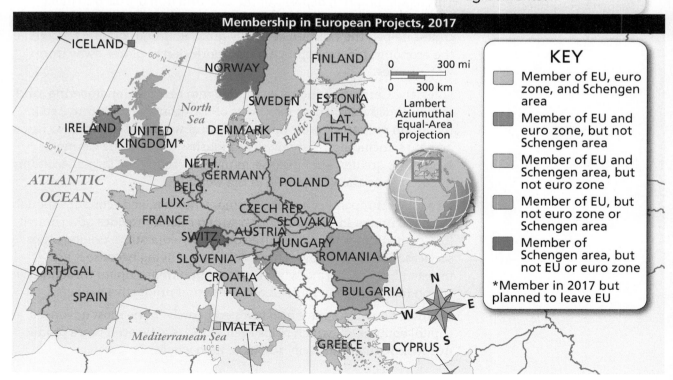

Membership in European Projects, 2017

KEY
- Member of EU, euro zone, and Schengen area
- Member of EU and euro zone, but not Schengen area
- Member of EU and Schengen area, but not euro zone
- Member of EU, but not euro zone or Schengen area
- Member of Schengen area, but not EU or euro zone

*Member in 2017 but planned to leave EU

Lambert Aziumuthal Equal-Area projection

Analyze Images
Many young Germans receive on-the-job training through apprenticeship programs, which makes them more productive. **Infer** What might happen if companies did not invest in their workers?

The German Economy

During the late 1800s and early 1900s, Germany, like other European countries, depended heavily on its natural resources. Germany built a strong steel industry in the northwestern Rhine–Ruhr region. This region had rich deposits of the coal and iron ore used to make steel. Water transport along the Rhine, other rivers, and a system of canals helped the German economy grow. Railroads greatly helped the economy, too, by improving transportation to places away from water routes.

Later, the German economy expanded into research, engineering, and technical activities. These new parts of the economy were centered in the urban areas that grew up along the railways and waterways. These activities, including Germany's car industry, are now the German economy's greatest strength. Germany is currently the largest economy in Europe and the fifth largest in the world.

Like other European countries, Germany has a mixed economy, though the government in Germany has a strong role. It provides government-funded health insurance and free university education, among other services. Germany enjoys a high standard of living because it has invested heavily. Germany's investment in human capital through education has resulted in high literacy rates and productive workers.

German companies have also invested heavily in the most advanced capital equipment, which helps their workers to be even more productive. This high productivity results in high wages.

Entrepreneurship is also very strong in Germany, which placed 14th out of 130 countries ranked on entrepreneurial strength in 2016. This means that German entrepreneurs have an easier time starting a business and are more likely to succeed than in many other countries. Strong entrepreneurship helps the German economy grow and stay strong.

☑ READING CHECK **Summarize** What is the role that entrepreneurship plays in Germany's economy?

The British Economy

The United Kingdom, also known as Britain, was the first country to industrialize. Its first industry was textile production, or the making of cloth. This industry relied heavily on water power, a natural resource readily available in England's wet and hilly northwest. (The industry also relied on cotton, which does not grow in Britain and had to be imported.) Water transport became another key factor in Britain's early industry. As an island country, Britain has many seaports. The British added to their water network by building many canals across the country in the 1700s and early 1800s.

Later in the 1800s, Britain relied on its rich coal and iron ore deposits to develop a steel industry. In the late 1900s, Britain benefited from yet another natural resource: the deposits of oil and natural gas in the North Sea.

By the early 2000s, both Britain's supply of natural resources and its economic dependence on them had decreased. Today, the British economy relies heavily on research, innovation, and financial services. Jobs in these areas depend on the highly educated British workforce.

🖑 **INTERACTIVE**

Northwestern Europe's Economies

Did you know?

In 1875, Britain produced almost 40 percent of the world's steel. Today, British steel makes up less than 1 percent of world production. Britain has shifted away from steelmaking and other heavy industries.

Analyze Images Container ships unload and take on cargo at a British port. **Recognize Cause and Effect** How did Britain's location lead to a reliance on trade?

▲ Students at the University of Cambridge in England, a part of Britain

Like other European countries, Britain has invested heavily in human capital. As a result, it has high literacy rates and a high standard of living. Major trading partners include the United States, Germany, France, and the Netherlands.

Like other European countries, Britain has a mixed economy. Britain's economy, however, has a stronger market orientation than most others in Europe. For example, while the government owns railroads in most European countries, Britain's are privately owned. Similarly, while university students in many European countries enjoy a free education, most students in Britain are expected to pay some of the cost.

In 2016, Britain placed ninth out of 130 countries ranked on entrepreneurial strength. This ranking is even higher than Germany's. It shows that Britain offers a good environment for starting and growing a business. This, in turn, helps keep its economy strong.

☑ READING CHECK Compare and Contrast How is Britain's mixed economy different from other mixed economies in Europe?

☑ Lesson Check

Practice Vocabulary

1. Why do businesses invest in **human capital**?

2. How can **entrepreneurship** make a country's economy stronger?

Critical Thinking and Writing

3. Identify Cause and Effect Name three ways in which the European Union has changed the economies of Europe.

4. Sequence What effect has access to water had on Europe's industry?

5. Compare and Contrast How do the economies of Germany and the United Kingdom differ?

6. Writing Workshop: Support Thesis with Details Add details in your ▤ Active Journal to support your thesis about the impact of cultural diversity on aspects of life in Europe. You will use the new details you add from this lesson as the supporting details of the explanatory essay you will write at the end of the topic.

Analysis Skills

Construct Charts and Graphs

Follow the steps below to construct a line graph for three countries of the growth in gross domestic product (GDP) per capita, or per person.

> INTERACTIVE

Create Charts and Maps

1 **To create a graph, first select a set of data.** Use a graph to display data visually. A set of data is a collection of related pieces of information.

2 **Research and find the data.** In this case, the data are provided in the chart below. Compare the growth rates of GDP per capita for France, Germany, and Britain from 2011 to 2015.

3 **Organize the data for your graph to show the information you want to highlight.** Think about how to present the growth in GDP per capita for one country. See the sample line graph of unemployment. A line graph makes sense because it shows a continuous change over time. For this graph, use a line with a different color for each country so that viewers can compare them.

4 **Draw and title the graph.** The symbol for each country's data is the colored line. After you choose a color for each country, create a key showing which color corresponds to each country. The key will make it easier for others to make sense of your graph. Then create a vertical axis with labels ranging from −0.5% to 3.0% and a horizontal axis with a label for each year. Finally, plot your data points and draw a line connecting them for each country. Include a title that describes the information shown. What would be a good title for this line graph?

Annual Growth in GDP per Capita, 2011–2015

	France	Germany	Britain
2011	1.6%	3.7%	0.8%
2012	−0.3%	0.4%	0.7%
2013	0.1%	0.4%	1.3%
2014	0.2%	1.5%	2.5%
2015	0.8%	1.7%	1.6%

SOURCE: United Nations Statistics Division

Unemployment and Underemployment, 1996–2012

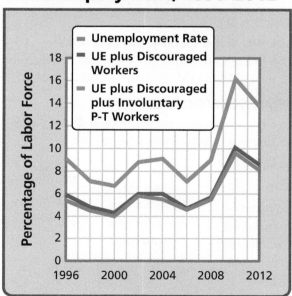

Analysis Skills • Constructing Charts and Graphs **177**

Government in Europe

BOUNCE TO ACTIVATE ▶ VIDEO

GET READY TO READ

START UP

Look at the photograph of a meeting of one of the houses of Germany's parliament. Write down three things you want to learn about Europe's governments and how they work.

GUIDING QUESTIONS

- What are the forms of government in Europe?
- How is the European Union run?

TAKE NOTES

Literacy Skills: Classify and Categorize

Use the graphic organizer in your 📓 Active Journal to take notes as you read the lesson.

PRACTICE VOCABULARY

Use the vocabulary activity in your 📓 Active Journal to practice the vocabulary words.

Vocabulary

dictatorship
theocracy
presidential democracy
parliamentary democracy
constitutional monarchy

Academic Vocabulary

coordinate
symbolic

There are 44 independent countries in Europe, not counting countries that are partly in Asia. Each has its own national government, the form of which varies from country to country. Most European governments are a type of democracy. In addition, 28 of the countries were members of the European Union (EU) in 2017. The EU is a governmental organization that helps **coordinate** action among its member nations.

Forms of Government in Europe

Most European governments are democracies. In a democracy, citizens control the government, usually by electing officials to make decisions. Belarus is not a democracy, but a dictatorship. In a **dictatorship**, or autocracy, citizens have little or no say in the direction of the government. They are simply forced to obey it. Belarus has been a dictatorship since 1994.

Another type of government is a **theocracy**, or a government controlled by a religious leader. The Vatican City, home to the Roman Catholic Church, is an example of this kind of government.

While all European countries besides Belarus and a few tiny states are democracies, they vary in the amount of freedom they allow. Some countries set limits on government power and protect freedoms such as the freedom of speech and free elections more strongly than others.

Presidential Democracies There are two main types of democracy: presidential and parliamentary. A **presidential democracy** has a president who leads the national government. The president is elected by the nation's citizens, and so is accountable to the people, not to the legislature. The president has powers in both domestic issues and foreign affairs. The president directs the government in carrying out laws the legislature enacts. The president also deals with foreign states and commands the nation's military forces.

Presidential democracies usually have a balance of power between the executive, controlled by the president, and the legislature. For example, the president may be able to veto, or reject, a law that the legislature has passed. In return, the legislature can override the veto. Although the president makes up a budget and names people to offices in the government, the legislature typically has to approve these plans.

Parliamentary Democracies Most European democracies have a parliamentary system. In a **parliamentary democracy**, the legislative branch, or parliament, has the most power. The parliament is made up of members elected by voters. The parliament makes laws for the country, as in a presidential democracy. In a parliamentary democracy, though, the government is led by a prime minister, who is usually elected by a majority of the members of parliament. As a result, the head of government is accountable to the parliament. The prime minister appoints other ministers who run the various government departments.

Parliamentary democracies fall into two groups, depending on who leads the country symbolically as head of state. In some, such as Germany, the head of state is a democratically chosen president with little or no control over government. The head of state is the **symbolic** leader of a country.

In other parliamentary democracies, such as the United Kingdom, the Netherlands, and Denmark, a monarch—a king or queen—inherits the role of head of state. In democracies with monarchs, the monarch's powers are limited by a constitution that rests power with the representatives elected by the people.

Academic Vocabulary
coordinate • v., to bring different elements into a relationship to ensure efficiency; organize
symbolic • adj., standing for an idea or a power, but with little practical role

Analyze Images Queen Margrethe, here with Prince Henrik, is queen of Denmark, a parliamentary democracy. **Draw Conclusions** What role does she play in Denmark?

Some European countries have governments that are a mix of parliamentary and presidential democracy. In these countries, including France, Portugal, and Ukraine, a prime minister chosen by parliament leads some parts of the government while a directly elected President leads others.

Government in the United Kingdom: Constitutional Monarchy

In 1215, King John signed the Magna Carta. This document limited the power of the king and gave rights to his people. It was the beginning of democratic government in England, which later joined with neighboring countries to form the United Kingdom, or Britain.

Today, the British government is a **constitutional monarchy**. This means that the monarch is subject to limits set by a constitution. Britain's monarch is the symbolic leader and head of state, but Parliament makes the laws under its constitution. Unlike the United States Constitution, the British constitution is not a single document, but a group of laws and court decisions. Britain's monarch in 2017 was Queen Elizabeth II.

The British legislature, or Parliament, is located in London, England. It is made up of the House of Lords and the House of Commons. Members of the House of Commons are elected by voters. At one time, members of the House of Lords inherited their seats. Today, most members of the House of Lords are appointed. These members include high-ranking clergy, judges, and national leaders. The elected House of Commons has most of the power. The head of the party in the House of Commons with the most members is the prime minister, the true head of the British government.

Since the 1990s, some lawmaking power has moved from the national to a regional level. The United Kingdom includes England, Wales, Scotland, and Northern Ireland. Scotland has its own parliament and government that handle laws specific to that country. The Welsh National Assembly can pass laws that directly affect Wales. Northern Ireland also has a separate assembly with its own powers.

German Government: A Parliamentary Democracy With a President Germany also has a parliament that makes laws. It is made up of two houses. Representatives to one house, the Bundestag, are elected by the people every four years. The members of the other house, the Bundesrat, are chosen by state governments.

The head of the government in Germany is the chancellor, who is similar to the prime minister in other parliamentary democracies. The chancellor, who is usually the leader of the political party with the most members in the Bundestag, is elected by a majority vote of Bundestag members. The chancellor sets the general policies of the government and appoints government ministers to carry out the policies and enforce laws.

However, the chancellor is not the head of state. That position is held by the president, who symbolizes the nation. The president is elected to a five-year term by a Federal Assembly. Half of this group are Bundestag members; the other half are state government representatives. The role of the president is largely symbolic. However, the president also has two powerful tools according to the German constitution.

The president may dissolve the Bundestag in case it no longer supports the government. This has happened three times in the history of the Federal Republic. If this happens, new elections are held.

The president also signs bills passed by the Bundestag into law. The president can refuse to sign a bill, in which case the bill is vetoed. Having a president with these responsibilities adds a balance of power to the German parliamentary system.

☑ **READING CHECK Compare and Contrast** How are the governments of the United Kingdom and Germany similar and different?

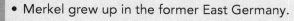

BIOGRAPHY
5 Things to Know About

ANGELA MERKEL
German politician (1954–)

- Merkel grew up in the former East Germany.

- She earned a doctoral degree in chemistry and worked as a research scientist.

- She first won election to the Bundestag in 1990, the year East Germany and West Germany were reunified.

- She is the leader of the Christian Democratic Union political party.

- Merkel was sworn in as chancellor of Germany in 2005 and was the first woman to hold the office.

Critical Thinking Summarize What prepared Angela Merkel to lead Germany?

How Is the European Union Run?

The European Union (EU) is a political and economic union of countries. The EU began as an effort by western European countries to ensure peace and improve their economies through a single market. After the collapse of the Soviet Union in 1991, many eastern European countries applied for entry to the EU. By 2014, the EU had grown to include 28 member nations.

The EU Government The EU has its own government with limited powers that member countries have accepted. These powers ensure that all members follow the same rules so that trade is free and fair. The rules also keep member countries from giving their businesses unfair advantages over businesses from other member countries.

The EU has a complex set of decision-making bodies, each made up of representatives from member nations. Only one of these bodies, the European Parliament, is directly elected by EU citizens. The European Parliament is part of the EU's legislative branch. The other decision-making bodies are made up of people appointed by the governments of member states. One of these, the European Commission, runs most EU agencies. The European Council includes the elected heads of government of the member countries. The Council has little formal power, but it resolves disputes among members.

Challenges to Union Not all European countries are members of the EU. Some countries do not meet its rules for membership. Others have decided against full membership. Many people in those countries are wary of the power of the EU's unelected decision-making bodies.

Quest CONNECTIONS

How might freedom of movement within the EU lead to increased cultural diversity in member countries? Record your findings in your 📓 Active Journal.

EUROPEAN UNION GOVERNMENT

POLICYMAKING

EUROPEAN COUNCIL:
- Function: sets EU policies
- Members: heads of government in charge of foreign affairs of each country, President of the European Council, and President of European Commission

LEGISLATIVE

EUROPEAN PARLIAMENT:
- Function: passes laws, adopts budget, approves members of European Commission
- Members: elected by EU citizens; number per country based on population

COUNCIL OF THE EUROPEAN UNION:
- Function: passes laws, adopts budget, coordinates policies among countries, and sets EU foreign policy
- Members: one government minister appointed by each country

EXECUTIVE

EUROPEAN COMMISSION:
- Function: proposes legislation, implements EU policies and budget, enforces EU law, represents EU globally
- Members: one commissioner appointed from each country

JUDICIARY

COURT OF JUSTICE:
- Function: ensures that EU legislation is applied the same way in all member countries
- Members: 28 judges appointed by country governments

Source: "How the European Union Works"

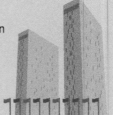

Analyze Charts The EU has a complex structure. **Synthesize Visual Information** Which body controls the EU's government?

EU members sometimes find economic growth affected by the addition of new members. For example, as one of the EU's poorer members, Portugal received financial help from the EU. Its EU development funding was cut by several billion euros when Romania and Slovakia entered the EU. These countries are poorer than Portugal and their workers earn lower wages.

Although the EU's members work together on most issues, conflict occurs. During the troubled economic times of 2008–2011, governments of poorer member countries struggled to pay back loans. In return for extending those loans, the richer members imposed strict spending limits on the poorer countries that caused hardship for many of their citizens.

The response by EU members to the Syrian refugee crisis of 2015 varied greatly. Germany declared an open door policy and resettled an estimated 300,000 refugees. In 2016, Poland, Germany's neighbor, refused to accept any refugees.

People in some EU member countries want to leave the EU. Britain, which had disagreements with the EU, voted to leave it in 2016. British voters wanted to end the EU's power over their country.

Europe's economic power is due in part to the EU's existence. However, differences over economic policy as well as migration have been pulling EU members apart. The biggest challenge for the EU is keeping its members together to find the best solutions to the problems of migration, terrorism, economic growth, and trade.

▲ People attempting to migrate to Europe from North Africa being rescued at sea

✓READING CHECK Identify Main Ideas How is the European Union representative of its member nations?

✓ Lesson Check

Practice Vocabulary

1. What is the most important feature of a **dictatorship**?

2. How can **constitutional monarchies** also be democracies?

Critical Thinking and Writing

3. **Infer** How can you tell that the legislature is the most powerful branch of government in a parliamentary democracy?

4. **Compare and Contrast** How does the role of the German president differ from that of the British monarch?

5. **Draw Conclusions** Why have most European countries become members of the European Union?

6. **Identify Main Ideas** What major challenge does the European Union face because of the way it is organized?

7. **Writing Workshop: Write an Introduction** Write a paragraph in your 📓 Active Journal that includes your thesis statement and a basic introduction to the impact of cultural diversity in Europe. This introduction will be the first paragraph of the explanatory essay that you will finish at the end of the topic.

The Debate Over Brexit

Through a vote held in 2016, British citizens decided that Britain should leave the European Union (EU). The vote in favor of *Brexit* (British exit from the EU) left some British citizens worried about the future of their country's economy and the stability of western Europe. Print and electronic media throughout Europe paid close attention to Brexit. Political cartoonists in Britain also addressed the issue.

◀ A British march opposing Brexit prior to the vote

Analyzing Geographic Sources

To analyze the cartoons, look for the symbols and other images the artists use to make their points. Consider what each figure in the cartoon stands for. Also look for irony and exaggeration.

1. **Analyze Political Cartoons** Explain what the cartoonist is suggesting about the British man stepping out of the EU plane while holding just the flag.

2. **Analyze Political Cartoons** Who are the refugees in the second cartoon, and why might they be coming to the EU?

3. **Support Ideas With Evidence** What images in the second cartoon indicate the view that Britain may regret the Brexit decision?

4. **Compare Authors' Treatment of Similar Topics** Compare the two cartoons. How are the messages in each cartoon alike? How are they different?

5. **Determine Author's Point of View** What clues in each cartoon show how the cartoonist feels about Brexit?

LESSON 4

Challenges Facing Europe

BOUNCE TO ACTIVATE · VIDEO

GET READY TO READ

START UP

Look at the photo of people playing a game in a French town. Many European countries have populations that are getting older, as people live longer and fewer Europeans have children. What problems might come up in a society where the number of elderly people is growing faster than the number of young workers?

GUIDING QUESTIONS

- What environmental challenges does Europe face?
- Why do demographics pose a challenge for Europe?
- What challenges does the European Union face?

TAKE NOTES

Literacy Skills: Draw Conclusions
Use the graphic organizer in your ▢ Active Journal to take notes as you read the lesson.

PRACTICE VOCABULARY

Use the vocabulary activity in your ▢ Active Journal to practice the vocabulary words.

Vocabulary		Academic Vocabulary
greenhouse gas	Kyoto Protocol	fertility
climate change	demographic	critical

Over the past hundred years, Europe has changed in several ways—the growth of its economies, the development of the European Union, and a changing population. These changes have brought a variety of challenges. Europeans must face issues of environmental harm, falling population, immigration, and tensions within the European Union.

Environmental Challenges

As you have read, Europe was the birthplace of the Industrial Revolution. More than 200 years later, the industries that helped so many countries to grow have left behind some unpleasant effects. Today, many European cities face air pollution. Countries are also working to develop energy sources such as wind and solar power that will not threaten the climate.

Air Pollution Given its many kinds of industry—most of which involve burning fossil fuels—Europe has long fought pollution. Vehicles, power plants, waste management, and even fertilized crops and livestock waste all contribute to the problem. Germany is among the nations most affected.

Air pollution is the largest environmental health risk in Europe. Ozone and unsafe chemicals in the air threaten people's health and harm the growth of crops and forests. Meanwhile, acid from air pollution is damaging culturally important buildings that are now centuries old.

Acid rain is a product of air pollution. The chemicals sent into the air from burning coal and other fossil fuels produce acid that mixes with rain. Germany and countries to its east are particularly affected by acid rain. In parts of Poland and the Czech Republic, forests have been destroyed by acid rain. Polluted water and soil have caused higher rates of birth defects, cancer, and other diseases.

Air pollution hurts Europe's economy, as well. Workers who are fighting pollution-related illnesses are often unable to work, resulting in lower productivity. These workers also bring increased health costs.

Nuclear Fears Some European countries have turned to nuclear power to supply their energy needs. A single nuclear power station can create a lot of power. When generated safely, nuclear energy produces much less air pollution than coal.

However, nuclear waste is very dangerous and can remain dangerous for thousands of years. A serious accident can spread radioactive pollution over a large area. For example, in 1986, an explosion occurred at one of the towers at the Chernobyl nuclear power plant in Ukraine. Winds spread radioactive pollution over a huge area in Europe. Many people became sick and died from the radiation. Farmland in Ukraine and Belarus was contaminated, and the food grown there was no longer safe to eat. More than 20 years later, the area around the power plant was still contaminated.

In 2014, there were 14 EU member countries operating nuclear power plants. These plants generate about 27 percent of the electricity produced in all of the European Union. Five countries alone—France, Germany, Sweden, Britain, and Spain—generate 82 percent of this nuclear-produced electricity.

Analyze Images This building stands in Pripyat, Ukraine, near the Chernobyl nuclear power plant. **Cite Evidence** What evidence can you see of the Chernobyl disaster?

Climate Change Burning fossil fuels also produces what scientists call **greenhouse gases**, or gases that trap heat in Earth's atmosphere and make the planet warmer. An overall temperature increase is one aspect of **climate change**, a process of long-term change in Earth's climate. Agriculture, livestock, landfills, forest clearing, and various industrial gases may also contribute to climate change.

There is already much evidence of the effects of climate change on Europe. The continent has seen several heat waves in recent years, and the five hottest years ever recorded in Europe have all occurred since 2000. Rainfall patterns have also changed. In central and eastern Europe, forests are predicted to have slow growth as rainfall decreases. In northern Europe, glaciers have been shrinking. Warming is also causing sea levels to rise. The sea level rise is a direct threat to some countries, especially the Netherlands, much of which is below sea level and could face serious flooding.

In 1997, the European Union signed the **Kyoto Protocol**, an international agreement to reduce the emission of greenhouse gases that contribute to climate change. The EU and its members joined the Paris Agreement to combat climate change in 2015. Under the agreement, the EU is trying to reduce greenhouse gas emissions and energy consumption, to switch to cleaner forms of transportation, and to use renewable energy, such as wind and bio-fuels.

✓ READING CHECK Identify Cause and Effect Name three ways in which air pollution and climate change can affect the economy.

Population Distribution by Age Group

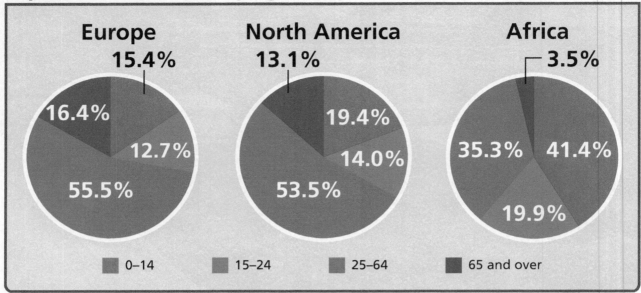

Europe
15.4%
16.4%
12.7%
55.5%

North America
13.1%
19.4%
14.0%
53.5%

Africa
3.5%
35.3% 41.4%
19.9%

■ 0–14   ■ 15–24   ■ 25–64   ■ 65 and over

Analyze Graphs Europe's share of elderly people is larger than that of children under 15. **Infer** What future problem might Europe face based on the age makeup of its population?

Academic Vocabulary
fertility • *n.,* the ability to have or likelihood of having children

Demographic Challenges

Europe is experiencing **demographic** change. *Demographic* means having to do with population trends and the different groups that make up the population of a place or region. An aging, shrinking population within Europe and increased immigration from outside Europe present challenges to Europeans.

An Aging Population For many years, European countries have experienced a declining birth rate. Women are not having as many children as in past decades. In developed countries, the total **fertility** rate—the average number of children born per woman—needs to be about 2.1 children per woman to keep the population steady. Yet the total fertility rate in most of Europe is much lower. For example, in Italy, the total fertility rate was only 1.43 in 2016.

As a result, Europe's population is shrinking. Population experts predict that populations may decline by more than 15 percent by 2050 in several countries, including Hungary, Bulgaria, and Lithuania.

While the number of children born in Europe is falling, the number of elderly people is increasing. Europeans are living longer. In fact, the percentage of people aged 80 years or older in EU countries is expected to more than double between 2015 and 2080.

Economic Effects As Europe's population is slowly shrinking, so is the number of people of working age. There is a growing shortage of workers in some European industries. It is difficult for European economies to grow when the number of people making products and earning wages is shrinking.

Yet for those in the workforce, taxes are also a concern. Governments around Europe must support their growing elderly populations, often by collecting higher taxes from workers.

The pension or retirement payments sent to the elderly are a huge expense. The costs of healthcare for older people are also high.

To cover these expenses without hurting living standards, European countries cannot afford for their economies to shrink along with their population. The strong demand for workers in some parts of Europe means that there are jobs available for immigrants. As you have read, this availability of jobs and a better way of life has drawn millions of immigrants to Europe. Immigration is a possible solution to Europe's demographic problems.

But as you have also learned, many Europeans do not welcome immigrants. Because of this lack of acceptance, immigrants often remain outside the mainstream of the European countries where they live. Due to discrimination, many children of immigrants miss out on the advanced education they would need for skilled jobs to help keep Europe's economies strong.

☑ READING CHECK **Compare and Contrast** How do the growth rates of younger and older populations differ in Europe?

Challenges Facing the European Union

Controversy over immigration is one of the challenges facing the European Union. Meanwhile, severe financial difficulties in some EU countries threaten the future of the euro, the EU's common currency, and may even threaten the survival of the EU.

Criticism of the European Union You have read that people in EU member countries can move freely to other EU countries. This freedom has resulted in increased migration from the east to wealthier western European countries. But people in these countries do not always welcome poorer eastern Europeans.

In recent years, millions of refugees have also been entering EU countries from Southwest Asia and Africa. The European Commission estimates that three million people arrived in the EU between 2015 and 2017. The cost of caring for, housing, and educating these refugees has caused tension between poorer and wealthier EU countries.

Adding to this conflict is a belief among some people that the EU does not represent ordinary Europeans. Most of the decisions in the EU are made by officials appointed by their governments and not elected by Europe's people.

Quick Activity

Follow instructions in your 📖 Active Journal to discuss with a partner the role of government spending and its effect on individual countries and on the EU.

▼ As workers move to Europe, new businesses have opened to serve them. In this store, signs in several languages cater to immigrants from a variety of backgrounds.

سوپر ایرانی ساوالان

POLISH , RUSSIAN , LITUANIAN
EAST EUROPEAN FOOD & DRINK

БОЛГАРСКИ СТОКИ

In the past few years, political parties that are **critical** of the EU have begun to win more support from voters. Frustration with EU rules led a majority of voters in Britain to vote to leave the EU in 2016. This British exit—"Brexit"—may not be finished before 2019, but it weakens the EU and may encourage other EU countries to leave the union.

The Euro Crisis When the euro was first adopted, countries using it agreed to follow common rules. For example, the public debt in a country was not supposed to be more than 60 percent of the country's gross domestic product.

Yet not all countries that use the euro—said to be in the euro zone—followed those rules closely enough. In some countries, additional problems, such as poor tax collection and loans that could not be repaid, worsened government finances.

Finally, a global financial crisis in 2008 caused the near collapse of world trade. Investment in business and demand for consumer goods fell. Nations' economies worldwide were at risk. Poor countries such as Greece were especially vulnerable.

By 2009, several countries using the euro faced a financial crisis. Their banks and governments faced a risk of bankruptcy, which would have destroyed some people's savings and threatened the value of the euro. From 2008 to 2009, the GDP in countries using the euro shrank by 4 percent. Unemployment increased, especially in Latvia, Lithuania, Ireland, Spain, and Greece.

Analyze Political Cartoons
The flag on the ATM machine is Greece's.
Analyze Images What message do you think the cartoonist is delivering?

In response, other countries using the euro—in particular, Germany—offered new loans to the countries in crisis. These loans came with strict conditions. Spending had to be cut and taxes had to be increased.

◀ Greek demonstrators opposed the restrictions placed on their economy by the EU during Greece's economic crisis.

Many people lost jobs or faced hardship. In Ireland and Spain, the age a person could retire and receive a pension was raised. In Greece, government employees' wages and payments to retirees were cut.

Some countries that received loans have still not recovered. Greece's economy has been crippled by debt and the restrictions imposed by other European countries. It may never be able to pay off its loans. The euro crisis has increased tensions among EU member countries.

✓ READING CHECK Identify Main Ideas Why are some Europeans dissatisfied with the EU?

Quest CONNECTIONS

Consider how cultural diversity and ethnic nationalism might conflict. Record your findings in your 📓 Active Journal.

✓ Lesson Check

Practice Vocabulary

1. How do scientists connect **greenhouse gases** to **climate change**?

2. What **demographic** challenges do many European countries face?

Critical Thinking and Writing

3. Summarize What are the main advantages and the main disadvantages of nuclear energy?

4. Understand Effects Why have some countries that suffered economic harm during the euro crisis still not fully recovered?

5. Identify Cause and Effect Why might immigration be necessary as many European countries' birth rates decline?

6. Writing Workshop: Clarify Relationships with Transition Words In your 📓 Active Journal, list transition words such as *additionally* or phrases such as *on the other hand* that you might use to help your reader follow connections between your ideas.

TOPIC 3

Review and Assessment

VISUAL REVIEW

Economies of Germany and United Kingdom

GERMANY
- Bigger government role in economy
- Higher education costs paid by government

BOTH
- Mixed economy
- Strong entrepreneurship
- Investment in human capital
- Most healthcare costs paid by government

UNITED KINGDOM
- Smaller government role in economy
- Some higher education costs paid by students

CHALLENGES IN EUROPE

Cause	Event	Effect
• War and poverty outside Europe • Weak economies in poorer European countries • Economic opportunities in wealthy European countries	• Immigration to Europe from other regions • Internal migration from poorer countries to wealthy countries within Europe	• Pressure on wealthy EU countries to integrate immigrants • Inability of poor European countries to maintain healthy economies • Resentment toward immigrants

READING REVIEW

Use the Take Notes and Practice Vocabulary activities in your Active Journal to help you to review the topic.

Quest FINDINGS

Present Your Project

Get help for creating and presenting your project in your Active Journal.

INTERACTIVE

Practice vocabulary using Topic Mini-Games.

ASSESSMENT

Vocabulary and Key Ideas

1. **Describe** What are people who are **bilingual** able to do?

2. **Explain** the relationship between natural or human resources and **specialization**. Give an example.

3. **Compare and Contrast** What is the difference between a **parliamentary democracy** and a **presidential democracy**?

4. **Identify Implied Main Ideas** How does a **constitutional monarchy** limit the power of the monarch?

5. **Check Understanding** Why did the EU sign the **Kyoto Protocol**?

6. **Recall** How have immigrants changed the age and size of the European workforce in the past century?

7. **Identify Cause and Effect** Why have residents of countries that are newer members of the European Union, such as Slovakia and Romania, moved to western Europe?

Critical Thinking and Writing

8. **Cite Evidence** How has geography influenced the diversity of Europe?

9. **Understand Effects** Describe the effects of governments' roles in mixed economies.

10. **Infer** What features of the European Union's structure make it difficult for the EU to address environmental issues in Europe?

11. **Use Evidence** See the Country Databank in the back of the book. Find the column for average annual real GDP growth rate.

What does that information show about the economies of Greece, Portugal, and Ukraine?

12. **Revisit the Essential Question** How do the unique cultures of Europe shape life in Europe?

13. **Writing Workshop: Write an Explanatory Essay** Following instructions in your 📓 Active Journal, answer the following question in a five-paragraph explanatory essay: What is the impact of cultural diversity on Europe?

Analyze Primary Sources

14. Which statement paraphrases the statement below by Olle Schmidt?
    A. Immigrants can slow economies.
    B. Immigrants can take jobs away from people born in a country.
    C. Immigrants can help the growth of economies.
    D. Immigrants can cost a lot of money.

"We have a lot of proof and we all know that Europe without migrants would have been a much less influential continent. The potential of immigrant entrepreneurs, for example, has been enormously important in the creation of new ideas and new jobs."

—Olle Schmidt, Swedish Member of the EU's European Parliament

Analyze Maps

Use the map to answer the following questions.

15. Which letter represents the capital of the European country led by Angela Merkel?

16. Which letter represents the constitutional monarchy that has Europe's leading financial sector today?

17. Which letter represents the country with Europe's largest economy?

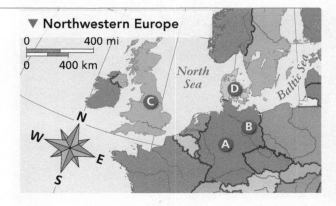

▼ **Northwestern Europe**

GO ONLINE
to access your
digital course

▶ VIDEO

◀) AUDIO

📖 ETEXT

👆 INTERACTIVE

✏ WRITING

🎮 GAMES

📄 WORKSHEET

☑ ASSESSMENT

Go to where Europe

meets Asia on the east in NORTHERN EURASIA. Visit the Russian capital, Moscow, and the city of Vladivostok on the Pacific Ocean. Journey through rugged mountains, vast plains, and an inland desert. The people of Northern Eurasia are as varied as the land. Its many ethnic groups have a rich, complex, and sometimes challenging history.

Explore The Essential Question

What role should people have in their government?

All of Northern Eurasia was controlled at one time by the Soviet Union. How does the Soviet legacy affect the region's people?

Unlock the Essential Question in your 📓 Active Journal.

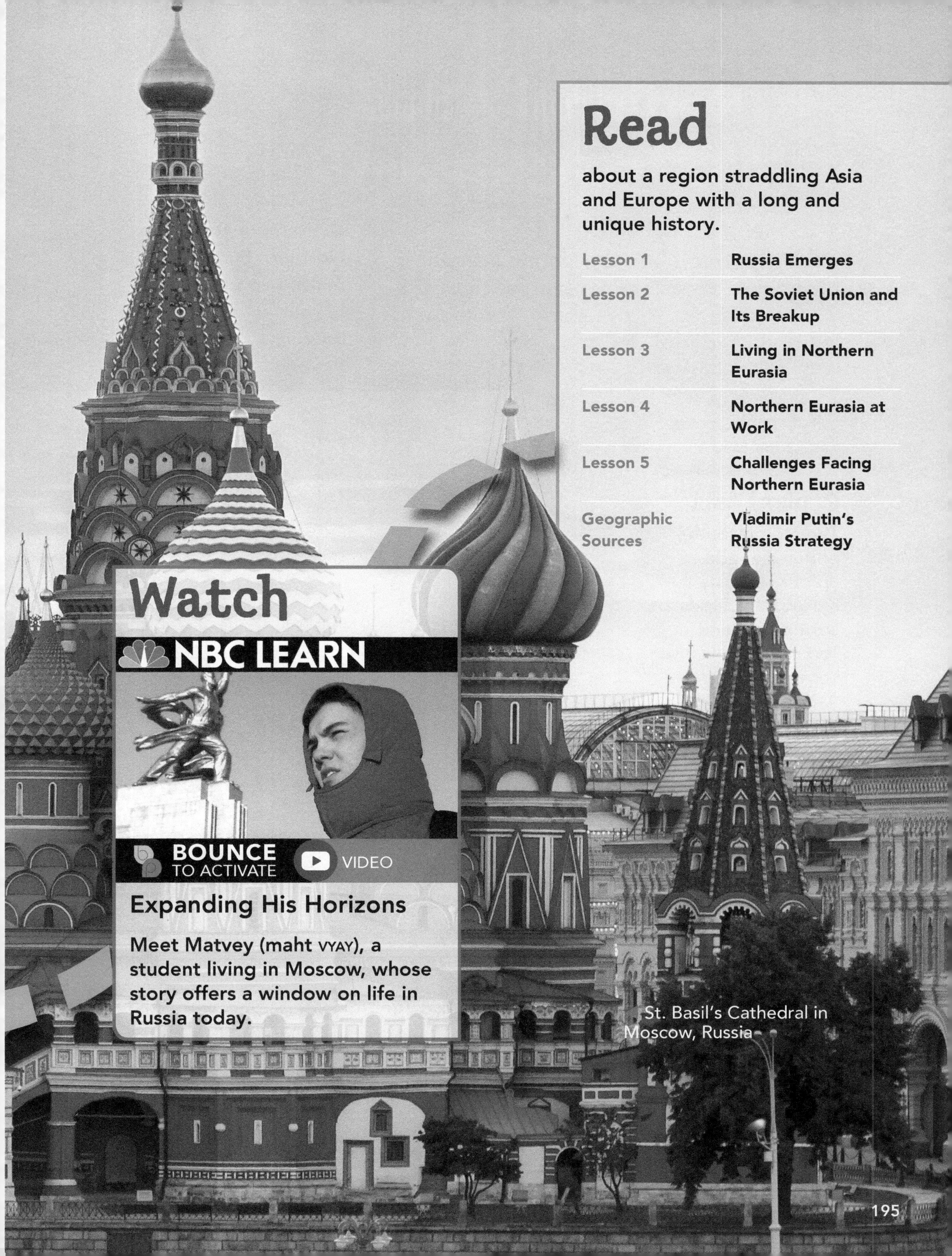

Read

about a region straddling Asia and Europe with a long and unique history.

Watch

NBC LEARN

BOUNCE TO ACTIVATE ▶ VIDEO

Expanding His Horizons

Meet Matvey (maht VYAY), a student living in Moscow, whose story offers a window on life in Russia today.

St. Basil's Cathedral in Moscow, Russia

Northern Eurasia: Political

RUSSIAN INFLUENCE

Russia has long been the dominant country in Northern Eurasia. However, each of the smaller countries to the south has its own traditions and identity.

Learn more about Northern Eurasia by making your own map in your 📓 Active Journal.

🖐 **INTERACTIVE**

Topic Map

Central Asia

The region south of Russia made up of Kazakhstan, Kyrgyzstan, Tajikistan, Uzbekistan, and Turkmenistan is often known as Central Asia. This area is populated by people who belong to several ethnic groups, such as these Uzbek girls.

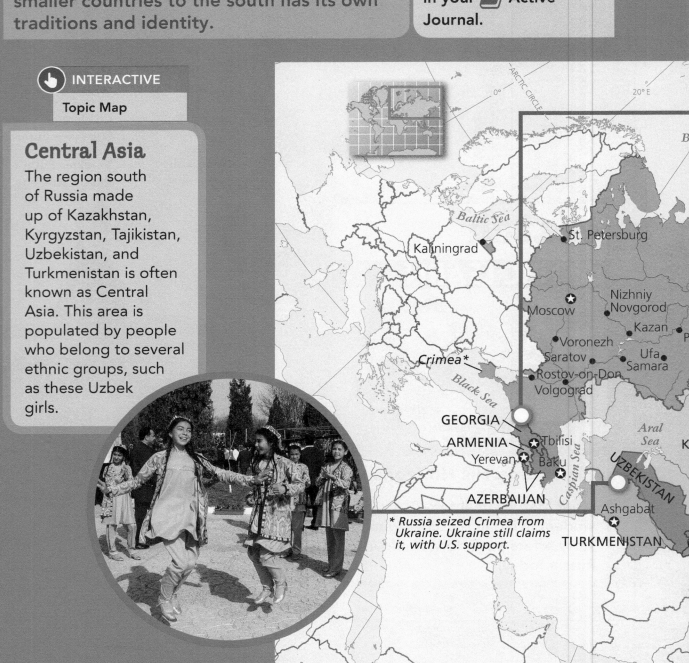

* Russia seized Crimea from Ukraine. Ukraine still claims it, with U.S. support.

The Caucasus
Because it lies within the Caucasus Mountains, the region made up of Georgia, Armenia, and Azerbaijan is often known as the Caucasus.

A World Giant
Russia is the world's largest country in area. It covers 6.6 million square miles, almost twice the size of the United States.

ARCTIC OCEAN

40° E   60° E   80° E   100° E   120° E   140° E   160° E   180°

Barents Sea

Kara Sea

Laptev Sea

East Siberian Sea

Bering Sea

60° N

RUSSIA

Sea of Okhotsk

od

Perm'

an

ara

a

Yekaterinburg

Chelyabinsk

Omsk

Novosibirsk

Krasnoyarsk

Irkutsk

L. Baikal

40° N

Astana ✪

KAZAKHSTAN

L. Balkhash

Vladivostok

TAN

Bishkek ✪   Almaty

Tashkent ✪

N   ✪ Dushanbe

KYRGYZSTAN

TAJIKISTAN

PACIFIC OCEAN

KEY
— Country border
✪ Capital city
• Other major city

0 ————— 600 mi
0 ————— 600 km

Lambert Conformal Conic Projection

N
W · E
S

TROPIC OF CANCER

20° N

197

Northern Eurasia: Physical

MOUNTAINS AND PLAINS

Mountains rim much of this region, with low plateaus and plains between them. Though Russia has a huge coastline, much of the coast is icebound for most of the year.

Learn more about Northern Eurasia by making your own map in your 📒 Active Journal.

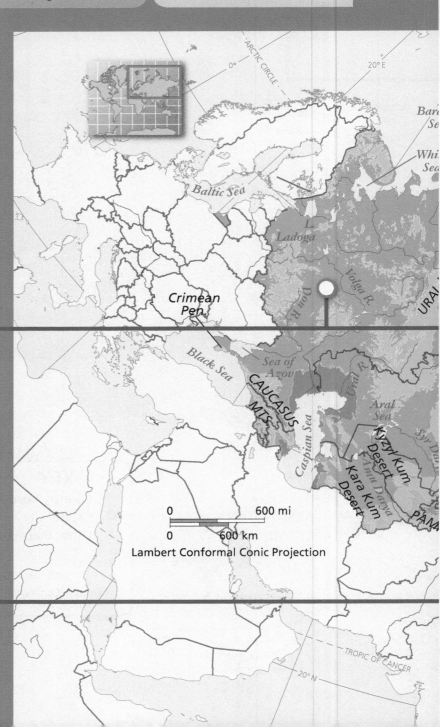

A Lowland Plain

The rolling plains of European Russia extend east to the Ural Mountains and south to the Caucasus Mountains. The Ural Mountains form the eastern boundary of Europe. The country of Russia extends from Europe across the Urals into Asia.

Soaring Mountains

Northern Eurasia's highest mountains are the ice-capped Pamir and Tian Shan (tyen shahn) ranges in Kyrgyzstan and Tajikistan.

Baltic Sea

L. Ladoga

Crimean Pen

Black Sea

Sea of Azov

CAUCASUS MTS.

Caspian Sea

Volga R.

Don R.

Ural R.

URAL

Aral Sea

Kyzyl Kum Desert

Kara Kum Desert

Amu Darya

Syr Darya

PAM

Bar Se

Whi Sea

ARCTIC CIRCLE

0°

20° E

0   600 mi
0   600 km
Lambert Conformal Conic Projection

TROPIC OF CANCER

20° N

A Vast, Cold Region

The vast region of Siberia extends from the Ural Mountains to the Chukchi Peninsula and the Pacific Ocean in the far east. This Asian part of Russia includes plains in the west, long rivers, and mountains and plateaus in the center and east. This area includes Lake Baikal (by KAHL), the world's deepest lake, shown in the photograph.

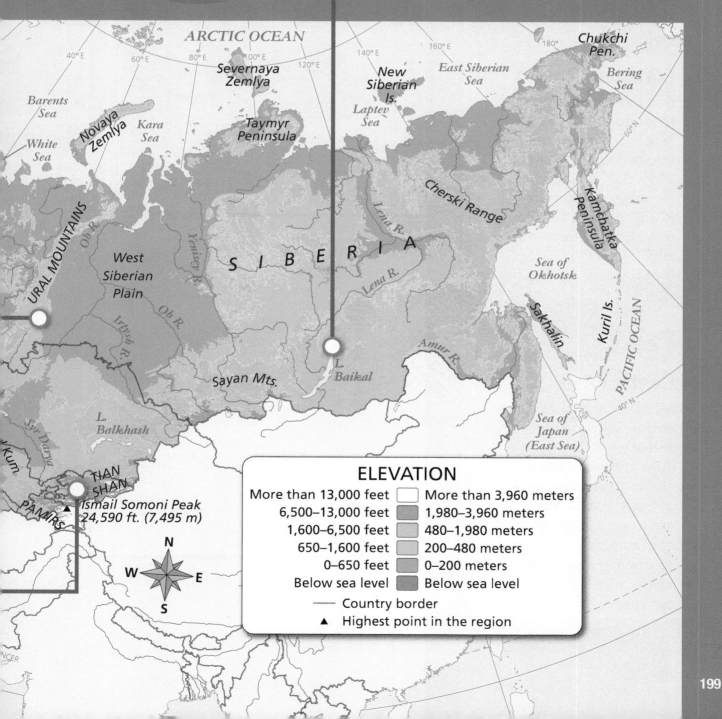

ARCTIC OCEAN

Chukchi Pen.

Severnaya Zemlya

New Siberian Is.

East Siberian Sea

Bering Sea

Barents Sea

Novaya Zemlya

Kara Sea

Laptev Sea

White Sea

Taymyr Peninsula

Cherski Range

Kamchatka Peninsula

URAL MOUNTAINS

Ob R.

Yenisey R.

Lena R.

S I B E R I A

West Siberian Plain

Irtysh R.

Ob R.

Lena R.

Sea of Okhotsk

Sayan Mts.

L. Baikal

Amur R.

Sakhalin

Kuril Is.

PACIFIC OCEAN

Syr Darya

Kum

L. Balkhash

Sea of Japan (East Sea)

TIAN SHAN

PAMIRS

▲ Ismail Somoni Peak 24,590 ft. (7,495 m)

CER

N W E S

ELEVATION

More than 13,000 feet		More than 3,960 meters
6,500–13,000 feet		1,980–3,960 meters
1,600–6,500 feet		480–1,980 meters
650–1,600 feet		200–480 meters
0–650 feet		0–200 meters
Below sea level		Below sea level

— Country border
▲ Highest point in the region

Northern Eurasia: Climate

A VERY COLD REGION

The interior location of this region gives it mainly continental climates, and its northern location means temperatures are generally low.

European Russia

The parts of Russia where most people live, such as Moscow, have continental cool summer climates. Moscow's average January temperature is 15°F (−9°C), and its average July temperature is 65°F (18°C).

Central Asia

Most of Central Asia has arid or semiarid climates. This means that there is little rainfall. In the north and in the mountains of Central Asia, there are frigid winters and cool summers, while in southern valleys, there are milder winters and hot summers.

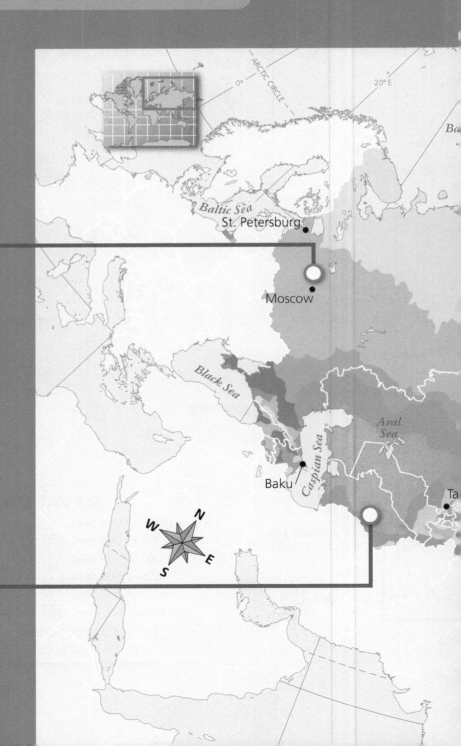

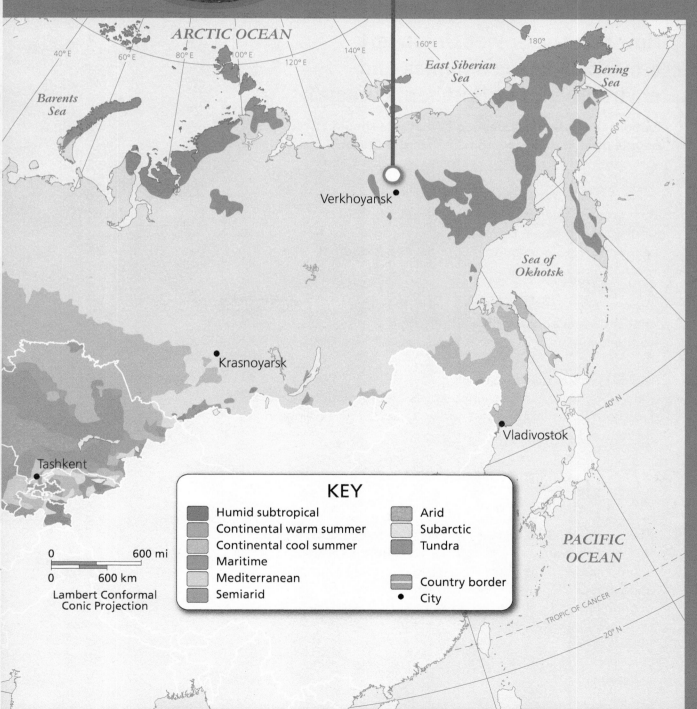

The Freezing North

Northern and eastern Russia have cold subarctic and tundra climates. On an average day in January, the high temperature in Verkhoyansk is a frigid −51°F (−46°C), and the low temperature drops to −57°F (−49°C). Farming is not possible in much of this area.

ARCTIC OCEAN

40° E 60° E 80° E 100° E 120° E 140° E 160° E 180°

Barents Sea

East Siberian Sea

Bering Sea

60° N

Verkhoyansk

Sea of Okhotsk

Krasnoyarsk

40° N

Vladivostok

Tashkent

PACIFIC OCEAN

0   600 mi
0   600 km

Lambert Conformal Conic Projection

KEY

Humid subtropical		Arid	
Continental warm summer		Subarctic	
Continental cool summer		Tundra	
Maritime			
Mediterranean		Country border	
Semiarid		• City	

TROPIC OF CANCER

20° N

Quest

Evaluating the Soviet Legacy

Quest KICK OFF

The rule of the Soviet Union left a lasting influence on the people of Northern Eurasia. Your quest will be to create a multimedia presentation that will inform and educate people about these long-term effects.

How has the Soviet Union left a mark on the economies and environments of Northern Eurasia?

Explore the Essential Question "What role should people have in their government?" in this Quest.

▲ Soviet policies led to the loss of most of the Aral Sea.

1 Ask Questions

First you will need to learn more about the effects of Soviet rule on the region. Begin by making a list of questions that you need to ask. Write your questions in your 📙 Active Journal.

2 Investigate

As you read the lessons in this topic, look for **Quest** CONNECTIONS that show the effects of Soviet rule on Northern Eurasia. Respond to them in your 📙 Active Journal.

3 Conduct Research

Find some valid and relevant sources of information on issues facing Northern Eurasian countries today. Record your findings in your 📙 Active Journal.

Quest FINDINGS

4 Create Your Multimedia Presentation

Make a multimedia exhibit including graphs, photos, and paragraphs that together answer the Guiding Question. Explain how Soviet economic decisions affected the region's natural environments and what challenges the Soviet system created for the region's economies.

LESSON 1
Russia Emerges

GET READY TO READ

Russia expanded from humble beginnings to become a vast empire. Powerful rulers such as Ivan III and Catherine the Great built the Russian empire. However, economic and social unrest eventually caused many Russians to rebel against their ruler.

On the Northern Fringes of Civilization

Many different peoples came to and settled in Russia during its early history. Areas around the Black Sea were known to the ancient Greeks and Persians. The Greeks set up trading settlements along that sea and profited from trade with people in the dense forests to the north. In those forests, small clan-based groups lived in scattered villages and survived through a combination of hunting, fishing, and farming. A **clan** is a group of families with a common ancestor.

A Cultural Crossroads East of the Caspian Sea is Central Asia. The Chinese played an influential role there in ancient times. Around 100 BCE the Chinese empire conquered parts of that region.

INTERACTIVE

Russia's Rulers

In the 300s CE, Christianity spread from the Roman empire into the kingdoms of the Caucasus, the area between the Black and Caspian seas where Europe and Asia meet. Armenia was the first country to adopt Christianity as its official religion, in 301. Christian kingdoms ruled most of the Caucasus for the next 1,400 years.

Around 500, a group known as the Slavs began spreading eastward from what are now Poland and Belarus into the Russian forests and the plains of Ukraine. These Slavs became known as East Slavs.

The Silk Road Crosses Eurasia As different peoples moved from place to place across the region, a trade network spread from east to west. The **Silk Road** was a group of trade routes that crossed Asia and connected China to the Mediterranean Sea. It was the most important trade network in Central Asia. It was named for silk, a type of cloth that was a highly prized trade good from China. Traders carried many other goods as well, including spices and fine pottery. In addition to goods, travelers brought new ideas, languages, tools, and customs.

In the 500s, nomadic Turkic tribes began spreading west into northern Central Asia. Meanwhile, forces from the Arab Muslim empire conquered the eastern Caucasus in the 600s. They brought Islam to southern Central Asia when they conquered it in the 700s. Islam spread and gradually became the dominant religion in Central Asia.

✓ READING CHECK **Identify Main Ideas** How did trade help shape Northern Eurasia's early history?

GEOGRAPHY SKILLS

The Silk Road connected Central Asia with areas to the east and west.

1. **Location** How many trade centers were located in Central Asian Muslim states?

2. **Use Visual Information** What regions could have influenced Central Asia through Silk Road trade?

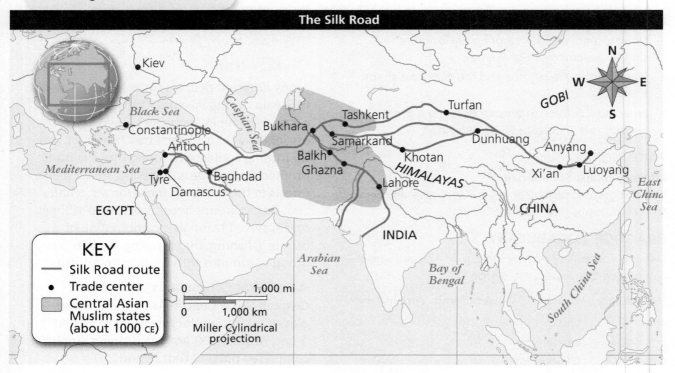

The Silk Road

KEY
— Silk Road route
• Trade center
▨ Central Asian Muslim states (about 1000 CE)

0   1,000 mi
0   1,000 km
Miller Cylindrical projection

How Did Russia Come Into Being?

Around 800, Vikings from northern Europe arrived in what is now western Russia. They set up trading posts with military defenses in villages of the East Slavs along rivers. From the East Slavs, the Vikings bought amber. This hard, gem-like fossil can be polished and used in jewelry. They also bought lumber, which they sold in the Byzantine and Islamic empires to the south of Russia.

In the late 800s, one family of Vikings conquered a kingdom covering parts of present-day European Russia, Belarus, and Ukraine. These Vikings married East Slavic people and adopted Slavic culture. They called themselves the Rus. The center of their kingdom, known as the Kievan Rus (KEE ev un ROOS), was the city of Kiev, now the capital of Ukraine.

The Kievan Rus Kiev's rulers grew rich from trade and united the East Slavic tribes. Under Vladimir I, the Kievan Rus formed close ties with the Byzantine empire starting around the year 1000.

Vladimir adopted Eastern Orthodox Christianity from the Byzantines. He converted all of Kiev to Christianity in a mass ceremony. Byzantine culture also influenced Russian language, art, and music as well as the architectural style of Russian churches.

The Mongol Invasion In the early 1200s, Mongol armies built a great empire. They conquered much of China, Central Asia, and southern Siberia. Part of the Mongol empire called the Golden Horde extended Mongol control westward, taking Kiev and European Russia. The Kievan Rus collapsed. Russian princes had to accept the authority of Mongol rulers. The Mongols brought Asian **models** of leadership and government to Russia. Trade between Russia and Southwest Asia increased.

The small town of Moscow gained wealth and power under the Mongols. Muscovy, the state centered in Moscow, came to dominate trade across the region. In the late 1300s, the princes of Muscovy and their allies defeated the Golden Horde, which had been weakened by fighting within the Mongol empire.

READING CHECK **Understand Effects** How did the arrival of the Mongols affect Russia?

How Did Russia Become a Great Power?

Over time, Muscovy expanded steadily. It conquered a region stretching from the Arctic Ocean to the Caspian Sea and east to the Ural Mountains. Rulers of Muscovy also established the practice of serfdom in Russia. **Serfs** were peasants who were bound to live and work on the land owned by a lord. They had few rights and lived difficult lives.

▲ This reconstruction of a Viking ship unearthed in Russia is an example of the swift trading ships that traveled Russia's many rivers.

Academic Vocabulary

model • *n.*, example; pattern of behavior to be followed

Did you know?

Russia's alphabet, called Cyrillic, was developed by missionaries who carried Eastern Orthodox Christianity to medieval Russia.

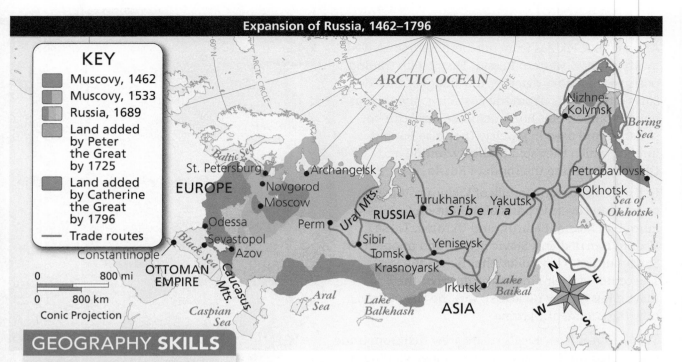

Expansion of Russia, 1462–1796

KEY
- Muscovy, 1462
- Muscovy, 1533
- Russia, 1689
- Land added by Peter the Great by 1725
- Land added by Catherine the Great by 1796
- Trade routes

0 800 mi
0 800 km
Conic Projection

GEOGRAPHY SKILLS

Between 1462 and 1796, Russia gained huge amounts of territory.

1. **Place** Which cities in western Russia could be used as ports? When did they become part of Russia?

2. **Use Visual Information** In which direction did Russia expand between 1533 and 1689?

The Beginnings of the Romanov Dynasty In 1613, an assembly of nobles elected a new **tsar**, or Russian ruler. The word *tsar* comes from the Latin *caesar,* or emperor. This new ruler was Michael Romanov, the 16-year-old son of an influential noble. His family, called the Romanov dynasty, ruled Russia for the next 300 years.

During Michael's rule, Russia increased contact with Western Europe. In addition, Russian explorers traveled thousands of miles across Siberia. They reached the Pacific Ocean in 1639 and founded settlements across Siberia.

Peter the Great The first great Romanov tsar was Peter the Great, who ruled from the late 1600s to 1725. He dreamed of making Russia a rival to the powerful countries of Europe. He **westernized** Russia; that is, he **adopted** Western ideas, technology, and culture. He conquered lands along the Baltic Sea and founded a new capital, St. Petersburg, on the Baltic. Peter chose this location, at the western edge of Russia, because it offered access to western Europe and its knowledge.

Catherine the Great Catherine II, known as Catherine the Great, took the throne in 1762. By the end of her rule in 1796, Catherine had greatly expanded Russia. She conquered the Black Sea coast, much of Ukraine, and parts of Poland. Russia gained recognition as one of Europe's great powers. By taking ports on the Black Sea, she gave Russia warm-weather ports that were open to shipping year-round. The waters of its northern ports often froze in winter, preventing trade.

Academic Vocabulary

adopt • *v.,* to make use of a new tool or idea

☑ READING CHECK **Draw Conclusions** How did the Romanov dynasty make Russia a great power?

The Russian Empire Expands but Weakens

In the early 1800s, Russia seized most of the Caucasus. However, by the early 1900s, Russian rulers faced unrest that eventually brought down the empire.

The Imperial Age Ends In spite of westernization, Russia lagged behind Western Europe in many ways. As Europe industrialized, Russia still depended on agriculture and serf labor. In 1856, Russia lost the Crimean War to Britain, Turkey, and France. Shocked, Russia's leaders aimed to modernize. Hoping to develop a more modern economy, Russia's leaders freed the serfs in 1861.

During the 1860s and 1870s, the Russian empire conquered most of Central Asia. Russian peasants settled the lands of southwestern Siberia and what is now northern Kazakhstan to farm. Russia finally began to industrialize in the late 1800s.

Unrest Grows While industry grew, most Russians remained desperately poor. During the late 1800s, Russia's large Jewish minority faced prejudice and resentment. Many of Russia's poor unjustly blamed Jewish people for their troubles. Their resentment resulted in a wave of pogroms, or anti-Jewish riots, in the late 1800s and early 1900s. Hundreds of Jewish people were killed, more were wounded, and many saw their possessions looted or destroyed. As a result, hundreds of thousands of Jewish people fled Russia. Many of these people migrated to the United States.

▼ In 1905, the tsar's troops attacked protesters on a day that came to be called Bloody Sunday.

The outbreak of World War I in 1914 put a huge burden on Russia. Because peasants had to leave farms to fight in the army, food production fell dangerously low. **Inflation**, or a general increase in prices, meant workers could not buy enough food. Tsar Nicholas II tried to prevent unrest, which grew intense.

✓ READING CHECK **Identify Cause and Effect** What was a main reason for unrest during the Russian imperial age?

☑ Lesson Check

Practice Vocabulary

1. What effects did the **Silk Road** have on the development of Russia?

2. How did poverty and **inflation** affect the **tsars'** rule in Russia in the late 1800s and early 1900s?

Critical Thinking and Writing

3. **Understand Effects** What are four changes the Mongol invasion brought to Russia?

4. **Compare and Contrast** How were Michael, Peter the Great, and Catherine the Great similar as rulers?

5. **Understand Effects** What effect did poverty have on Russia's Jewish population?

6. **Writing Workshop: Introduce Claims** Think about how Russia's history was affected by its citizens' role or lack of a role in government. What do you think the role of citizens in government should be? Record your thoughts in your 📓 Active Journal.

LESSON 2

The Soviet Union and Its Breakup

GET READY TO READ

START UP

This photograph shows a Soviet parade in 1977 celebrating the Russian Revolution. What does the photograph suggest about the Soviet Union?

GUIDING QUESTIONS

- How did Stalin's rule and the Cold War shape the Soviet Union?
- Why did the Soviet Union collapse?
- How did Russia and the other republics change after the Soviet Union broke up?

TAKE NOTES

Literacy Skills: Sequence

Use the graphic organizer in your 🗐 Active Journal to take notes as you read the lesson.

PRACTICE VOCABULARY

Use the vocabulary activity in your 🗐 Active Journal to practice the vocabulary words.

Vocabulary

Bolsheviks
communism
collectivization
Cold War

economic
oligarchy
sanction

Academic Vocabulary

emerge
condemn

A popular uprising ended the rule of the tsars in the Russian empire in the 1910s. A communist government took control and ruled the region for more than 70 years. Then that government fell due to economic and political problems. The communist state splintered into several new countries. Since 1991, Russians and other peoples across Northern Eurasia have built new governments and economies.

The Russian Revolution

As you have learned, World War I caused serious hardships for ordinary Russians. Unrest and public protests spread. Fearing that the people could become violent, Russia's parliament and military leaders forced Tsar Nicholas II to give up his throne in March 1917. The government that formed to replace him was weak, however.

The **Bolsheviks**, a well-organized Russian political group that called for workers to control private property, saw an opportunity. Led by Vladimir Lenin, they seized control of Russia in late 1917 in the Russian Revolution.

Lenin created a communist government. **Communism** is a way of organizing a society in which there is no private property and an authoritarian government owns the things that are used to make and move products. Lenin and the Bolsheviks built a state-controlled, communist economy.

☑ READING CHECK **Identify Cause and Effect** Why were the Bolsheviks able to replace the first government that followed the tsar?

Stalin's Rule and the Cold War

In 1922, after the communists won a civil war, they brought Russia and other parts of the former Russian empire together to form the Union of Soviet Socialist Republics (USSR), or the Soviet Union. Russia was the largest and most important of the republics.

Stalin Takes Control After Lenin died in 1924, Josef Stalin **emerged** as the new Soviet leader. Stalin wanted to transform the Soviet Union's economy. He used brutal tactics to enforce his policies and maintain power. He crushed all opposition and sent millions of people to prisons and labor camps called gulags, where many died.

Stalin believed that for communism to survive, the Soviet Union would have to become an industrial leader. He ordered a series of five-year plans. These government plans set economic goals for the next five years and detailed how to achieve them.

Stalin pushed for the development of industry and the collectivization of farms. **Collectivization** is a shift of control from an individual or company to a group called a collective.

A horrible famine from 1932 to 1933 showed how disastrous collectivization could be. Collectives in the Caucasus, Ukraine, and elsewhere were forced to send all their grain to the government. This left none for the farmers. More than six million people died of starvation. Stalin did nothing to help them.

Communism in the Smaller Republics The Soviets completely controlled the Caucasus and Central Asia. Government officials told the people of each republic what to produce. In Central Asia, many livestock herders were forced to settle on government farms, regardless of whether the land was suitable for farming.

Soviet leaders also wanted to unify the country. They built many new schools. These schools taught in Russian instead of in local languages. To control cultural life, the government closed churches and mosques. Many Russians also moved into the republics outside Russia.

👆 **INTERACTIVE**

From Russian Empire to Soviet Union, 1914–1923

Academic Vocabulary
emerge • *v.*, to rise or become known

Analyze Images Vladimir Lenin led the communist revolution and became dictator of the Soviet Union. **Infer** Who supported Lenin?

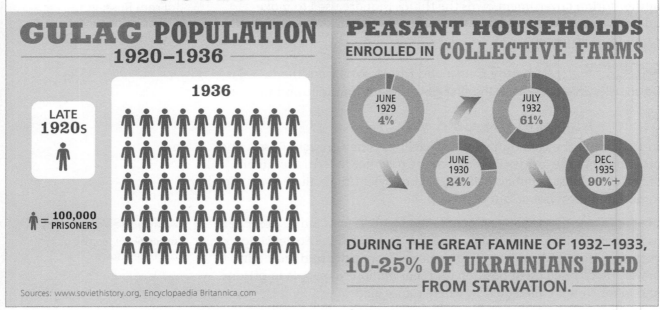

COSTS OF STALIN'S RULE

GULAG POPULATION
1920–1936

LATE 1920s

1936

= 100,000 PRISONERS

PEASANT HOUSEHOLDS
ENROLLED IN COLLECTIVE FARMS

JUNE 1929 4%

JULY 1932 61%

JUNE 1930 24%

DEC. 1935 90%+

DURING THE GREAT FAMINE OF 1932–1933, 10-25% OF UKRAINIANS DIED FROM STARVATION.

Sources: www.soviethistory.org, Encyclopaedia Britannica.com

Analyze Charts During the 1930s, Stalin sent 5 million people to the prison labor camps called *gulags.* **Draw Conclusions** How did collectivization lead to suffering?

The Cold War Begins Under Stalin's rule, the Soviet Union worked with Western powers to defeat the Axis powers during World War II. Soon, Soviet relations with the United States and its allies chilled.

Soviet troops occupied Eastern Europe during the war and remained after the war ended. The Soviet Union set up communist governments there, angering the United States. At the same time, Stalin objected to U.S. goals and actions after the war. This period of hostility between, on one side, the Soviet Union and its allies and, on the other side, the United States and its allies was called the **Cold War**. The Cold War went global when both sides tried to influence countries in Latin America, Asia, and Africa to follow their point of view.

☑ READING CHECK **Identify Main Ideas** Why did the Cold War develop?

The Soviet Union Collapses

During the Cold War, the Soviet Union built a huge and powerful military. Leaders neglected the rest of the economy, though. This neglect eventually led to the Soviet Union's collapse.

The Communist Economy Weakens To compete with the United States, Soviet government focused on building weapons and military vehicles. It failed to invest in new technologies. Meanwhile, the government-controlled command economy gave workers little reason to work hard. As a result, the Soviet Union struggled to pay for imported food and consumer goods. Shortages of basic goods were common.

During the 1980s, the Soviet Union lost a war to support a communist government in Afghanistan. The loss brought calls for reform. At the same time, the price of oil, a major export, fell sharply, hurting the economy. Soviet leaders knew that their system was in trouble.

Did you know?

During the Cold War, the Soviet Union and United States competed in a space race to win prestige. The Soviets put the first human in space, a man named Yuri Gagarin. The United States was the first to land people on the moon.

Openness and Restructuring A new leader, Mikhail Gorbachev (mee KYLE GAWR buh chawf) tried to fix the Soviet system. Coming to power in 1985, he introduced two new policies, glasnost (GLAHS nawst) and perestroika (pehr uh STROY kuh). Glasnost, or "openness," meant greater freedom of speech. Glasnost led to more discussion of Soviet economic and military failures. Perestroika, or "restructuring," reduced government control over the economy and provided for freer markets. Social freedoms expanded, too. More people were allowed to move around and out of Russia. This allowed a large number of Soviet Jews to emigrate.

The Collapse Comes Gorbachev also eased Soviet control over Eastern Europe. In 1989, several communist governments there collapsed in the face of widespread opposition from citizens.

Unrest reached East Germany, and people there elected their first democratic government. In 1990 East and West Germany were reunified as one nation. When Gorbachev made no move to oppose that change, world leaders knew that Soviet power was ending.

Angry over these events, some Soviet military leaders tried to stage a coup (koo), or government takeover. They wanted to restore the communist system. Russians resisted, and the coup failed. At the end of 1991, the Soviet Union officially broke apart, and the Cold War came to an end. All of the former Soviet republics gained independence. The largest of these was Russia.

☑ READING CHECK Draw Conclusions How did events in Germany contribute to the collapse of the Soviet Union?

Transition from Communism

Boris Yeltsin became the first president of a new Russia. He headed a nation on the verge of economic collapse. Economic change brought great hardship, inflation, and unemployment. Russia also had to deal with an armed rebellion in one region. Meanwhile, the republics of the Caucasus and Central Asia tried to forge their own identities.

Quick Activity

Hold a debate with a partner in which one of you is a supporter of communist tradition and the other is a supporter of glasnost and perestroika. Prepare for your debate using your 📓 Active Journal.

INTERACTIVE

The Fall of the Soviet Union

Analyze Timelines Russia's government went through major changes in the 1900s. **Synthesize Visual Information** How long did communist rule in the region last?

Key Dates of Soviet and Post-Soviet Russia

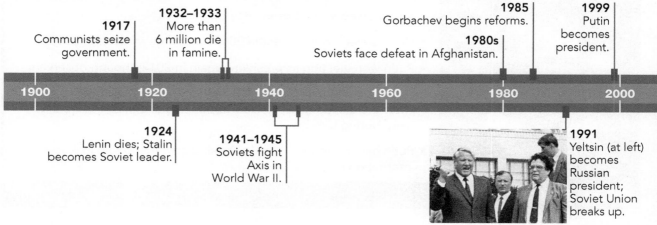

1917 Communists seize government.

1932–1933 More than 6 million die in famine.

1985 Gorbachev begins reforms.

1980s Soviets face defeat in Afghanistan.

1999 Putin becomes president.

1924 Lenin dies; Stalin becomes Soviet leader.

1941–1945 Soviets fight Axis in World War II.

1991 Yeltsin (at left) becomes Russian president; Soviet Union breaks up.

1900 — 1920 — 1940 — 1960 — 1980 — 2000

Quest CONNECTIONS

How did years under the Soviet command economy affect attempts to transition to a market economy after the breakup of the Soviet Union? Record your findings in your Active Journal.

Change in Russia Yeltsin oversaw a shift from the old Soviet command economy to a market economy. The change happened very suddenly. Many Russians saw their incomes drop sharply at first. The economy did not recover until the 2000s.

Some people benefited greatly from the shift. Some very powerful individuals gained control of what had been state-owned firms. They used the economic might of these new businesses to become very wealthy. They formed an **economic oligarchy**, a small group of people who control the economy and influence the government.

Yeltsin resigned in 1999, naming Vladimir Putin as acting president. One challenge both of these presidents faced was a breakaway region. Rebels in Chechnya wanted independence, which the Russians had been fighting since 1994. Putin forcefully ended the rebellion, but Chechnya was left in ruins.

Changes in the Other Republics The leaders of the other republics formed new governments. In Central Asia, though, former communist leaders continued to rule as dictators. Democracy had more success in Armenia and Georgia but was still not strong.

Economically, Azerbaijan (az ur by JAHN), Kazakhstan, Uzbekistan, and Turkmenistan had some success because they had valuable oil and gas resources that they could sell. Other republics struggled with the change to market economies.

✓ READING CHECK **Identify Main Ideas** How did the economy of Russia change under Yeltsin?

Putin's Russia

Putin moved to rebuild Russia through strong leadership and increased government control. Critics have charged that Putin's policies have taken away citizens' rights and threatened democracy and peace.

BIOGRAPHY
5 Things to Know About ▶ VLADIMIR PUTIN
Russian president (born 1952)

- Putin served in the Soviet secret police.

- He was elected president in 2000 and prime minister in 2008.

- Putin won election as president again in 2012, though observers claimed that he abused his power to win it.

- After the election, Putin jailed opponents and in 2014 invaded neighboring Ukraine.

- Putin has worked to increase Russia's power and role in international affairs.

Critical Thinking How did Putin attempt to ensure he retained control over the government?

Economic Growth From 2000, when Putin gained power in Russia, until 2014, Russia experienced an oil boom. Oil is Russia's most important export. High oil prices helped the Russian economy. Putin also put in place economic changes that promoted growth. Some of these policies increased government's control of the economy. Some cut the power of the oligarchy. Family income went up. The middle class grew, and the number of people living in poverty fell.

Russian Aggression Putin's relations with his neighbors were rocky. Russia has supported rebels in two regions of Georgia. When Georgia sent troops to one of them in 2008, Russian troops drove them out.

In 2013, the pro-Russian president of Ukraine, Viktor Yanukovich, rejected a trade deal with the European Union in favor of closer ties with Russia. In 2014, pro-European protesters and politicians in Ukraine forced Yanukovich out of office.

In response, Russians living in eastern Ukraine rebelled against Ukraine's government. Putin sent the rebels military aid. Russian troops also invaded Crimea, in southern Ukraine. Russia quickly annexed—or took over—Crimea.

Tough Times Return Russia's seizure of Crimea was **condemned** by the United States and United Nations. The United States and others placed economic sanctions on Russia. **Sanctions** are actions that attempt to force a country to follow international law. At the same time, world oil prices plunged in 2014. This change and the sanctions hurt Russia's economy.

Analyze Images In 2015 these Tatars and Ukrainians protested Russia's annexation of Crimea. **Infer** Why are these protestors waving the Ukraine flag?

☑ **READING CHECK** Identify Causes and Effects What contributed to Russia's economic troubles in the 2010s?

Academic Vocabulary
condemn • *v.*, to express public disapproval

☑ Lesson Check

Practice Vocabulary

1. What role did the **Bolsheviks** play in the birth of the **communist** Soviet Union?

2. How did the power of the Russian **economic oligarchy** change under Vladimir Putin?

Critical Thinking and Writing

3. **Synthesize** Why do you think it was so difficult to create democracies and market economies in the region after the fall of the Soviet Union?

4. **Distinguish Relevant Information** What factors weakened the Soviet Union?

5. **Compare and Contrast** How is Putin's rule similar to and different from the rule of the communists who led the Soviet Union?

6. **Writing Workshop: Support Claims** In your 📓 Active Journal, write several sentences on how the history of the Soviet Union and its breakup supports your argument about citizens' role in government. Provide evidence for your argument.

Solve Problems

 INTERACTIVE

Solve Problems

Use the sources and the steps below to practice the skill of solving problems.

1 Understand the problem. First, you need to identify the problem. What are the causes and effects of the problem? Who is involved?

a. What problem does Cheney identify?

b. How does he illustrate the problem?

2 Consider possible solutions and choose the best one. Once you have identified the problem and gathered some information, list and consider a number of possible options for solving it. Be sure to carefully consider the advantages and disadvantages of each option. Choose the solution whose benefits outweigh its drawbacks.

a. What does Allison say should be a condition for former Soviet republics to establish diplomatic relations with the United States?

b. How does Allison propose to solve the problem Cheney identifies?

3 Make and implement a plan. Choose and implement a solution and assign yourself a deadline for each step. Of course, there are many things that you cannot predict. Adjust your plan as necessary.

a. What problem might come up in implementing Allison's plan?

b. How might you solve this problem?

Primary Source

"If the Soviets do an excellent job at retaining control over their stockpile of nuclear weapons—let's assume they've got 25,000—and they are 99 percent successful, that would mean you could still have as many as 250 that they were not able to control . . ."

"Given the disintegration of their society, given the sad state of their economy, the only realistic thing for me to do as Secretary of Defense is to anticipate that one of the byproducts of the breakup of the Soviet Union will be the proliferation [spread] of nuclear weapons."

—Dick Cheney, U.S. Secretary of Defense, on Meet the Press (1991)

Primary Source

". . . Insist that the U.S. will establish diplomatic relations with new republics only on the basis of their . . . willingness to comply with international treaty commitments . . . ."

"Explore cooperative measures with the Soviet and Russian government to return all nuclear warheads to Russian territory immediately. . . ."

"Organize a strategy for military-to-military cooperation on . . . limiting the spread of nuclear weapons. . ."

"Explore [forming] a . . . [group] to limit the sale of . . . dangerous weaponry . . . to third parties. . ."

—Graham Allison, memo to General Colin Powell (1991)

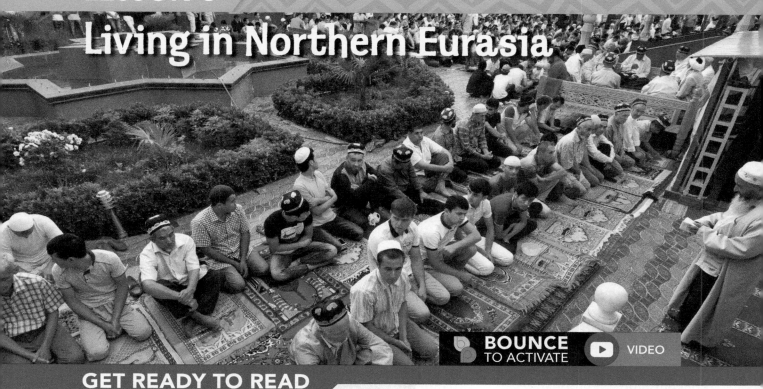

Living in Northern Eurasia

BOUNCE TO ACTIVATE   ▶ VIDEO

GET READY TO READ

START UP

Look at the photo of Muslims in Uzbekistan praying on the holiday Eid al-Fitr. Seeing the photo, what questions do you have about the cultures of Northern Eurasia? Write your ideas.

GUIDING QUESTIONS

- What explains where people live in Northern Eurasia?
- What is the cultural makeup of Northern Eurasia?

TAKE NOTES

Literacy Skills: Draw Conclusions
Use the graphic organizer in your ▤ Active Journal to take notes as you read the lesson.

PRACTICE VOCABULARY

Use the vocabulary activity in your ▤ Active Journal to practice the vocabulary words.

Vocabulary	Academic Vocabulary
permafrost	extract
tundra	cluster
taiga	

Northern Eurasia stretches from Europe to the Pacific Ocean and from the frozen Arctic to temperate forests, grasslands, and deserts. The hundreds of millions of people living in this vast region come from many ethnic and cultural backgrounds.

Where Do the People of Northern Eurasia Live?

Russia, the largest country on Earth in area, spans two continents. The region also includes three countries in the Caucasus and five in Central Asia. The diverse geography of Northern Eurasia has affected where people live and how they use their resources.

Physical Geography and Settlement

Most of Northern Eurasia lies far from the Equator. Most of it is continental—far from oceans. These factors make the climates of the region generally cold. Much of the region has a climate and soils that make farming difficult. Without a large rural population, cities and industry are slow to develop. Mountains and deserts also affect settlement patterns.

Northern Eurasia: Population Density

KEY

Population Density

Persons per sq. mile	Persons per sq. kilometer
500	195
300	115
150	60
25	10
1	1

Urban Areas
- ■ More than 3 million
- • 1 million–3 million

0   800 mi
0   800 km
Lambert Azimuthal
Equal-Area projection

GEOGRAPHY SKILLS

Most of Russia's people are concentrated in European Russia and areas along its southern border that support farming.

1. **Region** Where is population density the highest in the Central Asian republics?

2. **Synthesize Visual Information** Look at the climate map of the region in the Regional Atlas. What explains the very low population density of central and western Uzbekistan and Turkmenistan?

Settlement Patterns in Russia The European part of Russia has the greatest population density. That is, more people live there per square mile than live in other parts of the country. Russia's most densely settled areas are those that have the best climates and soils for agriculture. As in other countries such as Britain and Germany, the largest cities are located in areas that were attractive to farmers. Over time, surplus food produced by farmers enabled cities to rise. Today, cities draw people for a variety of reasons, including by providing jobs in offices and factories.

Russia is so vast you might think that many people live in rural areas. Actually, three-quarters of all Russians live in urban areas, similar to the distribution in Germany and Britain.

If you look at the population density map, you will see that Siberia, while huge, has few people. One of the many challenges for human settlement in this area is **permafrost**. This permanently frozen soil lies beneath the tundra and often beneath the taiga. The **tundra** is a plain with limited vegetation, such as moss and shrubs. The **taiga** is a thick forest of coniferous trees that covers much of Siberia. Permafrost makes construction of roads and buildings difficult.

Siberia is rich in natural resources. The harsh climate, however, limits economic opportunities. In addition, modern technologies allow people to **extract** resources with relatively few workers.

Settlement Patterns in Other Republics The Caucasus countries have higher population densities than Russia. But given their relatively warm climates, population density could be even higher were it not for

Academic Vocabulary

extract • *v.*, to take out or remove

the steep mountains that give the region its name. In the Caucasus, people have mainly settled in the valleys and plains beneath the mountains. These areas have fertile soils for agriculture. The warm climate allows farmers to grow fruits, vegetables, and cotton.

In Central Asia, deserts and mountains hold down population density. Traveling across the mountains and deserts is a challenge. Yet, for thousands of years, farmers and cities have thrived in the rich mountain and river valleys.

✓ READING CHECK **Draw Conclusions** What factors affect population distribution?

Cultural Diversity

Many groups of people have passed through and settled in Northern Eurasia over its long history. As a result, the region has considerable cultural diversity.

Ethnic and Religious Makeup The first Russians were East Slavs, who migrated into the area from east-central Europe. Today, about 80 percent of the population are Russian-speaking Slavs. However, Russia has at least 100 other ethnic groups. Each has a distinct culture.

Traditionally, Russian Slavs were Russian Orthodox Christians. Soviet leaders discouraged the practice of religion. Since the fall of communism, however, religious observance and church attendance have increased. Vladimir Putin has supported the role of the Russian Orthodox Church. He does so in part to build national pride. Russia's many Muslims, Jews, and Buddhists also enjoy more freedom to practice their faiths now than ever before.

Did you know?

The Caspian Sea is the largest salt lake and the largest inland body of water in the world. It is larger than the state of Montana.

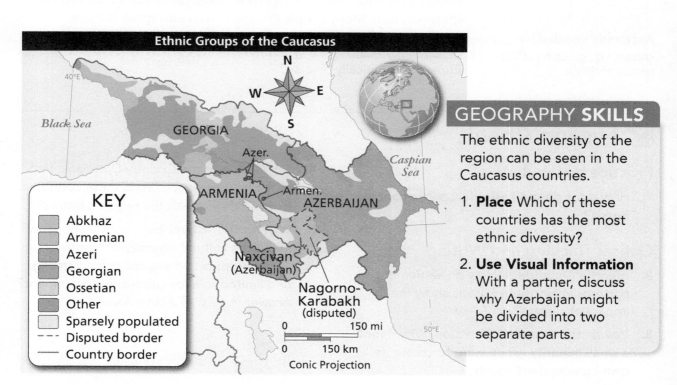

Ethnic Groups of the Caucasus

KEY
- Abkhaz
- Armenian
- Azeri
- Georgian
- Ossetian
- Other
- Sparsely populated
- - - Disputed border
- — Country border

Black Sea
40°E
GEORGIA
Azer.
ARMENIA — Armen.
AZERBAIJAN
Caspian Sea
Naxçivan (Azerbaijan)
Nagorno-Karabakh (disputed)
0   150 mi
0   150 km
50°E
Conic Projection

GEOGRAPHY SKILLS

The ethnic diversity of the region can be seen in the Caucasus countries.

1. **Place** Which of these countries has the most ethnic diversity?

2. **Use Visual Information** With a partner, discuss why Azerbaijan might be divided into two separate parts.

The Caucasus The people of the Caucasus practice a variety of religions. In Georgia, many people are members of an Eastern Orthodox Church. Most practicing Armenians attend another Orthodox church, the Armenian Apostolic Church. Azerbaijan is mostly Shia Muslim.

The Caucasus is also home to many ethnic groups. These ethnic groups tend to live in **clusters**. In some cases, a minority group lives mainly in one part of a country, where it may be a majority. Some of these areas wish to gain independence and form their own small countries. For instance, Nagorno–Karabakh is a small region within Azerbaijan that has an Armenian population. Armenia and Azerbaijan have clashed over this territory since before the Soviet breakup.

Analyze Images Monks of the Armenian Apostolic Church, the national church of Armenia, lead a procession in the mountains above Sevan Lake. **Draw Conclusions** What is the significance of having an official state church?

Central Asia As in the Caucasus, many different ethnic groups have settled in Central Asia. The ethnic majority in each country is the group for whom the country is named. For example, Tajiks are the largest ethnic group in Tajikistan and Uzbeks in Uzbekistan. Islam came to the region in the 700s. Today, most people in Central Asia practice Islam.

Languages While Russian is the most widely spoken language across Northern Eurasia, each of the other republics has its own national language. Many have several minority languages. Even within Russia, dozens of ethnic minorities speak their own languages. In total, more than 40 different languages are native to the Caucasus.

Most of Central Asia's major ethnic groups speak Turkic languages similar to Turkish. The Tajiks speak a language similar to the Persian spoken in Iran. Many people in Central Asia also speak Russian.

Academic Vocabulary
cluster • *n.*, grouping of like people or things

☑ READING CHECK **Identify Implied Main Ideas** Why is Northern Eurasia so ethnically diverse?

☑ Lesson Check

Practice Vocabulary

1. How does **permafrost** affect settlement in Russia?

Critical Thinking and Writing

2. **Identify Main Ideas** How do settlement patterns in Northern Eurasia show the impact of climate?

3. **Revisit the Essential Question** Why might a small minority group want to create its own independent country?

4. **Synthesize** In the Country Databank, look at the languages spoken in these countries. How do they reflect the region's history?

5. **Writing Workshop: Support Claims** How might the cultural diversity of Northern Eurasia support an argument for a strong or a limited role for citizens in government? Answer in your ▤ Active Journal.

Northern Eurasia at Work

BOUNCE TO ACTIVATE ▶ VIDEO

GET READY TO READ

START UP

Look at this photo of a subway station in Moscow. Write a few notes about what the image tells you about Russia's economy.

GUIDING QUESTIONS

- What kinds of governments rule the countries of Northern Eurasia?
- How have economies in Northern Eurasia changed since the Soviet breakup?
- What are the strengths and weaknesses of the Russian economy?

TAKE NOTES

Literacy Skills: Use Evidence
Use the graphic organizer in your 📕 Active Journal to take notes as you read the lesson.

PRACTICE VOCABULARY

Use the vocabulary activity in your 📕 Active Journal to practice the vocabulary words.

Vocabulary	Academic Vocabulary
authoritarian government	remote
reserves	internal
industrial goods	

Since the breakup of the Soviet Union, the people of Northern Eurasia have formed new governments and new economic patterns. Russians also have had to adjust to a new role in world affairs.

Government in Northern Eurasia

Since the fall of the Soviet Union, few governments in Northern Eurasia have become truly democratic. Most countries in the region have **authoritarian governments**. This means that they are controlled by one or more people who have not been chosen in a free and fair election.

Government in Russia Rising to power in 1999, President Vladimir Putin has limited or punished opposition and free speech in Russia. Vocal opponents of the government have been killed under suspicious circumstances. Russia does hold elections; however, the government's control of the media and limits on political action mean that its political system is not truly democratic. Citizens have few real rights.

Government in the Other Republics A few of the other republics, including Armenia, Georgia, and Kyrgyzstan, have imperfect democracies. Georgia has a presidential democracy, in which an elected president controls the government. Armenia and Kyrgyzstan have parliamentary democracies, in which the head of the leading party in parliament becomes the prime minister and controls the government. Even in these countries, however, free and fair elections are rare. Georgia, for example, has held more than 13 elections since 1991, but only a few have been considered free and fair.

The governments of the rest of Central Asia and Azerbaijan are dictatorships, often led by former communist officials. Citizens lack freedom of speech or any voice in politics. Uzbekistan had the same ruler, a former leader of the Communist party, from 1991 until his death in 2016.

☑ READING CHECK **Identify Main Ideas** What factors determine whether or not a government is truly democratic?

Analyze Images
The golden statue of Saparmurat Niyazov, dictator of Turkmenistan from 1991 to 2006, stands in Independence Square, Ashgabat. **Infer** Why do you think dictators glorify themselves?

How Have Economies Changed in the Region?

The former Soviet Union had a command economy, with the central government making most economic decisions. The government decided what to produce, how to produce it, and how goods and services would be distributed to people. Soviet planners proved unable to meet the citizens' desires for consumer goods and better living standards.

The Change to Mixed Economies After the fall of the Soviet Union, Russia and the other former Soviet republics developed mixed economies. A mixed economy combines elements of market and command economies. In a market economy, individual consumers and producers make all economic decisions.

In shifting away from a command economy, Russia and the other former Soviet republics privatized many state-run industries and collective farms. That is, they transferred ownership to private businesses and individuals. Many of these governments do still control some business activities. Governments tend to control energy-based industries, for example. But in other areas of the economy, they allow the market system to operate.

None of these countries are close to Britain or Germany in their reliance on markets. For instance, Russia's government does not control just the energy industries; it also owns transportation, banking, and defense-related businesses.

Quick Activity

Work with another student to create a table in your 📓 Active Journal that you can use to categorize the governments in Northern Eurasia.

In addition, people in **remote** areas of Siberia or Central Asia may live in a traditional economy. In a traditional economy, people make economic decisions based on custom.

The Region's Natural Resources Russia has rich mineral and energy resources, especially in Siberia. Its resources also include timber, fish, and hydroelectric power. About one-third of all of Earth's coal is located in Siberia. In spite of Siberia's extremes of climate and its distance from markets, vast reserves of oil and gas in West Siberia have contributed greatly to Russia's economy. **Reserves** are resources available for future use. Russia also has metal ores such as iron, gold, cobalt, nickel, and platinum.

Rich natural resources are also important to the economies of Azerbaijan and Central Asia. These regions have oil and natural gas. Large reserves of oil are located in Azerbaijan and Kazakhstan. The oil and gas is moved by pipelines from these inland areas that have no water access to world markets.

The Caucasus and Central Asia also have important mineral deposits. For example, Armenia has copper, lead, and zinc. Gold is mined in Kyrgyzstan. Exporting minerals plays an important role in the economies of all of these countries.

Specialization and Trade The countries of Northern Eurasia have different economic strengths and weaknesses. Like other countries, they specialize in producing what they are best able to produce. They trade with other countries to meet their other needs. For example, countries around the Caspian Sea specialize in producing oil and gas.

Academic Vocabulary
remote • *adj.,* distant

INTERACTIVE

Russia's Energy Production

GEOGRAPHY **SKILLS**

Because of its generally cold climates, Northern Eurasia has little farmland.

1. **Place** Which countries have oil resources?

2. **Synthesize Visual Information** Why is Siberia important to Russia?

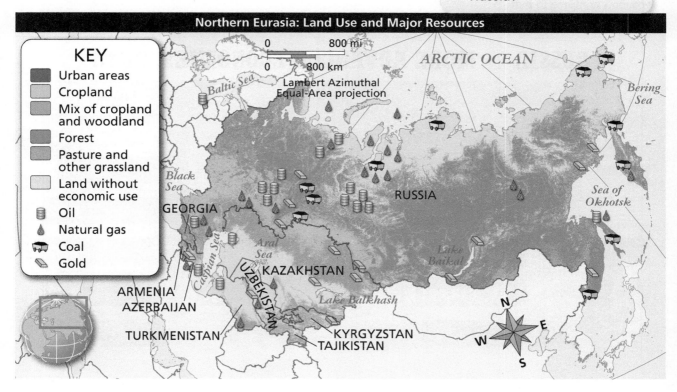

Northern Eurasia: Land Use and Major Resources

KEY
- Urban areas
- Cropland
- Mix of cropland and woodland
- Forest
- Pasture and other grassland
- Land without economic use
- Oil
- Natural gas
- Coal
- Gold

0   800 mi
0   800 km
Lambert Azimuthal Equal-Area projection

ARCTIC OCEAN
Bering Sea
Baltic Sea
Black Sea
GEORGIA
RUSSIA
Sea of Okhotsk
Aral Sea
Lake Baikal
Caspian Sea
KAZAKHSTAN
UZBEKISTAN
Lake Balkhash
ARMENIA
AZERBAIJAN
TURKMENISTAN
KYRGYZSTAN
TAJIKISTAN
N E W S

Quest CONNECTIONS

How does the Russian economy show the lingering effects of the Soviet system? Record your findings in your 📓 Active Journal.

Kazakhstan's plains and climate allow it to specialize in growing wheat. The rainier climate in Georgia lets farmers there grow fruits and vegetables for export. Herding has long been a way of life on the steppes of Central Asia. Many people in the region continue to raise livestock. They lead the animals to the mountains in the spring, when snow melts and grass grows. When the snows return in winter, they move down to the plains below.

✓ READING CHECK **Compare and Contrast** How does Russia's economy compare to those of Britain and Germany?

Russia's Economy

Russia has a fairly modern economy. It produces **industrial goods**, which are products or raw materials needed to produce other goods. For instance, some companies make machinery that is used to make other products. Office supplies are industrial goods as well. Russia also has many kinds of services that it provides to its **internal** market of more than 100 million Russians. However, Russia does not produce everything its people want.

Academic Vocabulary

internal • *adj.*, within a country

Major Industries Russia's most valuable natural resources are its large oil and gas deposits. They are also Russia's main exports. The economy was hurt by a drop in oil prices that began in 2014. Trade sanctions placed on Russia over its move to seize Crimea did not help the economy.

Analyze Diagrams Despite its vast size and resources, Russia's economy does not perform as well as others. **Compare** How does Russia's economy compare to that of the United States?

Some sectors, or areas of the economy, did benefit from the sanctions. Russia's economic troubles made its currency, the ruble, lose value. That made other goods it exports less expensive to buyers in other countries. As a result, steel exports increased.

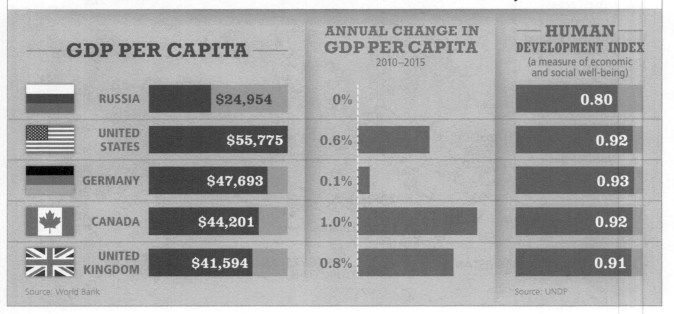

RUSSIA vs. MORE ADVANCED ECONOMIES, 2015

	GDP PER CAPITA	ANNUAL CHANGE IN GDP PER CAPITA 2010–2015	HUMAN DEVELOPMENT INDEX (a measure of economic and social well-being)
RUSSIA	$24,954	0%	0.80
UNITED STATES	$55,775	0.6%	0.92
GERMANY	$47,693	0.1%	0.93
CANADA	$44,201	1.0%	0.92
UNITED KINGDOM	$41,594	0.8%	0.91

Source: World Bank   Source: UNDP

Russia also has abundant supplies of timber, used for wood products such as lumber and paper. Wood products are major Russian exports. Russia's iron ore and coal, mined in the Ural Mountains, are the basis for its strong iron and steel industry.

Factors Affecting Economic Performance In Soviet times, the government invested little in capital, such as factories, machinery, and technology, except in military industries. Since the Soviet Union's breakup, investment has focused on the energy industry. Because of this history of low investment in some industries, consumer goods and other industries have old factories with out-of-date technology.

This lack of technology holds Russia's economic output lower than that of more advanced economies. As a result, Russia has a lower standard of living than these countries. Its factories cannot meet the people's demand for consumer goods. Russia imports such goods as vehicles, medicines, and plastic.

Russia has a skilled workforce due to its strong educational system. Literacy is near 100 percent. Investment in human capital through Russia's educational system helps make the economy more productive. It helps to explain why Russia's standard of living is higher than that of nations in Central Asia, where education systems are weaker.

Compared with other industrial nations, Russia does not do a good job at promoting entrepreneurship, or people's ability to start a business. Widespread corruption and heavy government regulation in Russia discourage people from taking this step. This lack of opportunities for entrepreneurs holds back Russia's economy.

Analyze Images Oil workers drill in the Volgograd region. **Identify Supporting Details** Where does Russia's oil go?

☑ READING CHECK **Identify Main Ideas** What are the strengths and weaknesses of Russia's economy?

☑ Lesson Check

Practice Vocabulary

1. In what ways does Russia have an **authoritarian government**?

Critical Thinking and Writing

2. Analyze Charts Use the Country Databank to compare the per capita GDP of the countries of Northern Eurasia. What might explain the differences?

3. Identify Main Ideas List some characteristics of governments in Northern Eurasia.

4. Identify Cause and Effect Why do the countries around the Caspian Sea, other than Russia, have the highest economic output?

5. Writing Workshop: Write an Introduction In your ▤ Active Journal, nail down your thesis statement and start the introduction to your essay about the role of citizens in government.

Challenges Facing Northern Eurasia

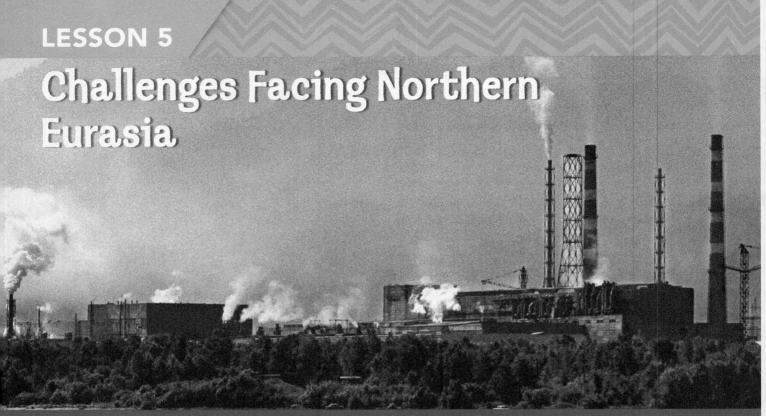

GET READY TO READ

START UP

Examine the photograph of pollution from a paper plant on Lake Baikal. What challenges might situations like the one shown here pose for the countries of the region?

GUIDING QUESTIONS

- What environmental problems did Soviet policies leave behind?
- What political challenges do the countries of Northern Eurasia face?

TAKE NOTES

Literacy Skills: Identify Cause and Effect
Use the graphic organizer in your 📕 Active Journal to take notes as you read the lesson.

PRACTICE VOCABULARY

Use the vocabulary activity in your 📕 Active Journal to practice the vocabulary words.

Vocabulary	Academic Vocabulary
Green Revolution	divert
Aral Sea	repressive
militant	

Environmental problems, ethnic conflict, and troubled governments are challenges in many Northern Eurasian countries today. People in this region face new challenges as well as the problems left behind by the Soviet Union.

Environmental Challenges

Many parts of Northern Eurasia face serious environmental problems. Air, water, and ground pollution threaten both the environment and the region's people.

The Green Revolution in Central Asia During the 1950s and 1960s, scientists introduced new disease-resistant crops to parts of the world that were facing the possibility of massive food shortages. This increase in agricultural production through improved technology is known as the **Green Revolution**. The new approach brought a dramatic increase in farm output. However, the Green Revolution also led to a huge expansion in irrigation and the heavy use of chemical pesticides and fertilizer.

The Aral Sea Shrinks One outcome of the Green Revolution was the dramatic shrinkage of the **Aral Sea**, once a large saltwater lake in Central Asia. During the 1960s, the Soviet government turned large amounts of land in Central Asia into irrigated farmland. To water the crops, including the key export, cotton, the government **diverted** water from the Syr Darya and the Amu Darya rivers. These two rivers are the main source of water for the Aral Sea. With less water coming into it, and sitting as it does in a dry climate, the water in the Aral Sea gradually evaporated.

That was not the only problem. What water remained became increasingly salty, and the fish living in the lake died off. Winds blowing over the dry lake bed picked up harmful chemicals from farm pesticides and fertilizers. The wind carried them to other areas, causing further damage. As a result, people living in the surrounding areas have much higher rates of cancer and other health issues.

Countries affected by the destruction of the Aral Sea have tried to work together to solve these problems, but they have seen few results. Cleaning up the pollution is expensive. In addition, some Central Asian countries still rely on cotton and still irrigate from the Syr Darya and Amu Darya rivers. Governments struggle to balance protecting the environment with their other responsibilities.

Pollution in Russia Heavy pollution is a problem in many parts of Russia as well. Pollution increased with Josef Stalin's attempts to industrialize the Soviet Union and has continued to the present day, mostly due to a lack of government concern with the problem and the few resources it has dedicated to addressing it.

In many cases, pollution is caused by Russian manufacturers' use of old equipment and techniques. Some of the most polluted cities in the world are in Russia. Industrial pollution in Norilsk, in northern Siberia, has released millions of tons of chemicals into the air.

Academic Vocabulary
divert • *v.*, to turn from one course to another

 INTERACTIVE

Before and After: Aral Sea

Analyze Images These boats were left behind when the Aral Sea disappeared from beneath them. **Sequence** What events led to the loss of the Aral Sea?

Academic Vocabulary
repressive • *adj.,* acting to control or limit dissent

Air pollution has reduced the life expectancy of Norilsk's citizens by ten years. It has also had a devastating effect on nearby forests.

In addition to air and water pollution from factories, leaking oil pipelines have contaminated the ground and water near them. In the Arctic, oil and gas extraction pose extreme environmental risks to an area that can be easily harmed.

✓ **READING CHECK** **Use Evidence** How did Soviet policies cause the Aral Sea to shrink?

Political Challenges

Though the former Soviet republics achieved their independence, they have continued to struggle to establish fair and just governments. One major problem is a lack of democracy and the accompanying risk of political violence. Ethnic conflict and terrorism are other issues that have affected the region.

Lack of Democracy When the Soviet Union collapsed, the countries in this region were left on their own. Often, people who had been part of the Soviet government became leaders in the new countries.

The leaders of the newly independent countries wrote new constitutions and laws that seemed to protect peoples' rights. Yet many of these leaders later acted to limit democracy.

The government of Turkmenistan is one of the most **repressive**. Like the Soviet government before it, it keeps strict control over its citizens and economy. The president holds most of the power. Only the president's political party is allowed in Turkmenistan, and the press is not free to criticize the president. The president elected in 2007 was re-elected in 2012 with 97 percent of the vote. A vote total that high indicates that no serious opposition was permitted.

Analyze Images This forest near a power plant in Norilsk, Russia, was destroyed by pollution. **Draw Conclusions** Why is it difficult to stop or improve pollution in Russia?

5 Things to Know About

ROZA OTUNBAYEVA
Former president of Kyrgyzstan (born 1950)

- Otunbayeva was born in Soviet Kyrgyzstan and educated in Russia.

- She served in the Soviet Foreign Ministry and as Soviet ambassador to Malaysia.

- She served as Kyrgyzstan's ambassador to the United States.

- Otunbayeva charged the governments of the first two Kyrgyzstan presidents with corruption.

- During her presidency, she brought stability to Kyrgyzstan during a violent uprising.

Critical Thinking Why was a peaceful transfer of power by Otunbayeva important to the stability of Kyrgyzstan?

While most Central Asian countries have authoritarian governments like Turkmenistan's, Kyrgyzstan became a democracy. However, it has struggled to establish a stable government. After independence, the first two administrations were accused of abusing power and overthrown. In December 2011, the interim president, Roza Otunbayeva, peacefully transferred power to President Almazbek Atambayev.

Across the region, progress has been uneven. In some countries, protests have brought greater democracy, as they did in Kyrgyzstan. Still, the political systems of most countries are not open and democratic.

Ethnic Conflict As you have read, different ethnic groups live side by side in this region. Minority groups are sometimes treated unfairly. For example, members of the ancient Central Asian Jewish communities faced harsh treatment. This prompted most of them to move to Israel and the United States.

In Uzbekistan, Tajiks have a harder time finding jobs than Uzbeks. Some Tajiks claim to be Uzbek because they fear they will not be treated fairly. While the Uzbek government promotes Uzbek traditions, the Tajik people in Uzbekistan may have to give up their identity.

In Kyrgyzstan, the majority of the population is Kyrgyz, but there is a large ethnic Uzbek minority. In 2010, clashes between Uzbeks and Kyrgyz in southern Kyrgyzstan became violent. The military was called in to stop the violence, but some witnesses accused the military of participating in violence against Uzbek people. While the violence quieted, ethnic tensions remain.

Meanwhile, in Georgia and Azerbaijan, ethnic tension has led to armed conflict when minority ethnic groups have tried to break away and form separate countries. Violence has also been common in the Russian regions bordering the Caucasus that are home to Muslim ethnic minorities, such as Chechnya. The Russian military has fought rebels in this region.

Quest CONNECTIONS

How did the Soviet system create many of the challenges facing the region? Record your findings in your Active Journal.

Terrorism Some Chechens and others have used acts of terrorism to pursue their goals. In recent years, terrorists have attacked planes, the Moscow subway, a movie theater, and even a school. In neighboring Dagestan, where tension has long existed among local ethnic groups, Islamist militants have struck. **Militants** are people who are aggressively active in a cause. These Islamists, influenced by those in Chechnya, have launched attacks against officials, police, and politicians. They have also bombed railways and a pipeline. Ingushetia, which was once united with Chechnya in the Soviet Union, has also suffered from terrorist attacks. Islamist terrorists there have carried out assassinations and bombings.

▲ In 2009, Chechen terrorists bombed this train in Russia, killing 27 travelers.

Corruption Political problems often create problems in the economy. Corruption is a serious problem in most countries of the region. Government officials often take money for themselves that is meant to provide government services. A lack of good schools, roads, and bridges due to corruption holds these economies back. The economy is also hurt when businesspeople avoid the region due to officials' demands for illegal payments.

☑ READING CHECK **Identify Main Ideas** What are some of the major political problems Northern Eurasians face?

☑ Lesson Check

Practice Vocabulary

1. How did the **Green Revolution** affect the **Aral Sea**?

Critical Thinking and Writing

2. **Draw Conclusions** Why might the Russian government be unwilling to tackle its environmental problems?

3. **Understand Effects** How does ethnic conflict pose problems for governments?

4. **Draw Conclusions** How does government corruption hold back economic development?

5. **Writing Workshop: Organize Your Essay** In your 📓 Active Journal, work on an outline of your essay on the role of citizens in government. Provide support for your claims, and address opposing claims.

Vladimir Putin's Russia Strategy

President Vladimir Putin is the leader of Russia. His government has engaged in aggressive actions against other countries in the region. Read the excerpt from an article that examines Putin's foreign policy and contrasts his actions with those of the United States government. Think about the goals Putin has, according to the writer. Then answer the questions.

▶ Russian troops after seizing Ukraine's naval headquarters in Crimea, 2014

Putin has what America lacks — a <u>comprehensive</u>, ① long-term strategy that is built precisely and firmly around his own perceptions of his nation's best interests. ② He wants to dominate . . . the independent and <u>quasi-independent</u> ③ countries of the former Soviet Empire that have attempted to move out of Russia's orbit. He wants to place Russia firmly in the <u>pantheon</u> ④ of the world's great powers. . . . In other words, he wants to "Make Russia Great Again.". . .

[Putin] understands exactly what his ally Iran understands—that the civilian leaders of his much stronger foes are the ones who are terrified of military conflict. . . .

Russia is [much] more powerful than Iran, and it displays a similar tolerance for risk. It's thus capable of <u>several orders of magnitude more international aggression</u>. ⑤ It's proven that it can invade a European nation without meaningful military consequence.

—David French, "Vladimir Putin's Russia Strategy: How Russia Wins," *National Review* (December 12, 2016)

Reading and Vocabulary Support

① complete

② Is the first sentence a fact or an opinion? How can you tell?

③ not completely independent

④ a respected group

⑤ What reason does the author give for his opinion that Russia is capable of "several orders of magnitude" —meaning "several times"—more aggression than Iran?

Analyzing Geographic Sources

Cite specific evidence from the source to support your answers.

1. **Identify Bias** What bias does the author show regarding Putin and his actions?

2. **Assess Credibility** Does the author provide adequate evidence to support his opinion about Putin? Explain.

3. **Analyze Style and Rhetoric** Does the author use fair language in evaluating Putin, or does he use biased language that leads readers to a specific conclusion?

☑ Review and Assessment

VISUAL REVIEW

Major Events in Russian History

Early Period (500s–700s)	Kievan Rus (late 800s–1240)	Mongol Rule (1240–1400s)
• Slavs move into modern Russia. • Turks move into Central Asia. • Islam spreads into Central Asia.	• Kievan Rus forms. • Eastern Orthodox Christianity is adopted. • Byzantine culture influences region.	• Mongols conquer Kievan Rus. • Asian government model spreads.

Russian Empire (1400s–1917)	Soviet Era (1917–1991)	Post-Soviet Era (1991–present)
• Romanov tsars rule Russia starting in 1613. • Serfdom lasts until 1861. • A centralized state develops. • The empire spreads through conquest.	• Bolsheviks gain power in revolution. • A Communist system is set up. • Soviets run a command economy. • Soviets oppose the West in Cold War.	• Russia shifts to a market economy. • Putin gains power.

The Peoples of Northern Eurasia

Russia	Caucasus	Central Asia
• Most Russians live in European Russia. • Most densely settled areas have good soil and climates. • About 80 percent of people are Russian Slavs. • At least 100 other ethnic groups exist. • Russian is the most common language.	• People live mainly in valleys and plains. • Region has many different ethnic groups. • Christians live in Armenia and Georgia; Muslims in Azerbaijan. • Many different languages are spoken.	• Desert and mountains limit population density. • People live in rich valleys. • Many different ethnic groups live here. • Most people practice Islam. • Most speak Turkic languages.

READING REVIEW

Use the Take Notes and Practice Vocabulary activities in your Active Journal to review the topic.

👆 INTERACTIVE

Practice vocabulary using the Topic Mini-Games.

Quest FINDINGS

Create Your Presentation

Prepare your multimedia exhibit about the continuing impact of the Soviet system on the region. Get help in your Active Journal.

ASSESSMENT

Vocabulary and Key Ideas

1. **Define** What is a **tsar**, and how was the tsars' rule an example of **authoritarian government**?

2. **Identify Main Ideas** How and why did Peter the Great **westernize** Russia?

3. **Identify** Who were the **Bolsheviks**, and how were they related to **communism**?

4. **Describe** How were the policies of the tsars and the Soviets similar?

5. **Describe** How does climate, including **permafrost**, affect where people settle in Northern Eurasia?

6. **Compare and Contrast** How was Stalin's approach to the economy similar to and different from Putin's?

7. **Check Understanding** Why is pollution a problem in Russia and Central Asia?

Critical Thinking and Writing

8. **Identify Main Ideas** See the Country Databank in the back of the book. Explain how the history of the region affected the degree of democracy in these countries.

9. **Identify Cause and Effect** How did the early history of Northern Eurasia affect its modern-day population?

10. **Draw Conclusions** What are the advantages and challenges that Siberia offers to Russia's economy?

11. **Revisit the Essential Question** What role did citizens have in the government of the former Soviet Union?

12. **Writing Workshop: Write Arguments** Using the outline in your 📓 Active Journal, write an argument or persuasive essay on the question: What role should citizens play in their government?

Analyze Primary Sources

13. Which of the following leaders might have made this statement?
    A. Vladimir Putin
    B. Mikhail Gorbachev
    C. Peter the Great
    D. Josef Stalin

"To [slow down] would mean falling behind. And those who fall behind get beaten. . . . Do you want our socialist fatherland to be beaten. . .? If you do not want this, you must . . . [be quick] in building up its socialist system of economy."

Analyze Maps

Use the map to answer the following questions.

14. What city is marked by the letter A? Why is that city important?

15. Which region is marked by the letter B? Why is it controversial?

16. What body of water is indicated by the letter D? What happened there due to Soviet rule?

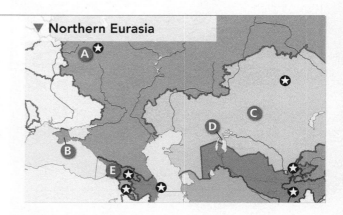
▼ **Northern Eurasia**

GO ONLINE
to access your
digital course

▶ VIDEO

🔊 AUDIO

📖 ETEXT

👆 INTERACTIVE

✍ WRITING

🎮 GAMES

📄 WORKSHEET

☑ ASSESSMENT

Let's take a journey

to **AFRICA**, a continent with dramatic landscapes and the biggest desert on Earth. Rich wildlife and stunning landscapes are not the only reasons Africa inspires wonder. Africa stretches from the Mediterranean Sea to the Southern Ocean and from the Atlantic Ocean to the Indian Ocean. It has more countries (54) than any other continent and its 1.2 billion people belong to more than 3,000 ethnic groups.

Explore

The Essential Question

Who should benefit from a country's resources?

For much of Africa's history, its own people did not gain from the continent's resources. Who should benefit when a country's oil, minerals, and precious metals are used or exported? How can a country's resources help all of its people?

Unlock the Essential Question in your 📓 Active Journal.

▲ Cape Town, South Africa

Watch

BOUNCE TO ACTIVATE ▶ VIDEO

A String of Dreams

Meet Evelyn and learn about her work in her grandmother's business and the role of markets in West African life.

Read

about a continent that scientists believe is the birthplace of our human species. Read about Africa's great civilizations and their achievements and trade networks. Study the impact of Europe on Africa and Africans' efforts to build independent countries. Learn how Africans have adapted to their environments, how they live and work today, and how they are dealing with challenges.

5 | Regional Atlas

Africa: Political

A CONTINENT OF VARIETY

Africa is Earth's second largest continent. The continent has great cultural diversity and a rich past.

Learn more about Africa by making your own map in your Active Journal.

The Northern Fringe

Most of the people of North Africa (Morocco, Algeria, Tunisia, Libya, and Egypt) live near its coast in cities like Tunis, Tunisia, shown here, or along the Nile River. The vast desert lands of the Sahara separate these countries from the rest of Africa.

👆 INTERACTIVE

Topic Map

The Colonial Legacy

Africa is divided into countries whose boundaries were drawn when they were colonies controlled by European countries. Those boundaries cut across ethnic areas and place rival ethnic groups in the same country.

The Congos

Africa has two Congos. The Democratic Republic of the Congo is Africa's second-largest country by area. The smaller Republic of the Congo lies across the Congo River.

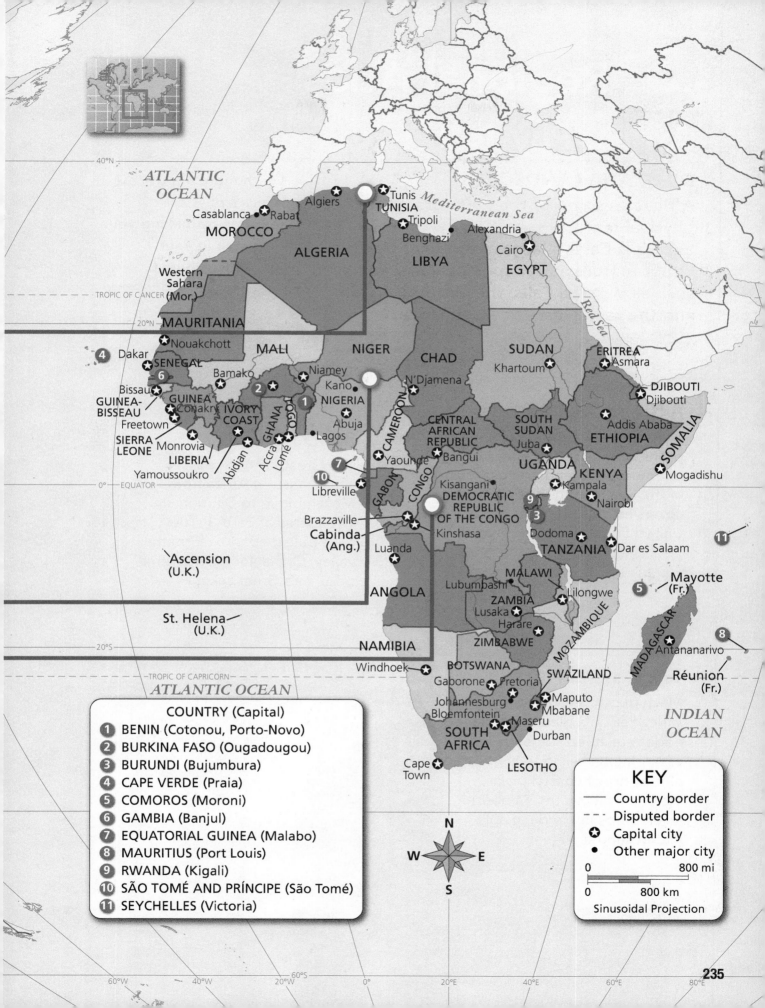

ATLANTIC
OCEAN

Mediterranean Sea

Tunis
TUNISIA
Algiers
Casablanca • Rabat
MOROCCO
Tripoli
Benghazi • Alexandria
ALGERIA
LIBYA
Cairo
EGYPT
Western
Sahara
(Mor.)
TROPIC OF CANCER

MAURITANIA
Nouakchott
MALI
NIGER
CHAD
SUDAN
ERITREA
Asmara
Khartoum
DJIBOUTI
Djibouti
④ Dakar
SENEGAL
Bamako
N'Djamena
Kano
⑥ Niamey
② NIGERIA
Bissau
GUINEA-
BISSEAU
GUINEA
Conakry
IVORY
COAST
GHANA
TOGO
① Abuja
Lagos
CAMEROON
CENTRAL
AFRICAN
REPUBLIC
SOUTH
SUDAN
Juba
Addis Ababa
ETHIOPIA
SOMALIA
Freetown
SIERRA
LEONE
Monrovia
LIBERIA
Yamoussoukro
Abidjan
Accra
Lomé
Yaoundé
Bangui
UGANDA
KENYA
Mogadishu
⑦
⑩
Libreville
GABON
CONGO
Kisangani
DEMOCRATIC
REPUBLIC
OF THE CONGO
⑨
Kampala
Nairobi
Brazzaville
Cabinda
(Ang.)
Kinshasa
③
Dodoma
TANZANIA
Dar es Salaam
⑪
EQUATOR
Luanda
Ascension
(U.K.)
ANGOLA
Lubumbashi
MALAWI
Lilongwe
⑤
Mayotte
(Fr.)
St. Helena
(U.K.)
ZAMBIA
Lusaka
Harare
MOZAMBIQUE
MADAGASCAR
Antananarivo
⑧
Réunion
(Fr.)
NAMIBIA
ZIMBABWE
Windhoek
BOTSWANA
SWAZILAND
Maputo
Mbabane
INDIAN
OCEAN
ATLANTIC OCEAN
TROPIC OF CAPRICORN
Gaborone • Pretoria
Johannesburg
Bloemfontein
Maseru
Durban
SOUTH
AFRICA
LESOTHO
Cape
Town

COUNTRY (Capital)
① BENIN (Cotonou, Porto-Novo)
② BURKINA FASO (Ougadougou)
③ BURUNDI (Bujumbura)
④ CAPE VERDE (Praia)
⑤ COMOROS (Moroni)
⑥ GAMBIA (Banjul)
⑦ EQUATORIAL GUINEA (Malabo)
⑧ MAURITIUS (Port Louis)
⑨ RWANDA (Kigali)
⑩ SÃO TOMÉ AND PRÍNCIPE (São Tomé)
⑪ SEYCHELLES (Victoria)

KEY
— Country border
--- Disputed border
✪ Capital city
• Other major city
0   800 mi
0   800 km
Sinusoidal Projection

N
W   E
S

5 Regional Atlas

Africa: Physical

DRAMATIC LANDSCAPES

Africa has some of the most dramatic physical features found on Earth. The Sahara is Earth's largest nonpolar desert. Other features offer spectacular scenery, such as Victoria Falls, the Great Rift Valley, and the rainforests of West Africa.

Learn more about Africa's physical features by making your own map in your Active Journal.

A Giant Desert

The vast Sahara covers mountains, plains, and plateaus—areas of high but mostly flat land—across much of the northern third of Africa. It covers an area about as big as the United States, including Alaska.

Splitting Plates

The Great Rift Valley slices across eastern Africa from Mozambique to Djibouti. Two plates of Earth's crust have pulled apart to form the valley. On its floor are several of Africa's Great Lakes.

The Central Plateau

Much of central and southern Africa lies on a plateau. At its edges are steep slopes called escarpments falling to a narrow rim of coastal plains. Victoria Falls, on the Zambezi River, drops into a deep split in that central plateau.

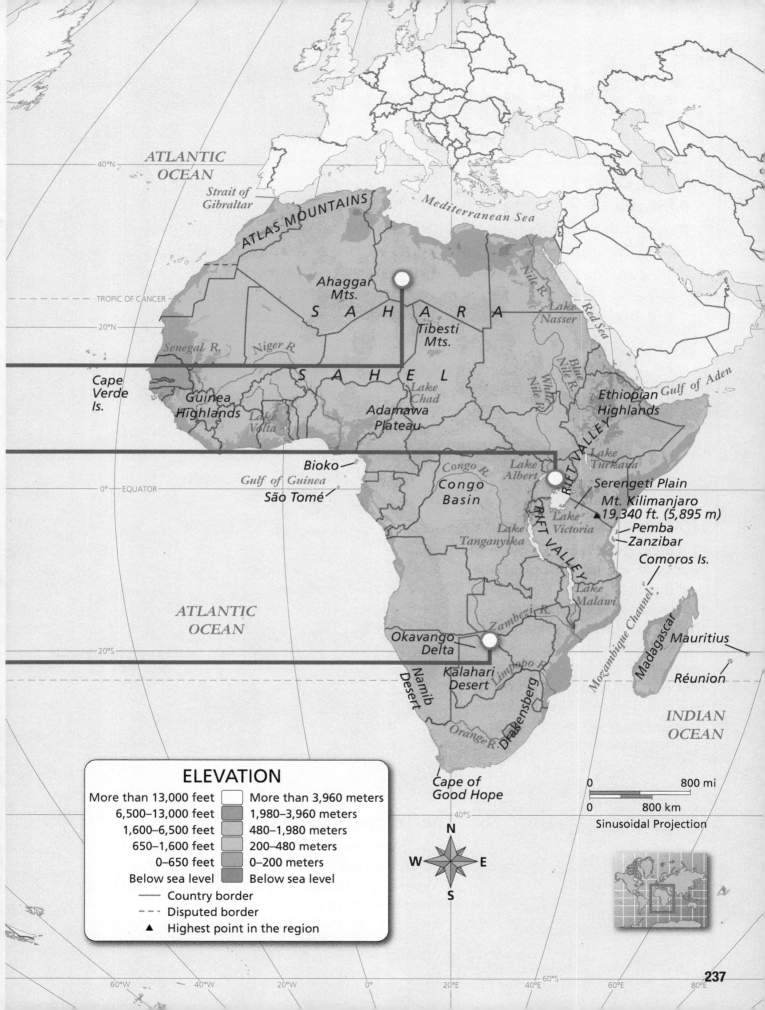

ELEVATION

More than 13,000 feet	More than 3,960 meters
6,500–13,000 feet	1,980–3,960 meters
1,600–6,500 feet	480–1,980 meters
650–1,600 feet	200–480 meters
0–650 feet	0–200 meters
Below sea level	Below sea level

— Country border

- - - Disputed border

▲ Highest point in the region

ATLANTIC OCEAN

Strait of Gibraltar

Mediterranean Sea

ATLAS MOUNTAINS

Ahaggar Mts.

S A H A R A

Tibesti Mts.

Nile R.

Lake Nasser

Red Sea

TROPIC OF CANCER

Senegal R.

Niger R.

S A H E L

Lake Chad

Blue Nile R.

White Nile R.

Gulf of Aden

Cape Verde Is.

Guinea Highlands

Lake Volta

Adamawa Plateau

Ethiopian Highlands

Bioko

Gulf of Guinea

São Tomé

Congo R.

Congo Basin

Lake Albert

RIFT VALLEY

Lake Turkana

Serengeti Plain

EQUATOR

Mt. Kilimanjaro
▲ 19,340 ft. (5,895 m)

Lake Victoria

RIFT VALLEY

Lake Tanganyika

Pemba

Zanzibar

Comoros Is.

ATLANTIC OCEAN

Lake Malawi

Mozambique Channel

Madagascar

Mauritius

Okavango Delta

Zambezi R.

Réunion

Namib Desert

Kalahari Desert

Limpopo R.

Drakensberg

INDIAN OCEAN

Orange R.

Cape of Good Hope

0   800 mi

0   800 km

Sinusoidal Projection

N
W   E
S

5 Regional Atlas

Africa: Climate

VERY DRY, VERY WET

Africa's climate zones include the massive, dry Sahara and the semiarid lands just south of it. Tropical wet climates cover the center of the continent, with dense rainforests that contrast sharply with the dry areas to the north.

The Hot, Dry North

Cairo, Egypt, has the same arid desert climate as neighboring parts of the Sahara. It gets very little rainfall and has very hot summers and mild winters.

Hot Tropics in the Center

The Serengeti Plain, like much of central Africa, has a tropical wet and dry climate. The weather here is hot and wet most of the year, but hot and dry from June to September. Savanna, providing food for vast herds of grazing animals, covers tropical wet and dry areas like the Serengeti. Rainforests cover wetter areas.

The Temperate South

Cape Town, South Africa, has a Mediterranean climate, with warm, dry southern hemisphere summers from October to March, and mild, wet winters from April to September.

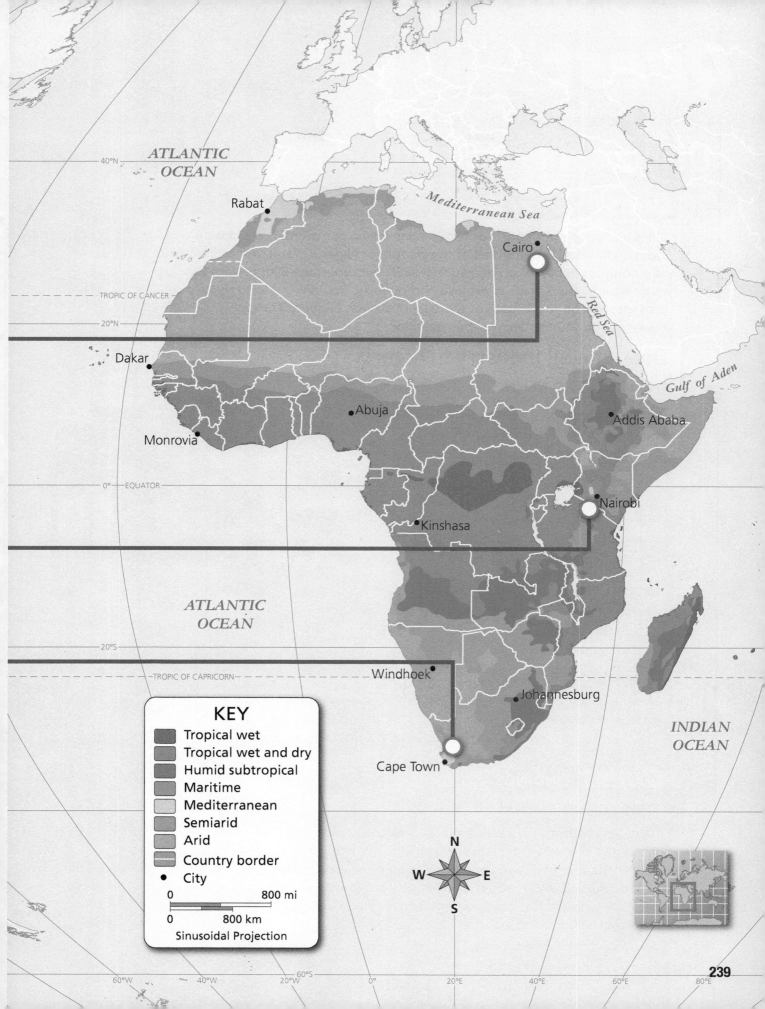

ATLANTIC
OCEAN

40°N

Rabat

Mediterranean Sea

Cairo

TROPIC OF CANCER

20°N

Red Sea

Dakar

Gulf of Aden

Abuja

Addis Ababa

Monrovia

0° EQUATOR

Kinshasa

Nairobi

ATLANTIC
OCEAN

20°S

TROPIC OF CAPRICORN

Windhoek

Johannesburg

INDIAN
OCEAN

Cape Town

KEY

Tropical wet
Tropical wet and dry
Humid subtropical
Maritime
Mediterranean
Semiarid
Arid
Country border
● City

0   800 mi
0   800 km
Sinusoidal Projection

N
W   E
S

60°W   40°W   20°W   60°S   0°   20°E   40°E   60°E   80°E

Quest

Discuss Nigeria's Oil Industry

Quest KICK OFF

Oil is an important export for Nigeria. However, some critics say the oil industry has not benefited all of the people of Nigeria. You are the director of a nongovernmental organization (NGO) that operates with private funding to deal with issues such as disease and poverty. You are going to make a presentation on the impact of the oil industry on Nigeria. Through your research you want to answer this question:

Does the oil Industry in Nigeria benefit the country as a whole?

Be ready! Other NGO directors will challenge your arguments. It's time to prepare!

1 Ask Questions

You are determined to understand the issue thoroughly. Get started by making a list of questions about Nigeria. Write the questions in your ▰ Active Journal.

2 Investigate

As you read the lessons in this topic, look for **Quest** CONNECTIONS related to your study. Respond to them in your ▰ Active Journal.

3 Examine Primary Sources

Next, explore a set of sources. They will support differing viewpoints about whether the oil industry in Nigeria benefits the country as a whole. Capture notes in your ▰ Active Journal.

▲ A Nigerian oil pipeline passes through a poor village in the Niger River delta.

Quest FINDINGS

4 Discuss

After you collect your clues and examine the sources, you will prepare to discuss this question: Does the oil industry in Nigeria benefit the country as a whole? Use your knowledge of Nigeria's needs and its oil industry as well as evidence from sources to make convincing arguments to answer the question. You may also come up with answers of your own.

LESSON 1
Human Origins

GET READY TO READ

START UP

Look at this photo of a prehistoric rock painting from the Sahara. Then preview the guiding questions below. Write a few sentences describing what scientists might learn from evidence such as prehistoric art.

GUIDING QUESTIONS

- How do scientists know about early humans?
- Where did humans originate and how did early people live?
- How did people spread around the world and adapt to different environments?

TAKE NOTES

Literacy Skills: Identify Main Idea
Use the graphic organizer in your 🗎 Active Journal to take notes as you read the lesson.

PRACTICE VOCABULARY

Use the vocabulary activity in your 🗎 Active Journal to practice the vocabulary words.

Vocabulary

artifact
fossil
hunter-gatherer

technology
pastoralism

Academic Vocabulary

determine
series

Scientists believe that the earliest humans originated in Africa, millions of years ago. Uncovering the history of the earliest people is a complicated, ongoing process.

The Study of Early Humans

Until about 5,000 years ago, there was no history, because people had not invented writing. To study early humans, archaeologists investigate the places where these ancient people once lived.

Hunting for Fossils To learn about the earliest humans, archaeologists study artifacts and fossils. **Artifacts** are objects made by human beings, such as a tool or weapon. **Fossils** are hardened remains or imprints of living things that existed long ago. These remains may include plants, feathers, bones, and even footprints that are millions of years old. Complete fossilized human remains are rare. Archaeologists can use a few teeth to show what kind of food early people ate. A few bones can reveal the size and structure of an early human's body.

INTERACTIVE

Piecing the Past Together

Archaeologists use several methods for **determining** the ages of fossils. One dating method is to compare objects found in similar layers of rock or soil. Objects found in lower layers are generally older. They can also test the chemicals in fossils and bones to determine their age.

Searching for Artifacts The earliest humans lived millions of years ago. To study them, archaeologists look for old settlements that can contain artifacts such as tools, pottery, or weapons. Archaeologists examine these artifacts to understand how early people lived.

☑ READING CHECK **Identify Supporting Details** What types of objects do archaeologists study to learn about the past?

African Beginnings

In 1960, British archaeologists Mary and Louis Leakey discovered a piece of a human-like skull in East Africa. Tests showed that the fossil was at least 1.75 million years old. From that point on, the search for the origins of humankind has largely focused on Africa.

Lucy In 1974, American fossil hunter Donald Johanson made a discovery in the East African country of Ethiopia that reshaped views of human origins. Johanson and his team found 40 percent of a human skeleton. They determined it had belonged to a 3.5-foot-tall woman and named her "Lucy." The bones indicated that Lucy had walked upright on two legs, 3.2 million years ago.

Academic Vocabulary
determine • *v.*, to figure out, or decide a question

▼ The discovery of "Lucy" in 1974 gave scientists evidence that humans walked upright as long as 3.2 million years ago.

Finding the "Oldest One" Most scientists now conclude that early humans first lived in East Africa about 4.5 million years ago. At that time, they believe, there was more than one early human species in Africa. Scientists are not sure which of these species are the ancestors of modern humans. They believe, though, that the first people were African.

☑ READING CHECK **Identify Implied Main Ideas** Why do scientists believe that the first humans lived in Africa?

How Early Hunter-Gatherers Lived

Archaeologists believe that early people were **hunter-gatherers**, or nomadic people who survived by hunting, fishing, and gathering wild plants. Life was harsh. To survive, early humans developed **technology**, tools and skills that people use to meet their needs and wants.

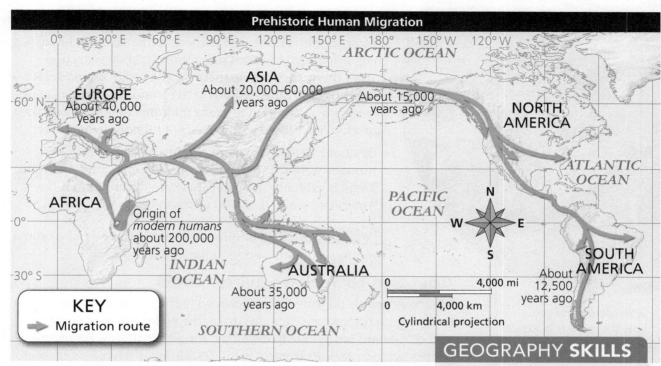

Prehistoric Human Migration

ARCTIC OCEAN

ASIA
About 20,000–60,000 years ago

About 15,000 years ago

NORTH AMERICA

EUROPE
About 40,000 years ago

AFRICA

Origin of *modern humans* about 200,000 years ago

PACIFIC OCEAN

ATLANTIC OCEAN

INDIAN OCEAN

AUSTRALIA
About 35,000 years ago

SOUTH AMERICA
About 12,500 years ago

0   4,000 mi
0   4,000 km
Cylindrical projection

KEY
Migration route

SOUTHERN OCEAN

Sources: Guy Gugliotta, Smithsonian Magazine, July 2008; Britannica Academic

The Development of Tools About 2.5 million years ago, during the Paleolithic Era, or Old Stone Age, early humans learned how to make tools out of stone. At first, the tools were simple and used for chopping trees or cutting meat. Over time, toolmakers became more skillful, making thinner and sharper blades for arrows and spears. With improved weapons, they could hunt larger animals such as deer.

The Use of Fire During the Paleolithic Era, people also learned how to use fire. With this technology, people could have light at night, when it was dark. They could cook meat and plants, making them easier to digest, and use flames to scare off dangerous animals. Fire also made it possible for hunter-gatherers to survive in cold places.

Wandering Bands The cultures of early societies were simple and focused on survival. Stone Age hunter-gatherers lived in bands of ten or twelve adults and their children. Bands moved from place to place with the seasons. They lived in caves, temporary huts made from branches, or tents made from animal skins, another major advance in technology.

Hunter-gatherers collected fruit, grains, seeds, and nuts. They harvested eggs and honey, hunted large animals, and caught small land animals or fish. They also may have picked herbs for medicine.

☑ READING CHECK **Use Evidence** How did technology help Paleolithic humans survive?

GEOGRAPHY SKILLS

Scientists think that modern humans arose first in Africa and migrated, or moved, from there to other regions.

1. **Movement** Scientists think modern humans migrated along the routes shown on the map. What could explain their movement?

2. **Draw Conclusions** How have archaeological discoveries helped anthropologists understand the first modern humans?

Migration from Africa

Most scientists think that modern humans, or *Homo sapiens*, originated in Africa more than 100,000 years ago. From there, they argue, these people began a long **series** of migrations to other regions of the world. The evidence suggests that as modern humans migrated to new places, they gradually replaced earlier kinds of humans living there.

By about 30,000 years ago, scientists believe, modern humans were living in Africa, Asia, Europe, and Australia. There is evidence that they had spread throughout the Americas by about 12,500 years ago.

READING CHECK **Sequence** What happened after some modern humans began to move out of Africa?

Adapting to Varied Environments

Wherever people migrated, they adapted to their new environments by changing their ways of life. In Africa, the wide variety of climates and ecosystems led people to develop a range of cultures. For example, people living in Africa's tropical rainforests or near rivers had regular access to water, animals, and plant life. These groups had ways of life that were different from those of people living in drier areas of Africa.

Between about 7000 and 5000 BCE, the evidence suggests that much of the present-day Sahara had a wetter climate. Hunter-gatherers began raising livestock and herding them across the area's grasslands. The climate changed, and Sahara became a desert during the 4000s BCE. These people moved to other parts of Africa.

The practice of raising livestock on open pastures is known as **pastoralism**. From prehistoric times to the present, many pastoralists in Africa have been nomadic. Nomadic pastoralists often migrate in a seasonal pattern to find the best pastures in each season.

READING CHECK **Draw Conclusions** Why did some Africans take up pastoralism?

▲ Herders guide cattle near their village in Kenya. Scientists think people have herded cattle in Africa for about 9,000 years.

Academic Vocabulary

series • *n.,* a group of related or similar things or events, often arranged in order

---

☑ Lesson Check

Practice Vocabulary

1. Why are **fossils** so important to learning about early humans?

2. How did **technology** help **hunter-gatherers** adapt to environments?

Critical Thinking and Writing

3. **Understand Effects** Why was the discovery of Lucy so important to archaeologists?

4. **Summarize** Name three characteristics of hunter-gatherer bands.

5. **Writing Workshop: Gather Information** At the end of the topic, you will write an informative essay explaining who has benefited from Africa's resources. Start by listing how early humans used resources in your ▤ Active Journal.

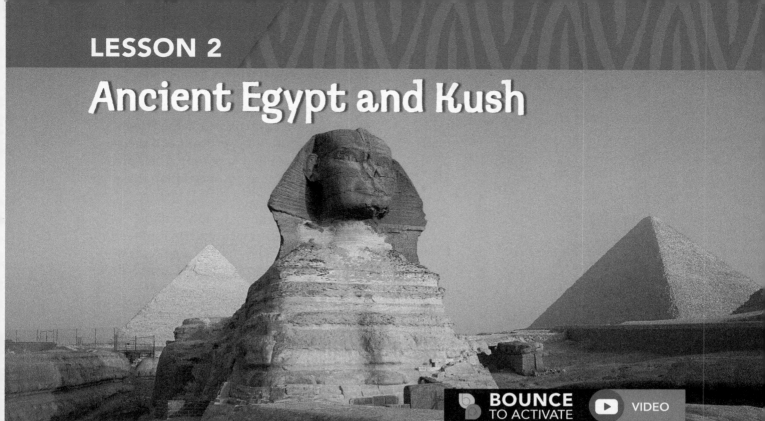

LESSON 2
Ancient Egypt and Kush

BOUNCE TO ACTIVATE ▶ VIDEO

GET READY TO READ

START UP
Look at the photograph of the Great Sphinx and the pyramids at Giza, Egypt. List two or three questions that you have about the people who built these impressive structures.

GUIDING QUESTIONS
- How did civilization develop in ancient Egypt?
- What were the beliefs and achievements of ancient Egyptians?
- What were the key features of Kushite civilization?

TAKE NOTES
Literacy Skills: Summarize
Use the graphic organizer in your ▤ Active Journal to take notes as you read the lesson.

PRACTICE VOCABULARY
Use the vocabulary activity in your ▤ Active Journal to practice the vocabulary words.

Vocabulary		Academic Vocabulary
pharaoh	hieroglyphic	artisan
dynasty	papyrus	preserve
bureaucracy	tribute	
mummy		

Egypt was home to one of the world's first great civilizations. With a complex society and culture, Egyptians made great achievements in writing, architecture, and various fields of science. Later civilizations, such as ancient Greece and Egypt's neighbor Kush, built on Egypt's accomplishments.

Civilization Develops

More than 7,000 years ago, people began growing grains in the Nile River Valley. The waters of the Nile and the fertile soil left behind by the yearly Nile floods allowed crops to grow in Egypt's arid climate.

Growing a Surplus Egyptian farmers built earthen walls around fields to trap the Nile's flood waters. The water soaked into the soil and allowed grains to grow. This simple form of crop irrigation allowed farmers to produce a food surplus, or an amount greater than their own family's needs.

The Birth of Cities Eventually, powerful people and families gained control over regions in Egypt. They began collecting some of the surplus crops as taxes.

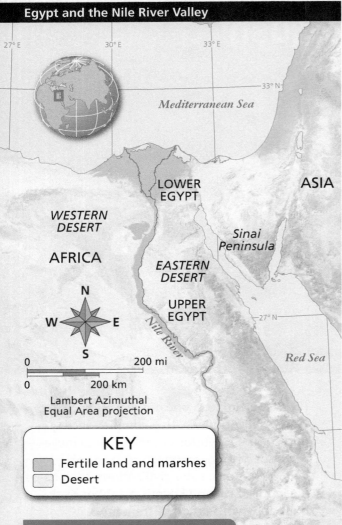

Egypt and the Nile River Valley

Mediterranean Sea

LOWER EGYPT

ASIA

WESTERN DESERT

Sinai Peninsula

AFRICA

EASTERN DESERT

UPPER EGYPT

Nile River

Red Sea

0   200 mi
0   200 km
Lambert Azimuthal
Equal Area projection

KEY
- Fertile land and marshes
- Desert

GEOGRAPHY **SKILLS**

The ancient kingdoms of Upper Egypt and Lower Egypt arose in northeastern Africa.

1. **Region** What geographic features may have helped rulers unite Upper and Lower Egypt?

2. **Infer** What geographic feature might have made it difficult to unite Egypt's two kingdoms?

Academic Vocabulary

artisan • *n.*, skilled worker who practices a handicraft

Rulers used the taxed crops to buy rich cloth, jewelry, and other luxury goods from merchants and **artisans**. The food that the artisans received as payment helped them to specialize as full-time artisans of a specific craft, such as weaving or pottery. Their products were much more advanced than those made by farmers.

Artisans and merchants began to settle around the homes of local rulers. These settlements grew into cities that became centers of culture and power. Skilled architects built impressive buildings decorated by artists who painted images and sculpted statues.

✓ READING CHECK Draw Conclusions Why could some Egyptians take jobs that did not involve farming?

The Kingdoms of Egypt

During the 3000s BCE, two kingdoms developed in Egypt: Upper Egypt and Lower Egypt. According to legend, a king named Narmer united the two kingdoms around 3000 BCE.

Uniting Egypt By uniting the kingdoms, Narmer became the first **pharaoh**, or king of a united Egypt. He also founded Egypt's earliest **dynasty**, or ruling family. Normally, pharaohs inherited their position from older members of the dynasty. Sometimes, however, a new dynasty gained power.

Historians divide Egypt's history into periods based on kingdoms and dynasties. A kingdom was a period when Egypt was unified. A series of dynasties ruled during each kingdom. Over its history, Egypt had three unified kingdoms, each lasting hundreds of years, and each followed by a period of warfare and division.

Three Kingdoms The first stable kingdom, the Old Kingdom, lasted from about 2686 BCE to 2181 BCE. After a period of civil wars, the Middle Kingdom lasted from about 2025 BCE to 1700 BCE. After another time of war, the New Kingdom arose about 1550 BCE.

The New Kingdom was Egypt's richest and most powerful kingdom. It conquered lands outside Egypt in Asia and Africa. It finally broke apart about 1070 BCE.

Egyptian Government The pharaoh relied on a **bureaucracy**, or a system of many government officials who carry out government rules. Heading this bureaucracy was an official called the vizier.

The bureaucracy collected taxes in the form of surplus crops from farmers. The bureaucracy took some of this surplus for itself. It distributed the rest to the pharaoh, to priests, and to artisans and merchants who worked for the pharaoh. Egypt's bureaucracy was a model that later governments followed.

☑ READING CHECK **Identify Supporting Details** Why was Egypt's New Kingdom considered the most powerful of the three kingdoms?

Egyptian Society

To control Egypt, pharaohs needed the loyalty and labor of the people. Egypt's society was supported by many farmers, servants, and slaves, who together did most of the work but had the lowest status.

Egyptian society was led by the pharaoh. Egyptians believed that gods controlled everything, and since the pharaoh controlled Egypt, people saw him as a god-king who deserved loyalty.

Just below the pharaoh were nobles, priests, and officials. They helped the pharaoh govern Egypt. So did scribes, who kept records for its bureaucracy. The scribes, along with merchants and artisans, made up two middle levels. In Egypt, painters, stonecutters, and builders spent their entire lives working on temples and tombs.

Analyze Charts Egyptian society was organized like a pyramid, with very few people at the top with high status and many people at the bottom with low status. **Compare and Contrast** Who had a higher status in ancient Egypt, artisans or farmers? Why?

EGYPT'S SOCIAL PYRAMID

Pharaoh

Nobles, priests, officials

Scribes

Merchants, artisans

Farmers, servants, slaves

▲ A mummy from the 300s
BCE found in Saqqara, Egypt

By far, most of the people of ancient Egypt were farmers. When not raising Egypt's food, many farmers worked as laborers on the pharaoh's building projects. Most did so willingly. They believed that if they helped the god-king, they would be rewarded after death.

Slaves were at the bottom of society. Many were prisoners of war or people who owed large debts. They were the property of their owners and did forced labor. Slaves were freed after serving for a period of time.

☑ **READING CHECK** **Identify Cause and Effect** Why were Egyptians loyal to the pharaoh?

Egyptian Religion

Religion played an important role in the life of Egyptians. They believed that their gods controlled everything from the flooding of the Nile River to the death of a child. Their gods could be kind or dangerous. To please the gods, Egyptians built them temples and offered them prayers and gifts.

Religion and Society Ancient Egyptians were polytheists, or people who worship many gods. Egyptians believed in hundreds of gods, many associated with animals. Egyptians thought that gods shared the qualities of these animals, such as their strength, speed, or bad temper.

People obeyed the pharaoh and his officials for fear of angering a god. Priests were also powerful, because Egyptians thought priests could help a person gain favor with the gods. The priests of the Temple of Amon-Re in the city of Thebes were especially powerful.

Preparing for the Afterlife Egyptians believed that life on Earth could lead to an afterlife, or life after death. However, this required preparation by living a good life. Egyptians believed that Osiris, god of the dead, decided who would have an afterlife. Those who had lived good lives would be allowed to live forever, but the sinful would be destroyed.

Preserving the Dead The second way that Egyptians prepared for the afterlife was by having their bodies **preserved** after death. They believed that their spirit would need to recognize their preserved body and use it as a home in the afterlife.

Egyptians went to great efforts to preserve the bodies of their dead. Poor people were buried in the desert, where the hot, dry sand quickly dried out their bodies. Wealthy Egyptians had their bodies made into mummies. A **mummy** is a body that has been preserved so that it will not decompose. Internal organs and the brain were removed, then the body was dried and wrapped in sheets of linen with chemicals to preserve it. The knowledge of this process was one of ancient Egypt's great achievements. From mummies, scientists have learned much about life and death in ancient Egypt.

☑ **READING CHECK** **Summarize** How did Egyptians prepare for the afterlife while still alive?

Egyptian Achievements

The contributions that ancient Egyptians made to their civilization and those that followed it were enormous. Many of the huge pyramids that the Egyptians constructed as tombs still stand today as reminders of the civilization's lasting influence. The writing system that Egyptians developed allowed them to record their knowledge of many other achievements.

Writing Ancient Egyptians developed early forms of writing by 3200 BCE using hieroglyphics. A **hieroglyphic** is a drawing or symbol that stands for a word, idea, or sound. Most ancient Egyptians did not know how to write. Scribes were therefore valued for their knowledge.

Egyptian scribes wrote with ink on **papyrus**, a paper-like material made from the papyrus reed that grew along the Nile. (Our word *paper* comes from the word *papyrus*.) Papyrus was easy to transport and could last a very long time in Egypt's dry environment. Many documents written on papyrus—including medical books, calendars, stories, poems, and prayers—have survived to the present.

With writing, Egyptians could share and preserve knowledge. This ability made Egypt's complex civilization and advanced technology possible.

The Pyramids The Egyptians created temples for their gods and tombs for their pharaohs. The tombs of early rulers were underground chambers, or rooms. The burial chamber contained items that the ruler might want in the afterlife.

An architect named Imhotep designed a new kind of tomb for his pharaoh in the 2600s BCE. This step pyramid had six stone mounds, one on top of the other. Later architects made the sides smoother to create a true pyramid.

During the Old Kingdom, three of these enormous structures with triangular sides were built at Giza for King Khufu, his son Khafre, and his grandson Menkaure. These pyramids were the largest structures on Earth. For nearly 4,000 years, the Great Pyramid of Khufu was the world's tallest building. Nearby stands the Sphinx, a famous statue. The Sphinx guarded Khafre's pyramid.

Building the pyramids required the labor of thousands of workers. Workers cut and placed the huge stones by hand. Scholars once thought that slaves had built the pyramids. They now think that hired, free workers built them.

The great age of pyramid building ended about 2200 BCE. Pharaohs who ruled after that time carved massive tombs from the cliffs at the edge of the Nile Valley.

INTERACTIVE

Egyptian Pyramids

Analyze Images
Hieroglyphics used more than 2,000 characters that represented common objects from ancient Egypt or ideas associated with the object. **Infer** What ideas might be associated with the image of an eye?

▲ The Abu Simbel temples in Upper Egypt were built by pharaoh Ramses II in the 1200s BCE. These huge statues depicted him as an Egyptian god.

Science and Mathematics The ancient Egyptians developed a solid understanding of mathematics. Their ability to construct the great pyramids proves their command of arithmetic and geometry and their knowledge of engineering concepts. No other civilization had been able to plan and build structures so large or so perfectly shaped. To bring the water of the Nile River to their fields, the ancient Egyptians also developed complex systems of irrigation.

Ancient Egyptians also made enormous advances in science. They had an advanced understanding of astronomy—the study of the stars and other objects in the sky. They used astronomy to help plan growing seasons and to develop a calendar similar to the one we use today.

The ancient Egyptians also made many of the earliest discoveries in chemistry. These discoveries led to several new inventions, including the earliest forms of glass and mortar for holding bricks together.

Work with mummies taught ancient Egyptians much about human anatomy, or the structure of the body and its organs. The ancient Egyptians became skilled surgeons. Egyptian doctors also studied diseases and developed effective medicines to treat or cure them.

☑ **READING CHECK** Draw Conclusions How did Egyptian writing influence the civilization's later achievements?

Egypt and Kush

Through trade, the Egyptians came into contact with Kush, a land up the Nile to the south. Kush was rich in resources, including gold.

Egypt Conquers Kush To gain control over these riches, Egypt conquered most of Kush during the Middle and New Kingdoms. The conquered Kushites had to pay tribute to the pharaoh. **Tribute** is payment from conquered peoples or to a more powerful country.

When Egypt weakened and the New Kingdom ended, Kush became an independent kingdom ruled by Kushite kings.

Kush Conquers Egypt In the mid-700s BCE, a Kushite king conquered the Egyptian city of Thebes. The next ruler of Kush, a king named Piye (PEE yeh), conquered the rest of Egypt. Finally, Piye declared himself pharaoh of a united Egypt and Kush.

Pharaohs from Kush ruled Egypt for almost a hundred years. Kushite rulers promoted the traditional Egyptian ways that their people had learned in the past. They built temples to honor Kushite and Egyptian gods. About 665 BCE, though, Assyrians from Southwest Asia drove the Kushites south out of Egypt and back into Kush.

INTERACTIVE

Art and Culture of Kush

✓ READING CHECK **Summarize** Why did Egypt conquer Kush?

The Civilization of Kush

Kush remained an advanced civilization for almost a thousand years after it lost Egypt. During this time, it developed its own system of writing, economy, and government.

Independent Kush In 591 BCE, the Egyptians destroyed Napata, the capital of Kush. The Kushites moved their capital south to the city of Meroë (MEHR oh ee), which was on a trade route from Central Africa and was easier to defend. Meroë was also located near iron deposits. It became Africa's first ironworking center. Kush's iron tools and weapons were much stronger than Egypt's softer bronze tools.

Analyze Images This painting shows Kushite princes and their servants paying tribute by bringing gold to Egypt. **Identify Cause and Effect** Why did Kush pay tribute to Egypt?

The Kushites built hundreds of pyramids at Napata and Meroë. Built at a steep angle, the pyramids held the tombs of the rulers of Kush.

The Kushites also created the Meroitic script, one of the world's first alphabets. While scholars have learned to read this alphabet, they still don't understand the words of the Meroitic language.

Kush's Links to Africa and the World Kush played an important role in ancient Africa. The kingdom may have controlled an area larger than the Egyptian empire. Kushites traded iron goods, cloth, gold, and slaves with other African peoples in return for ivory elephant tusks and ebony wood. Kushites also traded with the ancient Greeks and Romans.

Kush used irrigation to grow more food. It was still necessary to trade for some food and cloth. Ports on the Red Sea allowed the Kushites to trade with countries as far away as India.

By the 200s CE, war with the Roman empire in Egypt had weakened Kush. Desert peoples raided Kush's cities and disrupted its trade. Finally, in the 300s CE, Kush was conquered by the kingdom of Axum, centered in the present-day country of Ethiopia to the southeast.

Throughout its history, Kush had linked Africa south of the Sahara with other ancient civilizations. Kushites created patterns of trade and farming that continue in the region to this day.

Analyze Images Kushite pyramids were shaped differently from Egyptian pyramids. In front of each pyramid is the remains of a Kushite temple. **Use Visual Information** What do these pyramids suggest about the relationship of Kush to Egypt?

✔ READING CHECK **Recognize Multiple Causes** What were two advantages of Kushites moving their capital to Meroë?

☑ Lesson Check

Practice Vocabulary

1. What was the relationship between a **pharaoh** and a **dynasty**?

2. How did the invention of **papyrus** and **hieroglyphics** affect ancient Egypt?

3. What role did **mummies** play in Egyptians' plans for the afterlife?

Critical Thinking and Writing

4. **Understand Effects** How did food surpluses enable the ancient Egyptians to develop a complex civilization?

5. **Use Evidence** How did the kingdom of Kush connect Africa with other parts of the world?

6. **Writing Workshop: Develop a Clear Thesis** Using what you have learned about who benefited from resources in Egypt and Kush and in prehistoric Africa, develop a thesis in your 📓 Active Journal on who has benefited from Africa's resources.

Draw Conclusions and Make Generalizations

INTERACTIVE
Draw Conclusions

Follow these steps and use the sources to learn how to draw sound conclusions and make generalizations from sources.

1 **Study the facts and main ideas in a source.** Identify the facts and information in the text. Compare these to the visual information in the satellite image.

2 **Formulate questions about the sources.** Ask, "What is this text source telling me about river silt? Why is this information important to my understanding of ancient Egypt?"

3 **Draw conclusions from the sources.** Ask, "What conclusions do the sources suggest about the role the Nile River played in ancient Egyptian life?"

4 **Test any conclusions for soundness.** Ask, "Do the facts in the text and visual source support the conclusion? Is this the only reasonable conclusion that I could draw from the information?"

5 **Make a generalization about the information in the sources.** Ask, "What generalizations can I make about the importance of the Nile River and its annual floods to the people of ancient Egypt?"

Secondary Source

"The river carries silt—fine mineral particles that can form fertile soil—from its sources in East Africa. . . . A narrow strip of fertile soil lines both banks of the Nile and covers its delta. This rich, dark soil was so important to the Egyptians that they called their country Kemet, which means 'the Black Land.' The yearly flooding of the Nile created the Black Land. Each summer, heavy rainfall in East Africa poured into the Nile's sources. Flood waters surged through Egypt. When the flood waters drained away, they left behind a layer of fresh silt."

—Pearson, *World History*

Primary Source

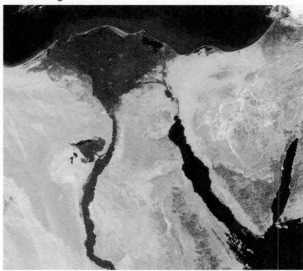

▲ This is a satellite image of the Nile River. The green you can see in the photo indicates the vegetation along the banks of the Nile. The tan indicates the desert areas on either side of the river.

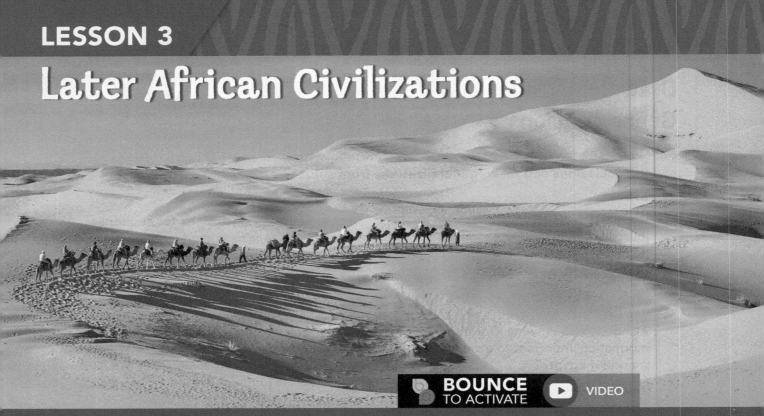

Later African Civilizations

BOUNCE TO ACTIVATE ▶ VIDEO

GET READY TO READ

START UP

Study the photo of the caravan crossing the Sahara. For hundreds of years, it took merchants months of desert travel to reach their markets. How do you think this affected the region's trade?

GUIDING QUESTIONS

- How did Islam affect North and West Africa?
- How did the empires of West Africa arise and grow wealthy?
- What civilizations and cultures developed in East Africa and southern Africa?

TAKE NOTES

Literacy Skills: Compare and Contrast
Use the graphic organizer in your 📔 Active Journal to take notes as you read the lesson.

PRACTICE VOCABULARY

Use the vocabulary activity in your 📔 Active Journal to practice the vocabulary words.

Vocabulary	**Academic Vocabulary**
stele	practice
monk	accommodate
stonetown	

Africa's unique geography shaped the growth of civilizations that followed the empires of ancient Egypt and Kush. Trade also influenced the development and culture of the continent.

Muslim North Africa

Soon after the religion of Islam began to spread in the 600s CE, Arab Muslim armies built an empire that stretched from Spain to Iran. North Africa was part of this empire.

Arab Muslim merchants and religious leaders came to North Africa. They built trading centers and mosques, or Islamic houses of worship. These Arabs spread the Arabic language and Islam to Egyptians and Berbers, the indigenous people of western North Africa. Most North Africans converted to Islam, but Jews and Christians continued to live in the region.

North Africa became a cultural center of the Islamic world. Arab rulers founded cities such as Kairouan in Tunisia and Cairo in Egypt that grew into centers of religion and learning. North Africans produced new works of art and literature.

While earlier conquerors had seen the Sahara as a barrier, the Muslim Arabs saw it as an opportunity. They quickly came to control the trans-Saharan (across the Sahara) camel caravan routes that linked North Africa, where they had settled, with West Africa. Merchants spread Arabic and Islam to peoples they traded with across the Sahara.

✓ READING CHECK Sequence How did Muslim North Africans spread ideas and beliefs to West Africa?

Western Trading Empires

Three great trading empires arose in West Africa between 600 CE and the mid-1600s. As in ancient Egypt, food surpluses had helped the population to grow. They allowed civilization to develop, with some people specializing in work besides farming.

The Kingdom of Ghana Ghana, the first of the great empires, flourished between 600 and 1200. Originally a kingdom founded between the Niger and Senegal rivers, Ghana grew into a full-fledged empire through its mastery of making iron weapons. These weapons helped Ghana to conquer other peoples.

Beginning around 750, Ghana began to develop trans-Saharan trade with North Africa. North Africans wanted gold to make into coins. West Africans were rich in gold, but they needed salt—a mineral necessary for good health—which was plentiful along trade routes across the Sahara. Eventually, the kings of Ghana grew rich from the gold-salt trade.

A growing population, though, strained resources. Then, around 1050, power struggles with peoples to the north weakened Ghana and disrupted trade and farming. In 1240, the leader of a newer empire called Mali (MAH lee) attacked Ghana's last strongholds. Soon, Mali swallowed up the old empire.

The modern country of Ghana took its name from the empire of Ghana. However, that empire lay in present-day Mali and Mauritania. It did not include present-day Ghana.

The Empire of Mali Arab trading partners brought more than salt to West Africa. They also carried learning, law, and the religion of Islam to the region. The trade networks gave birth to new cities. Rulers gained power by collecting taxes and tribute.

This was true in the empire of Mali, which controlled an even larger territory than Ghana. At its height, Mali covered an area about the size of Western Europe. Mali also controlled all of the gold-producing regions and trade routes.

Analyze Images A woman sells salt in a village market in modern-day Ghana. The salt-gold trade brought wealth to West Africa's empires. **Identify Supporting Details** Why was salt so important to West African peoples?

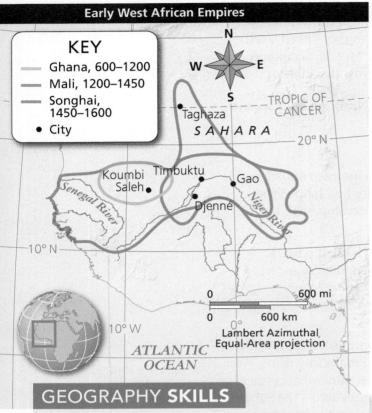

Early West African Empires

KEY
— Ghana, 600–1200
— Mali, 1200–1450
— Songhai, 1450–1600
• City

TROPIC OF CANCER
SAHARA
20° N
Taghaza
Koumbi Saleh
Timbuktu
Gao
Djenné
Senegal River
Niger River
10° N
10° W
0°
ATLANTIC OCEAN

0   600 mi
0   600 km
Lambert Azimuthal
Equal-Area projection

GEOGRAPHY SKILLS

This map shows the territory of the empires of Ghana, Mali, and Songhai.

1. **Region** What body of water was important to both Mali and Songhai?

2. **Use Visual Information** What role do you think the Niger River played in those two empires?

Academic Vocabulary

practice • v., to make use of, follow, or observe regularly

👆 **INTERACTIVE**

West African Trade, Empires, and Art

Mali's greatest emperor, Mansa Musa, ruled from about 1312 to 1337. He **practiced** Islam. He made a spectacular pilgrimage, or religious journey, to the Arabian city of Mecca in 1324. The trip strengthened Mali's ties with the Muslim world. It drew the world's attention to the empire and attracted many Muslim scholars and artists.

Among those who journeyed to Mali was a great traveler of the time, Ibn Battuta (IB un but TOO tuh) of Morocco. In 1352, Ibn Battuta spent months crossing the Sahara to get to Mali. Ibn Battuta's written accounts of his time in Mali offer some of the best descriptions of the great empire.

Mali, like Ghana, weakened and declined. Soon, the Songhai kingdom took its place as the most powerful West African empire.

The Songhai Empire In the mid-1400s, the empire of Songhai took over from Mali. It became the largest empire in African history. Songhai ruled the great trading cities of Timbuktu (also spelled Tombouctou) and Djenné (jen NAY). Timbuktu flourished as the center of the salt trade and of Islamic learning and culture in West Africa.

Songhai's strongest ruler was Askia Muhammad. Under Askia, the Songhai army controlled the empire's many lands. Askia established a stable system of government run by efficient officials. He also strengthened the role of Islam in the empire. This promoted heavier use of Arabic, the language of the Islam's holy book, the Quran.

In Songhai, as in earlier West African kingdoms, some people lived in slavery. Enslaved people were sometimes sold to traders from North Africa. In West African civilizations, though, enslaved people were mostly farmworkers who had some legal rights and protections.

By the late 1500s, competition between rulers had weakened Songhai. Soldiers from North Africa armed with guns invaded and defeated the empire. By the early 1600s, Songhai had split into smaller states.

✓ READING CHECK **Identify Cause and Effect** What was the impact of Arab trade on the three great empires of West Africa?

Axum and Ethiopia

You have already learned about the first civilization in Eastern Africa, Kush. The kingdom of Axum replaced Kush as the commercial hub of northeast Africa.

Axum was located in what is Ethiopia today. It had a port on the Red Sea. This location helped make Axum a center for trade in and beyond Africa. Axum's traders sold gold, ivory, and other goods from the interior of Africa for textiles, tools, jewelry, and steel. They traded with Rome to the northwest and India to the east.

Axum's wealth and power could be seen in its huge monuments. Great stairways led to altars honoring Axum's gods. A kind of grand stone pillar, called a **stele** (STEE lee), marked each grave of Axum's rulers. Each stele looked like a skyscraper. It had false doors and windows carved into the stone. Beneath the stele lay royal burial tombs.

Roman traders may have brought Christianity to Axum. By the mid-300s, Christianity had become the kingdom's leading religion. **Monks**, or men who dedicate themselves to worshiping God, traveled through the region to spread Christian beliefs. Ethiopia still is mostly Christian today.

Axum slowly began to weaken in the 600s due to economic problems. Another factor was the spread of Islam to the area. Eventually a new dynasty called the Zagwe appeared in what is now Ethiopia. The Zagwe rose to power in the mid-1000s and continued the Christian tradition. They promoted Christian officials. They also traded successfully with the Muslim world.

☑ READING CHECK **Sequence** How did Christianity affect East Africa?

Quick Activity

Suppose you are a trader in the year 1000. With a partner, discuss what you want to buy and sell in Africa. Record your findings in your 📓 Active Journal.

▼ A priest stands outside an Ethiopian Christian church in Lalibela, Ethiopia. The church was carved from solid rock in the late 1100s.

Quest CONNECTIONS

The leaders of trading empires and city-states once controlled Africa's resources. How much do you think that trade benefited all the people of those empires? Record your findings in your 📓 Active Journal.

East African City-States

Trade connecting East Africa, the Mediterranean, and India brought distant peoples together. Between the 800s and the 1400s, Muslim immigrants came to coastal East Africa. A mixed culture—combining features from Southwest Asia and East Africa—developed in more than three dozen ports along the coast of present-day Somalia, Kenya, Tanzania, Mozambique, and Madagascar.

The Swahili Culture Over time, this new Swahili culture formed in trading towns along the coast of East Africa. The Swahili imported ceramics, glassware, and silver and copper jewelry from Southwest Asia and silk from China. They adopted Islam by the 700s. Muslim traders and teachers of Islam had brought the religion to the area.

A Blending of Cultures By the 1000s, these coastal settlements had grown into city-states, centered on stonetowns. **Stonetowns** were Swahili cities with multistoried stone houses.

The Swahili imported trade goods from the interior of East Africa, which produced natural resources such as copper and ivory. They then traded these goods, as well as enslaved Africans, for goods found in distant lands, such as cotton cloth and sugar from India.

Contact through trade brought a multicultural mix to the East African coast. The Swahili language, for example, included words from East African languages as well as Arabic. Swahili is still a major African language today. Islam also became part of the blended culture of coastal East Africa.

👆 **INTERACTIVE**

Stonetowns

✓ READING CHECK Draw Conclusions How is the language of Swahili an example of East Africa's multiculturalism?

Bantu Peoples in Southern Africa

Southern Africa was not home to many early empires. Yet its open land attracted people from Central Africa. These peoples' cultures had an impact on Southern Africa that continues today.

Analyze Images The stonetown at Zanzibar, Tanzania, is an example of the Swahili coastal trading towns of East Africa. **Identify Main Ideas** How do these towns show the impact of trade?

Analyze Images These ruins were part of the city of Great Zimbabwe, which thrived in the 1400s. **Synthesize Visual Information** How would you describe the physical geography around the remains of this important city?

The Bantu Migration By about 1000 BCE, the population of the first Bantu people in western Africa had grown until their land could not **accommodate** them. They left their homeland and migrated into East and Central Africa. Then, around 1 CE, Bantu peoples began to spread into southern Africa. The Bantu introduced their farming methods to the people of the region, including the raising of cattle. They also brought skill at making iron tools.

The original language spoken by the Bantu developed into a variety of different languages. Today, millions of people across East, Central, and southern Africa speak languages that are members of the Bantu language family.

Great Zimbabwe In southern Africa, Great Zimbabwe thrived in the 1400s. It was a large trading city founded by Bantu-speaking people. Great Zimbabwe's traders took gold and ivory to Africa's east coast ports. There they traded for goods from China, India, and Southeast Asia.

☑ READING CHECK **Understand Effects** What was the result of the Bantu migration?

Academic Vocabulary
accommodate • *v.,* to have or make room for

☑ Lesson Check

Practice Vocabulary

1. What was the role of **monks** in the spread of Christianity in Axum?

2. What were Swahili **stonetowns**?

Critical Thinking and Writing

3. **Identify Main Ideas** How did Islam come to East and West Africa?

4. **Understand Effects** How did the East African city-states come to have a blend of cultures?

5. **Writing Workshop: Support Thesis With Details** Using your 📓 Active Journal, give details of how people from Africa and from outside Africa used and benefited from Africa's resources in the time covered in this lesson. Use these details to support the thesis you have written.

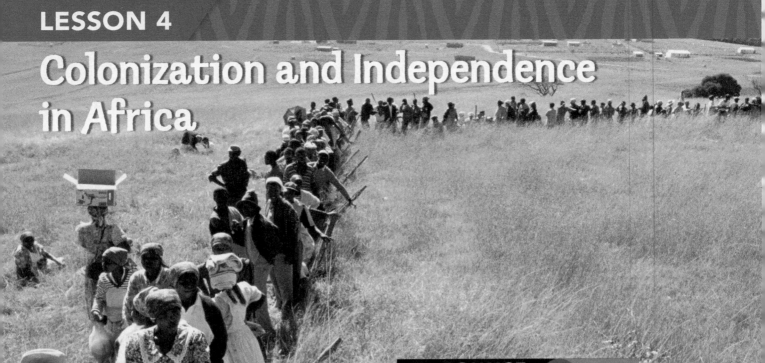

Colonization and Independence in Africa

BOUNCE TO ACTIVATE ▶ VIDEO

GET READY TO READ

START UP

Look at the South Africans waiting in line to vote when that country had its first fully democratic election in 1994. Write a list of questions you have about how modern Africa took shape.

GUIDING QUESTIONS

- What issues did Africa face under colonialism and during the struggle for independence?
- What challenges have African nations faced since gaining independence?
- How did the Arab Spring affect North Africa?

TAKE NOTES

Literacy Skills: Identify Cause and Effect
Use the graphic organizer in your 📓 Active Journal to take notes as you read the lesson.

PRACTICE VOCABULARY

Use the vocabulary activity in your 📓 Active Journal to practice the vocabulary words.

Vocabulary
Atlantic slave trade
colonialism
Pan-Africanism
apartheid
genocide
Arab Spring
Islamism

Academic Vocabulary
movement
discord

When Europeans began to make long sea voyages in the 1400s, they learned of the riches of Africa beyond the Sahara and began to set up colonies. European powers took control of and transformed most of Africa. In the 1900s, Africans regained power over their own lands.

European Rule

In the 1400s, Africans beyond the Sahara began trading with Europeans who had recently arrived on their coastlines. Gold drew Europeans to Africa, just as it had drawn Arab traders. Soon, Europeans became involved in the slave trade. Later, they would gain control of most of the continent.

Atlantic Slave Trade The trans-Saharan trade had long included enslaved people. However, Europeans greatly increased the impact of the slave trade on Africa.

In the 1500s, African traders began selling enslaved people for guns and other European goods. Europeans then brought the enslaved Africans across the Atlantic

Ocean to work on colonial plantations in the Americas. This trade, called the **Atlantic slave trade**, may have involved 13 million enslaved Africans. Hundreds of thousands of Africans died as they made this forced journey.

With European guns, slave-trading states could defeat neighboring peoples in war and capture more people to trade as slaves. These wars weakened the region and made it more vulnerable to European control.

Colonization The slave trade was mostly outlawed in the early 1800s, but European interference in Africa continued. Beginning in the 1500s, Europeans had built trading posts on the African coast. By the early 1800s, European powers began actively colonizing Africa. **Colonialism** is a policy by which one country seeks to rule other areas.

Europeans wanted full access to Africa's natural resources and control of important trade routes. Britain took control of Egypt, while France ruled most of western North Africa. Spain and Italy governed other parts of northern Africa.

Britain, France, Germany, and Portugal set up colonial rule along the west coast and then moved farther inland. Belgium colonized a large region of Central Africa. Southern and Eastern Africa were also colonized as early as the 1600s. Dutch and British trading companies built supply posts for traders traveling to Asia. One of these was Cape Town in present-day South Africa.

INTERACTIVE

European Imperialism in Africa

GEOGRAPHY **SKILLS**

Several European powers controlled different parts of Africa in the early 1900s.

1. **Location** Where were most French colonies in Africa at this time?

2. **Use Visual Information** Which European nation had the largest presence in southern Africa?

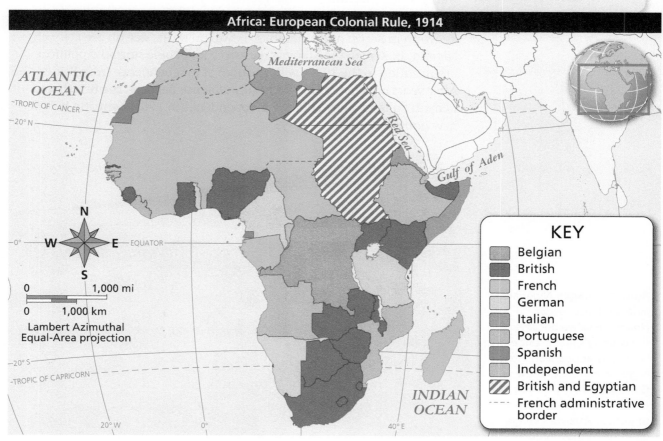
Africa: European Colonial Rule, 1914

ATLANTIC OCEAN

TROPIC OF CANCER

20° N

Mediterranean Sea

Red Sea

Gulf of Aden

N
W E
S

EQUATOR

0   1,000 mi
0   1,000 km
Lambert Azimuthal Equal-Area projection

20° S
TROPIC OF CAPRICORN

INDIAN OCEAN

20° W   0°   40° E

KEY
- Belgian
- British
- French
- German
- Italian
- Portuguese
- Spanish
- Independent
- British and Egyptian
- French administrative border

Academic Vocabulary

movement • *n.*, a group of people sharing and pursuing social or political goals

Impact of Colonialism By 1900, European nations had divided most of Africa into colonies. The only country that was never colonized was Ethiopia, though it was invaded by Italy in the 1930s.

Many Africans suffered under colonial rule. Some lost their land, and others were forced to work for little or no pay. When Africans fought back against colonizers, they were quickly defeated by the Europeans' modern weapons.

However, Europeans did make positive changes by outlawing slavery and introducing modern health care. They improved transportation, but mainly to help them ship natural resources to Europe. Europeans also built schools that gave Africans access to education.

✓ READING CHECK **Identify Main Ideas** Why did Europeans want to establish colonies in Africa?

Independence

Many Africans resented having little or no control over their own government. Some colonies did ask a few Africans to help run their governments. As these Africans became educated, leaders emerged. They grew frustrated with the unfair rule of colonial powers.

African independence **movements** gained momentum in the 1940s. In Ghana, a local political leader named Kwame Nkrumah (KWAH may un KROO muh), promoted the idea of **Pan-Africanism**. Pan-Africanism was a political and social movement to unite black Africans around the world. Ghana became independent in 1957.

Pan-Africanism influenced other independence leaders, including Jomo Kenyatta in Kenya and Nnamdi Azikiwe (un NAHM dee ah zee KEE weh) in Nigeria. In Kenya, the Kikuyu (kee KOO yoo) people started a political organization in the 1920s with the goal of independence from Britain. After years of negotiation and finally violence between the British and Kenyan fighters, Kenya gained independence in 1963. Kenyatta led the new nation.

Analyze Images Nigerian independence leader Nnamdi Azikiwe became the country's first president. His image appears on Nigerian currency. **Draw Conclusions** Why do you think Nigerians have chosen to include Azikiwe's image on some of their money?

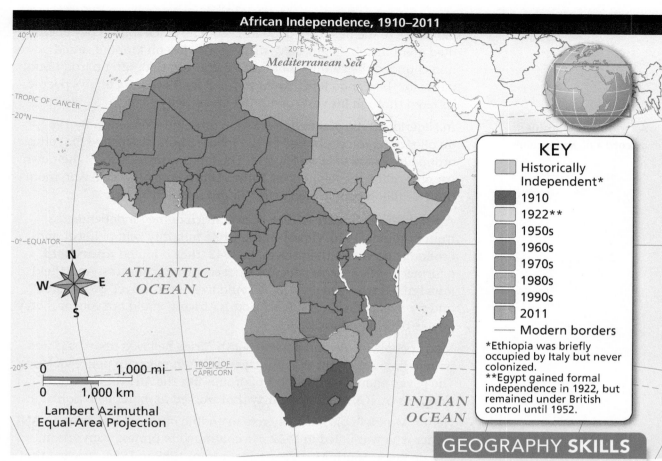

African Independence, 1910–2011

Mediterranean Sea

TROPIC OF CANCER
20°N

Red Sea

0° EQUATOR

N
W E
S

ATLANTIC
OCEAN

20°S

0   1,000 mi
0   1,000 km

TROPIC OF
CAPRICORN

Lambert Azimuthal
Equal-Area Projection

INDIAN
OCEAN

KEY

Historically
Independent*
1910
1922**
1950s
1960s
1970s
1980s
1990s
2011
—— Modern borders

*Ethiopia was briefly
occupied by Italy but never
colonized.
**Egypt gained formal
independence in 1922, but
remained under British
control until 1952.

In Nigeria, local leaders with growing government power united more than 40 ethnic groups to oppose British rule. Everyone from soldiers who had served in World War II to farmers and women working in the markets joined the call for freedom. Azikiwe, who had left Nigeria to pursue a U.S. education, returned to help the independence movement. Nigeria became independent in 1960.

Most of Africa gained independence in the 1950s and 1960s. In South Africa, independence came as early as 1910. However, as you will read, this did not immediately bring all the freedoms most South Africans desired.

✓ **READING CHECK** **Sequence** How did nationalist leaders in Nigeria build their movement?

After Independence

The transition to independence was difficult. Many Africans had not been involved in government in colonial times, and Europeans still controlled many economic activities. Locally owned businesses were few and small. To make matters more complicated, European powers had drawn the borders of countries without regard to ethnic divisions.

GEOGRAPHY SKILLS

African countries gained independence mainly during the mid-1900s.

1. **Region** Why might so many countries have won independence around the same time?

2. **Compare and Contrast** How do the boundaries on this map compare with those on the map of colonial Africa in 1914?

INTERACTIVE

Colonial Rule and Independence

Unrest in the Congo and Nigeria Belgium abruptly granted independence to the Belgian Congo in 1960. The quick shift in power created great instability. In 1965, army leader Joseph Mobutu seized power and changed the country's name to Zaire (zah EER), after a traditional name for the Congo River. Mobutu ruled for 32 years. Congo's people suffered through his vast corruption and cruelty.

Academic Vocabulary
discord • *n.,* strife, conflict

In Nigeria, ethnic **discord** arose soon after independence. By 1967, an oil-rich region controlled by the Igbo (IG boh, also called Ibo) ethnic group attempted to leave Nigeria. The Igbos wanted to form their own country called the Republic of Biafra. During a bloody civil war, more than a million people died before Biafra rejoined Nigeria.

Apartheid in South Africa South Africa gained independence from Britain in 1910. However, the white minority kept political and economic power for themselves. In 1948, they adopted **apartheid**, a former South African policy of strict separation of races. Apartheid laws limited where black people could live, work, travel, go to school, and receive medical care. Black South Africans could not vote or marry people of different races.

Many people inside and beyond South Africa believed apartheid was wrong. Protests within the country were often met with police violence. The government jailed leaders of groups like the African National Congress (ANC), a political party that worked for black civil rights.

Nelson Mandela played a key role in ending apartheid. He was an ANC leader who was jailed in 1962. He continued to protest from prison. F.W. de Klerk, South Africa's president from 1989 to 1994, realized that apartheid was destroying South Africa. In 1990, he released Mandela from prison and agreed to end apartheid. In 1994, South Africans of all races voted together and Mandela became president. South Africa was truly free and independent at last.

5 BIOGRAPHY Things to Know About

NELSON MANDELA
South African leader (1918–2013)

- Mandela chose to become a lawyer instead of becoming a clan chief like his father.

- He was arrested for protesting apartheid in 1962.

- While in prison, he rejected offers of freedom that would have required him to speak against his beliefs.

- He won the Nobel Peace Prize with F.W. de Klerk in 1993.

- His birthday, July 18, has been declared Nelson Mandela International Day by the United Nations.

Critical Thinking How did Nelson Mandela demonstrate his commitment to the task of ending apartheid in his country?

Conflicts in Sudan Sudan and South Sudan used to be part of one country called Sudan. In northern Sudan, which today is still called Sudan, most people are Arabs who practice Islam. In the southern part, now South Sudan, most people belong to other ethnic groups and are not Muslims.

Only a few years after Sudan gained independence in 1956, southerners rebelled against northern rule. Civil wars raged until 2005 and killed several million people. In 2011, South Sudan became independent.

In Darfur, a region in the west of Sudan, black farmers fought Arab herders over scarce water resources. The Sudanese government supported the herders, while it failed to protect black farmers. Hundreds of thousands of people, mostly black farmers, were killed in the early 2000s. Many more fled their homes. Some called the Darfur conflict a **genocide**, or an attempt to destroy a whole people.

Genocide in Rwanda Rwanda is divided between two main ethnic groups, the majority Hutu and the minority Tutsi. Before Belgium colonized the region, the Tutsi ruled the Hutu. The Belgians favored the Tutsi and used them to keep control of the Hutu. After independence, violence flared up against the Tutsi, and the Hutu took control.

The conflict exploded into a genocide. During a few months in 1994, Hutu military and militia groups killed an estimated 800,000 to 1 million Tutsis. Attempts by the United Nations to stop the killings failed.

The murders stopped when the Tutsi once again came to power. Millions of Hutus fled the country to neighboring Zaire, today called the Democratic Republic of the Congo. Fighting between the two groups continues in that country.

☑ READING CHECK **Compare and Contrast** What do the conflicts in Darfur and Rwanda have in common?

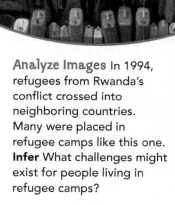

Analyze Images In 1994, refugees from Rwanda's conflict crossed into neighboring countries. Many were placed in refugee camps like this one. **Infer** What challenges might exist for people living in refugee camps?

Arab Spring

Long after gaining independence, many African countries had governments that were not democratic. In 2010, a movement for more democracy that came to be known as the **Arab Spring** began in Tunisia. This movement soon spread to many other North African and Southwest Asian countries, where it had mixed results.

Tunisia Tunisian protestors used social media to organize protests against government corruption, unequal treatment of citizens, and rising prices. Tunisia's dictator resigned in January of 2011 and a more democratic government was put in place.

The Arab Spring in Libya resulted in a civil war there.

Algeria and Morocco Protests in Algeria led to new policies that ensured fairer elections and protected freedoms. Similarly, the king of Morocco responded to peaceful protests. He issued a new constitution that voters approved in 2011. It limited the king's powers and strengthened the parliament.

Libya Protests in Libya against human rights abuses by dictator Muammar Qaddafi (moo AH mahr kah DAH fee) erupted into a civil war. Some other countries supported the rebels. Qaddafi was killed in October of 2011, but the new government that formed did not have the support of all the rebel groups. These armed groups fought over control of territory and valuable oil wells. Terrorists set up bases and carried out attacks.

Egypt In Egypt, President Hosni Mubarak led an often corrupt and tightly run dictatorship for 30 years. Arab Spring protests forced him to resign in 2011. Democracy was not the only issue in this revolt. Mubarak's government had been secular, or nonreligious. Many Egyptians wanted an Islamist government. **Islamism** is the belief that government and society should reflect Islamic law.

Egyptians elected an Islamist president, Mohammed Morsi, in 2012. A new Islamist constitution was put into place. Morsi's government set limits on opposition. But in 2013, the military imprisoned Morsi and banned his political party. Egypt's new government soon amended the constitution to give power to the military and police.

☑ READING CHECK **Classify and Categorize** What do Islamists want from government?

☑ Lesson Check

Practice Vocabulary

1. How might the **Atlantic slave trade** have helped Europeans **colonize** parts of Africa?

2. What did **Arab Spring** protestors wish to achieve?

Critical Thinking and Writing

3. **Identify Cause and Effect** Name five major effects of colonialism on Africa.

4. **Sequence** When did most African nations gain their independence?

5. **Writing Workshop: Revise Your Thesis** Considering what you have read about the role of resources in the colonization and independence of Africa, revise the thesis in your 📓 Active Journal about who has benefited from Africa's resources.

LESSON 5
Living in Africa

BOUNCE TO ACTIVATE ▶ VIDEO

GET READY TO READ

START UP

Look at the photo of market day in Jinka, Ethiopia. What does it suggest to you about everyday life in Africa? What would you like to know about the people and cultures of Africa?

GUIDING QUESTIONS

- Why do Africans live where they do?
- What is the relationship between culture and the environment in Africa?
- What patterns of religion and ethnicity exist in Africa?

TAKE NOTES

Literacy Skills: Draw Conclusions

Use the graphic organizer in your 📓 Active Journal to take notes as you read the lesson.

PRACTICE VOCABULARY

Use the vocabulary activity in your 📓 Active Journal to practice the vocabulary words.

Vocabulary		Academic Vocabulary
oasis	indigenous	prone
savanna		consider
Copts		

Africans have adapted to the continent's sometimes challenging environments for thousands of years. These cultural adaptations help to explain the continent's great ethnic and religious diversity.

Where Africans Live

Africa is the second largest continent. Its more than 1.2 billion people are not spread evenly across the continent. Geography and climate help determine population density in Africa.

Settlement Patterns Many of the most densely populated regions in Africa are found near sources of water or in climates with regular precipitation. In North Africa, population is highest along the Mediterranean coast and the Nile River Valley. The tropical wet and dry climates south of the Sahara also include several large population centers, especially in highlands and near coastlines.

However, regions of Africa with a tropical wet climate do not typically have large populations. The rainforests that grow in these areas are dense, and soils are poor.

Did you know?

Oases in the Sahara are created by underground rivers flowing out of mountains in and around the desert and bubbling to the surface. There are about only 800 square miles (2,071 sq. km.) of oases across the Sahara.

The Importance of Water Throughout Africa's history, people have chosen to live where they have access to water and a good climate for farming. For example, almost all Egyptians live along the Nile River. In Nigeria—Africa's most populated country—a tropical climate and regular summer rains have all supported agriculture. Today, 70 percent of Nigerians still farm for a living.

Many of Africa's cities have developed around harbors or rivers that made it possible to transport goods from Africa's interior to the rest of the world. Since the 1900s, these cities have attracted more and more Africans. People may move to cities to look for work because a season's crops have failed. Conflict forces others from their homes. While only around one-seventh of Africans lived in cities in 1950, today about two-fifths of the population is urban.

The Sahara's Great Divide Drier regions of Africa are much more sparsely populated. The world's biggest hot desert, the Sahara, separates the people of North Africa from those residing in the rest of the continent. Very few people live in the Sahara. Many of these people live and farm in oases. An **oasis** is a place in the desert where water can be found. Other people of the Sahara are nomads, who make a living in the desert by trading and herding sheep, camels, and goats.

☑ **READING CHECK** Identify Main Ideas Where are the most densely populated areas of Africa found?

Environment and Culture

In Africa, as in other places, different cultures have developed in different environments. North African cultures developed in the mild climate of coastal North Africa, with its rainy winter season. In the Sahara, people created very different cultures to adapt to the dry desert climate. Some developed a nomadic lifestyle, moving their livestock to different water sources depending on the season.

Look at the physical map of Africa in the Regional Atlas. The area just south of the Sahara is called the Sahel. Here, people developed still other cultures. They planned around the rainy and dry seasons. In

▼ Farmers in North Africa use irrigation to grow crops in dry areas. Center-pivot irrigation uses a rotating system to water crops. It creates circular fields like this one, in Libya.

Analyze Images A goat herder leads his flock in Niger's semiarid Sahel region. **Summarize** How does a nomadic lifestyle help people adapt to the environment of the Sahel?

summer, rains helped crops grow and made it possible for livestock to graze on the otherwise dry plains. In the dry winter months, people moved livestock into river valleys, with their supplies of water and dry pasture for livestock.

Farther south, peoples in the forests and **savannas**—park-like grasslands with scattered trees that can survive dry spells—developed cultures adapted to those environments. As time went on, people began shaping their environments. Irrigation brought water to dry land, but the grazing of livestock stressed grasslands **prone** to drought.

Academic Vocabulary
prone • *adj.,* having a natural tendency

☑ READING CHECK **Compare and Contrast** Why did the peoples of the Sahel develop a culture different from that of Saharan peoples?

Religion and Ethnicity

Along with geographic features, cultural ideas and practices unrelated to geography have sometimes affected cultures. The cultures that have developed in Africa are very diverse in both religion and ethnicity. European colonialism has also had an impact on Africa's cultures.

Religious Diversity Africa is home to great religious diversity. Islam is the dominant religion in the north, on the east coast, and in the northern parts of West Africa. Egypt, however, has a large Christian minority called the Copts. The **Copts** speak Arabic, like other Egyptians, but belong to an ancient Christian church. South of Egypt, most people in Ethiopia and Eritrea follow a Christian tradition.

Farther south, the people of coastal Kenya and Tanzania are mainly Muslims, but those living farther inland in East Africa are mainly Christian. There is also a mix of faiths in West Africa. The northern parts of the region—including the Sahel—are mainly Muslim. Yet most people living along the coastline of the Gulf of Guinea are Christian.

Much of central and southern Africa is Christian, though Muslim and other religious minorities exist. Some people practice traditional African religions. These religions are **indigenous**, or present in the region since ancient times. They are based on oral traditions such as legends and folktales, not written scriptures. They involve a belief in spirits, including those of ancestors.

Ethnic Diversity Africa is also ethnically diverse. Every African country includes ethnic minorities. In most African countries, there is no ethnic majority. This means that no single group makes up more than half the population. During the colonization of Africa, European powers drew the continent's borders without **considering** ethnic differences. As a result, most countries are home to multiple ethnic groups, some of which were split between countries. Ethnic tensions are common.

Analyze Images In Cairo, Egypt, the tower of a Coptic church rises behind the dome of a mosque. **Analyze Visual Information** What does this image suggest about religion in Egypt?

Ethnic groups are defined by a shared identity and shared cultural traits, which usually include language. Just as there are many ethnic groups in Africa, there are also many languages—an estimated 1,500. Most Africans speak more than one language.

Some ethnic groups share a common religion. For example, many traditional African religions were specific to a particular ethnic group. Today, though, members of the same ethnic group may belong to different religions. For example, some members of the Yoruba ethnic group of Nigeria and Benin practice the traditional Yoruba religion. Other Yorubas are Christians. Still others are Muslims.

Academic Vocabulary
consider • *v.*, to take into account

✔ READING CHECK **Identify Supporting Details** What different religions are practiced in Africa?

☑ Lesson Check

Practice Vocabulary

1. Why is knowing where to find an **oasis** so important to people living in the Sahara?

2. Who are the **Copts**?

Critical Thinking and Writing

3. **Identify Cause and Effect** Explain the connection between a culture and an environment, using an example from one of the areas of Africa.

4. **Draw Conclusions** Look at the column in the Country Databank showing official languages. What conclusions can you draw about the impact of history on these languages?

5. **Writing Workshop: Pick an Organizing Strategy** Based on what you have learned so far, create a structure in your 📓 Active Journal for your informative essay on who has benefited from Africa's resources.

LESSON 6

Africa at Work

GET READY TO READ

START UP

Many Africans rely on natural resources for a living. In the Democratic Republic of the Congo, many jobs depend on open pit mining of copper, as shown in this photo. Considering the role of natural resources in Africa's history, predict how they might affect Africa's economies today.

GUIDING QUESTIONS

- What kinds of governments and economies exist in Africa?
- How does trade affect African countries?
- How do the economies of Kenya, Nigeria, and South Africa compare?

TAKE NOTES

Literacy Skills: Use Evidence

Use the graphic organizer in your 📖 Active Journal to take notes as you read the lesson.

PRACTICE VOCABULARY

Use the vocabulary activity in your 📖 Active Journal to practice the vocabulary words.

Vocabulary		Academic Vocabulary
corruption	CFA franc	custom
call center		intensive

Since independence, many African countries have struggled to establish stable governments and economies. Civil war and political unrest made this difficult for many countries. Economic dependence on natural resources has also posed a challenge.

Governments of Africa

Some African nations have democratic governments, while others are autocracies, or governments ruled by dictators. Citizens have a say in their governments in democracies, but not in autocracies.

Democracy vs. Autocracy Today, one of Africa's more stable democracies is South Africa. South Africa is a parliamentary democracy, in which parliament chooses the head of government and a president is the symbolic head of state.

After the end of apartheid, free elections produced fairly stable governments in South Africa. The nation's limited government had a good record of respecting human rights, such as freedom of speech. However, critics of the government have accused it of corruption.

▲ Omar Hassan al-Bashir is the dictator of Sudan.

Some other African nations have democratic governments as well. For example, both Kenya and Nigeria have presidential democracies, so a directly elected president heads the government. Yet **corruption**, or the use of power for personal gain, has become widespread in Kenya and Nigeria. In some African democracies, limits on freedom of expression or unfair election practices limit citizens' power.

Some African governments are autocracies. In these cases, dictators rule in a one-party system with no limits on government power. For example, in the small, oil-rich country of Equatorial Guinea, the president has almost total control over the entire political system. Although Equatorial Guinea does have a constitution that allows opposition parties, corrupt and unfair elections have prevented a change in the presidency since 1979.

Citizen Participation The degree to which Africans can participate in and influence the political process varies by government. Autocracies severely limit citizen participation, and criticism of the government can be dangerous. But in democracies such as South Africa, citizens have the opportunity to participate in the political process by voting. They can also influence government decisions or policies by joining political parties or holding protests.

However, in weak democracies like Kenya and Nigeria, elections can be manipulated in favor of a certain candidate or against others. Violence has erupted during elections, as extremists or members of warring ethnic groups attempt to influence voters. Media outlets are often closely monitored by the government, and journalists can face punishment for criticizing the government.

☑ READING CHECK **Compare and Contrast** How are the governments of South Africa and Equatorial Guinea different?

Analyze Images
These South Africans are protesting against the government of their province. They support one party, but that government is run by another. **Identify Implied Main Ideas** How are protests a form of citizen participation in government?

How Do African Economies Work?

As you have read in previous topics, there are three types of economic systems: traditional, command, and market. These systems determine how people make and distribute goods and services in an economy.

Mixed Economies All African countries have mixed economies that include some features of market economies and command economies. Therefore, consumers and producers make economic decisions, and the government does, too. In some remote, rural parts of Africa, economic decisions are made based on **custom** in traditional economies.

Resource-Rich Africa Natural resources continue to play an all-important role in African economies. Africa is a resource-rich continent.

South Africa is a major source of uranium, as well as precious stones and metals like diamonds, gold, and platinum. Oil reserves are located in several countries, including Algeria, Libya, Nigeria, Gabon, Angola, Chad, and Cameroon. Zambia is a major copper producer.

African countries with rich soils produce large amounts of crops for export. Cacao from the Ivory Coast is used to make chocolate. Ethiopia and Kenya harvest and sell coffee for worldwide consumption.

☑ READING CHECK **Summarize** What kind of economic system do all African countries have?

Trade in Africa

In general, African countries have grown to depend on just a few major products for export. When prices of these goods fall on global markets, African economies suffer. As a result, many countries are looking for ways to move away from this dependence.

Specialization and Changing Economies Countries benefit when they specialize, or focus on making the products that they are best at making. Specialization encourages trade. For example, Nigeria has very large oil and natural gas reserves. Therefore, Nigeria trades its oil and gas with other countries to buy goods it does not produce enough of, such as rice. In fact, over 90 percent of the money Nigeria makes from exports comes from oil and natural gas production.

In recent decades, many countries have been trying to specialize in new activities, including the service sector. Kenya has had some success developing services such as **call centers**. These are businesses that have groups of workers who provide customer service by phone. Ghana, South Africa, and Mauritius also offer services to foreign companies. Additionally, tourism is slowly growing in Africa. The number of foreign tourists visiting Africa is predicted to double by 2030.

Analyze Images A young woman picks coffee in Ethiopia. **Identify Supporting Details** How are agricultural exports an example of the use of natural resources?

Academic Vocabulary
custom • *n.*, usual practice, especially of a group

Countries' environments can limit their ability to specialize and trade. For example, a country in the Sahara and Sahel such as Chad cannot export crops that depend on **intensive** use of water. Countries in savanna and rainforest ecosystems, such as Kenya, Ethiopia, Tanzania, and the Ivory Coast, are able to specialize in coffee and cacao production.

Trade Barriers As in other regions, African nations must deal with trade barriers. Tariffs, quotas, and embargoes can stand in the way of trade. Tariffs are fees that raise the cost of imports, while quotas limit imports by quantity, and embargoes block imports.

A key ingredient for trade is currency exchange. This allows people to buy goods from another country in their currency, and the company producing the goods to be paid in its currency. Since currency exchange can add to the cost of traded goods, it can be a barrier to trade.

To minimize these currency exchange costs, several West and Central African countries share a common currency called the **CFA franc**. This currency is linked to the euro, the currency of several European countries. These European countries remain West and Central Africa's main trade partners. The CFA franc also eases trade among member countries.

☑ READING CHECK **Identify Cause and Effect** How does the CFA franc remove a trade barrier within West and Central Africa?

Comparing Three Economies

Africa's economies vary widely. A comparison of Kenya, Nigeria, and South Africa shows how different factors affect economic development.

Natural Resources Kenya, Nigeria, and South Africa have different types and quantities of natural resources. These resources contribute to economic development.

Kenya's rich soils are good for farming. As you have learned, Nigeria has substantial supplies of oil, and oil is its leading export. South Africa has enormous mineral wealth. It exports gold, diamonds, chrome, platinum, and many other metal ores and other minerals.

Analyze Images A road construction crew builds a highway near Accra, Ghana. **Draw Conclusions** How does improving infrastructure with projects like this one help a country's economy?

World Oil Prices and Nigeria's Economy

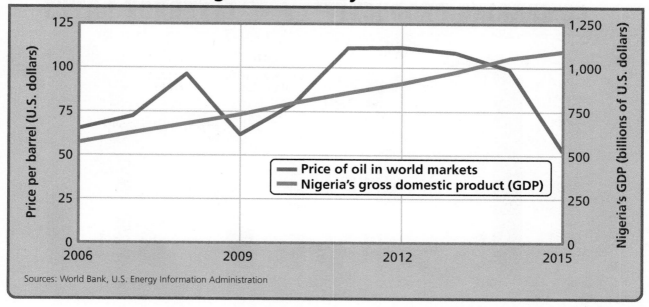

Sources: World Bank, U.S. Energy Information Administration

Capital Investment and Entrepreneurship Investment in productive capital, or the means of production, is another source of economic development. Productive capital can include machinery, factories, offices, and computers.

According to the World Bank, capital investment in 2014 totaled $301 per person in Kenya, $513 per person in Nigeria, and $1,294 per person in South Africa. The greater the investment in capital, the more productive an economy will be, and the higher its average standard of living.

Entrepreneurship, or the ability to start and grow companies, also affects economic success. According to a global comparison, it is much easier to start a company in South Africa than in Kenya or Nigeria.

Literacy Rates Literacy rates are a reflection of investment in human capital. One aspect of human capital is the quality of a country's educational system.

The literacy rate for adults in Kenya is 78 percent. In Nigeria, it is 60 percent, indicating a weaker educational system. In South Africa, the rate is 94 percent, reflecting a relatively strong educational system. Investment in human capital, including education, makes people more productive and allows them to earn a higher standard of living.

Effect on Standard of Living Gross domestic product (GDP) per capita is the value of goods and services produced in a country in a given year, divided by the country's population. GDP per capita is one way to measure a country's standard of living.

In 2015, GDP per capita was $3,083 in Kenya, $5,992 in Nigeria, and $13,278 in South Africa. This suggests that Nigeria's and South Africa's rich natural resources and capital investment result in higher standards of living.

Analyze Graphs Oil prices changed greatly from 2006 to 2015. **Synthesize Visual Information** How did changes in Nigeria's GDP compare to changes in oil prices over this time?

 INTERACTIVE

Literacy Rates in West and Central Africa

Quest **CONNECTIONS**

How might government instability and corruption result in the loss of revenue from natural resources? Record your findings in your 📓 Active Journal.

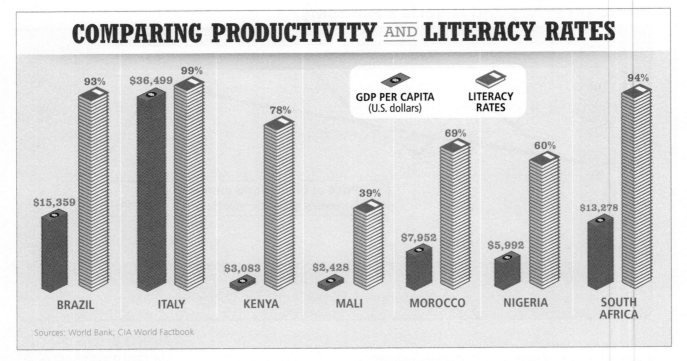

COMPARING PRODUCTIVITY AND LITERACY RATES

GDP PER CAPITA (U.S. dollars) | LITERACY RATES

BRAZIL: $15,359 — 93%
ITALY: $36,499 — 99%
KENYA: $3,083 — 78%
MALI: $2,428 — 39%
MOROCCO: $7,952 — 69%
NIGERIA: $5,992 — 60%
SOUTH AFRICA: $13,278 — 94%

Sources: World Bank; CIA World Factbook

Analyze Charts This chart shows the literacy rates and GDP per capita in seven countries. **Identify Main Ideas** From an examination of these seven countries, what connections can you see between literacy rates and GDP? Give examples.

South Africa's abundant resources, its investment in education, and its openness to entrepreneurship help explain its high GDP per capita. Yet, even without significant natural resources or strong entrepreneurship, Kenya has a little more than half of Nigeria's GDP per capita. Kenya's GDP per capita is also higher than that of neighboring countries such as Tanzania ($2,589) or Uganda ($1,825). In this case, Kenya's investment in education probably results in a higher standard of living than it would otherwise have.

READING CHECK Draw Conclusions What does Kenya's GDP, in comparison with neighboring countries, suggest about the roles of natural resources and human capital in African economies?

☑ Lesson Check

Practice Vocabulary

1. How can **corruption** affect government?

2. How might the **CFA franc** help the economies of the countries in West and Central Africa that use it?

Critical Thinking and Writing

3. **Draw Conclusions** What are the advantages and disadvantages of an economic focus on natural resources for many African nations?

4. **Compare** Using the Country Databank, compare South Africa's GDP to that of other large countries in Africa and suggest reasons for the difference.

5. **Writing Workshop: Include Graphics** In your 📓 Active Journal, add information from this lesson about the role of natural resources in many African economies. Think about how you can present some of this information to your reader in graphic form, such as a table or graph.

Nigeria's Resource Use

Many African economies depend on exports of natural resources. In most cases, a country exports a natural resource that it has in abundance and that it can easily access. African countries often specialize in a few exports that other countries need, and then import what they cannot or do not produce enough of themselves.

▶ An oil tanker docked in Lagos, Nigeria

Comparative Advantage and Trade

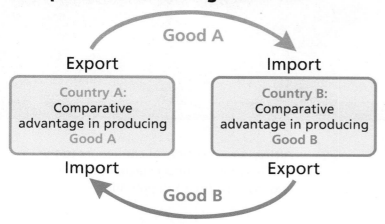

Good A

Export → Import

Country A: Comparative advantage in producing Good A

Country B: Comparative advantage in producing Good B

Import ← Export

Good B

Analyzing Geographic Sources

Examine the diagram and the two pie charts. Consider how the pie graphs help explain the ideas in the diagram using the example of the Nigerian economy.

1. **Analyze Diagrams** What does the diagram show about the reasons for trade?

2. **Compare and Contrast** How do the top three named Nigerian exports and the top three named Nigerian imports compare?

3. **Synthesize Visual Information** Refer to both the diagram and the graphs. What do they suggest about Nigeria's ability to make more advanced products from its natural resources?

Nigeria's Exports and Imports

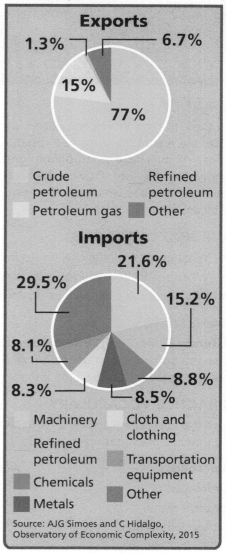

Exports

1.3% 6.7%
15%
77%

Crude petroleum   Refined petroleum
Petroleum gas   Other

Imports

21.6%
29.5%
15.2%
8.1%
8.8%
8.3%
8.5%

Machinery   Cloth and clothing
Refined petroleum   Transportation equipment
Chemicals   Other
Metals

Source: AJG Simoes and C Hidalgo, Observatory of Economic Complexity, 2015

LESSON 7
Challenges Facing Africa

GET READY TO READ

START UP

In some parts of Africa, the desert is slowly taking over the rest of the land. As a result, people in those regions have to struggle to get water, as shown in the photo. Preview the headings in this lesson to see what other kinds of challenges Africans face.

GUIDING QUESTIONS

- What environmental challenges face Africa?
- What political challenges exist in Africa?
- What economic challenges do Africans face?

TAKE NOTES

Literacy Skills: Analyze Text Structure
Use the graphic organizer in your ▱ Active Journal to take notes as you read the lesson.

PRACTICE VOCABULARY

Use the vocabulary activity in your ▱ Active Journal to practice the vocabulary words.

Vocabulary

deforestation

desertification

nongovernmental
  organization (NGO)

**Academic
Vocabulary**

nutrient

collaborate

Africa faces a variety of challenges in the 2000s. Africans must overcome these obstacles to reach their full potential.

Environmental Challenges

Africa struggles with serious environmental issues. Access to clean water is limited, and water-borne diseases are common. In recent years, a loss of trees has led to drier soils and a growth in desert. Frequent droughts only make survival more difficult in several countries.

Clean Water Most Africans do not have access to proper toilets or waste disposal systems. As a result, human waste often ends up in rivers and in groundwater that people use for drinking. Water-borne diseases such as cholera—an infection that causes acute dehydration and can kill someone within hours—then spread quickly. The World Health Organization estimates that 115 Africans die every hour from water pollution.

Only about one-sixth of Africans have access to a clean water supply for drinking, cooking, and hygiene. Given its scarcity, water is often stored in people's homes, where it can become contaminated and attract mosquitoes. These mosquitoes are common carriers of other diseases, including malaria.

The lack of clean water also makes it difficult to irrigate crops safely. This threatens both Africans' food supply and African efforts to export crops to other countries.

Deforestation and Desertification **Deforestation** is the loss of forest cover that results from so many trees being removed that trees cannot grow back. In a tropical rainforest, plants hold most of the environment's **nutrients**. When too many trees are cleared, nutrients in the soil wash away with rain. The poor soils that remain cannot support tree growth. Once a tropical rainforest is lost, it may be lost forever.

Traditionally, farmers cut down and burned small plots in the forest. They would farm these plots until soil nutrients were lost, then move on to a different region while the forest in the plot they had just farmed slowly grew back. Over the past 100 years, however, Africa's population has grown so much that farmers have been cutting down too many trees for the forests to recover. The Ivory Coast has a very high rate of deforestation. More than 90 percent of its forests have been cleared by the timber industry since the late 1900s. Deforestation is also a serious problem in the Democratic Republic of the Congo and in Burundi.

Desertification, the change from arable land to desert, is a major problem in the Sahel, a region just south of the Sahara. Here, livestock herders have grown in numbers.

GEOGRAPHY **SKILLS**

The UN and other groups have worked to improve the quality of drinking water in Africa.

1. **Interaction** Using the Africa: Political map in the Regional Atlas, identify the countries where people have the least access to improved water.

2. **Compare and Contrast** Compare water quality in Central Africa to that in the rest of the continent.

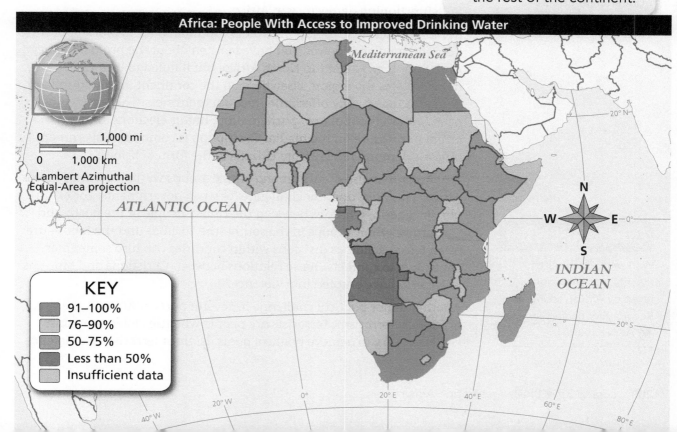

Africa: People With Access to Improved Drinking Water

0   1,000 mi

0   1,000 km

Lambert Azimuthal Equal-Area projection

Mediterranean Sea

ATLANTIC OCEAN

INDIAN OCEAN

N / W • E—0° / S

KEY
- 91–100%
- 76–90%
- 50–75%
- Less than 50%
- Insufficient data

Analyze Images The dry environment in many parts of Africa makes it necessary for farmers to work hard to find usable water. A well dug here in the Sahel of Sudan makes it possible to grow vegetables. **Understand Effects** Name three challenges that drought can cause.

Too many livestock now graze the fragile grasslands, and people have also chopped down trees for firewood. These actions, combined with drought, have caused parts of the Sahel to dry out and become desert. This leaves less land for farming and grazing and increases the risk of famine.

Drought Climate change may contribute to the increasing drought that Africans in the Sahel and other regions are experiencing. Between 2010 and 2012, for example, almost 260,000 people in Somalia died from drought and the resulting famine. Half of those who died were children under the age of five.

For many, drought makes it much harder to make a living. This difficulty causes other problems as well, as groups then often clash over control of territory. Livestock herders migrate from dry areas to agricultural regions, where farmers often resent their presence. In some regions, including Somalia and the Darfur region of Sudan, tensions among herders, farmers, and governments have led to long and bloody conflicts, which have driven millions of refugees from their homes.

✔ **READING CHECK Identify Cause and Effect** How and where does desertification occur?

Political Challenges

Many African countries became more democratic in the 1990s. But there are very few full democracies in Africa—governments in which civil liberties are respected and checks and balances on political power are in place. Mauritius, an island nation, is often considered the only fully functioning democracy in Africa.

In many other African nations, rulers continue to try to block opposition and hold onto power. You have learned about the pro-democracy Arab Spring movement in North Africa, but it failed to bring stable democracy to the region. Elsewhere on the continent, many so-called democracies actually offer little freedom or fairness. These typically have low levels of political participation, unfair elections, and government pressure on the media. Corruption is common. Government officials demand money from citizens in the form of bribes.

Ethnic conflict also occurs among ethnic groups within countries across Africa. This adds another challenge for weak governments. For example, in Nigeria, relations between the Hausa people of the north and the largest ethnic groups in the south—the Yorubas and the Igbos—are often tense. Religious divisions within countries can also sometimes contribute to conflicts. Tense relations between Christians and Muslims in Nigeria have erupted into violence.

Another major political challenge in several parts of Africa is the rise of Islamist terrorism. Terrorists are people who use violence against civilians to try to achieve political goals. Islamist terrorists use violence

Quick Activity

Work with a partner to identify four challenges faced by African countries. Record your findings in your Active Journal.

seeking to impose a harsh version of Islam. Most Muslims in Africa and elsewhere reject Islamist terrorists and their version of Islam.

In northern Nigeria, Islamist terrorists called Boko Haram have killed thousands and damaged the region's economy. An Islamist terrorist group called al-Shabaab has fought a civil war against Somalia's weak government for more than 10 years. Al Qaeda and ISIS, Islamist terrorist groups based in Southwest Asia, have waged attacks in Mali, Algeria, Tunisia, Libya, and Egypt.

Countries in the region have formed different organizations to **collaborate** in solving common problems. The African Union (AU) is the most important of these organizations. Recently, it has sent peacekeeping troops to Sudan and Somalia.

Academic Vocabulary
collaborate • *v.*, work together

☑ READING CHECK **Summarize** What problems do African governments face today?

What Holds Africa's Economies Back?

Africa is the poorest of the world's major regions. Many countries lack the equipment and roads to produce valuable goods and get them to markets. Many Africans do not receive proper education or decent health care. As a result, they are not as productive at work as they could be. Political conflicts have also hurt African economies.

Infrastructure Most African nations do not have machinery or energy supplies necessary for large-scale production of goods. For countries without large reserves of natural resources like oil, this lack of equipment and energy can be an obstacle to economic growth.

Africa also faces the challenge of a poor transportation infrastructure. Roads are not sufficient for getting goods to market.

▼ An African Union peacekeeper from Uganda stands outside the shelter of a Somali family who were displaced by fighting in their home country.

▲ The rainy season in parts of Africa turns unpaved roads into muddy paths that make travel difficult.

Almost half of all Africans live in areas without tarred or paved roads. Roads that are in good condition are often crowded with traffic, which hurts economies due to lost productivity. Studies estimate that clogged roads in Cairo cause a loss of $8 billion a year for Egypt.

However, foreign investors have begun to invest more in African industry. In 2014, foreign investment in Africa totaled $80 billion. While countries rich in natural resources received most of that money, more and more foreign dollars are going toward manufacturing and service industries.

Health Issues Of all the regions in the world, southern and eastern Africa have been hit hardest by AIDS, the often-deadly disease caused by the HIV virus. AIDS attacks the immune system and has killed up to 1.5 million people in Africa per year. Three out of every four HIV-related deaths in the world are in Africa.

Many countries are too poor to properly treat the sick. Also, when so many people get sick or die, work that is necessary to the economy does not get done. This holds back development and hurts everybody.

Foreign governments and **nongovernmental organizations (NGOs)**, groups, usually nonprofit, that operate with private funding, often help to deal with disease and poverty. The United Nations also provides aid to the region. Its World Food Programme distributes food to those in need. For example, when Somalia was hit by famine in 2011, the Programme provided aid to 1.5 million people.

Instability The lack of stable governments is a major obstacle to development in Africa. Also, conflicts harm economies as well as people. Wars destroy homes and businesses, force people to become refugees, and make it difficult to develop the economy.

BIOGRAPHY
5 Things to Know About

ELLEN JOHNSON SIRLEAF
Liberian leader (born 1938)

- Sirleaf's father was the first Liberian legislator not descended from African American colonizers.

- After studying economics and business administration in the United States, she returned to Liberia to work in government.

- When she was critical of other government officials, she was imprisoned and then exiled.

- She returned to Liberia and became Africa's first elected female head of state when she was elected president in 2005.

- She won the Nobel Peace Prize for resolving conflicts and promoting peace in Liberia in 2011.

Assessment How did Ellen Johnson Sirleaf make history in both Liberia and all of Africa?

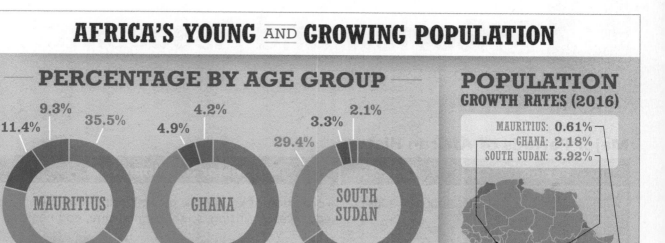

AFRICA'S YOUNG AND GROWING POPULATION

PERCENTAGE BY AGE GROUP

MAURITIUS
9.3%
11.4%
35.5%
43.9%

GHANA
4.9%
4.2%
34%
56.9%

SOUTH SUDAN
3.3%
2.1%
29.4%
65.2%

Under 25   25–54   55–64   65 and older

Source: CIA World Factbook

POPULATION GROWTH RATES (2016)

MAURITIUS: 0.61%
GHANA: 2.18%
SOUTH SUDAN: 3.92%

Less than 1%
1–2.5%
More than 2.5%

Even in Africa's more stable democracies, real economic problems persist. For example, while South Africa has one of the continent's strongest economies, many of its people have limited economic opportunities. The country has a history of unrest among workers, many of whom lack the education needed for good jobs. Big companies dominate some sectors and discourage new businesses from starting. In 2016, the unemployment rate in South Africa was almost 27 percent. Most unemployed persons were under the age of 35.

READING CHECK Identify Main Ideas What are four major obstacles to economic growth in Africa?

Analyze Graphs High birth rates in some countries cause rapid population growth. Economic growth can struggle to keep up, and poverty persists. **Draw Conclusions** What is the connection between high population growth rates and the percentage of people under the age of 25?

☑ Lesson Check

Practice Vocabulary

1. How can **deforestation** lead to **desertification**?

Critical Thinking and Writing

2. **Draw Conclusions** How can drought spark political conflicts in Africa?

3. **Identify Main Ideas** What is the state of democracy in Africa today?

4. **Identify Causes and Effects** Why is public health in Africa an economic issue?

5. **Writing Workshop: Write an Introduction** Add details, such as those about the value of natural resources to governments and economies, to your ▱ Active Journal. Then revisit your main ideas and decide how you want to introduce your essay. Remember that your introduction should draw readers into your topic and should include your thesis statement.

☑ Review and Assessment

VISUAL REVIEW

Major Periods of African History

Period	Time	Major Developments
Ancient Egypt and Kush	3000 BCE–300s CE	Formation of kingdoms; pyramids and mummies; advances in writing, sciences, medicine, engineering
Kingdoms and empires	300s CE–1400s	West African trading empires: gold, salt trade, Islam; East African kingdoms: trade with Arabia and India, Christianity and Islam
European influence	1400s–1900s	Slave trade; European colonial rule; end of slave trade
Independence	1910–2000s	Unstable governments; ethnic conflict; poverty; apartheid and its end; move toward democracy

COMPARISON OF THREE AFRICAN ECONOMIES

Kenya
- Few natural resources
- Capital investment: $301/person
- Literacy rate: 78%
- GDP per capita: $3,083

Nigeria
- Rich oil resources
- Capital investment: $513/person
- Literacy rate: 60%
- GDP per capita: $5,992

South Africa
- Rich in mineral resources
- Capital investment: $1,294/person
- Literacy rate: 94%
- GDP per capita: $13,278

READING REVIEW

Use the Take Notes and Practice Vocabulary activities in your 📓 Active Journal to review the topic.

👆 **INTERACTIVE**

Practice vocabulary using the Topic Mini-Games.

Quest FINDINGS

Discuss Nigeria's Oil Industry

Prepare for your discussion in your 📓 Active Journal.

ASSESSMENT

Vocabulary and Key Ideas

1. **Identify Supporting Details** How do **artifacts** teach us about prehistory?

2. **Check Understanding** How did **pastoralism** represent a change for **hunter-gatherers**?

3. **Trace** Explain how food surpluses in ancient Egypt led to the formation of a class of **artisans** and merchants.

4. **Describe** How do **nongovernmental organizations** help during crises in Africa?

5. **Explain** Why do many Africans not have access to clean water?

6. **Check Understanding** How are the Sahara and the Sahel similar and different?

7. **Identify Main Ideas** Why was the discovery of the skeleton of "Lucy" so important?

Critical Thinking and Writing

8. **Understand Effects** How did the spread of Islam affect Africa?

9. **Draw Conclusions** Why do you think Pan-Africanism appealed to so many Africans around the world?

10. **Infer** Why are many African countries looking for ways to diversify their economies?

11. **Draw Conclusions** How do the types of governments in Africa, shown in the Country Databank, reflect Africa's political challenges?

12. **Revisit the Essential Question:** Who deserves to benefit from a country's resources?

13. **Writer's Workshop: Write an Informative Essay** Following instructions in your 📕 Active Journal, write your informative essay. Include information you learned in the last two lessons and make sure that it has a clear structure and details that support your thesis about who has benefited from Africa's resources.

Analyze Primary Sources

14. What former South African policy was Nelson Mandela describing in this quote?
    A. colonialism
    B. apartheid
    C. industrialization
    D. slavery

"We are extricating [removing] ourselves from a system that insulted our common humanity by dividing us from one another on the basis of race and setting us against each other as oppressed and oppressor. That system committed a crime against humanity."

—South African President Nelson Mandela, 1998

Analyze Maps

Use the map to answer the following questions.

15. Which letter represents the river that flows north and once flooded its banks, creating fertile land in Egypt?

16. Which letter represents a country rich in oil resources?

17. Which letter represents Africa's newest country?

18. What is the name of the country labeled A?

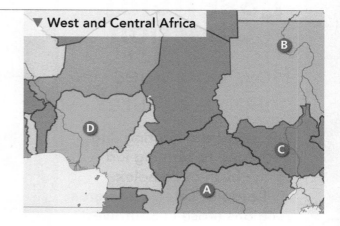

▼ West and Central Africa

GO ONLINE
to access your
digital course

▶ VIDEO

◀)) AUDIO

📖 ETEXT

👆 INTERACTIVE

✏️ WRITING

🎮 GAMES

📄 WORKSHEET

☑️ ASSESSMENT

Go back some 12,000 years,

to the region of SOUTHWEST ASIA. Why? You could witness the dawn of civilization. People in this region began to settle down as farmers around 12,000 years ago. They created the world's first civilizations.

Explore The Essential Question

How do values shape a culture?

The shift from hunting and gathering to farming led to the birth of complex civilizations. Later, three great religions arose in Southwest Asia that have helped shape the modern world.

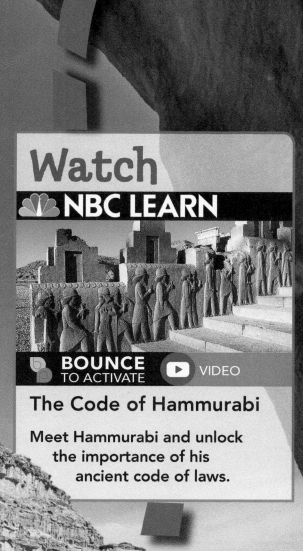

Watch

NBC LEARN

BOUNCE TO ACTIVATE ▶ VIDEO

The Code of Hammurabi

Meet Hammurabi and unlock the importance of his ancient code of laws.

Read

about a region where the first complex civilizations developed and then influenced other parts of the world over time.

◄ One of the remaining structures of Petra, the ancient capital of the Nabataean Kingdom, located in present-day Jordan

Southwest Asia: Physical

A CHALLENGING LANDSCAPE

The civilizations and religions of Southwest Asia developed in a region of vast deserts, high mountains, and fertile plains.

Learn more about Southwest Asia by making your own map in your Active Journal.

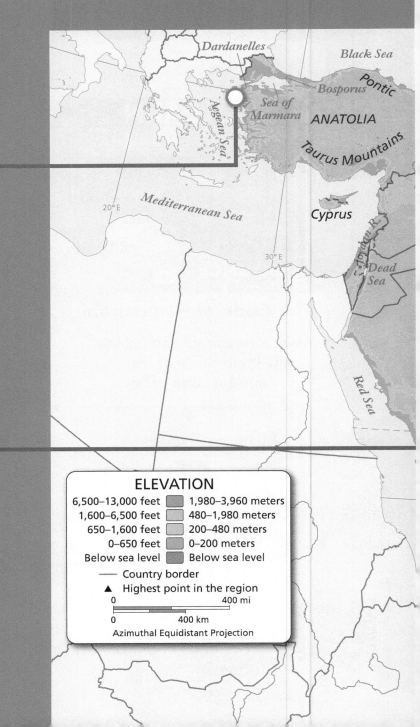

INTERACTIVE

Topic Map

A Key Trade Route

The Bosporus, Sea of Marmara, Dardanelles, and Aegean Sea form a water route linking the Black Sea and the Mediterranean Sea. This string of water routes forms the traditional boundary between Europe and Asia. It has been strategically important since ancient times.

A Desert Peninsula

The Arabian Peninsula is a region of vast deserts, from the Syrian Desert in the north to the Rub' al-Khali in the south. On this vast, dry peninsula, no permanent rivers flow to the sea.

ELEVATION

6,500–13,000 feet	1,980–3,960 meters
1,600–6,500 feet	480–1,980 meters
650–1,600 feet	200–480 meters
0–650 feet	0–200 meters
Below sea level	Below sea level

— Country border
▲ Highest point in the region

0   400 mi
0   400 km
Azimuthal Equidistant Projection

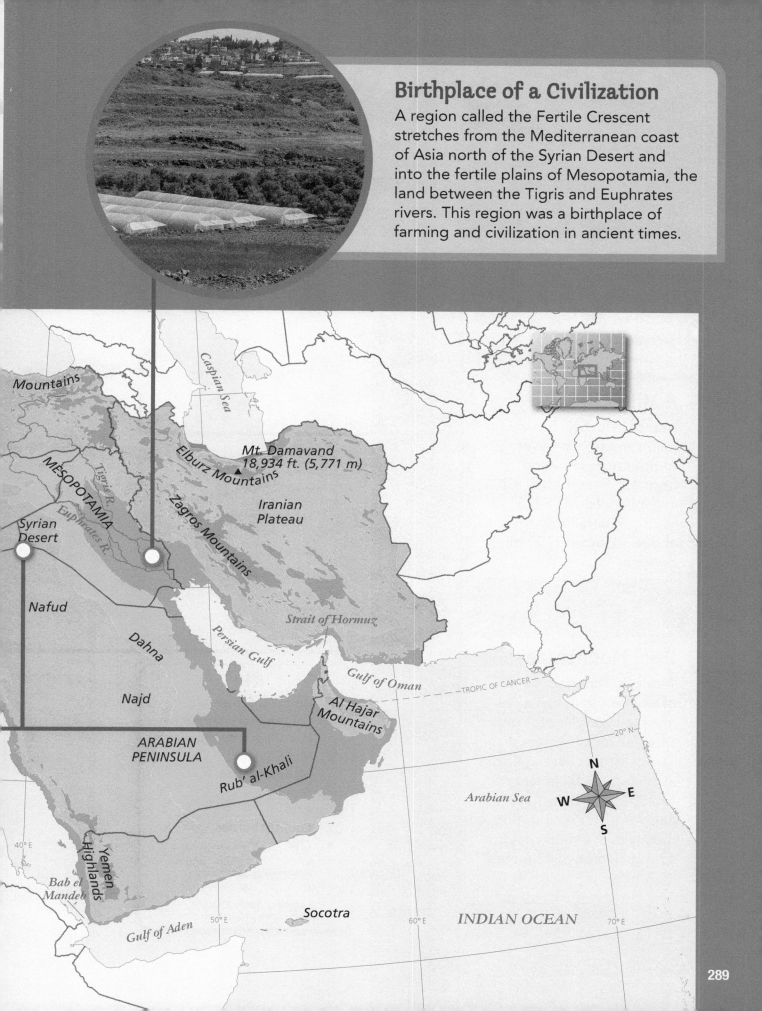

Birthplace of a Civilization

A region called the Fertile Crescent stretches from the Mediterranean coast of Asia north of the Syrian Desert and into the fertile plains of Mesopotamia, the land between the Tigris and Euphrates rivers. This region was a birthplace of farming and civilization in ancient times.

Mountains

Caspian Sea

Mt. Damavand
18,934 ft. (5,771 m)

Elburz Mountains

MESOPOTAMIA

Tigris R.

Euphrates R.

Zagros Mountains

Iranian Plateau

Syrian Desert

Nafud

Strait of Hormuz

Persian Gulf

Dahna

Gulf of Oman

TROPIC OF CANCER

Najd

Al Hajar Mountains

ARABIAN PENINSULA

Rub' al-Khali

20° N

Arabian Sea

N
W   E
S

40° E

Yemen Highlands

Bab el Mandeb

Socotra

INDIAN OCEAN

Gulf of Aden

50° E

60° E

70° E

Southwest Asia: Climate

A MOIST NORTH AND DRY SOUTH

While deserts cover the Arabian Peninsula in the south, mountains and valleys in the north get rain and snow, mainly in winter and spring.

 INTERACTIVE

Topic Map

A Mild Climate

Istanbul, Turkey, has a mild climate, with average temperatures ranging from 42° F (around 6° C) in January to 74° F (23° C) in July. Rainfall averages about 30 inches (750 mm) per year.

Cool Mountains

Tabriz, in the mountains of western Iran, has a much cooler climate, with snowfall most winters. Temperatures average from 30° F (−1° C) in January to 75° F (24° C) in July and August. Precipitation, mostly in the winter and spring, averages 13 inches (318 mm).

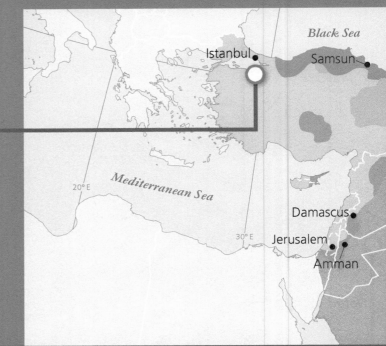

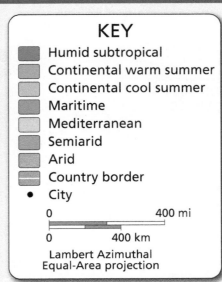

KEY

- Humid subtropical
- Continental warm summer
- Continental cool summer
- Maritime
- Mediterranean
- Semiarid
- Arid
- Country border
- • City

```
0                    400 mi
0          400 km
```

Lambert Azimuthal
Equal-Area projection

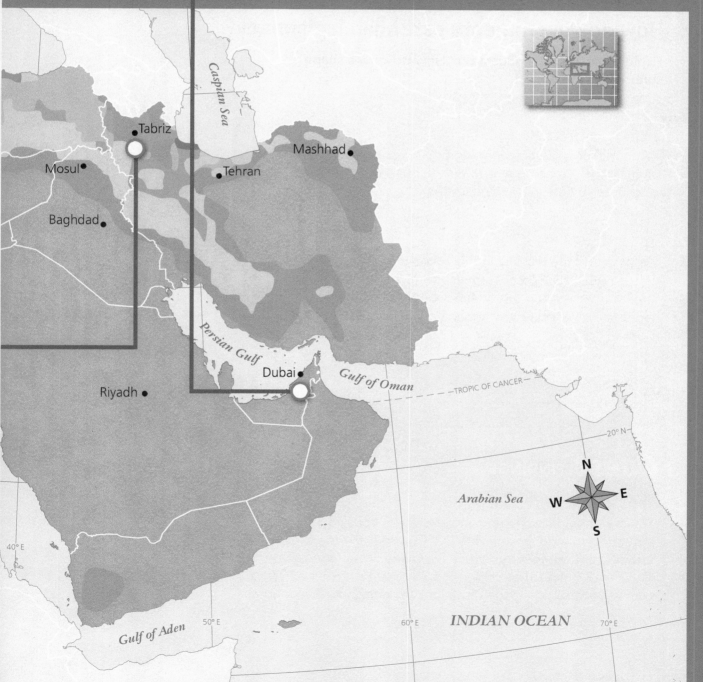

Hot, Dry Deserts

In this desert near Dubai, the coolest month is January, with an average temperature of 66° F (19° C). Average temperatures in July are 93° F (34° C), with highs averaging over 104° F (40° C). Rainfall averages just 4 inches (87 mm) per year.

Caspian Sea

Tabriz

Mashhad

Mosul

Tehran

Baghdad

Riyadh

Persian Gulf

Dubai

Gulf of Oman

TROPIC OF CANCER

20° N

Arabian Sea

N

W   E

S

Gulf of Aden

40° E

50° E

60° E

INDIAN OCEAN

70° E

Quest
Document-Based Writing Inquiry

Establishing a Government

▼ Stele of Naram-Sin, ruler of the Akkadian empire

Quest KICK OFF

You are writing a report to a leader who is seeking to form a new government for a country in Southwest Asia at the end of a civil war there. What issues do you need to consider when making recommendations?

How do governments establish legitimacy?

Explore the Essential Question "How do values shape a culture?" in this Quest.

1 Ask Questions
What makes a government legitimate, or seen as having a right to govern? Write your own questions in your 📓 Active Journal.

2 Investigate
As you read the lessons in this topic, look for **Quest CONNECTIONS** that investigate ways past governments in the region have established their legitimacy. Respond to them in your 📓 Active Journal.

3 Examine Primary Sources
Explore the sources provided for this Quest and take notes in your 📓 Active Journal.

Quest FINDINGS

4 Write Your Report
You are an expert advising the leaders of your country about how to form a government there. Consider the decisions others creating governments have made. What conditions did they face? What other choices could have been made? Write your report following the directions in your 📓 Active Journal.

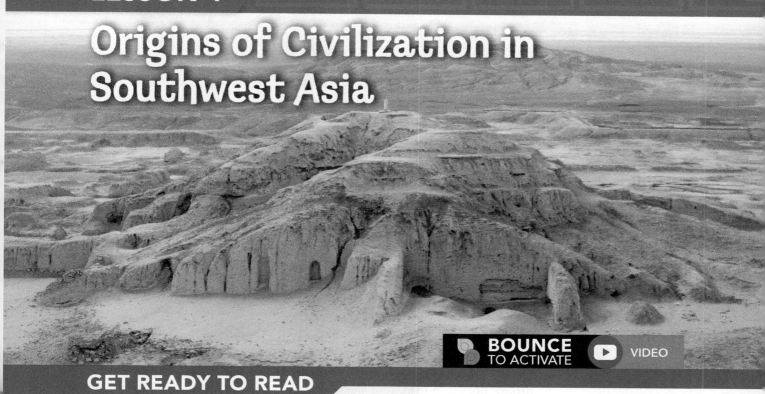

LESSON 1
Origins of Civilization in Southwest Asia

BOUNCE TO ACTIVATE ▶ VIDEO

GET READY TO READ

START UP
Look at this image of the ruins of the ancient city of Uruk in modern-day Iraq. What changes might have enabled hunters and gatherers to settle down and build cities like Uruk?

GUIDING QUESTIONS
- How did people begin farming in Southwest Asia?
- How did the farmers of Mesopotamia adapt to their environment?
- What were the key features of Sumer as a civilization?

TAKE NOTES
Literacy Skills: Identify Cause and Effect
Use the graphic organizer in your 📓 Active Journal to take notes as you read the lesson.

PRACTICE VOCABULARY
Use the vocabulary activity in your 📓 Active Journal to practice the vocabulary words.

Vocabulary

		Academic Vocabulary
domesticate	irrigate	
Neolithic	city-state	fertile
Revolution	polytheism	distinct
Mesopotamia	cuneiform	

Southwest Asia is the birthplace of the world's oldest civilization. Ideas and ways of living that developed here have helped shape modern cultures around the world.

The First Farmers
Around 12,000 years ago, hunters and gatherers in Southwest Asia began to settle in villages as Earth's climate became milder. As these nomads settled down, they began to notice that seeds from the crops they had gathered grew into plants they could eat. They planted those seeds and later harvested the crop. In this way, they learned how to farm.

These early farmers also learned how to capture animals, raise them in herds, and domesticate them. To **domesticate** is to train the growth of a plant or behavior of an animal in ways useful to humans. The period when the introduction of agriculture led people to move from nomadic to settled life is the **Neolithic Revolution**, or Agricultural Revolution. The development of agriculture, or farming, was a major turning point in human history.

Analyze Images The people of Çatalhöyük lived in rectangular houses made of mud brick. People entered the houses from the roof, using ladders. **Draw Conclusions** How might living close together in this way benefit the people of Çatalhöyük?

Southwest Asia was probably the first place where the Neolithic Revolution occurred. Most likely it happened in the hilly northern Fertile Crescent, in what are now northern Syria, central and eastern Turkey, northern Iraq, and western Iran.

The village of Çatalhöyük (chah TAHL huh yook), in what is today southern Turkey, was one of the largest Neolithic farming communities. It emerged around 7000 BCE. Çatalhöyük covered 34 acres and had a population of between 3,000 and 8,000 people.

✓ **READING CHECK** **Identify Cause and Effect** How did people's lives change when they learned to farm?

Farming in Mesopotamia

The Fertile Crescent was one of several places where early human farmers flourished. Its soil is rich and **fertile**. Some of the most productive land in the region is in Mesopotamia. **Mesopotamia** is the region that lies between the Tigris and Euphrates rivers.

Academic Vocabulary
fertile • *adj.,* capable of producing abundant crops

Mesopotamia's Rivers The Tigris and Euphrates rivers begin in the mountains of southeastern Turkey and flow south and east, through present-day Syria and Iraq. For many years, the rivers have carried fine, fertile material called silt down from the mountains. Each spring, the rivers flood their banks, spreading floodwaters and silt across the plain. When the floods end, they leave behind a fresh layer of moist, fertile earth.

Sumerian Farmers The rivers' runoff helped create rich soil that was good for growing grains and vegetables. As a result, thousands of years ago, the world's first civilization began to form here. This was the civilization of Sumer (SOO mur). In addition to crops, the Sumerians raised sheep, goats, and cattle.

Mesopotamia's geography also challenged Sumerian farmers. The heavy spring floodwaters could wash away crops and even villages.

Quick Activity

What was the social structure like in Sumer? Who ranked higher than whom? Explore these questions in your 📓 Active Journal.

During the summer, the hot sun baked the ground rock hard. With little rain for months, plants would die.

Sumerians turned to technology to make Mesopotamia into productive farmland. Technology is the use of tools and structures to do work.

Sumerians **irrigated**, or supplied water to, their crops by digging many miles of canals. They used the canals to water their crops during the hot, dry summer. They also developed a new way of planting that made the process faster and easier. They created a plow with a funnel attached in order to funnel seeds into the crop rows instead of planting them by hand.

☑ **READING CHECK** **Understand Effects** In what ways did technology make Sumerian civilization possible?

How Was Civilization Born in Sumer?

Better agricultural techniques helped the Sumerians produce more food. With a dependable food supply, the populations of villages began to grow. Soon, farmers grew more food than they needed. Religious and political leaders began to demand a share of that food in the form of taxes. For the first time, some people could specialize in crafts other than farming, as farmers and leaders paid craftspeople, such as tool makers, with food. Around 3400 BCE, cities started to form in southern Mesopotamia.

City-States Develop Uruk was possibly the world's first city. It had a population of more than 40,000 people. Other early cities were Ur, Lagash, and Nippur. Some cities grew large and powerful. They became the world's first city-states. A **city-state** is an independent political unit that includes a city and its surrounding territory. The city-states traded with one another and with lands farther away. They used trade to obtain goods they could not make.

Sumerian Society As Sumerian society grew, a social order with three classes developed. People of each class had **distinct** roles within Sumerian society. The upper class included the ruler, top officials, powerful priests, and wealthy merchants and landowners. Farmers and skilled workers made up the middle class. Slaves belonged to the lowest class.

Like most ancient peoples, the Sumerians practiced **polytheism**, the worship of many gods or deities. Sumerians believed these gods controlled every aspect of life, including rain, wind, and other elements of nature.

INTERACTIVE

Sumerian Civilization

Academic Vocabulary

distinct • *adj.*, recognizably different from something else

GEOGRAPHY **SKILLS**

Mesopotamia was located between the Tigris and Euphrates rivers.

1. **Location** In what part of Mesopotamia was Sumer located?

2. **Draw Conclusions** How did Sumerians likely interact with their environment?

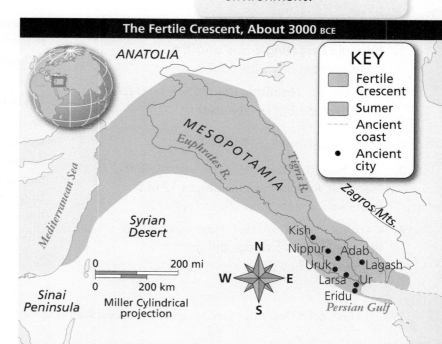

The Fertile Crescent, About 3000 BCE

ANATOLIA

MESOPOTAMIA

Euphrates R.

Tigris R.

Zagros Mts.

Mediterranean Sea

Syrian Desert

Kish

Nippur
Adab
Uruk
Lagash
Larsa
Ur
Eridu

Persian Gulf

Sinai Peninsula

0   200 mi
0   200 km
Miller Cylindrical projection

KEY
- Fertile Crescent
- Sumer
- Ancient coast
- • Ancient city

N / S / E / W

▲ The *Epic of Gilgamesh*, shown here, was written in cuneiform on a clay tablet.

Sumerian Government The first leaders of Sumerian city-states were priests, not kings. In times of war, priests helped choose a man to lead the city-state into battle. After the war was over, this leader was expected to give up his power. But some of these military leaders kept control of the city-states even after war ended. These military leaders became the first kings.

Kings were careful to respect the priests' rights and powers. In turn, priests declared that the gods had sent the king to rule the city.

Some kings collected city laws into a law code, or a written set of laws. The earliest known law code was issued around 2100 BCE by Ur-Nammu (uhr NAHM OO), the king of Ur.

Sumerian Writing Sumerian society gave the world its first system of writing. Sumerians drew pictographs on clay. Pictographs are simple pictures that represent objects. By 3400 BCE, these pictographs had developed into a new writing system called cuneiform. **Cuneiform** is a system of writing using wedge-shaped marks pressed into clay tablets to stand for ideas or sounds.

Cuneiform was originally used to record sales, taxes, and agreements. Later, Sumerians developed written literature. Around 2000 BCE, the long poem known as the *Epic of Gilgamesh* appeared. It is the earliest known literary work.

Other Sumerian Achievements Sumer was one of the first cultures to make bronze by mixing copper and tin. Bronze is a harder metal than copper, so it is better for making tools and weapons. Sumerians also made advances in mathematics and astronomy. Through trade, many Sumerian advances spread to other lands.

☑ READING CHECK Use Evidence What details indicate that Sumer was an advanced civilization?

Did you know?

The stories about Gilgamesh are myths, or made-up tales of gods and heroes. However, some scholars believe that Gilgamesh may have been a real king.

☑ Lesson Check

Practice Vocabulary

1. How did **irrigating** crops spur the development of civilization?

2. How did the **Neolithic Revolution** lead to the development of **city-states**?

Critical Thinking and Writing

3. **Understand Effects** How do you think the Neolithic Revolution that began 12,000 years ago affects your life today?

4. **Compare and Contrast** How was settled life in a Neolithic village different from nomadic life?

5. **Understand Effects** How did living in settlements change the way people thought and interacted with one another?

6. **Cite Evidence** What made the Neolithic Revolution a turning point?

7. **Writing Workshop: Generate Questions to Focus Research** In your 📖 Active Journal, make a list of questions about Sumerian civilization that you might use to guide research for an essay about the values of cultures in Southwest Asia through time.

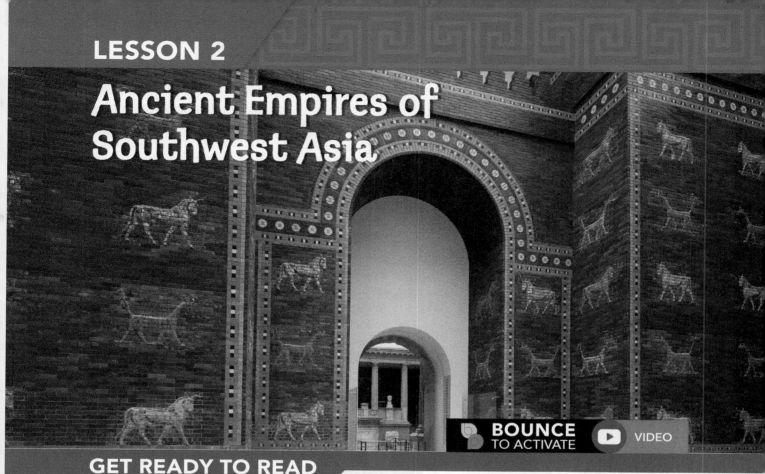

BOUNCE TO ACTIVATE ▶ VIDEO

LESSON 2
Ancient Empires of Southwest Asia

GET READY TO READ

START UP
Look at the structure from ancient Babylon. What does it suggest about the people who built it?

GUIDING QUESTIONS
- What was new and different about Sargon's empire?
- What were the main achievements of the Babylonians, Hittites, and Phoenicians?
- What did the Assyrian, Neo-Babylonian, and Persian empires accomplish?

TAKE NOTES
Literacy Skills: Compare and Contrast
Use the graphic organizer in your 🗐 Active Journal to take notes as you read the lesson.

PRACTICE VOCABULARY
Use the vocabulary activity in your 🗐 Active Journal to practice the vocabulary words.

Vocabulary	Academic Vocabulary
empire	ally
Hammurabi's Code	appoint
navigation	

As the city-states of Sumer grew, they often fought among themselves. In time, strong rulers emerged and conquered the whole region. They created the world's first **empires**—territories containing several countries and ruled by a single government.

The First Known Empire
Years of fighting made Sumerian city-states grow weaker. Their weakness led to the conquest of Sumer.

Conflict in Sumer The fighting between the city-states of Umma and Lagash is one example of the conflict in Sumer. For many years, Umma and Lagash and their **allies** fought to control a fertile region on their shared border.

Around 2450 BCE, armies from Umma and Lagash met in a major battle. Thousands of troops died in the fighting before Lagash won the battle. Lagash soldiers looted and burned Umma. They captured prisoners and sold them as slaves. It took years for Umma to recover from its defeat.

Sargon Builds an Empire While the Sumerian city-states struggled for power, a new society arose in Mesopotamia, northwest of Sumer. Akkadians spoke a different language from the Sumerians and had different customs.

During the 2300s BCE, an Akkadian named Sargon became king of the Sumerian city-state of Kish. He changed the language used by the government to Akkadian. Under Sargon's rule, the Akkadian army conquered other city-states in Sumer and other parts of Mesopotamia, creating the world's first known empire. Sargon placed loyal Akkadians in important government and religious positions. These moves helped him solidify his power. Akkadian troops and traders moved throughout the Fertile Crescent, spreading Akkadian and Sumerian culture.

The End of an Empire To control his large empire, Sargon **appointed** local rulers. Each local ruler served as king of the land he oversaw. Sargon was able to control the Akkadian empire for more than 50 years.

After Sargon's death in 2279 BCE, internal rebellions and outside invasions weakened the Akkadian empire. Within 100 years, the empire had collapsed. Warriors from the east took control of the region.

▲ Most of what is known about Sargon, above, comes from stories written about him during 2,000 years of Southwest Asian history, rather than from historical documents written during his rule.

Around 2100 BCE, Sumerian kings were able to unite the region again, this time under Ur Nammu, the ruler of Ur. Ur prospered for about 100 years. Then, an uprising of rebels ended Ur's rule over Sumer and renewed fighting between Sumerian city-states. Over the next few hundred years, Sumer faced invasions by a series of enemies, including the Amorites. The Amorites took control of several Sumerian cities, including Babylon (BAB uh lahn).

✓ **READING CHECK** **Understand Effects** Why did Southwest Asian empires tend to weaken and fall apart during this period?

The Babylonian Empire

Academic Vocabulary

ally • *n.*, an independent country or empire that works with other countries or empires to achieve a shared military or political goal

appoint • *v.*, to assign an official position or role to someone

When the Amorites invaded, Babylon was a small, unimportant city on the Euphrates River near present-day Baghdad, Iraq. But under a king named Hammurabi (hah muh RAH bee), Babylon became the center of a new Mesopotamian empire.

Hammurabi Builds an Empire Hammurabi became king of Babylon around 1792 BCE. He solidified his power, built up his army, and led the Amorites in attacks against other Mesopotamian city-states.

He united southern Mesopotamia into what we now call the Old Babylonian (bab uh LOH nee uhn) empire, or Babylonia.

Hammurabi was a skilled ruler. He created a strong government by sending his own governors, tax collectors, and judges to rule distant cities. He stationed troops throughout the empire. Hammurabi also made Babylon into a great city. He oversaw a number of public building projects and encouraged the growth of trade. Hammurabi also established a set of laws known as **Hammurabi's Code**. Hammurabi states the purpose of the code in its introduction.

Quest CONNECTIONS

How does Hammurabi's stated goal for his law code establish his legitimacy as ruler? Record your observations in your ▱ Active Journal.

Primary Source

"bring about the rule of righteousness in the land, to destroy the wicked and the evil-doers; so that the strong should not harm the weak—so that I should . . . further the well-being of mankind."

—Hammurabi's Code

The code governed life in the Babylonian empire.

Legacy of Sumer and Babylonia The Babylonians built on the mathematical work of Sumerians. They made advances in geometry and an early form of trigonometry. Their work formed the basis for later developments in mathematics and were a lasting contribution of Mesopotamian civilization.

The Babylonians also built on Sumerian work in astronomy. They made detailed calculations of the movements of the sun, moon, planets, and stars.

The Babylonian empire eventually collapsed after Hammurabi's death in 1750 BCE. In the years that followed, the once-great civilization of Sumer slowly faded away. However, Sumerian and Babylonian advances in technology, farming, writing, learning, and the law lived on.

✓ READING CHECK Understand Effects How would the accomplishments of the Babylonians and Sumerians survive to influence the modern world?

Analyze Visuals
Hammurabi (left) receives the Code of Laws from the sun god. The Code of Laws is carved on the bottom of the stele. **Use Visual Information** How is the sun god portrayed?

The Hittites

During the time of the Sumerians and Babylonians, ideas and people moved through trade to the northwest and the east, into present-day Turkey and Iran. A people called the Hittites had settled in central Turkey by the 1800s BCE.

Key Events in Ancient Southwest Asia, 2500 BCE–50 CE

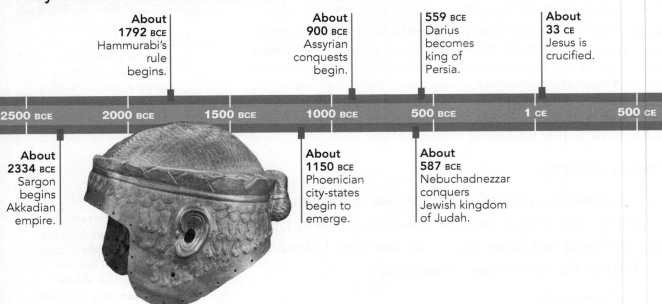

About 1792 BCE Hammurabi's rule begins.

About 900 BCE Assyrian conquests begin.

559 BCE Darius becomes king of Persia.

About 33 CE Jesus is crucified.

| 2500 BCE | 2000 BCE | 1500 BCE | 1000 BCE | 500 BCE | 1 CE | 500 CE |

About 2334 BCE Sargon begins Akkadian empire.

About 1150 BCE Phoenician city-states begin to emerge.

About 587 BCE Nebuchadnezzar conquers Jewish kingdom of Judah.

Analyze Timelines
Over a few thousand years, Southwest Asia saw a succession of empires.
Compare and Contrast How did the Phoenician city-states differ from the other states shown in this timeline?

INTERACTIVE

Development of Civilizations

The Hittites defeated the peoples around them and developed a kingdom. The Hittites relied on bronze for tools and weapons but eventually learned to use iron. Iron was a much harder metal and made better weapons and tools.

By the 1300s BCE, the Hittites had established an empire that covered most of present-day Turkey and northern Syria. The empire lasted until the 1100s BCE, when massive invasions destroyed it.

READING CHECK **Understand Effects** What effect might the ability to use iron have on a region's people?

The Phoenicians

During the time of the Hittites, the lands along the Mediterranean coast of Southwest Asia, known as Canaan, developed a culture of city-states like that of Mesopotamia. The people living along the northern coast of Canaan, in a region stretching from modern Syria through Lebanon to northern Israel, are known as the Phoenicians.

Egypt controlled parts of Canaan off and on for many years, beginning around 1500 BCE. Phoenician society began to emerge when Egyptian rule ended around 1150 BCE. Independent Phoenician city-states soon prospered through trade with the Egyptians, Hittites, and other peoples.

The Phoenicians were experts at **navigation**, the art of steering a ship from place to place. For hundreds of years, they dominated sea trade across the Mediterranean.

Phoenician Traders Phoenician traders brought back many imports, including gold, silver, tin, copper, iron, ivory, and precious stones.

Phoenician traders also exported goods, such as silver bowls, weapons, jewelry, and pine logs.

Trade also allowed the Phoenicians to build colonies around the Mediterranean Sea. One trading post was Cyprus, where the ancient Greeks also had trading colonies.

Phoenician Achievements Through trade, the Phoenicians linked the diverse cultures around the Mediterranean region and beyond. In the process, Phoenician ideas spread. The Phoenicians passed parts of their culture on to the Greeks. For example, the Greeks used the Phoenician standard of weights and measures.

The Phoenicians also developed the first phonetic writing system, in which each character corresponded to a spoken sound. The Greeks adapted this writing system to create an alphabet, which later evolved into the Roman alphabet. The Roman alphabet is used today for English and many other languages.

☑ READING CHECK **Understand Effects** How did Phoenician trade affect other cultures?

The Assyrian and Neo-Babylonian Empires

Assyria (uh SEER ee uh) lay north of Babylon, along the Tigris River. Like much of Mesopotamia, it fell under the influence of Sumer. Later, Assyria was part of the Akkadian and Babylonian empires.

An Empire Built on Iron The Assyrians learned iron-making from the Hittites and began forging iron tools and weapons, beginning the Iron Age. The Assyrians also developed a powerful military state.

INTERACTIVE

Mesopotamian Empires

GEOGRAPHY **SKILLS**

Phoenicians traded with people all around the Mediterranean Sea.

1. **Interaction** What information on the map supports the claim that the Phoenicians were skilled sailors?

2. **Use Visual Information** On which continent were most Phoenician colonies located?

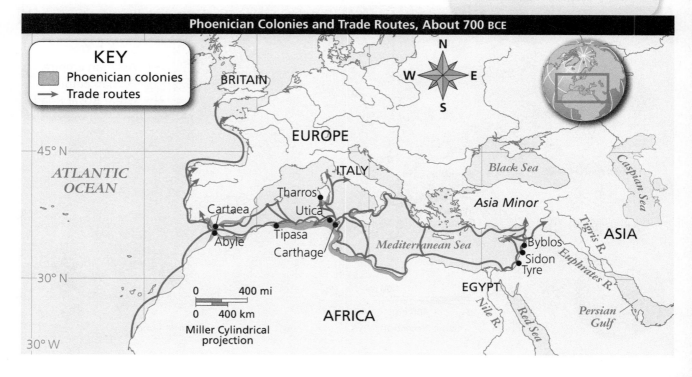

Phoenician Colonies and Trade Routes, About 700 BCE

KEY
- ▢ Phoenician colonies
- → Trade routes

BRITAIN

EUROPE

ATLANTIC OCEAN

ITALY

Black Sea

Asia Minor

Caspian Sea

Tharros

Cartaea
Utica
Tipasa
Abyle
Carthage

Mediterranean Sea

Byblos
Sidon
Tyre

Tigris R.
Euphrates R.

ASIA

EGYPT

Nile R.
Red Sea

Persian Gulf

AFRICA

0   400 mi
0   400 km
Miller Cylindrical projection

45° N
30° N
30° W

With their iron weapons, the Assyrians conquered neighboring regions in the 900s BCE. By the 700s BCE, the Assyrian empire was the largest empire yet known, covering the entire Fertile Crescent and extending into present-day Turkey and Iran. In the early 600s BCE, the Assyrians conquered Egypt.

Assyrian rulers divided the empire into around 70 smaller units of government called provinces that were led by a governor. Each governor reported directly to the Assyrian ruler. This helped the ruler keep control of distant lands.

Babylon Rises Again Civil wars and attacks from present-day Iran in the late 600s BCE caused the Assyrian empire to collapse. Around this time, Babylon once again rose to power. Its rulers built another empire, called the Neo-Babylonian empire. *Neo* is Greek for "new."

Babylon conquered Judah, the homeland of the Jewish people, in what is now Israel. The Babylonians drove the leadership of the Jews out of Judah and forced them to live in Babylonia. This period of Jewish history is called the Babylonian Captivity. The Neo-Babylonian empire eventually fell to attacks by the Persians from what is now Iran, in 539 BCE.

✔ READING CHECK Identify Supporting Details What two factors helped the Assyrians develop a powerful empire?

Who Were the Persians?

The Persians lived in what is now southwestern Iran. They established a mighty standing army that conquered neighboring lands.

GEOGRAPHY **SKILLS**

The Assyrian empire began from a base in northern Mesopotamia. The Persian empire originated further east and expanded west.

1. **Region** Which empire mainly occupied the Fertile Crescent?

2. **Use Visual Information** What did the Great Royal Road connect?

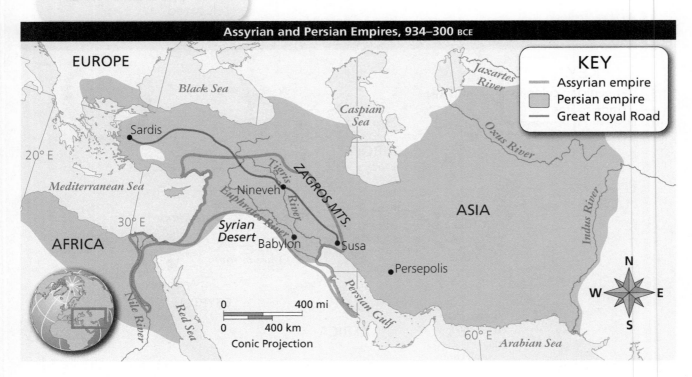

Assyrian and Persian Empires, 934–300 BCE

KEY
— Assyrian empire
▢ Persian empire
— Great Royal Road

In 559 BCE, a ruler named Cyrus became king of Persia. During his reign, Cyrus created a vast empire even larger than the former Assyrian empire. It covered nearly all of Southwest Asia, as well as parts of South and Central Asia. In the late 500s, the Persians conquered Egypt.

Like the Assyrians, the Persians ruled their empire effectively by dividing it into provinces ruled by governors. A strong army, a network of roads, and a standard currency tied the empire together. Other later empires borrowed these ideas in organizing their empires.

In the late 400s, the Persians tried to conquer the Greek city-states but failed. Still, the Persians dominated the region until 331 BCE, when a Greek army led by Alexander the Great defeated and conquered the Persian empire.

☑ READING CHECK **Identify Main Ideas** Why did empires like the Persian empire find it useful to have standing armies?

Analyze Images These archers decorated the palace of a Persian emperor. **Infer** What can you conclude about the Persian armies from this image?

☑ Lesson Check

Practice Vocabulary

1. How did Phoenician **navigation** influence the history of the world?

2. How can an **empire** hold together different peoples?

Critical Thinking and Writing

3. **Summarize** How did Sargon exert control over his empire?

4. **Identify Cause and Effect** How did Sumerian culture spread?

5. **Compare and Contrast** In what ways were Hammurabi and Sargon alike in how they governed?

6. **Identify Cause and Effect** How did the Assyrians become militarily powerful?

7. **Writing Workshop: Support Ideas with Evidence** In your ▱ Active Journal, take notes and write a paragraph describing one of the cultures you have just read about. Make sure you are introducing specific facts about that culture. Be thinking about how the details you included reflect the values of your chosen culture. You will use these notes to help write an essay on the values of a Southwest Asian culture.

Analyze Sequence and Chronology

INTERACTIVE

Sequence

Follow these steps and use the timeline to analyze events and their relationship in a chronology. A chronology is a list of events in sequence, or the order in which they happened.

1 **Identify the scope and subject of the chronology.** A timeline or a text presenting a chronology might have information spanning a huge amount of time. Begin by identifying the span of time covered and the subject covered by the list or timeline.

a. What is the span of time shown in this timeline?

b. What are most of the entries about?

2 **Look for clues about time.** Important clues include information about key events. When you see the letters BCE, that means Before Common Era, or the time before the era in which our years are numbered. Because these years are counted backward from 1 BCE, years BCE with larger numbers are earlier. Years BCE with lower numbers are later and closer to the present. So, as time passes during the period BCE, the number of the year goes down.

a. Which dates are approximate?

b. What do these dates have in common?

c. How would you explain why those dates are approximate?

3 **Look for relationships between events.** Entries with the same key words may be about the same person or group. See what the wording of the entry can tell you about how the events are related. What does the span of time between the entries tell you about the person or group?

a. Which empire ruled the longest? Which was the shortest?

b. How are the dates of the Assyrian and Neo-Babylonian empires related? What can you conclude from that relationship?

c. What two other empires are related in a similar way?

Ancient Southwest Asia

About 2334 BCE
Beginning of Akkadian empire; lasts to about 2154 BCE

About 626 BCE
Beginning of Neo-Babylonian empire; lasts to 539 BCE

539 BCE
Beginning of Persian empire; lasts to 330 BCE

| 2500 BCE | 2000 BCE | 1500 BCE | 1000 BCE | 500 BCE | 1 CE |

About 1850 BCE
Beginning of Babylonian empire; lasts to about 1595 BCE

About 934 BCE
Beginning of Assyrian empire; lasts to about 627 BCE

Origins and Beliefs of Judaism

BOUNCE TO ACTIVATE ▶ VIDEO

GET READY TO READ

START UP

This illustration shows Moses—considered by Jews to be a prophet, or messenger of God—holding the Ten Commandments. What impact might laws such as the Ten Commandments have on a society?

GUIDING QUESTIONS

- How do Jews believe their religion began?
- What are Judaism's sacred writings and teachings?
- What happened to the Jews during ancient times?

TAKE NOTES

Literacy Skills: Summarize

Use the graphic organizer in your 🗐 Active Journal to take notes as you read the lesson.

PRACTICE VOCABULARY

Use the vocabulary activity in your 🗐 Active Journal to practice the vocabulary words.

Vocabulary

monotheism   commandment
ethics   rabbi
Torah   Talmud
covenant   Sabbath
Exodus   Diaspora

Academic Vocabulary

compel
commentary

Judaism first emerged as a religion more than 3,000 years ago in the Fertile Crescent. It was the first religion based on belief in one God, who set down laws about right and wrong. Judaism helped shape the religions of Christianity and Islam, as well as modern ideas about law and human rights.

The Ancient Israelites and Their God

The ancient Israelites practiced **monotheism**, or the belief in a single God. The Israelites believed that God created each person in God's image and that God called on them to act based on **ethics**, or beliefs about what is right and wrong. Their teachings and practices became known as Judaism, the religion of the Jews.

Sources Most of what Jews believe about the origins of their religion comes from the Torah (TOH ruh). The **Torah** consists of the first five books of the Hebrew Bible. The archaeology and history of biblical sites in Egypt and the Fertile Crescent also help us understand the world of the Torah.

▲ This Christian illustration of Abraham shows him as the first patriarch of the Jews. Abraham is revered by Jews, Christians, and Muslims.

Academic Vocabulary

compel • *v.*, to force someone to do something

INTERACTIVE

The Origins of Judaism

Abraham's Covenant The Torah tells about a man named Abraham. According to the Torah, God told Abraham to leave Ur and travel with his family to a land called Canaan (KAY nun) on the Mediterranean coast. The Torah says that God made a **covenant**, or binding agreement, with Abraham. Under the covenant, if Abraham and his descendants remained faithful to God, Canaan would belong to them, so it became known as the Promised Land.

Primary Source

"I will maintain My covenant between Me and you, and your offspring to come, as an everlasting covenant throughout the ages, to be God to you and your offspring to come."

—Genesis 17:7

Abraham, his son Isaac, and Isaac's son Jacob are known as the patriarchs, or the forefathers, of the Jews. According to the Torah, God later gave Jacob the name Israel. For this reason, his descendants were known as Israelites.

✓ **READING CHECK** **Summarize** According to Jewish belief, what were the terms of the covenant that Abraham made with God?

The Exodus

Scholars believe that the stories of the Israelites were eventually written down in Genesis, the first book of the Torah. Genesis describes a famine that occurred in Canaan. Because Egypt had great supplies of grain, Jacob's family moved there and continued to grow.

The book of Exodus (EKS uh dus) comes after Genesis in the Torah. Exodus describes how the pharaoh, or king of Egypt, enslaved and mistreated the Israelites and **compelled** them to do harsh work.

Moses According to the Torah, the pharaoh ordered that all boys born to Israelites be thrown into the Nile. The life of Moses (MOH zuz), an Israelite baby, was at risk. He was found at the shore by the pharaoh's daughter, who then adopted him. The Torah states that, when Moses grew up, God told him to rescue his people from slavery in Egypt. The pharaoh refused to let Moses lead the Israelites out of Egypt, and so God sent plagues to the Egyptians.

Finally, says the Torah, the pharaoh allowed the Israelites to leave Egypt. The escape of the Israelites from slavery in Egypt is called the **Exodus**. Jews celebrate the holiday of Passover each year to remember the Exodus.

The Desert Experience According to the Torah, after the Israelites left Egypt, they lived in the Sinai desert for 40 years. There, God prepared them for life in the Promised Land.

The Israelites faced harsh conditions and occasionally battled other peoples. Some questioned the leadership of Moses or even of God. However, they came to believe that if they obeyed God's commands, God would provide for them. According to the Torah, after Moses died, the Israelites returned to the Promised Land and conquered it.

☑ READING CHECK **Summarize** What was the role of Moses in the Exodus, according to the Torah?

The Ten Commandments

The book of Exodus says that during the Israelites' journey, they stopped at Mount Sinai. Moses went up the mountain to meet with God. God gave Moses laws, known as the Ten Commandments. A **commandment** is an order to do something.

According to the Hebrew Bible, the Ten Commandments and other laws told the Israelites how to behave toward God and one another. They are still important to Jews today. According to the laws, behaving well toward one another is a duty to God. If people believe in God and obey God's laws, God will protect them and support them.

Because they believe that each person is created in the image of God, Jews have a strong sense of each person's worth. They also believe that people have a responsibility to do what is right.

☑ READING CHECK **Identify Main Ideas** According to the Hebrew Bible, what is the purpose of the Ten Commandments?

▶ INTERACTIVE

The Ten Commandments and Modern Laws

GEOGRAPHY **SKILLS**

According to the Bible, the Israelites spent 40 years traveling across the Sinai Peninsula.

1. **Place** Where is Mount Sinai?

2. **Understand Effects** What was the result of the Exodus?

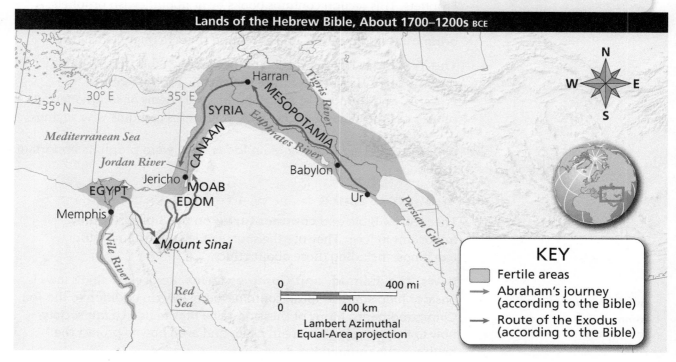

Lands of the Hebrew Bible, About 1700–1200s BCE

KEY
- ▢ Fertile areas
- → Abraham's journey (according to the Bible)
- → Route of the Exodus (according to the Bible)

0 — 400 mi
0 — 400 km
Lambert Azimuthal Equal-Area projection

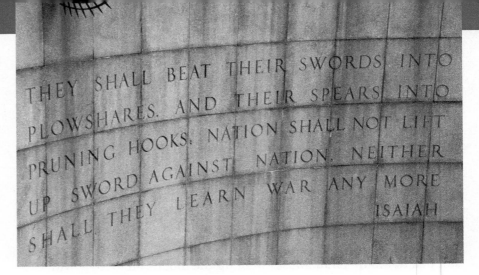

THEY SHALL BEAT THEIR SWORDS INTO PLOWSHARES. AND THEIR SPEARS INTO PRUNING HOOKS. NATION SHALL NOT LIFT UP SWORD AGAINST NATION. NEITHER SHALL THEY LEARN WAR ANY MORE
ISAIAH

The Hebrew Bible

The Torah and the larger Hebrew Bible are Jewish sacred writings and the source of Jewish teachings. The Hebrew Bible is also known as the Tanakh in Hebrew. To Jews, the Bible reveals God's will as carried out in human events. This shared account unites Jews all over the world. The Hebrew Bible also forms the basis for the Christian Old Testament, which is made up of the books of the Hebrew Bible. By tradition, the books of the Hebrew Bible are divided into three sections.

The Torah The Torah begins with the story of God's creation of the world. It continues to tell of the life of Abraham and God's covenant with him.

The Torah then focuses on Abraham's son Isaac, his grandson Jacob, and Jacob's descendants, the Israelites. It tells the story of the Exodus. The Torah contains not only the Ten Commandments but also many other rules and laws.

The Prophets The next section of the Hebrew Bible is called the Prophets. This section contains books by or about Jewish prophets. A prophet is a person believed to be chosen by God as a messenger to bring truth to the people and to remind them to obey God's laws.

The Writings The last section of the Hebrew Bible, the Writings, includes great Hebrew literature such as the Psalms (sahmz), the Proverbs, and the Song of Songs. Psalms are poems or songs offering praises or prayers to God. The book of Proverbs contains wise sayings.

✓ **READING CHECK** Identify Main Ideas Why were prophets important to Judaism?

The Importance of Law and Learning

The Hebrew Bible and **commentaries** on the Bible are vitally important to Jews. They are the source of Jews' most important teachings, including those about ethics.

Laws, the Talmud, and Commentaries Respect for God's laws is basic to Judaism. The Torah contains many laws in addition to the Ten Commandments. Many of these describe how to have a fair society, how to help people who are in need, and even how to protect the health of the community.

Academic Vocabulary
commentary • *n.*, a set of comments or a recorded discussion about something

Many centuries after the time of Moses, prominent Jewish **rabbis** (RAB yz), or religious teachers, recorded and commented on oral laws that they believed had come down from the teachings of Moses. Around 600 CE they put together their discussions in the Talmud. The **Talmud** is a collection of oral teachings and commentaries about the Hebrew Bible and Jewish law. Jews still study and discuss it.

The Need to Study The Hebrew Bible and the Talmud are central to Jewish teaching and practice. Jewish scholars still write commentaries on these writings today.

The Hebrew Bible is written mostly in the Hebrew language. As a result, many Jews try to learn to read Hebrew. Some also learn Aramaic, the language of most of the Talmud.

☑ READING CHECK Summarize Why do Jews value the Hebrew Bible and Talmud?

Basic Teachings

Jews' idea of God was unique in the ancient world. In most other early religions, people worshiped many gods. They had images of these gods made of wood, stone, pottery, or metal. Some believed that each god lived in a certain place. In contrast, the Israelites believed that their God was invisible and yet present everywhere.

Many of the teachings of the Torah and the Talmud have to do with ethics. Ethical monotheism is probably the most important teaching of Judaism. This is the idea that there is one God who sets down ethical rules, or rules about right and wrong. Being faithful to God means following these rules.

Analyze Charts Several beliefs are central to the teachings of Judaism. **Identify Main Ideas** Why does the belief in ethical monotheism come first?

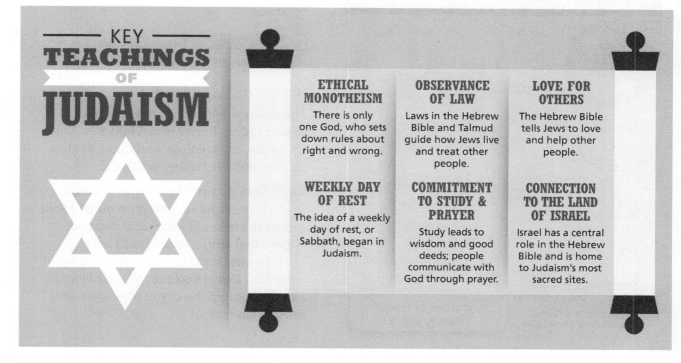

KEY TEACHINGS OF JUDAISM

ETHICAL MONOTHEISM
There is only one God, who sets down rules about right and wrong.

OBSERVANCE OF LAW
Laws in the Hebrew Bible and Talmud guide how Jews live and treat other people.

LOVE FOR OTHERS
The Hebrew Bible tells Jews to love and help other people.

WEEKLY DAY OF REST
The idea of a weekly day of rest, or Sabbath, began in Judaism.

COMMITMENT TO STUDY & PRAYER
Study leads to wisdom and good deeds; people communicate with God through prayer.

CONNECTION TO THE LAND OF ISRAEL
Israel has a central role in the Hebrew Bible and is home to Judaism's most sacred sites.

Ethics, Justice, and Law Ethical monotheism calls on Jews to know the difference between right and wrong. For Jews, actions should be based on ethics and justice.

As you have learned, Jews believe that each person has value and worth because he or she is created in the image of God. Along with individual worth comes individual responsibility to God. Each individual has the responsibility to act righteously in God's eyes.

The Jewish idea of individual responsibility means that God's laws and commandments apply equally to every Jew. This idea of equality in the eyes of God helped shape modern systems of law and justice.

Love for Others The Hebrew Bible commands, "Love your fellow [human being] as yourself." Jews are required to help others. As a result, Jews have been involved in many efforts to fight discrimination. Jews also give charity in response to this teaching. These ideas have influenced modern thinking about human rights.

Other Key Teachings Another important Jewish teaching is to observe the **Sabbath**, or a weekly day of rest, free from work. For Jews, the Sabbath is the seventh day of the week, or Saturday.

Jewish teaching also stresses the importance of study and prayer. You have learned about the importance of studying the Hebrew Bible and the Talmud. Jews also value prayer as a way of communicating with God.

Jewish teachings also include Jews' ties to the Land of Israel. This includes the modern state of Israel.

READING CHECK Draw Conclusions Why is prayer essential to Judaism?

Kingdoms and Exile

The Hebrew Bible is our main source for Jewish history before about 900 BCE. After that date, archaeology and other written sources provide further evidence.

Saul, David, and Solomon According to the Hebrew Bible, a warrior named Saul united the tribes of Israel and became Israel's first king. One of Saul's best fighters was David, a young shepherd and musician. David became the next king. David captured the city of Jerusalem and made it his capital.

GEOGRAPHY SKILLS

This map shows the extent of David's kingdom by 966 BCE.

1. **Location** Which regions outside of Israel were controlled by Israel under King David?

2. **Use Visual Information** Which empire lay to the east of Israel?

Israel Under King David, 966 BCE

36° N

Euphrates River

ARAM

PHOENICIA

ASSYRIA

Mediterranean Sea

Sea of Galilee

Shechem
Jerusalem

Jordan River

32° N
32° E

PHILISTIA

Dead Sea

ISRAEL

EGYPT

N
W   E
S

KEY

Kingdom of Israel

Other regions controlled by Israel

Border of David's empire, 966 BCE

0   200 mi
0   200 km

Lambert Azimuthal Equal-Area projection

David's son Solomon ruled after him. According to the Hebrew Bible, Solomon commissioned the great First Temple in Jerusalem, the holiest shrine for the Israelites. According to tradition, Solomon also wrote many of the wise sayings in the Bible's Book of Proverbs.

The Kingdom Divides When Solomon died around 900 BCE, the Hebrew Bible states that Israel split into two parts. Solomon's descendants ruled the kingdom of Judah in the south. From the name *Judah*, the religion of the Israelites became known as Judaism, and the descendants of the Israelites became known as Jews.

A competing kingdom in the north kept the name of the kingdom of Israel. About 722 BCE, the Assyrian empire conquered the kingdom of Israel. Thousands of Israelites were sent to distant parts of the empire. Others fled south to Judah.

More than 100 years later, Babylon, in present-day Iraq, rebelled against Assyria and began the second Babylonian empire. Babylonian emperor Nebuchadnezzar conquered Judah. About 587 BCE, the Babylonians destroyed Jerusalem, including the First Temple.

The Babylonian Captivity The Babylonians forced thousands of people out of Judah into Babylon. Most of them wished to return to their homeland.

Persian king Cyrus the Great later conquered the Babylonian empire. In 538 BCE, Cyrus allowed the Jews to go home. Jewish leaders built the Second Temple in Jerusalem and rebuilt the walls of Jerusalem.

The Diaspora The Babylonian Captivity was a turning point in Jewish history. Communities of Jews lived throughout the Babylonian empire. They came to be known as the Diaspora. The **Diaspora** (dy AS puh ruh) refers to the Jewish communities outside of their ancient homeland. Today, Jews live around the world.

Analyze Visuals The Assyrians conquered the kingdom of Israel about 722 BCE. **Use Visual Information** Which figures in the relief are Assyrian officers? How do you know?

▲ The Western Wall is all that remains of the Second Temple of Jerusalem. It is a sacred site to Jews, where many people come to pray.

The Jews who remained in the former kingdom of Israel, including Judah, later came under the rule of the Persian empire, the empire of Alexander the Great, and the Roman empire.

Greek and Roman Rule After the Babylonian Captivity ended, Jews in the Land of Israel tried to live according to their religion. However, they faced harsh and unfair treatment by Greek and Roman rulers.

During the 100s BCE, a family known as the Maccabees rebelled against their Greek rulers and won independence. The Jewish holiday of Hanukkah celebrates the victory of the Maccabees and their reclaiming of the Temple.

In 6 CE, the Land of Israel became part of the Roman empire. By this time, it was called Judea, or "land of the Jews." Roman disrespect toward Judaism led Jews to rebel against Rome. In response, in 70 CE, the Romans destroyed Jerusalem, including the Second Temple.

The Romans also killed or enslaved thousands of Jews. Thousands more fled to other lands inside and outside of the empire.

After another Jewish rebellion, the Romans banned Jews from Jerusalem and changed the name of the province in 135 CE to Palestine, after the ancient Israelites' enemies the Philistines.

☑ READING CHECK **Identify Main Ideas** Why did the Jewish Diaspora occur?

☑ Lesson Check

Practice Vocabulary

1. What are the **Torah** and the **Talmud**?

2. According to the Hebrew Bible, what role did God's **covenant** with Abraham play in the creation of Judaism?

Critical Thinking and Writing

3. **Draw Conclusions** Why might ethical monotheism be considered the most important Jewish teaching?

4. **Identify Main Ideas** What are the three main parts of the Hebrew Bible, and how do they differ?

5. **Compare and Contrast** How did the Israelites' idea of God differ from those of other people living in the region at that time?

6. **Writing Workshop: Support Ideas with Evidence** In your 📓 Active Journal, write a paragraph about how the text in this lesson presents the values of the Israelites. Support your claims with evidence from the lesson.

LESSON 4

Origins and Beliefs of Christianity

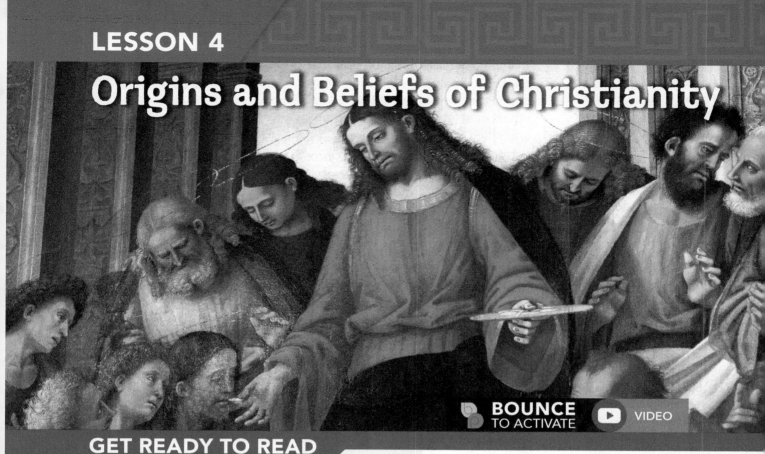

BOUNCE TO ACTIVATE   ▶ VIDEO

GET READY TO READ

START UP

Look at the painting of Jesus, the founder of Christianity, and some of his followers. Write three questions you have about the origins and spread of Christianity.

GUIDING QUESTIONS

- What are the main components of the Christian Bible?
- What are the main beliefs and practices of Christianity?
- How and why did Christianity spread?

TAKE NOTES

Literacy Skills: Determine Central Ideas
Use the graphic organizer in your 📓 Active Journal to take notes as you read the lesson.

PRACTICE VOCABULARY

Use the vocabulary activity in your 📓 Active Journal to practice the vocabulary words.

Vocabulary

		Academic Vocabulary
resurrect	epistle	oppression
crucifixion	apostle	circulate
New Testament	Trinity	
Gospel	conversion	
parable		

The Romans built a powerful empire. They conquered many lands. In Judea, many Jews opposed Roman rule. Some opposed the power of leading Jews in enforcing Roman rule. As the political fires grew hotter in Judea, according to the Christian Bible, a Jewish spiritual leader named Jesus emerged there. Eventually, the Romans would execute him. Nevertheless, a new religion sprang up based on his teachings and the writings of his early followers. Today, Christianity is the world's most widely practiced faith.

A Religion Is Born

In 63 BCE, the Romans established control over the Jewish kingdom of Judea, centered in Jerusalem. In 6 CE, they made Judea part of the Roman empire. Many Jews opposed Roman rule. They saw the Romans as foreigners who occupied their land and treated them cruelly.

Jewish Groups Under the Romans, Jews were divided into groups with different approaches to Judaism. One group believed that good people could be resurrected after death.

To **resurrect** means to come back to life. Others hoped that God would send a savior called a Messiah to save the Jews from **oppression**. They hoped the Messiah would drive the Romans from their homeland. Still others actively opposed the Romans. The Zealots refused to pay taxes and killed Roman officials.

During this period of upheaval, according to the Christian Bible, a Jewish man named Jesus of Nazareth lived and taught. He attracted a large following. After his execution by the Romans, a new religion emerged in Judea. It was called Christianity.

Jesus the Teacher The Christian Bible is our main source on the origins of Christianity. Part of the Bible tells the story of a young Jewish religious teacher named Jesus. According to these writings, Jesus began to attract many followers in Judea. Evidence in the Bible suggests that Jesus taught during the late 20s and early 30s CE.

Opposition, Arrest, and Death The Christian Bible says that Jesus went to Jerusalem around 33 CE to celebrate the Jewish holiday of Passover. Roman authorities in Jerusalem worried about the large holiday crowds. Local Jewish leaders also feared trouble. A riot might provoke the Romans into destroying the city.

The Christian Bible says that in response to these concerns, Roman governor Pontius Pilate acted. He had Jesus arrested, beaten, and crucified. **Crucifixion** was a slow and painful Roman method of execution. The victim was nailed or tied to a large wooden cross and left to hang until dead.

Analyze Visuals
According to the Christian Bible, the night before he was crucified, Jesus washed the feet of his closest followers. Today, many Christian churches hold special ceremonies recognizing this event.
Use Visual Information
How do you know this is a Christian service?

The Resurrection According to the Christian Bible, after Jesus died, his body was taken down from the cross and laid in a tomb. The Romans sealed the tomb and posted guards around it. The Bible then tells how some disciples, or followers, of Jesus visited the tomb three days later. They found the guards gone and the tomb empty. They ran to tell the other disciples. Many claimed to see and speak to Jesus after his death. They believed that God had resurrected Jesus and that he was indeed the Messiah.

Jesus and his early followers, like others in Judea, were Jews. But those who believed Jesus was the Messiah came to form a new religion known as Christianity. The Greek word for Messiah is *Christos*, or *Christ* in English. Followers of Jesus became known as Christians.

☑ **READING CHECK** **Identify Main Ideas** According to the Christian Bible, what event showed that Jesus was the Messiah?

The Christian Bible

In the years after the death of Jesus, Christians wrote down the story of Jesus and other teachings. They also worked to develop their faith.

The Old and New Testaments Because Jesus and his first followers were Jews, the Hebrew Bible was the Christians' only sacred text at first. Then they began to add their own writings. Christians called the Hebrew Bible the Old Testament. They named the new body of work the **New Testament**. It tells the story of Jesus, his early followers, and their beliefs. Christians read both testaments together as their scriptures.

The works that became the New Testament were written down between 50 and 150 CE. By the 300s they were collected and began **circulating** in the form that Christians recognize today. Jesus and his early followers probably spoke Aramaic, although the New Testament was written in Greek. Greek was the most widely spoken language in the eastern part of the Roman empire. The New Testament contains 27 separate documents, called books.

The Gospels The first four books of the New Testament are the **Gospels**. They describe the life and teachings of Jesus from four different points of view. The Gospels do not all describe the same events in exactly the same way. Together, however, they create a powerful portrayal of Jesus and his teachings.

▲ This is a page from the *Book of Kells*, an illuminated manuscript created in the British Isles around 800. It contains the Gospels and other material.

Academic Vocabulary
circulate • *v.*, to move from place to place

 **INTERACTIVE**

Early Christian Symbols

Many teachings of Jesus are presented in the form of **parables**, or stories with a religious moral. Jesus often used parables to explain important lessons.

Other Writings After the Gospels come a number of other books. Most of them are **epistles**, or formal letters. These are letters that the **apostles**, the core group of early followers of Jesus, and other early leaders wrote to the newly established churches.

Most epistles were written to explain Christian teachings or to solve problems in the church. The apostle Paul wrote many of these epistles to churches he had started himself. His letters explained many Christian beliefs in great detail.

☑ READING CHECK **Recognize Multiple Causes** Why did the apostles of Jesus write letters to the newly established churches?

What Do Christians Believe?

Christians base many of their beliefs on the New Testament. Most Christians today share some basic beliefs.

The Son of God The Gospels refer to Jesus as the Son of God. Christian belief holds that Jesus was God in human form. Christians see God's sacrifice of his son on the cross as a result of human sin, or error. They believe that the resurrection of Jesus proves God's forgiveness of human sin and promise of life after death. They also believe that because of the resurrection, Christians can have faith that they, too, will be resurrected after death. Christians believe that faith in God, and in Jesus, will bring the reward of eternal, or endless, life in the presence of God.

Analyze Visuals
The central beliefs of Christianity include the idea of the Trinity. **Use Visual Information** According to Christians, which of the three members of the Trinity shows the power of God on Earth?

✚ CHRISTIAN BELIEFS ✚

GOD THE FATHER
creator

THE TRINITY

JESUS CHRIST THE SON
God in human form

HOLY SPIRIT (HOLY GHOST)
the power of God on Earth

- There is only one God.
- God exists in three forms (the Trinity).
- Jesus died on the cross for people's sins.
- His resurrection shows God's forgiveness for those sins.
- People's souls live forever.
- The Bible is the revealed source of God's word.

The Soul and Salvation Christians believe that everyone has a soul, or spirit. What happens to the soul after death depends for Christians on whether a person believes in God and Jesus. They believe that people need God to forgive their sins, or wrongdoings, so that their souls can live on in the presence of God after death. Most believe that God will forgive people who are truly sorry for their sins and choose to follow Jesus.

Many Christians view the death and resurrection of Jesus as key to forgiveness. In the ancient world, some peoples atoned, or made up for sins, by offering animal sacrifices to their gods. Many Christians believe that Jesus, by being crucified, became the sacrifice for everyone's sins.

The Trinity Like Jews and Muslims, Christians are monotheists—they worship one God. Most Christians, however, believe that God exists as three forms. Together, these three forms are known as the **Trinity**. The Trinity includes God the Father, Jesus the Son, and the Holy Spirit.

Christians, Jews, and Muslims all believe that God created the universe. Christians also believe that Jesus is God's son and is God in human form. The Holy Spirit, also called the Holy Ghost, is described as the power of God as experienced on Earth. Early Christians believed that the Holy Spirit allowed them to sense the presence of God after Jesus was no longer with them.

☑ READING CHECK **Compare and Contrast** How does Christian monotheism differ from that of Islam and Judaism?

The Practice of Christianity

In daily life, Christians try to follow the teachings of Jesus. Most Christians also observe similar rituals and holidays.

Following Jesus The teachings of Jesus often involve ethics, or issues of right and wrong and how to treat people. Christians today try to live according to these ethical teachings. Jesus urged his followers to treat others as they would like to be treated. This is called the "Golden Rule."

Primary Source

"In everything, do to others as you would have them do to you."

—Matthew 7:12

Jesus also showed great concern for poor and humble people. He accepted even those with the lowest social standing among his followers.

Analyze Visuals Many Christian churches have stained-glass windows that illustrate stories from the Christian Bible. This window illustrates the baptism of Jesus as described in the Gospels. **Draw Conclusions** Which part of the image most likely represents the Holy Spirit?

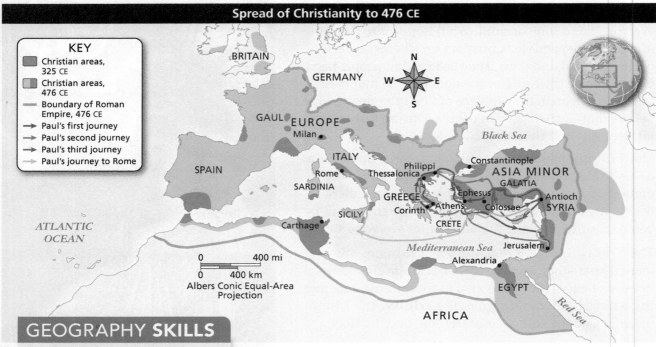

Spread of Christianity to 476 CE

KEY
- Christian areas, 325 CE
- Christian areas, 476 CE
- Boundary of Roman Empire, 476 CE
- Paul's first journey
- Paul's second journey
- Paul's third journey
- Paul's journey to Rome

BRITAIN
GERMANY
GAUL
EUROPE
Milan
ITALY
SPAIN
Rome
SARDINIA
ATLANTIC OCEAN
Carthage
SICILY
GREECE
Corinth
Athens
CRETE
Thessalonica
Philippi
Ephesus
Colossae
Constantinople
ASIA MINOR
GALATIA
Antioch
SYRIA
Black Sea
Mediterranean Sea
Jerusalem
Alexandria
EGYPT
Red Sea
AFRICA

0   400 mi
0   400 km
Albers Conic Equal-Area Projection

GEOGRAPHY **SKILLS**

Christianity spread rapidly under Roman rule because of the empire's safe roads and sea routes.

1. **Interaction** Did Christianity spread first in Asia Minor or Britain? Why do you think this might be so?

2. **Use Visual Information** Paul wrote epistles to the Ephesians, Thessalonians, Colossians, Corinthians, Philippians, and Romans. Based on the map, which of their cities did Paul visit on his second journey?

INTERACTIVE

The Spread of Christianity

Besides following Jesus' ethical teachings, Christians believe it is important to have faith. To most Christians, Christianity means believing in Jesus, in his sacrifice for other people's sins, and in his resurrection.

Rituals and Holidays Most Christians observe Sunday, the day of the resurrection according to the Gospels, as a day of rest and prayer. At worship services, many Christians participate in a ritual meal called Holy Communion or Eucharist. This usually includes bread and wine or grape juice. Many Christians are baptized, either as infants or adults. To baptize is to dip or immerse someone in water as a sign of entry into a church or Christian community.

Christmas and Easter are two important Christian holidays. Christmas celebrates the birth of Jesus. Easter celebrates the resurrection of Jesus.

READING CHECK Draw Conclusions How are the teachings of Christianity similar to the teachings of Judaism?

The Spread of Christianity

During his life, Jesus chose 12 trusted followers, the apostles. According to the Gospels, one of them betrayed him to the Romans. The others spread his teachings after his death.

The Early Church The apostle Peter became a leader of the new church. The word *church* can refer to the community of all Christians, a specific group of Christians, or a building Christians worship in.

Peter and other apostles spread the belief in Jesus as the Messiah. They carried their faith to many parts of the world. They visited Europe, Asia, and North Africa.

Christians and Jews The first Christians still considered themselves Jews. They respected most Jewish laws and traditions. They read the Hebrew Bible and prayed in synagogues—Jewish religious buildings.

But differences grew between Jewish followers of Christianity and other Jews. Christians began sharing their beliefs with non-Jews outside of Judea. Peter even traveled to Rome itself. People from different backgrounds heard the apostles' message. More and more gentiles, or non-Jews, became Christians.

The Apostle Paul The apostle Paul helped spread Christianity throughout the Roman empire. Paul is called an apostle, though he was not one of the original 12 followers that Jesus had chosen.

Early in his life Paul was opposed to Christianity. However, he had an experience that led to his conversion to Christianity. A **conversion** is a heartfelt change in one's opinions or beliefs. Paul believed that Jesus had appeared to him and told him to spread the new faith.

Paul traveled to Greece and other areas. He founded churches and preached. Paul helped spread the belief that non-Jews did not need to follow all Jewish laws to become Christians. As more gentiles came into the church, Christianity and Judaism became separate religions.

Reasons for Growth Christianity spread between 30 and 200 CE, although it remained a minority faith in the Roman empire. Several factors helped the new faith grow.

For one thing, new roads built by the Romans allowed Christians to move more easily from place to place, spreading their beliefs. Paul's journeys, for example, might not have been possible in an earlier period.

Just as important, Greek was widely spoken in the eastern half of the empire, and by educated people everywhere. Christian scriptures were in Greek, so a large number of people could understand them.

Many people appreciated Christianity's moral teachings and its promise of salvation. Some were also attracted by the Christian belief that all people are equal in God's sight, including slaves and women.

☑️ **READING CHECK** Identify Cause and Effect How did improved transportation help the spread of Christianity?

▼ Throughout history, the Christian church has recognized many saints, or holy people. Many, including Saint Perpetua, shown here, died for their beliefs.

Christianity in Southwest Asia

Because Christians would not worship Roman gods or the emperor, they were often mistreated and even killed by Roman officials. However, in 313 CE, the Roman emperor Constantine became a Christian. Others soon began to embrace the religion.

The Romans and Christianity By the late 300s, Christianity had become the official religion of the Roman empire. Many people in western Southwest Asia, which was controlled by the Roman empire, also began to embrace Christianity. These people lived in present-day Turkey, Cyprus, Syria, Lebanon, Israel, and Jordan. Nevertheless, many people in the region continued to follow Judaism and other religions.

▲ Christianity spread into Southwest Asia under the Roman empire. This Christian church is in Jerusalem.

The Spread of Christianity Christianity became dominant in these parts of Southwest Asia under the Roman empire's successor, the Byzantine empire, during the 500s and early 600s. Christianity also spread eastward into the Parthian empire, which controlled modern Iraq, Iran, part of the Arabian Peninsula, and some surrounding regions. Christianity continued to spread under the Sassanid empire, which followed the Parthian empire and covered a similar territory.

Christianity also spread beyond the borders of these empires into the Arabian Peninsula. It soon became the dominant religion of Mesopotamia and the eastern Arabian Peninsula, in addition to Byzantine Southwest Asia. However, in Iran and in the western Arabian Peninsula, Christianity was a minority religion.

☑ READING CHECK **Use Evidence** What led to Christianity becoming the dominant religion of the Roman empire?

☑ Lesson Check

Practice Vocabulary

1. What is the relationship between the **crucifixion** and **resurrection** of Jesus, according to Christian belief?

2. What was the impact of the **Gospels** and the **New Testament**?

Critical Thinking and Writing

3. **Draw Conclusions** Why might the Roman authorities have feared Jesus?

4. **Identify Main Ideas** Why did many people find the teachings of Christianity so appealing?

5. **Cite Evidence** What does Christianity have in common with Judaism?

6. **Writing Workshop: Support Ideas with Evidence** In your 🗐 Active Journal, write a paragraph about the rise and spread of Christianity and the values reflected in Christian teachings.

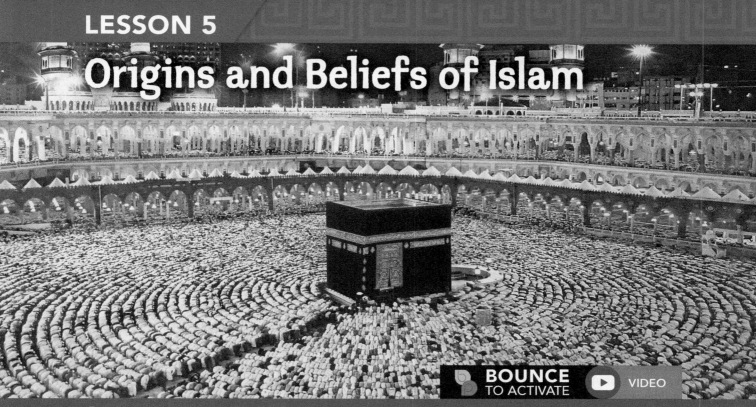

LESSON 5
Origins and Beliefs of Islam

BOUNCE TO ACTIVATE   ▶ VIDEO

GET READY TO READ

START UP
Look at the photo of Muslim pilgrims at a holy site in Mecca. What does the photo suggest about the importance of this site to Muslims? Explain your answer.

GUIDING QUESTIONS
- What factors shaped life in Arabia in ancient times?
- What are the main sacred text, beliefs, and practices of Islam?
- How does Islam shape life in Muslim countries?

TAKE NOTES
Literacy Skills: Analyze Text Structure
Use the graphic organizer in your 📓 Active Journal to take notes as you read the lesson.

PRACTICE VOCABULARY
Use the vocabulary activity in your 📓 Active Journal to practice the vocabulary words.

Vocabulary		Academic Vocabulary
Bedouin	Sunnah	revelation
Kaaba	hajj	submission
Quran	mosque	
Hijra	Sharia	

Arabia, or the Arabian Peninsula, has one the harshest climates in the world. In its deserts, water is scarce. Temperatures can soar to more than 122° Fahrenheit (50° Celsius). It was here, however, that Islam emerged in the 600s CE. Today, only Christianity has more followers worldwide than Islam.

Arabia Before Islam
Arabia is a huge peninsula. It is nearly five times the size of Texas. It lies south of modern-day Iraq and Jordan and across the Red Sea from eastern Africa. The geography of Arabia influenced its history and culture.

Ancient Arabia Before Islam arose in Arabia, the peninsula was largely on the sidelines of ancient history. Persia to the northeast fought against Rome to the northwest for influence in northern Arabia. Southern Arabia was closely connected to Axum and other kingdoms in East Africa.

In the center of the peninsula, the harsh desert climate kept large kingdoms from developing. As a result, the area was home to a scattering of independent Arab tribes.

▲ Bedouins today are still nomadic and typically migrate to the desert during the winter months and to farmland during the summer months.

Nevertheless, these Arabs traded and migrated across the region. As a result, they came into contact with the surrounding civilizations. Consequently, some Arabs adopted religions such as Judaism and Christianity.

Living in Arabia Many ancient Arabs were nomads. They had no fixed homes. Others were settled in oases, or places in the desert with water supplies. Both nomadic and settled Arabs belonged to tribes. Their loyalties lay with tribe and family. They worshiped many gods and tribal spirits.

Arab nomads, known as **Bedouins** (BED oo winz), lived in the deserts. They herded sheep, goats, and camels. They traveled from oasis to oasis with their flocks. Bedouins were skilled warriors. Tribes raided one another for animals and goods.

Sedentary Arabs lived as farmers and merchants. Farmers tended fields watered by oases. Merchants set up shop in oasis towns along Arabia's trade routes. The most important route passed along the mountainous western region of the peninsula called the Hijaz. Camel caravans carrying trade goods stopped at these towns for water, food, and supplies.

Trade brought wealth and attracted settlers. The largest town in the Hijaz, Mecca, became a trading center. It was there, around 570, that Muhammad (muh HAHM mad) was born. Muhammad was the first person to preach the religion of Islam.

READING CHECK Draw Conclusions How did trade and migration in ancient Arabia affect people's religious beliefs?

How Did Islam Begin?

Muslims, people who practice Islam, consider Muhammad the prophet of their religion. Muslims believe that he was the messenger of God.

Mecca When Muhammad was born in Mecca, it was a religious center. It had an important shrine called the Kaaba where Arabs came to worship their gods. Every year, a religious fair attracted thousands of people. Today, the **Kaaba** is the most important Islamic holy site.

Muhammad's Early Life Muhammad was orphaned at an early age. He was raised by close relatives. At 25, he married a wealthy, widowed merchant named Khadija. Muhammad did well in business, but he was critical of Meccan society. All around him, he saw greed, corruption, and violence.

Seeking peace of mind, Muhammad often retreated to a cave outside Mecca to pray and reflect. Muslims believe that one night, in the year 610, the angel Gabriel appeared to Muhammad in the cave. Gabriel told him to recite, or say out loud, messages from God.

Did you know?

Another ancient trading city on the Arabian Peninsula was Petra, in modern-day Jordan. Though the area was occupied as early as the Paleolithic period, an Arab tribe called the Nabataeans later made Petra the capital of its kingdom. Under Nabataean rule, Petra became an important center of the spice trade. The Nabataeans were later conquered by the Romans.

Primary Source

"Recite in the name of your Lord who created—
created man from clots of blood.

Recite! Your Lord is the Most Bountiful One, who
by the pen taught man what he did not know."

—Quran 96:1–5

INTERACTIVE

The Origins of
Islam

Muslims believe that Gabriel brought more messages from God.
Muhammad passed these on to his followers. They were later written
down in the **Quran** (koor AHN), Islam's holy book.

Preaching a New Message Muhammad began to preach in the
streets of Mecca. He told Arabs to worship only one God and to change
many of their behaviors. He said that he had received **revelations**
from God. He said that this was the same God who had spoken to
Abraham, Jesus, and prophets and religious figures of Judaism and
Christianity. Muhammad respected those religions. But Muslims believe
he was the final prophet.

Muhammad began to win believers. However, many Meccans opposed
Islam. They feared that the beliefs preached by Muhammad would
reduce their status and wealth as keepers of the Kaaba. They also
feared he would anger the gods they worshiped. They began to persecute Muhammad and other Muslims.

The Hijra In 622, Muhammad and his fellow Muslims fled Mecca to
escape this persecution. They moved to the town of Medina, about 275
miles to the north. Muhammad's migration with his followers from
Mecca to Medina is called the **Hijra**.

Academic Vocabulary
revelation • *n.*, the act of
communicating a divine
truth

Analyze Visuals The
Prophet's Mosque, built
in 706 on the site of
Muhammad's home and
where he led prayer, is
one of the three most
sacred sites in Islam.
Infer What might be the
purpose of the large
open space shown in
the photograph?

▲ Because Islam prohibits the depiction of either humans or animals in religious art, Muhammad is often represented by his name in calligraphy.

In Medina, Muhammad continued his preaching. He became Medina's political and military leader. The Muslims of Medina fought with the people of Mecca. The Meccans tried to conquer Medina, but Muhammad defeated them. After several Muslim victories, Mecca's resistance crumbled.

In 630, Muhammad returned to Mecca as its ruler. He banned worship of the old gods and organized the Muslim community. Muhammad destroyed statues of the gods at the Kaaba and rededicated it as an Islamic holy site. The Kaaba became a place for Muslim pilgrims, or people who travel for religious reasons, to visit.

Quickly, the Muslims united most of Arabia under their rule. Muhammad died, but his death did not halt the spread of his faith. United by Islam, Arabs preached their religion and expanded their rule across Southwest Asia and to many other parts of the world.

✓ **READING CHECK** **Identify Main Ideas** How do Muslims believe Muhammad was different from earlier prophets?

Sources of Islamic Teachings

The Quran is the main source of Islamic teaching. Muslims believe that the Quran is the record of God's revelations to Muhammad.

The Quran According to Islamic tradition, Muhammad recited the words that had been revealed to him. His followers memorized what Muhammad told them. They compiled them into the Quran after Muhammad's death. It has remained unchanged since then.

The Quran consists of 114 chapters in verse form. The verses discuss the nature of God, creation, and the human soul. They also address moral, legal, and family issues. Much of the Quran is written in a poetic style that many Arabic speakers find beautiful.

To Muslims, the Quran is the word of God. They recite its passages during daily prayers and on special occasions. They believe that it must be studied in Arabic, the language in which it is written. Although most Muslims today are not Arabs and do not speak Arabic in daily life, the Arabic language of the Quran unites all Muslims.

Muslims treat the Quran with great devotion. They take special care of copies of the book. They commit passages to memory. Children often first learn reading and writing from the Quran.

The Sunnah Another key source of Islamic thought is the **Sunnah** (SOON nah), or traditions believed by Muslims to come from the prophet Muhammad and his companions. The Sunnah refers to the words and actions of Muhammad. He is considered the best role model. The Sunnah provides Muslims with guidelines for living a proper life. It also helps believers interpret difficult parts of the Quran.

Muslims believe the Sunnah is based on the sayings and actions of Muhammad and his associates. They were recorded in writings called the Hadith. Many of its passages deal with Islamic law.

☑ READING CHECK **Classify and Categorize** How are the Quran and the Sunnah related?

What Do Muslims Believe?

A number of core beliefs are central to Islam. They are stressed in the Quran and in Islamic tradition.

Monotheism The word *Islam* means **"submission"** in Arabic. A Muslim is one who has submitted to God's will. The principal belief of Islam is that there is only one God who created the universe and all things in it. Muslims believe this is the same God that Jews and Christians worship. Muslims usually refer to God as *Allah,* which is simply the word for "God" in Arabic.

Academic Vocabulary
submission • *n.,* the act of being obedient

Muslims also believe that Muhammad was a prophet but that he had no divine, or godlike, power himself. Muslims believe that important Jewish and Christian religious figures such as Abraham, Moses, and Jesus were also prophets and that Muhammad is part of this tradition. Muslims believe that Muhammad is the last in the line of prophets of the Jewish and Christian Bibles.

The Soul and Afterlife Islam teaches that each person has a soul that keeps living after a person dies. Each person also has the freedom to choose between good and evil. The choices a person makes in life affect what happens to his or her soul after death.

☑ READING CHECK **Compare and Contrast** What is a major similarity between Christianity and Islam?

◀ A copy of the Quran in Arabic

The Five Pillars of Islam

Muslims have five key religious duties. These duties are known as the Five Pillars of Islam.

- **Belief** The first pillar is stating a belief that "there is no god but God, and Muhammad is the messenger of God."
- **Prayer** The second pillar is prayer. It is a religious duty for Muslims to pray five times a day.
- **Charity** The third pillar of Islam is giving charity to the needy. Muslims must share their wealth with the less fortunate.
- **Fasting** The fourth pillar is fasting during Ramadan, a month in the Islamic calendar. Fasting means not eating or drinking for a period of time. During Ramadan, Muslims fast between daybreak and sunset. Muslims believe that fasting tests their commitment to God and reminds them of the hunger of the poor. The end of Ramadan is marked by Eid al-Fitr (eed ahl FIT ur), or Festival of the Breaking of the Fast. This is an important holiday.
- **Pilgrimage** The fifth pillar is the **hajj**, or the pilgrimage made by Muslims to the holy city of Mecca. A pilgrimage is a journey to a sacred place or shrine. The Quran instructs every Muslim to make the hajj at least once, if possible. Bringing Muslims from all parts of the world together every year strengthens the global community of Muslims.

☑ READING CHECK **Summarize** Why do Muslims fast?

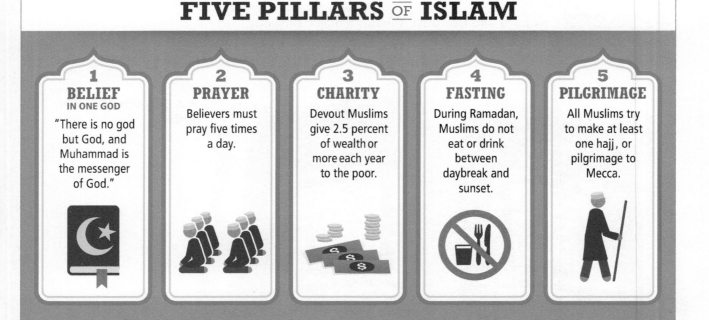

FIVE PILLARS OF ISLAM

1 BELIEF IN ONE GOD	2 PRAYER	3 CHARITY	4 FASTING	5 PILGRIMAGE
"There is no god but God, and Muhammad is the messenger of God."	Believers must pray five times a day.	Devout Muslims give 2.5 percent of wealth or more each year to the poor.	During Ramadan, Muslims do not eat or drink between daybreak and sunset.	All Muslims try to make at least one hajj, or pilgrimage to Mecca.

Analyze Charts Examine the infographic that explains the Five Pillars of Islam.
Identify Main Ideas Which of these pillars do you think Muslims would consider the most important? Why?

▲ This photograph shows a mosque in Shiraz, Iran. Muslims gather at a mosque for worship on Fridays.

Prayer, Pilgrimage, and Law

Islam plays a large role in the daily lives of Muslims. It helps shape society in Muslim-majority nations.

Worship Prayer and worship are key elements of daily life for Muslims. At five specific times each day, devout Muslims stop what they are doing to pray. Before praying, Muslims remove their shoes and wash their hands and feet. This is called an ablution. They may bow several times. Then, facing in the direction of Mecca, they kneel and pray.

A Muslim house of worship is called a **mosque** (mahsk). At a mosque, the community participates in group prayer and other religious activities. Mosques are usually found at the heart of Muslim-majority towns or cities. All mosques contain a prayer hall facing in the direction of Mecca. They usually include a special place for the imam (ee MAHM), or religious leader, to stand to give sermons. A minaret is attached to most mosques. Minarets are towers from which a man called a muezzin (moo EZ un) sings the call to prayer. On Fridays, Muslims gather at a mosque for group worship and to hear a sermon.

The Hajj As you have read, the hajj is a pilgrimage to Mecca. During the hajj, pilgrims take part in many rituals. The most important is walking in a circle around the Kaaba. The Kaaba is a cube-like building in the courtyard of the Grand Mosque in Mecca. Muslims believe that in ancient times, Abraham and his son Ishmael built the Kaaba as a place to worship God. During the hajj, Muslims also visit the place where Muhammad gave his last sermon. The hajj reminds Muslims of Abraham, Ishmael, and Muhammad. It connects Muslims to their religious history.

Analyze Visuals Muslim scholars converse outside a religious college in Iran. **Identify Main Ideas** What is the basis of law codes in secular nations?

Law Muhammad taught that everyday life was no different from religious life. Living a proper life meant following God's laws as revealed in the Quran and the Sunnah. These laws are collected in the Islamic law code known as the **Sharia** (shuh REE uh). The Arabic word *Sharia* means "the way," as in the right way to act.

The Quran and the Sunnah served as sources for the Sharia. But those sources could not cover every possible situation. Religious scholars also judged new situations based on reason, consensus, and other sources.

By the 900s, Muslim scholars had established the Sharia as a fixed body of law. In this form it was used by Muslim societies for centuries. In the 1800s, however, governments in some Muslim lands began replacing parts of Sharia law with law codes based on European models. Other parts of the Sharia were reformed. Today, law codes in some Muslim nations are closely based on the Sharia. Others have a more secular, or nonreligious, basis.

Rules of Proper Conduct The Sharia provides Muslims with specific rules of personal conduct. The most important rules concern the basic duties of every Muslim—the Five Pillars of Islam. Other rules list things that Muslims should not do. For example, the Sharia forbids Muslims from gambling, stealing, eating pork, or drinking alcohol. The Sharia also includes rules that give guidance for resolving family issues and for doing business ethically.

☑ READING CHECK **Identify Main Ideas** What is the purpose of the hajj?

☑ Lesson Check

Practice Vocabulary

1. What is the connection between the **Sharia**, the **Quran**, and the **Sunnah**?

2. What role do **mosques** play in the lives of Muslims?

Critical Thinking and Writing

3. **Compare and Contrast** What is the main similarity between Islam, Judaism, and Christianity?

4. **Identify Main Ideas** Why do Muslims consider Mecca sacred?

5. **Summarize** How does the word *Islam* reflect one of the core beliefs of the faith?

6. **Writing Workshop: Support Ideas with Evidence** In your 📓 Active Journal, write a paragraph about the values of Islam and other religions that originated in Southwest Asia. Decide how you might incorporate these values into your essay.

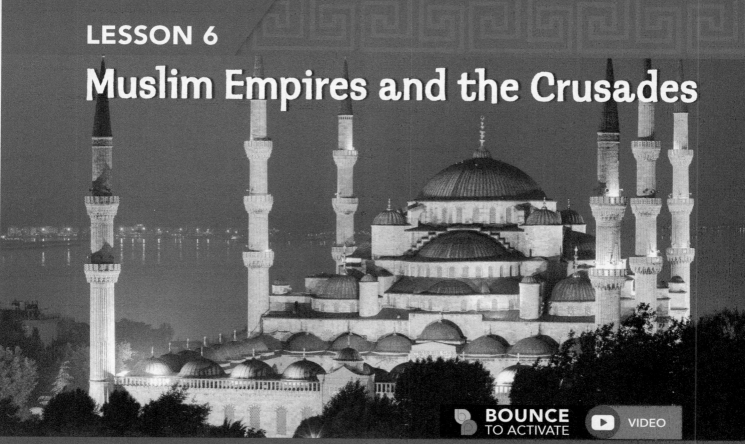

LESSON 6
Muslim Empires and the Crusades

BOUNCE TO ACTIVATE · VIDEO

GET READY TO READ

START UP
Look at the picture of the Blue Mosque in Istanbul, built during the time of the Ottoman empire. What does it suggest about the achievements of Muslim empires?

GUIDING QUESTIONS
- How did Islam and Muslim rule spread across Southwest Asia?
- How did the caliphate lead to both divisions among Muslims and great cultural achievements?
- How did Southwest Asia change after medieval invasions?

TAKE NOTES
Literacy Skills: Use Evidence
Use the graphic organizer in your ▣ Active Journal to take notes as you read the lesson.

PRACTICE VOCABULARY
Use the vocabulary activity in your ▣ Active Journal to practice the vocabulary words.

Vocabulary	Academic Vocabulary
caliph	convert
sultan	install

At the time of Muhammad's death in 632, many tribes of Bedouin warriors had **converted** to Islam. These Arab tribes formed a powerful and skilled army and began to expand Arab Muslim rule across three continents.

The Arab Muslim Empire and the Spread of Islam

Arab Muslim armies first aimed to conquer all of Arabia. After Muhammad's death, some Arab tribes rebelled against Muslim rule, but the Muslims were able to defeat them.

Early Conquests After securing Arabia, the Arab Muslims defeated greater rivals in nearby lands. In the 630s and 640s, these armies conquered the Persian empire and much of the Byzantine empire. Arab Muslims took Mesopotamia, Palestine, Syria, Egypt, and Persia. Later, they conquered Afghanistan, northern India, North Africa, and Spain. By 800, the Muslims ruled a vast empire.

Academic Vocabulary

convert • *v.*, to cause to change in form or function

INTERACTIVE

The Dome of the Rock

GEOGRAPHY SKILLS

By 800, Islam had spread west into North Africa and Spain and northeast into Central Asia.

1. **Movement** How did trade routes affect the spread of Islam?

2. **Use Visual Information** What are three regions conquered by Arab Muslims?

Islam Spreads As the Arab Muslims built their empire, Islam spread in the region. At first, most of the conquered non-Arab peoples retained their existing religions, such as Christianity. As the religion of the empire's rulers, however, Islam offered opportunity for advancement. After a few hundred years, most people in the region had converted to Islam. The Arabic language also spread widely.

Islam spread through trade as well as conquest. Muslim merchants traveled outside the empire, carrying their faith with them. Over time, many people in South Asia, Southeast Asia, and Africa turned to Islam.

Reasons for Success Arab Muslims built a massive empire in a short period of time. Several factors led to Muslim success. One was the decline of the Persian and Byzantine empires. Years of warfare had left those large empires weak and vulnerable.

A second factor was the ability and devotion of Muslim warriors. They were great fighters, and their belief that God was on their side may also have spurred them to fight with great zeal.

Relative religious toleration also helped the Arab Muslim empire expand. Muslims conquered lands where large numbers of Jews and Christians lived. Muslims generally did not force their religion on these groups. This policy made conquered peoples less likely to rebel. Still, non-Muslims faced discrimination in the Muslim empire, such as having to pay a special tax and being forced to wear special clothing.

READING CHECK Summarize Why did Jews, Christians, and others in the Muslim empire tolerate Islamic rule?

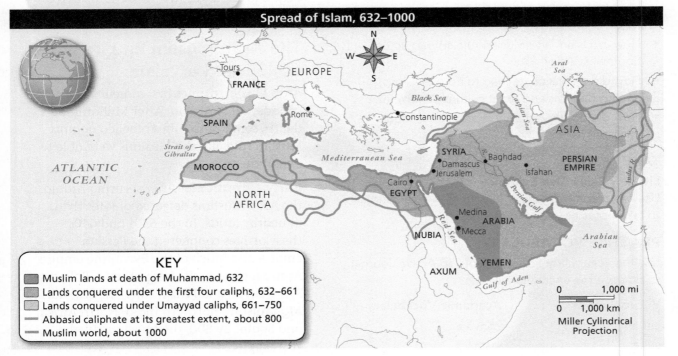

Spread of Islam, 632–1000

Tours
FRANCE
EUROPE
SPAIN
Rome
Black Sea
Constantinople
Aral Sea
ASIA
Strait of Gibraltar
ATLANTIC OCEAN
MOROCCO
Mediterranean Sea
SYRIA
Damascus
Jerusalem
Baghdad
Isfahan
PERSIAN EMPIRE
NORTH AFRICA
Cairo
EGYPT
Medina
Mecca
ARABIA
NUBIA
Red Sea
Persian Gulf
Arabian Sea
AXUM
YEMEN
Gulf of Aden
Caspian Sea
Indus R.

0   1,000 mi
0   1,000 km
Miller Cylindrical Projection

KEY
- Muslim lands at death of Muhammad, 632
- Lands conquered under the first four caliphs, 632–661
- Lands conquered under Umayyad caliphs, 661–750
- Abbasid caliphate at its greatest extent, about 800
- Muslim world, about 1000

Shias and Sunnis

SHIAS

- Believe only descendants of Muhammad should be chosen as caliphs
- Are a minority of Muslims

- Allah as only God
- Quran
- Five Pillars of Islam
- Imams are divinely inspired religious leaders

SUNNIS

- Believe any pious male member of the Muslim community can be chosen as a caliph
- Are the majority of Muslims

The Caliphs

As you read, Muhammad was the first Muslim leader. After he died, rulers called caliphs (KAY lifs) led the Muslim community and then the empire. In Arabic, **caliph** means "successor," as in the successor of Muhammad. A government run by a caliph is called a caliphate.

Two Competing Groups But who was to be the first caliph? Who could follow a man who Muslims viewed as the messenger of God? This difficult issue split Muslims into two competing groups.

Most Muslims believed that the community needed a leader with political skills. They supported Muhammad's main advisor, Abu Bakr, who became the first caliph. Members of this group became known as Sunnis (soo neez) because they hold the Sunnah in high regard.

A minority of Muslims believed that only Muhammad's relatives should become caliph. They supported Ali, Muhammad's cousin and son-in-law. They were called Shias (SHEE uz), which means supporters, because they supported Ali.

The split between Sunnis and Shias still exists today. Most Muslims—at least 85 percent—are Sunnis. Shias are the largest minority Islamic group and are the majority of Muslims in a few countries, such as Iran.

The "Rightly Guided" Caliphs Each of the first four caliphs had close ties to Muhammad. Each was guided by Muslim principles. For these reasons, Sunni Muslims came to refer to these leaders as the "rightly guided caliphs." They ruled the growing empire from the city of Medina, in Arabia.

Muhammad's cousin Ali, favored by Shias, finally became the fourth caliph in 656. But by then, he had many enemies. He was soon assassinated. After that, the caliphate passed to the powerful Umayyad family. Shias saw Ali as a martyr, a person killed for his or her religion.

Analyze Diagrams
This diagram shows how Sunni and Shia beliefs are alike and different.
Compare and Contrast
What beliefs do Sunni and Shia Muslims share? In what ways are they different?

Quest CONNECTIONS

How did the caliphs establish their legitimacy, or right to rule? Reflect on the question in your Active Journal.

The Umayyad Dynasty The Umayyads founded the first Muslim dynasty. A dynasty is a family that passes down political power from one relative to another. The Umayyads moved the empire's capital from Medina to Damascus, an ancient city in Syria.

Under the Umayyads, the Arab Muslim empire reached its greatest size. Muslim armies conquered North Africa, Spain, and parts of South and Central Asia. Expansion brought Arabs into contact with other cultures. Many non-Arabs adopted Islam, and some began to speak Arabic. In turn, non-Arab cultures influenced the Arab conquerors. Over time, a distinct, blended Islamic civilization emerged.

The Abbasid Dynasty In 750, rebel Arab forces overthrew the Umayyads and **installed** a caliph from the Abbasid family. The Abbasids built a new capital city called Baghdad, in present-day Iraq. Baghdad became the center of a golden age of art, science, and learning.

But as Islamic civilization flourished, the Abbasids were slowly losing control of their empire. In 756, Spain became an independent Muslim state under the Umayyads.

Power slowly passed from Arabs to non-Arabs. Starting in the 900s, Turks migrated into Muslim lands. The Turks were a nomadic people from Central Asia who became Muslims. The Abbasid caliphs hired Turks as soldiers. Eventually, a group of Turks gained control of Baghdad. They allowed the Abbasid caliphs to remain on the throne but stripped them of all real power.

☑ READING CHECK Compare and Contrast How do Sunni Muslims differ from Shia Muslims?

Crusaders and Mongols

Islam gradually became the dominant religion across Southwest Asia. After 1000, however, the region faced invasions from non-Muslim outsiders, including Christian Crusaders from Europe.

Analyze Visuals This illustration of a camel caravan at an oasis shows life during the Abbasid dynasty. **Use Visual Information** What elements of the image suggest that this was a golden age of Islamic civilization?

5 Things to Know About

SALADIN
Founder of the Ayyubid Dynasty (1137/38–1193)

- Saladin's uncle was an important military commander.
- Saladin believed in jihad, the idea of a holy war.
- He supported the creation of Muslim schools.
- As a military commander, Saladin was able to unite various groups against the Europeans.
- When he captured Jerusalem, he let the city's Christians pay a ransom rather than face death.

Critical Thinking What does Saladin's career suggest about his devotion to Islam?

The Crusades The Crusaders invaded and conquered regions on Southwest Asia's Mediterranean coast, including the area Christians knew as the Holy Land, the birthplace of Judaism and Christianity, once known as Judea. Crusaders also took control of Cyprus.

The main goal of the Crusaders was to free Jerusalem from Muslim control. This city was where they believed Jesus had been crucified and resurrected. The Crusaders conquered Jerusalem in 1099 and established the Kingdom of Jerusalem. The Crusaders killed many of the city's Jewish and Muslim residents and turned Islamic shrines into churches and palaces.

The Kingdom of Jerusalem was one of four Crusader states founded on the mainland of Southwest Asia. During the 1100s, the Crusader states began to face defeat by Muslim armies. Muslims resented Christian domination of a region that was home to many Muslims. In 1187, a Muslim general named Saladin defeated the Crusader armies and regained control of Jerusalem.

Mongol Invasion The Mongols, a non-Muslim people from Central Asia, also invaded Southwest Asia. In 1258, they destroyed Baghdad, the city of the caliphs, and killed many of its people. Later, the Mongol rulers of Southwest Asia adopted Islam, and the region slowly recovered.

Trade and the Spread of Ideas The creation of an Islamic empire that stretched from South Asia to Spain led to the spread of ideas and technologies across the region. These ideas included advanced mathematics from India, including a system of numerals, later called Arabic numerals, that we still use today.

At the same time, the Silk Road, a trade route crossing Asia, and Indian Ocean trade routes linked the Muslim empire to China. Trade with China brought many new technologies to the Islamic world.

 INTERACTIVE

Muslim Advances in Technology, Math, and Science

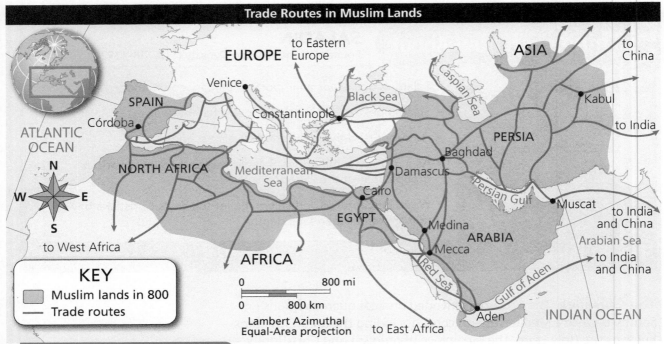

Trade Routes in Muslim Lands

EUROPE
to Eastern Europe
ASIA
to China
Venice
SPAIN
Córdoba
Black Sea
Caspian Sea
Kabul
to India
ATLANTIC OCEAN
Constantinople
PERSIA
N
W E
S
NORTH AFRICA
Mediterranean Sea
Baghdad
Damascus
Persian Gulf
Muscat
to India and China
Cairo
to West Africa
EGYPT
Medina
Mecca
ARABIA
Arabian Sea
to India and China
AFRICA
Red Sea
Gulf of Aden
Aden
INDIAN OCEAN
to East Africa

0   800 mi
0   800 km
Lambert Azimuthal
Equal-Area projection

KEY
Muslim lands in 800
— Trade routes

GEOGRAPHY SKILLS

Trade routes crisscrossed Southwest Asia, North Africa, Europe, and beyond, which expanded trade and the exchange of ideas.

1. **Movement** What city might be a starting point for a merchant traveling to East Africa?

2. **Use Visual Information** Through which cities did trade and ideas from Muslim-ruled areas pass to West and East Africa?

The conquest and occupation by European crusaders also opened up trade routes to Europe. As a result, ideas and technologies spread from Southwest Asia and other parts of Asia to Europe. These included the compass, paper, and later, gunpowder.

The Mongol conquest brought devastation to Southwest Asia, but it also connected the Muslim world to the rest of the Mongol empire, including China. This spurred the exchange of still more ideas and technologies between east and west.

✓ **READING CHECK** Draw Conclusions How did foreign conquests affect both Southwest Asia and other regions?

Non-Arab Muslim Empires

The Mongol invasion ended the caliphate and the golden age of Islamic civilization. But individual Muslim states survived, many ruled by non-Arab dynasties. The leaders of many of these states called themselves **sultans**, or rulers of a Muslim country.

The Ottoman Empire The largest of these states became the Ottoman empire, which lasted into the early 1900s. The Ottomans were a Turkish dynasty. They founded their empire in Anatolia, the Asian part of what is now Turkey.

Ottoman expansion was powered by a strong military, particularly the janissary corps. Ottoman armies eventually conquered territory from southeastern Europe to northern Africa and the Arabian Peninsula.

The Ottoman sultan declared himself caliph, and the Ottoman empire reunited much of Southwest Asia.

New Persian Empires You have already read about the rich culture of the ancient Persian empire. Persian culture continued to develop after the ancient Persian empire fell.

After the Arab conquest, most Persians converted to Islam but kept the Persian language. Persian culture also survived.

In the 1500s, the Safavid dynasty took control of Persia. The Safavids were Shias and made Shia Islam the official religion of Persia. Although the Safavid dynasty lost power in 1722, other dynasties continued to rule Persia and neighboring territories into modern times. Today, Persia is called Iran, and it remains a majority Shia country.

☑ **READING CHECK** **Identify Main Ideas** How did the Ottomans and Safavids change the region?

▲ This Persian miniature shows a lavish reception at a Safavid prince's palace.

☑ Lesson Check

Practice Vocabulary

1. How does the term *caliph* relate to Muhammad?

2. How do **sultans** and **caliphs** differ?

Critical Thinking and Writing

3. **Compare and Contrast** How did the issue of Muhammad's successor split Muslims into Sunni and Shia?

4. **Identify Cause and Effect** How did non-Muslims and non-Arabs affect the Umayyad empire?

5. **Understand Effects** How did the Mongol invasion of Southwest Asia affect the region?

6. **Draw Conclusions** According to the Country Databank, what is the standard language in most countries in the region? What might explain this?

7. **Writing Workshop: Develop a Clear Thesis** Begin developing a thesis statement for your essay based on the work you have already done on this topic. Your thesis statement should reflect the most important thing you have learned about the values of cultures in Southwest Asia. Write your thesis in your ▱ Active Journal.

Building Modern Nations in Southwest Asia

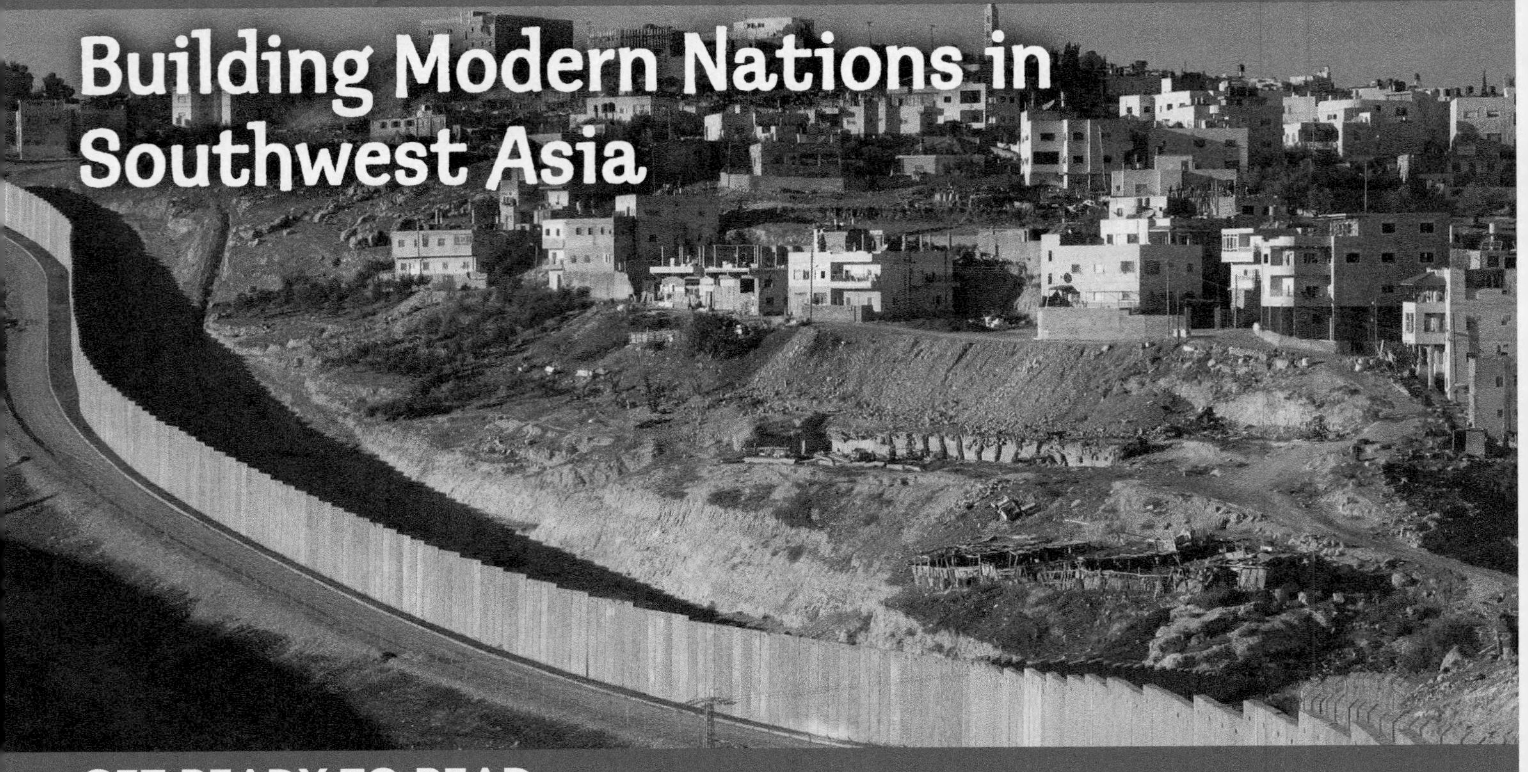

GET READY TO READ

START UP
The photograph above shows the security barrier cutting through communities in Jerusalem and throughout the West Bank. Why do you think this wall was built?

GUIDING QUESTIONS
- How did Europeans reshape Southwest Asia?
- Why was there conflict between Israel and neighboring Arabs?
- How did the Iranian Revolution transform Iran?
- Why did Iraq and Lebanon face conflict?

TAKE NOTES
Literacy Skills: Sequence
Use the graphic organizer in your ▰ Active Journal to take notes as you read the lesson.

PRACTICE VOCABULARY
Use the vocabulary activity in your ▰ Active Journal to practice the vocabulary words.

Vocabulary
mandate   nation-state
anti-Semitism   secular
Zionism

Academic Vocabulary
modernize
armistice

For much of modern history, the people of Southwest Asia have struggled to find peace and stability. Often, the region faced conflict.

European Colonialism
At its height, the Ottoman empire included most of Southwest Asia outside of Persia, as well as parts of Europe and Africa. The Ottomans remained in control of this area until World War I ended in 1918.

European Mandates After Britain and France defeated the Ottoman empire in World War I, they declared mandates over what are now Syria, Lebanon, Israel, Jordan, and Iraq. A **mandate** was a territory controlled by an Allied power after World War I. Syria and Lebanon were the French mandate. British mandates included what are today the nations of Israel, Jordan, and Iraq. Britain also controlled colonies and protectorates on Cyprus and the Arabian Peninsula, which it had established in the 1800s to protect trade routes to India.

Mandates Generate Conflict The borders of the mandates ignored religious and ethnic divisions. For example, the Kurdish people were split among Iran, the French and British mandates, and Turkey. This left the Kurds without a country. In addition, Arabs had helped the Allies fight Ottoman forces in World War I and expected independence. Feeling betrayed, they organized revolts and protests.

Another center of conflict was the Palestine Mandate, including present-day Israel and Jordan. During World War I, the British had sought Arab support by promising Arabs control over Ottoman lands in Southwest Asia. They also tried to win Jewish help by declaring support for a homeland for the Jewish people in the same lands.

For centuries, the Jews of Europe had faced cruel and often violent **anti-Semitism**, or discrimination against Jews. In the late 1800s, Jews in Europe formed a movement called **Zionism**. Its goal was to create an independent Jewish country in Jews' historic homeland in Palestine. Having such a state would give Jews a safe haven.

The British did establish Arab kingdoms in Iraq and in Transjordan, the eastern part of the Palestine Mandate. Both Arabs and Jews were unhappy, however, believing wartime promises had been broken. The Arabs wanted to rule the entire mandate. Jews wanted a country of their own. Conflict developed as more Jews and Arabs moved into the area.

✓ READING CHECK **Identify Cause and Effect** How did splitting Southwest Asia into mandates lead to conflict?

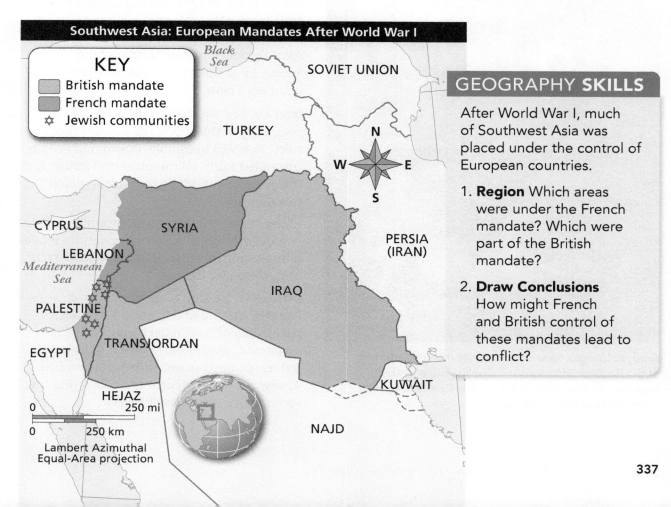

Southwest Asia: European Mandates After World War I

KEY
- British mandate
- French mandate
- ☆ Jewish communities

GEOGRAPHY **SKILLS**

After World War I, much of Southwest Asia was placed under the control of European countries.

1. **Region** Which areas were under the French mandate? Which were part of the British mandate?

2. **Draw Conclusions** How might French and British control of these mandates lead to conflict?

337

New Nation-States

While the British and French controlled some parts of the region, changes were taking place elsewhere. Peoples resisting foreign domination began founding new nation-states in the region. A **nation-state** is a country that is independent.

Modern Turkey Forms European powers tried to take control of present-day Turkey following World War I and divide it among Greece and other nations. The Turks fought this plan, hoping to establish their own nation. A Turkish army officer named Mustafa Kemal led forces fighting for independence. Turkish nationalists defeated Greek forces and declared Turkish independence in 1923.

Mustafa Kemal became the first president of the Turkish Republic. Kemal tried to **modernize** Turkey and to westernize it. Kemal made Turkey a **secular**, or nonreligious, state. Women were given more rights than before. People were encouraged to wear European clothes. The Latin alphabet was used for the Turkish language.

Kemal ruled using undemocratic methods. Still, many of his reforms won great respect from the Turkish people. He called himself Atatürk, which means "Father of the Turks." Most Turks today consider him a national hero.

Iran Under the Shahs Around the beginning of the 1900s, the dynasty that ruled Iran was in trouble. Russia and Britain controlled Iran's oil resources and influenced the government. Many Iranians resented this situation.

In the 1920s, a military leader named Reza Pahlavi overthrew the government. He made himself shah, or ruler. He tried to modernize and westernize Iran.

After 1941, his son, Mohammad Reza Pahlavi, continued this work. He became a close ally of the United States. In 1953, an elected government threw out the shah, but he regained power with American help. Afterward, the shah arrested critics, and his secret police were greatly feared.

Analyze Images Mustafa Kemal was the first president of the Republic of Turkey. He took the name Atatürk, meaning "Father of the Turks." **Draw Conclusions** Why might he have picked this name?

A Fractured Region After the Ottoman empire collapsed at the end of World War I, two new kingdoms—Saudi Arabia and Yemen—emerged on the Arabian Peninsula.

 **INTERACTIVE**

Religious Diversity in the Middle East

In the 1700s, Sunni fundamentalists known as Wahhabis allied with kings of the Saudi dynasty to create a new state. In 1932, this dynasty conquered most of the Arabian Peninsula to form the Kingdom of Saudi Arabia.

Yemen had been controlled by two imperial powers—the Ottomans in the north and Britain in the south—until the end of World War I. After the fall of the Ottoman empire, the north became independent, while the south remained under British control until the 1960s. The two parts of Yemen were not unified until 1990.

Oil became the focus of the region's economy beginning in the early 1900s. Foreign companies began to move into Saudi Arabia, British-occupied Iraq, and elsewhere to exploit the fuel that powered factories, power plants, and cars.

At the same time, Southwest Asia was becoming more volatile. Iraq, Syria, and Lebanon won their independence in the 1930s and 1940s. Each of these new countries had deep ethnic and religious divisions, however. Britain allowed a large part of the Palestine Mandate, Transjordan, to become a kingdom, later known as Jordan.

☑ **READING CHECK** **Summarize** How did Mustafa Kemal change Turkey?

How Did Conflict Develop in Israel?

After Nazi Germany murdered millions of Jews during World War II in the Holocaust, international support increased for an independent homeland in the Palestine Mandate. In 1947, the United Nations set up a plan to divide the Palestine Mandate into two states, one Arab and one Jewish. Jews accepted the plan, but the Arabs did not.

Quick Activity

Work with classmates to make a timeline of Southwest Asian history. Refer to your 📓 Active Journal.

BIOGRAPHY

5 Things to Know About

GOLDA MEIR
Prime minister of Israel (1898–1978)

- Golda Meir grew up in Milwaukee, Wisconsin.

- Meir and her husband, Morris Myerson, immigrated to Palestine in 1921.

- During World War II, Meir was a strong spokesperson for Zionism.

- She was one of the signers of Israel's Declaration of Independence.

- As Israeli prime minister, Meir worked to defend Israel and make peace with the Arab states.

Critical Thinking What impact did Meir have on the creation of Israel?

Quest CONNECTIONS

Why did the founders of Israel declare independence? Reflect on the situation in your 📓 Active Journal.

Academic Vocabulary

armistice • *n.,* a temporary agreement made by opposing sides in a war to stop the fighting

▼ The Ayatollah Khomeini speaks to a crowd in 1979.

Independence Brings War In 1948, Britain withdrew from the Palestine Mandate. The Jews who were living there declared their part of the region under the UN plan the State of Israel.

Once Israel declared its independence, neighboring Arab states attacked the new country. Palestinian Arabs fled or were driven from their homes in Israeli territory, settling as refugees in the West Bank of the Jordan River and in the Gaza Strip. Some moved to UN camps in nearby countries. Meanwhile, Jewish refugees forced out by Arab states or fleeing persecution there moved to Israel. This war ended in an **armistice**. Jordan took control of the West Bank and East Jerusalem, and Egypt took control of the Gaza Strip. Israel joined Great Britain and France in attacking Egypt in a second war in 1956, after Egypt blockaded the Suez Canal.

Further Conflicts and a Fragile Peace In June 1967, Egyptian forces mobilized along the Israeli border. This led to another war between three Arab countries—Jordan, Egypt, and Syria—and Israel. When the fighting ended, Israel had won control of the West Bank and East Jerusalem from Jordan. Israel also gained control of the Sinai Peninsula and Gaza from Egypt and the Golan Heights from Syria. Egypt and Syria attacked Israel in 1973, hoping to regain their lost territories. However, Israel defeated them.

In 1979, the United States helped Egypt and Israel reach a peace agreement, the first Israel signed between an Arab state and Israel. Israel returned the Sinai Peninsula to Egypt in exchange for formal recognition and peace. This meant that Egypt officially acknowledged Israel as an independent country. Israel and Jordan signed a peace treaty in 1994.

✅ READING CHECK **Summarize** What was the United Nations partition plan? What was the reaction to it in the region?

The Iranian Revolution

During the 1960s, a high-ranking Shia religious leader named Ruhollah Khomeini became a leading critic of the pro-western, harsh rule of the shah of Iran. Khomeini wanted Iran to follow Islamic law and traditions. The shah forced Khomeini to leave Iran, but the Ayatollah continued to speak out against the shah.

In 1978, a revolution broke out. The shah and his family fled, and his government collapsed. In February 1979, Khomeini returned and took power. In 1980, war broke out between Iran and Iraq. The war was started by Iraq's dictator, Saddam Hussein, who wanted Iran's oil-rich lands. Iraq had the open support of Saudi Arabia, Kuwait, and other Arab states. The United States also quietly supported Iraq. The deadly Iran–Iraq War dragged on until 1988.

✅ READING CHECK **Recognize Multiple Causes** What sparked the Iranian Revolution?

Conflicts Between Iraq and the West

After 1990, a series of conflicts devastated parts of Southwest Asia. Iraq and Lebanon were among the countries affected.

Wars in Iraq Saddam Hussein started another war in 1990. His troops invaded neighboring Kuwait and took control there. Saddam wanted its oil. The United States organized a large group of countries opposed to this action. In 1991, they forced Iraqi troops to leave Kuwait.

In 2003, U.S. President George W. Bush claimed that Iraq was a threat to the world because it had weapons of mass destruction. These are dangerous weapons that can kill large numbers of people at once.

That year, the United States and some allies invaded Iraq. United States-led forces quickly removed Saddam Hussein from power. No weapons of mass destruction were found. The United States and its allies supported the creation of a democratic Iraqi government in 2005.

Continued Fighting Saddam's overthrow did not end the conflict, however. Some Iraqis resisted U.S.-led forces. Fighting also broke out among Iraq's three main ethnic and religious groups: the Kurds, Sunni Arabs, and Shia Arabs. Violence continued, and American troops stayed in Iraq to keep the peace. The United States maintained a close relationship with Iraq's government.

Violence in Iraq remained a problem, much of it caused by conflict between the Sunni Arab minority and the Shia Arab majority. Sunni Muslims complained of unfair treatment by the Shia-led government.

READING CHECK **Draw Conclusions** Why do you think the old rivalry between Sunni and Shia Muslims continued in Iraq?

Analyze Visuals Iraqi civilians and U.S. and allied soldiers take down a statue of Saddam Hussein in Baghdad in 2003. **Draw Conclusions** Why do you think people wanted to get rid of the statue?

Analyze Visuals This photograph was taken in Beirut, Lebanon, in 1976. **Use Visual Information** Judging from the image, what effect did the civil war have on Beirut?

Civil War in Lebanon

When Lebanon gained independence in the 1940s, Christians were the largest religious group and held the most power. Over time, Muslims became the largest group. They demanded more power.

In 1975, civil war broke out between Muslims and Christians. Palestinian Arabs who had fled to Lebanon from the 1948 war and from conflict in Jordan in 1970 also took part in the war. Syrian troops invaded Lebanon in response for its own security interests and to help its allies there.

In 1982, Israel also invaded Lebanon to stop terrorist attacks on its people launched by Palestinians in that country. Israel withdrew most of its troops from Lebanon, but the civil war in Lebanon continued until 1990. Peace during the 1990s allowed Lebanon to rebuild. Israeli troops had left by 2000. Syrian troops remained until 2005. However, tensions among Lebanese groups continued.

☑ READING CHECK **Summarize** What factors led to the civil war in Lebanon?

☑ Lesson Check

Practice Vocabulary

1. How does **Zionism** relate to **anti-Semitism**?

2. What does it mean to make a country **secular**?

Critical Thinking and Writing

3. **Summarize** How did the end of World War I lead to regional conflict in Southwest Asia?

4. **Sequence** What steps led to the establishment of the modern State of Israel in 1948?

5. **Draw Conclusions** Why did independence in some Arab states lead to conflict?

6. **Synthesize Visual Information** How does the Degree of Democracy column in the Country Databank reflect this region's history?

7. **Writing Workshop: Write an Introduction** In your 📓 Active Journal write an introductory paragraph that supports your thesis about the values of a culture you have studied in this topic.

Geographic Sources

The Syrian Refugee Crisis

In 2011, a civil war broke out in Syria. The conflict created a refugee crisis as millions fled the country. Several countries allowed the refugees to enter and stay, but when the numbers of refugees swelled, this policy faced growing opposition.

▶ These Syrians escaped the war in their country by fleeing to an island in Greece.

"According to an April 2016 <u>UN</u> ① estimate, the death toll among Syrian Government forces, opposition forces, and civilians had reached 400,000. As of December 2016, approximately 13.5 million people were in need of <u>humanitarian assistance</u> ② in Syria, with 6.3 million people <u>displaced</u> ③ <u>internally</u>, ④ and an additional <u>4.8 million Syrian refugees</u>, ⑤ making the Syrian situation the largest humanitarian crisis worldwide."

—CIA World Factbook

Reading and Vocabulary Support

① United Nations

② *Humanitarian assistance* is medical, food, housing, or other aid people need in order to survive.

③ *Displaced* means forced out of one's home.

④ What does "displaced internally" mean?

⑤ What share of Syria's 18.5 million people were homeless because of the crisis?

Analyzing Geographic Sources

Read the article and study the political cartoon. Then answer the questions that follow.

1. **Determine Author's Purpose** The signs around the refugees represent the countries of the European Union. What point was the cartoonist making?

2. **Determine Author's Point of View** Why does the cartoonist show just one refugee family?

3. **Compare Authors' Points of View** What aspect of the problem is more clear from the secondary source than from the cartoon?

☑ Review and Assessment

VISUAL REVIEW

MAJOR RELIGIONS OF SOUTHWEST ASIA

Judaism
- Oldest monotheistic religion
- Hebrew Bible; Talmud (commentaries)
- Abraham, Moses, David
- Ethical monotheism; helping others; observing Sabbath; study and prayer

Christianity
- Jewish roots
- Bible
- Jesus, Paul
- Monotheism (God in three persons); soul; salvation through the death of Jesus, resurrection; ethical behavior; faith

Islam
- Built on Jewish and Christian traditions
- Quran, Sunnah (traditions)
- Muhammad
- Monotheism; submission to God; Five Pillars: belief, prayer, charity, fasting, pilgrimage

History of Southwest Asia

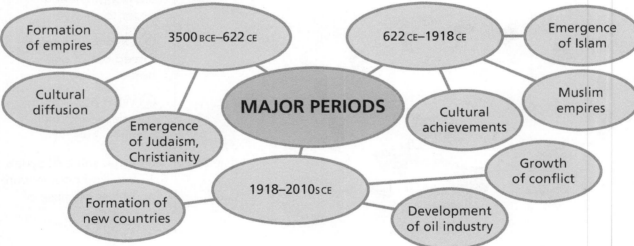

Formation of empires

Cultural diffusion

3500 BCE–622 CE

Emergence of Judaism, Christianity

622 CE–1918 CE

Emergence of Islam

Muslim empires

MAJOR PERIODS

Cultural achievements

Growth of conflict

Formation of new countries

1918–2010s CE

Development of oil industry

READING REVIEW

Use the Take Notes and Practice Vocabulary activities in your 📖 Active Journal to review the topic.

👆 INTERACTIVE

Practice vocabulary using the Topic Mini-Games.

Quest FINDINGS

Writing Your Report

Use the notes you have taken to prepare your report recommending a new government for your country. Prepare your report in your 📖 Active Journal.

ASSESSMENT

Vocabulary and Key Ideas

1. **Identify Main Ideas** How was the **Neolithic Revolution** related to the formation of **city-states** and **empires**?

2. **Identify** Name civilizations of the region that practiced **polytheism** and three religions that believe in **monotheism**.

3. **Identify Supporting Details** How are **parables** related to the **Gospels**?

4. **Identify** How is the **Sunnah** related to the **Quran**?

5. **Compare and Contrast** What is the difference between a **caliph** and a **sultan**?

6. **Recognize Multiple Causes** How did the region between the Tigris and Euphrates rivers attract people to settle down and become farmers?

7. **Trace** How did trade and empire-building contribute to the spread of Judaism, Christianity, and Islam?

Critical Thinking and Writing

8. **Identify Main Ideas** What helped establish the unity of the Muslim world under the Umayyad and Abbasid empires?

9. **Identify Supporting Details** Why are law and morality important in Judaism?

10. **Compare and Contrast** What beliefs and practices of Judaism, Christianity, and Islam are similar?

11. **Identify Cause and Effect** How did World War I create an environment that contributed to conflict in Southwest Asia?

12. **Revisit the Essential Question** How did a dispute over who was to be the first caliph affect Muslim society from the 600s to the present?

13. **Writing Workshop: Use Technology to Produce and Publish** Using the research that you carried out and the notes you made in your ⬛ Active Journal, write a research essay that explores the values of a culture you studied in the topic.

Analyze Primary Sources

14. Which religious leader delivered this message?
    A. Abraham
    B. Jesus
    C. Moses
    D. Muhammad

"I am the good shepherd; the good shepherd lays down His life for His sheep."

Analyze Maps

Use the map at right to answer the following questions.

15. Which letter represents an area that was part of the French mandate?

16. Which letter represents a region where early farming civilizations thrived?

17. Why did the area labeled with the letter C become a source of conflict?

18. Which letter represents a country that became a kingdom after the fall of the Ottoman empire?

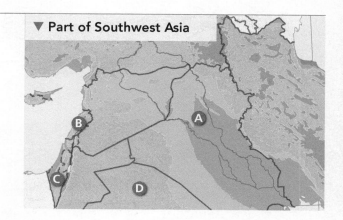

▼ **Part of Southwest Asia**

Southwest Asia Today

GO ONLINE
to access your
digital course

▶ VIDEO

 AUDIO

 ETEXT

 INTERACTIVE

 WRITING

GAMES

WORKSHEET

✓ ASSESSMENT

Travel to

MODERN SOUTHWEST ASIA,
a complex region with many
challenges. It is ethnically
and religiously diverse, it
has traditional and modern
influences, and its water and
oil are both precious.

Explore
The
Essential
Question

How should we handle conflict?

Southwest Asia is home to Muslims,
Jews, and Christians. How is this
diversity connected to conflict?
Unlock the Essential Question
in your 📖 Active Journal.

▲ Palm Island, a community
in Dubai

Read

about the different ethnic and religious groups as well as the economic and political systems of Southwest Asia.

Watch

BOUNCE TO ACTIVATE ▶ VIDEO

Maayan and Muhammad

Meet Maayan, a young Jewish Israeli woman, and Muhammad, an Arab Israeli boy, and learn about life in this complex land.

7 Regional Atlas

Southwest Asia: Political

SOUTHWEST ASIA

The region has seen a lot of conflict. Some countries dispute, or disagree about, their borders. Some countries are divided into areas held by different armed groups.

Learn more about Southwest Asia by making your own map in your 📓 Active Journal.

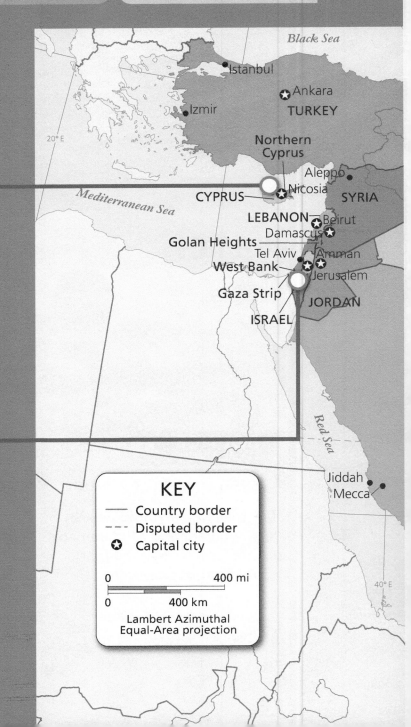

A Divided Cyprus

In 1975, the Turkish people of northern Cyprus broke away from the rest of Cyprus to form a separate republic with military backing from Turkey. Other countries do not recognize the independence of Northern Cyprus, however.

Disputed Borders

Many of the borders around Israel and the Golan Heights, West Bank, and Gaza Strip are disputed between Israel and its neighbors.

KEY
—— Country border
- - - Disputed border
⭐ Capital city

0	400 mi
0	400 km

Lambert Azimuthal
Equal-Area projection

Shifting Control

Conflict within both Syria and Yemen, shown in the photograph, has divided those countries among armed groups that control shifting territories.

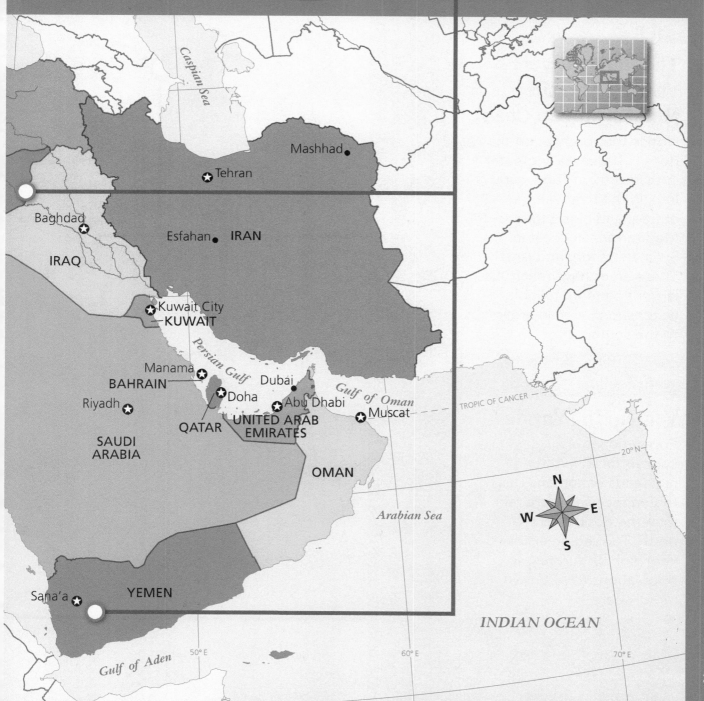

Caspian Sea

Mashhad •

⭐ Tehran

Baghdad
⭐

IRAQ

Esfahan • **IRAN**

Kuwait City ⭐
KUWAIT

Persian Gulf

Manama
BAHRAIN ⭐   Dubai
⭐ Doha •   Gulf of Oman

Riyadh ⭐   ⭐ Abu Dhabi   TROPIC OF CANCER

QATAR   ⭐ Muscat

**UNITED ARAB
EMIRATES**

**SAUDI
ARABIA**   20° N

OMAN

Arabian Sea

N
W ✦ E
S

Sana'a ⭐   **YEMEN**

INDIAN OCEAN

50° E   60° E   70° E

Gulf of Aden

349

Southwest Asia: Population Density

WHERE DO PEOPLE LIVE?

Southwest Asia is densely populated along its coasts. People live in these areas because higher rainfall permits farming and ports give access to trade. Population density is also high in traditional areas of settlement.

The North, River Valleys, and the Mediterranean Coast

Notice that population density is generally greater in the north, in Turkey and Iran, in the river valleys of Iraq, and along the Mediterranean coast in Syria, Lebanon, and Israel. These areas have much larger and more reliable water supplies than areas to the south.

Yemeni Highlands

Population is also concentrated in the highlands of Yemen. This region receives more rain than the deserts to the north. The region also has very high birth rates, so populations have grown rapidly here.

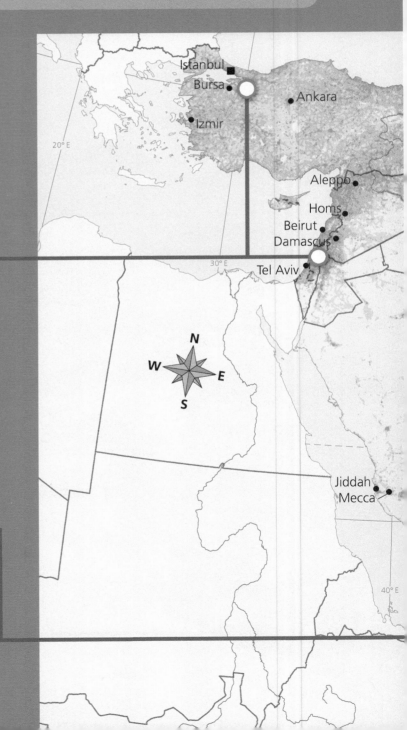

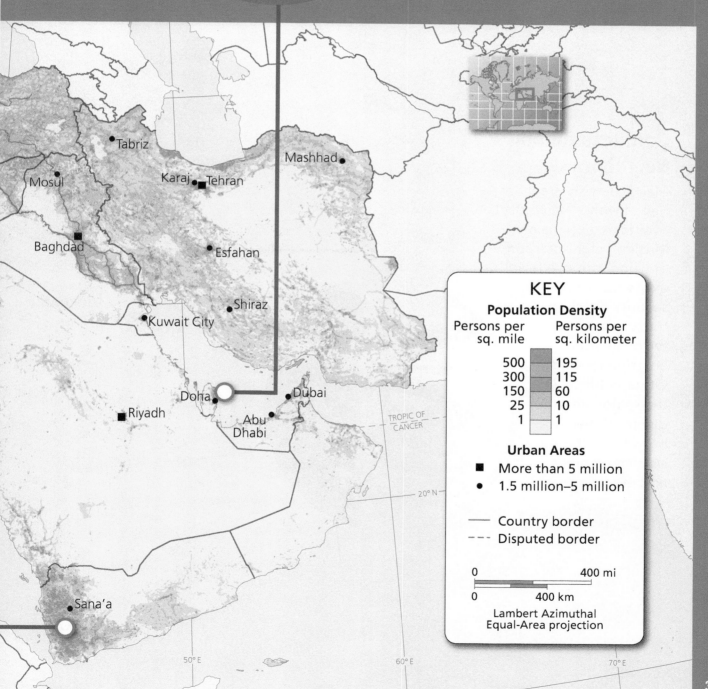

The Persian Gulf and Arabian Peninsula

Other areas of high population densities are the cities lining the Persian Gulf such as Doha, Qatar. People have migrated to these cities for jobs in the oil industry.

Tabriz

Mashhad

Mosul

Karaj • Tehran

Baghdad

Esfahan

Shiraz

Kuwait City

Doha

Dubai

Riyadh

Abu Dhabi

TROPIC OF CANCER

20° N

Sana'a

50° E

60° E

70° E

KEY

Population Density

Persons per sq. mile	Persons per sq. kilometer
500	195
300	115
150	60
25	10
1	1

Urban Areas

■ More than 5 million

● 1.5 million–5 million

——— Country border

- - - Disputed border

0   400 mi

0   400 km

Lambert Azimuthal Equal-Area projection

Regional Atlas

Southwest Asia: Governments and Conflicts

SOUTHWEST ASIA TODAY

Southwest Asia is a region of diverse governments. Several countries are involved in bloody internal conflicts.

Conflicts Among Neighbors

Mainly Jewish Israel has been involved in conflicts over land with mainly Muslim neighbors, some of whom oppose Israel's existence. Israel has security checkpoints to try to prevent terrorists from entering its land. Other conflicts in the region involve disputes over land between different Muslim religious and ethnic groups.

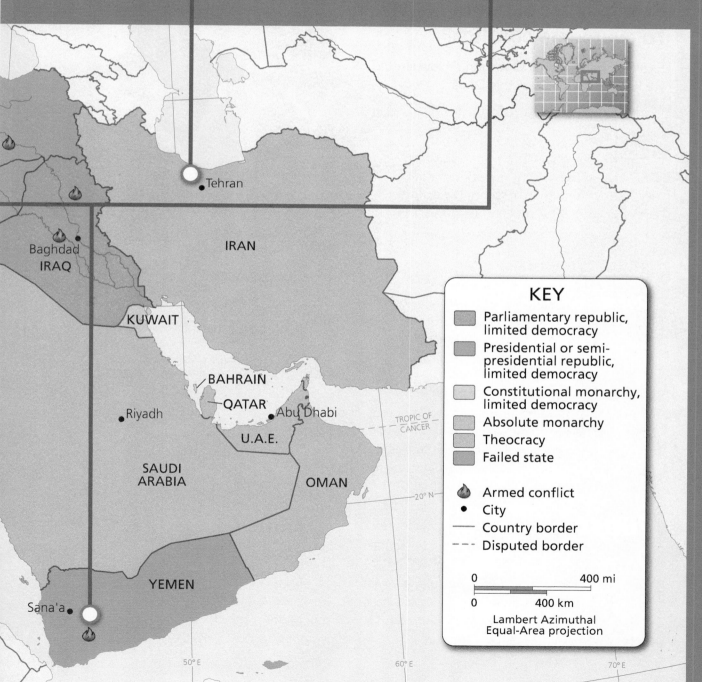

Distinct Governments

Southwest Asia has a wide variety of governments, most of them not very democratic. The region includes types of government not found in most regions, including absolute monarchies and a theocracy in Iran.

Complex Conflicts

The conflicts in Syria and Yemen are complex, involving three or more groups, ethnic or religious conflicts, and soldiers from other countries.

Tehran

Baghdad
IRAQ

IRAN

KUWAIT

BAHRAIN

QATAR

Riyadh

Abu Dhabi

TROPIC OF
CANCER

U.A.E.

SAUDI
ARABIA

OMAN

20° N

YEMEN

Sana'a

KEY

Parliamentary republic, limited democracy

Presidential or semi-presidential republic, limited democracy

Constitutional monarchy, limited democracy

Absolute monarchy

Theocracy

Failed state

Armed conflict

● City

Country border

--- Disputed border

0   400 mi

0   400 km

Lambert Azimuthal
Equal-Area projection

50° E

60° E

70° E

Quest
Project-Based Learning Inquiry

Plan a Youth Peace Summit

Quest KICK OFF

You are a planner for a peace summit, or meeting. Your summit will consider the following question:

How can people work together to overcome conflict?

Explore the Essential Question, "How should we handle conflict?" in this Quest.

1 Ask Questions

What are the goals of a peace summit? Get started by writing questions that will help you plan your summit. Capture notes in your 📙 Active Journal.

2 Investigate

As you read the lessons in this topic, look for **Quest CONNECTIONS** that provide information on how people have handled conflict. Record your responses in your 📙 Active Journal.

3 Conduct Research

Next, do research to find and study sources about Southwest Asia. They'll help you learn even more about how people have handled conflict in this region. Take notes on your findings in your 📙 Active Journal.

▲ Students in Pakistan attend a Model UN meeting, an event in which young people hold a simulated conference among the world's nations.

Quest FINDINGS

4 Plan Your Youth Peace Summit

Your plan should include a schedule, a list of issues, and a list of rules for productive dialogue. You will also need to create a flyer and a brochure to promote your summit. Get help preparing these materials in your 📙 Active Journal.

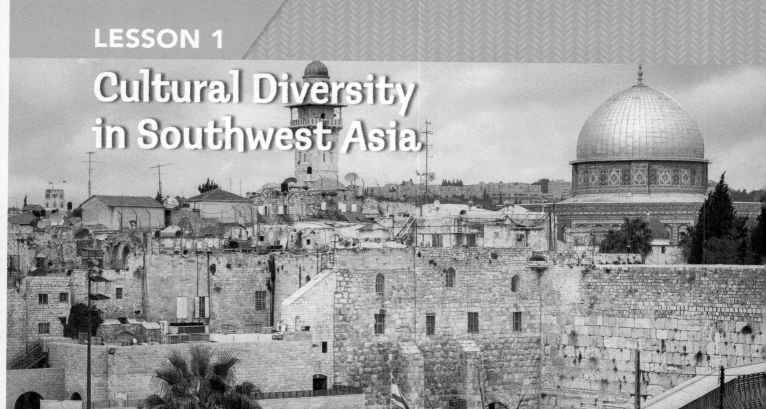

LESSON 1
Cultural Diversity in Southwest Asia

GET READY TO READ

START UP

Examine the image from Jerusalem of the Dome of the Rock, sacred to Muslims, and the Western Wall, sacred to Jews. Write down three things this image tells you about life in Southwest Asia.

GUIDING QUESTIONS

- What are the main religions in Southwest Asia?
- What ethnic groups live in Southwest Asia?
- How have people in the region responded to cultural change?

TAKE NOTES

Literacy Skills: Analyze Text Structure
Use the graphic organizer in your 📓 Active Journal to take notes as you read the lesson.

PRACTICE VOCABULARY

Use the vocabulary activity in your 📓 Active Journal to practice the vocabulary words.

Vocabulary	Academic Vocabulary
ethnic group	predominantly
fundamentalism	interpretation
Islamism	
Sharia	
hijab	

All of the countries in Southwest Asia have religious diversity. That is, the people of these countries practice more than one religion or follow more than one tradition within the same religion. All of them also have people from more than one ethnic group. An **ethnic group** is a group of people who share a distinct language, culture, and identity. While Southwest Asians from different religious and ethnic groups often live peacefully side by side, there has also been conflict. While the region has a long history, it has also been affected by the modern world.

A Region of Many Faiths

Most people in Southwest Asia are Muslim, but their religion, Islam, has many different faith traditions. Each of these traditions has its own group of followers. While they all agree on certain core principles of Islam, they have different beliefs and practices.

Athough Islam has the most followers in the region, most countries in Southwest Asia have significant religious minorities. In fact, two small countries have non-Muslim majorities.

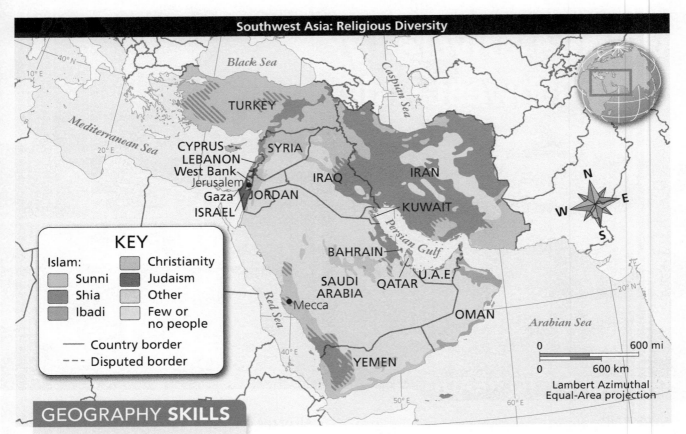

Southwest Asia: Religious Diversity

KEY

Islam:
- Sunni
- Shia
- Ibadi
- Christianity
- Judaism
- Other
- Few or no people

— Country border
--- Disputed border

0 — 600 mi
0 — 600 km
Lambert Azimuthal Equal-Area projection

Cyprus is **predominantly**, or mainly, Christian, and Israel has a Jewish majority. Christian minorities exist throughout the region, except in Iran, Saudi Arabia, and Yemen. Jewish minorities used to exist in many countries, but most Jews in the region have moved to Israel.

Sunnis, Shias, and Ibadis Most people in the region are Muslims who follow the Five Pillars of Islam, the basic principles of Islamic belief. Islam shapes many parts of Muslims' daily life. Still, all Muslims do not view their faith or its influence on daily life in the same way. Beliefs and practices vary.

Islam has two main varieties: Sunni Islam and Shia Islam. These two varieties have different beliefs. Sunnis make up about 75 percent of Muslims around the world. In Oman, most people follow a third branch of Islam, called Ibadism.

Mainstream Shias live mainly in Iran, Iraq, Lebanon, and eastern Saudi Arabia. Groups such as the Alawites of Syria have many Shia beliefs, but also other beliefs that are different from other Shias. Most Shia Muslims in Yemen also have different beliefs from the Shias who live in other countries.

Academic Vocabulary
predominantly • adv., mainly

Most Sunnis follow a moderate tradition that has developed over the centuries and that tolerates modern culture. In countries north of Saudi Arabia, most Sunni Muslims follow a moderate form of Islam.

Wahhabism and Islamism Other Sunnis, mainly on the Arabian Peninsula, follow a branch of Sunni Islam called Wahhabism. Wahhabis believe in returning to the original teachings of Islam and rejecting all modern interpretations of the Quran (koo RAHN), the holy book of Islam. Wahhabism is a form of **fundamentalism**, or the belief that holy books should be taken literally, or word for word.

Wahhabis also believe that government should be based on the original teachings of Islam. Wahhabism is one form of **Islamism**, or the belief that government and society should reflect Islamic law. The rulers of Saudi Arabia are Wahhabis. Wahhabism determines much of the kingdom's politics. Most Muslims in Southwest Asia are neither Wahhabis nor Islamists.

✅ READING CHECK **Identify Main Ideas** How do Muslims differ in their religious faith?

A Region of Many Peoples

In addition to religious diversity, Southwest Asia also has great ethnic diversity. As you have read, ethnic groups are groups of people who share cultural traditions such as language and group identity. Religious beliefs may be a part of ethnic identity, but members of an ethnic group may also belong to different religions.

Arabs The largest ethnic group in Southwest Asia is Arabs. Arabs are the majority in every country in the region except Turkey, Iran, Cyprus, and Israel. However, Arabs are divided by religion. Most Arabs are Muslims, but some are Sunni, others are Shia, and others follow other traditions. There are also Christian Arabs.

Other Groups In Turkey, Turks are the largest ethnic group. Most Turks are moderate Sunni Muslims, though some are Alevis, who share some beliefs with the Shias.

Did you know?

Iran still has a small community of Zoroastrians. This ancient religion began in Persia more than 3,500 years ago.

Analyze Images People of different ethnic and religious groups shop in a market in Jerusalem, Israel. **Infer** How do people's differences sometimes spark conflict? What advantages are there to living among people who are different?

▲ Shia Muslims gather before dawn at a shrine in Najaf, Iraq, for a religious festival. The shrine is the burial place of Ali, Muhammad's son-in-law. It is one of the holiest sites in Shia Islam.

INTERACTIVE

Jerusalem

In Iran, Persians are the largest ethnic group. Most Persians are Shia Muslims, though some follow an ancient religion called Zoroastrianism.

Jewish Israelis form the largest ethnic group in Israel. Arabs are a minority in Israel. Christian Greeks form the largest ethnic group in Cyprus, where Muslim Turks are a minority, living mainly in the north.

One of the larger ethnic groups in the region is the Kurds. Kurds are mainly Sunni Muslims. Kurds are not the majority in any country, but they occupy a large region covering parts of Syria, Turkey, Iraq, and Iran.

Some oil-rich countries have large numbers of people from outside the region. About three out of every ten people living in Saudi Arabia, for instance, is a foreign-born worker. Many of these people are from South Asia or Africa. They cannot become citizens, however. In Qatar and the United Arab Emirates, the majority of the people are not Arabs. In these countries, foreigners make up most of the population. Immigrants come from such countries as India, Sri Lanka, Pakistan, Bangladesh, and the Philippines. These people are not citizens of the country where they live. Immigrants form nearly half of the population of Kuwait as well.

Religious and Cultural Traditions Although most people in the region are Muslims, they have different ideas about politics and everyday life. For example, some Muslims believe that women should not mix with unrelated men in public. Others believe that Islam allows unrelated men and women to work together.

There are differences among Israeli Jews as well. Some Israeli Jews are more religiously observant, while others are less so. Most Israeli Jews, even if they are not religious, identify with the culture and history of Judaism. This is a cornerstone of their identity.

This region is home to many cultural traditions as well. Some traditions concern the foods that people eat or the importance of tribal membership. Others concern how to welcome guests, treat elders with respect, or give gifts.

Religion and Conflict Tensions among ethnic and religious groups have led to conflicts within and among the region's countries. For example, Lebanon suffered through years of war among its Christian, Druze, Sunni, and Shiite groups. Some Kurds wish to form an independent Kurdish country. The governments of the countries where Kurds live strongly oppose that idea. These differences have led to conflict.

The word *jihad* in Arabic means "struggle." For some Muslims, it means a struggle against one's evil inclinations. For some Muslim extremists, it refers to a violent holy war to defend or spread Islam. Muslim extremist groups in the region see European and American influence as a threat. They support the use of violence against Westerners or Muslims who do not share the same **interpretation** of Islam.

READING CHECK Recognize Multiple Causes Why have there been conflicts within Southwest Asia?

How Has Modern Life Affected the Region?

Income from oil changed society in the region. From the mid-1900s, people in the region met Westerners working in the oil industry. Many bought televisions and computers. Wealthier Southwest Asians traveled to foreign countries or sent their children to study there. They were exposed to Western and global culture.

Modern, Western, or global culture appealed to many people in the region. They have adopted some aspects of modern global culture. Some of the region's people work for Western firms. Others work for local firms using Western business practices.

Quest CONNECTIONS

Different ethnic and religious groups have lived together in the region for hundreds of years. Why might conflict arise among them? Record your findings in your 📓 Active Journal.

Academic Vocabulary
interpretation • *n.*, way of viewing the meaning of a text, rules, or belief

Analyze Visuals In the early 2000s, many new buildings and skyscrapers were built in Dubai, a city in the United Arab Emirates. **Infer** Why are some countries in Southwest Asia able to afford so many modern buildings?

The region has become part of the modern world. However, not all people in the region are comfortable with this change.

Cultural Diffusion In modern times, Southwest Asia, like other parts of the world, has experienced cultural diffusion, or the spread of aspects of culture from one place to another. Diffusion has brought many ideas from Europe and other Western countries to the region, including modern technologies and ways of life.

Different groups have reacted to modern ideas in different ways. Christians and Jews have embraced many modern ideas. Many have ways of life similar to people in Europe or the United States. Many moderate Muslims have also adopted new ideas and ways of life.

Some conservative Muslims, however, accept many modern technologies but view other modern practices as a threat to their faith. For example, the government of Iran enforces strict observance of **Sharia**, or the Islamic law code. Other countries in the region have strict laws based on Islamic tradition that women must follow.

The Status of Women in the Region Traditionally, women in the Arab world have had to obey men. In Saudi Arabia, they cannot travel without the permission of a father, husband, or other male relative. In much of the region, Muslim women are expected to cover their hair and sometimes their faces. They are expected to wear concealing, conservative garments known as **hijab**, or a veil that covers the head and chest. Unrelated men and women are not permitted to interact.

Analyze Images People shop at a market in Istanbul, Turkey. **Use Visual Information** How does this image show people following both traditional and more modern ways of life?

Despite the attraction of modern global culture for some people in the region, tradition still shapes the lives of men and especially women in this region. In most countries, women face more restrictions than they do in the United States or other Western countries. The most restrictive country is Saudi Arabia, where women are forbidden to drive cars or ride bicycles. They cannot legally meet with unrelated men in public. Many Saudi women cannot pursue certain careers, since that would mean working with unrelated men.

However, attitudes are changing in many parts of the region. In some countries, such as Iraq, women are free to work outside the home and to have their own careers. In some countries, women can dress as they wish. Even in Saudi Arabia, some women are finding ways to pursue careers.

Women in Israel enjoy full civil rights. Women serve in the military, and women have served as prime minister and as Supreme Court president. Most Israeli women work, some in executive positions.

▲ Many women in the region, such as these women shopping in Lebanon, wear headscarves to cover their hair. For many Muslim women, wearing the hijab is a source of pride in their religious heritage.

READING CHECK **Identify Cause and Effect** How has the Western world influenced Southwest Asia?

☑ Lesson Check

Practice Vocabulary

1. How are a religious group and an **ethnic group** different?

2. What is a **hijab**, and why is it important to many Muslims?

3. What is **Sharia**, and how does it affect life in Iran?

Critical Thinking and Writing

4. **Summarize** Describe the diversity of religions in Southwest Asia.

5. **Summarize** Describe the diversity of **ethnic groups** in Southwest Asia.

6. **Identify Cause and Effect** How have Westernization and modernization affected the culture of Southwest Asia?

7. **Writing Workshop: Gather Information** When you complete this topic, you will write an explanatory essay about causes of conflict in the region. Start preparing for this task by gathering information. What religious and ethnic issues are the causes of conflict in the region? Are these conflicts within countries or between countries or both? Why do these issues lead to conflict? Record your ideas in your 📓 Active Journal.

Construct Charts and Tables

Use the example, the data provided, and the steps below to create a pie chart that reflects the religious makeup of the population of Lebanon.

INTERACTIVE

Create Charts and Maps

1 **To create a chart, first select a set of data.** You are studying the people of Southwest Asia, so your chart should focus on data about the people there.

2 **Research and find the data you would like to present in the chart.** Your choice of data will be based on the theme you wish to explore and what your research uncovers.

a. What is the subject of the data in the pie chart on this page?

b. What is the subject of the data in the second source?

3 **Organize the data according to the specific format of your chart.** For the information on the religious groups of Lebanon, a pie chart is the best way to show data, as was the case with the Iraqi data. Pie charts are very good at showing the share of a whole amount represented by each of its components or parts. Notice that Lebanon has more than one Muslim

group and more than one Christian group. Make sure that the size of each segment of the pie chart reflects the percentage that it represents.

a. How are the data on Iraq organized?

b. How will you organize the religious data on Lebanon?

4 **Create symbols, patterns, or a color scheme, a key (as needed), and a title for your chart.** Create symbols or a color or pattern to represent each piece of data you want to show. For your chart, you can use different colors or patterns to represent each religious group in the population of Lebanon.

a. What colors or patterns will you choose?

b. What title will you give your pie chart?

c. Create your pie chart on another sheet of paper.

Secondary Source
Ethnic Diversity in Iraq

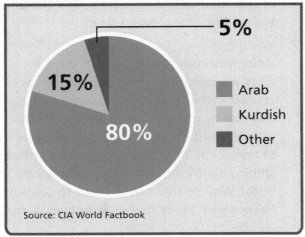

5%

15%

80%

Arab
Kurdish
Other

Source: CIA World Factbook

Primary Source
Religion in Lebanon

- Muslim 54% (27% Sunni, 27% Shia)

- Christian 40.5% (includes 21% Maronite Catholic, 8% Greek Orthodox, 5% Greek Catholic, 6.5% other Christian)

- Druze 5.6%

- Very small numbers of Jews, Baha'is, Buddhists, Hindus, and Mormons
  —CIA World Factbook

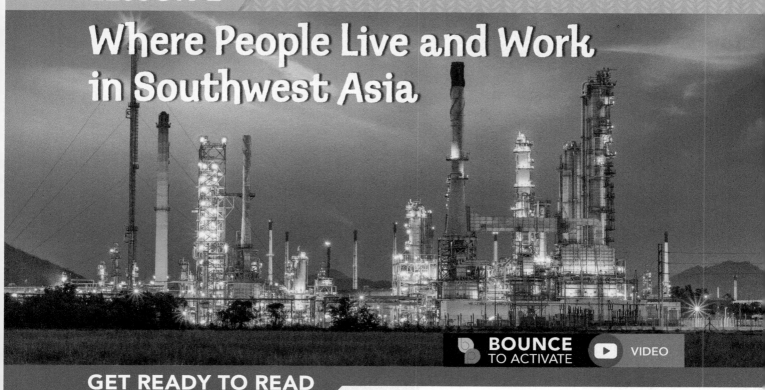

LESSON 2

Where People Live and Work in Southwest Asia

BOUNCE TO ACTIVATE ▶ VIDEO

GET READY TO READ

START UP

Study the image of an oil refinery in Southwest Asia. Write three things you want to know about resources in Southwest Asia.

GUIDING QUESTIONS

- How does geography shape where people live in Southwest Asia?
- What factors have shaped the economies of Southwest Asia?
- What are the strengths and weaknesses of the Saudi, Turkish, and Israeli economies?

TAKE NOTES

Literacy Skills: Summarize

Use the graphic organizer in your 📓 Active Journal to take notes as you read the lesson.

PRACTICE VOCABULARY

Use the vocabulary activity in your 📓 Active Journal to practice the vocabulary words.

Vocabulary

desalination   subsistence
nationalize   farming
capital
oasis

Academic Vocabulary

prosper
entrepreneur

The first civilization arose in Southwest Asia thousands of years ago in the Fertile Crescent because the Tigris and Euphrates rivers supported farming. Water, fertile land, and other resources made this area ideal for civilization to flourish.

How Does Geography Affect Where People Live?

People live where there are opportunities to make a good living. Before the 1900s, most people lived where soils and water supplies allowed farming. Look at the population density map of the region in the Regional Atlas. What conclusion can you draw about the areas with very low population density?

Settlement in Southwest Asia As you have read, major cities in the region arose in the Fertile Crescent, which supported farming. Today, much of the region's population still lives in that region.

Some areas of Southwest Asia, like Turkey and northern and western Iran, have moister climates. These areas have higher population densities than most of the region.

Analyze Images Crops grow at an oasis in Saudi Arabia. An oasis is a place in the desert where water can be found. **Compare and Contrast** Compare the land growing crops with the land in the distance.

Effects of Technology Modern irrigation methods, such as those practiced in Israel and Saudi Arabia, allow farming in places that were once too dry for farming. People have used technologies such as electric pumps to solve the problem of access to water. That has brought people to regions that had not been settled before.

Because of the arid climate in much of the region, access to water has always been a key issue. With few rivers in some areas, irrigation and clean drinking water are in short supply. Pollution has also damaged the quality of the water in rivers such as the Euphrates. New technology has helped with this problem.

Besides pumps, some countries in this region use a technology called **desalination**, which is the removal of salt from sea water. This technology has enabled population growth in desert regions, though poorer countries such as Yemen and Jordan cannot afford enough technology to meet all of their needs for water. According to a Saudi prince,

Primary Source

"Currently, Saudi Arabia is the largest producer of desalinated water in the world, and the kingdom continues to invest in research and development to make access to fresh water more affordable."

—Prince Dr. Turki Al Saud Al Faisal, from ibm.com

Effects of Resources The world today depends on oil to power cars, trucks, and other vehicles. Oil and natural gas are fuels for heating homes. Oil is also a raw material for plastics and other products. Many Southwest Asian countries are rich in oil and natural gas. Jobs in the oil and gas industries have attracted people to live in the oil-rich region around the Persian Gulf.

The discovery of oil in Saudi Arabia in the early 1900s led to the gradual development of a vast oil industry. During the mid-1900s, the government gradually **nationalized**, or took ownership of, the oil industry.

In 1960, many of the world's largest oil producers formed OPEC, or the Organization of Petroleum Exporting Countries. They formed this group to have control over oil pricing and profits. Members include Saudi Arabia, Iran, Iraq, other Persian Gulf countries, and countries from outside the region.

Oil has helped the region **prosper**, but it poses a risk, too. Because water supplies are so limited in this region, the threat of water pollution from the oil industry or other industries is a very serious challenge. Heavy irrigation can lead over time to a buildup of salt in soils, ruining farmland. Also, as populations grow, rivers can be so heavily tapped for human use that they no longer flow as rivers.

☑ READING CHECK **Identify Main Ideas** What are the region's main resources? How are they used?

Academic Vocabulary
prosper • *v.*, to enjoy success

GEOGRAPHY SKILLS

Oil deposits in the region are concentrated along the Persian Gulf.

1. **Place** Which countries have the least oil?

2. **Synthesize Visual Information** Which waterway is likely the most used for shipping oil from the region?

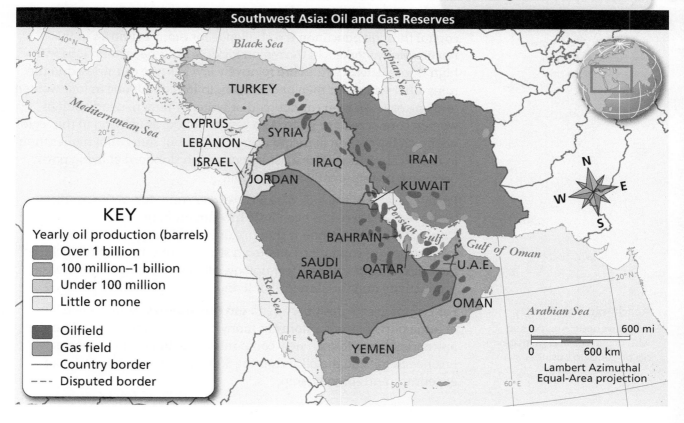

Southwest Asia: Oil and Gas Reserves

KEY
Yearly oil production (barrels)
- Over 1 billion
- 100 million–1 billion
- Under 100 million
- Little or none

- Oilfield
- Gas field
- — Country border
- - - - Disputed border

Lambert Azimuthal Equal-Area projection

Analyze Visuals People live in poverty in this slum located in Yemen. **Demonstrate Reasoned Judgment** What factors may account for the poverty seen in this photograph?

Economies of Southwest Asia

The economies of Southwest Asia vary in many ways. Several countries are dominated by the oil industry, but others have no oil deposits. Some are very wealthy, and some are poor. All take part in the world economy.

Economic Systems In Iran, Saudi Arabia, and other oil-rich states, oil companies and other major sectors of the economy are government-owned. Government officials make decisions, as is the case in a command economy. In these countries, smaller businesses are privately owned and operate in more of a market economy.

In other countries, such as Lebanon and Israel, the government has a smaller role. The mixed economies in these countries are closer to market economies.

In remote parts of the region, some people still live in small tribal groups. These groups practice a traditional economy, in which custom and habit determine economic activity.

Investment and Living Standards A lack of investment in human capital through education is a challenge for many countries in this region. Many workers in the region lack the skills needed for jobs with high wages. Literacy rates are relatively low in some countries, and the rates differ widely for men and women. In Iraq about one in four women and one of seven men cannot read or write. In Yemen, nearly half of women cannot read or write. As a result, standards of living in the region are much lower than in neighboring Europe, but somewhat higher than in many countries in Africa. Israel has a high standard of living partly because it invests greatly in education.

Partly because of the lack of skilled workers and due to the conflict in the region, there has been little investment in productive capital. **Capital** is money or goods that are used to make products. Israel's large supply of capital has created a strong economy. Capital includes factories, machinery, and technology, all of which can help increase productivity and the standard of living.

Academic Vocabulary

entrepreneur • *n.,* person who organizes and manages his or her own business

For economies to grow, they need **entrepreneurs**. State ownership of large parts of the economy in many countries limits possibilities for entrepreneurs to launch new companies. Seeking to encourage new businesses outside the oil sector, the Saudi government has tried to encourage entrepreneurship.

Specialization and Trade Many economies in the region specialize in the oil industry. Israel has specialized in technology and other industries. When countries specialize, they need to trade with other countries specializing in different products. For instance, some oil-rich countries like Saudi Arabia cannot grow their own food. They must import their food. Because most countries have their own currencies, trade requires a process for exchanging different currencies.

Some government policies can hinder trade. Trade barriers, such as tariffs (fees on imports), quotas (limits on imports), or embargoes (bans on imports) can hurt trade and specialization.

Turkey's economy shows the benefits of free trade. Its economy was held back in the past by trade barriers meant to protect Turkish producers. In the late 1900s, Turkey removed these trade barriers and became more active in specializing and trading. As a result, the country's economy has grown rapidly in recent years, especially in cities. People are more productive and enjoy higher incomes.

☑ READING CHECK **Identify Main Ideas** What factors have shaped the economies of Southwest Asia?

The Economy of Saudi Arabia

Like most countries in the region, Saudi Arabia has a mixed economy. Yet it has more of a command economy than most countries in the region because the government largely controls its most valuable resource—oil. About 20 percent of the world's known oil reserves are located in Saudi Arabia.

Analyze Diagrams Government plays a very strong role in the Saudi economy, but that is less true of Turkey or Israel. **Identify Cause and Effects** What impact has the nationalized oil industry had on entrepreneurship in Saudi Arabia?

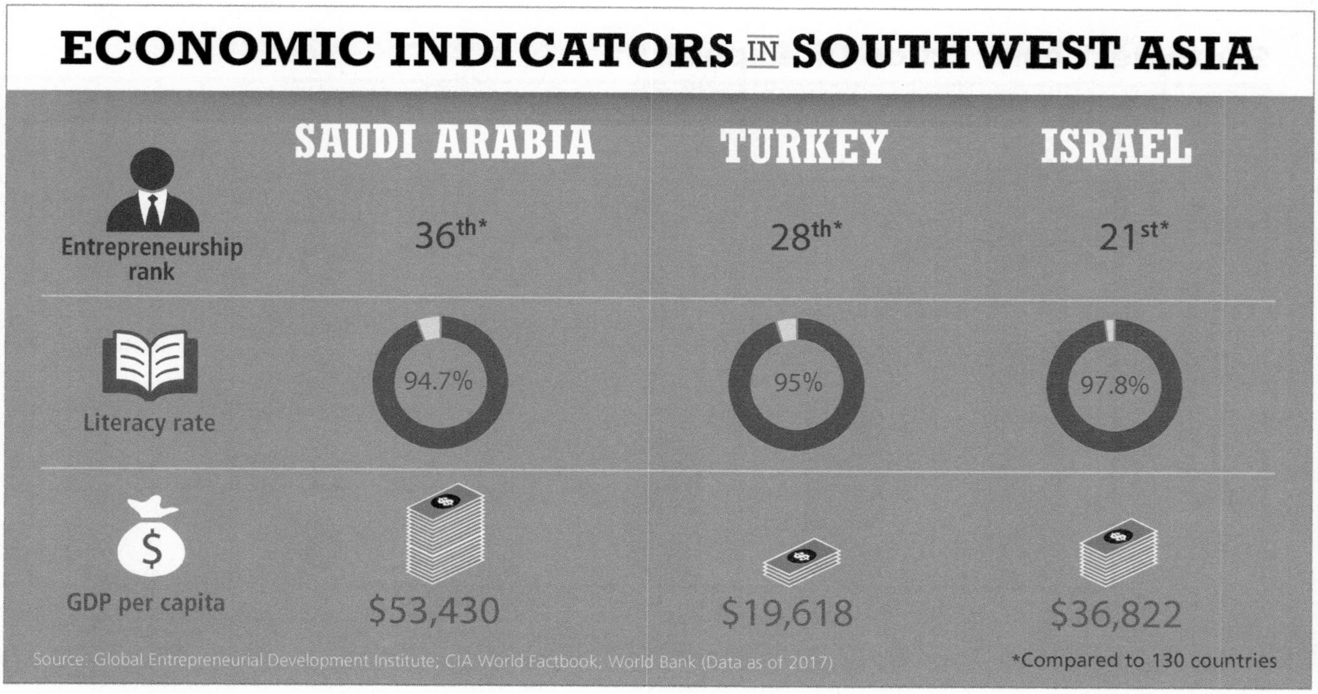

ECONOMIC INDICATORS IN SOUTHWEST ASIA

	SAUDI ARABIA	TURKEY	ISRAEL
Entrepreneurship rank	36th*	28th*	21st*
Literacy rate	94.7%	95%	97.8%
GDP per capita	$53,430	$19,618	$36,822

Source: Global Entrepreneurial Development Institute; CIA World Factbook; World Bank (Data as of 2017)

*Compared to 130 countries

Before the 1900s, what is now the country of Saudi Arabia was a poor desert region, with most of its people raising livestock or growing a few crops in desert oases. An **oasis** is a place in the desert where water can be found. They could produce only enough to survive. Development of the oil industry greatly changed the Saudi economy.

Citizens of Saudi Arabia today have a relatively high standard of living. They are practically guaranteed high incomes from oil earnings. There are few incentives to work outside of the oil sector or in government jobs. Migrants from India, Pakistan, and other poor South Asian, African, and Southeast Asian countries work in less desirable jobs for low wages.

In recent years, Saudi Arabia has tried to invest in other industries. It has had little success. Saudi Arabia has invested heavily in productive capital for the oil industry and in an educational system that produces high literacy rates, but Saudi Arabia offers few advantages to businesses that produce products other than oil. Government control of much of the economy leaves little room for entrepreneurship.

✓ READING CHECK **Summarize** What are the strengths and weaknesses of the Saudi economy?

The Economy of Turkey

Turkey bridges Southwest Asia and Europe. This mostly Muslim country has strong connections to Europe. Turkey's economy has grown in recent years.

Turkey has a diverse economy, with agriculture, industry, and services all playing important roles. It also is much more of a market-oriented

Analyze Graphs Oil plays a major role in many economies of Southwest Asia. **Compare and Contrast** How much oil does Saudi Arabia export compared to the other countries shown?

Southwest Asia: Crude Oil Exports

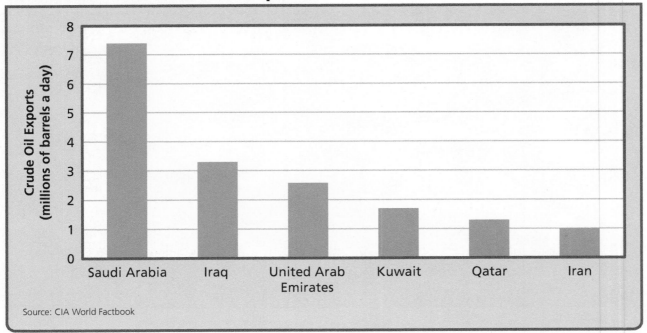

Source: CIA World Factbook

country than Saudi Arabia because most of its businesses are privately owned. That was not the case in the past, when the government ran many industries. In the late 1900s, the government cut its role in the economy and made it easier for entrepreneurs to start new businesses and form private companies.

For many decades, Turkey has lagged behind European countries economically. One reason is that Turkey's educational system is not as strong as that of most European countries. As a result, Turkey's workers are less productive, have lower literacy rates, and earn lower incomes.

In recent years, Turkey has invested heavily in productive capital to develop its industries. Turkey's main industries are textiles, steel, shipbuilding, and defense, along with agricultural production of fruits, nuts, and vegetables.

✅ **READING CHECK** **Identify Cause and Effect** How does investment in human capital through education affect Turkey's economy?

The Israeli Economy

Israel has few natural resources. Unlike many countries in Southwest Asia, Israel does not export oil, though natural gas has recently been discovered. Most Israelis are employed in the service sector. Israel also has a large industrial sector, with a high concentration of high-tech businesses. In fact, Israel has been called the "start-up nation" because of its high-tech entrepreneurship.

Israel has a mixed economy. As in many European countries, the government plays a key role in providing health care and education. In other sectors of the economy, a market economy exists.

Before the 1900s, the region that became Israel was relatively poor. Farmers practiced **subsistence farming**, or farming mainly to feed the farmer's family with little left over to send to market.

Quick Activity

What economic challenges do people in Southwest Asia face? Record your ideas in your 📓 Active Journal.

INTERACTIVE

Turkey's Trade

▲ A diamond cutter at work in Israel

During the early to mid-1900s, when the country of Israel was created, hundreds of thousands of Jewish people arrived from Europe and other world regions. Many of these new immigrants were highly educated. With their help, Israel invested in a strong school system. As a result, Israel has highly literate, skilled workers. Today, Israeli males and females typically have 16 years of schooling, which is comparable to that of highly developed economies like the United States. Israel's educated, skilled workers produce valuable products that allow them to earn high incomes.

Israel's skilled workforce has also attracted investment in productive capital from other countries. The country's large supply of capital has further boosted its productivity and living standards.

Because Israel has few natural resources of its own, it needs trade. Israel trades its people's skills for resources by selling its goods and services and buying natural resources. For example, one of Israel's most valuable exports is cut diamonds. These are mined in other countries, then cut and polished in Israel before being exported. Israel also sells fruit and produce to Europe. Its main source of income, however, is technologically advanced goods and software. Because of Israel's high-tech entrepreneurship, Israel has been called the "start-up nation."

☑ READING CHECK Recognize Multiple Causes Why does Israel have a highly productive economy?

☑ Lesson Check

Practice Vocabulary

1. Why is **desalination** in Southwest Asia important?

2. In what ways have Saudi Arabia, Turkey, and Israel invested **capital**?

Critical Thinking and Writing

3. Use Evidence Give an example of each type of economic system in Southwest Asia.

4. Infer How is the importance of entrepreneurship shown by Israel's economy?

5. Compare and Contrast Look at the per capita GDP figures in the Country Databank for Saudi Arabia and Israel. Based on that information and what you have read in the lesson, which economy do you think is stronger? Explain your answer.

6. Writing Workshop: Gather Information Continue gathering information to use in your essay on conflict in the region. What economic issues are or could be causes of conflict in Southwest Asia? Why do these issues lead to conflict? Are the conflicts being addressed? Record your ideas in your 📓 Active Journal.

Geographic Sources

Oil Dependence in Southwest Asia

Several countries in Southwest Asia are rich in fossil fuels. Look at the map of oil and gas reserves in Lesson 2 to identify them. The economies of some of these countries depend heavily on oil and gas exports. The chart on this page shows the share of petroleum, or oil, and natural gas in total exports for six countries in the region. The graph shows changes in the average price of oil over the early 2010s. Use the map in Lesson 2 and the data here to answer the questions below.

▶ An oil derrick pumps oil from the ground in Oman.

Oil and Gas Exports, 2015

Country	Oil and Gas % of Exports
Iraq	99%
Qatar	93%
Kuwait	90%
Saudi Arabia	84%
Iran	75%
United Arab Emirates	66%

Source: The MIT Observatory of Economic Complexity

Crude Oil Prices, 2011–2015

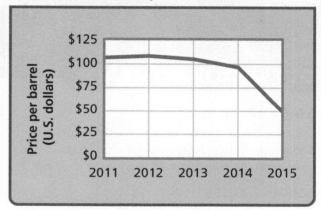

Source: OPEC Annual Statistical Bulletin 2016

Analyzing Geographic Sources

1. **Synthesize Visual Information** What does the map in Lesson 2 suggest about the value of each country's oil exports?

2. **Compare and Contrast** Which country would be most affected by changes in oil prices from year to year? Why?

3. **Generate Explanations** Which of these oil-rich countries has had the most success in reducing its dependence on oil and gas? Why do you think so?

 **Quest CONNECTIONS**

How might natural resources such as oil lead to conflict? How might such conflicts be resolved? Record your thoughts in your 📓 Active Journal.

Governments in Southwest Asia

BOUNCE TO ACTIVATE ▶ VIDEO

GET READY TO READ

START UP

Examine the photo of female members of parliament in Iran. How might it affect a country to have both male and female lawmakers?

GUIDING QUESTIONS

- What kinds of democratic governments exist in Southwest Asia?
- How are Southwest Asia's monarchies different from one another?
- What other forms of government are present in the region?

TAKE NOTES

Literacy Skills: Classify and Categorize
Use the graphic organizer In your 🗐 Active Journal to take notes as you read the lesson.

PRACTICE VOCABULARY

Use the vocabulary activity in your 🗐 Active Journal to practice the vocabulary words.

Vocabulary

authoritarian
  government
theocracy
secular

compromise
failed state

Academic Vocabulary

flawed
ultimate

Southwest Asia has many different kinds of government. Few countries in the region are strong democracies. Undemocratic forms of government in the region include dictatorships, absolute monarchies, and theocracies.

Many Forms of Government

Southwest Asia has a wider range of governments than most regions in the world. Several governments in the region are based on religion or tradition.

Today, the region's governments range from democracies to authoritarian governments. An **authoritarian government** is one in which all power is held by a single person or a small group. The ruler's power is unlimited. Authoritarian governments include absolute monarchies and outright dictatorships.

Democracies in the Region While the region has some democracies, ethnic and religious tensions have weakened democracy in many countries. Lebanon's leaders, for example, are chosen based on their religion and not by a purely democratic vote.

Monarchies in the Region Historically, the region was ruled by monarchs, such as kings or sultans, or by military leaders who took power. In ancient Mesopotamia, kings ruled city-states and empires. When Muslim empires rose after the spread of Islam, caliphs ruled a vast empire. Since caliphs had religious as well as civil authority, they had great power. Monarchs still rule many countries today, particularly on the Arabian Peninsula.

Saudi Arabia is an absolute monarchy, which means that the king rules and controls the government alone. Saudi citizens have little or no say in politics. There are no legal limits to the ruler's power.

Dictatorship in the Region In the 1900s, some countries in the regions had dictatorships, where one leader seized and wielded total power. Both Iraq and Syria had dictators for many years. Saddam Hussein lost power in the wake of the U.S.-led invasion of Iraq. Bashar al-Assad's rule in Syria has been challenged by a civil war. While Turkey has an elected government, its president took so many powers and set so many limits on opposition in 2016 that some feared the country was moving toward dictatorship.

Other Forms The region also has a theocracy in Iran. A **theocracy** is a government run by religious power. Two countries—Syria and Yemen—faced civil war in the 2010s, with competing rulers or groups controlling parts of their territory.

☑ READING CHECK **Draw Conclusions** What are the different forms of government in Southwest Asia?

Analyze Diagrams
Governments in Southwest Asia differ in how much power they have over their citizens. **Compare and Contrast** Which government do you think gives its people the most freedom? Why?

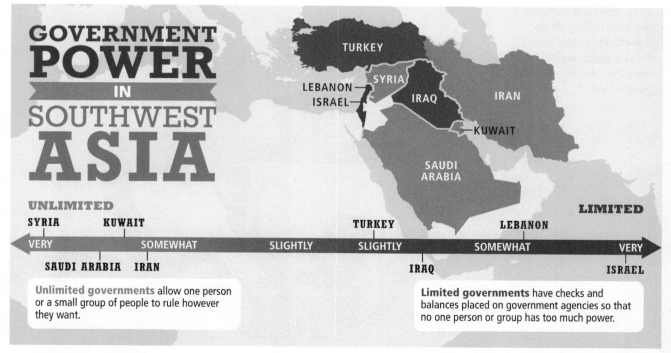

GOVERNMENT POWER IN SOUTHWEST ASIA

TURKEY
SYRIA
LEBANON
ISRAEL
IRAQ
IRAN
KUWAIT
SAUDI ARABIA

UNLIMITED
SYRIA   KUWAIT   TURKEY   LEBANON   **LIMITED**
VERY   SOMEWHAT   SLIGHTLY   SLIGHTLY   SOMEWHAT   VERY
SAUDI ARABIA   IRAN   IRAQ   ISRAEL

Unlimited governments allow one person or a small group of people to rule however they want.

Limited governments have checks and balances placed on government agencies so that no one person or group has too much power.

What Kinds of Democracy Exist in Southwest Asia?

Some countries in Southwest Asia have taken steps toward democracy. Even on the Arabian Peninsula, where monarchies are dominant, a limited democracy exists in Kuwait. Strong democracies in the region are present in Cyprus and Israel. As in all democracies, citizens in these countries have a key role in electing representatives to their governments.

Parliamentary and Presidential Democracies Israel is a parliamentary democracy, like Canada and Great Britain. In a parliamentary democracy, the head of the largest party in parliament becomes prime minister and runs the government. Israel has a president who serves as its symbolic head of state.

Cyprus is a presidential democracy like the United States. In this type of democracy, an elected president serves as both the head of state and the head of government.

Flawed Democracies Turkey became a republic in 1923. Some Turks favor a **secular**, or nonreligious, government. From its founding, Turkey's military leaders strongly supported this vision of a secular state. In the past, they have forced out a government if they did not think it was secular enough.

In recent years, however, a political party that is less secular began to gain strength. The party is called the Justice and Development Party (AKP). In the 2010s, Tayyip Erdogan of the AKP was elected prime minister and then president. He and members of his party in the legislature have passed laws limiting freedom of the press and other civil rights.

Analyze Images People in Turkey march in support of President Erdogan in 2016. They are carrying the Turkish flag. **Draw Conclusions** How would these supporters likely view the idea of a secular government?

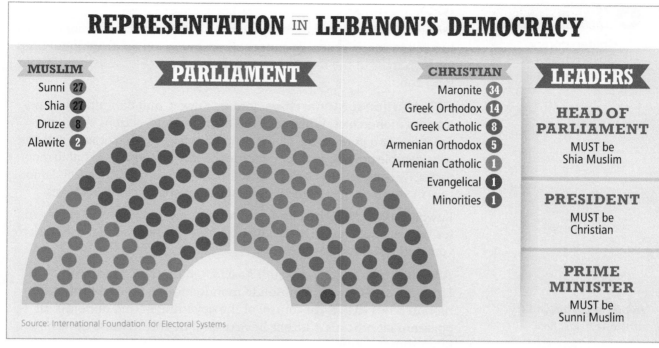

REPRESENTATION IN LEBANON'S DEMOCRACY

PARLIAMENT

MUSLIM
Sunni 27
Shia 27
Druze 8
Alawite 2

CHRISTIAN
Maronite 34
Greek Orthodox 14
Greek Catholic 8
Armenian Orthodox 5
Armenian Catholic 1
Evangelical 1
Minorities 1

LEADERS

HEAD OF PARLIAMENT
MUST be Shia Muslim

PRESIDENT
MUST be Christian

PRIME MINISTER
MUST be Sunni Muslim

Source: International Foundation for Electoral Systems

They also put their political opponents in jail. These changes have made Turkey a **flawed** democracy.

Iraq started to take steps toward democracy in the early 2000s. However, the government has been led by members of the Shia Arab majority. They have often discriminated against or attacked Iraq's Kurdish and Sunni Arab minorities.

In addition, violent opposition, including an invasion by the terrorist so-called Islamic State (IS, or ISIS), has hurt the government. For these reasons, Iraq is a flawed democracy.

Other Democracies Many countries in the region have had to balance ethnic and religious differences in forming a government. Leaders of one country chose an unusual solution.

Lebanon's government has democratic elections and a parliamentary democracy, but tensions among the religious groups have made it hard for them to govern together. Its government involves a compromise among its religious groups. A **compromise** is a an agreement in which each side gives up some demands to achieve others. According to its constitution, Lebanon's president must be a Christian, its prime minister must be a Sunni Muslim, and the head of its parliament must be a Shia Muslim. This structure calms tensions but limits democratic choice.

A number of seats in the parliament are set aside for different ethnic or religious groups. This ensures that they have a voice, but it means that Lebanon is not a full democracy.

✓ **READING CHECK** Compare and Contrast How are the democratic governments in Southwest Asia different?

Analyze Diagrams
Lebanon's democracy is carefully constructed to ensure representation for all groups. **Use Visual Information** What are the two main divisions of the parliament's members?

Academic Vocabulary
flawed • adv., marked by problems; not perfect

Quest CONNECTIONS

Based on the text, how does Lebanon's constitution reflect compromise as a response to conflict? Write your findings in your 📓 Active Journal.

INTERACTIVE

Contemporary
Governments of
Southwest Asia

Monarchies

Many of Southwest Asia's Arab countries retain traditional monarchies headed by kings, emirs, or sultans. *Emir* and *sultan* are traditional titles for monarchs in the region. Most of these monarchies were established long ago.

Constitutional Monarchies Jordan, Kuwait, and Bahrain are constitutional monarchies. While each has a king or emir, citizens elect representatives to a parliament. However, in all three, the king or emir still has considerable powers, so these countries cannot be considered full democracies. By contrast, Britain is a constitutional monarchy with a full democracy in which the government decisions are made by elected officials.

Kuwait has strengthened its democracy. Its elected assembly is known for its lively debates. In 2005, the assembly granted women the right to vote and run for office.

Academic Vocabulary
ultimate • *adj.,* final

Absolute Monarchies Saudi Arabia, Qatar, the United Arab Emirates, and Oman are absolute monarchies. In these countries, the monarch has **ultimate** control of the government and appoints all government officials. Citizens have almost no role in these governments other than to obey.

Saudi Arabia's government is an authoritarian monarchy. There is no written constitution that defines the powers of the monarch. There are no national elections. The king chooses the members of the Consultative Council. The 150 members of this body serve four-year terms. In 2013, former King Abdullah chose 30 women. This was the first time in the kingdom of Saudi Arabia's history that women had served in this role.

▼ Leaders of Saudi Arabia, Lebanon, and Bahrain meet in Riyadh, Saudi Arabia's capital. Saudi Prince Salman, now King Salman, is seated second from the left.

✓READING CHECK Compare and Contrast How do monarchies in Southwest Asia differ?

A Theocracy and Failed States

The remaining governments in the region are of two different types. Unlike other countries in the region, Iran's government is controlled by religious leaders. As a result of political strife and terrorism, two countries in the region have little or no government.

Iran's Theocracy After the 1979 revolution in Iran, a new government dedicated to following Islamic law and anti-Western policies came into power. Iran is one of the world's few theocracies, or governments run by religious leaders. Iran's supreme leader, who is also a Shia religious leader, appoints a council also made up of religious leaders. They, in turn, appoint the next supreme leader. As a result, the system is self-perpetuating, with no citizens involved in choosing the leader.

Iran does have an elected president and parliament. Citizens cannot choose their representatives freely, however. The religious leaders of the government decide who can run for seats. They only allow candidates who support strict religious and anti-western policies. They also have the power to veto, or overrule, laws passed by the parliament.

▲ The Ayatollah Ali Khamenei, a Muslim religious leader, has been the ultimate leader of Iran since 1989.

Failed States Syria has been led by dictators since the mid-1900s. For about 50 years, Syria has had a family-centered dictatorship. From 1971 to 2000, Hafez al-Assad ruled as president, with absolute power. His son, Bashar al-Assad, assumed power after Hafez's death.

In 2011, during what is known as the Arab Spring, many Syrians, like people in several Arab countries, rose up to demand democracy. Bashar al-Assad responded by carrying out a war against Syrians who oppose his dictatorship. Large parts of the country came under the control of rebel groups and terrorists, including ISIS. For these reasons, Syria is considered by many to be a failed state. A **failed state** is a country with a government that cannot control its territory or provide effective government services to its citizens.

While one armed group or another, including the Assad government, controls each part of Syria, none of them can provide effective government services. The ongoing warfare among these armed groups makes it impossible to protect the safety of Syrians or maintain effective rule of law. Instead, in a failed state like Syria, everyday life takes place under a constant threat of violence.

Analyze Images Syrian refugees live in a camp in Turkey. **Draw Conclusions** What kinds of challenges could large numbers of people living in conditions such as this pose for local governments?

Yemen, although legally a democracy, is also a failed state because it does not have an effective government. The country has been divided since 2015 into regions controlled by different armed groups or terrorists.

As in Syria, the ongoing state of war makes it impossible for any group in this failed state to deliver effective government. Attacks by one armed group or another kill innocent civilians and shift parts of Yemen from the control of one group to another. These armed groups are focused on military goals and have little interest in effective government.

☑ READING CHECK Identify Cause and Effect What causes have led to the failed states of Yemen and Syria?

☑ Lesson Check

Practice Vocabulary

1. How is a democracy different from an **authoritarian government**?

2. Why do you think Iran is one of the few **theocracies** in the world?

Critical Thinking and Writing

3. **Draw Conclusions** Why does Southwest Asia have such different forms of government, as compared to other regions?

4. **Classify and Categorize** Based on the information in the Country Databank, which countries in Southwest Asia are democracies? Which of them do you think are more democratic?

5. **Identify Cause and Effect** What effect do terrorist groups have on governments in the region?

6. **Writing Workshop: Develop a Clear Thesis** Based on what you have read, think about a thesis statement for your essay. What generalization can you make about the causes of conflict in the region? What can you say about how these conflicts are being addressed? Write your thesis statement in your 📓 Active Journal.

LESSON 4
Conflicts in Southwest Asia

BOUNCE TO ACTIVATE ▶ VIDEO

GET READY TO READ

START UP

Look at the photograph of soldiers preparing to fight the terrorist organization ISIS in Iraq. Make a list of three reasons why you think there has been conflict in this region of the world.

GUIDING QUESTIONS

- Why has the Palestinian–Israeli conflict persisted?
- What are the main issues in the Iraqi civil conflict?
- Why are the civil wars in Syria and Yemen so complex?

TAKE NOTES

Literacy Skills: Sequence

Use the graphic organizer in your 📙 Active Journal to take notes as you read the lesson.

PRACTICE VOCABULARY

Use the vocabulary activity in your 📙 Active Journal to practice the vocabulary words.

Vocabulary	Academic Vocabulary
Israeli settlement	civilian
Intifada	outrage
caliphate	

Southwest Asia is a region with worldwide importance. It is also a region torn by conflicts among different religious, ethnic, and political groups.

Conflict and Peace

During the Arab-Israeli War of 1967, Israel took control of the West Bank and Gaza. These areas were home to many Palestinian Arabs who now lived under Israeli control.

By 2015, about 6.2 million Muslims and Christian Arabs lived in Israel, Gaza, and the West Bank. This included 1.8 million Arabs who lived in Israel and were Israeli citizens. About 6.4 million Jews lived in Israel and the West Bank in that year.

Both Jews and Palestinian Arabs see the same region as their homeland. Most Israelis want to live in a Jewish state. Most Palestinians want to live in an Arab-dominated state. Some Jews have settled in the West Bank. Many Israeli Arabs want to remain in Israel. Meanwhile, many Palestinians would like to take back land that once belonged to their families.

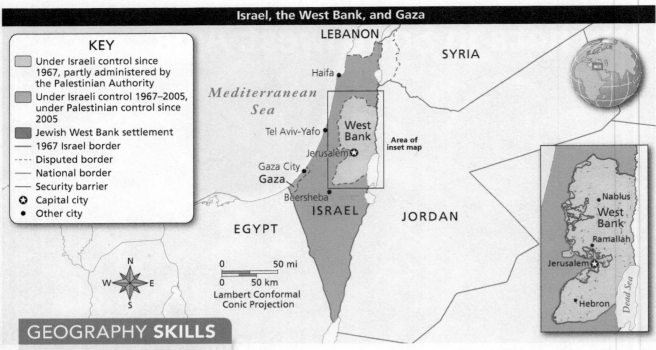

Israel, the West Bank, and Gaza

KEY

- ☐ Under Israeli control since 1967, partly administered by the Palestinian Authority
- ☐ Under Israeli control 1967–2005, under Palestinian control since 2005
- ☐ Jewish West Bank settlement
- — 1967 Israel border
- --- Disputed border
- — National border
- — Security barrier
- ✪ Capital city
- • Other city

LEBANON
SYRIA
Haifa
Mediterranean Sea
Tel Aviv-Yafo
West Bank
Area of inset map
Jerusalem ✪
Gaza City
Gaza
Beersheba
ISRAEL
JORDAN
EGYPT

0   50 mi
0   50 km
Lambert Conformal Conic Projection

Nablus
West Bank
Ramallah
Jerusalem ✪
Hebron
Dead Sea

GEOGRAPHY SKILLS

The majority of Palestinians live in the West Bank and the Gaza Strip.

1. **Place** Where are the West Bank and Gaza Strip in relation to each other?

2. **Draw Conclusions** What elements on the map indicate conflict in this region?

Obstacles to Peace As you have read, Arab leaders refused to negotiate peace with Israel after the 1967 war. In 1973, Egypt and Syria attacked Israel on Yom Kippur, the holiest day of the year in Judaism.

Israelis defeated the Arab armies in this war as well. After the war, Israelis worried about their ability to defend their borders in the future.

During the 1970s and 1980s, Israeli Jews built a growing number of Israeli settlements in the West Bank and Gaza. **Israeli settlements** are places in the West Bank or Gaza where Israelis have settled, or built communities. Many Israelis moved to settlements for economic reasons. Israel withdrew its settlers from Gaza in 2005.

Some Israeli Jews think it was wrong to build Jewish settlements on disputed land. Others want these areas to be part of Israel. Most other nations have opposed the settlements. Israeli settlements in the West Bank are still an area of disagreement between Palestinians and Israelis.

Palestinians accused Israel of diverting most of the West Bank's water. Israel maintains that most underground water deposits, or aquifers, lie under both Israel and the West Bank, that Israel is abiding by its agreements with the Palestinians, and that water loss is caused by leaks and illegal connections.

The Intifada During this time, Palestinians living in Arab countries launched repeated terrorist attacks against Israel. Many attacks targeted Israeli **civilians**.

In the late 1980s, some Palestinians began the First Intifada. This **Intifada** was a campaign of violent resistance against Israeli control. Israel used military force to contain the violence. More than 1,000 people died, mainly young Palestinians.

A Peace Agreement Frustrated Starting in 1993, Israel signed agreements with the Palestine Liberation Organization, or PLO, which represented Palestinians. These agreements—the Oslo Accords—created the Palestinian National Authority to rule parts of the West Bank and Gaza. Israel agreed to withdraw military forces from Gaza and parts of the West Bank. The PLO recognized Israel's right to exist.

Over time, however, each side accused the other of violating the peace agreement, and the Oslo Accords failed. In 2000, Palestinians launched a Second Intifada. The new attacks brought the peace process to a halt, and Israel again fought back. The fighting died down around 2005.

Israel built security barriers around Gaza and the West Bank in the 2000s to prevent attacks on Israel. The barrier also separates some Palestinian villages from each other and blocked some Palestinians' access to their farmland. The barriers succeeded in reducing attacks on Israel but made life more difficult for Palestinians.

During the 2010s, Israel continued to expand settlements on land in the West Bank. Other nations protested these expansions.

Ongoing Conflict and Hopes for Peace In 2005, Israel withdrew completely from Gaza, leaving it under a Palestinian government. In the next year, a Palestinian group called Hamas won the most seats in the Palestinian parliament. Hamas is an organization that has stated a goal of eliminating the State of Israel. It is classified as a terrorist

Analyze Images Trucks from the United Nations bring food supplies to Palestinians. **Draw Conclusions** Why might some Palestinians living around Gaza and the West Bank need food aid?

5 Things to Know About

YITZHAK FRANKENTHAL
Israeli peace activist, born 1951

- In 1994, Yitzhak Frankenthal's son, Arik, an Israeli soldier, was kidnapped and killed by Palestinian fighters.

- He spent months doing research to find the names of other Israeli families that had experienced the same type of loss.

- Frankenthal started Parents Circle—Families Forum as a way to bring together Israeli and Palestinian families who lost a loved one in the Arab–Israeli conflict.

- He founded the Arik Institute for Reconciliation, which has Palestinians speak to Israelis about to enter military service.

- Frankenthal also leads the Fund for Reconciliation, Tolerance, and Peace, which funds peace efforts.

Critical Thinking Why do you think Frankenthal decided to work for peace and reconciliation after his son was murdered?

organization by many nations, including the United States. Hamas fighters took control of Gaza in 2007. Hamas began shooting rockets into Israel, which killed more than a dozen Israeli civilians.

In response to rocket attacks against Israeli cities, Israel bombed Hamas targets in Gaza for one month in late 2008 and early 2009, and sent troops to kill or capture Hamas fighters. Hundreds of Hamas fighters were killed, as well as hundreds of Palestinian civilians.

Israel and Egypt also imposed a blockade on Gaza, blocking all traffic by air, sea, or land. This blockade damaged the economy of Gaza.

Fighting has also occurred between Israel and a Lebanese Shia group called Hezbollah. Hezbollah is considered a terrorist group by Israel, the United States, and other countries and is supported by the government of Iran. It has both a political wing and a military wing and holds seats in Lebanon's parliament. Hezbollah has launched many rocket attacks into northern Israel. In response to a cross-border raid, Israel briefly invaded southern Lebanon to attack Hezbollah in 2006.

In 2014, once again rockets from Gaza were fired into Israel, and Israel sent troops into Gaza to eliminate the threat to Israel. In this conflict, 7 civilians in Israel and 66 Israeli soldiers died. According to the United Nations, more than 2,100 Palestinians in Gaza died.

Most Palestinians and Israelis want peace. Many support creating an independent Palestinian state in the West Bank and Gaza, alongside Israel. This is called a two-state solution to the conflict. However, violence must end for this solution to work.

INTERACTIVE

Regional Conflicts

READING CHECK **Draw Conclusions** Why has the Palestinian–Israeli conflict persisted?

The Conflict in Iraq

After Saddam Hussein was removed from power in Iraq in 2003, violence continued. Rival groups fought for power. Shia and Sunni rebels attacked civilians and people who worked for the government. The forces of the United States and its allies also faced attacks. American troops stayed in the war-torn country in an effort to train some Iraqis so that they were prepared to keep the peace.

Ethnic and Religious Conflict Meanwhile, civil war broke out between different ethnic and religious groups. Shia Arabs and Sunni Arabs fought for control of land around the capital, Baghdad, and in other parts of Iraq. In the north, Arabs fought against Iraqi Kurds.

Kirkuk, an oil-rich city, was the focus of a tug-of-war battle between Arabs and Kurds for many years. The Kurdish government has long contended, or argued, that Kirkuk is their capital. Kurds and the Arab-led government also disagreed over who should benefit from oil taken from the Kurdish region.

The Rise of ISIS In the midst of turmoil in Iraq and Syria, the Islamic State in Iraq and Syria (ISIS), an Islamist terrorist group, arose and became a serious threat. In April 2013 ISIS began to invade and occupy territory in Iraq. By June 2014, ISIS announced the formation of what it called simply the Islamic State (IS). It called that state a **caliphate**, a region controlled by a caliph, or an Islamic religious and political leader. ISIS proclaimed that its caliphate included Muslim lands around the world. Though no Muslim countries follow the Islamic State's ideology, ISIS members all over the world have spread terror.

ISIS captured Iraq's second largest city, Mosul, and attacked other parts of Iraq. As a result, Kurdish leaders and the Iraqi government agreed to work together to defeat ISIS. The United States joined this effort. By 2016, combined forces had won back Iraqi territory and towns from ISIS.

READING CHECK Identify Main Ideas What are the main issues in the Iraqi civil war conflict?

Did you know?

Peshmerga means "Facing Death." Peshmerga forces are Kurdish fighters with roots in tribal groups that have fought for an independent Kurdish state for over a century.

Analyze Images
Firefighters put out a fire from a car bomb in Baghdad, Iraq. **Draw Conclusions** Why is setting off bombs in crowded areas a common terrorist action?

The term *spring* has been used to describe moments in history characterized by peaceful revolution. Why do you think the word *spring* is applied to movements like the Arab Spring? Record your thoughts in your Active Journal.

Academic Vocabulary

outrage • *n.*, shock and anger at a violation of principles

The Conflict in Syria

In March 2011, as part of the Arab Spring, many Syrians demonstrated against the authoritarian government of President Bashar al-Assad. The government, hoping to crush the opposition and preserve its power, responded with a military crackdown. This began a civil war between pro-Assad and anti-Assad forces.

The conflict has been a costly one. Hundreds of thousands of civilians have been killed in the fighting. Several million Syrian refugees have fled to other countries in Southwest Asia and to Europe since the civil war began.

The Assad government has used chemical weapons against civilians, violating international law. The Assad government received support from Iran and Russia. Leaders of the United States and other countries expressed **outrage** at this action. They threatened air strikes against Syria, a move that was criticized by Russia, China, and Iran. The Americans and their allies then negotiated an agreement with Russia and Syria for the Assad government to give up its chemical weapons. By late 2013, weapons inspectors from the United Nations had removed them.

In early 2014, ISIS launched an attack on Syria. It fought both pro-Assad government forces and anti-Assad rebels, the two sides who were still locked in their own civil war. In 2015, Russia began to take a more active role in the conflict. It helped the Assad forces with air strikes that it claimed were aimed at ISIS forces. Often, though, these strikes hit rebels seeking democracy rather than ISIS. With Russian assistance, Assad's government made progress against the rebels.

In 2017, the government once again struck with chemical weapons. The United States attacked a Syrian air base in response.

READING CHECK Summarize Why is the Syrian civil war so complex?

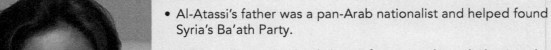

BIOGRAPHY
5 Things to Know About

SUHAIR AL-ATASSI
Human Rights Activist (born 1971)

- Al-Atassi's father was a pan-Arab nationalist and helped found Syria's Ba'ath Party.

- In 2001, she created a dialogue for peace through the Jamal al-Atassi Forum, named for her father.

- In 2011, she was arrested for asking for the release of political prisoners during the Arab Spring and later moved to France.

- In 2012, al-Atassi was elected as a vice president of the National Coalition of Syrian Revolutionary and Opposition Forces.

- Al-Atassi has a master's degree in French literature, which she earned at the University of Damascus.

Critical Thinking Why do you think al-Atassi has worked for human rights in her country?

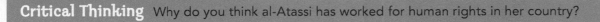

The Conflict in Yemen

Yemen had been divided into two separate countries with different governments until 1990, when they united. Differences between the regions remained, however. Southern rebels tried more than once to reestablish a separate country.

In 2011, during the Arab Spring, protesters in Yemen succeeded in removing President Ali Abdullah Saleh from office. Forces that wanted democracy and the political opposition were helped by the Gulf Cooperation Council (GCC), a political and economic organization of countries on the Arabian Peninsula, including Saudi Arabia. The GCC helped make a deal to end the violence.

In February 2012, Saleh's former vice president, Abd Rabbuh Mansur Hadi, became president of Yemen under the agreement sponsored by the GCC. The new government established under Hadi included the political opposition in an effort to gain unity. Anti-government protests continued, however, and in 2014 a rebel group backed by Iran, known as the Houthis (HOO theez), took control of much of Yemen. They installed their own government.

Beginning in 2015, ISIS entered the conflict in Yemen. Its forces took control of parts of Yemen. Meanwhile, the Saudi-led forces launched deadly air strikes against rebel territory. As the fighting continued, Yemen became a failed state.

Analyze Images Anti-government protesters in Yemen march in 2011, during the Arab Spring. **Main Idea and Details** What was the result of these protests in Yemen?

☑ **READING CHECK** **Use Evidence** Why is Yemen's civil war so complex?

☑ Lesson Check

Practice Vocabulary

1. What was the **Intifada**?

2. Why did the so-called Islamic State declare a **caliphate**?

Critical Thinking and Writing

3. **Compare and Contrast** How are the conflicts in Southwest Asia similar and different?

4. **Sequence** How did ISIS take advantage of the civil unrest in Syria and Iraq to launch its attacks? What events did those attacks follow?

5. **Draw Conclusions** Look at the information about Yemen in the Country Databank. Based on that information and what you read in this lesson, why was Yemen affected by the protests of Arab Spring when most of the region's governments were not?

6. **Writing Workshop: Make an Outline** Decide on the three or more main ideas you will present in your essay. For each main idea, write three or four details in your ▱ Active Journal.

☑ Review and Assessment

VISUAL REVIEW

Comparing Israel, Saudi Arabia, and Turkey

Country	Government	Economy	Cultures
Israel	Parliamentary republic	High-tech economy, high GDP	Ethnic, religious mix
Saudi Arabia	Absolute monarchy	Oil-rich economy, high GDP	Largely Arab, Muslim population
Turkey	Parliamentary republic	Diversified economy, low GDP	Turks, Kurds, and others; chiefly Muslim

CAUSES OF CONFLICT IN SOUTHWEST ASIA

Territorial Claims

- Israeli-Palestinian conflict
- Kurdish claims in Turkey, Iraq, Iran

Religious and Political Differences

- Sunni-Shia conflict in Iraq
- ISIS, Islamist conflict with more moderate Muslims
- ISIS attempts to set up caliphate

Political Conflict

- Sunni-Shia conflict in Iraq
- Syrian civil war
- Yemen civil war
- Pro-democracy movements in region

READING REVIEW

Use the Take Notes and Practice Vocabulary activities in your 📔 Active Journal to review the topic.

INTERACTIVE

Practice vocabulary using the Topic Mini-Games.

Quest FINDINGS

Create Your Peace Summit Plan

Get help for creating your plan in your 📔 Active Journal.

ASSESSMENT

Vocabulary and Key Ideas

1. **Check Understanding** How is the **theocracy** of Iran connected to **Sharia**?

2. **Trace** What are the historical reasons for Southwest Asia's religious diversity?

3. **Explain** How does **Islamism** differ from a **secular** outlook?

4. **Identify Main Ideas** How has the oil industry been both helpful and harmful to some countries in the region?

5. **Identify Main Ideas** What role have entrepreneurship and investment in **capital** played in the region's economies?

6. **Explain** How have Palestinians and Israelis responded to conflict over water in the region?

7. **Define** How has the use of **desalination** affected settlement patterns in the region?

Critical Thinking and Writing

8. **Identify Cause and Effect** How has cultural diffusion affected the region?

9. **Synthesize** Look at the types of government for all the countries in the region listed in the Country Databank, and consider what you have learned about Southwest Asia. What might explain why there are so few democracies in the region?

10. **Summarize** What purpose does OPEC serve?

11. **Compare and Contrast** How is the situation in Syria in the 2010s similar to and different from the situation in Iraq since 2003?

12. **Revisit the Essential Question** Describe an effort by people of Southwest Asia to resolve conflict peacefully. Why did it succeed or fail?

13. **Writing Workshop: Write an Explanatory Essay** Using the thesis and plan you wrote in your 📓 Active Journal, answer the following question in a multi-paragraph essay: What are the roots of conflict in Southwest Asia?

Analyze Primary Sources

14. Between what groups does the quotation predict conflict?
    A. ISIS and Israel
    B. Kurds and Arabs
    C. Palestinians and Israelis
    D. Shia Muslims and Sunni Muslims

"I can promise that if there is not sufficient water in our region, if there is scarcity of water, if people remain thirsty for water, then we shall doubtless face war."

—*Meir Ben Meir, Israel's former Water Commissioner*

Analyze Maps

Use the map at right to answer the following questions.

15. a) In which area did Israel grant the Palestinian Authority limited control? b) In which area do Palestinians exercise full internal control?

16. Which country has a democratic government with a power-sharing arrangement?

17. Which letter marks the scene of a long and difficult civil war in the 2000s?

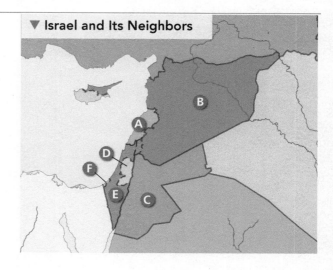

▼ Israel and Its Neighbors

GO ONLINE
to access your
digital course

▶ VIDEO

◀)) AUDIO

📖 ETEXT

👆 INTERACTIVE

✎ WRITING

🎮 GAMES

📄 WORKSHEET

☑ ASSESSMENT

Some of the world's oldest civilizations and empires developed

in SOUTH ASIA. It is the birthplace of Hinduism and Buddhism, which shaped the region's history and culture along with Islam. Today, South Asia is home to more than 1.7 billion of the world's people.

Explore
The Essential Question

What should governments do?

Governments in South Asia face many challenges. What role should they take in helping the region solve its problems?

Unlock the Essential Question in your 📖 Active Journal.

◀ Taj Mahal

Read

about the religions and cultures that have shaped South Asia, as well as the major challenges that it faces today.

Watch

BOUNCE TO ACTIVATE ▶ VIDEO

Nancy's Fruitful Loan

Meet Nancy, who is helping her mother start a new business in a mountainous region of India.

389

8 Regional Atlas

South Asia: Political

MANY PEOPLE

South Asia is one of the smaller world regions in size but the largest in population. The region shares a common history and many cultural features.

Learn more about the physical features of South Asia by making your own map in your Active Journal.

Mountain Countries

Centered in the foothills of the Himalayas, Nepal and Bhutan are two small mountain countries in South Asia.

Muslim Neighbors

Afghanistan, Pakistan, and Bangladesh are all mainly Muslim countries. Though smaller in population than India, Pakistan and Bangladesh have huge populations of more than 160 million people each.

INTERACTIVE

Topic Map

A Giant Country

India is home to around 1.3 billion people. It has about four times the population of the United States in about one third as much land area. By 2022, India's population is expected to surpass China's to become the largest of any country in the world. India has a Hindu majority and a large Muslim minority.

Island Countries

Sri Lanka and the Maldives are island countries located south of India in the Indian Ocean.

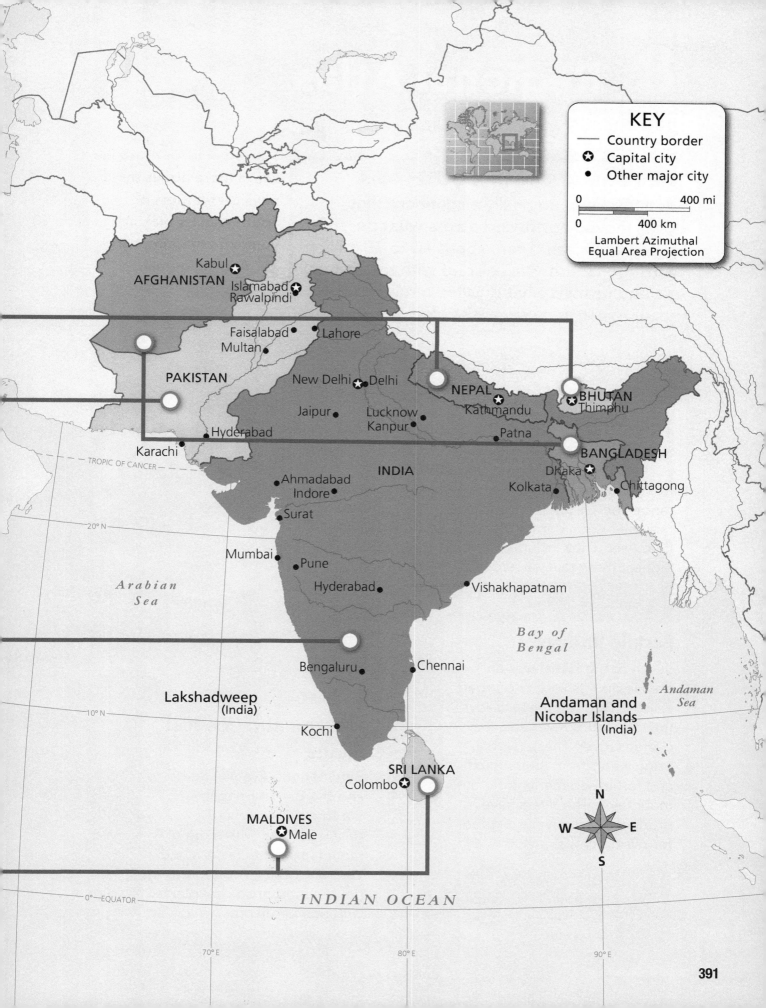

South Asia: Physical

THE FORMATION OF SOUTH ASIA

South Asia was originally a continent that slowly moved northward across what became the Indian Ocean. Then, about 40 to 50 million years ago, South Asia collided with the rest of Asia and formed what is called a subcontinent.

Learn more about the physical features of South Asia by making your own map in your Active Journal.

Towering Mountains

South Asia's collision with the rest of Asia pushed Earth's crust up to form the Hindu Kush and the Himalayas, the highest mountain ranges on Earth. The Himalayas—the highest range—form a barrier between South Asia and East Asia. They include Mount Everest, Earth's highest mountain, shown in the photograph.

Fertile Valleys

South of the Himalayas and the Hindu Kush are two broad valleys. Through these valleys flow the Indus River and the Ganges River. These rivers bring water from melting ice and fertile sediments from the mountains. The rivers have produced fertile valleys good for raising crops.

Plateau and Coastal Plains

Between the Arabian Sea and the Bay of Bengal, South Asia consists of a rolling plateau with a rim of mountains—the Eastern and Western Ghats. Around this rim is a strip of coastal plains with rich farmland.

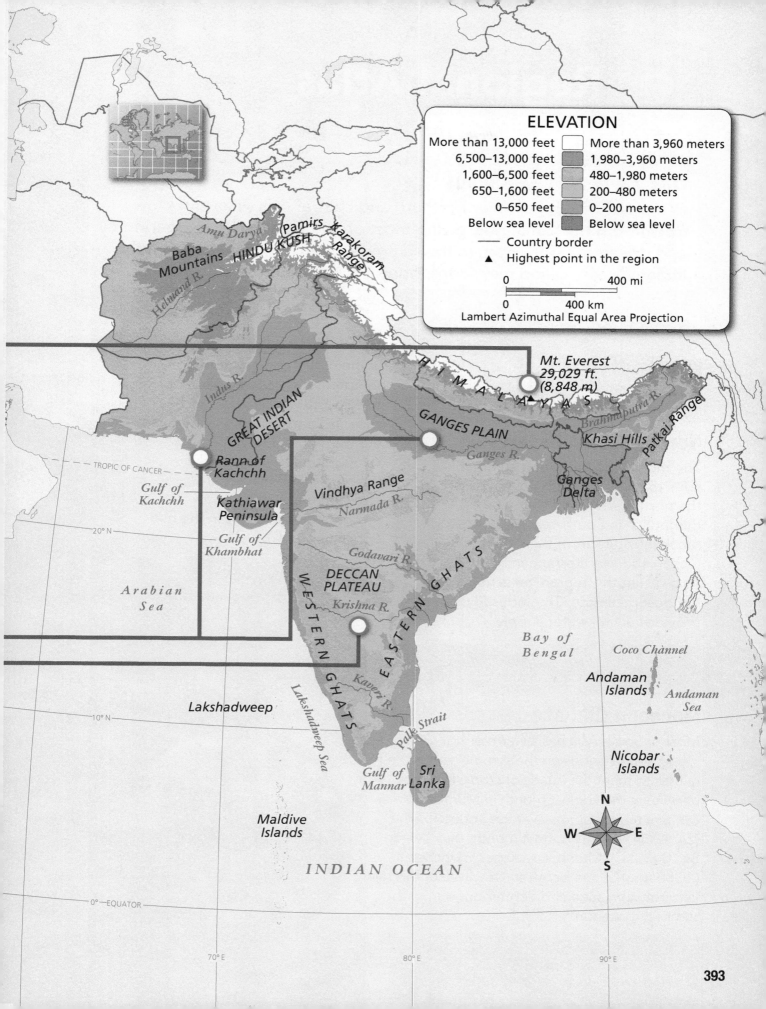

ELEVATION

More than 13,000 feet		More than 3,960 meters
6,500–13,000 feet		1,980–3,960 meters
1,600–6,500 feet		480–1,980 meters
650–1,600 feet		200–480 meters
0–650 feet		0–200 meters
Below sea level		Below sea level

—— Country border

▲ Highest point in the region

0   400 mi

0   400 km

Lambert Azimuthal Equal Area Projection

Amu Darya

Baba Mountains   HINDU KUSH   Pamirs   Karakoram Range

Helmand R.

Indus R.

HIMALAYAS

Mt. Everest
29,029 ft.
(8,848 m)

GREAT INDIAN DESERT

GANGES PLAIN

Brahmaputra R.

Khasi Hills   Patkai Range

TROPIC OF CANCER

Rann of Kachchh

Ganges R.

Ganges Delta

Gulf of Kachchh

Vindhya Range

Kathiawar Peninsula

Narmada R.

Gulf of Khambhat

20° N

Godavari R.

DECCAN PLATEAU

EASTERN GHATS

Arabian Sea

WESTERN GHATS

Krishna R.

Bay of Bengal

Coco Channel

Andaman Islands

Andaman Sea

Lakshadweep

Lakshadweep Sea

Kaveri R.

10° N

Palk Strait

Nicobar Islands

Gulf of Mannar

Sri Lanka

N
W   E
S

Maldive Islands

INDIAN OCEAN

0°—EQUATOR

70° E

80° E

90° E

393

South Asia: Climate

DRY AND WET SEASONS

In the winter, cold air over northern and central Asia sinks and blows down from the Himalayas, giving most of South Asia mild temperatures and dry air during winter. In the summer, warm, moist winds from the Indian Ocean, called monsoons, bring South Asia most of its rainfall.

Cool Mountains

In the mountains around Gilgit, temperatures are well below freezing all winter. A few inches of snow fall most winters. Summers are warmer, but daytime high temperatures average only in the mid-70°s F (mid-20°s C), and summer nighttime low temperatures average in the mid-50°s F (around 12° C).

Northwestern Deserts

The monsoons that bring summer rains to most of South Asia bypass the northwest. At the same time, mountains in Southwest Asia block moisture from the Atlantic Ocean and Mediterranean Sea. As a result, this region has a hot, dry desert climate. The Indus River provides a vital water supply.

Monsoon Climate

Most of South Asia has a warm or hot climate year-round and depends on the summer monsoon for rainfall to meet the needs of crops, livestock, and people. In the coolest month in Mumbai, India, January temperatures average about 75° F (24° C). In May, its hottest month, they average 86° C (30° C). Mumbai averages 93 inches (2,386 mm) of rain per year. Nearly all of this rain falls between June and September during the summer monsoon.

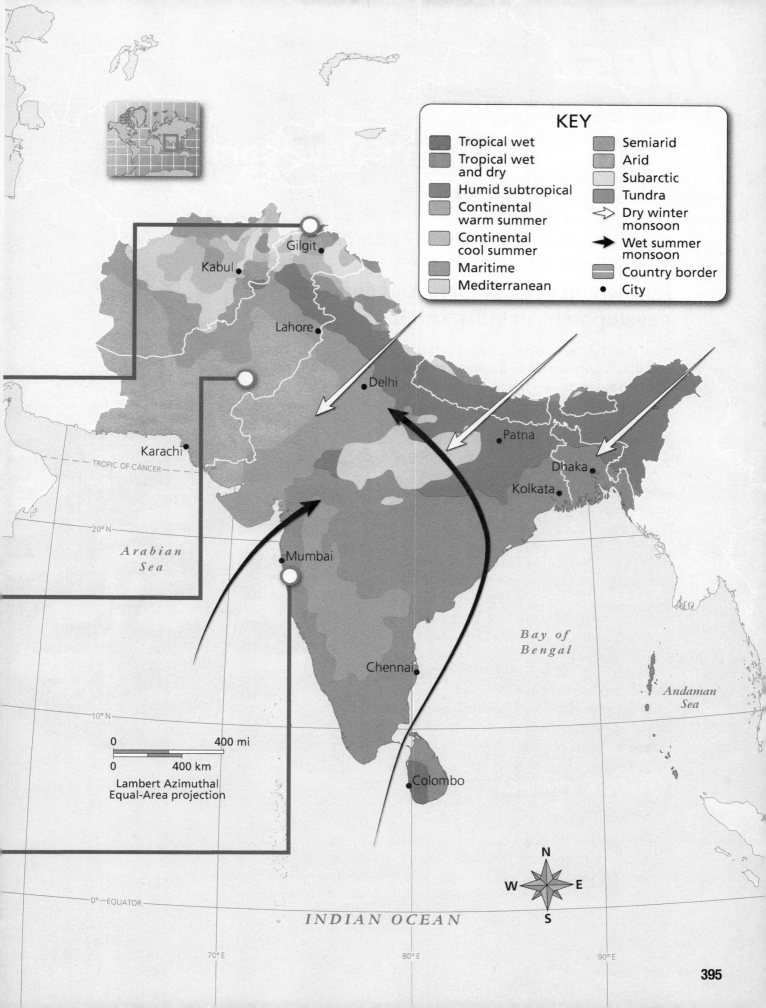

KEY

- Tropical wet
- Tropical wet and dry
- Humid subtropical
- Continental warm summer
- Continental cool summer
- Maritime
- Mediterranean
- Semiarid
- Arid
- Subarctic
- Tundra
- ⇨ Dry winter monsoon
- ➡ Wet summer monsoon
- Country border
- • City

Gilgit

Kabul

Lahore

Delhi

Karachi

TROPIC OF CANCER

Patna

Dhaka

Kolkata

20° N

Arabian Sea

Mumbai

Chennai

Bay of Bengal

Andaman Sea

10° N

0   400 mi

0   400 km

Lambert Azimuthal
Equal-Area projection

Colombo

N
W   E
S

0° EQUATOR

INDIAN OCEAN

70° E

80° E

90° E

Quest

Comparing Economic Development

Quest KICK OFF

You will learn about the development of and challenges facing two of the most populous countries in the world, India and Bangladesh.

How would you compare and contrast development in India and Bangladesh?

How did their economies, transportation systems, health care, and education develop? Explore the Essential Question "What should governments do?" in this Quest.

▼ Heavy traffic fills a street in New Delhi, India.

1 Ask Questions

One of the challenges that a developing country faces is meeting the basic needs—food, clothing, and shelter—of its people. What other challenges do governments face? Write the questions in your ▣ Active Journal.

2 Investigate

As you read the lessons in this topic, look for **Quest** CONNECTIONS that provide information on how these two countries have developed. Capture notes in your ▣ Active Journal.

3 Examine Geographic Sources

Next, explore a set of primary sources about India and Bangladesh. They'll help you learn more about development in these countries in the past and in the present. Take notes on the sources in your ▣ Active Journal.

Quest FINDINGS

4 Write Your Essay

At the end of the topic, you'll write an essay in which you compare and contrast the development of India and Bangladesh. In writing your essay, you will gain a better understanding of how these neighboring countries developed in similar or different ways. Get help for writing your essay in your ▣ Active Journal.

LESSON 1
Early Civilizations of South Asia

GET READY TO READ

START UP
Examine this sculpture of the Vedic and Hindu god Indra. Write three questions that you have about the civilization that created this artwork.

GUIDING QUESTIONS
- What were the key features of the Indus Valley civilization?
- How did the Indo-Aryans shape the culture of South Asia?
- What were the achievements of the Maurya and Gupta empires?

TAKE NOTES
Literacy Skills: Analyze Text Structure
Use the graphic organizer in your 📓 Active Journal to take notes as you read the lesson.

PRACTICE VOCABULARY
Use the vocabulary activity in your 📓 Active Journal to practice the vocabulary words.

Vocabulary		Academic Vocabulary
Veda	Dalit	evidence
ahimsa	guild	ancestor
tolerance	citizenship	
caste		

The Indus River valley in northwestern South Asia nurtured the development of one of the world's first civilizations. It offered fertile agricultural land, while mountains and oceans provided natural barriers for protection from invaders. A series of civilizations developed here and in the Ganges River valley to the east.

A Complex Civilization
Farmers began growing crops in hills near the Indus River valley around 7000 BCE. With a steady food supply, the population grew. After 3000 BCE, cities began to develop on the broad plains of the Indus Valley. By about 2500 BCE, these cities were the centers of the complex Indus Valley civilization. However, by around 1700 BCE, the civilization had largely disappeared.

In the 1920s, archaeologists discovered the ruins of two great Indus Valley cities: Harappa and Mohenjo-Daro. Since then, archaeologists have found more than 1,000 other towns and villages that were part of this civilization.

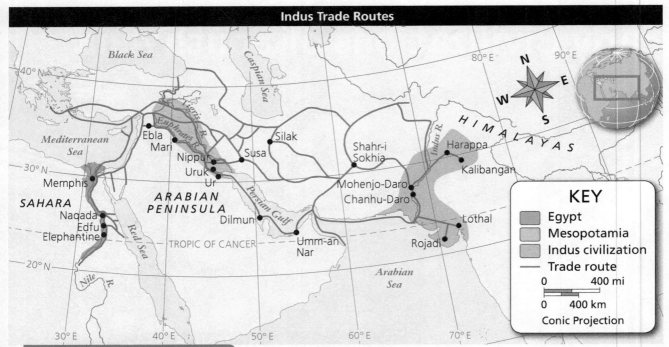

Indus Trade Routes

KEY
- Egypt
- Mesopotamia
- Indus civilization
- Trade route

0 — 400 mi
0 — 400 km
Conic Projection

GEOGRAPHY **SKILLS**

Trade was important to early civilizations that arose in the Indus Valley. Trade strengthened their economies and gave them a way to exchange goods and ideas.

1. **Location** What is similar about the location of the three civilizations on this map?

2. **Use Visual Information** What waterways would be used to trade goods between the Indus Valley civilization and Mesopotamia?

Farming the Indus Valley Farmers in the dry Indus Valley could not always depend on the monsoon rains. Therefore, they built irrigation channels and ditches to bring river water to their wheat and barley fields.

Indus Valley farmers also raised cattle, sheep, goats, and chickens for food. They used oxen or cattle to pull carts. Animals seem to have been important to the Indus Valley people. They carved wooden animals and painted pictures of animals on the pottery they made.

Trade The Indus Valley environment was rich in resources for trade. Jewelers there used precious stones to make beautiful jewelry, which was sold as far away as Mesopotamia. Traders also sold cotton cloth woven in the Indus Valley and teak, a valuable wood from a tree that grows in India.

Indus Valley traders used stone seals with writing to identify their goods. They stamped their seals on soft clay squares attached to their goods.

Technology Indus Valley cities were well planned and organized. The people of the Indus Valley built thick walls around their cities. In these cities, they built huge raised mounds of earth and brick. During floods, these mounds remained above the rising water.

Many houses in these cities had a bathroom and toilet. Waste water from houses flowed into brick-lined sewage channels. These were the world's first sewer systems.

The Indus Valley people had an advanced knowledge of mathematics. Their cities were built with wide, straight streets in a grid pattern. They also had a system of weights and measurements using multiples of ten, like the modern metric system. Accurate weights and measures supported trade.

Indus Valley Mysteries The careful planning of cities and standard system of weights and measures suggest that the Indus Valley people had a strong central government. Yet, no royal statues or tombs have been found, and we do not know what kind of government existed. While the civilization seems to have had a system of writing, no one can read it today.

The greatest mystery is what caused this civilization to disappear. Before 1700 BCE, the Indus Valley people began to abandon their cities. The civilization declined rapidly after that. Some **evidence** suggests that a disease may have killed many people. Some scholars think that flooding, drought, or overgrazing might have made farming difficult.

☑ READING CHECK **Summarize** What economic activities supported the Indus Valley civilization?

Who Were the Indo-Aryans?

By 1600 BCE, another group of people were living in the Indus Valley. They called themselves Aryans. This meant "the noble ones" in their language. The Aryans, whom scholars also call Indo-Aryans, introduced a new language. They also brought a new religion with them. They expressed their beliefs in a collection of hundreds of sacred hymns known as **Vedas**. For this reason, this period of Indian history is called the Vedic age.

Origins of Indo-Aryan Culture Over many years, most scholars believe that the Indo-Aryans migrated into India from Central Asia

Quest CONNECTIONS

What kinds of development took place in the Indus Valley? Record your findings in your 📓 Active Journal.

Academic Vocabulary
evidence • *n.,* something that provides information about something unknown

Analyze Images Mohenjo-Daro included the large structure shown here that archaeologists call the Citadel. **Use Visual Information** What evidence of planning do you see in this photo?

with their livestock. In India, they mixed with local people and adopted local beliefs. Local people adopted the mixed Aryan language and religion and called themselves Aryans, too.

The Indo-Aryans settled in India, many of them choosing to live in the Ganges River valley. They developed a complex civilization, including trade and specialization.

For a thousand years, Indians passed the Vedas down by word of mouth. They sang or chanted them in an Indo-Aryan language called Sanskrit, which is a distant relative of English. Today, Sanskrit remains a language of sacred literature. Sanskrit is the **ancestor** of many modern Indian languages. Around 500 BCE, Indians began to collect the Vedas and put them into writing.

The oldest of the Vedas is the *Rig Veda*. It includes more than 1,000 hymns. Most of them praise Indo-Aryan Gods and Goddesses representing natural forces such as the sky, sun, and fire.

Indo-Aryan Life Most of what we know about Indo-Aryan life in South Asia comes from the Vedas. The earliest Indo-Aryans lived as nomadic herders. Cattle held special importance for them since the herds provided both food and clothing.

The Vedas also mention that the Indo-Aryans settled in villages and practiced agriculture. They planted crops such as barley, wheat, and lentils and grazed cattle and horses on pastures around their villages.

The Vedas show that the Indo-Aryans found joy in their day-to-day lives. They loved music and dancing. They held chariot races and enjoyed gambling. They also questioned the meaning of life in their texts. The following passage from the *Rig Veda* describes the connection between the human body and God:

▼ Page of Sanskrit from the *Rig Veda*, or "Knowledge of the Hymns of Praise"

Primary Source

"The human body is the temple of God. One who kindles the light of awareness within gets true light. The sacred flame of your inner shrine is constantly bright."

—*Rig Veda*

✓ READING CHECK **Summarize** Why are the Vedas important to understanding Indo-Aryan civilization?

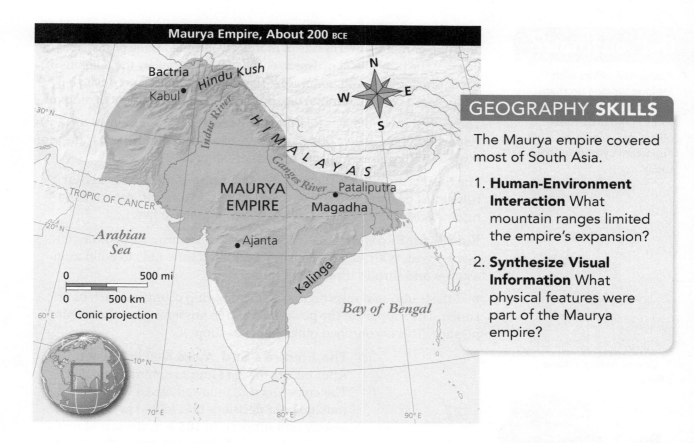

Maurya Empire, About 200 BCE

Bactria
Kabul
Hindu Kush
Indus River
HIMALAYAS
Ganges River
MAURYA EMPIRE
Pataliputra
Magadha
TROPIC OF CANCER
Arabian Sea
Ajanta
Kalinga
Bay of Bengal
0   500 mi
0   500 km
Conic projection

GEOGRAPHY SKILLS

The Maurya empire covered most of South Asia.

1. **Human-Environment Interaction** What mountain ranges limited the empire's expansion?

2. **Synthesize Visual Information** What physical features were part of the Maurya empire?

The Maurya Empire

By the end of the Vedic age, many kingdoms and chiefdoms covered India. The strongest of these kingdoms was Magadha (MUH guh duh). Around 321 BCE, a rebel army overthrew the king of Magadha. The leader of the rebels was Chandragupta Maurya (chun druh GOOP tuh MOWR yuh).

By 305 BCE, Chandragupta ruled much of the Indian subcontinent. Chandragupta's Maurya empire stretched from the Bay of Bengal to present-day Afghanistan.

As Chandragupta grew older, he became a Jain—a follower of Jainism (JY niz um). Jainism is an Indian religion that stresses doing no harm to any living creature. According to legend, Chandragupta gave up being emperor to enter a Jain monastery.

Power passed to his son, Bindusara. Bindusara expanded the Maurya empire farther across India. Then Bindusara's son Asoka took power.

Asoka Changes Course Asoka spent his first eight years as emperor strengthening his hold on power. Then, he went to war again. His target was the kingdom of Kalinga, which had resisted conquest. Eventually, Asoka conquered Kalinga, but with a terrible loss of life.

The suffering that Asoka saw during the war made him think hard about how he wanted to rule. Asoka adopted nonviolence. Nonviolence was a key value of the religion of Buddhism, another religion that had developed in India since Vedic times.

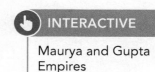

INTERACTIVE

Maurya and Gupta Empires

Whenever possible, Asoka replaced rule by force with rule based on dharma, or moral law. His rule of moral law included three principles. The first was the principle of **ahimsa**, or the belief—shared by the religions of Hinduism, Jainism, and Buddhism—that one should not hurt any living thing. Asoka gave up hunting and banned the cruel treatment of animals.

The second principle was tolerance. **Tolerance** is a willingness to respect different beliefs and customs. Asoka was a Buddhist, but he respected Hinduism, Jainism, and other religions.

The third principle was the people's well-being. Asoka believed that a ruler must be careful to rule his people well. As a result, Asoka made many decisions to make his empire a better place to live.

Buddhism Expands Asoka's support for Buddhism helped the religion spread. With Asoka's backing, Buddhists were able to build monasteries and shrines throughout India.

Buddhists also sent missionaries to neighboring countries, such as Sri Lanka. The support of the powerful Maurya emperor gave the religion prestige. This encouraged other rulers to adopt it.

▼ One of Asoka's stone pillars

The Empire's End Asoka died in 232 BCE. After his death, the Maurya empire struggled. The emperors that followed Asoka were weak, making poor decisions and failing to command loyalty and support. In 185 BCE, the last Maurya ruler was murdered. After 136 years, the Maurya empire had come to an end.

✓ READING CHECK **Recognize Multiple Causes** Why did Asoka turn away from violence and practice tolerance?

The Gupta Empire

After the collapse of the Maurya empire, India broke into many small kingdoms. Armies from the north and west invaded India repeatedly. Meanwhile, trade brought Indians into contact with China, Southeast Asia, and Europe. Invaders and traders brought new ideas from the ancient Greeks and other peoples. Indians built on these ideas to make their own advances in art, literature, math, and science. During this time, Hinduism, a religion derived from the Vedic religion, was practiced alongside Buddhism, and a new social structure began to develop.

The Caste System Over hundreds of years, India developed a social structure based on caste. A **caste** is a fixed social class into which a person is born. People inherited their caste from their parents. They stayed in that caste for their entire lives.

Members of different castes did not usually mix socially. They rarely married across caste lines. This social structure is known as a caste system. Social classes began to develop in India in ancient times but may not have become fixed castes until modern times.

The most basic grouping was by occupation. Some scholars think that occupation-based castes or communities began as extended families that had a family business or occupation. There are hundreds of such communities today.

The Vedas identify four caste groupings based on religious status. Priests were known as Brahmins. Another grouping was the Kshatriyas, or the rulers and warriors. A third was the Vaishyas, or landowners, bankers, and merchants. The fourth was the Sudras, who did farm work and other manual work.

Later, a fifth caste grouping developed. Known today as **Dalits**, people in this caste had to do jobs that no one else wanted, such as cleaning toilets or butchering animals. Members of the higher castes avoided contact with people in this group for fear of being made unclean. Although these caste groupings came to involve inequality, that inequality did not derive from Vedic teachings.

A New Empire in India Meanwhile, about 500 years after the Mauryas, the Gupta dynasty again united northern India. Chandra Gupta I, the first Gupta ruler, may have been named after the founder of the Maurya empire, Chandragupta. Like the first Maurya emperor, Chandra Gupta I dreamed of building an empire. He gained power over a kingdom in the Ganges basin and ruled from about 320 to 335 CE. He expanded his territory across the Ganges basin through alliances and wars of conquest.

His son Samudra Gupta conquered most of the remaining small kingdoms of northern India. Samudra Gupta also conquered lands to the south and west.

Under Samudra's son, Chandra Gupta II, the Gupta empire reached its greatest size. Like Asoka, he tried to bring peace and prosperity to India. Unlike the Mauryas, the Guptas did not try to rule their entire empire directly. Instead, they left most decisions in the hands of local leaders. Governors controlled provinces. Village and city councils made decisions at the local level.

In each village, the leading families sent representatives to the council. In the cities, **guilds**, or groups of merchants or craftsmen working in the same line of business, sent representatives to the city council.

Analyze Images The Ellora Caves in India feature temples carved out of solid rock. The site dates from the 600s to the 800s CE. **Draw Conclusions** What can you conclude about the culture that built these temples?

 INTERACTIVE

A Golden Age in the Arts

Origins of Arabic Numerals

Late Gupta (India, 500s)	Gwalior (India, 800s)	Western Arabic (North Africa and Spain, 900s)	Western Arabic (Worldwide, Today)
O	o	o	0
—	1	1	1
=	2	2	2
☰	3	7	3
४	8	⅌	4
h	Ч	5	5
६	し	6	6
フ	7	7	7
S	ſ	8	8
フ	9	9	9

Analyze Diagrams
Indians created numerals, or symbols representing numbers, that evolved into the Arabic numerals that we use today. **Compare** Which late Gupta symbol is closest to the modern numeral?

People living in the Maurya empire were subjects, with a duty to obey. The people of the Gupta empire were also subjects, but many also had a kind of **citizenship**, or a membership in a state or community that gives a person civil and political rights and obligations.

Under later Gupta rulers, the empire faced new invaders from the west. Parts of the empire broke away. The last Gupta ruler died around the year 540.

Gupta Achievements During the Gupta period, Indians built many impressive temples and monasteries. Just after the empire ended, they carved temples and monasteries into the rocks of cliffs. The rock-cut shrines of Ellora contain brilliant sculptures and paintings.

Trade had brought the learning of Persia and Greece to India. Indian scholars drew on this learning to make advances of their own in mathematics. Two great advances were the idea of zero as a number and the decimal system. The decimal system and the use of zero led to further advances in algebra and trigonometry.

During this time, Indians also made great advances in science. Indian astronomers were the first to describe the movement of the sun, Earth, and moon correctly. They also made advances in medicine and metalworking.

READING CHECK Compare and Contrast How were people treated differently under the Mauryas and the Guptas?

☑ Lesson Check

Practice Vocabulary

1. What were the **Vedas**?

2. What place did **Dalits** have in the **caste** system?

Critical Thinking and Writing

3. **Explain** Name two advances of the Indus Valley civilization.

4. **Synthesize** What advances made in the Gupta period still affect life today?

5. **Identify Main Ideas** How did Asoka spread Buddhism throughout India?

6. **Writing Workshop: Generate Ideas** Write your thoughts about challenges that the Indus Valley civilization faced and how they were met in your 📓 Active Journal. You will use these ideas in a persuasive essay about challenges in South Asia at the end of the topic.

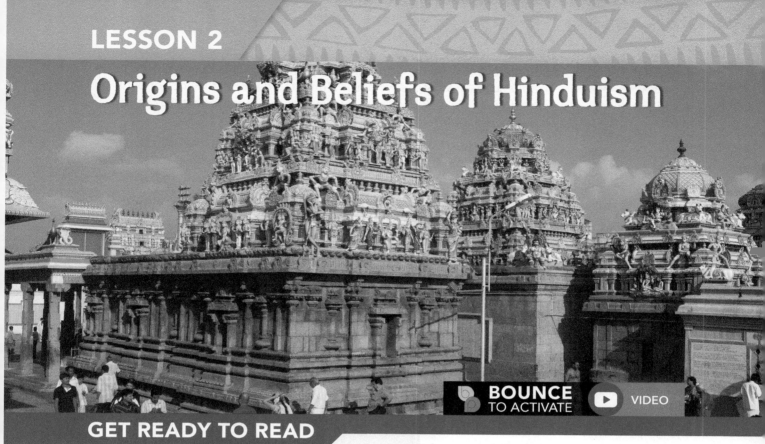

LESSON 2

Origins and Beliefs of Hinduism

BOUNCE TO ACTIVATE · ▶ VIDEO

GET READY TO READ

START UP

Examine the image of the Hindu temple and review the headings in the lesson. Based on this information, what do you think are two features of Hinduism?

GUIDING QUESTIONS

- How did Hinduism develop?
- What are the main beliefs of Hinduism?
- How has Hinduism affected India and the world?

TAKE NOTES

Literacy Skills: Determine Central Ideas
Use the graphic organizer in your 🕮 Active Journal to take notes as you read the lesson.

PRACTICE VOCABULARY

Use the vocabulary activity in your 🕮 Active Journal to practice the vocabulary words.

Vocabulary	Academic Vocabulary
guru	righteous
Brahman	cosmic
reincarnation	
karma	
dharma	
moksha	

Hinduism is one of the oldest religions in the world. It began in India during the Vedic age. Then it slowly grew and changed into modern Hinduism.

What Are the Roots of Hinduism?

Hinduism has been the main religion of India since ancient times. In fact, the word *Hinduism* means "the religion of the people of India."

Early Hinduism As you have learned, the Vedas are India's oldest religious texts. The Vedas contain hymns to many Gods. They also describe rituals, including offerings of food to specific Gods such as Agni, the God of fire.

Early Hinduism was a religion based on studying sacred texts and carrying out rituals, particularly sacrifices to the Gods. Brahmins studied the Vedas and were also the only ones who could perform the rituals. They believed that they had to perform rituals perfectly to avoid angering the Gods. This gave the Brahmins authority in early Indian society.

INTERACTIVE

The Origins of
Hinduism

New Teachings Beginning about 500 BCE, people began asking questions such as: Why are we born? How should we live? What happens to us when we die? Hinduism evolved from Indians' efforts to answer these difficult questions.

To find those answers, thinkers and teachers known as **gurus** left their homes to live in the forest, to think, and to talk about religious ideas. In a sense, these gurus and their students were founders of modern Hinduism.

Their ideas survive in writings known as the Upanishads (oo PAN uh shadz). The Upanishads made connections between heavenly forces and people's lives. Alongside the Vedas, the Upanishads became Hindu holy scriptures. The oldest Upanishads date to around 800 or 700 BCE.

Epic Poems Later, two epic poems helped define Hinduism. An epic poem is a long story of heroes told in verse. Both poems took shape within a few hundred years of 1 CE. These epic poems are the *Ramayana* (rah MAH yuh nuh) and the *Mahabharata* (muh hah BAH ruh tuh). They helped explain how people should live their lives as Hindus.

The *Ramayana* is the story of a king named Rama and the rescue of his beautiful wife, Sita, from kidnappers. This epic stresses the importance of dharma, or **righteous** action. The *Mahabharata* tells the story of two families at war for control of a kingdom. It also deals with moral issues.

The best-known section of the *Mahabharata* is the *Bhagavad-Gita* (BUG uh vud GEE tuh). This means "Song of the Lord." Some scholars consider the *Bhagavad-Gita* to be Hinduism's most important religious text. This text deals with key Hindu beliefs. These beliefs have to do with the nature of the soul, its relationship to God, and ways to live a good life.

✅ **READING CHECK** **Identify Main Ideas** What was the role of gurus?

Academic Vocabulary
righteous • *adj.,* according to moral law

Analyze Images Priests perform religious rituals at a shrine of the God Shiva. **Infer** What can you infer about the practice of Hinduism today from this photo?

Analyze Images An illustration from the *Bhagavad-Gita* showing Krishna and Radha, who often symbolize the love of Brahman. **Identify Main Idea** Why is the *Bhagavad-Gita* important to Hindus?

Hindu Beliefs About God

Hinduism is like a great river. Over thousands of years, many beliefs and traditions have flowed into it. As a result, Hindus may have different practices, but Hindus share certain basic beliefs.

The Upanishads contain two beliefs that lie at the heart of Hinduism. The first is that there is one supreme **cosmic** consciousness, spiritual force, or God, known as **Brahman**. The Upanishads teach that all of the Gods that Indians worship are forms of Brahman. Brahman, they say, is the source of all things.

Many Hindus worship individual Gods or Goddesses as forms of Brahman. Some Hindus worship Brahman as Vishnu. Others worship Brahman as Shiva. Still others worship Brahman as the Goddess Shakti. These Gods and Goddesses may have other named forms. For example, the God Krishna is a form of Vishnu.

The second core Hindu belief is that every person is born with a soul, which is also a form of Brahman. According to the Upanishads:

Academic Vocabulary

cosmic • *adj.,* relating to the whole universe

Primary Source

"This soul of mine within the heart is smaller than a grain of rice. . . . This soul of mine within the heart is greater than the earth, . . . greater than the sky. . . . This soul of mine within the heart, this is Brahman."

—*The Thirteen Principal Upanishads*

✓ **READING CHECK** **Summarize** What do Hindus believe about God and the soul?

Hindu Beliefs About Life

Hindu scriptures such as the Upanishads and the *Bhagavad-Gita* also teach important Hindu beliefs about life.

Reincarnation and Karma Hinduism teaches that when people die, most will undergo reincarnation. **Reincarnation** is the rebirth of a soul in a new body.

In the *Bhagavad-Gita,* the God Krishna explains the process of reincarnation to Arjuna, the hero of the *Mahabharata:*

Primary Source

"As a man discards worn-out clothes to put on new and different ones, so the embodied self (soul) discards its worn-out bodies to take on other new ones."

—*Bhagavad-Gita*

The law of karma determines how a person is reborn. **Karma** is the effect of a person's actions in this and in previous lives. Hindus believe that bad karma—evil deeds—will bring rebirth into more suffering in the next life, while good karma will lead to a clearer path to liberation from rebirth.

GEOGRAPHY SKILLS

Hinduism eventually spread to areas outside of India, including Pakistan, Bangladesh, Nepal, and parts of Southeast Asia.

1. **Movement** In which direction did Hinduism expand between 1 and 1100 CE?

2. **Cite Evidence** Based on the map, do you think that Hinduism expanded during that time mainly by land or mainly by sea? Explain.

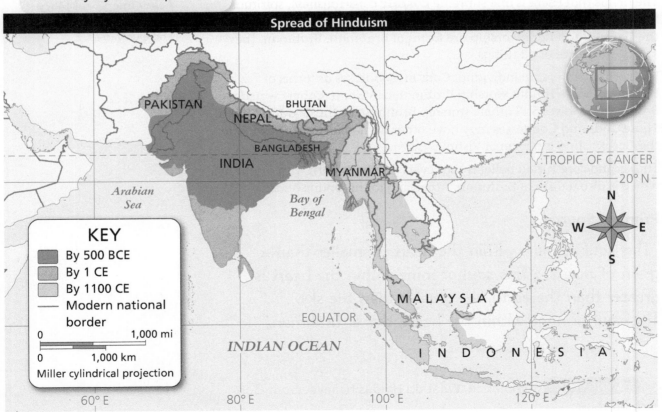

Spread of Hinduism

KEY
- By 500 BCE
- By 1 CE
- By 1100 CE
- Modern national border

0   1,000 mi
0   1,000 km
Miller cylindrical projection

Four Goals Hindus believe that people have four basic goals in life. People should pursue all four, but not everyone achieves all of these goals in one lifetime.

The first goal is doing what is right. For Hindus, **dharma** is a person's duty or what is right for him or her. Dharma includes the duties that come with one's age or one's position in life. Dharma also includes the rule of ahimsa, or avoiding doing harm to any living thing. Following dharma brings good karma. Violating dharma brings bad karma.

The second goal is striving for well-being, or earning a livelihood with dignity. This goal can involve raising a family. It can involve starting or running an honest business. However, Hindus say, material well-being by itself does not bring true happiness.

The third goal is pleasure. This includes physical pleasures such as eating good food. However, seeking nothing but pleasure, Hindus believe, can leave a person feeling empty.

The final goal is **moksha**, or liberation from reincarnation. When this happens, a person's soul becomes one with Brahman. For Hindus, the purpose of human life is to achieve moksha. A soul that achieves moksha is free from want, fear, and pain. It lives forever in a state of joy.

Hindus believe there are different ways to achieve moksha. The first path is the way of knowledge. The second is the way of works. The third is the way of devotion. The fourth path is meditation. Hindus may try to follow any or all of these four paths.

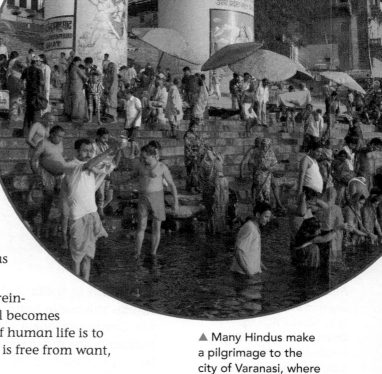

▲ Many Hindus make a pilgrimage to the city of Varanasi, where they perform religious ceremonies along the Ganges River on stone steps called ghats.

✔ **READING CHECK** Identify Main Ideas What are the four paths to moksha in Hinduism?

What Was the Impact of Hinduism?

Long ago, the people of India lived under many separate rulers. They spoke many different languages. They worshiped many different Gods. Yet, most Indians practiced Hinduism.

The Growth of Hinduism Several things helped the growth of Hinduism in India. One was Hinduism's flexibility. Because Hinduism views all Gods as forms of a single, supreme God, it can accept the worship of new Gods. People did not have to give up their old religion when they became Hindus. Instead, Hinduism adopted their traditions and Gods or viewed their Gods as forms of existing Hindu Gods.

INTERACTIVE

Holi Festival

Hinduism also did not require regular attendance at religious services. Instead, Hindus could pray or make offerings to the Gods at a local temple during special celebrations or whenever it was convenient. They could also pray or make offerings in their own homes.

Over time, Hinduism spread to other lands. For more than a thousand years after 1 CE, Indian traders and priests carried Hinduism to Southeast Asia. Hinduism left a lasting influence on countries such as Thailand and Indonesia, where epic poems such as the *Ramayana* remain popular. Today, most people on the Indonesian island of Bali are Hindus.

Indians also took Hinduism with them when they moved overseas. Many migrated to Britain, the United States, and Canada. More than a million Hindus now live in the United States.

Analyze Images People worship at a Hindu temple in London, England. **Draw Conclusions** What conclusions can you draw from this photograph?

Hinduism in India Today Hindus live in some 150 countries, but most Hindus still live in India. Hindu traditions remain important in Indian life. One festival takes place on the Ganges River. Every year, millions of Indians bathe in the river. They believe that its waters can wash away bad karma and cure disease.

Hinduism's openness to all religions has shaped India's political system. It guarantees religious freedom.

✓ READING CHECK **Draw Conclusions** What aspects of Hinduism helped it to spread?

✓ Lesson Check

Practice Vocabulary

1. What is **karma?**

2. Define **Brahman**.

Critical Thinking and Writing

3. **Compare and Contrast** Moral behavior is important in Hinduism. What other major religions share that same belief?

4. **Identify Cause and Effect** How is dharma related to moksha?

5. **Identify Main Ideas** How did Hinduism spread?

6. **Writing Workshop: Generate Ideas** Brainstorm a list of possible challenges facing South Asia in your 🗐 Active Journal. You will revise this list as you work through the topic. Be sure to include possible solutions.

LESSON 3

Origins and Beliefs of Buddhism

BOUNCE TO ACTIVATE ▶ VIDEO

GET READY TO READ

START UP

Look at this photo of Buddhist monks gathering outside a temple in Bhutan. Write down what you already know about Buddhism and what you would like to know.

GUIDING QUESTIONS

- How did Buddhism begin?
- What are the main beliefs of Buddhism?
- How has Buddhism affected the world?

TAKE NOTES

Literacy Skills: Draw Conclusions
Use the graphic organizer in your 🗐 Active Journal to take notes as you read the lesson.

PRACTICE VOCABULARY

Use the vocabulary activity in your 🗐 Active Journal to practice the vocabulary words.

Vocabulary

meditate   monastery
enlightenment   missionary
ascetic   bodhisattva
nirvana

Academic Vocabulary

consequence
illusion

Buddhism, like Hinduism, arose in ancient India. Buddhism is a religion based on the teachings of Siddhartha Gautama (sid DAHR tuh GOW tuh muh), an Indian spiritual leader who became known as the Buddha. We call his followers Buddhists.

Who Was the Buddha?

Siddhartha Gautama was probably born during the 500s BCE in what is now Nepal. The story of his life comes mainly from Buddhist texts. They state that he was a Hindu prince. His father shielded him from everything unpleasant and disturbing.

When Siddhartha was in his 20s, he left his father's palace. He saw people who were old, sick, and suffering. He decided to give up his life as a prince and begin a search for the truth about life and death.

Siddhartha spent years of studying with Hindu teachers and searching for answers, but he was not satisfied with what he learned. Then, according to Buddhist texts, he sat under a tree to meditate. To **meditate** means to calm or clear the mind, often by focusing on a single subject.

He meditated for 49 days and nights. Finally, he achieved **enlightenment**—a state of perfect wisdom, free of suffering. Siddhartha had become the Buddha, which means "the Enlightened One."

Buddhist texts say that the Buddha then traveled across India, sharing his message with followers. Texts say that his dying words were these:

Primary Source

"This is my last advice to you. All . . . things in the world are changeable. They are not lasting. Work hard to gain your own salvation."

—The Buddha, in Rev. Siridhamma, *Life of the Buddha*

☑ READING CHECK **Identify Supporting Details** How did Buddhism begin?

What Are Key Buddhist Beliefs?

Buddhists believe that when the Buddha gained enlightenment, he had a flash of insight. He understood why people suffer. He also saw how people could escape the cycle of death and rebirth.

Analyze Images The Buddha meditates beneath the bodhi, or bo, tree. **Use Evidence** What details in the painting point to the Buddha having reached a state of peace and enlightenment?

The Buddha accepted the Hindu idea of karma—the idea that a person's actions have **consequences** in this or in future lives. He believed that a "self" might be reborn in a new body, but he thought that the "self" was an **illusion**. He believed that it would disappear and cease to exist when a person achieved enlightenment.

The Buddha moved away from some Hindu beliefs. For example, the Buddha did not believe in the existence of any god. He also did not accept the caste system.

The Middle Way The Buddha had lived in luxury, as a wealthy prince. He had also lived in poverty, as an **ascetic**, or a person who tries to achieve spiritual purity through self-denial. Neither way of life had led him to enlightenment. To gain enlightenment, the Buddha advised people to follow a Middle Way. That way of life called for accepting four truths.

The Four Noble Truths These Four Noble Truths were among the insights the Buddha had when he achieved enlightenment.

The First Noble Truth is that all of life involves suffering. Birth, sickness, old age, and death bring suffering.

The Second Noble Truth is that wanting or desiring things for oneself causes suffering.

Academic Vocabulary

consequence • *n.*, result

illusion • *n.*, something unreal or misleading

The Third Noble Truth is that people can end their suffering. The way to do this is to give up all selfish desires.

The Fourth Noble Truth is that there is a way to overcome selfish desires. The way to overcome those desires is to follow the Eightfold Path.

The Eightfold Path was another of the Buddha's insights. The Buddha taught that this path was open to anyone. People of any caste could follow it.

The Eightfold Path The Eightfold Path takes its name from its eight steps. These steps lead to Three Qualities.

The first two steps are Right Belief and Right Purpose. They involve preparing one's mind for spiritual growth. These steps produce the first of the Three Qualities, wisdom.

The next three steps are Right Speech, Right Conduct, and Right Livelihood (or profession). These steps call for taking charge of one's behavior. They include respect for all living things and compassion for others. These steps produce the quality of morality, which is also called right action.

The last three steps are Right Effort, Right Mindfulness (awareness of one's thoughts and actions), and Right Meditation or Concentration. They help train the mind to gain enlightenment. The third quality is the same as the eighth step—meditation.

Reaching Nirvana The goal of a person who follows the Eightfold Path is to reach nirvana. **Nirvana** is a state of blissful peace without desire or suffering. Those who reach nirvana are at peace with themselves. They are also freed from having to go through reincarnation, or rebirth.

Analyze Diagrams Hinduism and Buddhism share some similarities, as seen in the chart. **Use Visual Information** How do the goals and focus of Hinduism and Buddhism differ?

COMPARING HINDUISM AND BUDDHISM

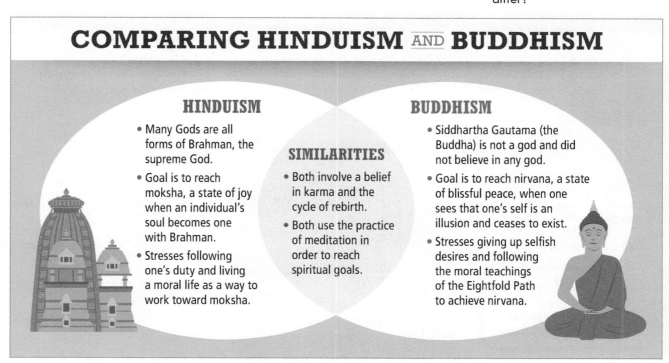

HINDUISM
- Many Gods are all forms of Brahman, the supreme God.
- Goal is to reach moksha, a state of joy when an individual's soul becomes one with Brahman.
- Stresses following one's duty and living a moral life as a way to work toward moksha.

SIMILARITIES
- Both involve a belief in karma and the cycle of rebirth.
- Both use the practice of meditation in order to reach spiritual goals.

BUDDHISM
- Siddhartha Gautama (the Buddha) is not a god and did not believe in any god.
- Goal is to reach nirvana, a state of blissful peace, when one sees that one's self is an illusion and ceases to exist.
- Stresses giving up selfish desires and following the moral teachings of the Eightfold Path to achieve nirvana.

INTERACTIVE

The Origins and Spread of Buddhism

Buddhists believe that they can find enlightenment by carefully following the Eightfold Path. Enlightenment is the moment when nirvana is achieved. Each branch of Buddhism stresses different ways to find enlightenment and nirvana.

READING CHECK **Understand Effects** What do Buddhists hope to achieve by following the Eightfold Path?

The Spread of Buddhism

For hundreds of years, the Buddha's followers memorized his teachings. Eventually, they wrote those teachings down. Those written teachings make up the sacred scriptures of Buddhism today. Different branches of Buddhism accept different collections of these scriptures. However, all Buddhists accept the Four Noble Truths and the Eightfold Path.

Monasteries and Missionaries As the Buddha preached, he gained many followers. At first they followed him from place to place. After a while, the Buddha found places for them to stay during the rainy season. These became Buddhist **monasteries**, or religious communities. In monasteries, Buddhists had time to study and meditate. Other monasteries were begun in other locations as well.

The Buddha urged his followers to carry his teachings to all corners of Earth. After he died, **missionaries**, or people who seek to spread their religion, carried Buddhism across India and to Sri Lanka. Later, missionaries carried his teachings throughout Asia.

GEOGRAPHY **SKILLS**

Buddhism spread outside of India to some of the same countries as Hinduism.

1. **Place** In which present-day country did Buddhism originate?

2. **Use Visual Information** Through which present-day countries did Buddhist missionaries travel before they reached Japan?

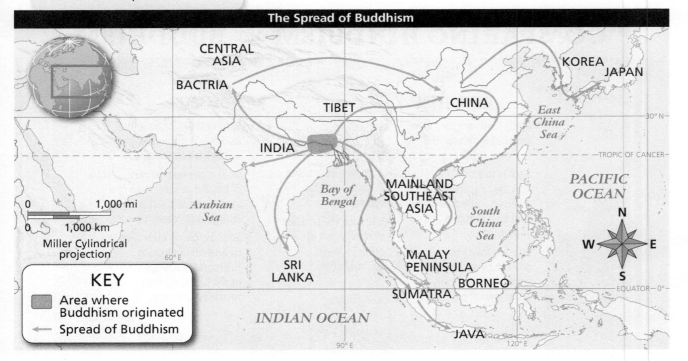

The Spread of Buddhism

KEY

▢ Area where Buddhism originated

← Spread of Buddhism

Two Schools of Buddhism As Buddhism spread, its followers split into two major branches, or sects. The two branches share basic beliefs, but they see the Buddha's life and teachings differently.

One branch is Theravada (thehr uh VAH duh) Buddhism. This sect focuses on the wisdom of the Buddha and his achievement of enlightenment and nirvana.

Mahayana Buddhism (mah huh YAH nuh) is the other branch. It focuses on the Buddha's compassion. For its members, the Buddha's greatest achievement was returning from nirvana to share his wisdom with others out of compassion. Its members also revere, or hold sacred, **bodhisattvas** (boh dih SUT vuz), or beings who have gained enlightenment and, out of compassion, try to help others.

The Legacy of Buddhism Today, there are about 400 million Buddhists. Most live in Asia. Theravada Buddhism is the main religion of Sri Lanka, Myanmar (or Burma), Thailand, and Cambodia. Mahayana Buddhism is widespread in Bhutan, Vietnam, China and Taiwan, Mongolia, North Korea, South Korea, and Japan.

More than 2 million Buddhists live in the United States. Although few Buddhists remain in India, the religion's birthplace, the Buddha's teachings made a lasting impact on Hinduism.

Buddhism has inspired beautiful art and architecture. It has been a source of wisdom even for some non-Buddhists.

▲ The Dalai Lama addresses a crowd in Germany. The Dalai Lama is an important figure in Buddhism and is seen by many Tibetans as their spiritual leader.

✔ READING CHECK **Compare and Contrast** How are the two branches of Buddhism similar and different?

☑ Lesson Check

Practice Vocabulary

1. In Buddhism, how is **enlightenment** related to **nirvana**?

2. Why do Buddhists **meditate**?

Critical Thinking and Writing

3. **Draw Conclusions** How does the message of the Four Noble Truths connect to Siddhartha's life before he became the Buddha?

4. **Sequence** How did Buddhism spread?

5. **Compare and Contrast** How is Buddhism similar to and different from Hinduism?

6. **Writing Workshop: Generate Ideas** Continue to brainstorm and revise your list of challenges facing South Asia in your 📕 Active Journal. Be sure to include possible solutions.

Later History of South Asia

BOUNCE
TO ACTIVATE
▶ VIDEO

GET READY TO READ

START UP

Study the painting of Akbar, an emperor who ruled much of South Asia around 1600. Write three questions you have about the later history of South Asia.

GUIDING QUESTIONS

- How did the spread of Islam affect South Asia?
- How did British colonial rule change South Asia?
- How have the countries of South Asia fared since independence?

TAKE NOTES

Literacy Skills: Sequence
Use the graphic organizer in your 📖 Active Journal to take notes as you read the lesson.

PRACTICE VOCABULARY

Use the vocabulary activity in your 📖 Active Journal to practice the vocabulary words.

Vocabulary	Academic Vocabulary
Punjab	flourish
nonviolent resistance	concentrated
discrimination	
partition	
nonalignment	

After the Gupta empire declined in the 500s CE, Islam came to South Asia. Most of the region became part of the Mughal empire and later, the British empire.

South Asia After the Guptas

After the fall of the Gupta empire, South Asia was divided among several kingdoms and empires. These kingdoms and empires were mainly Hindu. Each was centered in a different part of South Asia. Each of these kingdoms or empires ruled part of South Asia for a period. Eventually, each of them broke apart or faced conquest by a neighboring empire.

As kingdoms rose and fell, South Asia's culture continued to develop and **flourish**. South Asians built impressive new Hindu temples. These temples showed strong engineering skills. Many contained beautiful sculptures. South Asians also continued to make advances in science and mathematics.

☑ READING CHECK Identify Main Ideas How was South Asia's culture affected by the fall of the Gupta empire?

How Did Islam Arrive in South Asia?

The Muslim empire of Southwest Asia began a rapid expansion in the 600s and conquered much of what are now Afghanistan and Pakistan in the early 700s. Muslim soldiers brought their new religion, Islam, with them to the region. However, Hindus and Buddhists resisted Muslim rule for several hundred years in the rest of South Asia.

Muslim Rule Spreads Muslim traders also brought Islam to South Asia by sea. They built Muslim communities in seaports and on the islands. Then, in the 900s, Turkic Muslim kings gained power in present-day Afghanistan. These kings launched raids into what is now northern Pakistan to seize the wealth that was stored in Hindu temples. In the 1100s, they began to conquer territory.

By the 1200s, one group of Turkic invaders established the Muslim-ruled Delhi sultanate. It covered much of what are today Pakistan and northern India. Muslims ruled parts of South Asia for the next 600 years. However, Hindu rajas, or rulers, continued to control kingdoms in southern India.

Hindus and Muslims were often rivals. While they sometimes came in conflict, there was a great deal of cultural exchange. Many people migrated from Muslim Baghdad to Delhi, some of whom were scholars. They helped to stimulate learning, art, and architecture.

✓ **READING CHECK** Sequence When and how did Islam arrive in South Asia?

Academic Vocabulary
flourish • v., to thrive

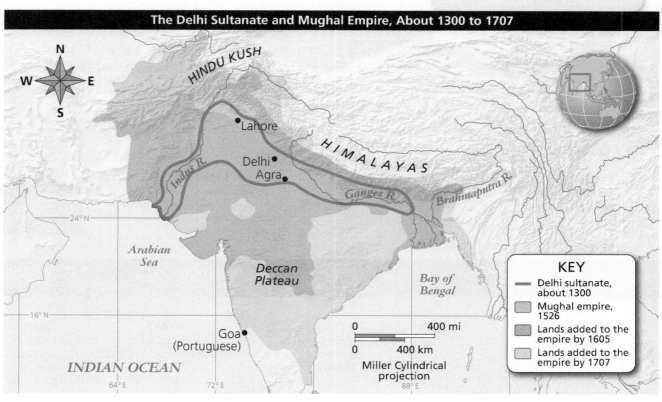

The Delhi Sultanate and Mughal Empire, About 1300 to 1707

HINDU KUSH

Lahore

Delhi
Agra

HIMALAYAS

Indus R.

Ganges R.

Brahmaputra R.

24° N

Arabian
Sea

Deccan
Plateau

Bay of
Bengal

16° N

Goa
(Portuguese)

0   400 mi
0   400 km
Miller Cylindrical
projection

INDIAN OCEAN

64° E   72° E   88° E

KEY
— Delhi sultanate, about 1300
■ Mughal empire, 1526
■ Lands added to the empire by 1605
■ Lands added to the empire by 1707

The Mughal Period

In 1526, a Muslim from Central Asia named Babur overthrew a weakened Delhi sultanate and founded the powerful Mughal empire. This new empire was centered in Agra, a city in what is now northern India. The Mughal empire was the most important Muslim state in South Asia.

The Mughal Empire Babur's grandson, Akbar, was a tolerant ruler who conquered much of South Asia. Akbar included Hindus in his army and government and protected other religions.

In 1658, Aurangzeb seized power. Aurangzeb ended religious tolerance. He began persecuting Hindus and other non-Muslims. Despite a series of uprisings against him, Aurangzeb continued to expand Mughal territory. However, his military campaigns weakened the empire. After Aurangzeb's death, the Mughal empire declined.

Hindu Kingdoms The Mughal empire never conquered what is now far southern India. Hindu kings continued to rule in that region. Beginning in the 1700s, Hindu rebels in what is now central India rose up against the Mughal empire. They formed their own kingdoms.

The Rise of Sikhism As Islam spread in the north, a new religion called Sikhism was born. Most followers of Sikhism, known as Sikhs, live in an area of what is now northern Pakistan and India called the **Punjab**.

The founder of Sikhism was a guru, or spiritual leader, named Nanak, who lived in the 1400s. Nanak taught the belief in one God and the equality of all people. Sikhs follow the teachings of Nanak, nine additional gurus, and the scripture called the *Guru Granth Sahib*. Sikhs view the *Guru Granth Sahib* as their present-day guru. It contains the teachings of the Sikh gurus and spiritual leaders from other faiths.

Analyze Diagrams From the 1500s until today, South Asia has been under the control of very different rulers. **Use Visual Information** How many years passed between the creation of East and West Pakistan and Bangladesh declaring independence?

✓ READING CHECK **Compare and Contrast** How was the Mughal emperor Akbar different from his great-grandson Aurangzeb?

Key Dates in South Asian History, 1526–2001

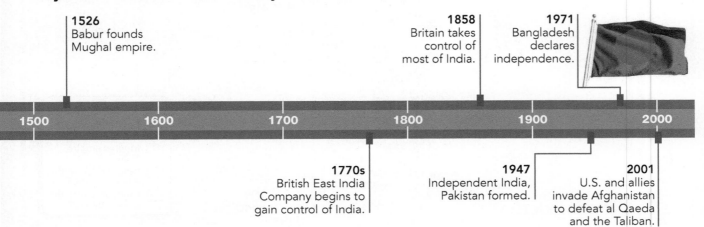

1526
Babur founds Mughal empire.

1858
Britain takes control of most of India.

1971
Bangladesh declares independence.

1770s
British East India Company begins to gain control of India.

1947
Independent India, Pakistan formed.

2001
U.S. and allies invade Afghanistan to defeat al Qaeda and the Taliban.

1500   1600   1700   1800   1900   2000

European Colonialism

During the Mughal period, the Portuguese, Dutch, British, and French set up trading ports in South Asia. They came in search of spices, especially pepper, as well as cotton, silk, and indigo for dyeing cloth.

Trading Ports to Empire The British government used the powerful East India Company as its trading agent in South Asia. By the mid-1700s, the Company had pushed its European rivals out of most of the subcontinent. To protect its trade, the Company also took over some Indian states by force. It slowly gained more power as the Mughal empire lost power. By the 1820s, the Company controlled most of the area that is now India.

In 1858, the British government took control of the East India Company's territories. At that point, most of South Asia was a British colony. As part of the British empire, the region provided Britain with tea, coffee, grain, and raw materials such as cotton. Britain used Indian cotton to make inexpensive cloth in its factories.

Analyze Images An Indian servant waits on an English man. **Use Visual Information** What does this image tell you about relationships and power in India during the time of British colonialism?

Because of the British takeover, India's textile industry collapsed. Its craftspeople could not compete with British factory-made cloth. Instead of exporting cloth and other finished goods, India became a market for those goods.

Struggle for Independence In the early 1900s, a movement arose to force Britain out of India. Its greatest leader was Mohandas Gandhi (moh HAHN dus GAHN dee). Gandhi organized boycotts of British goods and led protest marches. Inspired by the Hindu principle of ahimsa, or nonviolence, Gandhi urged **nonviolent resistance**, or peaceful protest against laws considered unjust.

Gandhi hoped to pressure the British to abandon colonial rule and grant independence to India, including what are now Pakistan and Bangladesh. Gandhi believed that a nation should not be built around only one religion or ethnic group. He called on Hindus and Muslims to unite as one nation.

Not all South Asians agreed with Gandhi's vision, however. While he called for a single country for both Hindus and Muslims, others favored dividing South Asia along religious lines. An organization called the Muslim League supported two separate states, one with a Muslim majority and one with a Hindu majority.

Quest CONNECTIONS

How did the British develop India during their colonial rule? Record your findings in your *Active Journal.*

☑ READING CHECK **Identify Cause and Effect** How did British rule affect South Asia's economy?

Quick Activity

Using your Active Journal, work with classmates to identify the major contributions of key figures in South Asian history.

INTERACTIVE

Indian Independence and Partition

South Asia After Independence

In 1947, facing widespread resistance, Britain decided to withdraw from South Asia. Like Gandhi, many Indian leaders were Hindu and had hopes for a unified India that would include both Muslims and Hindus. But Muslims in the northwest and in the northeastern region of Bengal feared that they would face **discrimination**, or unfair treatment, if they remained in Hindu-dominated India. Britain decided to **partition**, or split, British India into two states, India and Pakistan. At the time, Pakistan was divided into two regions, East Pakistan and West Pakistan, with 1,000 miles separating the two. On August 15, 1947, the nations of India and Pakistan were finally free and independent of Britain.

Partition and After With partition, a massive migration began. Millions of Hindus and Sikhs moved from Pakistan to India, while millions of Indian Muslims moved to Pakistan. People lost all that they owned, and families were split up. Many people died of starvation and other difficulties experienced on the journey. Violence erupted between ethnic and religious communities, and around one million people were killed. Gandhi himself was shot and killed by a Hindu extremist on January 30, 1948, for insisting on fair treatment for Muslims. As the world mourned his death, the worst of the violence came to an end.

After partition, relations between India and Pakistan were tense. Both countries claimed the region of Kashmir, located in the northern part of the Indian subcontinent. In 1947 and again in 1965, India and Pakistan went to war over Kashmir. Kashmiris supporting separation from India have often battled with Indian troops, and the region continues to be a source of conflict between the two countries.

India's prime minister from independence into the 1960s was Jawaharlal Nehru (juh WAH hur lahl NAY roo). Nehru sought to modernize India and tried to keep religion out of politics.

BIOGRAPHY

5 Things to Know About

MOHANDAS GANDHI
Indian Activist (1869–1948)

- Many people in India called Gandhi "Mahatma," which means "great soul."

- Gandhi often fasted, or went without eating for a period of time, as a form of protest.

- To boycott British goods such as cotton cloth, Gandhi spun his own cotton thread to make his clothing.

- Gandhi developed nonviolent protest, called satyagraha, to resist imperialist policies that discriminated against Indians.

- Gandhi's methods of nonviolence and civil disobedience were used by Dr. Martin Luther King Jr. and others in the American civil rights movement in the 1950s and 1960s.

Critical Thinking Why do you think Gandhi relied on nonviolent protest?

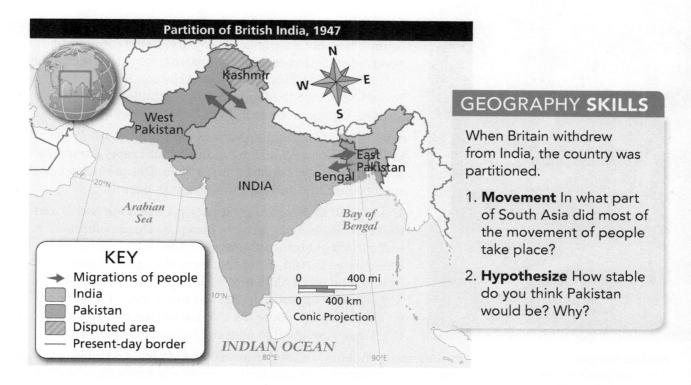

Partition of British India, 1947

GEOGRAPHY SKILLS

When Britain withdrew from India, the country was partitioned.

1. **Movement** In what part of South Asia did most of the movement of people take place?

2. **Hypothesize** How stable do you think Pakistan would be? Why?

In foreign affairs, Nehru forged a policy of nonalignment. **Nonalignment** was a policy of not allying with either of the superpowers—the United States or the Soviet Union—during the Cold War.

Nehru died in 1964. Two years later his daughter, Indira Gandhi, became prime minister of India. She oversaw yet another war with Pakistan in 1971. Though India still followed a policy of nonalignment, it developed nuclear weapons in the 1970s. Pakistan soon did as well, and the existence of the weapons alarmed people watching the hostilities between the two nations.

Independence for Bangladesh Meanwhile, the leading political party in East Pakistan demanded independence. The people of East Pakistan outnumbered those in West Pakistan, but the government was **concentrated** in West Pakistan. A thousand miles separated the two parts of the country, making trade and governing difficult. Because the government invested more in West Pakistan, East Pakistan remained deep in poverty.

At the demand for independence, the Pakistani government attacked East Pakistan in March 1971. Some 10 million people, mostly Hindus, fled from East Pakistan into India. Most of them settled in the Indian region of Bengal.

India helped East Pakistan gain independence. In December 1971, East Pakistan became the nation of Bangladesh (BAHNG luh desh).

Other Conflicts Civil war also struck Sri Lanka, where the majority are Buddhists who speak Sinhala. Some members of the Hindu minority, which speaks Tamil, began fighting for a separate state in 1983. In 2009, the Sinhala-dominated government took control of rebel areas and declared victory. The war killed an estimated 70,000 people.

Academic Vocabulary
concentrated • *adj.,*
focused on or gathered in

In Afghanistan, the king was overthrown in 1973, and the country became a republic. Five years later, a communist government seized control. In response, rebellions broke out throughout the country. To support the communists, the Soviet Union invaded Afghanistan. The United States gave arms to Afghan rebels to fight its Cold War rival.

After a decade of fighting various rebel groups, the Soviet Union withdrew. A Muslim fundamentalist rebel group, the Taliban, took over Afghanistan in 1996. This group imposed strict Islamic law and ruled Afghanistan harshly.

The Taliban sheltered and supported Osama bin Laden and the al Qaeda Islamist terrorist group. Al Qaeda planned and carried out terrorist attacks on the United States on September 11, 2001. Later that year, the United States, Britain, and other allies attacked the Taliban. They helped Afghans who opposed the Taliban take power. Taliban fighters continued to oppose the U.S.-backed government, and U.S. forces continued to fight the Taliban into the 2010s.

Analyze Images Girls raise their hands in class at an Afghan school. **Make Connections** Girls have not always been able to receive an education in some South Asian countries. Why is the education of girls a significant step in the development of the region?

Ever since independence, Pakistan has struggled to build a stable government. Power shifted back and forth between elected civilian leaders and military rulers. Tensions among the country's diverse ethnic groups posed challenges. People living in the remote northwest of the country were left largely on their own, outside of government control.

The activities of Islamic fundamentalists also created problems in Pakistan. The fundamentalists wanted the government to follow strict Islamic principles, while other Pakistanis wanted greater separation between religion and state. Because of the shared border with Afghanistan, many Taliban fighters fled into Pakistan once the United States went to war with them.

☑ READING CHECK **Synthesize** How did the 1947 partition affect later events in South Asia?

☑ Lesson Check

Practice Vocabulary

1. Which religious group is centered in the **Punjab**?

2. How did fear of **discrimination** lead to the partition of India?

Critical Thinking and Writing

3. **Understand Effects** How did the introduction of Islam affect South Asia?

4. **Recognize Multiple Causes** How did the Mughal empire in India decline?

5. **Identify Cause and Effect** How did Gandhi's belief in nonviolence affect the course of India's history?

6. **Writing Workshop: Gather Evidence** Add to your list of challenges in your 🗐 Active Journal by considering how South Asia's history has led to challenges for South Asians today. Include how these challenges can be met.

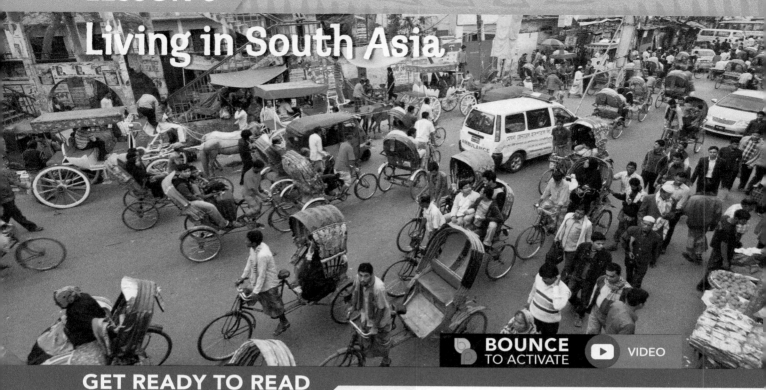

Living in South Asia

BOUNCE TO ACTIVATE · VIDEO

GET READY TO READ

START UP

Examine the photograph showing a street in Dhaka, Bangladesh. How does this scene compare to ones you have seen of other cities?

GUIDING QUESTIONS

- What explains the population distribution of South Asia?
- What is the religious landscape of South Asia?
- How ethnically diverse are South Asian countries?

TAKE NOTES

Literacy Skills: Use Evidence

Use the graphic organizer in your 📓 Active Journal to take notes as you read the lesson.

PRACTICE VOCABULARY

Use the vocabulary activity in your 📓 Active Journal to practice the vocabulary words.

Vocabulary	Academic Vocabulary
topography	sparse
monsoon	overwhelmingly

South Asia is home to more than 1.7 billion people. It is a region of dense populations and high birth rates. South Asia is home to people who adhere to many different religions. It is also culturally diverse.

Where Do South Asians Live?

South Asia has been a center of civilization for thousands of years. The region is also very much a part of the modern world. South Asia's cities are growing rapidly, as people pursue the job opportunities and better education that urban areas offer.

Geography and Population

Topography, or the physical features of an area, has been an important factor in the settlement of South Asia. Landforms such as mountains, deserts, coasts, and river valleys have long had a profound effect on settlement patterns. Seasonal winds and weather patterns, called **monsoons**, also affect the climate of South Asia. They bring heavy rains in summer and dry air in winter.

Since ancient times, people have settled in areas where rainfall supported agriculture.

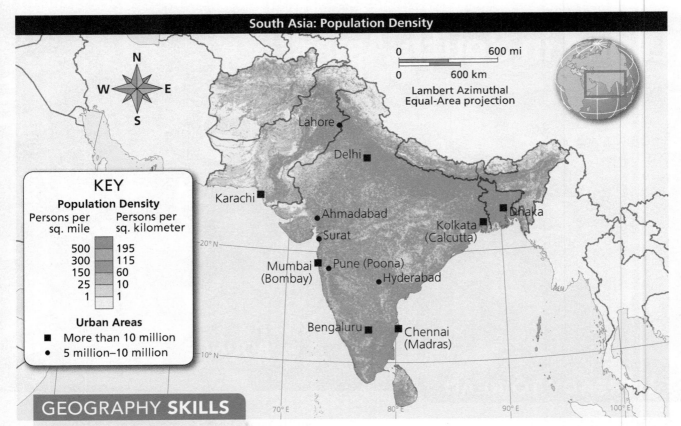

South Asia: Population Density

0 — 600 mi
0 — 600 km
Lambert Azimuthal
Equal-Area projection

KEY

Population Density

Persons per sq. mile	Persons per sq. kilometer
500	195
300	115
150	60
25	10
1	1

Urban Areas
- ■ More than 10 million
- ● 5 million–10 million

Cities labeled: Lahore, Delhi, Karachi, Ahmadabad, Surat, Mumbai (Bombay), Pune (Poona), Hyderabad, Kolkata (Calcutta), Dhaka, Bengaluru, Chennai (Madras)

GEOGRAPHY SKILLS

South Asia is one of the most densely populated areas of the world.

1. **Region** What physical features explain why the northeastern part of South Asia is densely populated?

2. **Draw Conclusions** What might explain differences in population density in India's interior?

A substantial portion of the region's population lives in the humid temperate climate region, in the Ganges River valley, and on both sides of the Indus River. Lahore, Delhi, and Dhaka are major cities in these river valleys. These cities grew as centers of trade for the fertile farmland that surrounds them.

Some coastal areas have excellent harbors, which enabled people to trade. Over time, as trade expanded, trading posts grew into towns and cities. Today, the coastal cities of Karachi, Mumbai, Kolkata, and Chennai are among the region's largest cities.

Bengaluru, one of India's biggest cities, lies on the Deccan Plateau in southern India. The people in this city have relied on nearby rivers for water. Its major growth has come since the late 1900s. Government policies promoted the development of manufacturing and computer jobs that attracted people there.

Less Populated Areas Parts of South Asia have an arid climate and cannot support farming or trade. As a result, these areas have **sparse** populations. These areas include the Great Indian Desert and the arid and the semiarid western parts of Afghanistan and Pakistan. While mountain valleys have attracted settlement, the rugged terrain of the Hindu Kush and Himalayas also make farming and trade very difficult.

Academic Vocabulary

sparse • *adj.*, few and scattered

✓ READING CHECK **Draw Conclusions** How has geography affected trade and settlement and population growth in South Asia?

Religion in South Asia

South Asia is religiously diverse. Hinduism has the largest number of followers in the region, and Islam has the second largest.

Major Religions Most people in India and Nepal are Hindu. In Pakistan, Afghanistan, Bangladesh, and the Maldives, Muslims form the largest religious group. Most Muslims in South Asia are Sunnis, but Afghanistan has large Shia minorities.

The partition of British India in 1947 created Muslim majorities in what are now Pakistan and Bangladesh. Many Hindus in these areas feared mistreatment and fled to India. As a result, Pakistan and Bangladesh are **overwhelmingly** Muslim, though Bangladesh has a significant Hindu minority. While some Muslims fled from India to Pakistan at partition, millions remained in India. Today, nearly 200 million Indians, or about one in every seven persons, are Muslims. It is the largest religious minority in the region.

Other Religions In addition to Hinduism and Islam, other religions are practiced in South Asia. Sikhism dominates in the Punjab area of northwest India. Jainism and Zoroastrianism are also found in India. Buddhism is mainly practiced in Bhutan and Sri Lanka, but there is also a significant Buddhist minority in Nepal. Sri Lanka also has large Hindu and Muslim minorities.

An ancient Christian community in southern India has existed for more than 1,500 years. Small Christian minorities can also be found in other parts of South Asia.

☑ READING CHECK **Summarize** What are the major religions of South Asia?

Academic Vocabulary
overwhelmingly • *adj.,* superior by a large margin

Analyze Diagrams The countries of South Asia have both religious and language diversity. **Contrast** Which country has the greatest diversity of languages? Which has the least?

A CROSSROADS OF CULTURE

RELIGION ■ Buddhist ■ Christian ■ Hindu ■ Muslim ■ Sikh ■ Other/Unspecified

INDIA

PAKISTAN

SRI LANKA

LANGUAGE HUNDREDS OF LANGUAGES ARE SPOKEN THROUGHOUT SOUTH ASIA.

INDIA 41% HINDI — THERE ARE 22 OFFICIAL LANGUAGES IN INDIA TODAY.

PAKISTAN 48% PUNJABI — MOST PAKISTANIS SPEAK URDU AS A SECOND LANGUAGE.

SRI LANKA 74% SINHALA — 18% OF SRI LANKANS SPEAK TAMIL.

Sources: CIA World Factbook, Encyclopaedia Britannica

Ethnic Diversity

As you have learned, ethnic groups are groups of people who share common cultural traits. One of the cultural traits shared by an ethnic group may be a common religion. In South Asia, however, most major religions have followers from more than one ethnic group. Also, some ethnic groups have members who follow different religions. For example, ethnic Bengalis may be Hindu, Muslim, Buddhist, or Christian.

South Asia is ethnically diverse. The hundreds of different languages spoken in India reflect its great ethnic diversity. Within many Indian states, there is a majority ethnic group, and this group speaks the state's official language. While about two out of five people speak Hindi, India has fourteen other official languages. Many people speak English.

▲ In Pakistan, a Pashtun family in traditional clothes stays in a camp after losing their home to an earthquake.

Punjabis, Sindhis, Pashtuns, Mohajirs, and Baluchis are the main ethnic groups of Pakistan. Most people in Bangladesh are Bengali. A small Bihari minority also lives in the country.

Afghanistan's two largest ethnic groups are Pashtuns and Tajiks. Nepal, Bhutan, and Sri Lanka are ethnically diverse. Sri Lanka has a Sinhalese majority with Tamil and Moor minorities. Most people in Maldives belong to just one ethnic group.

✓ READING CHECK **Compare and Contrast** How is ethnicity similar to and different from religion?

☑ Lesson Check

Practice Vocabulary

1. How have South Asia's **topography** and climate influenced its settlement?

2. Why is the **monsoon** important to the people of South Asia?

Critical Thinking and Writing

3. **Identify Cause and Effect** How did trade affect settlement in South Asia?

4. **Draw Conclusions** Why is South Asia ethnically and religiously diverse?

5. **Synthesize** What cultural characteristic do Afghanistan, Bangladesh, and Pakistan have in common?

6. **Writing Workshop: Gather Evidence** Add to your list of challenges in your 📔 Active Journal by considering how South Asia's diversity contributes to the region's challenges. Be sure to brainstorm possible solutions.

LESSON 6
South Asia at Work

BOUNCE TO ACTIVATE ▶ VIDEO

GET READY TO READ

START UP
Study this image of Indian workers at a technical support call center for an American company. What do you know about India that explains why American companies might open call centers there?

GUIDING QUESTIONS
- What kinds of governments exist in South Asia?
- What factors shape South Asia's economies?
- What are the strengths and weaknesses of India's economy?

TAKE NOTES
Literacy Skills: Compare and Contrast
Use the graphic organizer in your ▤ Active Journal to take notes as you read the lesson.

PRACTICE VOCABULARY
Use the vocabulary words in your ▤ Active Journal to practice the vocabulary words.

Vocabulary	Academic Vocabulary
federal system	eradicate
microlending	impede
outsourcing	

South Asia has a growing workforce of around 700 million people. The governments of this complex region face the challenges of assuring order and stability and of fostering economic growth to provide jobs for these people.

Governments of South Asia
All of the governments of South Asia claim to be democracies. Several countries are not full democracies, however. In Afghanistan, Bangladesh, the Maldives, and Sri Lanka, governments have limited freedom of expression, have held elections that were not free, or forced out political opponents.

Democracy in South Asia India has the region's strongest democracy. India is also the world's largest democracy.

India has a parliamentary democracy, in which voters elect members of parliament, and parliament then elects the prime minister, usually the leader of the largest party in parliament. India's president, who is elected by parliament, is the symbolic leader of the nation but has very limited powers. Instead, the prime minister controls the government.

Analyze Images Female students cast ballots in an election in Afghanistan. **Infer** What kind of political system do these women live under?

Like the United States, India has a **federal system**, in which power is divided among central, regional, and local governments.

Afghanistan and the Maldives are presidential democracies like the United States. In this form of government, the president is directly elected by voters and is both a symbolic leader and the head of the government. Power is shared between the president and the legislature or parliament.

Sri Lanka uses a mix of parliamentary and presidential democracy. Different parts of its government are controlled by either the president or the prime minister.

Other Forms of Government India is a secular state, in which government and citizens' rights are not based on religion. Still, parties identified with religion are an important part of the political system. In other nations, religion defines the state. Even though Afghanistan has a presidential democracy, it is also an Islamic republic. Pakistan is an Islamic republic as well. Since Islam is the dominant and official religion in both countries, it plays an important role in the governing of both countries. Some laws are based on Islamic law, for instance.

Bangladesh and Sri Lanka have had democratic rule for a long time, but their citizens do not always enjoy the same level of rights and freedoms as citizens do in India. Nepal recently ended its monarchy. It is now a democratic republic. Bhutan also holds democratic elections, but it is a constitutional monarchy, in which there are an elected parliament and limits on the monarch's power.

☑ READING CHECK **Identify Main Ideas** What is the role of citizens in India's political system?

Economies of South Asia

All South Asian countries have developing economies, with per capita GDPs below the world average and widespread poverty. Parts of the region remain very poor, despite efforts to industrialize and diversify economies. India, however, has experienced strong economic growth in recent years.

Even though most countries in South Asia are poor by world standards, most have areas that are relatively prosperous. These are generally areas that produce goods or services that have value in world markets and can be traded with other countries.

Factors Driving South Asian Economies All countries of South Asia have mixed economies with market elements. In a market economy, businesses and individuals make the basic economic decisions. Pakistan has more features of a command economy, as the government owns some businesses.

Although Pakistan's economy has grown in recent years, its population is growing nearly as fast, limiting the gains for each Pakistani. Many live in poverty. Industrialized areas around Karachi and Lahore contrast sharply with the poverty of more rural areas.

Bangladesh is poorer than Pakistan. However, it has a strong textile industry. Microcredit banks such as Grameen Bank have helped pull many people in that nation out of poverty. Microcredit banks focus on **micro-lending**, or making small loans to people with their own small businesses. In the 1990s, the government began building software technology parks. Here, workers create computer software for worldwide export.

Quick Activity

Think of a small business you could start. Role play asking for and granting a microloan. Follow the directions in your Active Journal to plan your business and request your microloan.

INTERACTIVE

South Asia's Population and Economies

BIOGRAPHY

5 Things to Know About

SHEIKH HASINA WAZED
Prime Minister of Bangladesh (born 1947)

- Hasina's father, Sheikh Mujibur Rahman, helped lead the separation of Bangladesh from Pakistan in 1971, but was assassinated with her mother and brothers in 1975.

- After living in exile for six years, Hasina returned to Bangladesh in 1981 and called for democracy during the autocratic rule of Mohammad Ershad.

- She was elected as president of the Bangladesh Awami League, a political party, in 1981.

- Hasina has worked with world leaders to address clean drinking water and sanitation issues and was appointed by the United Nations to serve on a panel on water.

- Hasina became prime minister of Bangladesh in 1996 and returned to that office in 2009.

Critical Thinking What do you think drove Hasina to push for democracy?

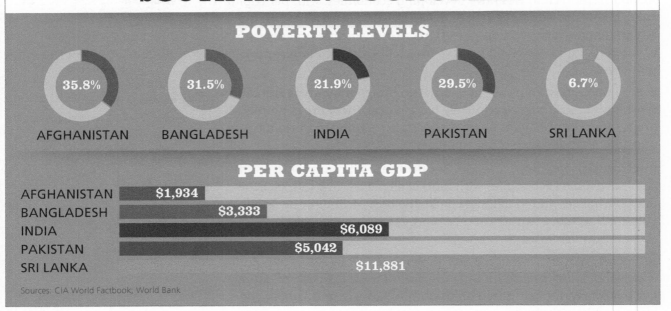

SOUTH ASIAN ECONOMIES

POVERTY LEVELS

35.8%	31.5%	21.9%	29.5%	6.7%
AFGHANISTAN	BANGLADESH	INDIA	PAKISTAN	SRI LANKA

PER CAPITA GDP

AFGHANISTAN	$1,934
BANGLADESH	$3,333
INDIA	$6,089
PAKISTAN	$5,042
SRI LANKA	$11,881

Sources: CIA World Factbook; World Bank

Analyze Graphs High populations and low economic development keep many people in the region mired in poverty. **Infer** Why would low economic development be linked to poverty?

India also provides software services to companies all over the world. For example, companies in Europe and the United States have found it cheaper to send many computer-related tasks to workers outside the company. The practice of hiring outside firms or workers to perform specific tasks for a company is called **outsourcing**. India's economy and its skilled workforce have benefited from this practice.

India has put its high-tech skills to work in another area—space. The country has launched many satellites into orbit around Earth for many nations. In the 2000s, India successfully landed a space probe on the moon and launched a probe into orbit around Mars.

Resources Natural resources play a role in the economies of South Asia. Deposits of coal and iron are crucial to India's energy supply and steel industry. Generally, though, the region is not rich in natural resources other than soil and water. Instead, the region relies on the skills of its people to earn the money it needs to buy resources from other countries.

Most South Asian countries rely heavily on agriculture. Though population density is high in the region, and many cities are huge, most people live in rural areas.

✓ **READING CHECK** **Compare and Contrast** Explain how outsourcing benefits both India and the companies that do the outsourcing.

Trade in South Asia

Countries benefit when they specialize in producing what they are capable of making most efficiently. Then they trade with other countries for what they need or cannot produce efficiently. Pakistan,

Bangladesh, and Sri Lanka specialize in producing cloth and clothing. They have workers who are skilled at producing these goods for a lower wage than in other countries. They sell these goods on global markets in order to buy other goods and services from other countries. India sells a variety of manufactured and agricultural goods on global markets.

Trade barriers such as tariffs, quotas, and protective regulations can stand in the way of trade. In India, tariffs and regulations have sometimes limited trade between different states within the country.

☑ READING CHECK **Draw Conclusions** Why is it beneficial for a South Asian country to produce what it specializes in, rather than try to produce everything that it needs?

India's Economy

Indians in government and industry have focused on boosting the country's economic growth in recent years. They have invested in productive capital, such as machinery, factories, offices, and computers. As a result, India's GDP has grown. By 2016, India's economy surpassed that of Britain, its former colonizer, and was ranked among the most productive economies in the world. While India's output was far behind that of China or the United States, it produces more goods and services than Germany and Japan combined. The lives of many middle-class Indians have improved, with millions now able to afford goods such as refrigerators and televisions.

Yet despite recent economic growth, India has failed to **eradicate** poverty and illiteracy. As the middle class experiences growing prosperity, millions of people still lack basic services such as clean water supplies. Illness and malnutrition are also still significant and ongoing problems.

Quest CONNECTIONS

What development efforts are underway in India and Bangladesh today? Record your findings in your 📕 Active Journal.

Academic Vocabulary
eradicate • *v.*, to eliminate

Analyze Images Workers harvest rice crops in India. **Draw Conclusions** How does having a large number of workers in agriculture affect India's economic growth?

India's soil and climate are valuable resources, and India takes advantage of them by producing rice and other crops. Through the use of technology, India has been able to produce more than it needs. As a result, rice has become a major export for India.

India's major cities—Delhi, Mumbai, Kolkata, Chennai, and Bangalore—have all received capital investment in recent years. This, in turn, has boosted their economies by making them more productive. However, compared to developed countries in Europe and the United States, investment in capital goods in India is still very low. India's infrastructure—its built networks such as roads, power supply, and schools—is poorly developed. This holds the economy back because capital goods, including infrastructure, help businesses and workers be more productive.

Literacy rates are a reflection of investment in human capital, for example through education. Though India's literacy rate has risen since independence, the average literacy rate for adults in India is still only 71 percent, well below the world average. Dividing the statistic between men and women shows a greater disparity, as the literacy rate for adult women is only 63 percent. Investment in human capital, including education

GEOGRAPHY **SKILLS**

The countries of South Asia trade widely around the world.

1. **Place** What is India's most important trade partner?

2. **Infer** Why do you think Saudi Arabia and the United Arab Emirates are important sources of imports for several countries in the region?

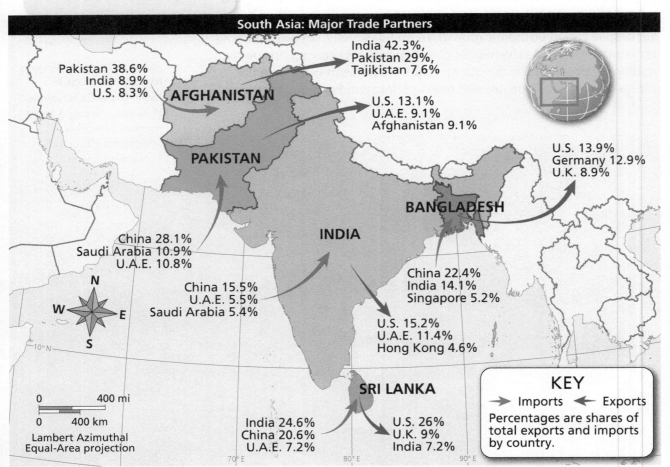

South Asia: Major Trade Partners

Pakistan 38.6%
India 8.9%
U.S. 8.3%

AFGHANISTAN

India 42.3%,
Pakistan 29%,
Tajikistan 7.6%

U.S. 13.1%
U.A.E. 9.1%
Afghanistan 9.1%

PAKISTAN

U.S. 13.9%
Germany 12.9%
U.K. 8.9%

China 28.1%
Saudi Arabia 10.9%
U.A.E. 10.8%

BANGLADESH

INDIA

China 15.5%
U.A.E. 5.5%
Saudi Arabia 5.4%

China 22.4%
India 14.1%
Singapore 5.2%

U.S. 15.2%
U.A.E. 11.4%
Hong Kong 4.6%

N
W E
S

SRI LANKA

0   400 mi
0   400 km
Lambert Azimuthal
Equal-Area projection

India 24.6%
China 20.6%
U.A.E. 7.2%

U.S. 26%
U.K. 9%
India 7.2%

KEY
→ Imports ← Exports
Percentages are shares of total exports and imports by country.

70° E   80° E   90° E

and training, makes people more productive and allows them to achieve a higher standard of living. India's government is trying to address this need.

India ranks about average worldwide on the strength of its entrepreneurship. Countries where it is easier for entrepreneurs to start new businesses tend to have higher economic growth. In India, many small businesses have sprung up, but they do not have the financing that they need to survive. Indian businesses also often face heavy government regulations and corruption from officials that **impede** their growth.

As you have learned, GDP is a measure of the value of goods and services produced in a country in a given year. In 2015, GDP per capita in India was $6,089. This is far below the figure for fully developed economies like those of the United States or western Europe. Still, India ranks higher than most other countries in South Asia. Because India has limited natural resources and must rely on its peoples' skills, India's investment in education and other forms of human capital probably results in a higher standard of living than it could have achieved otherwise.

▲ Students attend class in a school located in North Sikkim, India.

READING CHECK **Identify Cause and Effect** What factors have led to economic growth in India? What factors are impeding further development and prosperity?

Academic Vocabulary
impede • *v., to* slow or block the movement of something

☑ Lesson Check

Practice Vocabulary

1. Why has India benefited from **outsourcing**?

2. How has **microlending** affected the region's economies?

Critical Thinking and Writing

3. **Compare and Contrast** How is India's economy similar to and different from other economies in the region?

4. **Compare and Contrast** How does the literacy rate affect the standard of living in India?

5. **Identify Cause and Effect** How do India's natural resources affect its economy?

6. **Writing Workshop: Gather Evidence** Add to your list of challenges in your 📓 Active Journal by considering the challenges posed by South Asia's economy and possible solutions.

Economic Growth and Poverty in India

Graphs and diagrams can provide useful information in a visual format. They can make data easy to understand and analyze. When you analyze data, you examine it carefully, thinking about what you already know and using the data to help you make an informed judgment. The graphs below show two categories of data about India.

◄ A family in rural India

India's GDP, 1990–2015

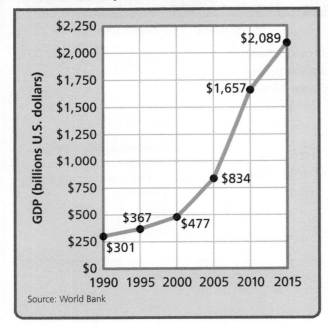

Source: World Bank

India: People Living in Poverty
(% of population)

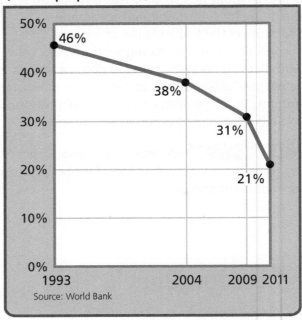

Source: World Bank

Analyzing Geographic Sources

Examine the two graphs carefully. Then answer the questions.

1. **Analyze Graphs** How has India's GDP changed since 1990?

2. **Synthesize Visual Information** When did most of that growth occur?

3. **Analyze Charts** How has the poverty level in India changed as the economy has grown?

4. **Draw Conclusions** What conclusions can you draw about poverty in India based on the graph and diagram?

LESSON 7
Challenges Facing South Asia

GET READY TO READ

Examine the image of people using boats to navigate flooded streets in Bangladesh. How does this image reveal challenges that South Asia faces?

GUIDING QUESTIONS
- What economic challenges do South Asian countries face?
- How have South Asian countries dealt with conflicts?
- What environmental challenges face South Asia?

TAKE NOTES
Literacy Skills: Identify Cause and Effect
Use the graphic organizer in your 🗐 Active Journal to take notes as you read the lesson.

PRACTICE VOCABULARY
Use the vocabulary activity in your 🗐 Active Journal to practice the vocabulary words.

Vocabulary	Academic Vocabulary
sexism	overtax
regulation	compensate

Rapid population growth has contributed to poverty and pollution, which are among the challenges facing South Asia. Many South Asians also face a lack of clean water. In addition, these countries struggle with social and political conflicts. South Asia's governments have tried to address these issues, but finding solutions is not necessarily easy.

What Economic Challenges Does South Asia Face?

The biggest economic challenge in the region is poverty. Large populations, high population growth rates, and unequal treatment of women all are obstacles to solving this issue.

Poverty and Inequality To overcome poverty, countries need to provide better education for their people. One economic obstacle facing many South Asian countries is sexism. **Sexism** is the unfair treatment of people based on their gender. Some parents in these countries will not send their daughters to school. This limits women's contribution to the economy, and the economies suffer as a result.

Birth Rates in Afghanistan, India, and Pakistan

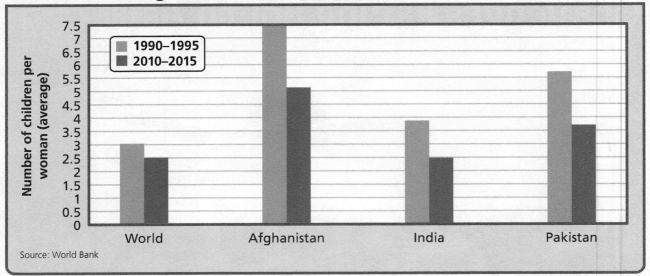

Source: World Bank

Analyze Graphs
The birth rate for the three largest countries in South Asia tends to be higher than the world average. **Synthesize Visual Information** Which country in the region is closest to the world average?

Academic Vocabulary
overtax • *v.*, to strain through overuse

Because they lack education and power, women in some countries may be pressured to have many children. This practice limits women's ability to go to school or work outside the home and can result in continued poverty as the population grows faster than the economy. In Afghanistan, for example, a woman can be expected to have an average of more than five children during her lifetime.

Infrastructure and Government The region suffers from poor infrastructure, or the body of public works—such as roads, bridges, and hospitals—that a country needs to support a modern economy. The public works that do exist are **overtaxed** by a large and rapidly growing population. Governments need to invest more in infrastructure to make workers and businesses more productive.

Another challenge that South Asian economies face is heavy **regulation**, or government rules that set limits or standards for businesses. Government corruption also makes it hard to start or grow businesses.

☑ READING CHECK Identify Cause and Effect What major economic challenges does South Asia face, and what is one cause?

Social and Political Challenges

South Asia is often caught between traditional ways of life and the demands of the modern world. It faces a variety of social, religious, and political tensions.

Overcoming Caste The caste system has persisted into the present, although India and Pakistan have both outlawed discrimination based on caste. While discrimination still occurs, government programs in India set aside places in universities for students from low castes, and some government jobs are also reserved for people from low castes. These programs aim to **compensate** for the way unfair treatment in the past limited opportunities for whole groups of people.

Academic Vocabulary
compensate • *v.*, to make up for

Political Conflicts Several countries face internal religious and political conflicts. The Afghan government continues to fight the Islamic fundamentalist Taliban. Taliban fighters can easily cross the Pakistani border to hide in the mountains of northwestern Pakistan.

There have also been ongoing tensions between Pakistan and India over the region of Kashmir, an Indian state with a Muslim majority. In the past, Pakistan's government has backed Kashmiri groups fighting for independence. These armed rebel forces have clashed with Indian troops. Pakistani and Indian troops also occasionally exchange fire.

Sri Lanka suffered a long conflict between the government, controlled by the Sinhalese majority, and rebels from the Tamil minority. The government won the war in 2009, but members of the Tamil minority still complain of unfair treatment.

In India, armed rebel groups called Naxalites have fought the government. These rebels generally operate in rural eastern India. The Naxalites call for a communist dictatorship. In addition, ethnic rebel groups also operate in far northeastern India.

There are also conflicts in India between the Hindu majority and Muslim minority. Narendra Modi was governor of India's state of Gujarat in 2002 when Hindus attacked Muslim communities and killed hundreds of Muslims. Modi was accused of encouraging the violence. He did little to stop it. In 2014, Modi became prime minister of India. This worried many Muslims.

✓ READING CHECK **Summarize** How has India dealt with discrimination as a result of the caste system?

Environmental Challenges

South Asia faces major environmental challenges, especially with regard to water. Pollution, water scarcity, and flooding from heavy monsoon rains all contribute to these problems. Air quality is also a major challenge.

Air Quality Air pollution is a major problem that affects much of South Asia. In northern India, particularly, air pollution is extremely high. By 2016, Delhi was found to have the worst air quality of any major city in the world. The air pollution causes lung disease and kills thousands of people each year. Causes of the pollution include exhaust from motor vehicles and industry; the burning of wood, charcoal, and cow dung for cooking and heat; and the burning of dead plants in nearby farm fields to fertilize them.

Some strides have been made in improving air quality. Delhi's city government has restricted

Analyze Images People in Delhi, India, wear face masks to protect themselves against air pollution. **Infer** What other precautions do you think people might take when living in a place with high air pollution?

▲ A woman in India retrieves water from a river to use at home. Many South Asian households lack running water.

car travel. The Indian government has also encouraged use of more efficient stoves that produce little smoke.

Water Problems Millions of people in the region lack clean drinking water. Raw sewage and farm runoff flows into the Ganges and its tributaries from cities along their banks. Yet people rely on the Ganges for drinking water. As a result, the river water spreads diseases.

Flooding brought on by the summer monsoons causes the polluted Ganges to overflow its banks and damage crops. These natural disasters affect the food supply and contribute to poverty.

India's government has tried to reduce water pollution, with limited success. Local non-governmental organizations are helping to reverse the damage caused by pollution. The Environmental Protection Act that India passed in 1986 had limited success, and even though in 2014 India's government initiated a new anti-pollution program, the Ganges River remains a polluted body of water.

Climate Change Climate change and rising sea levels also pose long-term threats to the region. Climate change could disrupt the summer monsoon rains that South Asians depend on as a source of water.

Most of Bangladesh is in or near the Ganges Delta, an area just a few feet above sea level. If sea levels rise as a result of climate change, large parts of Bangladesh could be flooded. Tens of millions of people could be left homeless.

As with most of South Asia's environmental issues, poverty is the main roadblock in overcoming these challenges. Rapid population growth, especially in cities, adds to these challenges. Even though some economic growth in the region has reduced poverty, it is still the main challenge that South Asia faces in the 2000s.

☑ **READING CHECK** **Identify Cause and Effect** What are the causes of air and water pollution in South Asia?

☑ Lesson Check

Practice Vocabulary

1. Why is **sexism** a problem in South Asia?

2. What is an example of **regulation**?

Critical Thinking and Writing

3. **Identify Cause and Effect** What are three of the effects of air and water pollution in South Asia?

4. **Draw Conclusions** How do you think political conflicts have affected South Asian governments' ability to solve environmental problems?

5. **Writing Workshop: Prepare to Write** Review your list of challenges and solutions In your 📔 Active Journal and revise based on new information or new thinking. Then write a thesis statement for your essay.

Solve Problems

Follow these steps and use the sources provided to learn how to understand a problem and determine the best solution for that problem.

INTERACTIVE

Solve Problems

1 **Understand the problem.** Gather as much information as possible in order to identify the problem and its causes. Try not to jump to conclusions or make assumptions.

   a. Based on the chart, how has reduced water flow affected the Ganges River?

   b. What are the sources of pollution of the Ganges River?

   c. What issues have prevented previous solutions from working?

2 **Consider possible solutions and choose the best one.** List and consider a number of possible options. Be sure to consider carefully the advantages and disadvantages of each option. Then choose the solution you think is best.

   a. What issue does the government's plan focus on?

   b. Are the proposed steps good ideas? Why or why not?

   c. What issues does that plan not address?

3 **Make and implement a plan.** Make a detailed step-by-step plan to implement your solution. Try to think of any problems that might come up and what you will do to address those problems. Evaluate the effectiveness of the solution and adjust it as needed.

   a. What other steps are needed?

   b. How would you address those issues?

Primary Source

"'Namami Gange' will focus on pollution [reduction] namely interception, diversion [and] treatment of wastewater flowing through the open drains through . . . appropriate . . . treatment / use of innovative technologies / sewage treatment plants (STPs) / . . . rehabilitation and [improvement] of existing STPs and immediate short term measures for arresting pollution at exit points on river."

—Government of India

Secondary Source

Causes of Ganges River Pollution

- Reduced water flow from irrigation and dam construction results in less water to use downriver and lower ability of river to clean itself.

- Farm runoff, untreated human sewage from cities, industrial pollution, and trash all dirty the river, causing disease.

- Poor government control and corruption cause money to be wasted.

☑ Review and Assessment

VISUAL REVIEW

Major Events in South Asia's History

Ancient South Asia (2500s BCE–1500s BCE)
• Harappa and Mohenjo-Daro thrive in Indus Valley. • Indo-Aryans migrate into India.

Religions and Empires (500s BCE–320 CE)
• Hinduism emerges. • Siddhartha Gautama founds Buddhism. • Maurya empire rules. • Gupta empire rules.

Islamic Rule (700s CE–1700s CE)
• Islam arrives in India. • Delhi Sultanate rules India. • Mughal empire conquers most of India, then faces Hindu revolts.

Colonialism and Independence (1700s–1971)
• British colonial rule begins. • India and Pakistan gain independence in 1947. • Bangladesh gains independence in 1971.

Snapshot of South Asia

Major Religions	Major Ethnic Groups		Businesses	Challenges
• Hinduism • Islam • Buddhism • Sikhism	• Hindi • Punjabi • Sindhi • Pashtun • Tajik	• Bengali • Sinhalese • Telugu • Marathi • Tamil	• Agriculture • Trade • Outsourcing • Manufacturing • Software and technical support	• Poverty • Low literacy rate • Pollution • Sexism • Inequality • Water issues

READING REVIEW

Use the Take Notes and Practice Vocabulary activities in your Active Journal to review the topic.

👆 **INTERACTIVE**

Practice vocabulary using the Topic Mini-Games.

 **Quest FINDINGS**

Write Your Essay

Get help for writing your essay in your 📓 Active Journal.

ASSESSMENT

Vocabulary and Key Ideas

1. **Define** How have **monsoons** been both helpful and damaging to Indian civilization?

2. **Describe** What are **castes**, and how have they changed over time?

3. **Explain** What is one similarity between Hinduism and Buddhism?

4. **Describe** Where did Hinduism and Buddhism spread?

5. **Define** What is **karma**, and why is it important to Hinduism and Buddhism?

6. **Explain** How has **outsourcing** helped strengthen India's economy?

7. **Define** What is **infrastructure**?

Critical Thinking and Writing

8. **Synthesize** How did Asoka use principles of Buddhism as a leader?

9. **Analyze Cause and Effect** Why were the Indo-Aryans important to the development of Indian civilization?

10. **Compare and Contrast** Use the information in the Country Databank to compare and contrast the governments of South Asia.

11. **Identify Cause and Effect** What strategy did Mohandas Gandhi use to try to win independence for India? How effective was it?

12. **Revisit the Essential Question** Give an example of a government action in South Asian history that you think was wise or unwise, and explain why.

13. **Writing Workshop: Write a Persuasive Essay** Choose one or more of the challenges you noted in your ▰ Active Journal for a persuasive essay explaining a challenge faced in South Asia and steps for meeting the challenge.

Analyze Primary Sources

14. Which figure from South Asia expressed this idea?
    A. Asoka
    B. Buddha
    C. Gandhi
    D. Nehru

"This is my last advice to you. All . . . things in the world are changeable. They are not lasting. Work hard to gain your own salvation."

Analyze Maps

Use the map to answer the following questions.

15. Which label on the map shows the location of Afghanistan?

16. What capital city is indicated by the label A?

17. What is the name of the disputed region labeled B?

▼ **Regions of South Asia**

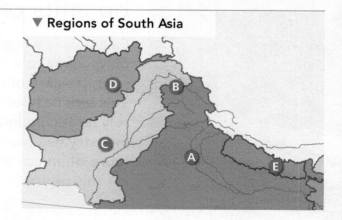

East Asia

GO ONLINE
to access your
digital course

▶ VIDEO

◀)) AUDIO

📖 ETEXT

👆 INTERACTIVE

✎ WRITING

🎮 GAMES

📄 WORKSHEET

☑ ASSESSMENT

Travel across the Pacific Ocean

to **EAST ASIA**, a region rich in history and economic strength. This region, home to ancient civilizations, also contains some of the world's richest and fastest-growing economies.

Explore The Essential Question

What are the costs and benefits of technology?

East Asia is a region where high technology plays a key role in the economy. Natural resources are not abundant in the region. This lack has pushed some countries to rely on technology and skilled workers. Yet industry has caused pollution. Is technology more of an advantage or a disadvantage for this region?

Unlock the Essential Question in your 📘 Active Journal.

▲ A section of the Great Wall of China

Watch

Xiao's Lake

Meet Xiao and learn about the benefits and costs of economic change in China.

Read

about a region that is home to ancient and influential civilizations and that is still important today.

East Asia: Political

ECONOMIC POWERS

East Asia is a global economic powerhouse. By some measures, China has the world's largest economy. Japan, South Korea, and Taiwan also have very productive economies.

Learn more about East Asia by making your own map of its countries in your Active Journal.

INTERACTIVE

Topic Map

A Regional Leader

More than 1.3 billion people live in China, the world's largest country by population in 2017. China's people and its giant cities, such as Shanghai, shown here, are concentrated in eastern China.

An Island Country

Taiwan was once part of China. China still considers Taiwan part of China, although China does not control it.

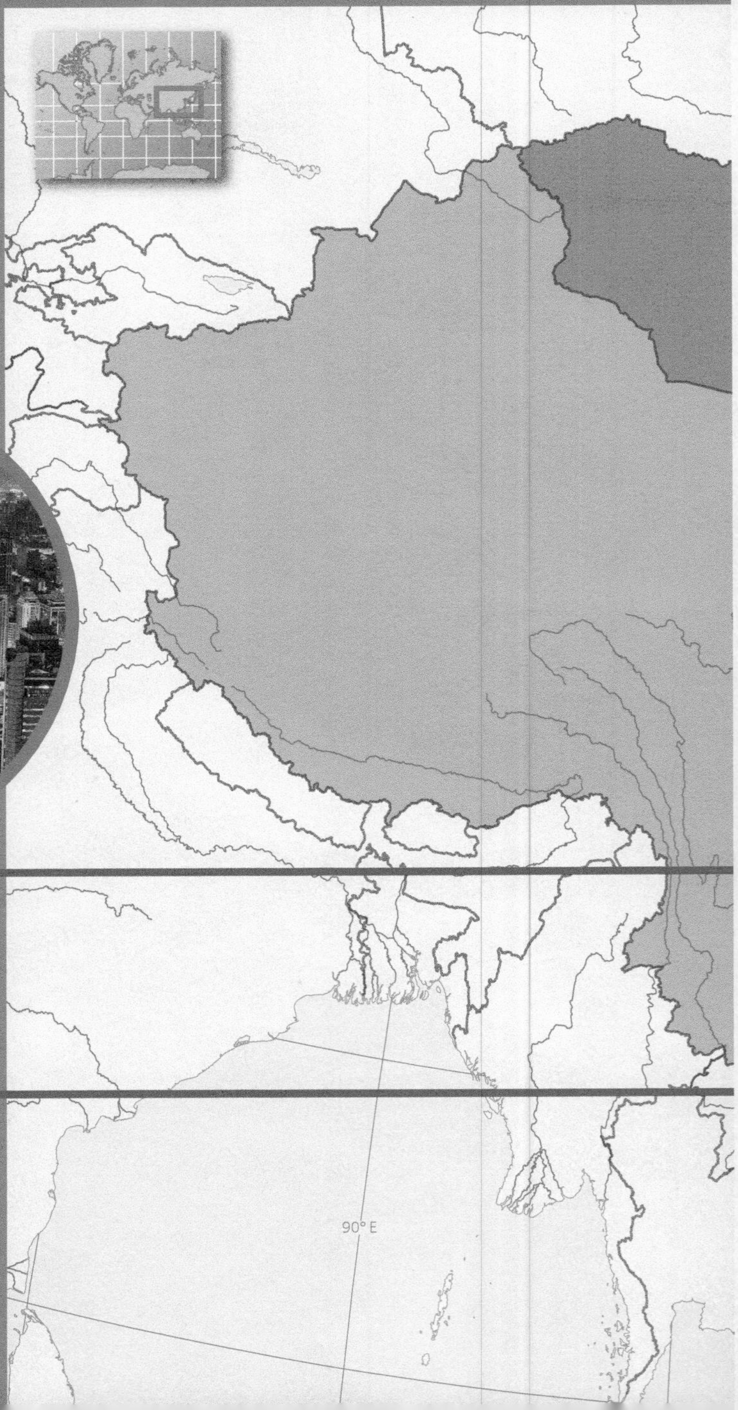

90° E

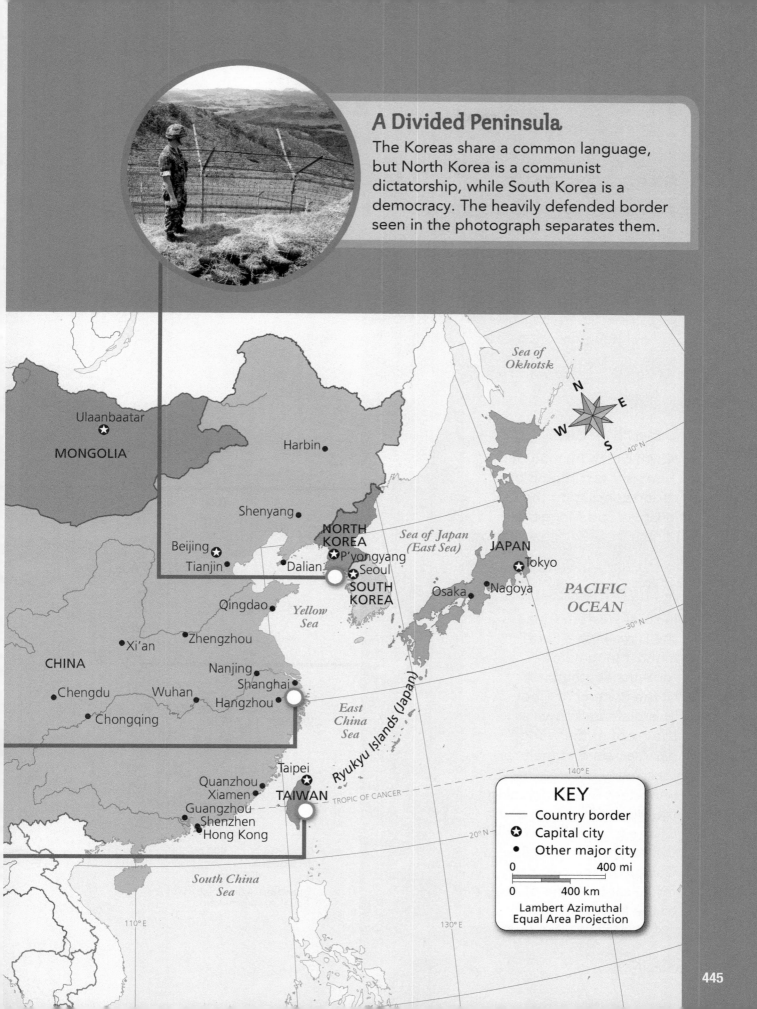

A Divided Peninsula

The Koreas share a common language, but North Korea is a communist dictatorship, while South Korea is a democracy. The heavily defended border seen in the photograph separates them.

MONGOLIA
Ulaanbaatar

Harbin

Shenyang

Beijing
Tianjin
Dalian

NORTH KOREA
P'yongyang
Seoul
SOUTH KOREA

Sea of Okhotsk

Sea of Japan
(East Sea)

JAPAN
Tokyo

Osaka
Nagoya

PACIFIC OCEAN

Qingdao

Yellow Sea

CHINA

Xi'an
Zhengzhou

Chengdu
Wuhan
Nanjing
Shanghai
Hangzhou

Chongqing

East China Sea

Ryukyu Islands (Japan)

Quanzhou
Xiamen
Guangzhou
Shenzhen
Hong Kong

Taipei
TAIWAN

TROPIC OF CANCER

South China Sea

40° N

30° N

140° E

20° N

130° E

110° E

KEY

— Country border

✪ Capital city

• Other major city

0 ———— 400 mi

0 ———— 400 km

Lambert Azimuthal
Equal Area Projection

East Asia: Physical

SHARP CONTRASTS

East Asia stretches from the world's highest mountain, Mt. Everest, across deserts and fertile plains to the Pacific island countries of Japan and Taiwan.

Learn more about East Asia by making your own map of its countries in your Active Journal.

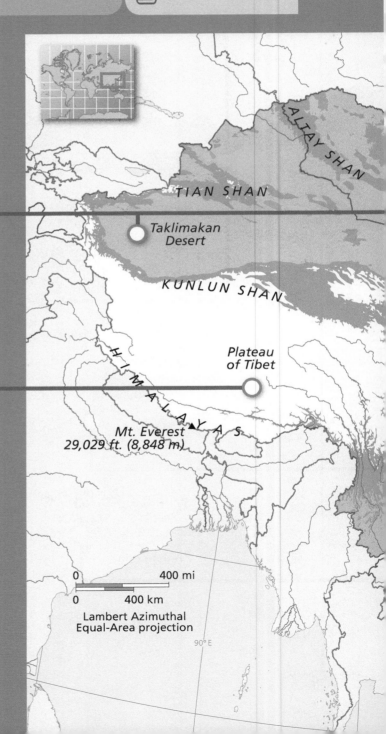

Desert Areas

North of the Plateau of Tibet is a vast region of deserts, including the Gobi in China and Mongolia.

A High Plateau

In southwestern China, the Himalayas—Earth's highest mountains—form the southern rim of the Plateau of Tibet. This plateau, known as the "roof of the world," has glaciers that melt to feed many of Asia's most important rivers, including the Huang (hwahng) and Chang (chahng) (also called the Yangtze or Yangzi) of China. These rivers carry fertile silt from the plateau to the North China Plain.

ALTAY SHAN

TIAN SHAN

Taklimakan Desert

KUNLUN SHAN

Plateau of Tibet

HIMALAYAS

Mt. Everest
29,029 ft. (8,848 m)

0   400 mi
0   400 km
Lambert Azimuthal
Equal-Area projection

90° E

On the Ring of Fire

Japan and Taiwan are parts of volcanic island chains. Here, Pacific Ocean crust slides beneath the continental crust of Asia. Molten rock rises to form volcanoes, such as Japan's Mount Fuji, shown here.

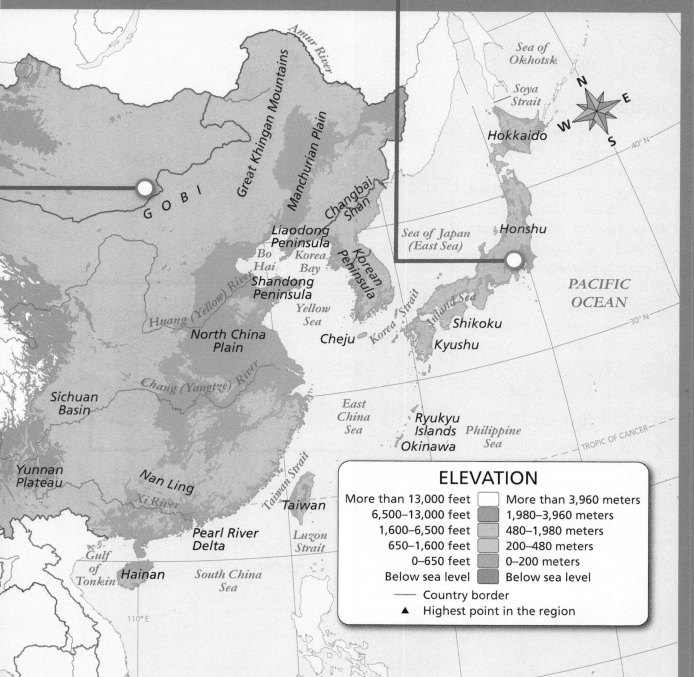

Amur River

Sea of Okhotsk

Soya Strait

Hokkaido

Great Khingan Mountains

Manchurian Plain

Changbai Shan

G O B I

Liaodong Peninsula

Bo Hai

Korea Bay

Korean Peninsula

Shandong Peninsula

Sea of Japan (East Sea)

Honshu

Huang (Yellow) River

Yellow Sea

North China Plain

Cheju

Korea Strait

Inland Sea

Shikoku

Kyushu

PACIFIC OCEAN

Chang (Yangtze) River

Sichuan Basin

East China Sea

Ryukyu Islands

Philippine Sea

Okinawa

TROPIC OF CANCER

Yunnan Plateau

Nan Ling

Xi River

Taiwan Strait

Taiwan

Luzon Strait

Pearl River Delta

Gulf of Tonkin

Hainan

South China Sea

40° N

30° N

110° E

ELEVATION

More than 13,000 feet	More than 3,960 meters
6,500–13,000 feet	1,980–3,960 meters
1,600–6,500 feet	480–1,980 meters
650–1,600 feet	200–480 meters
0–650 feet	0–200 meters
Below sea level	Below sea level

—— Country border
▲ Highest point in the region

East Asia: Climate

REGIONAL VARIETY

East Asia is a region of sharp contrasts in climate. The frigid tundra climate of the Plateau of Tibet is just a few hundred miles (or kilometers) from the tropical climate of the island of Hainan.

Moderate Climates

Most of East Asia's people live in areas with a humid subtropical climate like that of Tokyo, Japan. The coldest month there is January, with an average temperature of about 41° F (about 5° C). The hottest is August, with an average temperature of about 81° F (27° C). Tokyo averages about 56 inches (1,435 mm) of rain in a year.

Frigid Highlands

On the Plateau of Tibet, the town of Nagqu (nahg choo) has a cold tundra climate. The daily average temperature there is 10° F (−12° C) in January and just 49° F (9° C) in the warmest month, July.

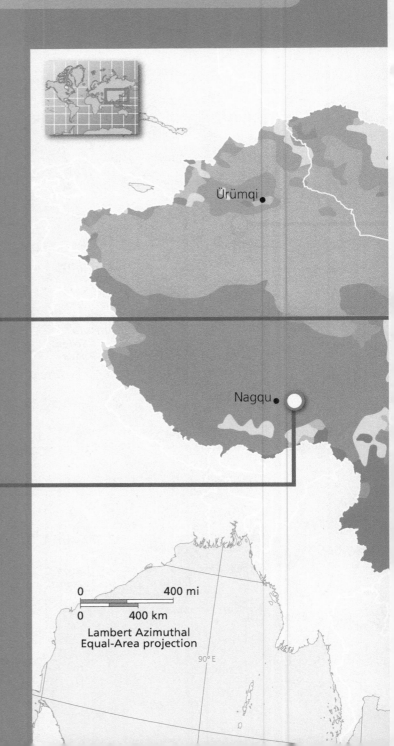

Ürümqi

Nagqu

0   400 mi

0   400 km

Lambert Azimuthal
Equal-Area projection

90° E

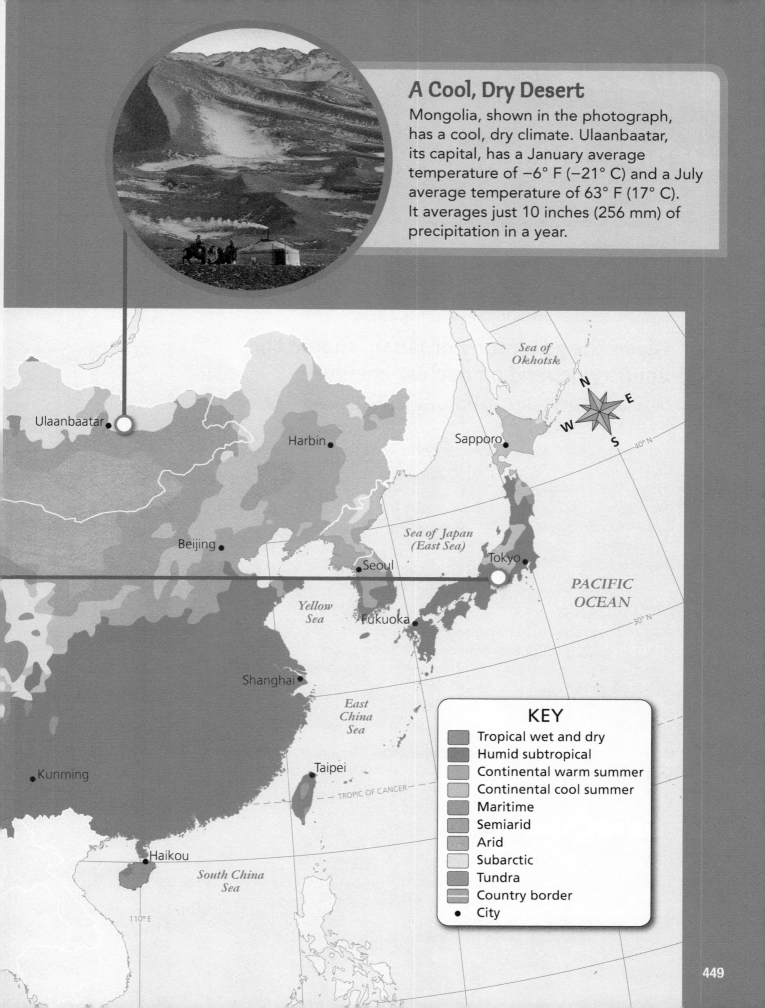

A Cool, Dry Desert

Mongolia, shown in the photograph, has a cool, dry climate. Ulaanbaatar, its capital, has a January average temperature of −6° F (−21° C) and a July average temperature of 63° F (17° C). It averages just 10 inches (256 mm) of precipitation in a year.

Sea of
Okhotsk

Sapporo

40° N

Ulaanbaatar

Harbin

Sea of Japan
(East Sea)

Tokyo

PACIFIC
OCEAN

Beijing

Seoul

30° N

Yellow
Sea

Fukuoka

Shanghai

East
China
Sea

Kunming

Taipei

TROPIC OF CANCER

Haikou

South China
Sea

110° E

KEY

- Tropical wet and dry
- Humid subtropical
- Continental warm summer
- Continental cool summer
- Maritime
- Semiarid
- Arid
- Subarctic
- Tundra
- Country border
- • City

Quest
Discussion Inquiry

Debate Nuclear Power for Japan

Quest KICK OFF

After an earthquake and tsunami in 2011 led to a meltdown at a Japanese nuclear power plant, the country closed most of its nuclear power plants. Japan's parliament is considering whether these plants are safe. As an engineer on a team reporting to the parliament, your task is to answer this question:

Given the geography of Japan, should the country depend on nuclear energy?

Be ready! Other experts will challenge your arguments. It's time to prepare!

▼ Onagawa Nuclear Power Plant in Japan

1 Ask Questions

You want to give the best possible advice to Japan's government. Get started by making a list of questions about Japan's geography. Write the questions in your 📓 Active Journal.

2 Investigate

As you read the lessons in this topic, look for **Quest CONNECTIONS** that provide information about energy policy in East Asia. Respond to these examples in your 📓 Active Journal.

3 Examine Primary Sources

Next, explore sources addressing the issue. Capture notes in your 📓 Active Journal.

Quest FINDINGS

4 Discuss

After you collect your ideas and examine the sources, prepare to discuss this question: Given the geography of Japan, should the country depend on nuclear energy? Use your knowledge of Japan's geography and evidence from the sources to make convincing arguments.

Early Civilizations of East Asia

BOUNCE TO ACTIVATE ▶ VIDEO

GET READY TO READ

START UP
Examine the image of pottery soldiers in the tomb of China's first emperor. What words might describe the society that produced this tomb?

GUIDING QUESTIONS
- How was ancient China united and governed?
- What were the greatest achievements of the ancient Chinese?
- How did the Korean and Japanese civilizations develop?

TAKE NOTES
Literacy Skills: Analyze Text Structure
Use the graphic organizer in your 📓 Active Journal to take notes as you read the lesson.

PRACTICE VOCABULARY
Use the vocabulary activity in your 📓 Active Journal to practice the vocabulary words.

Vocabulary

Mandate of Heaven
Great Wall
Legalism
civil service
Silk Road
acupuncture
clan

Academic Vocabulary

exempt
distinctive

By around 5000 BCE, farmers had settled in villages near the Huang (hwahng) River, also called the Yellow River, in China. Over time, powerful rulers united these villages to create large kingdoms.

How Did Government Emerge in China?

In the farming villages, people used stone tools at first and made pottery and silk cloth. Some villages had chiefs, or rulers, who organized workers and commanded warriors. Strong chiefs led their warriors to take control of nearby villages, creating small kingdoms.

Around 1700 BCE, one of those kingdoms began to expand. A ruler from this kingdom founded the Shang dynasty. A dynasty is a ruling family that holds power for many years. This dynasty lasted some 600 years.

New Technologies The Shang dynasty gained power as the Chinese were learning how to make bronze weapons and tools, which were stronger than earlier ones made of wood or stone.

▲ Bronze coins from the Zhou dynasty

The Shang also changed their environment by building dikes, or walls to hold back water, along the Huang River. The dikes helped prevent damaging floods.

In addition, the Chinese were developing a system of writing that began as drawings of objects or actions. Over time, the drawings were simplified into characters, or letters representing an entire word. This system of writing is still in use in China and Japan today.

A New Dynasty Claims the Right to Rule Around 1050 BCE, a group called the Zhou (joh) overthrew the Shang. Zhou leaders declared that their success proved they had heaven's support. They called this right to rule the **Mandate of Heaven**, which they said was given by heaven, the highest force of nature.

According to this idea, to stay in power, rulers had to act virtuously. They would have to be kind and just and serve the interests of the people. The concept of the Mandate of Heaven became a tradition of Chinese government. If a ruler performed his role well, there would be harmony between heaven and earth. To stay in power, the rulers of the new dynasty had to serve the interests of the people.

Zhou China developed or adopted several new technologies. An important invention was the crossbow. Chinese craftsmen also learned to make tools and weapons from iron, which is stronger than bronze. Coins were introduced as a form of money.

Warring States In the early 700s BCE, some nobles in the Zhou kingdom rebelled. They took power over their own territories and became more independent. At the same time, Chinese noble states spread south, into the valley of the Chang River. By the early 400s BCE, war had broken out among the noble states once ruled by the Zhou.

Stronger states conquered weaker ones. Loyalty to the Zhou dynasty disappeared. In 256 BCE, the last Zhou ruler was overthrown. Fighting continued for years before a new dynasty managed to unite China.

☑ READING CHECK **Sequence** Which dynasty ruled China first, the Shang dynasty or the Zhou dynasty? Which dynasty lasted longer?

The First Chinese Empire

The Warring States period came to an end when the king of Qin (chin) unified China in 221 BCE. King Zheng (jung), who had come to power in Qin in 247 BCE, was determined to build a great empire. He was skilled and ruthless. He defeated rival kingdoms and united China.

Quest CONNECTIONS

What efforts did the Chinese make to control the Huang River? Were they successful? Record your findings in your 📕 Active Journal.

Forming an Empire Zheng decided that *king* was too small a title for the ruler of such a vast territory, so he declared himself *Shi Huangdi* (shur hwahng DEE), or the "First Emperor" of China. To unite the empire, the emperor created a central governing system. He organized China into 36 provinces, each divided into counties. County leaders were responsible to the heads of provinces. Province heads reported to the central government and the emperor. The emperor dismissed any official who failed to carry out his policies.

The First Emperor also began work on one of the largest public works projects in history—the **Great Wall**, a long wall running east and west along the Chinese empire's northern border. The purpose of the wall was to defend the empire from invasion. It was meant to prevent attacks from nomads living on the vast grasslands to the north of the Qin empire.

Qin Government Qin rulers had brought in advisors from other kingdoms to help make Qin stronger. Shang Yang (shahng yahng) was one important advisor. He belonged to a school of thought called Legalism. According to **Legalism**, a strong leader and a strong legal system, not moral values, are needed to create social order.

The First Emperor agreed. He believed that strict rules were necessary to unite the empire. He imposed harsh rules on the common people. Heavy taxes and required labor service increased the emperor's wealth. The emperor also put in place a single set of laws across the empire. The kingdom became stronger and more orderly.

The Fall of the Qin Dynasty The Qin Dynasty was undone by its unbending enforcement of its harsh laws. A rebellion was sparked by a soldier named Chen Sheng. As news of Chen's uprising spread, thousands rose up to support him. The rebels joined together long enough to overthrow the Qin but then began fighting among themselves. Once again, China slid into chaos.

☑ READING CHECK **Draw Conclusions** Why is Shi Huangdi known as the First Emperor of China?

INTERACTIVE

The Terracotta Army of Shi Huangdi

Analyze Images The painting shows Qin soldiers burning books and burying scholars as the emperor sits on his throne. **Infer** What does this image suggest about Shi Huangdi's opinion of learning?

The Han Dynasty

The next Chinese ruling family was the Han (hahn). The Han emperors built on the successes of the Qin to create a dynasty that served as a model for future Chinese governments.

Reuniting and Expanding China A rebel general named Liu Bang (lyoh bahng) founded the Han dynasty in 206 BCE. The Han ruled China for about 400 years. Today, ethnic Chinese—the largest ethnic group in China—still call themselves the *Han.*

The first Han emperor came from a poor family, but he surrounded himself with capable advisors. He encouraged learning, lowered taxes, and relaxed the Qin's harsh rules.

The Han expanded China's territory. Much of this expansion took place under the fifth Han emperor, Wudi (woo DEE), who ruled for more than 50 years. Wudi sent his armies west to conquer lands far into Central Asia. He extended his empire north to the Korean peninsula and south into what is now Vietnam.

The Structure of Government Han emperors followed the example of the Qin by creating a strong central government. The Han government was organized like a pyramid. At the base were the chiefs of China's many towns and villages. At the top of the pyramid were the emperor and his chief advisors.

Han emperors tried to make sure that local leaders remained too weak to challenge the emperor's authority. When the Han emperors conquered new lands, they administered this land directly rather than giving it to a nobleman.

The strength of the Han government lay in its civil service. A **civil service** is a system of government employees mainly selected for their ability. Emperor Wudi created exams to find talented people for the civil service. In later dynasties, the exam system would become even more important for selecting officials.

The Silk Road and Buddhism The **Silk Road** is a series of trade routes that crossed Asia and connected China to the Mediterranean Sea. Trade routes across Central Asia had existed before the Han, but during the reign of Wudi contact between China and regions to the west increased. The name "Silk Road" comes from China's most important export: silk. The Chinese exchanged silk and other luxury goods for a wide range of other products.

The Silk Road was also a path for the exchange of ideas. Chinese inventions, such as paper, spread west along the trade routes. Foreign ideas, such as Buddhism, entered China during the late Han along the Silk Road as well. Buddhism spread from India to Central Asia and from there reached China. Over time, Buddhism became very popular in China. Chinese Buddhists also brought new ideas and practices to the religion.

Analyze Images This sculpture from the Han period shows an official in the government civil service. **Contrast** How did the Han government's treatment of scholars differ from that of the Qin?

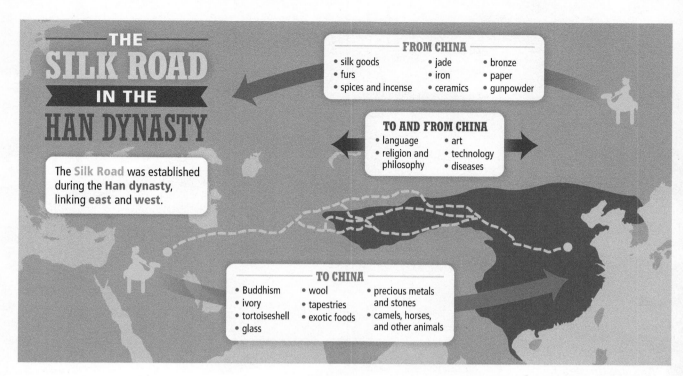

THE SILK ROAD IN THE HAN DYNASTY

The **Silk Road** was established during the **Han dynasty**, linking **east** and **west**.

FROM CHINA
- silk goods
- furs
- spices and incense
- jade
- iron
- ceramics
- bronze
- paper
- gunpowder

TO AND FROM CHINA
- language
- religion and philosophy
- art
- technology
- diseases

TO CHINA
- Buddhism
- ivory
- tortoiseshell
- glass
- wool
- tapestries
- exotic foods
- precious metals and stones
- camels, horses, and other animals

Along with Confucianism and Daoism, Buddhism is one of the most influential belief systems in China. You will learn about Confucianism and Daoism in the next lesson. Chinese scholars mixed ideas from the three belief systems in their writings and art.

☑ READING CHECK Compare and Contrast How was Han rule similar to and different from Qin rule?

Life in Ancient China

The Han dynasty was a time of innovation and economic development. Production and trade flourished. More Chinese worked as craftspeople and merchants. Many important inventions date to this dynasty.

Family Life and Women Confucian teachings about family loyalty and respect for elders were key values. During the Han, people continued to revere—honor and admire—ancestors. People made offerings to ancestors to show respect and gain support from them.

Also, the Han legal code enforced values promoted by the philosopher Confucius. Parents could report children who did not show proper respect. Adult children would be punished harshly. Younger children, though, were usually **exempt** from punishment.

The status of women was generally lower than that of men. Most worked in the home, cooking, weaving, and caring for their children and elderly family members.

Analyze Diagrams
Travelers on the Silk Road brought goods and ideas to and from China. **Draw Conclusions** What religion came to China as a result of the Silk Road?

 **INTERACTIVE**

The Silk Road Connects East and West

Academic Vocabulary
exempt • *adj.*, free from, not subject to

Han Achievements The prosperity of Han China helped support many cultural achievements. Artists painted colorful murals. Sculptors created beautiful works in stone, clay, and bronze. Poets wrote poems expressing emotion with images from the Chinese countryside. Musicians created works of beauty, and music and dancing were common at public festivals and ceremonies.

Scientists also made important advances. Astronomers studied the sky and made precise calculations of the length of the solar year. Han doctors made progress in medicine. They developed new theories to explain and treat illness. Herbal medicines were one important treatment. Another was **acupuncture**, a therapy that uses needles to cure sickness and stop pain.

Han inventors produced important new tools. One was a tool called the seismometer, which could detect earthquakes. Another invention was the wheelbarrow. This human-powered cart appeared in China about 100 BCE. It was so useful for moving heavy loads that it was called the "wooden ox."

Perhaps the most important innovation of the Han was paper. Early paper was made from rags and bark. Paper was probably not widely used at first. In later dynasties, printing on paper became a way to make cheap books. More people could afford books, and new ideas spread quickly.

✓READING CHECK **Identify Cause and Effect** How did prosperity under the Han dynasty affect Chinese culture?

Early Korean Civilization

Farmers were settled in villages by 3000 BCE in Korea, the peninsula that is divided today between North and South Korea. These people probably belonged to **clans**, or groups of families with a common ancestor that were part of larger tribes. Bronze-making technology spread to Korea from Shang China.

During the 300s BCE, a league of tribes formed a state called Choson in northern Korea. The use of iron weapons and tools spread from China to Choson. Meanwhile, other tribal states developed in southern Korea. Han China conquered Choson, but the other Korean states remained independent of Chinese control.

Eventually, northern Korea regained independence from China. Here the kingdom of Koguryo was established around 40 BCE. The kingdoms of Paekche and Silla developed in southern Korea around the same time. These kingdoms shared cultural features. They also waged frequent wars with one another.

☑ READING CHECK Draw Conclusions How do you think technology such as weapons and tools spread from China to Korea?

Early Japanese Civilization

Japan arose in the shadow of its powerful neighbor, China. Early Japanese culture and society often borrowed from China and Japan's other neighbor, Korea.

The first groups of people in Japan arrived many thousands of years ago. Historians have identified one culture group, the Jomon (JOH mun), by its **distinctive** pottery. The Jomon migrated to Japan some 11,000 years ago. They lived by hunting and fishing.

Academic Vocabulary
distinctive • *adj.,* setting a person or thing apart

BIOGRAPHY
5 Things to Know About ▸ MURASAKI SHIKIBU
Japanese author (about 978–1014 CE)

- Murasaki Shikibu was a woman of the Japanese imperial court; her real name is not known.

- Lady Murasaki wrote *The Tale of Genji,* probably the world's oldest full-length novel.

- *The Tale of Genji* tells about the life of a prince in the Japanese imperial court.

- The heroine in her epic novel is named Murasaki, and there are more than 400 other characters in her book.

- Lady Murasaki's father and grandfather were both poets who encouraged her to write at a time when few women were taught to read or write.

Critical Thinking Why do you think Lady Murasaki is remembered today?

A Farming Culture By 250 BCE, a new group had appeared in Japan—the Yayoi (YAH yoy). They probably came from Korea. In time, the Yayoi merged with or pushed out the Jomon. Unlike the Jomon, the Yayoi farmed, wove cloth, and worked bronze and iron.

Most important, the Yayoi introduced the technique of growing rice in irrigated fields. Rice became Japan's most important crop. A diet based on seafood and rice helped boost the population of Japan.

The Yamato Clan Triumphs Local clans ruled Japan by the 200s CE. The head of a clan was also a religious leader. Part of his job was to show respect to the clan's *kami,* or spirit being, so that the clan would have good harvests.

From the 200s to the 400s, warlike clans competed for land and power. The winner of this struggle was the Yamato clan from the plains of southern Honshu, Japan's largest island.

The Yamato first gained control over lands to the north and west. They eventually built a small state. Sometimes, they went to war against neighboring clans. More often, they made alliances through marriage or other ties.

The Yamato used iron tools to till the land. They also found better ways to level and flood rice fields. These improvements added to their wealth and power.

✓ READING CHECK **Compare and Contrast** In what way were the Yamato similar to the early dynasties in China?

✓ Lesson Check

Practice Vocabulary

1. What effect did **Legalism** have on how the Qin ruled?

2. How did the **Silk Road** get its name, and what was exchanged on it?

Critical Thinking and Writing

3. **Identify Cause and Effect** What lasting effects did the First Emperor's rule have on later dynasties in China?

4. **Identify Main Ideas** How and why did the ancient Chinese change their environment?

5. **Draw Conclusions** Why do you think Japan and Korea borrowed aspects of culture from China?

6. **Writing Workshop: Generate Questions to Focus Research** Write two questions in your 📓 Active Journal on the issue of the costs and benefits of technology in East Asia based on what you read in this lesson. You will use these questions to begin your research for a topic essay.

Chinese Religions and Philosophies

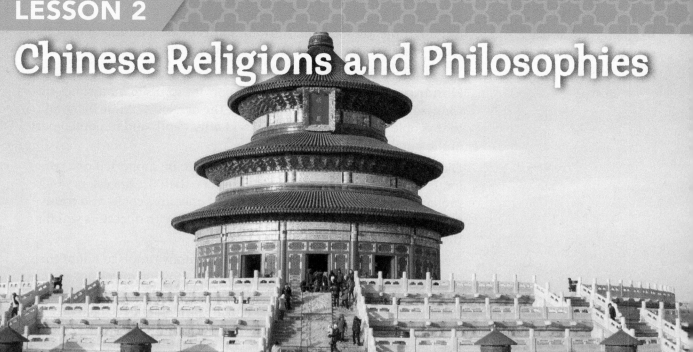

GET READY TO READ

START UP
Examine the photo of the Temple of Heaven in Beijing, China. Write three questions you have about Chinese beliefs and traditions.

GUIDING QUESTIONS
- What did Confucius teach?
- What do Daoists believe?
- What other traditions form part of traditional Chinese spirituality?

TAKE NOTES
Literacy Skills: Compare and Contrast
Use the graphic organizer in your 📓 Active Journal to take notes as you read the lesson.

PRACTICE VOCABULARY
Use the vocabulary activity in your 📓 Active Journal to practice the vocabulary words.

Vocabulary	Academic Vocabulary
philosophy	populate
Confucianism	stable
filial piety	
Daoism	

Two important belief systems, Confucianism and Daoism, developed during China's Zhou dynasty. Each is a **philosophy**, a system of beliefs about the world and how to live. Religious practices, such as the worship of gods, became connected to these philosophies. Later, Buddhism became an important religion in China. Today, Daoist, Confucian, and Buddhist temples are found across China.

Spiritual Traditions

Before Confucianism and Daoism appeared, the Chinese followed ancient spiritual traditions. Ancient Chinese viewed Earth as a flat square. Heaven stretched above. They believed that both heaven and Earth were **populated** by a variety of spirits.

Many Spirits The ancient Chinese viewed heaven as the home of the spirits of the sun, moon, stars, and storms. On Earth, spirits lived in hills, rivers, rocks, and seas. These spirits ruled the daily lives of people. Good spirits made the rains fall and crops grow. They helped sailors travel safely at sea.

Academic Vocabulary
populate • *v.*, to inhabit, or
live in

Not all spirits were so kind. Harmful spirits made it unsafe to walk the roads at night. They might hide in a house, bringing bad luck to all who lived there.

Honoring Ancestors The most important spirits to many ancient Chinese were those of their ancestors. The ancient Chinese believed that people lived on in the spirit world after death and remained part of the family.

Like any family member, the ancestors had to be supported and cared for. If the living took care of their ancestors, then the ancestors would protect and guide them. But the spirits of ancestors could also cause people trouble. The key to a good relationship with ancestors was for the living to honor the dead.

Over the centuries, the Chinese developed many rituals to honor their ancestors. Families had shrines with tablets showing ancestors' names. They set out food for their ancestors on special occasions. After paper money came into use, they burned fake "spirit" money to give the ancestors income in the afterlife. Many of these rituals are performed in China today.

☑ READING CHECK **Draw Conclusions** Why was it important to the Chinese to honor and respect their ancestors?

The Teachings of Confucius

Confucianism, a belief system based on the ideas of the thinker Confucius, is one of the most important philosophies that developed in China. Confucius lived just before the time of the Warring States. He and later thinkers during the late Zhou dynasty looked for solutions to China's problems. Among these thinkers, Confucius had the greatest effect on Chinese culture. He is known as the "First Teacher" and is honored for his great wisdom.

Analyze Images People pay their respects to Huangdi, or Yellow Emperor, a mythological emperor seen as an ancestor of the Chinese people. **Use Visual Information** What Chinese spiritual traditions does this practice reflect?

Life of a Philosopher Confucius was born into a poor family in 551 BCE. He held several low-level jobs in government. He saw firsthand some of the problems of his time, such as greed and cruelty. Officials often did not enforce the law. Some took bribes, or illegal payments, to do favors for the rich. Peasants starved while rulers taxed them to pay for wars.

Confucius believed that the cause of the disorder was that the Chinese had turned away from the traditional roles and values of the early Zhou. Only a return to those ideals could bring order to China. Confucius made his life's work teaching the wise ways of the ancestors.

To carry out this work, Confucius started his own school. Students of Confucius collected his teachings in a book called the *Analects*. In later centuries, this book became central to political and ethical thought in China and across East Asia. Chinese students still memorize passages from it today. The book includes the following saying:

Primary Source

"What I do not wish men to do to me, I also wish not to do to [other] men."

—Confucius, *Analects*

Five Relationships The heart of Confucianism lay in the ideal of a **stable**, orderly society based on five relationships: (1) ruler and subject, (2) father and son, (3) husband and wife, (4) older and younger brothers, and (5) two friends.

Especially important was the relationship between father and son, or parents and their children. Elders are supposed to care for and teach younger family members. In return, children respect and obey their elders. The devotion of children to their parents is called **filial piety**.

The relationship between parents and children was the model for the other relationships. The person of higher status, in traditional Chinese terms, in each of the relationships—that is, the ruler, elder, or husband—must fulfill the responsibilities of his or her role. The person of lower status—that is, the subject, younger person, or wife—should respect the senior person. Confucius believed order and harmony would come to society once all people acted according to their roles.

✓ **READING CHECK** **Infer** Why were the *Analects* studied across East Asia?

Analyze Images Confucius, shown in this painting, influenced Chinese society for hundreds of years. **Use Visual Information** What qualities does the artist give to Confucius in this image?

Academic Vocabulary
stable • *adj.*, unchanging; not likely to give way

What Are the Beliefs of Daoism?

Confucius and his students were not the only scholars affected by the chaos in China during the late Zhou dynasty. Another group of thinkers saw the disorder and responded differently. These thinkers developed a belief system called Daoism. **Daoism** is a philosophy of following the Dao (dow), that is, the natural way of the universe. It is an ancient Chinese way of living that emphasizes a simple and natural existence.

The Legend of Laozi According to legend, a man named Laozi (LOW dzuh) founded Daoism. Laozi is known as a sage, or wise person. He is said to have written down his beliefs in a book called the *Dao De Jing* (dow duh jing).

Historians do not know whether Laozi actually lived. They believe that the *Dao De Jing* was probably written by many people. It is a small book, made up mostly of poems. People throughout the world still read the *Dao De Jing* for its wisdom.

Yin and Yang Daoism reflects ancient Chinese beliefs about the world. The ancient Chinese saw quiet order in the changing seasons. They also saw the violence of nature in floods and storms.

Daoists believe that two great forces are at work in nature. These forces are called yin and yang. They are opposites yet work together. Yin is a female force. It is dark, cool, and quiet. Yang is a male force. It is bright, warm, and active. Daoists believe balance between yin and yang is key to harmony in the universe.

The Dao Daoists see the Dao, which means "the way" or "the path," as the source of yin and yang. The Dao is mysterious and impossible to define clearly. However, Daoists think people should try to follow the Dao. They frequently see evidence of the Dao in natural things, often connecting it with water:

Analyze Images The Daoist belief in harmony among natural elements can be found in Chinese landscape paintings such as this one. **Use Visual Information** What elements of the natural world do you see in this painting?

Primary Source

"There is nothing in the world more soft and weak than water, and yet for attacking things that are firm and strong, nothing is better than it. . . ."

—Laozi, *Dao De Jing*

Water, through consistent action over time, can even wear away rock. By acting like water, people are following the Dao.

People can upset order with their actions. Order comes when people keep to a simple life, instead of competing for wealth and power. Daoists believe that a good leader takes little action, letting people live a simple life. Daoists are less concerned with the morals, rituals, and learning that Confucians value.

Despite the differences between Confucianism and Daoism, most Chinese thinkers studied both philosophies. They freely used ideas from both. Throughout Chinese history, Confucianism and Daoism influenced Chinese culture even as new ideas came from abroad.

☑ READING CHECK **Compare and Contrast** What is one difference between Confucianism and Daoism?

Chinese Buddhism

Soon after the fall of the Han dynasty, during the 300s CE, a new religion, Buddhism, spread rapidly in China. You learned about its development in South Asia and its spread along the Silk Road in the last lesson.

Buddhism retained its most important teachings and practices when it spread across China. Chinese Buddhists, however, developed a uniquely Chinese version of the religion. Chinese Buddhism adopted beliefs and practices from Confucianism, Daoism, and China's older spiritual traditions.

☑ READING CHECK **Draw Conclusions** Why do you think the Chinese incorporated other beliefs and practices into Buddhist tradition?

▲ This figure of the Buddha at Longmen, China, was carved into rock in the 400s CE.

☑ Lesson Check

Practice Vocabulary

1. Name one Chinese **philosophy** and explain its influence on China.

2. What is an example of **filial piety**?

Critical Thinking and Writing

3. **Compare and Contrast** How are Buddhism and Hinduism different from Confucianism and Daoism?

4. **Identify Cause and Effect** What did Confucius think had caused disorder in China?

5. **Infer** Which of the five relationships that Confucius emphasized probably had the greatest impact on Chinese civilization? Why?

6. **Writing Workshop: Find and Use Credible Sources** Conduct a search for credible sources that you can use for your topic research paper. List three examples in your 📕 Active Journal.

Later History of East Asia

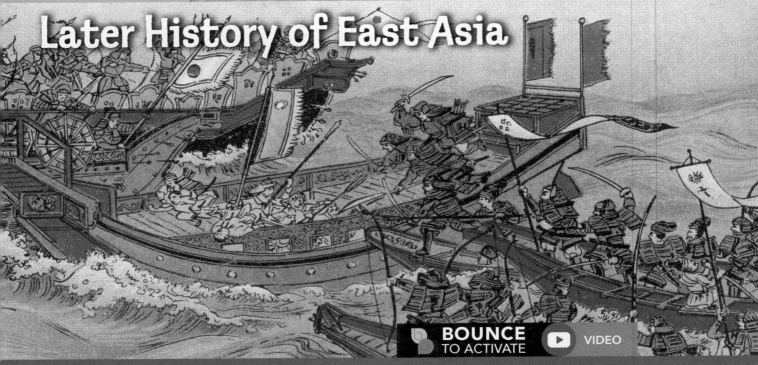

BOUNCE TO ACTIVATE ▶ VIDEO

GET READY TO READ

START UP

This painting shows a sea battle between Mongols and Japanese off Japan during the 1200s. Write two questions about East Asia's history that you have after viewing this painting.

GUIDING QUESTIONS

- How did China, Korea, and Japan develop before modern times?
- How did East Asian countries respond to Western expansion?
- How did East Asia develop after World War II?

TAKE NOTES

Literacy Skills: Sequence
Use the graphic organizer in your 📓 Active Journal to take notes as you read the lesson.

PRACTICE VOCABULARY

Use the vocabulary activity in your 📓 Active Journal to practice the vocabulary words.

Vocabulary
bureaucracy Meiji Restoration
tribute
Shinto

Academic Vocabulary
commercial
restore

For centuries, China, Korea, and Japan developed their own rich civilizations. Later, European expansion forced the region to confront new challenges. The countries of East Asia adopted new technologies and forms of government. Some emerged as leading economic and political powers.

The Tang and Song Dynasties

After the fall of the Han dynasty in 220 CE, many kingdoms competed for power in China. The Sui (sway) dynasty reunited China between 581 and 618. The Sui built the Grand Canal linking northern and southern China. It is still the world's longest human-built waterway.

Two Strong Dynasties By 624, the Tang (tahng) dynasty had won control of China. During the 630s, the Tang conquered much of Central Asia and controlled a territory larger than any earlier dynasty. Under the Tang, Islam first spread to China.

The Tang lost power in the early 900s. In 960 the Song reunited China. The Song ruled all of China until the early 1100s.

Then, the foreign Jin conquered northern China. The Song retreated into southern China, where they ruled until the late 1200s.

Strong Governments and Economies To help them govern, the Tang and Song relied on a **bureaucracy**, a system of many government officials who carry out government rules and regulations. They used exams to select people for jobs in the bureaucracy. Bureaucracies created stronger governments than the loose networks of nobles that earlier dynasties had used.

During the Tang and Song periods, trade along the Silk Road and Grand Canal made China rich. Cities such as the capital, Chang'an, became thriving cultural and **commercial** centers. Increased irrigation produced more crops, leading to population growth. Chinese artists and writers produced works of great beauty for wealthy merchants and officials.

☑ **READING CHECK** Summarize How did China become wealthy during the Song and Tang dynasties?

A Mongol Empire

Throughout history, China had been threatened from the north by nomads, or people who move from place to place. In the 1200s, the nomadic Mongols, led by Genghis Khan (GENG gis kahn), swept out of present-day Mongolia.

The Mongols conquered an empire stretching across Asia and part of Europe. They finished their conquest of China in 1260. Their vast empire opened up increased trade between China and other parts of Asia.

INTERACTIVE

Technology in the Tang and Song Dynasties

Academic Vocabulary
commercial • *adj.,* used for trade or other business

GEOGRAPHY **SKILLS**

At its greatest extent, the Mongol empire stretched all the way to Russia.

1. **Region** How far did Mongol territory extend from east to west?

2. **Use Visual Information** How did physical features affect Mongol expansion?

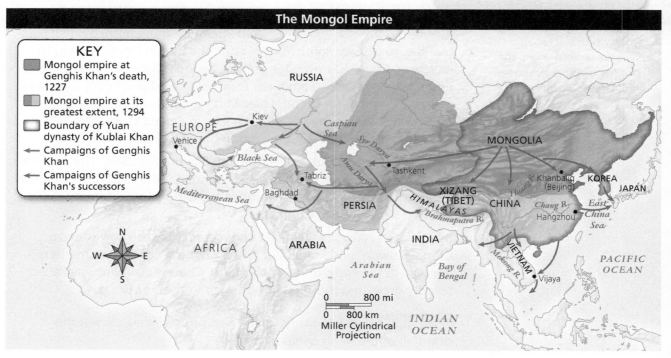

The Mongol Empire

KEY
- Mongol empire at Genghis Khan's death, 1227
- Mongol empire at its greatest extent, 1294
- Boundary of Yuan dynasty of Kublai Khan
- ← Campaigns of Genghis Khan
- ← Campaigns of Genghis Khan's successors

RUSSIA

EUROPE
Venice
Kiev
Caspian Sea
Syr Darya
MONGOLIA
Black Sea
Amu Darya
Tashkent
Khanbaliq (Beijing)
KOREA
JAPAN
Tabriz
XIZANG (TIBET)
CHINA
Chang R.
East China Sea
Mediterranean Sea
Baghdad
PERSIA
HIMALAYAS
Brahmaputra R.
Hangzhou

AFRICA
ARABIA
INDIA
Arabian Sea
Bay of Bengal
VIETNAM
Mekong R.
PACIFIC OCEAN
Vijaya

N W E S

0   800 mi
0   800 km
Miller Cylindrical Projection
INDIAN OCEAN

Analyze Images The Ming dynasty was at its most powerful under Yongle, the third Ming emperor, shown here. **Draw Conclusions** How do you know which figure in this painting is the emperor?

Chinese technologies spread west. Marco Polo, who traveled from Europe to China under the Mongols, described China's riches for Europeans in his writing.

Kublai Khan, the grandson of Genghis Khan, became emperor of China. He continued relying on the bureaucracy to rule China but filled government jobs with his followers. Chinese rebels overthrew the Mongols in the mid-1300s.

☑ READING CHECK **Understand Effects** What were the effects of the Mongols' conquest of China?

The Ming and the Manchus

In 1368, the Ming dynasty defeated the Mongols. The Ming returned to the use of examinations to choose government officials. They built a magnificent capital in Beijing.

Early Ming emperors were strong rulers, but later Ming emperors lost interest in government and focused on living in luxury. Corruption among officials grew, and as a result, the government was weak.

To strengthen China's trade connections, in the early 1400s the Ming emperor sent Zheng He (jung huh), a naval commander, to explore Southeast Asia and the Indian Ocean. Zheng He increased Chinese knowledge of these regions. Wherever Zheng went, he collected **tribute**, a payment from conquered peoples or to a more powerful country, for China. Later Ming rulers, however, restricted trade and closed many of China's ports. To defend China, the Ming rebuilt the Great Wall of China along their northern border.

As the Ming grew weaker, the wall failed to protect them. The Manchus, an ethnic group from the northeast, invaded China and overthrew the Ming in 1644. The Manchus founded the Qing (ching) dynasty and restored strong rule to China.

By the late 1700s, the Qing had conquered what are now western China, Taiwan, and Mongolia. Their conquests set China's modern borders. In the early 1800s, though, the Chinese economy weakened, poverty grew, and the Qing government lost some of its power.

☑ READING CHECK **Identify Cause and Effect** What caused the downfall of the Ming dynasty?

Chinese Achievements

Through trade, Chinese technologies and ideas spread far beyond China. Chinese culture had an especially strong influence on other parts of East Asia.

Chinese Technologies Chinese inventions that transformed the world include paper, printing, compasses, gunpowder, porcelain, and rudders and sealed compartments for ships. Europeans adopted these Chinese technologies. Chinese technologies also brought China wealth through trade. Foreign demand for Chinese silks and porcelains was high.

China's Cultural Reach China also had great artistic achievements. These included elegant paintings, ornate architecture, and powerful poetry. Chinese art and writing influenced artists and writers throughout East Asia and the world.

Chinese culture had an especially deep influence on neighboring countries. Korea and Japan adopted China's writing system. Chinese philosophies and Buddhism also reached Korea and Japan. Ideas from China helped shape the cultures of those countries.

READING CHECK Identify Cause and Effect How did Chinese technology affect the world?

Korean and Japanese Civilizations

To the east of China lie Korea and Japan. Both countries borrowed ideas from China but also created their own unique cultures.

Korea and Its Culture When the Tang dynasty came to power in China, Korea was divided into three kingdoms. In 668, the kingdom of Silla conquered the other two kingdoms and pushed Chinese forces out of Korea. Korea remained a united kingdom for most of the next 1,200 years.

During the 1200s, Koreans invented movable-type printing. Before this, Chinese printing required an entire page of characters to be carved from wood to print a page. With movable type, printers used one block of carved wood for each character. They could assemble these blocks to prepare a page for printing, and then take them apart and use them again in new combinations to make new pages. During the 1400s, Koreans invented an alphabet called Hangul. This alphabet was easier to use than the Chinese writing system.

Japan and Its Culture Around the same time that Korea unified, Japan became a unified country under an emperor. For much of Japan's history, the emperors were not strong. Instead, powerful military leaders called shoguns controlled Japan's government. The emperors were religious and symbolic leaders. During the 1400s and 1500s, Japan became fragmented. Power was divided among warlords, or military leaders who controlled a particular territory.

Analyze Images Korean printers used woodblocks with individual characters. **Draw Conclusions** How did this innovation make printing easier?

In 1600, Japan was reunified under the Tokugawa (toh koo GAH wah) shoguns. The Tokugawa ruled Japan for more than 200 years. The country prospered during this time of peace.

From the 700s to the 1100s, Japan had borrowed heavily from Chinese culture. Japan adopted the Chinese writing system. However, the Japanese also developed their own unique culture. For instance, the Japanese added new characters to the Chinese writing system and developed unique styles in art and architecture.

Japan had its own religious traditions. The traditional Japanese religion, called Shinto, is unique to Japan. **Shinto** is based on the worship of spirits and ideas of purity. Over time, though, the Japanese combined elements of Shinto and Buddhism to develop uniquely Japanese forms of Buddhism.

☑ READING CHECK **Draw Conclusions** Why do you think Tokugawa rule brought prosperity?

The Age of Imperialism

Beginning in the 1500s, Europeans began coming to East Asia to trade. European missionaries also brought Christianity to the region. Fearing that European ideas would disrupt their countries, the governments of Japan and Korea limited contact with the rest of the world. China also tried to restrict trade.

China Faces Foreign Domination Britain had been trading opium from its colony in India for Chinese tea. Opium is an addictive drug. Opium use was hurting Chinese families and communities. China tried to ban the drug, but Britain sent warships to bomb Chinese cities. Overpowered by a stronger military, China had to accept opium sales.

Analyze Diagrams
Confucianism and Shinto developed in East Asia. Buddhism came to the region from South Asia. **Compare** What feature of Shinto is similar to an important part of Confucianism?

COMPARING CONFUCIANISM, SHINTO, HINDUISM, AND BUDDHISM

CONFUCIANISM
- Ethical belief system to promote social order
- Five key relationships
- Filial piety

SHINTO
- Belief that spirits exist in natural forces
- Reverence for the spirits of ancestors

HINDUISM
- Many Gods as forms of cosmic God
- Karma and reincarnation
- Worship with ritual, meditation, doing duty

BUDDHISM
- Meditation as path to enlightenment
- Karma and reincarnation
- Life seen as suffering

Analyze Images Britain fought China's imperial forces in conflicts called the Opium Wars. **Use Visual Information** Based on this painting of Chinese ships in the foreground and a British vessel in the right background, which side had more powerful technology?

Meanwhile, European powers forced China to give them special privileges. These powers carved China into spheres of influence that they dominated economically. China's government was left with little power.

Angry at their government's weakness, the Chinese overthrew the Qing emperor in 1912. Still, foreign powers dominated the country. Mongolia declared independence from China but soon came under the control of the Soviet Union. In the 1920s, civil war broke out in China between Communists and a group called the Nationalists. Taking advantage of this conflict, Japan invaded China in the 1930s and ravaged the country during World War II.

Imperialism in Japan and Korea In 1853, American warships forced Japan to open its ports to trade. Alarmed at Western military superiority, Japanese rebels overthrew the shogun and **restored** the emperor. This time in Japanese history from 1868 to 1912 is called the **Meiji Restoration**, after Emperor Meiji. It marks the return to leadership of Japan's emperor. Japan's new government aimed to modernize Japan and its military and to industrialize.

Japan, in turn, forced Korea to open to trade in 1876. In 1910, Japan took full control of Korea. Under Japanese rule, Koreans had no political rights. The Japanese seized Korean land, forced Koreans to take Japanese names, and limited the use of the Korean language. Japan's harsh control of Korea continued through World War II.

During World War II, Japan occupied much of East and Southeast Asia and many Pacific islands. It attacked the United States in 1941. In response, the United States declared war on Japan. Japan was initially successful but was defeated in 1945, after the United States dropped two atomic bombs on Japanese cities.

✓ READING CHECK **Sequence** When and how did Japan take control of Korea?

Academic Vocabulary
restore • *v.*, to return to a former condition

 INTERACTIVE

The Meiji Restoration, 1868–1912

Quick Activity

What role has trade played in Chinese history? Use your Active Journal to reflect on this question.

The Cold War in East Asia

After World War II, the Cold War divided the region's countries into two groups: communist countries and those with market economies. Communist countries have command economies, based on government planning and control. The communist countries were China, North Korea, and Mongolia. These countries were allied with one another or with the Soviet Union.

Asian countries with market economies—Japan, South Korea, and Taiwan—were allied with the United States. Their market economies grew and eventually prospered.

China During the Cold War After Japan's defeat in 1945, Nationalists and Communists resumed their civil war in China. The Communists, led by Mao Zedong (mow dzuh doong), won in 1949. The Nationalists fled to Taiwan and established a dictatorship there with a market economy.

In Communist China, the government mismanaged the economy. The result was years with little economic growth. Millions died of starvation during the Great Leap Forward, a disastrous government program. To strengthen his grip on power, Mao launched what was called the Cultural Revolution in the 1960s. Mao's supporters killed opponents and further damaged the country's economy.

Korea and Japan After defeating Japan in World War II, the United States helped it rebuild. Japan began to recover quickly. An economic boom made Japan the second-largest economy in the world, after the United States, by the 1980s.

After Japan's defeat, Soviet troops occupied northern Korea. U.S. troops occupied the south. When North Korea attacked South Korea, the Korean War broke out. U.S. troops supported South Korea, while Chinese troops backed North Korea. When fighting ceased in 1953, Korea was divided. North Korea had a brutal communist dictatorship. South Korea had a dictatorship with a market economy.

☑ READING CHECK **Identify Cause and Effect** What impact did communism have on China?

▼ Car factories like this one helped drive Japan's economic growth in the late 1900s.

New Challenges for East Asia

Economic growth in South Korea and Taiwan brought demands for democracy. South Korea became a democracy in the 1980s, and Taiwan did so in the 1990s. The fall of the Soviet Union led to the end of communism in Mongolia, which had democratic elections in 1990.

Beginning in the late 1970s, China opened its economy to market forces. In 1989, protesters demanded political rights. Thousands gathered in Tiananmen (tyen ahn mun) Square in China's capital, Beijing. The communist government's brutal crackdown on this protest showed that it would not allow democracy or more freedoms for the Chinese people. Thousands of protesters were killed.

A growing market economy and a focus on manufacturing for export brought economic prosperity to China, however. By 2017, China had become the world's leading manufacturer and its largest economy by some measures.

North Korea's government-run economy continued to decline. North Koreans faced periods of starvation while their government imprisoned or killed its critics. In addition, North Korea developed nuclear weapons, which threatened the region.

☑ **READING CHECK** **Identify Main Ideas** What challenges have the region's countries faced since World War II?

Analyze Images In 1989, Chinese students demanded political rights in Tiananmen Square. **Draw Conclusions** What principle lay behind the Chinese government crackdown on the Tiananmen Square protests?

☑ Lesson Check

Practice Vocabulary

1. How did a **bureaucracy** improve government for China's rulers?

2. What changes did the **Meiji Restoration** bring to Japan?

Critical Thinking and Writing

3. Summarize What role did the United States play in Japan after World War II?

4. Identify Main Ideas Why did the United States get involved in the Korean War?

5. Synthesize Visual Information How does the Type of Government column in the Country Databank reflect the region's history after World War II?

6. Writing Workshop: Support Thesis With Details Write a thesis in your 📓 Active Journal that is supported by evidence in your sources. List these details to explain the costs and benefits of technology in East Asia for the report that you will write at the end of the topic.

Ming Porcelain

The Chinese first developed porcelain, a type of very fine pottery, during the Han dynasty. Later dynasties created porcelain using new technologies, colors, and methods. The porcelain created during the Ming dynasty became highly valued for its beauty. It was a trade good that was carried to Southwest Asia and Europe.

◄ Porcelain was a luxury item. Blue-and-white porcelain created during the Ming dynasty was valued for its elegance.

Reading and Vocabulary Support

① *Indigenous* means originally from a place.

② To *impose* something means to require it or force it to be.

③ What does this indicate about the reach of the emperor's government?

④ *Eclectic* means diverse, or drawing on many sources.

⑤ What explains the Mongol dynasty's openness to foreign influences?

"The early Ming dynasty was a period of cultural restoration and expansion. The reestablishment of an <u>indigenous</u> ① Chinese ruling house led to the <u>imposition</u> ② of <u>court-dictated styles in the arts</u> ③ ....

Early Ming decorative arts inherited the richly <u>eclectic</u> ④ legacy of the Mongol Yuan dynasty, which <u>included both regional Chinese traditions and foreign influences</u>. ⑤ For example, the fourteenth-century development of blue-and-white ware ... arose, at least in part, in response to lively trade with the Islamic world, and many Ming examples continued to reflect strong West Asian influences. A special court-based Bureau of Design ensured that a uniform standard of decoration was established for imperial production in ceramics, textiles, metalwork, and lacquer."

—Metropolitan Museum of Art, Heilbrunn Timeline of Art History (2002)

Analyzing Geographic Sources

Cite evidence from the primary source—the porcelain vase—and the secondary source—the art history text—to support your answers.

1. **Draw Conclusions** Why do you think porcelain was such a popular luxury trade good?

2. **Vocabulary: Use Context Clues** According to the secondary source, what influenced the style of Ming dynasty porcelain?

3. **Determine Author's Point of View** How does the author of the secondary source view the Ming government?

BOUNCE TO ACTIVATE ▶ VIDEO

GET READY TO READ

START UP
Examine the photograph of Shanghai, a Chinese city. What do you think it would be like to live in an environment like this?

GUIDING QUESTIONS
- Why are East Asia's people concentrated in certain areas?
- What religions do East Asians follow?
- What ethnic groups live in East Asian countries?

TAKE NOTES
Literacy Skills: Determine Central Ideas
Use the graphic organizer in your 📙 Active Journal to take notes as you read the lesson.

PRACTICE VOCABULARY
Use the vocabulary activity in your 📙 Active Journal to practice the vocabulary words.

Vocabulary	Academic Vocabulary
arable	corridor
steppe	confine
indigenous	
homogenous	

East Asia is a land of diverse landscapes that affect where and how people in the region live. The climates of the region range from arid desert and tundra to humid temperate and tropical. These climates affect settlement as well.

Where Do East Asians Live?
People are not evenly spread across countries in this region. They have been attracted to areas with opportunities to make a living.

China The environment partly explains patterns of population in China. Only about 15 percent of the country's area is **arable**, or able to grow crops. Most of this arable land is in eastern China. This is where people settled long ago to farm. China's big cities all developed here, originally to serve as markets for the farming population.

More than nine-tenths of China's people live in the east, and this area can be very crowded. Many of its cities are very large. Beijing and Shanghai both have more than 20 million people.

Other big cities have grown along the coast. A coastal location provides access to overseas trade.

Deserts and mountains cover much of central and western China. Those areas did not support farming in the past and offer little economic opportunity today. These regions are distant from markets and are not well located to serve as trade centers. For these reasons, these parts of China have fewer people than the heavily populated east.

Due to fewer opportunities for education and employment in rural areas, millions of Chinese people have been moving to cities. This movement of people has made China's cities grow faster. As a result, China's population has become even more concentrated in huge coastal cities.

Mongolia Much of Mongolia is covered by vast areas of grasslands called **steppes**. About half of all Mongolians are nomadic, living in tents and moving to follow herds of livestock across these plains. About a third of the population lives in the capital city of Ulaanbaatar, located in north-central Mongolia.

In Mongolia, cities have grown in recent years as herders have abandoned the steppes. Climate change has led to droughts and unusually harsh winters. Millions of livestock have died as a result, and herders have had to seek jobs in Ulaanbaatar and other cities.

North and South Korea In North and South Korea, most people live on the coastal plains because the interiors are mountainous. Population density is strikingly different in these two countries, however. South Korea has more than twice the population of North Korea, though it is smaller in size. As a result, it has a much higher population density than North Korea.

GEOGRAPHY **SKILLS**

Some areas of East Asia have very high population density.

1. **Region** Where are most of mainland China's largest cities located?

2. **Use Visual Information** Outside of mainland China, where is the population density greatest?

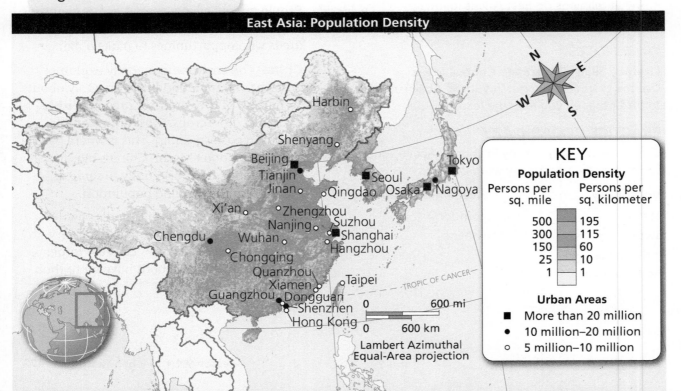

East Asia: Population Density

KEY

Population Density

Persons per sq. mile	Persons per sq. kilometer
500	195
300	115
150	60
25	10
1	1

Urban Areas

- ■ More than 20 million
- ● 10 million–20 million
- ○ 5 million–10 million

Lambert Azimuthal Equal-Area projection

Taiwan Like China, some parts of Taiwan are very crowded. Mountains cover much of the island, so most cities and farms are located on the plains along the west coast of the island. Almost three-quarters of Taiwan's population lives in coastal cities, including the capital of Taipei.

Japan Most Japanese people now live in coastal cities as well. Tokyo is the world's largest urban area. The Tokaido **corridor** holds more than three-fifths of the country's population. Tokyo, along with other cities such as Yokohama, Nagoya, Osaka, and Kobe, are located on this corridor. Hokkaido, the island nation's northernmost island, has cold winters, limited opportunities, and a small population.

In Japan, overcrowding in urban areas has resulted in creative space solutions. Skyscrapers and underground shopping centers hold large numbers of people. Pushers help push people into crowded subway cars. Capsule hotels enable travelers to get a night's sleep in a **confined** area.

▲ Public transportation, such as these high-speed trains in Taiwan, moves people efficiently in areas with high population density.

✓ **READING CHECK** Identify Cause and Effect How has East Asia's geography affected where people live?

Religion in East Asia

East Asia has many different religions. As you have learned, some of these religions developed internally, while others arrived through trade, missionaries, and travelers. Traditionally, most East Asians are Buddhist; followers of folk religion; Daoists; or, in Japan, followers of Shinto. Many East Asians combine elements of two or more of these religious traditions.

Islam, which began spreading from Southwest Asia in the early 600s, came to China hundreds of years ago. Traditionally, Muslims have formed a significant minority in China. Muslims form a majority in many communities in northwestern China.

In modern times, Christianity also spread to East Asian countries through missionaries and trade. Christianity is especially strong in South Korea, where about one-third of the people are Christian. Buddhism is also a major religion in South Korea. The Buddha's birthday is celebrated as a national holiday there. Religious freedom is a right in South Korea.

Partly because communist governments discouraged religion, many East Asians do not follow any religion. The Chinese government has made rules that control cultural and religious life in China. People cannot freely form groups to practice religion. The government limits the number of churches and religious organizations.

Academic Vocabulary
corridor • *n.*, a narrow, confined strip connecting one or more places
confine • *v.*, to limit or restrict

✓ **READING CHECK** Identify Main Ideas What religions have most East Asians historically followed?

👆 **INTERACTIVE**

Tokyo Living

Ethnic Diversity

Each of the countries of East Asia has one ethnic group that forms the majority. In Japan, a vast majority are ethnic Japanese. In both North Korea and South Korea, ethnic Koreans form an overwhelming majority. In Mongolia, Mongols make up the majority. In China and Taiwan, a majority of the population belongs to the Han ethnic group, sometimes called ethnic Chinese. The Han people are named after the Han dynasty of ancient China.

China While the majority of China's people are Han, China recognizes 55 ethnic minority groups. There are several more groups without official recognition. China's different ethnic groups are not evenly spread across the country. People of the Han ethnic group live mostly in the east. Many people who belong to minority groups live near the borders of the country, in western China, and in the hilly country of southern China. Mongols, Manchus, and ethnic Koreans live in China's north and northeast.

While some ethnic minorities, such as the Muslim Hui (hway), speak Chinese, many have their own languages. Each has a distinctive culture. Tibetans, while a minority in China as a whole, are a majority of the population of the Tibet region. The Muslim Uighurs (WEE gurz)—the largest ethnic group in the Xinjiang (shin jahng) region of northwestern China—have a language and culture similar to groups in Central Asia.

Taiwan Most of the people of Taiwan are Han Chinese. Han people migrated to the island in the 1600s. Taiwan also has indigenous ethnic groups. **Indigenous** means living in a region since ancient times.

▼ Muslims worship in the north-central Chinese province of Ningxia.

These groups lived on the island for thousands of years before the ethnic Han arrived. The indigenous people comprise only a small percentage of the total population.

Japan Japan is ethnically **homogenous,** meaning almost all people belong to the same ethnic group. The Japanese ethnic group is more than 98 percent of the population.

The northernmost island of Japan, Hokkaido, has a minority group called the Ainu who may have lived in Japan longer than the ethnic Japanese. The Ainu largely migrated north as ethnic Japanese farmers gradually expanded north over hundreds of years. Japan also has a small ethnic Korean minority. With such an ethnically uniform population, the country has experienced little ethnic conflict.

North and South Korea North and South Korea are similar to Japan in that they are essentially homogenous. In fact, they are among the most homogenous countries on Earth. The ancestors of Koreans have lived on the peninsula for thousands of years. North Korea's population includes small numbers of Chinese and Japanese who migrated to the country in the mid-1900s. South Korea's population also has a small Chinese minority. The vast majority in both Koreas, though, is ethnic Korean.

☑ READING CHECK **Use Evidence** Why are the majority ethnic groups in Korea and Japan even more dominant than the Han in China?

▲ An Ainu ritual expressing gratitude for nature in Hokkaido

☑ Lesson Check

Practice Vocabulary

1. How has the location of **arable** land in China affected population density in the past and present?

2. How do the **steppes** in Mongolia affect how people live?

Critical Thinking and Writing

3. **Compare and Contrast** How does East Asia's climate affect settlement patterns?

4. **Recognize Multiple Causes** Which country in the region has the greatest ethnic diversity? Why might this be so?

5. **Identify Main Ideas** Which religions entered East Asia from outside the region?

6. **Writing Workshop: Support Ideas with Evidence** Write examples in your 🗐 Active Journal of ways that technology is connected to population in East Asia. Think of both costs and benefits.

East Asia at Work

BOUNCE TO ACTIVATE ▶ VIDEO

GET READY TO READ

START UP

Study the image of manufacturing workers in China and quickly preview the headings in the lesson. What do the image and the headings tell you about the economies of East Asia?

GUIDING QUESTIONS

- What kind of government does each East Asian country have?
- How do the economies of China, North Korea, South Korea, and Japan compare with one another?

TAKE NOTES

Literacy Skills: Classify and Categorize

Use the graphic organizer in your 📔 Active Journal to take notes as you read the lesson.

PRACTICE VOCABULARY

Use the vocabulary activity in your 📔 Active Journal to practice the vocabulary words.

Vocabulary

autocracy   sanction

veto   malnutrition

hydroelectric
  power

Academic Vocabulary

reliant

orient

Since the 1970s, several countries of East Asia have seen rapid economic growth, changing their people's lives. Some have also moved toward democracy. Although China's economy has changed dramatically, China and North Korea remain firmly under the control of communist governments.

Governments of East Asia

As you have learned, East Asia has a long history of rule by monarchs and military leaders. Contact with the Western world exposed the region to democratic ideas beginning in the 1800s. Today, East Asian governments fall into two main categories: autocracies and democracies.

Autocracies China and North Korea are communist autocracies. An **autocracy** is a government controlled by one person who has not won a free election. Citizens have no real voice in choosing government officials or policies. In China and North Korea, unelected communist leaders control the government. They appoint government officials and make policy decisions.

Democracies The other countries in the region are democracies. There are two main types: presidential and parliamentary. Japan is a parliamentary democracy, so voters choose representatives in parliament. The party in parliament with the most seats chooses the prime minister, who runs the government. Japan is also a constitutional monarchy. The emperor of Japan has no real power in the government, but he serves as the symbolic leader of the country.

South Korea is a presidential democracy like the United States. Voters elect a president, who is both head of the government and head of state, or the symbolic leader of the country. They also elect members of a parliament that makes laws, just like the U.S. Congress.

Taiwan and Mongolia have what are called semi-presidential democracies. In their systems, a president is elected and suggests someone to be prime minister. Parliament must approve that person for him or her to take office. The prime minister is in charge of the government, while the president has some powers. In Mongolia, for instance, the president can veto laws passed by the legislature. To **veto** is to stop or cancel the action of a government official or body.

☑ READING CHECK **Compare and Contrast** Describe the types of government in power in East Asia.

Economies of East Asia

Trade is important to all of the economies of East Asia. Japan, China, Taiwan, and South Korea have achieved rapid economic growth by building export industries. Mongolia has focused on exporting raw materials to China. With little trade, North Korea remains impoverished.

Types of Economies Most of the economies in East Asia are mixed economies, yet the roles of government and markets vary widely.

BIOGRAPHY
5 Things to Know About

XI JINPING
Chinese leader (born 1953)

- Xi Jinping (shee jin ping) became leader of the Chinese Communist Party in 2012 and president of China in 2013.

- Xi has largely been a party loyalist known for acting carefully.

- Xi Jinping was a teen during the Cultural Revolution and was forced to move to the countryside for six years, where he worked alongside peasants.

- His father was a high Communist Party official who criticized party leadership and was frequently imprisoned.

- Xi received a college degree in chemical engineering from Tsinghua University in Beijing in 1979.

Critical Thinking How might Xi Jinping have found a place in the Communist Party leadership despite his father's history?

In North Korea, a command economy controls most aspects of economic life, with markets playing a minor role. The government makes all three economic decisions: what to produce, how to produce it, and for whom it will be produced. China also has a command system controlled by the government. However, China's system has more elements of a market economy, in which individuals make these economic choices. For instance, heads of businesses have some power to make decisions about the firms they run. In addition, the government allows some private ownership, and most prices are set in markets.

South Korea, Japan, and Taiwan all have mixed economies in which markets play a dominant role. However, governments have worked closely with industries to try to promote economic growth. Governments have enacted policies aimed at keeping prices low on imported raw materials and to discourage consumer spending. The goal has been to boost production of goods for export.

Natural Resources Natural resources play a key role in China and Mongolia. Both have large deposits of coal, on which they are largely **reliant** for their energy. North Korea has ample coal supplies, as well. North Korea and China also rely heavily on hydroelectric power. **Hydroelectric power** is the power produced by water-driven turbines to generate electricity.

Academic Vocabulary
reliant • *adj.,* dependent

China's steel industry depends on its coal and iron ore deposits, though China also imports these and many other natural resources. Mining is a key industry in Mongolia, where copper, gold, and metals are taken from the earth in addition to coal. North Korea, like China, has iron ore deposits. These deposits support its steel industry. However, in the other East Asian countries, natural resources are limited. Japan, Taiwan, and South Korea have to rely on imports because they have few natural resources.

Human Resources Many countries in East Asia have turned to a different type of resource: human resources. East Asians value education and invest heavily in it. Most East Asians learn valuable skills.

Analyze Images Workers and shoppers throng a busy street in Seoul, South Korea. **Use Visual Information** How does the image show that South Korea has a productive mixed economy?

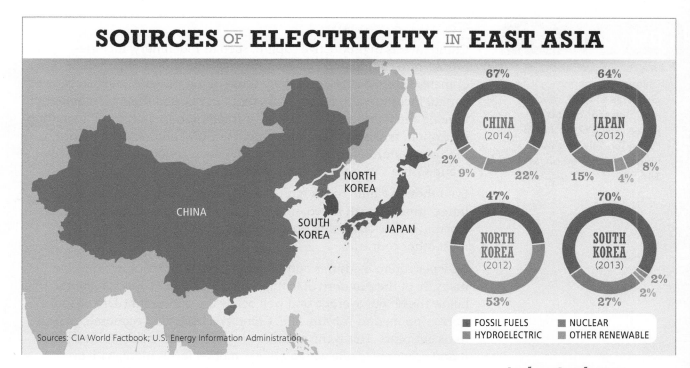

SOURCES OF ELECTRICITY IN EAST ASIA

CHINA (2014): 67%, 22%, 9%, 2%

JAPAN (2012): 64%, 8%, 4%, 15%

NORTH KOREA (2012): 47%, 53%

SOUTH KOREA (2013): 70%, 27%, 2%, 2%

- ■ FOSSIL FUELS
- ■ HYDROELECTRIC
- ■ NUCLEAR
- ■ OTHER RENEWABLE

Sources: CIA World Factbook; U.S. Energy Information Administration

Japan, South Korea, and Taiwan rely on the knowledge and skills of working people to make products that can be sold in other countries. This revenue in turn can buy resources from other countries.

Most East Asian economies depend on manufacturing and service industries. In fact, East Asia has more manufacturing jobs than any other region in the world. China's manufacturing sector is larger than that of any other country.

✔ **READING CHECK** Classify and Categorize List the type of economy found in each country in East Asia.

Trade in East Asia

Countries benefit when they specialize in producing what they are best at producing and trade with other countries for other products. For example, several East Asian countries, including Japan, South Korea, Taiwan, and China, specialize in producing electronic consumer goods. They have workers and companies that are skilled in producing these goods and can do so more efficiently than other countries. They sell the goods they produce in a global market and buy the goods and services they cannot produce efficiently from other countries.

Trade barriers such as tariffs, quotas, embargoes, and protective regulations can stand in the way of trade. As such, several of the countries in East Asia have made trade agreements with one another or with other countries to reduce trade barriers and increase trade.

✔ **READING CHECK** Summarize What are factors that encourage and limit trade?

Analyze Graphs East Asian countries depend on different energy sources to generate electricity. **Classify and Categorize** Which two countries depend most on hydroelectric power?

Quest CONNECTIONS

Why is China's demand for energy soaring? How will this affect its need for natural resources? Record your findings in your ▤ Active Journal.

Analyze Images Eastern China has benefited from specialization and trade. Many schools there have technology in the classroom. **Compare and Contrast** What aspects of this school are similar to yours? What are different?

China's Economy

China invests in productive capital, such as machinery, factories, offices, and computers. This investment is one source of economic development. Chinese cities, especially those along the coast, have received capital investment in recent years that has boosted their economies by making them more productive. Investment in human capital, including education, makes people more productive and allows them to earn a higher standard of living. Literacy rates are a reflection of such investment. China's 96 percent literacy rate is very high.

Even though China ranks high globally on a global entrepreneurship index, Japan, South Korea, and Taiwan are even more highly ranked. Starting a new business is easier in these four countries than it is in most other countries.

GDP per capita measures output per person in an economy. It is one measure of the standard of living. China's GDP per capita is slightly below the global average and well below the per capita GDPs of South Korea, Japan, and Taiwan. Still, China has had rapid economic growth in recent years. This is the result of the government's shift from a command economy to one with a greater market focus, along with an emphasis on rapid economic growth that began in the 1970s.

In the 2010s, however, China's growth slowed, due in part to limits on freedom and overinvestment in less productive, government-owned parts of the economy. Corruption on the part of government officials has been another problem for the economy. Extreme economic inequality has also hurt the economy. A few very rich Chinese have built huge fortunes, while most Chinese have low incomes that limit the development of a consumer economy.

☑ READING CHECK **Understand Effects** What does China's literacy rate say about its economy?

Analyze Images Few North Koreans can take advantage of this road, one of many large government infrastructure projects. **Draw Conclusions** Why do you think there are so few cars on the road?

North Korea's Economy

North Korea's command economy has shown very poor results over the years. Because North Korea's economy is so weak, there is little money available to invest in productive capital. Meanwhile, the government invests its limited resources in its unproductive military. As a result, North Korea has many weapons and much military equipment, including nuclear weapons, but it cannot manufacture many other products. Its factories and workers are among the least productive in the world.

North Korea's economy has also been hurt by sanctions placed on it due to its nuclear weapons program. **Sanctions** are actions that attempt to force a country to follow international law. They have limited the country's ability to trade. Unlike other countries in the region, entrepreneurship is not allowed in North Korea. This has also limited business and economic growth.

North Korea claims to have a 100 percent literacy rate, which would reflect a significant investment in human capital. However, experts question this claim because there is no evidence to support it. The educational system in the country is not strong.

The GDP of North Korea is far below the global average and well below any other country in East Asia. Despite the country's wealth in natural resources, North Koreans have a low standard of living and often face severe food shortages and even death from starvation. **Malnutrition**, or lack of enough nutrients from food, remains a problem for many North Koreans.

✓ **READING CHECK** Identify Cause and Effect Why is North Korea's economy weak?

South Korea's Economy

Academic Vocabulary
orient • *v.*, to tend toward; to adjust or adapt to

Even though South Korea has a limited supply of natural resources, it has a strong, market-**oriented** economy. Since the 1940s, when the Koreas were divided, South Korea has outperformed North Korea, showing the advantage of a market-driven economy over a command economy. Unlike North Korea, South Korea's businesses have invested heavily in productive capital. This has led to strong economic growth.

South Korea's literacy rate is higher than that of China, making it higher than the global average. South Korea has one of the best educational systems in the world. Because of the country's investment in education, people are more skilled and productive and earn a higher standard of living. South Korea's workforce is able to produce expensive, technologically advanced goods more efficiently than workers elsewhere.

Entrepreneurship is encouraged. In fact, South Korea ranks high among world countries for the ease of starting new businesses. Within the region, it is ahead of China and just behind Japan and Taiwan.

✔ READING CHECK **Compare and Contrast** Why has South Korea's economy grown since it was separated from North Korea, while North Korea's economy has remained weak?

Japan's Economy

Analyze Diagrams
This diagram shows how government control over the economy varies in the region. **Synthesize Visual Information** Why is China's economy farther to the left of the diagram than Japan's or South Korea's?

Japan has very few natural resources beyond its soil and water. Even the supply of arable land is limited. Much of the country is covered by mountains where farming is not possible. Japan imports most of the natural resources it uses and has had to develop other strengths.

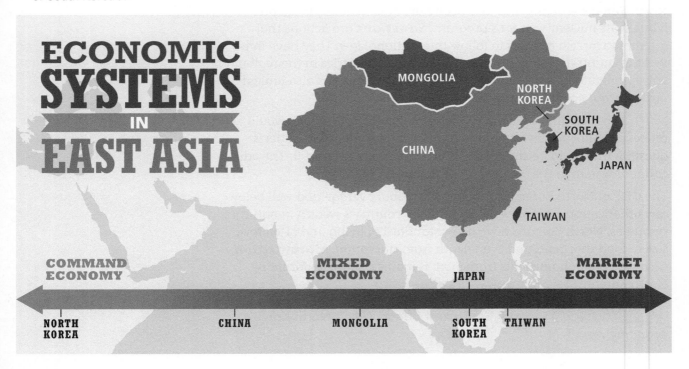

ECONOMIC SYSTEMS IN EAST ASIA

MONGOLIA
NORTH KOREA
SOUTH KOREA
CHINA
JAPAN
TAIWAN

COMMAND ECONOMY — MIXED ECONOMY — JAPAN — MARKET ECONOMY

NORTH KOREA   CHINA   MONGOLIA   SOUTH KOREA   TAIWAN

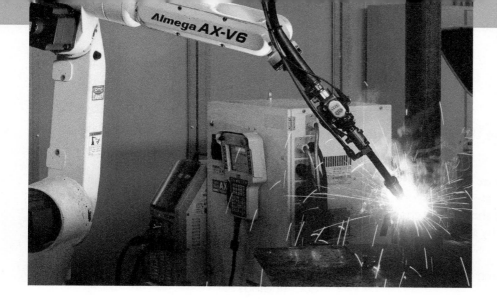

◄ Investment in advanced technology like this robot has boosted the success of economies in East Asia.

Lacking resources and surrounded by water, Japan has relied on trade. Its location also led Japan to develop one of the largest fishing industries in the world.

Investment in human and productive capital has been very important to Japan. Japan's skilled workforce is able to produce goods and services while taking advantage of advanced technologies more efficiently than workers elsewhere. This has made Japan one of the world's most successful producers of high-value products. Because of this investment, Japan also has one of the world's most productive economies.

The literacy rate in Japan is 99 percent, which is above the global average and the highest in the region. Investment in education and skills training has enabled many people in Japan to earn high wages and enjoy a high standard of living. Japan also encourages entrepreneurship. It is prosperous partly because it is so easy to start businesses there.

 **READING CHECK** **Draw Conclusions** Why is Japan's GDP so high?

☑ Lesson Check

Practice Vocabulary

1. Why is **malnutrition** a problem in North Korea?

2. Why is **hydroelectric power** an important energy source?

Critical Thinking and Writing

3. **Draw Conclusions** What conclusion can you draw about the connection between investing in productive and human capital and a country's GDP? Which countries in East Asia have invested wisely with good results?

4. **Compare and Contrast** What are the literacy rates in East Asia, and how do they affect the standard of living?

5. **Use Evidence** What explains the difference between North Korea's per capita GDP (from the Country Databank) and those of neighboring countries?

6. **Writing Workshop: Choose an Organizing Strategy** Based on what you have learned from this lesson and your sources about the costs and benefits of technology in East Asia, create a structure for your research paper in your ▱ Active Journal.

Analyze Data

Follow these steps and use the sources to analyze data and draw conclusions.

INTERACTIVE

Analyze Data and Models

1 **Read the title and look at the data given.** Starting with this step helps you learn about the data set shown in a chart or graph. Think about why these data are shown.

    a. What is the title of each graph?

    b. What does each graph show?

2 **Study the numbers, lines, or colors.** Taking this step will help you find out what the graphs or data show. Look for patterns such as similarities or differences in the data.

    a. What patterns do you see in the first graph?

    b. What pattern do you see in the second graph?

    c. How would you relate those two findings?

3 **Interpret the graphs or data sets by comparing them.** Break down the data to compare. What conclusions can you draw from comparing them?

Secondary Source

Per Capita GDP, Selected Countries, 2015

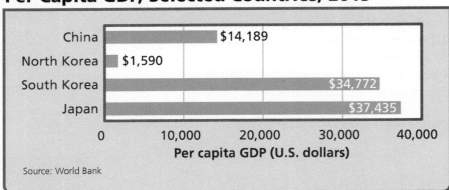

Source: World Bank

Secondary Source

Education, Selected Countries

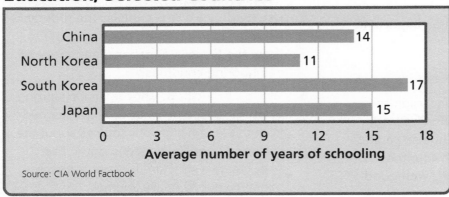

Source: CIA World Factbook

LESSON 6
Challenges Facing East Asia

GET READY TO READ

START UP
Study the photo of people in China's capital, Beijing. How would living in this environment affect people's lives?

GUIDING QUESTIONS
- What are the main economic challenges facing East Asia?
- What political issues pose threats to East Asia?
- What environmental challenges do people in East Asian countries face?

TAKE NOTES

Literacy Skills: Use Evidence
Use the graphic organizer in your 📓 Active Journal to take notes as you read the lesson.

PRACTICE VOCABULARY
Use the vocabulary activity in your 📓 Active Journal to practice the vocabulary words.

Vocabulary	Academic Vocabulary
demography	strain
reservoir	dispute
tsunami	

Many East Asian countries have strong economies, but they still face challenges. Several face economic risks, and tensions between countries threaten peace in the region. The region also faces serious environmental challenges, some of which result from economic activity.

What Economic Challenges Does the Region Face?

Some countries in East Asia face economic risks due to their dependence on exports. Others have aging workforces and shrinking populations, which make it hard for their economies to grow.

Relying on Exports The largest East Asian economies have all grown rapidly by producing goods for export outside the region. Investment has poured into export businesses. Government policies have also favored exporters.

Because workers in China and other countries receive relatively low pay and benefits, consumers in these countries have less to spend than those in the United States and Europe.

INTERACTIVE

Japan's Aging
Population

These countries lose out on growth that could take place through increased consumption by consumers at home. At the same time, their dependence on exports makes them vulnerable to economic downturns in Europe and the United States.

Trade East Asian economies are also hurt by trade barriers they have created. These barriers were meant to protect each country's businesses and to make sure that these countries exported more than they imported. Trade barriers block the potential for growth by letting countries specialize in what they make best.

A trade agreement among East Asian countries would help boost growth within the region. Political tensions among the countries in the region, however, have prevented them from making an agreement.

Demography Japan faces a serious problem with its **demography**, or population trends. Its population is shrinking, and so is the country's workforce. The number of babies born each year is lower than the number of people retiring. Japan has an aging population, or one in which a growing share of the population is elderly and retired. As a result, more and more elderly people must be supported by a shrinking workforce. These factors mean that economic growth faces **strains**. Economic growth is more difficult to achieve when the number of workers is falling.

Academic Vocabulary
strain • *n.*, pressure, stress

In response to this problem, businesses have increased the use of robots and computers, and the government has increased the retirement age. It could also remove restrictions on trade and other forms of economic activities, or make it easier for foreign workers to immigrate to Japan. Japanese voters are opposed to this idea, however.

✓ **READING CHECK** **Use Evidence** What economic issue do you think is the biggest challenge for the region to overcome? Use text evidence to support your response.

▼ A container ship loaded with trade goods is docked in Qingdao harbor in China.

What Political Challenges Does the Region Face?

Serious tensions among nations in the region pose an ongoing risk of conflict. The most serious issue in the region is North Korea's development of dangerous nuclear weapons and missiles.

Nuclear Weapons All countries in the region have condemned North Korea's nuclear weapons program, which threatens peace in the region. Any military action against North Korea's nuclear facilities, however, would likely result in a North Korean attack on South Korea that could kill millions of people.

World leaders have tried to persuade North Korea to stop developing nuclear weapons. The United States and other countries have pressured North Korea to give up these weapons, but its leaders have refused.

Land Claims Tensions exist between Japan and other countries in the region because of Japanese aggression during World War II. Conflicting land claims in the region are another source of conflict. Japan claims certain islands that are also claimed by China or South Korea. These **disputes** over territory could erupt into fighting.

Chinese claims to islands in the South China Sea also conflict with claims by Southeast Asian countries. China has been building military facilities on some of these islands in violation of international law.

Control of these islands would give China control of important shipping routes. By threatening U.S. naval power in the Pacific Ocean, China's claims also threaten world peace.

Political Freedom Both China and North Korea have authoritarian governments that limit people's freedom. North Korea's government is by far the harsher of the two, imprisoning many of its people in grim detention camps. Both governments limit people's access to information sources such as the Internet.

At the same time, in both China and North Korea, people face many injustices and unresponsive governments. Hong Kong, a former British colony, was promised democracy when China took possession of it in 1997, but China's government has blocked real democracy there.

✓ READING CHECK Compare and Contrast How does political freedom in North Korea and China differ from that in other countries in the region?

▲ North Korea has pushed to develop nuclear weapons and missiles like this one.

Academic Vocabulary
dispute • *n.,* a disagreement or debate

▲ Three Gorges Dam in central China was built in the 1990s and 2000s. It generates as much power as 15 coal power plants, but it caused damage to the environment and displaced more than a million people.

Quick Activity

How has technology affected East Asia? Write an answer in your 📕 Active Journal, based on one of these categories: economy, transportation, daily life, environment. Label your answer with the correct category.

Quest CONNECTIONS

How do you think the disaster at Fukushima has affected Japan's energy policy? Record your findings in your 📕 Active Journal.

What Environmental Challenges Does the Region Face?

East Asian governments have often pursued fast economic growth without considering the impact of their actions on the environment. The result is widespread serious pollution of the region's air, soil, and water supplies.

Water and Energy A serious problem in China is a shortage of clean water. Northern China has a fairly dry climate. As a result, it does not have enough water to meet the needs of its farmers, its hundreds of millions of people, and the industries where people work. Plans to address the water shortages in North China by pumping water from South China threaten to damage the environment.

China also faces a risk of flooding. Throughout the country's history, flooding from rivers has caused much damage to crops and homes and millions of deaths.

The Chinese government built the Three Gorges Dam along the Chang (or Yangzi) River to control flooding and produce hydroelectric power. The dam produces nearly 10 percent of China's total energy. Newly built ship canals also make transport along the river easier.

However, building this dam was disruptive and expensive. A 400-mile-long **reservoir**, or storage pool of water, now extends behind the dam. More than a million people had to be moved because their homes were flooded by the reservoir. The rising waters of the reservoir covered many historic sites along the river. China's leaders had to balance these costs with the need for new sources of energy.

China is also the world's largest producer of greenhouse gases, or gases that scientists believe are raising temperatures worldwide. This temperature rise threatens to melt ice sheets and raise sea levels worldwide. That endangers millions of people in East Asia who live in coastal lowlands.

Plate Tectonics The position on Earth's crust of Japan, the Koreas, and Taiwan also poses a challenge to these countries. Four tectonic plates meet in the region. The plates are slowly moving together. The result is great pressure that causes earthquakes.

Earthquakes that occur under the sea can make huge waves. These **tsunamis**, or tidal waves, can flood coastal areas.

In 2011, a powerful earthquake hit near the northeastern coast of Honshu, Japan's largest island. Tsunamis surged onshore and caused major damage, killing about 18,500 people. The two disasters caused an even worse problem. A nuclear power plant in Fukushima was damaged, contaminating the water, air, and soil with radioactivity. Because it has few fossil fuel resources, Japan had turned to nuclear power. The accident at Fukushima showed how earthquakes and tsunamis made this a risky choice.

The movement of tectonic plates poses another threat. As the Pacific Plate sinks beneath Japan, it releases gases that melt rock above it. The molten rock rises to Earth's surface, creating volcanic eruptions. Japan has 108 active volcanoes.

Pollution Environmental problems are especially severe in China, where farm fertilizers, industry, and sewage have polluted the water supplies that cities and farmers depend on. This pollution has affected the Chang River, the largest river in East Asia.

Air pollution from coal-burning factories and power plants and from vehicle exhaust in China has resulted in some of the world's worst air pollution. Studies suggest that millions of Chinese die early because of air pollution. The land around Beijing is so dry that sandstorms blow into the city, adding to the problem.

The Chinese government has made some attempts to control pollution. It has ordered industrial plants in and around Beijing to close for short periods. Long-term solutions have not yet been put in place.

▲ A scene of devastation in northern Japan left by the 2011 earthquake and tsunami

☑ **READING CHECK** **Identify Cause and Effect** What are the causes and effects of pollution in China?

☑ Lesson Check

Practice Vocabulary

1. Why is the **demography** of Japan a challenge to that country?

2. Why did building the Three Gorges Dam and filling its **reservoir** cause problems?

Critical Thinking and Writing

3. **Identify Cause and Effect** What are the causes and effects of water pollution in China?

4. **Identify Main Ideas** How does North Korea pose a political challenge for the region?

5. **Use Evidence** Is producing hydroelectricity from dams a good solution to China's energy challenges? Base your response on evidence from the text.

6. **Writing Workshop: Write an Introduction** Write an introductory paragraph in your 📖 Active Journal for your essay on the costs and benefits of technology in East Asia. Include your thesis sentence.

☑ Review and Assessment

VISUAL REVIEW

Chinese Achievements

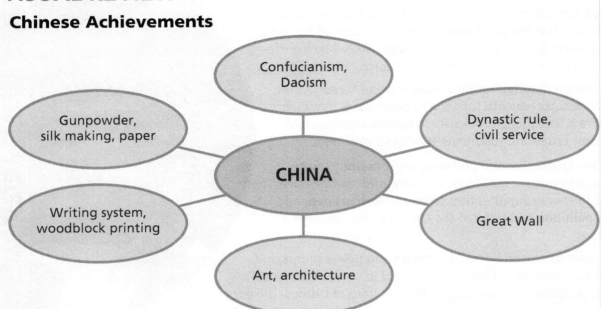

Comparing Governments and Economies in East Asia

Country	Government	Economy
China	Authoritarian communist state	Mixed, with strong command component; export orientation
Japan	Constitutional monarchy; parliamentary democracy	Mixed market; highly productive
North Korea	Authoritarian communist state	Command system; low output and living standard
South Korea	Presidential democracy	Mixed market; highly productive

READING REVIEW

Use the Take Notes and Practice Vocabulary activities in your 📕 Active Journal to review the topic.

 **INTERACTIVE**

Practice vocabulary using the Topic Mini-Games.

 **FINDINGS**

Discuss Your Opinion

Get help preparing for your discussion in your 📕 Active Journal.

ASSESSMENT

Vocabulary and Key Ideas

1. **Identify Main Ideas** How did **filial piety** relate to **Confucianism**?

2. **Describe** What traveled on the **Silk Road**?

3. **Identify Main Ideas** Explain the significance of the **Meiji Restoration**.

4. **Explain** How does the presence of **arable** land affect where China's people live?

5. **Describe** How is a changing **demography** affecting Japan?

6. **Recall** How has **hydroelectric power** helped China limit its use of fossil fuels?

7. **Check Understanding** In which economic sector does East Asia lead the world?

Critical Thinking and Writing

8. **Draw Conclusions** Why do you think that the United States wished to help rebuild Japan after World War II?

9. **Compare and Contrast** How is the role of citizens in government similar and different among the countries in East Asia?

10. **Use Evidence** Using the Country Databank, compare GDP per capita among the countries of East Asia. Use evidence from the text to explain the differences.

11. **Identify Main Ideas** How did the Japanese and Korean people borrow parts of Chinese culture and then change them?

12. **Revisit the Essential Question** How has technology both benefited and harmed the countries of East Asia?

13. **Writing Workshop: Conduct a Research Project** Using the questions and notes you wrote in your 📓 Active Journal, answer the following question in a three-paragraph research paper: What are the costs and benefits of technology in East Asia?

Analyze Primary Sources

14. From what source does this excerpt most likely come?

    A. the Mandate of Heaven
    B. the *Dao De Jing*
    C. the *Analects*
    D. Buddhist scripture

"Master, You said: It is rare to find a person who is filial to his parents and respectful of his elders, yet who likes to oppose his ruling superior. And never has there been one who does not like opposing his ruler who has raised a rebellion."

Analyze Maps

Use the map at right to answer the following questions.

15. Where did Chinese civilization begin?

16. Which is the vast plain where China's most populous cities are found?

17. Which region was the site of a military conflict during the Cold War?

18. Where did tsunamis following a powerful earthquake kill thousands of people in 2011?

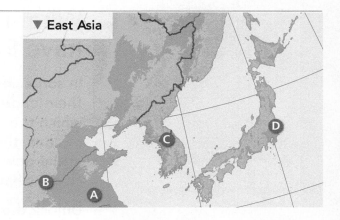

▼ East Asia

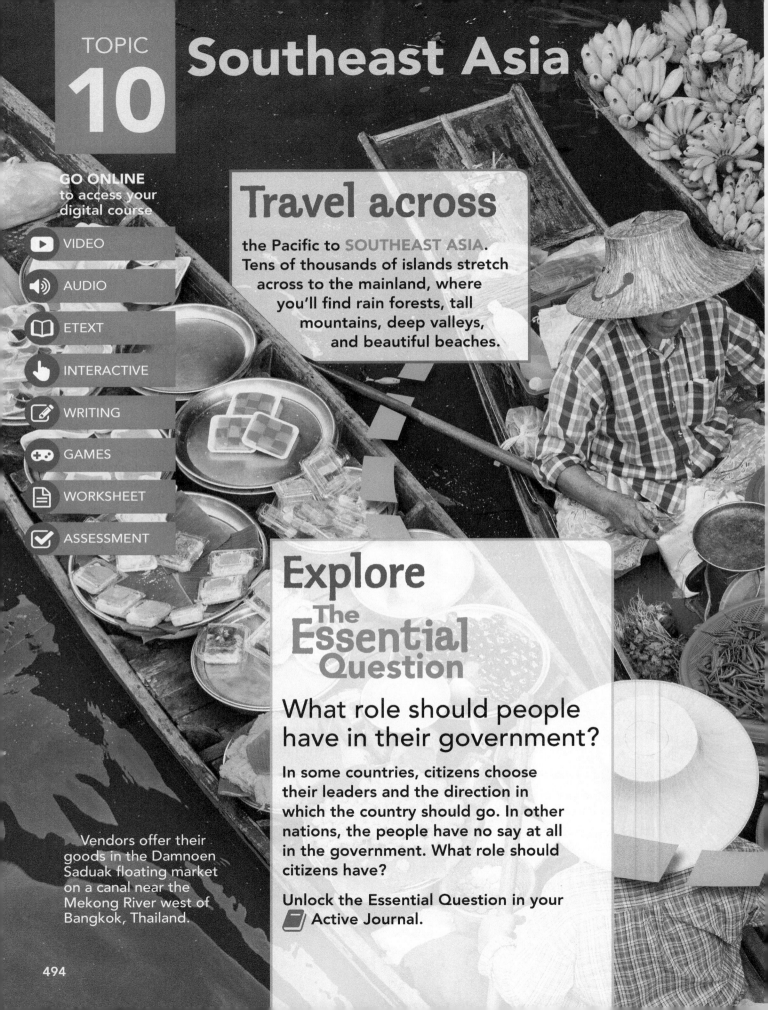

Southeast Asia

Travel across

the Pacific to SOUTHEAST ASIA.
Tens of thousands of islands stretch
across to the mainland, where
you'll find rain forests, tall
mountains, deep valleys,
and beautiful beaches.

Explore
The
Essential
Question

What role should people have in their government?

In some countries, citizens choose
their leaders and the direction in
which the country should go. In other
nations, the people have no say at all
in the government. What role should
citizens have?

Unlock the Essential Question in your
📓 Active Journal.

Vendors offer their
goods in the Damnoen
Saduak floating market
on a canal near the
Mekong River west of
Bangkok, Thailand.

Read

about a region where you can find many kinds of people, from rice farmers to giants of international finance.

Watch

BOUNCE TO ACTIVATE ▶ VIDEO

A Minangkabau Wedding

Meet Ridwan, an Indonesian boy who is helping friends and family prepare for his cousin's wedding.

10 Regional Atlas

Southeast Asia: Political

MAINLAND AND ISLANDS

Southeast Asia lies between the Indian and the Pacific oceans. It consists of a mainland area to the north and thousands of islands to the south.

Learn more about Southeast Asia by making your own map in your 📓 Active Journal.

INTERACTIVE

Topic Map

A Cultural Crossroads

Mainland Southeast Asia contains six countries wedged between its giant neighbors, India and China. Over the centuries, trade with India brought South Asian culture to the region, as shown by this Buddhist site in Thailand. The culture of China had a strong impact on Vietnam.

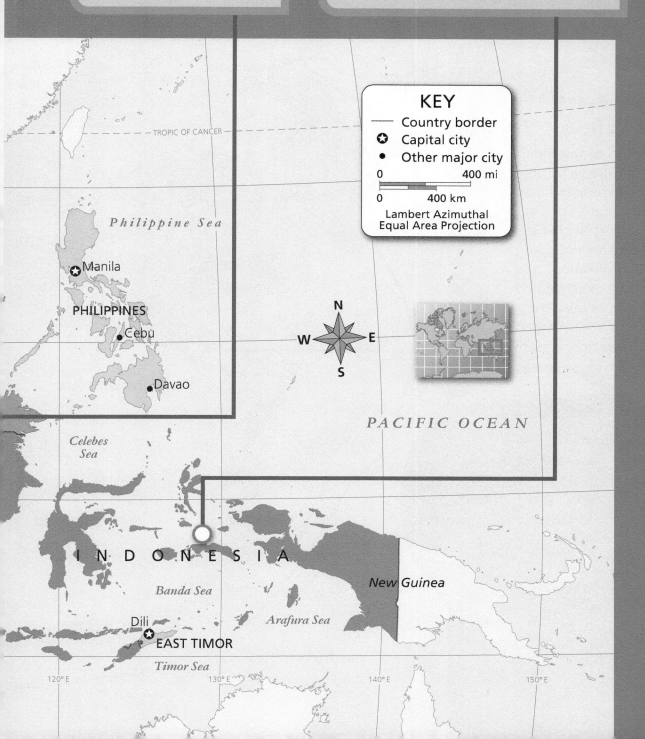

A Divided Country

Most of Malaysia's people live in the western part of the country, in mainland Southeast Asia, but the country also includes territory on the island of Borneo in island Southeast Asia.

An Island Country

The region's largest country is Indonesia, stretching thousands of miles or kilometers across thousands of islands. Indonesia, with 260 million people, ranks just behind the United States in population.

KEY
— Country border
⊛ Capital city
• Other major city

0   400 mi
0   400 km
Lambert Azimuthal
Equal Area Projection

TROPIC OF CANCER

Philippine Sea

⊛ Manila

PHILIPPINES

• Cebu

• Davao

Celebes Sea

N
W   E
S

PACIFIC OCEAN

I N D O N E S I A

Banda Sea

New Guinea

Arafura Sea

Dili
⊛ EAST TIMOR

Timor Sea

120° E   130° E   140° E   150° E

Southeast Asia: Physical

PLATE TECTONICS

Southeast Asia lies mainly on the Eurasian plate of Earth's crust, which is squeezed between the Pacific, Australian, and Indian plates.

Learn more about Southeast Asia by making your own map in your 📔 Active Journal.

INTERACTIVE

Topic Map

Fertile Valleys

The collision of the Indian plate with Eurasia formed the highest mountains of mainland Southeast Asia. This area's fertile plains and valleys saw the rise of its first civilizations and are home to most people today. River valleys like this one in Vietnam are used to grow rice, a staple food in the region.

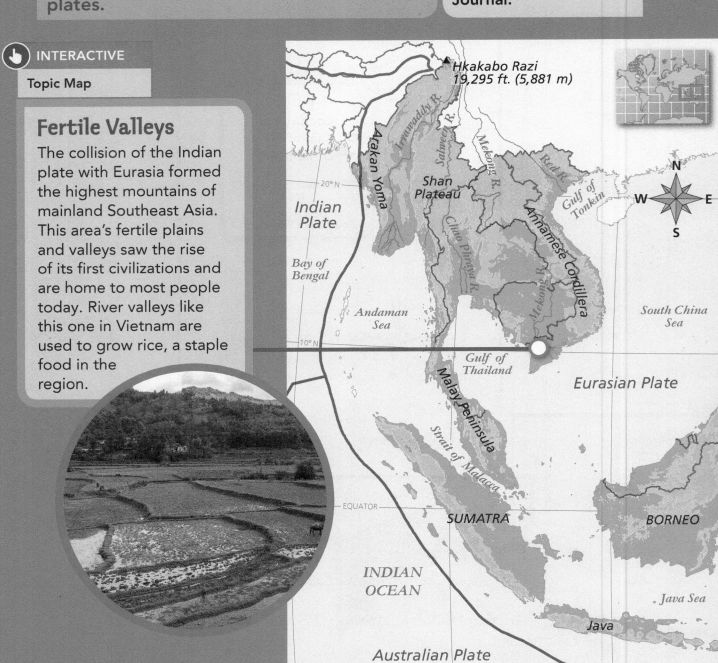

Hkakabo Razi
19,295 ft. (5,881 m)

Arakan Yoma
Irrawaddy R.
Salween R.
Mekong R.
Red R.
Gulf of Tonkin

Shan Plateau

Indian Plate

Chao Phraya R.

Annamese Cordillera

South China Sea

Bay of Bengal

Andaman Sea

Mekong R.

Eurasian Plate

Gulf of Thailand

20° N

10° N

N
W E
S

Malay Peninsula
Strait of Malacca

SUMATRA

BORNEO

EQUATOR

INDIAN OCEAN

Java Sea

Java

Australian Plate

10° S

90° E   100° E   110° E

Volcanic Islands

Where oceanic crust is forced beneath continental crust, the friction melts rock, which rises to the surface to form volcanoes. This process has shaped volcanic islands such as Java, Sumatra, Mindanao, and Luzon.

A Separate Island

New Guinea, at the southeastern edge of the region, is not on the Eurasian plate. It shares the Australian plate with Australia.

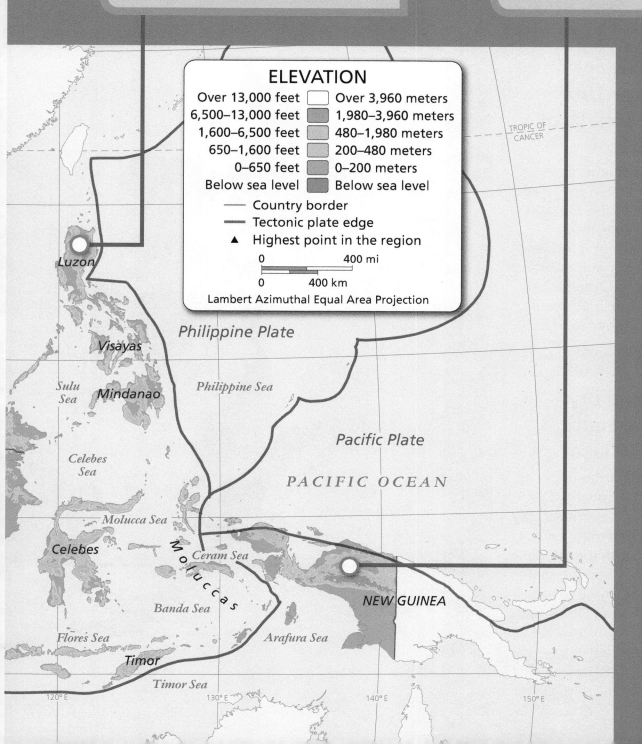

ELEVATION

Over 13,000 feet		Over 3,960 meters
6,500–13,000 feet		1,980–3,960 meters
1,600–6,500 feet		480–1,980 meters
650–1,600 feet		200–480 meters
0–650 feet		0–200 meters
Below sea level		Below sea level

— Country border
— Tectonic plate edge
▲ Highest point in the region

0 ——— 400 mi
0 ——— 400 km

Lambert Azimuthal Equal Area Projection

TROPIC OF CANCER

Luzon
Visayas
Sulu Sea
Mindanao
Philippine Plate
Philippine Sea
Philippine Plate
Celebes Sea
Pacific Plate
PACIFIC OCEAN
Molucca Sea
Celebes
Moluccas
Ceram Sea
Banda Sea
NEW GUINEA
Flores Sea
Arafura Sea
Timor
Timor Sea

120° E   130° E   140° E   150° E

Regional Atlas

Southeast Asia: Climate

A Tropical Region

Almost all of Southeast Asia lies within the tropics. A band of heavy rainfall called the intertropical convergence zone (ITCZ) forms a belt around Earth within the tropics. The ITCZ shifts north from May to September and south from November to March.

Rainy and Dry Seasons North of the Equator

Tropical wet and dry climates exist to the north and south of the Equator. Bangkok, Thailand, averages about 8 inches (200 mm) of rain per month from May to October but less than 1 inch (25 mm) from December to March.

Rainy and Dry Seasons South of the Equator

The pattern is the opposite south of the Equator. Dili, in East Timor, averages only 2 inches (50 mm) of rain or less per month from June to November, but more than 5 inches (125 mm) of rain per month from December to March.

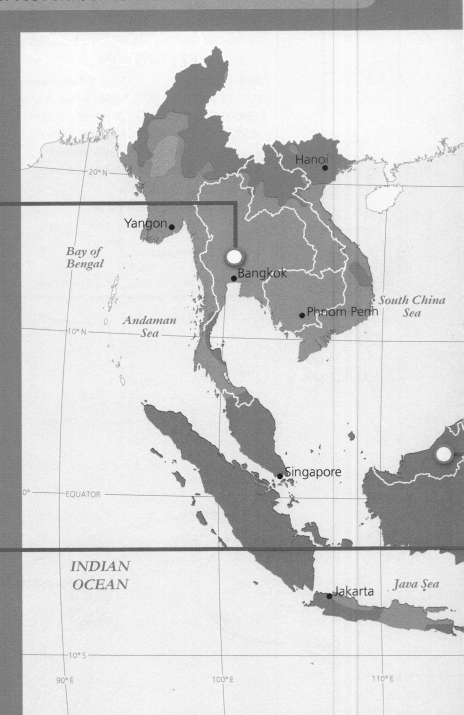

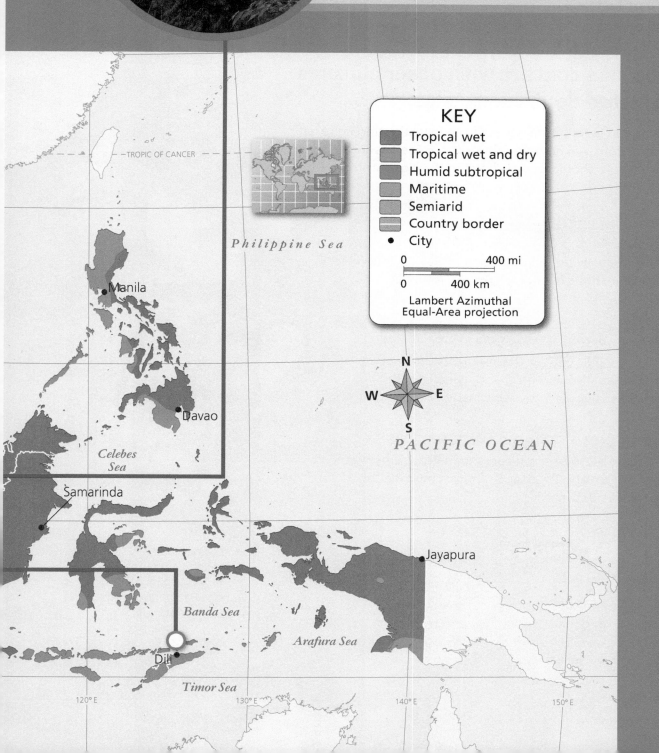

A Warm, Rainy Zone

Temperatures in the tropics are very warm all year, and the ITCZ gives Southeast Asia plenty of rain, especially near the Equator. This climate supports the growth of tropical rainforests, such as this forest in Sarawak, Malaysia.

KEY

- Tropical wet
- Tropical wet and dry
- Humid subtropical
- Maritime
- Semiarid
- Country border
- City

```
0          400 mi
0          400 km
```

Lambert Azimuthal
Equal-Area projection

TROPIC OF CANCER

Philippine Sea

Manila

Davao

Celebes Sea

Samarinda

Banda Sea

Jayapura

Arafura Sea

Dili

Timor Sea

N W E S

PACIFIC OCEAN

120° E   130° E   140° E   150° E

Quest
Document-Based Writing Inquiry

Studying Cultural Connections

Quest KICK OFF

Southeast Asia today is home to a blend of cultures. This blend is a product of history. Over thousands of years, traders, explorers, and other travelers have brought their languages, religions, and systems of government to Southeast Asia.

How has contact with other cultures affected Southeast Asia?

What you learn in this Quest from investigating cultural interactions will help you think about the Essential Question, "What role should people have in their government?"

1 Ask Questions

Preview the topic to come up with questions you have about cultural interaction in this region. Record your questions in your 📔 Active Journal.

2 Investigate

As you read the lessons in the topic, look for **Quest CONNECTIONS** that illustrate cultural interaction in the region and its results. Record notes in your 📔 Active Journal.

3 Examine Primary Sources

Next, explore primary sources that document cultural interaction and its effects. Collect information in your 📔 Active Journal.

Quest FINDINGS

4 Write Your Informative Essay

After your investigation is complete, write an essay explaining your observations and drawing a conclusion from them. Get help for writing your essay in your 📔 Active Journal.

▲ A dancer in Bali, Indonesia, performs a scene from the *Ramayana*, an ancient epic poem of India.

Early History of Southeast Asia

GET READY TO READ

START UP

Look at the image of Angkor Wat, a temple complex built in the 1100s in Angkor, the capital of the Khmer empire. Preview this lesson to find out what modern-day country Angkor is in.

GUIDING QUESTIONS

- When did people first come to Southeast Asia?
- How did geography and trade shape the early cultures of Southeast Asia?
- How did Europeans change Southeast Asia?

TAKE NOTES

Literacy Skills: Sequence
Use the graphic organizer in your ✍ Active Journal to take notes as you read this lesson.

PRACTICE VOCABULARY

Use the vocabulary activity in your ✍ Active Journal to practice the vocabulary words.

Vocabulary	Academic Vocabulary
empire	incorporate
sultanate	crucial
Indochina	
ethnic group	

Southeast Asia was a crossroads for sea trade routes between South Asia and East Asia. Its ancient civilizations borrowed from those neighboring cultures while they also developed unique features of their own.

The First Civilizations in Southeast Asia

The human history of Southeast Asia stretches back many thousands of years. The first people came by boat. Later arrivals came by land. Over time, complex civilizations developed in the region.

Early Arrivals The first Southeast Asians arrived tens of thousands of years ago. By 5,000 years ago, people were farming in fertile valleys and plains of mainland Southeast Asia. Small villages spread across the region.

A group called the Austronesians migrated across island Southeast Asia and the Malay Peninsula around 2000 BCE. The Austronesians were skilled seafarers and rice farmers. Austronesian languages are still spoken in Malaysia and island Southeast Asia today.

👆 INTERACTIVE

Angkor Wat

China Expands City-states and kingdoms began to develop on the Southeast Asian mainland. They appear for the first time in Chinese and Indian records around 200 BCE. Less than a hundred years later, Han China had conquered the northern and central parts of what is now Vietnam.

For around 1,000 years, the Chinese controlled much of Vietnam. The Vietnamese people adopted Buddhism, Confucianism, and Daoism from the Chinese.

Trade Brings New Ideas Southeast Asians traded with peoples to both the northeast and the west. Trade with South Asia began around 200 BCE. South Asian traders were attracted by the gems, ivory, and valuable timber of mainland Southeast Asia and by the valuable nutmeg and other spices produced in the Spice Islands.

Traders and travelers brought new ideas as well. Religions such as Hinduism and Buddhism spread to kingdoms and empires across Southeast Asia. Southeast Asian cultures also **incorporated** the writing systems and architectural styles of South Asia.

Academic Vocabulary
incorporate • v., to blend or merge

The Birth of Empires Southeast Asian city-states thrived based on rice farming. Kingdoms arose and conquered other groups, becoming **empires**, or states containing several countries.

The most powerful of these empires was the Khmer empire. Its center was the city of Angkor in what is now Cambodia. Around 1200 CE, Khmer Buddhists built a spectacular group of monasteries and temples called Angkor Wat.

Another major empire was called Srivijaya (shree vee JY uh). Like the Khmer empire, Srivijaya was mostly Hindu and Buddhist.

GEOGRAPHY SKILLS

This map shows the locations of the Srivijaya and Khmer empires and important trade routes connecting them to the rest of the world.

1. **Place** The Khmer empire comprised all or part of which present-day countries?

2. **Infer** Which empire do you think produced more and better sailors? Explain your answer.

Southeast Asian Empires and Trade Routes Around 1000

to India, Sri Lanka, and Africa

CHINA

Mekong River

Angkor

South China Sea

PACIFIC OCEAN

Philippine Islands

N W E S

KEY
Srivijaya empire
Khmer empire
Trade route

Malacca

Borneo

The Moluccas (Spice Islands)

Sumatra

Palembang

INDIAN OCEAN

0   600 mi
0   600 km
Lambert Azimuthal Equal-Area projection

Java

Starting in the 500s CE, Srivijaya became wealthy and powerful because it controlled the **crucial** trade routes between the Indian and Pacific oceans.

☑ READING CHECK **Identify Main Ideas** How did economics affect the cultures of Southeast Asia beginning around 200 BCE?

Buddhist and Muslim Monarchies

The Chinese, Khmer, and Srivijaya empires were not the only political powers in Southeast Asia. Other governments— some smaller, some larger—also made their way into the area.

Buddhist Kingdoms on the Mainland Beginning in the 800s, a series of Buddhist kingdoms controlled much of what is now Myanmar. They shaped a culture that continues to this day.

In the 900s, the Vietnamese finally regained independence from China. The Vietnamese kingdom existed until the 1800s.

In Thailand, the first Buddhist Thai kingdom developed in the 1200s. A later Thai kingdom defeated the Khmer empire and united most of Thailand in the 1400s.

Muslim Sultanates in the Islands Islam came from South and Southwest Asia along Indian Ocean trade routes. During the 1200s, Islam began to spread along these routes through the Malay Peninsula and the islands of Southeast Asia.

Then, in the 1400s, Muslim sultanates spread across the area. A **sultanate** is a monarchy headed by a sultan. The Sultanate of Malacca controlled much of the Malay Peninsula. The Sultanate of Brunei controlled much of the island of Borneo. Other sultanates controlled the rest of Borneo, the island of Java, and parts of other islands, including the Philippines.

☑ READING CHECK **Compare and Contrast** How did the Buddhist and Muslim states differ?

How Did Westerners Affect the Region?

In the late 1400s and 1500s, European explorers roamed across the globe. Like earlier travelers, they came to Southeast Asia because of its rich spice trade.

European Conquests The first Europeans to reach Southeast Asia were Portuguese. They arrived in the 1500s and conquered Malacca, a Muslim sultanate, in 1511. In the 1600s, the Dutch came to the region and gradually took over most of the Portuguese territory.

During the 1800s, the British conquered what are now Myanmar, Malaysia, and Singapore, and the French conquered the region called **Indochina**. Indochina is the peninsula that includes the countries of Cambodia, Laos, and Vietnam.

Analyze Images This photograph shows a gamelan, a type of musical group that originated on the Indonesian islands of Java and Bali. **Compare and Contrast** How does this gamelan differ from a traditional Western orchestra?

Academic Vocabulary
crucial • *adj.*, essential, decisive

Quest CONNECTIONS

How might European colonists have contributed to the culture of Southeast Asia? Record your thoughts in your 📓 Active Journal.

Imperialism in Southeast Asia, 1900

Western Power	Modern Countries Occupied
United Kingdom	Myanmar (Burma), Malaysia, Singapore, Brunei
Netherlands	Indonesia
France	Laos, Cambodia, Vietnam
Portugal	East Timor
United States	Philippines

Analyze Charts This chart shows the European powers that colonized Southeast Asia and the nations those colonies became after they achieved independence. **Synthesize** Which is the only Southeast Asian country that was not conquered by Europeans?

The only part of Southeast Asia that avoided conquest by Western powers was the kingdom of Thailand.

Filipinos rebelled against their Spanish rulers starting in the late 1800s. In 1898, during the Spanish–American War, the United States invaded the Philippines. It defeated Spain and made the Philippines a U.S. colony.

Populations on the Move The Western powers aimed to profit from their control. They built railroads, seaports, and cities to export resources from the region to Europe and the United States.

During the colonial period, large numbers of Chinese and Indian people migrated to Southeast Asia. These groups formed ethnic minorities in the region. An **ethnic group** is a group of people who share a distinct culture, language, and identity.

☑ READING CHECK **Draw Conclusions** Why was the United States the last Western power to colonize Southeast Asia?

☑ Lesson Check

Practice Vocabulary

1. What outside **ethnic groups** came to or had an influence on Southeast Asia before 1800?

2. What modern countries were in **Indochina**?

Critical Thinking and Writing

3. **Sequence** In what order did these peoples come to southeast Asia: Austronesians, Chinese, Europeans, Muslims, traders from South Asia?

4. **Classify and Categorize** What are the major religions in Southeast Asia? Where did they come from?

5. **Identify Cause and Effect** Why did Western powers want colonies in Southeast Asia?

6. **Writing Workshop: Narrow Your Topic** At the end of the topic, you will write an explanatory essay about how the role of citizens in Southeast Asian governments has changed over time. Work on narrowing your topic in your 📔 Active Journal.

LESSON 2
Independent Southeast Asia

GET READY TO READ

START UP

The Philippines gained independence in 1946. In 1986, Corazon Aquino (shown here wearing yellow) became the country's first democratically elected president. Do you think 40 years is a long time to establish democracy?

GUIDING QUESTIONS

- How did Southeast Asian countries win independence?
- Why did the Vietnam War take place?
- How have Southeast Asian political systems changed?

TAKE NOTES

Literacy Skills: Analyze Text Structure
Use the graphic organizer in your 📖 Active Journal to take notes as you read this lesson.

PRACTICE VOCABULARY

Use the vocabulary activity in your 📖 Active Journal to practice the vocabulary words.

Vocabulary
Cold War   Vietnam War
communist   coup
containment

Academic Vocabulary
collaborate
equip

By the end of the 1800s, almost all of Southeast Asia was a colony of one or another of the Western powers. In most of these colonies, independence movements developed in the early 1900s, but independence did not come until after World War II.

World War II and Independence

In the 1930s, Japanese troops invaded China and then kept moving south. By 1942, Japan occupied nearly all of Southeast Asia.

Nations Gain Independence During the war in many areas, resistance groups fought for both independence and an end to Japanese occupation. With Japan's defeat in 1945, Southeast Asians demanded independence from Western colonial powers.

The United States granted independence to the Philippines in 1946. Myanmar, Malaysia, and Singapore were all British colonies. They won independence, with little bloodshed, between 1948 and 1965.

Even before the end of World War II, Indonesian nationalists had declared independence from the Netherlands.

Winning Independence, 1945–1965

1946
Republic of the Philippines gains independence.

1948
Myanmar granted independence.

1953–1954
Laos and Cambodia gain independence.

1965
Singapore leaves Federation of Malaysia, becomes independent.

| 1945 | 1950 | 1955 | 1960 | 1965 |

1949
Indonesia wins independence.

1957
Federation of Malaya granted independence, expands to become Malaysia in 1963.

1945
Led by Ho Chi Minh, Vietnam declares independence, faces war and division until 1975.

Sources: CIA World Factbook; The Commonwealth

Analyze Timelines Most Southeast Asian countries achieved independence soon after World War II ended. **Identify Supporting Details** Which country entered into a voluntary union upon independence but later left that union?

Academic Vocabulary
collaborate • *v.*, to work jointly

👆 **INTERACTIVE**

Vietnam, 1945–1965: From Independence Struggle to Cold War Battleground

A war of independence began, lasting four years. The Dutch gave up and acknowledged Indonesian independence in 1949.

East Timor did not win independence from Portugal until 1975. It was quickly seized by Indonesia and remained part of that country until 2002. Meanwhile, the sultanate of Brunei gained independence in 1984.

Trouble Begins in Indochina In French Indochina, communist leaders declared the independence of Vietnam in 1945. In an attempt to retain control, France sent in troops to fight the communists. In 1953, the French granted independence to Cambodia and Laos.

In 1954, the French acknowledged communist control of northern Vietnam. They withdrew their forces from the north. Several countries, including France and the United States, **collaborated** to set up an anti-communist government in southern Vietnam. This left Vietnam divided between two rival governments. The government in the south quickly became a dictatorship.

✓ READING CHECK **Compare and Contrast** How was Indonesia's path to independence different from Malaysia's?

Why Was the Vietnam War Fought?

French withdrawal from North Vietnam did not resolve the conflict there. Instead, Vietnam became a battleground in a bigger conflict.

The Domino Theory The period after World War II was dominated by the **Cold War**. This was a struggle between **communist** countries, led by the Soviet Union, and countries with market economies, led by the United States. Communism was a political and economic system in which the state owns all property and the government makes all economic decisions. In the Cold War, the United States and the Soviet Union competed for influence over other countries. They did not fight each other directly, but they sponsored wars around the world between countries under each side's influence.

American leaders and their allies believed that a communist government in one country would force communism on its neighbors. One country after another would become communist, like a row of dominoes tipping over. The United States adopted a policy of preventing communism from spreading, called **containment**. In Southeast Asia, the United States pursued containment by assisting the anti-communist dictatorship in South Vietnam.

Meanwhile, North Vietnam was backed by China and the Soviet Union. Together, they promoted communist rebels in South Vietnam, Cambodia, and Laos.

The Conflict Escalates On August 2, 1964, an American naval ship exchanged gunfire with several North Vietnamese patrol boats. In response, Congress authorized direct military action. Over the next decade, hundreds of thousands of American troops were sent to fight the communist Vietnamese in the **Vietnam War**.

Starting on January 31, 1968, communist forces carried out a major series of attacks in the South. Americans and South Vietnamese suffered heavy losses. It became clear that the communists could not be defeated and that the government of South Vietnam lacked the support of its people. In the United States, the public turned against the war.

Moving Toward Peace Starting in 1969, the United States tried to **equip** South Vietnam to handle its own defense. The number of U.S. troops was gradually reduced.

In 1973, the Paris Peace Accords were signed. U.S. combat troops completed their withdrawal in 1973, but fighting continued.

In 1975, communist forces overran South Vietnam and overthrew its government. U.S. diplomats and advisors struggled to escape the South Vietnamese capital as communist troops closed in. The following year, Vietnam was reunited under a communist government.

INTERACTIVE

Fighting a Different War

Academic Vocabulary
equip • *v.*, to supply with the necessary items; to prepare

Analyze Images During the Vietnam War, U.S. soldiers often came in contact with Vietnamese civilians. **Infer** What do you think these soldiers are doing? Why are they doing it?

Also in 1975, communist forces won power in Cambodia and Laos. The communist Cambodians, known as the Khmer Rouge, slaughtered their enemies and many other people as well. By 1978, at least 1.5 million people—one fifth of the country's population—had been killed. Vietnamese forces overthrew the Khmer Rouge and created a new communist government in Cambodia under Vietnamese control.

✔ **READING CHECK** **Identify Cause and Effect** Why did the United States begin to look for a peaceful solution to the war?

Authoritarian Government or Democracy?

After the war, Western powers' involvement in Southeast Asia lessened. Each country could chart its own path. Communist governments held power in some countries. Others had governments that were authoritarian but not communist. Some developed democracies.

Types of Dictatorships Laos and Vietnam have lived under authoritarian communist dictatorships since the 1970s. Hun Sen, a former communist, has been the president of Cambodia since the 1980s. The country has held elections since 1993, but Hun has always won. He has retained power by limiting freedom of speech and controlling elections.

Malaysia and Singapore also have had regular elections, but the same political party has remained in power in both countries since independence. They stay in control by enacting laws that limit democratic freedoms. When Indonesia won independence, it formed a democratic government, but its first president, Sukarno, imposed authoritarian rule.

The tiny country of Brunei has been a sultanate since it gained independence. The sultan is an absolute monarch who has total control of the country.

BIOGRAPHY
5 Things to Know About

SUKARNO
President of Indonesia from 1949 to 1966 (1901–1970)

- Sukarno was a leader of Indonesia's independence movement and its first president.

- He played a large role in creating the modern Indonesian language.

- He had great charisma and was an inspiring speaker.

- In the late 1950s, Sukarno canceled elections, dismissed the parliament, and set up a government-run economy.

- Sukarno was forced from office after the military put down a coup attempt and then seized power itself.

Critical Thinking The economy Sukarno established in the late 1950s was similar to the economies of which other Southeast Asian countries?

Struggles for Democracy Other countries in the region have alternated between democratic and authoritarian government. In many countries, the military is a strong political force. When military leaders have felt their power threatened, they have seized control of the government. The sudden seizure of a government, often by force, is known as a *coup d'état* (koo day TAH), or **coup** (koo).

Popular opposition has removed some dictators from power or forced them to hand over control to an elected government. This happened in the Philippines and Indonesia during the 1980s and 1990s.

Analyze Images Troops occupy a neighborhood in Yangon, the largest city in Myanmar, in 2007. **Identify Main Ideas** How does the government of Myanmar differ from the government of the United States?

In other cases, military governments have allowed elections. But they have imposed constitutions that give them veto power over the actions of democratically elected governments. Military governments in Myanmar and Thailand imposed constitutions like these on their countries during the 2010s. Thailand's constitution moved it away from democracy, but Myanmar's constitution was actually a step toward democracy. Elections gave Myanmar's people some voice in the government, though the military still held much of the power.

☑ READING CHECK **Identify Supporting Details** What evidence shows that the nations of Southeast Asia have very different political systems?

☑ Lesson Check

Practice Vocabulary

1. What is the main difference between a **communist** economy and a market economy?

2. Why is the conflict between the United States and the Soviet Union in the second half of the 1900s called a **Cold War**?

Critical Thinking and Writing

3. **Summarize** the political events in Southeast Asia since World War II.

4. **Compare and Contrast** How are elections in Singapore different from elections in the Philippines?

5. **Revisit the Essential Question** What role did the people of the Philippines and Indonesia have in their governments in the 1980s and 1990s?

6. **Writing Workshop: Develop a Clear Thesis** In your 📓 Active Journal, write a sentence that expresses how the role of citizens in government has changed over time, based on your reading of Lessons 1 and 2. This sentence will become the thesis statement for an essay.

The End of the Vietnam War

By 1975, the United States had withdrawn all combat troops from Vietnam and greatly reduced the flow of money and weapons. On April 21, South Vietnamese President Nguyen Van Thieu gave a speech to his parliament announcing his resignation.

◀ Nguyen Van Thieu

Reading and Vocabulary Support

① Why does Nguyen make this comparison?

② Whose lives is Nguyen referring to here?

③ ARVN stands for Army of the Republic of Vietnam, South Vietnam's army.

④ Constituents are people represented by an elected official.

⑤ What do you think NVA stands for?

Primary Source

"You don't fight by miracles. You need high morale and bravery. But even if you are brave, you can't just stand there and bite the enemy. And we are fighting against Russia and China. We're having to bargain for aid from the United States like haggling for fish in the market ① and I am not going to continue this bargaining for a few million dollars when your lives ② are at stake. . . . You Americans with your 500,000 soldiers in Vietnam! You were not defeated . . . you ran away!"

—Nguyen Van Thieu, speech to parliament, April 21, 1975

Secondary Source

"In early March the North Vietnamese launched . . . what was expected to be a two-year offensive to secure South Vietnam. As it happened, the South's government and army collapsed in less than two months. Thousands of ARVN ③ troops retreated in disorder. . . . [U.S. President] Gerald R. Ford . . . pleaded in vain with Congress for additional military aid . . . . But members of Congress, like most of their constituents ④, were ready to wash their hands of a long and futile war. On April 21 [Nguyen Van] Thieu resigned and flew to Taiwan. On April 30 what remained of the South Vietnamese government surrendered unconditionally, and NVA ⑤ tank columns occupied Saigon without a struggle."

—Encyclopaedia Britannica, "Vietnam War"

Analyzing Geographic Sources

1. **Distinguish Fact From Opinion** Find one opinion, one fact, and one reasoned judgment in the sources quoted above.

2. **Compare Authors' Treatment of Similar Topics** How do the primary source and the secondary source treat Nguyen Van Thieu's resignation differently?

LESSON 3
Living in Southeast Asia

GET READY TO READ

START UP
Over 2,000 years ago, farmers dug terraces into these hillsides in the Philippines to create flat spaces for planting. Why do you think this is not done in the United States?

GUIDING QUESTIONS
- Why do people live where they do in Southeast Asia?
- How do cultures differ within Southeast Asia?

TAKE NOTES
Literacy Skills: Summarize
Use the graphic organizer in your 📓 Active Journal to take notes as you read this lesson.

PRACTICE VOCABULARY
Use the vocabulary activity in your 📓 Active Journal to practice the vocabulary words.

Vocabulary	Academic Vocabulary
terrain	factor
delta	characteristic
indigenous	

The natural resources of a region are one **factor** that influences where people choose to live. In ancient times, newcomers to Southeast Asia were attracted to areas of rich soil on the mainland and the volcanic islands. Today, large populations are concentrated in the same areas that attracted settlement in ancient times.

Where People Live in Southeast Asia

Why do Southeast Asians live where they do? Compare the population density map with the physical and climate maps in your Regional Atlas to find out.

Water: Too Much or Too Little? Notice on the climate map that no part of Southeast Asia has an arid climate. This means that population growth is generally not limited by a lack of water.

Notice, though, that much of the region has a wet, tropical climate. The heavy rains that are part of this type of climate can produce the opposite problem: swamps and thick rainforests.

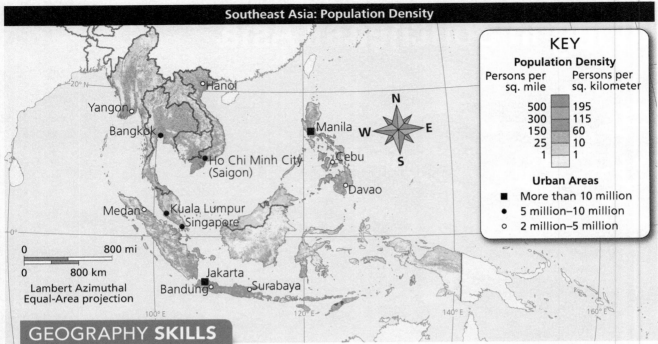

KEY

Population Density

Persons per sq. mile	Persons per sq. kilometer
500	195
300	115
150	60
25	10
1	1

Urban Areas

■ More than 10 million

● 5 million–10 million

○ 2 million–5 million

0 · 800 mi
0 · 800 km

Lambert Azimuthal Equal-Area projection

GEOGRAPHY SKILLS

This map shows how population density varies across Southeast Asia.

1. **Region** Which areas of Southeast Asia are the least densely populated?

2. **Synthesize Visual Information** Based on this map and the physical map in your Regional Atlas, do mountainous areas tend to be densely populated or sparsely populated?

Because these environments are not suitable for farming, they can support few people. This is true of much of Indonesia, including the islands of Sumatra and Sulawesi and the western part of New Guinea.

Farming: Easy or Difficult? A physical map shows a place's **terrain**, or physical features. On the physical map, find the rugged mountains of mainland Southeast Asia. Notice the steep terrain of much of the Philippines and the Indonesian island of Sulawesi. Now look at those same areas on the population density map. The rough terrain makes travel and farming difficult, so fewer people have settled there.

Notice that some of the greatest population densities are in the coastal plains and inland valleys. The coastal plains are the site of river **deltas**. River deltas form at the mouths of rivers, where fertile sediment washed down from the mountains is deposited. This creates flat areas with good water supplies that are ideal for farming. The Mekong River delta covers much of southern Vietnam and has a very high population density. Coastal areas have also attracted people seeking opportunity through trade.

There are also high population densities in areas surrounding the volcanic mountains of Java and Sumatra, the biggest islands of southwestern Indonesia. This is because volcanic ash produces very fertile soil that attracted farmers. Later, cities grew to serve those farmers and handle trade for those rich regions.

☑ READING CHECK **Identify Main Ideas** What factors determine whether a given area can support a large population?

Cultural Diversity in Southeast Asia

Southeast Asia has great cultural diversity. Waves of migration from the north have brought Burmese, Thai, and Lao peoples into mainland Southeast Asia. The ancient Austronesian migration brought settlers to the region by sea. Today, Chinese, Indians, Malays, Vietnamese, Thai, Khmer, and many other ethnic groups all call the region home. Some groups are **indigenous**, which means originally from a place. Indigenous Southeast Asian peoples have mixed customs and ideas from many cultures with their own local cultural traditions.

Many Different Religions In ancient times, Buddhism and Hinduism spread across the region. They were brought from the west by traders. They spread along trade routes and into the countryside.

Vietnam adopted Chinese forms of Buddhism, while the rest of mainland Southeast Asia adopted forms from India. Buddhism is still the major religion in mainland Southeast Asia, except in Malaysia.

A few hundred years ago, Islam came to the region along those same trade routes. It spread into what are now Malaysia, Brunei, Indonesia, and the southern Philippines. For many years, Indonesia has had the largest Muslim population of any country in the world. Today, several other Southeast Asian countries have Muslim minority populations.

Later, European colonial powers brought Christianity to the region. Christianity is the dominant, or main, religion of the Philippines and East Timor and is a minority religion in other countries.

Ethnic Diversity In mainland Southeast Asia, each country has a majority ethnic group. For example, ethnic Thais are the largest group in Thailand, and ethnic Vietnamese are the largest group in Vietnam.

Quest CONNECTIONS

Think about how the cultures of ethnic minorities influence other cultures. Record your findings in your ▱ Active Journal.

Analyze Charts As this chart suggests, Southeast Asian countries are very diverse. **Draw Conclusions** Of the five nations on this chart, which has the greatest ethnic diversity? Explain your answer.

ETHNIC AND RELIGIOUS DIVERSITY IN SOUTHEAST ASIA

ETHNIC DIVERSITY

INDONESIA	JAVANESE 41%	SUNDANESE 15%	OTHER 44%
MALAYSIA	MALAY 50%	CHINESE 23%	OTHER 27%
MYANMAR	BURMAN 68%	SHAN 9%	OTHER 23%
PHILIPPINES	TAGALOG 28%	CEBUANO 13%	OTHER 58%
THAILAND	THAI 75%	CHINESE 14%	OTHER 11%

RELIGIOUS DIVERSITY

Legend: ■ Buddhist ■ Christian ■ Hindu ■ Muslim ■ Other or None

INDONESIA	87%			10%	2% 1%
MALAYSIA	61%	20%	9%	6%	4%
MYANMAR	88%		6%	4%	2%
PHILIPPINES	92%			5%	3%
THAILAND	94%			5%	1%

Source: CIA World Factbook

In each of these countries, though, there are also minority ethnic groups. In Myanmar, for example, there are over 100 different ethnic groups.

Ethnic minorities are sometimes also religious minorities. For example, the Cham people are an ethnic minority in Vietnam and Cambodia. Both countries are mostly Buddhist, while most of the Cham follow Islam.

There has long been a strong Chinese presence in Southeast Asia. Today, Chinese communities thrive in every country in the region. In East Timor, Chinese are a tiny minority, while 77 percent of the people in Singapore are ethnic Chinese.

Analyze Images
Sundanese, an ethnic minority on the island of Java, celebrate their traditional planting festival, Ngarot. **Infer** Why might it be difficult for an ethnic minority to keep alive their traditions?

In Indonesia, the Philippines, and East Timor, no one ethnic group forms a majority. Instead, these countries are made up of a mosaic of different ethnic groups, each with its **characteristic** language and traditions. One way the governments of the Philippines and Indonesia are trying to tie their countries together is to promote a national language.

Cultural Blending Cultural mixing is a feature of Southeast Asian life. An example is the Minangkabau people of Indonesia, whose homeland is the mountains of Sumatra. In ancient times, the Minangkabau became merchants and travelers, pursuing the knowledge and wealth of the wider world. Along the way they absorbed Indian, Chinese, and Western customs and beliefs, including Islam. Later, they adopted the educational system of the Dutch, who colonized Indonesia.

The Minangkabau's openness to other cultures has served them well. Today, they are among the wealthiest, most educated, and most powerful groups in Indonesia.

Academic Vocabulary
characteristic • *adj.*, distinguishing, unique

☑ READING CHECK **Summarize** How did Buddhism and Hinduism first appear in and then spread through Southeast Asia?

☑ Lesson Check

Practice Vocabulary

1. What types of **terrain** are home to most of Southeast Asia's people?

2. In which large Southeast Asian country is Christianity the **dominant** religion?

Critical Thinking and Writing

3. **Compare and Contrast** Use the Country Databank to compare Southeast Asian countries' population growth rates. What explains the differences?

4. **Understand Effects** How does too much rainfall affect human habitation?

5. **Draw Conclusions** Is an ethnic minority in a given country always a religious minority as well? Explain your answer.

6. **Writing Workshop: Support Thesis with Details** In your 📓 Active Journal, write several details that support your thesis. As you gather more information, you may decide to adjust your thesis statement before you write the essay at the end of the topic.

Analyze Graphs and Diagrams

Graphs and diagrams put information into a visual form. Follow these steps and use the sources to analyze graphs and diagrams.

INTERACTIVE

Read Charts, Graphs, and Tables

1 **Determine the subject of each visual by reading titles, headings, and labels.**

   a. Look at the diagram. What is its main idea? How do you know?

   b. Examine the graph. What labels on the graph tell you what values it compares?

2 **Gather information from the visuals.**

   a. What does the diagram tell about why people choose to live in a certain place?

   b. Which country has the greatest population density? Which two countries have about the same population density as one another?

3 **Synthesize the information.**

   a. Of the four countries shown, which do you think has the best farmland or the most jobs?

   b. Explain how you came up with your answer.

Secondary Source

People Deciding Where to Live

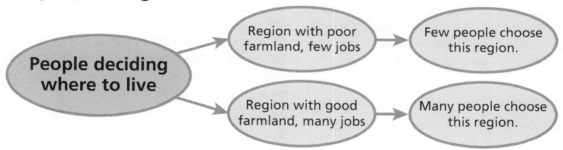

Secondary Source

Population Density of Selected Countries, 2014

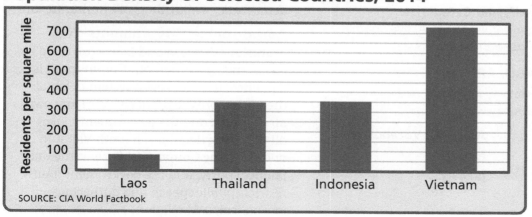

SOURCE: CIA World Factbook

Southeast Asia at Work

BOUNCE TO ACTIVATE ▶ VIDEO

GET READY TO READ

START UP

The skyline of Kuala Lumpur, Malaysia, shows the Petronas Towers. From 1998 to 2004, they were the tallest buildings in the world. Write a short paragraph describing how people in Kuala Lumpur might make a living.

GUIDING QUESTIONS

- How are Southeast Asian governments organized?
- What explains the success of Southeast Asia's economies?

TAKE NOTES

Literacy Skills: Classify and Categorize

Use the graphic organizer in your 🗐 Active Journal to take notes as you read this lesson.

PRACTICE VOCABULARY

Use the vocabulary activity in your 🗐 Active Journal to practice the vocabulary words.

Vocabulary	Academic Vocabulary
absolute monarchy	exercise
semiconductor	primary
exchange rate	

In the United States, voters elect officials to represent them in government. The U.S. economy is also based on individuals making decisions. If a business makes something, its managers decide what price to ask for it, and individual customers decide whether they are willing to pay that.

These are not the only forms of government and economy that exist in the world, though.

Governments of Southeast Asia

Southeast Asia alone has several different types of governments. Some are more or less democratic, while others are authoritarian.

Authoritarian Governments Two countries—Vietnam and Laos—are ruled by communist governments. Communism is a political and economic system in which there is no private property. The state owns all property, and the government makes all economic decisions. In both Vietnam and Laos, the Communist Party is the only political party, and the government tightly restricts public speech and gatherings, journalism, and religion.

Brunei is a sultanate. The sultan rules in an **absolute monarchy**, one in which the leader's power is hereditary and unlimited. Brunei's citizens have no say in government.

Military Governments In two countries, Myanmar and Thailand, the military controls the government. Elections are held, but military leaders have the right to overrule the will of the people.

Still, democratic elections are an improvement in Myanmar. Until 2010, it was under authoritarian military rule. The country's most widely supported politician, Aung San Suu Kyi (ong sahn soo tchee), opposed the military government. Because of this, the government held her under house arrest, or imprisoned her in her home, for many years. In 2010, the government allowed the first election in 20 years. Elections in 2015 gave Suu Kyi's party a majority in parliament. After winning power, the new government arrested citizens who criticized its policies.

Varying Degrees of Democracy In Cambodia, Malaysia, and Singapore, elections are held, but the government limits democratic freedoms. Election laws and procedures are designed to keep the ruling party in office. As a result, in each of these countries the same political party has held power for more than 35 years.

In Indonesia, the Philippines, and East Timor, citizens **exercise** the right to vote in relatively free and fair democratic elections. Even so, some elections have been disrupted by violence. Undemocratic actions, such as paying people to vote for a given candidate, have been reported.

Two Types of Democratic Government The governments of the Philippines and Indonesia are presidential democracies. They are similar to the government we have in the United States. An elected president heads the government, and elected representatives serve in a parliament, a citizen-elected, lawmaking body.

Quick Activity

With a partner, discuss how to answer the Essential Question, "What role should people have in their government?," for one country in the region. Write your results in your 📓 Active Journal.

Academic Vocabulary

exercise • *v.*, to use a privilege or discharge an official duty

---

5 BIOGRAPHY Things to Know About

AUNG SAN SUU KYI
Political Activist and Opposition Leader (born 1945)

- Aung San Suu Kyi attended university in Britain, where she married and raised her two sons.

- When she returned to Myanmar to care for her sick mother, the political upheaval of the time inspired her to act.

- She was under house arrest for a total of 15 years.

- Under Myanmar's constitution, drafted by its military, she cannot become president because her children are not citizens of Myanmar.

- She won the Nobel Peace Prize in 1991.

Critical Thinking Aung San Suu Kyi has been called "an outstanding example of the power of the powerless." What do you think that means?

Governments of Southeast Asia

GOVERNMENT	COUNTRY			
Constitutional Monarchy	Brunei	Cambodia	Malaysia	Thailand
Republic	East Timor	Indonesia	Myanmar	Singapore
	Philippines			
Communist Oligarchy	Laos	Vietnam		

Analyze Charts This chart groups the nations of Southeast Asia by type of government. **Synthesize Information** Does having a written constitution ensure that a nation's people are free and able to participate in their government? Explain.

In East Timor, the president is elected but has limited power. Instead, voters elect members to parliament, and the parliament chooses a prime minister, who heads the government. Several European countries, including Britain, have governments led by a prime minister.

☑ READING CHECK **Compare and Contrast** How are the governments of Myanmar and Thailand similar? How are they different?

Economies of Southeast Asia

Southeast Asia is one of the most economically diverse and dynamic areas in the world. In most of the region, economic growth has been faster than the world average for the past 20 years.

Traditional Economies Traditional economies still exist in remote mountain regions of mainland Southeast Asia. They can also be found in the Indonesian provinces on the island of New Guinea. In these economies, decisions about what to produce, how to produce it, and how to distribute it are made according to centuries-old customs.

The Market Decides Across Southeast Asia, markets play the **primary** role in economic life. In a market economy, consumers and producers make decisions based on prices set in competitive markets. These decisions determine what is produced, how it is produced, and how it is distributed.

Academic Vocabulary
primary • *adj.*, first or most important

Market economies contrast with command economies, in which the government decides what to produce, how to produce it, and how to distribute it. Market economies generally grow faster than command economies. This is because markets reward efficiency and productivity. Because government decision-making is centralized and political, command economies are generally less efficient and productive.

Vietnam clearly demonstrated this principle. In the 1980s, the government gave markets a greater role in the economy. As a result, Vietnam's economy began to grow much faster.

Mixed Economies All the countries of Southeast Asia have mixed economies. In a mixed economy, both government decisions and market decisions play a role. In most Southeast Asian countries, markets dominate the economy. In Vietnam and Laos, the governments have large roles, but markets are also important.

☑ READING CHECK **Summarize** Describe the economies found in Southeast Asia.

The Region's Role in the World Economy

Economic activity in Southeast Asia is concentrated in its booming cities. These cities originally grew up along trade routes. Because most long-distance trade has been carried out on ships, most of these cities are on or near coastlines.

Low Wages for Low-Skilled Labor Most Southeast Asian countries have experienced rapid economic growth. Many countries have done this by offering relatively cheap labor. They also promote investment to make that labor more productive.

For example, Vietnam has attracted companies that make clothing and shoes for Western consumers. It has done that by encouraging investment in factories and machinery. In addition, Vietnamese workers accept lower wages than the workers in neighboring China do.

Educated, Skilled Labor A few Southeast Asian countries have promoted economic growth in a different way. Instead of unskilled labor, they offer highly educated workers who can provide advanced goods and services. They often outcompete workers in wealthy countries such as the United States. Malaysia and Singapore are two countries that have followed this path.

Malaysia is one of the world's leading producers of **semiconductors**. Those are the computer chips that run smart phones, tablets, computers, and even appliances and cars.

Singapore is a leading financial center. It has become one of the richest countries in the world.

👆 INTERACTIVE

Ethnicities and GDP

Analyze Images In 2016, a factory worker in Cambodia earned about $150 in U.S. dollars a month. **Synthesize Visual Information** What are these workers making? Do you think they will buy any of the goods they make? Explain.

A country's economic success is commonly measured by its gross domestic product (GDP), the total value of all goods and services produced in the country in a year. Singapore's per capita GDP, or GDP per person, is higher than that of the United States.

The Importance of Trade You have read how trade shaped Southeast Asia's economies and the locations of its cities. Trade remains crucial to the region today. The Strait of Malacca is a major global shipping lane. Roughly 60,000 ships pass through it each year —an average of 164 a day. This represents one third of the world's trade, including 17 percent of the world's oil supply. The ports of Singapore, Malaysia, and Indonesia benefit greatly from this traffic.

Southeast Asia's economic growth has been driven by exports. Many of the region's most successful industries produce goods and services meant for customers in other countries. For example, electronic equipment made in Thailand is sold in the United States.

Southeast Asia's reliance on trade means that the region needs to be able to exchange different countries' currencies. For example, a Thai company selling products to a company in Cambodia doesn't want to be paid in Cambodian currency. The buyer has to first exchange the Cambodian money for Thai currency of equal value.

The value of one country's currency in terms of another's is called the **exchange rate**. Some countries try to decree what their currency is worth. Most exchange rates, though, are determined by the market—what people are willing to pay in order to purchase the currency. That, in turn, depends on a number of factors, including the country's rate of inflation, interest rates, and the relative value of its exports and imports.

Analyze Charts This chart compares the economies of three Southeast Asian nations. **Use Visual Information** Of these three countries, which has seen the greatest increase of exports since 2000?

TRADE IN SOUTHEAST ASIA

EXPORTS 2000–2015

Source: UN Comtrade

INDUSTRIAL GROWTH RATE 2016

SINGAPORE	1%
INDONESIA	3.5%
VIETNAM	7%

Source: CIA World Factbook

TOP EXPORTS 2016

SINGAPORE	INDONESIA	VIETNAM
machinery and equipment, pharmaceuticals	fuels, animal and vegetable fats, machinery	clothes, shoes, electronics

Source: CIA World Factbook

Currency exchange is carried out by banks. Singapore is a major banking center; it handles a large share of Southeast Asia's need for currency exchange.

▲ The giant cranes at the Port of Singapore move containers on and off the many container ships that pass through the port.

Southeast Asian Economic Success A successful economy needs a stable government; natural resources or skilled workers; and reliable banking, transportation, and communication systems. Singapore and Brunei meet these conditions and are the most successful countries economically in the region. More than half of Brunei's income comes from oil and natural gas production. Singapore's economy is based on exports of consumer electronics and information technology.

Meanwhile, countries without transportation networks, stable governments, or free markets have difficulty in attracting foreign investments. Nations such as Laos continue to struggle to develop their economies.

☑ **READING CHECK** Identify Cause and Effect Why might American companies make products in Vietnam rather than in the United States?

☑ Lesson Check

Practice Vocabulary

1. Which country in the region is an **absolute monarchy**?

2. Why would you check the **exchange rate** before travelling to a foreign country?

3. Why are **semiconductors** important in today's world?

Critical Thinking and Writing

4. Compare and Contrast What do Vietnam and Malaysia offer to foreign investors?

5. Classify and Categorize Which Southeast Asian countries have some form of democracy? How are some of these democracies limited?

6. Writing Workshop: Draft Your Essay Write a draft of your essay. Be sure to state your thesis clearly and present facts to support it. Refer to the notes in your 🗐 Active Journal

Challenges Facing Southeast Asia

GET READY TO READ

START UP

What challenges do you think the people who live in these neighborhoods of Jakarta, Indonesia, are facing?

GUIDING QUESTIONS

- What environmental challenges does Southeast Asia face?
- What political and economic challenges does Southeast Asia face?

TAKE NOTES

Literacy Skills: Use Evidence

Use the graphic organizer in your 📖 Active Journal to take notes as you read this lesson.

PRACTICE VOCABULARY

Use the vocabulary activity in your 📖 Active Journal to practice the vocabulary words.

Vocabulary	Academic Vocabulary
typhoon	contend
incentive	eventually
trade barrier	

Southeast Asia is a region of great economic and cultural vitality. The region also faces a variety of challenges.

Environmental Challenges

Throughout history, people have addressed problems by changing their environment. Since the 1800s, though, humanity has gained the power to affect the environment on a global scale. As in other parts of the world, this situation is presenting challenges in Southeast Asia.

The Climate Is Changing Climate change threatens to cause sea levels to rise all over the world. The impact would be especially great in Southeast Asia. Much of the region's population live on river deltas or coastal plains. Their homes are only a few feet or meters above sea level. Rising sea levels could destroy valuable property and leave millions homeless.

In recent years, Southeast Asia has also been experiencing more intense **typhoons**.

Typhoons are tropical cyclones similar to hurricanes. Some scientists believe that climate change has been increasing the destructive power of these storms.

Forests Are Dwindling Deforestation, or the destruction of trees faster than they can grow back, has eaten away at tropical rainforests across the region. This is especially true on Sumatra and Borneo, two large islands mainly in Indonesia. Scientists believe that deforestation contributes to climate change. In addition, deforestation threatens species that live in and depend on the rainforest.

A major cause of deforestation is humans burning forest to clear land for farming. On Sumatra and Borneo, such burning has caused serious air pollution across the region. Tropical winds carry the smoke from these fires hundreds of miles or kilometers, affecting people far away.

The Ring of Fire As you have learned, Southeast Asia lies along boundaries between tectonic plates that make up Earth's crust. As a result, it experiences earthquakes, tsunamis, and volcanic eruptions that sometimes cause great damage and loss of life. Indonesia and the Philippines are particularly hard hit, while mainland Southeast Asia experiences fewer seismic disasters.

✓ **READING CHECK** Identify Cause and Effect What are some ways climate change affects Southeast Asia?

Political and Economic Challenges

Southeast Asia has undergone rapid political and economic change in modern times. What political and economic challenges will Southeast Asia confront in the years ahead?

Cities Are Growing Southeast Asia as a whole is mainly rural. However, more people are moving to urban areas in search of jobs and higher living standards. Jakarta, Bangkok, Manila, and Ho Chi Minh City have all become huge cities with growing urban challenges.

Rapid growth places great strain on a city's infrastructure, or public works and structures, such as roads and hospitals, which a country needs to support a modern economy. Water supply, electricity, garbage disposal, and sewage facilities may not keep up with the increased demand. Housing, healthcare, and other services may also fall short.

Social Instability Population issues can affect a country as a whole. Countries whose populations are growing quickly must **contend** with the challenges that change in population brings. But the opposite is also true. Countries with low population growth are also concerned about the future.

> **INTERACTIVE**
>
> 3-D Model: Volcano

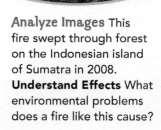

Analyze Images This fire swept through forest on the Indonesian island of Sumatra in 2008. **Understand Effects** What environmental problems does a fire like this cause?

Academic Vocabulary
contend • *v.*, to struggle, as in a contest

As people grow older, they stop working. If not enough young people enter or are born into the country, **eventually** there will not be enough workers to keep the economy running.

Singapore's birth rate is quite low, which means couples are having few children. To encourage population growth, the government provides financial **incentives**. An incentive is something of value that encourages people to behave in a certain way. Singapore offers couples thousands of dollars of tax reductions for every child they have.

In contrast, Indonesia faces the problem of overcrowding. Nearly 60 percent of the country's huge population live on one island, Java. The government has offered financial incentives to families to migrate to other islands.

Another social issue concerns ethnic minorities, who sometimes feel they have been treated unfairly by their national government. In several countries—including Myanmar, the Philippines, Indonesia, and Thailand—ethnic minorities have waged armed rebellions. These rebellions are an ongoing source of instability and loss of life.

Indonesia has the largest Muslim population in the world. Even so, Islamist terrorists have carried out attacks there, as well as in Thailand. These countries, and possibly other countries in the region, face an ongoing risk of Islamist terrorism.

Military Rule and Political Instability

In Thailand, a military government changed the country's constitution in 2016. Under the new constitution, the military appoints all of the country's senators. It also has the power to veto all democratic decisions and to pass laws without the senate's consent.

Thailand has experienced violent protests in the past over threats to democratic rights. In the past 85 years, there have been 19 coups.

Analyze Images In Bangkok, Thailand, supporters of one political group rally outside city hall. **Draw Conclusions** Do you think protests such as this one are an effective way to bring about change in Thailand? Explain.

It is possible that Thailand will continue to see instability in the future. Other countries in Southeast Asia without democratic rule also face a risk of political instability.

Trade Issues For a region so dependent on trade, Southeast Asia has a surprising level of **trade barriers**—laws and taxes that make it more difficult or more expensive to import goods. Unlike Europe or some other parts of the world, Southeast Asian countries have not benefited much from trade agreements with one another. One trade agreement, signed in 1967, created the Association of Southeast Asian Nations (ASEAN). Its goal was to boost trade within the region. But disagreements within the group have prevented it from accomplishing many of its goals.

China Looms China claims a number of small islands in the South China Sea. These islands are far from China, but close to Vietnam, the Philippines, and Malaysia. These countries also claim some of the islands claimed by China. The United States has supported the Southeast Asian countries. An international court rejected China's claims in 2016. China ignored the ruling, however, and continues to assert ownership of the islands. It has even built military installations on some of the disputed islands.

Most of Southeast Asia depends on trade through the South China Sea. The United States has called for freedom of navigation. China's actions in the sea could pose military and economic threats to the entire region.

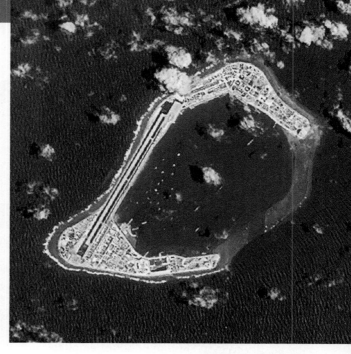

▲ China has strengthened its position in the South China Sea by constructing artificial islands like the one shown here. These islands serve as naval bases.

 **READING CHECK** Identify Main Ideas What are the primary political and economic challenges facing Southeast Asia today?

Quest CONNECTIONS

How do countries like China and the United States continue to influence Southeast Asia today? Record your findings in your 📝 Active Journal.

☑ Lesson Check

Practice Vocabulary

1. What do we call a tropical cyclone like a **typhoon** that develops in the Atlantic Ocean?

2. Give two examples of **trade barriers**.

Critical Thinking and Writing

3. **Identify Problems** Refer to the Country Databank. Which countries of Southeast Asia face the greatest challenges related to population? Explain the challenges.

4. **Identify Cause and Effect** What causes earthquakes in Southeast Asia?

5. **Summarize** What environmental challenges do the countries of Southeast Asia face?

6. **Writing Workshop: Revise** Review your draft essay and look for ways to improve it. Is your thesis supported? Is the writing clear? Be sure to check spelling, grammar, and punctuation as well.

☑ Review and Assessment

VISUAL REVIEW

From Empires to Independence

Year	
by 2000 BCE	Austronesians have settled in the region.
by 200 BCE	Trade begins between South Asia and Southeast Asia.
600s CE–1200s	Srivijaya empire
800s–1300s	Khmer empire
800s	Rise of Buddhist empires
1200s	Islam begins to spread through the region.
1500s	European conquests begin.
1940s–Present	After World War II, nations win independence from colonial powers.

Life in Southeast Asia

Major Religions

Buddhist: Thailand, Myanmar, Laos, Cambodia, Singapore
Muslim: Indonesia, Malaysia, Brunei
Christian: Philippines, East Timor
None: Vietnam

Ethnicities

Dozens including Chinese, Indian, Indonesian, Malay

Economic Development

High-income, developing: Brunei, Singapore
Middle income, developing: Indonesia, Malaysia, Philippines, Thailand, Vietnam
Least developed: Cambodia, Laos, Myanmar, East Timor

READING REVIEW

Use the Take Notes and Practice Vocabulary activities in your 📕 Active Journal to help you to review the topic.

INTERACTIVE

Practice vocabulary using the Topic Mini-Games.

Quest FINDINGS

Write Your Essay
Prepare the final version of your essay using your 📕 Active Journal.

ASSESSMENT

Vocabulary and Key Ideas

1. **Explain** What is the Malay Peninsula?

2. **Describe** the area of the Mekong **delta** and how it was formed.

3. **Recall** How is a country's **GDP** determined?

4. **Explain** How have **typhoons** changed recently?

5. **Check Understanding** Why did the United States enter the conflict in Vietnam?

6. **Identify Supporting Details** What two types of labor force are available in the different countries of Southeast Asia?

Critical Thinking and Writing

7. **Compare and Contrast** How did outsiders who arrived in Southeast Asia before the 1500s relate to the indigenous cultures? How did that change in the 1500s and 1600s?

8. **Classify** Is it possible for a government to be a monarchy but not authoritarian? Explain.

9. **Compare and Contrast** What are the differences between a communist and a market economy?

10. **Classify** What is an ethnic group? Is Austronesian an ethnic group? Explain.

11. **Revisit the Essential Question** What roles do the people of Southeast Asia have in their government? Give examples, using information from the Country Databank.

12. **Writing Workshop: Write an Explanatory Essay** Using information about Southeast Asia, finish your three-paragraph explanatory essay in answer to the following question: How have citizens' roles in the government changed over time? Consult the work you've already done in your ▣ Active Journal.

Analyze Primary Sources

13. Read this remark by a government official of a Southeast Asian country. Dr. Koh is most likely speaking about which country?

   A. Thailand
   B. Singapore
   C. Cambodia
   D. Vietnam

   "The Precision Engineering (PE) industry is a critical enabler for our manufacturing sector.

   In 2015, it employed around 90,000 workers. . . . The PE industry supports the production of complex equipment and highly precision-engineered components required in industries ranging from electronics and aerospace, to oil and gas and medical technology."
   —*Dr. Koh Poh Koon, speech on January 17, 2017*

Analyze Maps

Use the map to answer the questions.

14. Which two countries are shown in yellow?

15. What color is Malaysia?

16. Which letter indicates Singapore?

17. The Strait of Malacca lies between lands of which two countries?

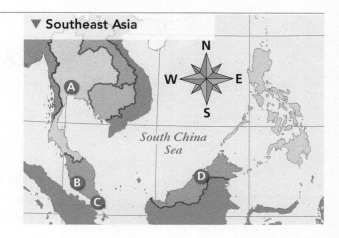

▼ **Southeast Asia**

Australia and the Pacific

GO ONLINE
to access your
digital course

▶ VIDEO

◀)) AUDIO

📖 ETEXT

👆 INTERACTIVE

✍ WRITING

🎮 GAMES

📄 WORKSHEET

☑ ASSESSMENT

Sail away to

AUSTRALIA AND THE PACIFIC, a continent and a multitude of islands spread across the vast expanse of the Pacific Ocean. Amid coral reefs and aquamarine seascapes, you will discover how peoples from distant lands have settled and shaped the region.

Explore
The Essential Question

How much does geography affect people's lives?

Other than Australia and New Zealand, much of the Pacific region is made up of small islands spread far apart. The whole region is far from most parts of the world. How does this isolation affect culture? Unlock the Essential Question in your 📔 Active Journal.

▶ The harbor of Sydney, Australia

Read

about the past and present of Australia and the Pacific, as well as the geography and mystery of Antarctica.

Watch

 BOUNCE TO ACTIVATE   VIDEO

Jack Connects to His Culture

Meet Jack, a New Zealand student who is eager to learn more about his ancestors' Maori culture.

Australia and the Pacific: Political

A MIX OF CULTURES
The diverse peoples of this region include hundreds of different Pacific island peoples, Australian Aborigines, and people of European and Asian heritage.

Learn more about Australia and the Pacific by making your own map in your  Active Journal.

INTERACTIVE

Topic Map

A Continental Country
Australia is the largest country in this region, and the sixth-largest country in the world in area. It is also Earth's smallest continent. Most of this region's people live in Australia. Most Australians speak English. To Australia's north is Papua New Guinea, the second-most populated country in the region, with hundreds of different ethnic groups.

Two Islands
New Zealand is another mostly English-speaking country. It consists of two main islands. Its capital is Wellington, but its largest city is Auckland.

Philippine Sea

120°E   135°E   150°E

Northern Mariana Islands (U.S.)

Guam (U.S.)

Melekeok ★
PALAU

FEDERATED STATES OF MICRONESIA

PAPUA NEW GUINEA
★
Port Moresby

Coral Sea

INDIAN OCEAN

AUSTRALIA

Brisbane ●

Perth ●

Adelaide ● ● Sydney
★ Canberra
● Melbourne

N
W   E
S

Small Islands

The rest of the region consists of mostly small Pacific islands. Many island groups are small independent countries. Some are dependencies, or areas controlled by another country. A few are U.S. dependencies, such as American Samoa, shown here.

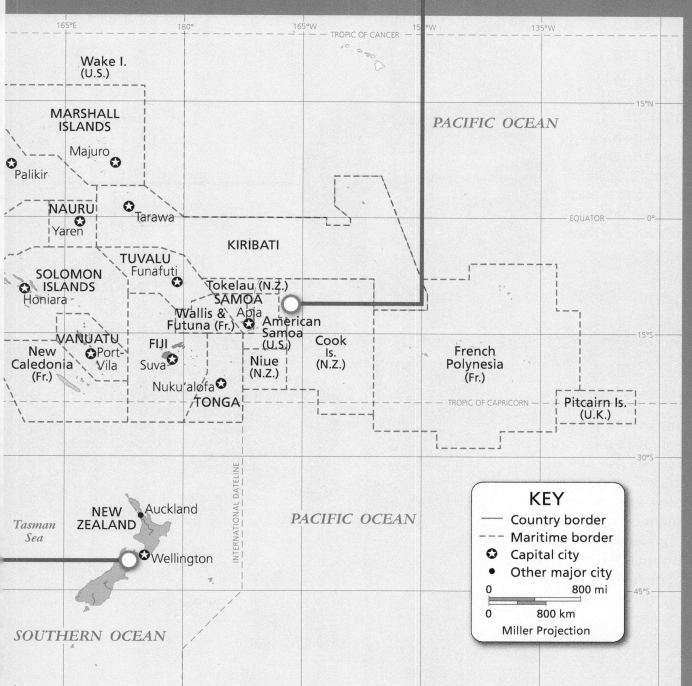

TROPIC OF CANCER

165°E · 180° · 165°W · 15°W · 135°W

Wake I.
(U.S.)

PACIFIC OCEAN

15°N

MARSHALL
ISLANDS
Majuro

Palikir

NAURU
Yaren

Tarawa

EQUATOR — 0°

KIRIBATI

TUVALU
Funafuti

SOLOMON
ISLANDS
Honiara

Tokelau (N.Z.)

SAMOA
Wallis &   Apia
Futuna (Fr.)   American
Samoa
(U.S.)

VANUATU
New
Caledonia
(Fr.)

FIJI
Port-
Vila
Suva

Niue
(N.Z.)

Cook
Is.
(N.Z.)

French
Polynesia
(Fr.)

15°S

Nuku'alofa

TONGA

TROPIC OF CAPRICORN

Pitcairn Is.
(U.K.)

30°S

INTERNATIONAL DATELINE

PACIFIC OCEAN

*Tasman
Sea*

NEW
ZEALAND

Auckland

Wellington

KEY
— Country border
- - - Maritime border
⊛ Capital city
● Other major city

0   800 mi
0   800 km
Miller Projection

45°S

SOUTHERN OCEAN

Australia and the Pacific: Physical

A FAR-FLUNG REGION

This region stretches about 8,000 miles (12,875 km) from west to east. Since the Pacific Ocean dominates the region, it is sometimes called Oceania.

Learn more about Australia and the Pacific by making your own map of its physical features in your Active Journal.

Melanesia

Melanesia, in the center of the region, includes New Guinea, other relatively large islands, and small coral atolls, such as Vonavona Island in the Solomon Islands, shown here.

Australia

Narrow coastal plains on Australia's east and west coasts rise quickly to mountain ranges and plateaus. The center of the continent consists of low-lying basins with some large rock formations, such as Uluru, or Ayers Rock, which is sacred to some Australian Aborigines.

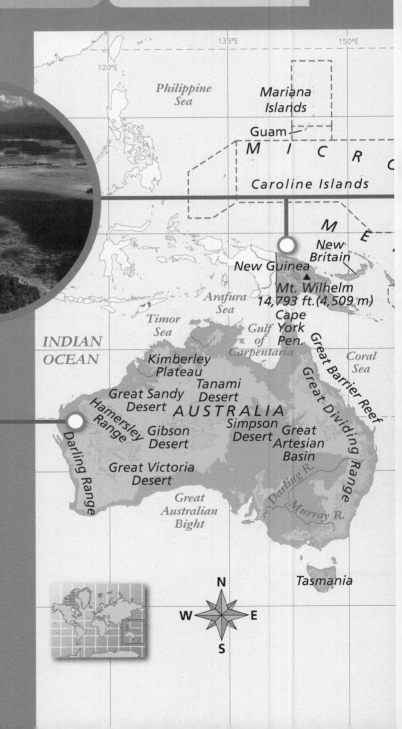

135°E   150°E
120°E

Philippine Sea

Mariana Islands

Guam

M   I   C   R   O

Caroline Islands

M   E

New Guinea   New Britain

Mt. Wilhelm 14,793 ft. (4,509 m)

Arafura Sea

Timor Sea

Cape York Pen.

Gulf of Carpentaria

Coral Sea

INDIAN OCEAN

Kimberley Plateau

Great Sandy Desert

Tanami Desert

AUSTRALIA

Great Barrier Reef

Hamersley Range

Gibson Desert

Simpson Desert   Great Artesian Basin

Darling Range

Great Victoria Desert

Great Dividing Range

Darling R.

Murray R.

Great Australian Bight

N

W   E

S

Tasmania

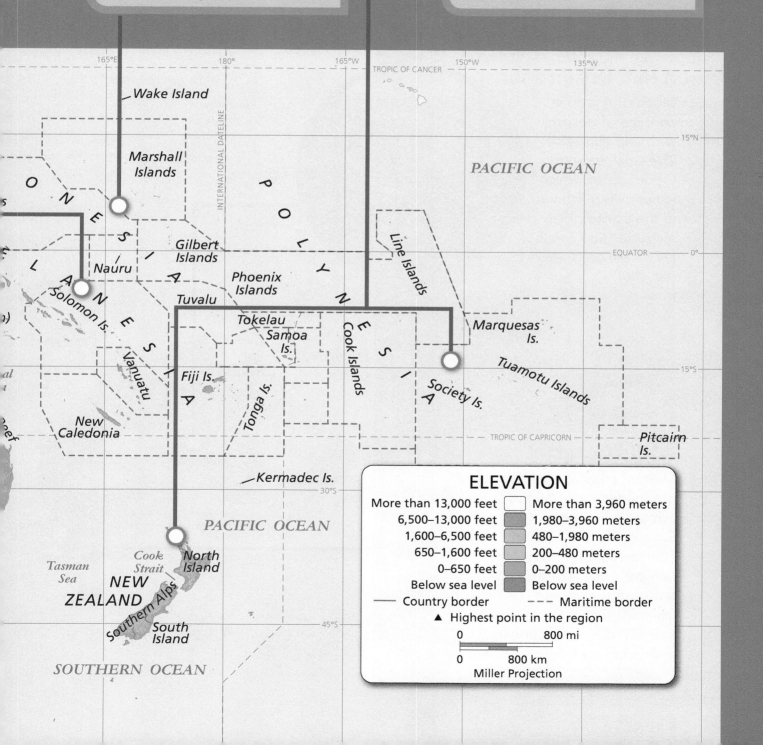

Micronesia

The Pacific islands belong to three large cultural and physical regions. Micronesia stretches across the northern part of this region and consists mainly of very small islands.

Polynesia

Polynesia consists of mostly small islands scattered across the eastern part of this region, as well as the large islands of New Zealand.

165°E   180°   165°W   TROPIC OF CANCER   150°W   135°W

Wake Island

INTERNATIONAL DATELINE

Marshall Islands

15°N

PACIFIC OCEAN

O N E S I A

P O L Y N E S I A

Gilbert Islands

EQUATOR   0°

Nauru

L

Solomon Is.

Phoenix Islands

Tuvalu

Line Islands

Tokelau

Samoa Is.

Cook Islands

Marquesas Is.

15°S

Vanuatu

Tuamotu Islands

Fiji Is.

Society Is.

Tonga Is.

New Caledonia

TROPIC OF CAPRICORN   *Pitcairn Is.*

Kermadec Is.

30°S

PACIFIC OCEAN

Tasman Sea

Cook Strait   *North Island*

NEW ZEALAND

Southern Alps

South Island

45°S

SOUTHERN OCEAN

ELEVATION

More than 13,000 feet	▢	More than 3,960 meters
6,500–13,000 feet	▢	1,980–3,960 meters
1,600–6,500 feet	▢	480–1,980 meters
650–1,600 feet	▢	200–480 meters
0–650 feet	▢	0–200 meters
Below sea level	▢	Below sea level
—— Country border		- - - Maritime border

▲ Highest point in the region

0   800 mi

0   800 km

Miller Projection

Australia and the Pacific: Climate

FROM TROPICAL TO FREEZING

The region covers a large area of the Pacific from north to south. Most of the islands in the region lie in the tropics, but southern areas have temperate climates. New Zealand even has glaciers in its high mountains.

A Hot, Dry Interior

Much of Australia consists of deserts with arid climates. The small town of Oodnadatta, which is near Uluru (shown in the photo), averages just 7 inches (176 mm) of rainfall per year.

A Mild Coast

Most of coastal Australia has milder, more humid climates. For example, Sydney averages about 52 inches (1,309 mm) of rain per year. Average temperatures range from 54° F (12° C) in July to 72° F (22° C) in January and February.

A Tropical Island

Papeete, on the island of Tahiti, has a tropical wet climate, like most of the tropical Pacific islands. It averages about 68 inches (1,728 mm) of rain a year, almost half of which falls from December to February. Temperatures average about 79° F (26° C) year-round.

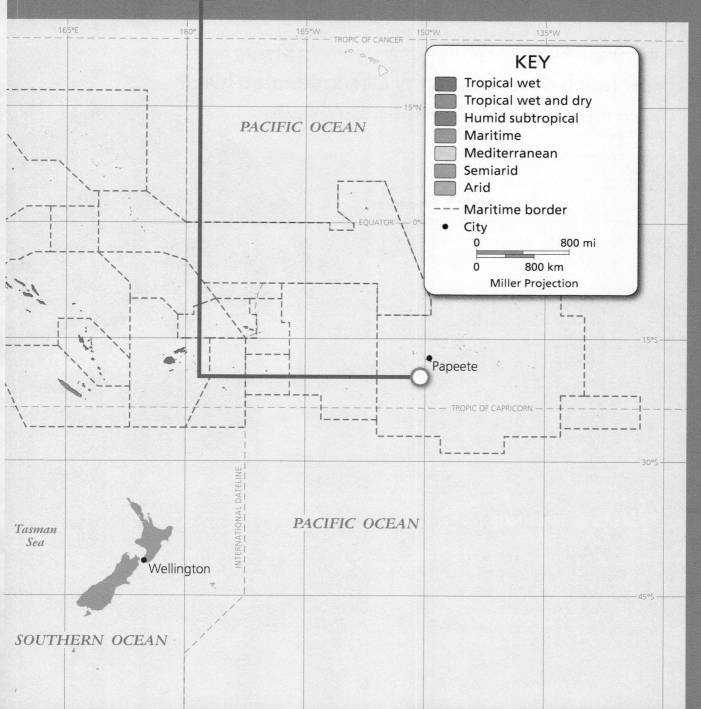

165°E   180°   165°W   TROPIC OF CANCER   150°W   135°W

PACIFIC OCEAN

15°N

KEY

- Tropical wet
- Tropical wet and dry
- Humid subtropical
- Maritime
- Mediterranean
- Semiarid
- Arid
- - - Maritime border
- • City

0	800 mi

0	800 km

Miller Projection

EQUATOR   0°

15°S

• Papeete

TROPIC OF CAPRICORN

30°S

INTERNATIONAL DATELINE

PACIFIC OCEAN

Tasman
Sea

• Wellington

45°S

SOUTHERN OCEAN

Quest

Write a Petition to Encourage Environmental Action

Quest KICK OFF

It's time to try to change the world! Australia and the rest of the Pacific region struggle with several environmental issues. It's up to you to research and write a petition, or a formal request, that will convince officials to help prevent even more damage to an important part of the environment. Your petition will highlight answers to the following question:

How much does geography affect people's lives?

Explore the Essential Question, "How much does geography affect people's lives?" in this Quest.

1 Ask Questions

What do you need to include in your petition to convince people to read and support it? Start by thinking about how you will write your petition. Outline your strategy in your ⬛ Active Journal.

2 Investigate

As you read the lessons in this topic, look for **Quest** CONNECTIONS about the many environmental challenges facing the region. Record your responses in your ⬛ Active Journal.

3 Conduct Research

Use reliable sources to learn more about one of these environmental issues you read about in the topic. Record and interpret your findings in your ⬛ Active Journal.

▲ A damaged coral reef

Quest FINDINGS

4 Write Your Petition

Use what you have learned about your issue to write your petition in your ⬛ Active Journal. Your petition should identify your audience (such as a government agency or industry leader), describe the issue, explain why it is a problem, and outline your solution.

Early Cultures of Australia and the Pacific

GET READY TO READ

START UP

Look at the photo of the traditional boat like those used by the people who settled the Pacific islands. What might be some of the challenges of traveling long distances over ocean waters on such a craft?

GUIDING QUESTIONS

- Who were Australia's first people?
- Who were the first settlers of New Guinea and the other Pacific islands?
- Who were the Polynesians and what were their achievements?

TAKE NOTES

Literacy Skills: Summarize

Use the graphic organizer in your 📖 Active Journal to take notes as you read the lesson.

PRACTICE VOCABULARY

Use the vocabulary activity in your 📖 Active Journal to practice the vocabulary words.

Vocabulary		Academic Vocabulary
Aborigine	Maori	oral tradition
Polynesian	marae	inhabitant

People settled Australia and the Pacific islands through several waves of migration. Migrants first came to Australia and New Guinea. Much later, other people settled various Pacific islands. All of these groups developed societies with distinct cultures, which formed partly in response to the region's geography.

Australia's First Peoples

The first people came to Australia about 60,000 years ago. Sea levels were much lower at that time than they are today. At that time, humans were able to use a land bridge to reach what is now Bali. Another land bridge connected New Guinea to Australia. Some would have used boats or rafts to safely cross short stretches of ocean water.

The Aborigines Australia's original people are known as **Aborigines** (ab uh RIH juh neez). These people belonged to hundreds of different ethnic groups. Each group had its own language, way of life, and beliefs. Aborigines lived throughout the continent, but most lived in the temperate southeast part of Australia.

Quick Activity

Plan how to prepare for a long ocean voyage in your 📒 Active Journal.

Most Aborigines were nomadic. Farming was not known in Australia—Aborigines were strictly hunter-gatherers. In order to balance limited resources with population, Aborigines lived in small groups and moved to a new area when necessary. Aborigines had a complex society without chiefs or other formal leaders.

Aboriginal Culture People in different parts of Australia had cultures adapted to their environments. For example, coastal peoples and those living along rivers relied on fishing. Inland peoples relied more on hunting. Aborigines in all parts of Australia gathered plant foods, but the plants that they gathered in desert regions were different from those in wetter coastal regions.

Throughout Australia, Aborigines built shelter frames using sticks. In wooded regions, they covered the frames with bark. In deserts, they covered them with dry grass. Aborigines had strong religious convictions about nature, believing that it was their responsibility to care for the land.

Australia's first people produced a rich oral literature. Storytellers recorded history, legends, religious beliefs, and knowledge about the world in songs and chants that were passed down from generation to generation. Today, historians study this **oral tradition** to learn more about what Australia looked like thousands of years ago.

Academic Vocabulary
oral tradition • *n.*, a community's cultural and historical background, passed down in spoken stories and songs

☑ READING CHECK **Identify Supporting Details** Describe how most Aborigines lived.

Analyze Images This example of Aboriginal housing shows the characteristic frame of sticks. **Draw Conclusions** Why would housing like this have fit a nomadic lifestyle?

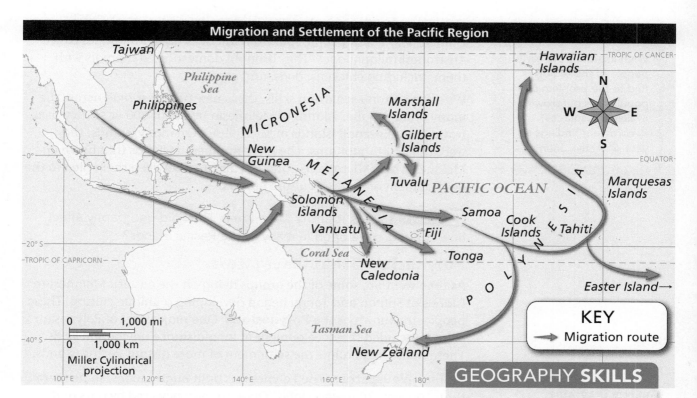

Migration and Settlement of the Pacific Region

Taiwan
Philippine Sea
Philippines
MICRONESIA
New Guinea
MELANESIA
Solomon Islands
Vanuatu
Coral Sea
New Caledonia
Marshall Islands
Gilbert Islands
Tuvalu
Fiji
Tonga
PACIFIC OCEAN
Samoa
Cook Islands
Tahiti
POLYNESIA
Hawaiian Islands — TROPIC OF CANCER
Marquesas Islands
Easter Island →
EQUATOR
N W E S
Tasman Sea
New Zealand
TROPIC OF CAPRICORN
0   1,000 mi
0   1,000 km
Miller Cylindrical projection
100° E   120° E   140° E   160° E   180°
-0°
-20° S
-40° S

KEY
→ Migration route

Early Cultures of Melanesia and Micronesia

If you look at the political map in this topic's Regional Atlas, you will see that the area making up the Pacific island region is vast. The islands can be broken down into three general groupings: Melanesia, Micronesia, and Polynesia.

Historians believe that people probably first settled in New Guinea around the same time they arrived in Australia. Descendants of these people then spread to the nearby Solomon Islands about 30,000 years ago.

Early New Guineans lived much as Australian Aborigines did, by hunting, fishing, and gathering. However, New Guineans were among the first people in the world to discover farming. They grew taro, a root crop, at least 10,000 years ago. They later grew yams, coconuts, sugarcane, and other crops. Many of these crops were made possible by the irrigation systems that New Guineans built, often by strategically draining wetlands and swamps.

Like the Australian Aborigines, the people of New Guinea and the Solomon Islands were divided into hundreds of distinct ethnic groups. Each group had its own language and culture, which was adapted to fit the various island environments. For example, groups living on the coast developed customs much different than groups isolated in the islands' inland valleys.

Between 3,000 and 4,000 years ago, a new group of people arrived on the coast of New Guinea. These people were also farmers. They had spread over time from the island of Taiwan, off the coast of China.

INTERACTIVE

Migration to Australia and the Pacific

Quest CONNECTIONS

What solutions did early people of the region find to the problem of populations outgrowing available resources? Record your findings in your ▱ Active Journal.

They migrated through the islands of Southeast Asia to New Guinea. These new people spoke a related group of languages called Austronesian languages. They brought domesticated animals with them, including chickens, dogs, and pigs.

With their strong seafaring skills, these new people spread across the many other, smaller islands of Melanesia by about 800 BCE. They also traveled to the small islands of Micronesia. On many islands, they were the first inhabitants. The huge number of islands that make up Melanesia and Micronesia—and the distance between them—led to the development of isolated culture groups.

☑ READING CHECK Identify Main Ideas How did geography affect how cultures developed in many of the Pacific islands?

Polynesia's Great Navigators

As time went on, some of the groups living on the eastern Melanesian islands of Samoa and Tonga began developing a unique culture. These people are known as the **Polynesians**. One major part of Polynesian culture included the development of long-distance navigation skills. These skills would allow the settlement of more distant Pacific islands.

Skillful Navigators The Polynesians built huge canoes, some more than 100 feet (30 meters) long. These canoes, powered by oars and sails, could travel long distances across the ocean.

To navigate more precisely, the Polynesians created maps of ocean swells and winds using twigs. They also memorized directions from one island to another, navigating by the positions of stars at night, the ocean currents, and even the flight patterns of birds.

Analyze Diagrams
The skills of Polynesian navigators enabled these people to travel long distances across the Pacific. **Analyze Effects** How did these navigation skills affect settlement patterns in the region?

POLYNESIAN NAVIGATION

THE BOATS

- Polynesians built double-hulled canoes connected by a central platform used for living and storage space.
- The canoes were powered by sails and paddles.
- Each boat could carry several families, livestock, and supplies. Even just medium-sized canoes could carry about 25 people and their belongings.

NAVIGATION ("WAYFINDING")

- By day, navigators used the rising and setting of the sun to find direction. By night, they used stars.
- Polynesian sailors completed ocean voyages over 2,000 miles (3,218 km) in distance.
- They observed the patterns and movement of clouds, waves, driftwood, and birds to find direction and their nearness to land.
- They passed this knowledge down over generations by oral tradition.

Historians today believe that the Polynesians first spread from Samoa and Tonga to the previously unsettled Society Islands of French Polynesia, including Tahiti, around the year 1000. This migration would have required an ocean journey of 1,700 miles (2,700 km), a voyage that would have taken weeks. The Polynesians were the first people in the world to carry out voyages of this length.

The Maori During the 1100s and 1200s, Polynesians spread thousands of miles from the Society Islands to the rest of Polynesia, including New Zealand and Hawaii. Unlike the islands of Melanesia, the high, volcanic islands of Polynesia did not have an isolating landscape that separated groups of settlers. Larger societies began to form on these newly settled islands.

The **Maori** are the original **inhabitants** of New Zealand and the Cook Islands. Like other Polynesians, the Maori lived in small settlements. The Maori fished, hunted, and farmed. Chiefs were at the top of Maori society. At the bottom of society were slaves, usually captured during warfare.

The center of Maori society is a **marae**, an enclosed area of land that functions as the center of Maori culture. Art became an important part of Maori culture. The Maori carve decorations into their buildings, canoes, weapons, and other objects. As you will read later in this topic, the Maori remain in New Zealand, though they changed their culture to adapt to the modern world.

☑ READING CHECK **Summarize** Why was the Polynesian migration to the Society Islands such a major achievement?

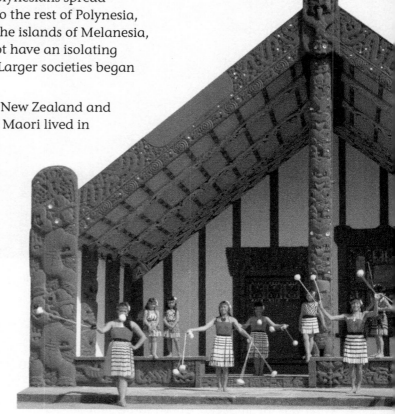

▲ Maori dancers perform in a marae meeting house on the North Island of New Zealand.

☑ Lesson Check

Practice Vocabulary

1. Why is the settlement of the **Aborigines** in Australia important to early human history?

2. What was the connection between **Polynesians** and the **Maori**?

Critical Thinking and Writing

3. **Compare and Contrast** How were the lifestyles of the Aborigines and the New Guineans different?

4. **Draw Conclusions** Why was it easier for the Polynesians to form larger societies than islanders living in Melanesia?

5. **Writing Workshop: Gather Evidence** When you complete this topic, you will write a persuasive essay about the impact of geography on people's lives in the region. Begin by gathering evidence from Lesson 1. How did geography affect early peoples? Record your thoughts in your 🗐 Active Journal.

Modern History of Australia and the Pacific

BOUNCE TO ACTIVATE ▶ VIDEO

GET READY TO READ

START UP

Look at the image of British ships bringing settlers to Australia. What do you think the Aborigines thought when they saw the British ships? How might the British settlers have reacted to them?

GUIDING QUESTIONS

- What was the impact of British settlement on Australia and New Zealand?
- How did colonialism affect the other Pacific islands?
- How did Australia, New Zealand, and the other Pacific island countries gain independence?

TAKE NOTES

Literacy Skills: Sequence
Use the graphic organizer in your 📓 Active Journal to take notes as you read the lesson.

PRACTICE VOCABULARY

Use the vocabulary activity in your 📓 Active Journal to practice the vocabulary words.

Vocabulary		Academic Vocabulary
penal colony	dominion	expedition
assimilation	dependency	restock

Australia and the Pacific began to attract European explorers and settlers in the 1600s and 1700s. As Europeans arrived, their interactions with the region's original settlers often sparked tension and violence.

European Exploration of the Pacific

Hundreds of years after the Polynesians first crossed the Pacific Ocean to settle many Pacific islands, Europeans learned to sail across oceans. They began exploring the Pacific Ocean in the early 1500s.

Early Exploration The first European to cross the Pacific was Ferdinand Magellan, sailing for Spain in 1521. He called the ocean *pacific*, or peaceful, because the winds were favorable when his ships crossed into the ocean.

The Spanish soon began sailing regularly across the Pacific, carrying precious metals from their colony in Mexico to China. Spain established colonial control over most of Micronesia in the 1500s. They also explored some Melanesian islands during the 1500s.

During the 1640s, Dutch sailors became the first Europeans to reach Australia and New Zealand. Yet the Dutch never claimed the region, failing to see its value for trade or further exploration.

British Claims European knowledge of Australia and the Pacific region remained limited until James Cook, a British sailor, explored the Pacific Ocean. In 1769, Cook navigated from the island of Tahiti to New Zealand. After spending 328 days mapping the New Zealand coast, he sailed west across the Tasman Sea. Cook reached the southeast coast of Australia in 1770.

Cook claimed both New Zealand and Australia for Britain. His **expeditions** increased European interest in the region.

☑ READING CHECK **Identify Supporting Details** Who were the first Europeans to reach Australia?

Academic Vocabulary
expedition • *n.,* a journey made for exploration, research, or war

British Settlement of Australia and New Zealand

Soon after Captain Cook claimed Australia and New Zealand, British settlers began arriving in the region. Their sudden presence, their attitude about land ownership, and their disrespect and aggression angered many Australian Aborigines and Maori.

Early British Settlement In 1788, the British sent a fleet of ships to Australia to establish a colony on the present-day site of Australia's largest city, Sydney. Of the approximately 1,000 people on these ships, about 730 were convicts. These convicts were sent to create a new **penal colony**, or a place where convicted prisoners could be sent for punishment, far from their homelands. These prisoners were forced to work, and they built the first buildings of the colony.

Britain continued to send prisoners to Australia into the 1800s. As convicts completed their sentences, many stayed in Australia to work for wages. Free settlers also arrived to start farms and businesses. Sheep raising to produce wool became a profitable industry. In 1851, the discovery of gold attracted many more settlers.

Analyze Timelines It took a long while for Europeans to settle in New Zealand after exploring it. They settled Australia much more quickly. **Sequence** How much time passed between Captain Cook claiming Australia for Britain and Britain putting settlers there?

European Exploration and Colonization of Australia and New Zealand

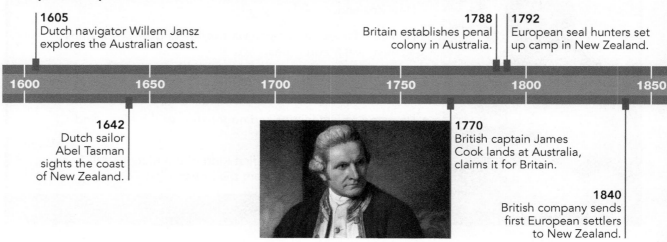

1605
Dutch navigator Willem Jansz explores the Australian coast.

1788
Britain establishes penal colony in Australia.

1792
European seal hunters set up camp in New Zealand.

1600   1650   1700   1750   1800   1850

1642
Dutch sailor Abel Tasman sights the coast of New Zealand.

1770
British captain James Cook lands at Australia, claims it for Britain.

1840
British company sends first European settlers to New Zealand.

Aboriginal Resistance British settlers drove many Aborigines off their land. Some Aborigines tried to resist, but the British seized their land, taking control of Australia's most fertile regions. As British colonists forced Aborigines off their lands, fighting broke out. Meanwhile, many Aborigines died from European diseases.

The British also practiced forced assimilation. **Assimilation** is the process by which one group takes on the cultural traits of another. British colonists took Aboriginal children away from their families and forced them to live in institutions or with white families where they were required to speak English and learn British culture. This practice continued into the 1960s. As a result many Aboriginal languages died out. Meanwhile, Aborigines were left isolated in deserts and tropical forests where white Australians did not want to settle. Their rights were often ignored, and the poor quality services they received resulted in relatively high death rates and low rates of literacy.

Interactions with the Maori In the early 1800s, British settlers had begun arriving in New Zealand, home to the Polynesian Maori people. New Zealand's harbors and rich soil attracted more British settlement. The Maori were alarmed at their loss of land. In the 1860s and 1870s, some Maori fought against British control, yet they failed to stop the British.

✓ READING CHECK **Summarize** What was the purpose of the first British settlers in Australia?

Colonialism in the Pacific

During the late 1800s, Western nations divided the Pacific islands among themselves, just as they divided Africa around the same time. Different island groups were controlled by Britain, France, Germany, and the United States.

BIOGRAPHY
5 Things to Know About

POTATAU TE WHEROWHERO
Maori King (?–1860)

- He was a descendant of the original Polynesians who settled New Zealand.

- He was a famous and fierce warrior, leading several battles against rival Maori tribes.

- He wrote to Britain's Queen Victoria in 1847 protesting the loss of Maori land.

- He acted as a mediator and negotiator for the Maori and the British.

- He agreed to become the first King of the Maori in 1858 to help protect Maori land from the British.

Critical Thinking Why did the Maori name a king for themselves?

European Colonization of Australia and the Pacific

Colony	Colonized by	Year Colonized	Year Independent
Australia	Britain	1788	1901
New Zealand	Britain	1840	1907
French Polynesia	France	1842	Never
Fiji	Britain	1874	1970
Vanuatu	Jointly by Britain and France	1887	1977
Solomon Islands	Britain	1893	1978
Papua New Guinea	Germany, Britain, Australia	1899, 1906, 1921	1975
Tonga	Britain	1900	1970

Source: Encyclopaedia Britannica

Colonizers claimed some islands because of their natural resources. Other islands were taken because of their strategic location. For example, the Micronesian islands, midway between North America and Asia, served as supply stations. Trading ships could use them to refuel and **restock** supplies during lengthy ocean voyages.

After World War I, in 1918, Japan took over Germany's possessions in Micronesia. Australia and New Zealand, which by that time were independent, gained Germany's possessions on New Guinea and other islands.

READING CHECK **Draw Conclusions** Why were some islands claimed simply because of their location?

New Nations Gain Independence

The Pacific region underwent major changes in government in the 1900s. Many of these changes were a result of World Wars I and II. Many Pacific islands gained independence peacefully.

Australia and New Zealand Australia became a **dominion**, or part of the British empire with internal self-rule, in 1901. New Zealand became a dominion in 1907. Both had democratic governments.

During World War I, Australia and New Zealand fought on Britain's side. In 1926, Britain recognized both colonies as equals to Britain under the British crown. Each country gained full independence from Britain in the 1940s. Today, Australia and New Zealand belong to the British Commonwealth of Nations, which includes 51 former British colonies.

As you will read, Australia and New Zealand developed strong economies with high standards of living. Both were allies of the United States during World War II and remained American allies after the war.

Analyze Charts Most colonies in the region were established in the late 1800s and early 1900s. **Compare and Contrast** How is French Polynesia different from other countries on this chart? How is Papua New Guinea different?

Academic Vocabulary
restock • *v.*, to obtain fresh supplies

▲ Australian troops led the invasion to retake the island of Borneo from the Japanese in July 1945 near the end of World War II.

Other Pacific Islands During World War II, Japan seized control of many Pacific islands. Most battles between Japan and the United States, such as the Battle of Guadalcanal, took place on and around those islands. After Japan surrendered in 1945 to end the war, the United States took possession of Japanese Micronesia.

After World War II, many Pacific islanders began to seek independence. During the 1960s and 1970s, most islands peacefully won independence from their former colonial powers.

American Samoa, Guam, and the Northern Mariana Islands remained U.S. **dependencies**, or self-governing territories controlled by the government of another country. France kept control of New Caledonia and much of eastern Polynesia. Several other small island groups remained under the control of Britain and New Zealand.

After gaining independence, some island nations struggled for economic and political stability. Many islands lacked strong economies and faced issues of poverty. Military leaders seized control from elected governments on some islands. However, many island nations do have democratic governments today.

☑ READING CHECK **Sequence** When did most Pacific island nations gain independence from colonial powers?

☑ Lesson Check

Practice Vocabulary

1. Why did the British try to **assimilate** Aborigines?

2. How did Australia and New Zealand's relationships with Britain change when they became **dominions**?

Critical Thinking and Writing

3. **Summarize** Which European country first claimed Australia and New Zealand?

4. **Use Evidence** How did Aborigines and the Maori react to British settlement?

5. **Sequence** When were many Pacific islands colonized, and by whom?

6. **Writing Workshop: Gather Evidence** Continue taking notes in your 📓 Active Journal for your topic essay. How did geography affect people in the years covered in Lesson 2? What other factors affected their lives?

Identify Cause and Effect

INTERACTIVE

Analyze Cause and Effect

Follow these steps and use the sources—a petition by an Aborigine and a poster inviting Europeans to move to Australia—to learn how to identify the causes and effects of changes.

1 Identify the change. Choose one event, process, or condition that involved change. Once you have chosen it, you can look for its possible causes and effects. If you're reading a primary source like the poster, you might look at the emphasized words.

a. What process is the poster advertising?

b. Why is this process taking place?

2 Study earlier events or conditions as possible causes of the change. A cause of the change must happen before the change. Look for earlier events, processes, or conditions by asking, "What led to the change?"

a. What earlier process prompted the process advertised on the poster?

b. What can you infer about the earlier process from this poster?

3 Study later events, processes, or conditions as possible effects of the change. Changes often have their own effects, either in the short term or over longer time. To identify effects, use prior knowledge and ask "What was a result of the change?"

a. What effect of the change and others like it does the petition indicate?

b. What future effect does the petition imply?

Primary Source

Primary Source

"To the King's Most Excellent Majesty in Council. The humble petition of the undersigned Aboriginal Inhabitants of the Continent of Australia showeth: That whereas it was not only a moral duty, but also a strict injunction [order] included in the commission issued to those who came to people Australia that the original occupants and we their heirs and successors should be adequately cared for . . . Your petitioners humbly pray that Your Majesty will intervene on our behalf . . . and grant us power to propose a member of parliament in the person of our own blood . . . ."

—*Australian Aborigine William Cooper's Petition to King George V, 1934*

Living in Australia and the Pacific

BOUNCE TO ACTIVATE ▶ VIDEO

GET READY TO READ

START UP
Look at the picture of New Zealanders on a hike through the mountains. How do you think life in an area like this would differ from life along a Pacific island coast?

GUIDING QUESTIONS
- Where do most people live in Australia and the Pacific islands?
- What cultures exist in Australia and New Zealand?
- What cultures exist in Melanesia, Micronesia, and Polynesia?

TAKE NOTES

Literacy Skills: Draw Conclusions
Use the graphic organizer in your 📓 Active Journal to take notes as you read the lesson.

PRACTICE VOCABULARY
Use the vocabulary activity in your 📓 Active Journal to practice the vocabulary words.

Vocabulary	Academic Vocabulary
station	scattered
pidgin language	background

Australia, New Zealand, and the other Pacific islands are home to many peoples. A blend of traditional and modern cultures have shaped life in Australia and on the thousands of islands across the Pacific that make up the region.

Where Do People Live in Australia and the Pacific?
Because it stretches across vast areas of ocean, the population of Australia and the Pacific is **scattered** widely. However, a few regions have attracted dense populations due to their geographic advantages.

Australia and New Zealand Examine the population density map of Australia, Papua New Guinea, and New Zealand. Compare it with the climate map in the Regional Atlas. Also look at the ecosystems map in Topic 1. As you can see, most of this region's population lives in Australia, primarily along the eastern coast of the continent.

European settlers were originally attracted to this part of the country for its mild, humid climate, which was good for farming.

Coastal locations also made it easier to conduct overseas communication and trade. Cities soon developed up and down Australia's eastern coast, where nearly 90 percent of the country's 22 million people live today. Few people live in Australia's vast and extremely dry interior, despite its wealth of natural resources. Mining companies can extract those resources with fairly small workforces.

New Zealand is also home to a predominantly urban population. Three-fourths of the country's 4.5 million people live on North Island, which includes the cities of Auckland and Hamilton and the country's capital, Wellington.

Pacific Islands Population varies in the Pacific islands. The highlands of central Papua New Guinea are an area of relatively high population density. As you learned, people in this region have been farming for thousands of years. The rich soils of the highlands continue to support much of the country's population. Almost 90 percent of Papua New Guinea's population is rural.

The population of many Pacific islands is also rural. While there are some large cities, such as Nouméa on the island of New Caledonia, most people live in small villages in hilly regions or on the coastline. Population is scattered and depends on the land available for farming, opportunities for fishing, or access to other jobs that will provide them with an income. Since most Pacific island nations are small, none besides Papua New Guinea have large populations.

✓ **READING CHECK** **Use Evidence** Describe population density in Australia, New Zealand, and the Pacific islands.

Academic Vocabulary
scattered • *adj.,* distributed or occurring in widely spaced areas

GEOGRAPHY SKILLS

Population density in Australia is influenced by the dry climates of the interior.

1. **Region** How does population density vary on Papua New Guinea's main island?

2. **Compare and Contrast** How does the population density of New Zealand's two islands compare ?

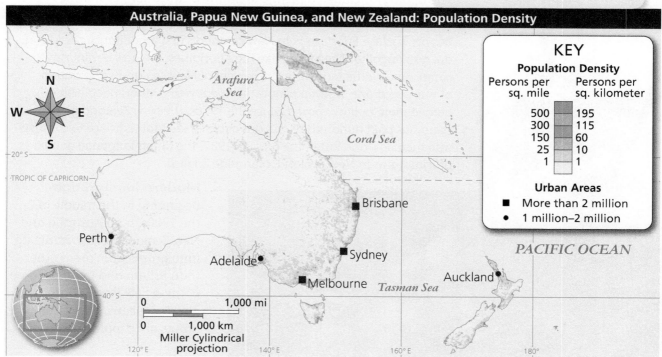

Australia, Papua New Guinea, and New Zealand: Population Density

KEY
Population Density

Persons per sq. mile		Persons per sq. kilometer
500		195
300		115
150		60
25		10
1		1

Urban Areas
■ More than 2 million
• 1 million–2 million

Quick Activity

Use your ☐ Active Journal to work with your classmates to represent the space between islands in the Pacific region.

Academic Vocabulary
background • *n.*, trait, such as ethnic heritage, that people inherit from their parents

Analyze Images A group of Australians celebrates Chinese New Year. **Identify Effects** What population trend does this celebration reflect?

Cultures of Australia and New Zealand

European settlement in Australia and New Zealand permanently changed both countries' population and cultures. Australian Aborigines and the Maori lost land and died from disease after Europeans arrived. Descendants of Europeans now greatly outnumber the original inhabitants of both countries. Immigrants from other regions of the world are also beginning to influence both island nations.

Cultural Characteristics Most of the people living in Australia and New Zealand are descended from the many British and Irish people who migrated there over the past 200 years. Each country has a unique culture that includes many British traditions but also reflects the country's own history and environment. For example, Australians and New Zealanders celebrate holidays exclusive to their own countries, and even their regions. In both countries, nearly everyone speaks English. Religion is more diverse, though the majority religion is Christianity.

Aborigines Today Australian Aborigines, the country's original inhabitants, are now a minority in Australia, where they make up about 2 percent of the population. British settlers and the Australian government mistreated Aborigines for many years. As you read, the British often took Aboriginal children from their families. Additionally, many Aborigines were forcibly moved to **stations**, or parcels of land put aside by the government, often in remote areas, on which some Aborigines were forced to live. By doing so, the government kept Aborigines apart from Australians with European **backgrounds**.

In recent years, the Australian government has begun to recognize the historical injustices done to Aborigines. In 2008, Australia's prime minister officially apologized for the unjust treatment of Aborigines. The apology included a pledge to improve education, economic opportunity, and living standards for Aborigines.

Maori Today Efforts to help New Zealand's first inhabitants, the Maori, are also ongoing. The Maori, like the Aborigines, are now a minority, comprising a little more than 14 percent of New Zealand's population, or one about one in seven people. In recent years, Maori people have gained more political power. Since the 1970s, the New Zealand government has paid hundreds of millions of dollars to Maori groups to compensate them for land lost in the past. In 1987, the Maori language gained official status in New Zealand, alongside English.

Modern Immigration Beginning in the middle of the 1900s, both Australia and New Zealand began attracting immigrants from areas other than Britain and Ireland. Some of these new immigrants are also Europeans. Many immigrants are people from Asia.

Because of Asian immigration, about one in ten Australians and New Zealanders are of Asian descent.

READING CHECK Summarize How have the Australian and New Zealand governments attempted to make up for past wrongs inflicted on the Aborigines and Maori?

Cultures of Melanesia, Micronesia, and Polynesia

Most Pacific islands are still home to the indigenous, or original, cultures and ethnic groups that were in place before Europeans arrived. Many Pacific islanders still practice traditional forms of art, dance, and music. Yet their cultures have also adapted to modern ways of life.

Each Pacific island group has its own culture and language. Some of the larger islands, such as those within the Solomon Islands, include several ethnic groups who speak different languages. On those islands and in Papua New Guinea and Vanuatu, people have developed national pidgin languages. A **pidgin language** is a simple language used for interaction between people who speak different languages. A pidgin language is usually based on one language but influenced by others. In the Pacific region, many pidgin languages are based on English, but they also use words and grammar from indigenous languages.

While the people on most Pacific islands are indigenous, some of the islands have ethnic minorities due to immigration. For example, about 38 percent of people in Fiji are descended from immigrants from India, and 16 percent of Palau's population have a Filipino background.

READING CHECK Identify Main Ideas Describe the cultures of most Pacific islands.

Analyze Images The British sport of rugby is popular on many Pacific islands. In this photo, Fiji rugby fans cheer on their team. **Draw Conclusions** What does Fiji's participation in rugby tell you about the country's culture?

☑ Lesson Check

Practice Vocabulary

1. Why did the Australian government create **stations**?

2. Why are **pidgin languages** useful?

Critical Thinking and Writing

3. Draw Conclusions Why have the highlands of Papua New Guinea maintained a dense population for so long?

4. Compare and Contrast Use the Country Databank to compare the population densities of countries in the region. What would explain the differences?

5. Writing Workshop: Introduce Claims Think about what you have learned about the effect of geography on people's lives in the region. In your ▱ Active Journal, write one or more claims about those effects that you think the evidence supports.

LESSON 4

Australia and the Pacific at Work

GET READY TO READ

START UP

Look at the photo of Australian cowhands. Write three questions you have about how geography shapes economic activities in Australia and the Pacific.

GUIDING QUESTIONS

- What forms of government exist in Australia and New Zealand?
- What forms of government exist in the other Pacific islands?
- What factors shape the economies of Australia, New Zealand, and the other Pacific islands?

TAKE NOTES

Literacy Skills: Compare and Contrast
Use the graphic organizer in your 📓 Active Journal to take notes as you read the lesson.

PRACTICE VOCABULARY

Use the vocabulary activity in your 📓 Active Journal to practice the vocabulary words.

Vocabulary	Academic Vocabulary
governor general	customary
remittance	quota

The governments and economies of the Pacific region vary greatly. Australia and New Zealand both have stable democratic governments and strong economies. Some of the other Pacific islands have weaker economies and democracies.

Government in Australia and New Zealand

Both Australia and New Zealand have parliamentary democracies that are also constitutional monarchies like Britain's. The head of government in a parliamentary democracy is chosen by the majority party in the legislature. That leader is called the prime minister. Australia's federal structure includes a national government and individual state governments, as in the United States. In New Zealand, most government decisions are made at the national level.

Both countries recognize Britain's monarch as head of state, but the monarch has only a symbolic role. The monarch's representative in each country, the **governor general**, has duties that are mostly ceremonial.

In both Australia and New Zealand, citizens' roles are to be informed about the issues affecting their nation and to elect representatives to parliament who represent their points of view. In New Zealand, citizens have a responsibility to vote but are not legally required to do so. In Australia, citizens can be fined for failing to vote.

READING CHECK **Classify and Categorize** What is the role of the monarch in Australia and New Zealand?

Government in the Pacific Islands

The Pacific island countries have a wide range of governments. This variety means that some governments are more democratic than others. For some Pacific islands, their territorial status means that government is both local and far away. Some remain dependencies, under the full or partial control of another country.

Types of Governments Most Pacific islands have democratic governments. Some governments—including those of the Solomon Islands, Tuvalu, and Papua New Guinea—are parliamentary constitutional monarchies like Australia and New Zealand.

Several other island countries, including Fiji and Nauru, are parliamentary republics. In this system of government, an elected parliament elects a prime minister as the head of government, and a president serves as a symbolic head of state. Still other island countries, such as Kiribati, are presidential republics like the United States. Presidential republics have an elected parliament that passes laws and a president elected by voters who serves as both head of government and head of state.

Some of these countries have healthy democracies, but others have flawed democracies. For example, powerful groups in Papua New Guinea have interfered with the country's free elections and the rule of law. Political leaders at many levels of the government have been accused of corruption. In Fiji, a military leader named Voreqe Bainimarama seized power from the elected government in 2006. Bainimarama was then named prime minister in 2014, after his party won a parliament majority in Fiji's first election in years. That election followed tight restrictions on the freedom of the press.

▼ The indigenous people of the Pacific region participate in government to protect their rights. Here, Maori people in Auckland, New Zealand, march to maintain their representation in city government.

Quest CONNECTIONS

Coal mining helps Australia's economy but causes pollution. Research this issue and record findings in your ▣ Active Journal.

Academic Vocabulary
customary • *adj.,* according to custom or usual practices

Territorial Governments Most of the Pacific islands that are dependencies or territories have elected governments that handle many internal matters. Other areas, such as defense and foreign relations, are handled by the dominant country. For example, American Samoa is a U.S. territory. Its people elect a governor and a legislature to handle most areas of government. However, its legal system and defense are under the control of the U.S. government, and it is subject to laws passed by the U.S. Congress. American Samoa follows a legal system made up of both **customary** law and U.S. common law.

☑ READING CHECK **Summarize** What types of government can be found in the Pacific islands?

Economies of Australia and New Zealand

Australia and New Zealand, like most countries, have mixed economies. Market forces, such as the preferences of consumers and producers, determine what is produced, how it is produced, and by whom. However, the Australian and New Zealand governments also play a decision-making role in some areas of economic life, as they do in command economies. Traditional economies, where economic decisions are based on custom, still exist on some Pacific islands.

Resources and Trade As in the rest of the world, Australia and New Zealand's natural resources affect what each country is best at producing. Australia has abundant deposits of coal and minerals, including iron ore. It is also home to vast grasslands that serve as pasture for livestock. As a result, Australia has an advantage at producing coal, iron ore, and other minerals, as well as wool from sheep. It exports these products, mainly to China and other Asian countries, for use in their growing steel and textile industries.

BIOGRAPHY
5 Things to Know About ▸ JULIA GILLARD
Australian Prime Minister (born 1961)

- Gillard was born in Wales, in Britain, but moved to Australia at the age of five.

- An active member of her university's student government, she eventually became president of the Australian Union of Students.

- In the 1980s and 1990s, she became an influential member of the Australian Labor Party (ALP) and was elected to parliament in 1998.

- She was elected deputy prime minister, ALP leader, and, in 2010, the first female prime minister of Australia.

- In 2013, after losing her party's vote for prime minister, she voluntarily retired from politics.

Infer What party led the government when Julia Gillard became prime minister?

New Zealand also has ample pastures for live-stock. As a result, it specializes in producing wool, meat, and dairy products for trade.

Australia and New Zealand have negotiated agreements with their trading partners—including each other—to reduce trade barriers, such as tariffs and **quotas**. Embargoes, or bans on trade, are another kind of trade barrier. For example, Australia imposes embargoes on North Korea, Russia, and Iran as punishments for actions their governments have taken. Both Australia and New Zealand have systems of currency exchange to make sure their overseas sales can easily be changed into Australian dollars (AUD) or New Zealand dollars (NZD).

Economic Investment Australia's strong economy shows the important connection between investment in human and productive capital and a country's standard of living.

In Australia, the government's investment in human capital through education boosts the skills of its workforce. Australia has a high literacy rate, with 96 percent of adults able to read and write. This high literacy rate is a sign of an educated, productive workforce that supports Australia's high gross domestic product (GDP) per person and its high standard of living.

Australia also has a high rate of investment in capital goods, such as computers, technical equipment, and workplaces. Capital goods allow workers to be even more productive. Again, increased productivity translates into a high standard of living. As you have learned, GDP per person is one way to measure standard of living. Australia's GDP per person is similar to that of Canada and the United States.

Entrepreneurship also plays an important role in Australia's economy. According to the Global Entrepreneurship and Development Institute, Australia is the third-best country in the world for people to start and grow a business. Only the United States and Canada rank higher.

▲ Tourism is a major sector of the economies of Pacific island countries. Tourists in Tonga can explore Swallow's Cave and other local landmarks.

Academic Vocabulary

quota • *n.,* a fixed quantity set by limits

✔ **READING CHECK** Use Evidence What advantages do Australia's and New Zealand's natural resources offer those countries' economies?

Economies of the Pacific Islands

The other Pacific island countries do not enjoy the same economic advantages as Australia and New Zealand. Most of these countries have few natural resources and all are far from global markets, leading to very little investment in capital goods. Weak economies also make it more difficult to invest in education. Therefore, many countries in the region have low literacy levels and, as a result, low productivity rates. All of these facts contribute to a relatively low standard of living.

INTERACTIVE

GDP by Economic Sector of Australia and the Solomon Islands

Analyze Graphs GDP per capita is one measure of a country's standard of living. **Draw Conclusions** Based on the information in the graph, what conclusions can you make about Palau's standard of living as compared to the standard of living in other Pacific island nations?

GDP per Capita in Australia and the Pacific

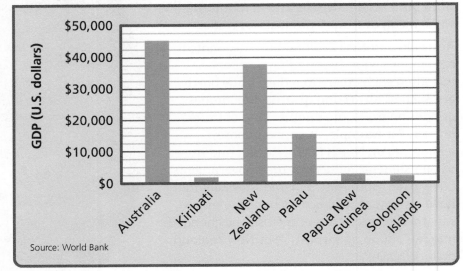

Source: World Bank

However, the isolation that hinders the region's economies also help them. Every year the islands attract thousands of tourists who travel to see the region's coral reefs, lagoons, and volcanoes. The money these tourists spend is crucial to many island economies. Some island countries also take advantage of their tropical location to produce tropical crops, such as sugarcane that can be processed into sugar and exported.

For many countries, the main resource is their people. Citizens of many Pacific island countries leave to work in Australia, New Zealand, the United States, or other wealthy countries. The money that they send home to their families, known as **remittances**, is important to the economies of their homeland.

☑ READING CHECK **Draw Conclusions** Why do many Pacific island countries lack the funds to invest more in education?

☑ Lesson Check

Practice Vocabulary

1. What is the role of the **governor general** in Australia and New Zealand?

2. How do **remittances** help Pacific island economies?

Critical Thinking and Writing

3. **Compare and Contrast** Explain the difference between the monarchy's role and the prime minister's role in Australia and New Zealand.

4. **Cite Evidence** Use the Country Databank to explain the connection between geographical size and GDP for countries in the Pacific region.

5. **Writing Workshop: Distinguish Claims from Opposing Claims** Review the claims about the effects of geography in the region that you wrote in your ▣ Active Journal. What opposing claims can be made using the evidence? How would you respond to those opposing claims?

Geographic Sources

The Refugee Issue

In recent years, Australia has experienced a large increase in the number of refugees seeking safety on its shores. Often, before these people can reach Australia, they are detained for years in processing centers on other Pacific islands. Some Australians believe that these offshore processing centers are necessary. Other Australians believe that the centers are run badly and cruel to refugees.

▶ A boat-load of asylum seekers is transferred to Christmas Island.

[T]he approach of this government is not going to change. We are not going to allow people to settle in our country who seek to come here by boat. We've been absolutely consistent in relation to that message and the same message applies to those who are on Manus and Nauru ① now. . . . We have restored integrity ② to our borders and I promise you this: we are not going to step back from that position. We are going to make sure, particularly in this day and age with national security as such an important issue, . . . that our borders remain secure so that we can keep our community in Australia as safe as possible. ③

—Australia's Minister for Immigration Peter Dutton, ABC News Australia interview, April 28, 2016

The conditions at the [Papua New Guinea] center, and at another on Nauru, a tiny island nation, have come under scrutiny. The United Nations has said that Australia's treatment of asylum seekers ④ at the offshore centers is cruel, inhuman and degrading, and that it violates international law. . . . "Australia's international reputation has been enormously damaged by the establishment of offshore camps," said Tim O'Connor, acting chief executive of the Refugee Council of Australia, which represents 200 groups that support asylum seekers. "It has done enormous damage to the thousands of individuals who have been trapped in this system. The refugees should immediately be brought to Australia." ⑤

—"Australia Will Close Detention Center on Manus Island, but Still Won't Accept Asylum Seekers," by Brett Cole, *New York Times*, August 17, 2016

Analyzing Geographic Sources

Consider the differences in how the two texts refer to the centers.

1. **Determine Author's Point of View** According to the author of the first text, why are restrictions on refugees necessary?

2. **Compare Authors' Treatment of Similar Topics** How does the tone of the first text compare with the tone of the second text?

3. **Assess Credibility** Why is it important to know the position in government held by the author of the first text?

Reading and Vocabulary Support

① Manus and Nauru are the sites of two of Australia's offshore detention centers.

② The state of being whole and undivided

③ What does the author say is Australia's policy toward refugees who seek to move to the country by boat?

④ People looking for the protection granted by a nation to those who have left their native country as political refugees

⑤ How does the quote support the United Nations' claim that the offshore centers treat asylum seekers cruelly?

Challenges Facing Australia and the Pacific

GET READY TO READ

START UP

Look at the photo of the sea wall constructed on the island of Tarawa in Kiribati. Predict the environmental challenge you think this wall was built to meet. How well has it done the job?

GUIDING QUESTIONS

- How do rising sea levels threaten Australia and the Pacific islands?
- What other environmental challenges does the region face?

TAKE NOTES

Literacy Skills: Identify Main Ideas
Use the graphic organizer in your 📕 Active Journal to take notes as you read the lesson.

PRACTICE VOCABULARY

Use the vocabulary activity in your 📕 Active Journal to practice the vocabulary words.

Vocabulary	**Academic Vocabulary**
atoll	catastrophic
coral reef	toxic
coral bleaching	

The economies of Australia and the Pacific partly depend on the environment. Tourism relies on the region's beaches and clear blue water. Agriculture and fishing use natural resources. But the region still faces environmental challenges that threaten these economies—and the region's people.

The Threat of Rising Sea Levels

One of the greatest challenges facing the region is rising sea levels. Scientists believe this rise is the result of climate change.

Climate Change As you have read, climate change is a long-term change. The United Nations and the Intergovernmental Panel on Climate Change point to human activities—such as burning fossil fuels that produce greenhouse gases—as the main force behind climate change.

As Earth's climate has slowly become warmer, the world's glaciers and massive ice sheets have begun to melt. This melted ice has raised sea levels. Additionally, warmer temperatures have caused ocean waters to warm, which causes them to expand.

Many scientists expect that the sea level will continue to rise in coming years, perhaps by as much as several feet by 2100.

Effect on Australia and New Zealand Rising sea levels in coastal areas of Australia and New Zealand threaten to ruin property and make parts of the coastline unlivable. With 85 percent of Australia's population living on or near the coast, the predicted increase in damaging high tides and storm surges may cause **catastrophic** damage.

In New Zealand, where sea levels have increased an average of 1.7 millimeters a year (or an inch every 15 years) for the past 40 years, the government has begun preparing for future increases. Laws limit new construction in areas already prone to coastal erosion.

Effect on Pacific Islands The threat of rising oceans is even more serious in many smaller island nations. Most of the islands of Micronesia and many of the islands of Polynesia are coral atolls. **Atolls** are low, sandy islands that have formed on top of extinct volcanoes that have eroded and sunk below the sea surface. Some atolls rise no more than a few feet above sea level.

By the year 2100, these atoll island nations, such as Tuvalu, could disappear completely. Even now, some smaller islands are beginning to vanish. Five of the islands within the Solomon Island group have slipped completely under water. On many other islands, surges of water during strong storms are washing away land needed for tourism, fishing villages, and subsistence farming.

☑ READING CHECK **Identify Main Ideas** Why are sea levels rising?

Academic Vocabulary
catastrophic • *adj.*, involving or causing sudden great damage or suffering

Analyze Diagrams Rising sea levels pose many threats to low-lying Pacific islands. **Analyze Data** What does the diagram tell you about sea level change and its effects?

THE **THREAT** OF **RISING SEA LEVELS** TO **PACIFIC ISLANDS**

RISE IN SEA LEVEL, 1996-2016

Increase since 1993 (mm)

Year	Value
1996	10.9
2000	27.3
2004	42.3
2008	51.5
2012	70.6
2016	85.6

SPECIFIC THREATS

Rising, warmer water damages coral reefs, which reduces their ability to protect the island from tides.

Higher tides flood homes and streets and erode beaches that attract tourists.

Ocean water fouls freshwater supplies and food crops.

People must move to higher ground, if available, or to another island.

ISLANDS AT SERIOUS RISK

- **Solomon Islands** (five islands had disappeared by 2014)
- **New Caledonia**
- **Fiji**
- **Kiribati**
- **Tuvalu**
- **French Polynesia**
- **Marshall Islands**
- **Cook Islands**

Sources: NASA, Scientific American, New York Times, National Geographic

Other Environmental Challenges

The region is struggling with other environmental issues. Among these problems are drought, damage to coral reefs, overfishing, and pollution.

Drought Australia, the world's driest inhabited continent, has often experienced severe drought. Some climate scientists predict that warmer temperatures will lead to an even drier climate. If this happens, water supplies in both rural farming regions and Australia's cities will be threatened.

Wildfires are also a concern in drought-prone countries, including New Zealand. There and in Australia, fires can spread rapidly across the countryside during a dry season. These destructive fires are made worse by the grasses that grow during a rainy season and then dry out.

Although many Pacific islands receive heavy rainfall, some places still do not have enough fresh water for drinking or other human use. Low-lying atolls and other low, sandy islands have very little fresh water.

Coral Bleaching The Great Barrier Reef, located off Australia's northeast coast, is the world's largest grouping of coral reefs. A **coral reef** is a living formation of rock-like material made up of the skeletons of tiny sea creatures. The Great Barrier Reef is home to an astounding variety of ocean plants and animals that depend on the reef environment.

In recent years, climate change has threatened the Great Barrier Reef and smaller reefs. When coral is healthy, microorganisms live inside it and provide the coral with a food source and color. But when coral is stressed—due to warmer ocean waters, exposure to the sun, or pollution—it expels the microorganisms living inside it. As a result, the coral weakens and lightens in color. This process is called **coral bleaching**. Another major cause of coral bleaching is rising carbon dioxide levels. Carbon dioxide from the atmosphere settles in the oceans, making the water more acidic.

Stressed coral can recover if conditions return to normal. However, if the coral remains bleached, it can starve to death. In 1998 and then again in 2002, over 50 percent of the Great Barrier Reef became bleached. About 5 percent of the reef was severely damaged each time. Coral bleaching threatens many sea creatures that live in reefs with extinction. It is another threat to atolls, which depend on healthy coral reefs.

▼ The arid climate regions of Australia are prone to wildfires. Lightning sparked this wildfire in northern Western Australia.

Overfishing The sea life of the Pacific region has also been threatened by overfishing. Fishing is one of the most important economic activities in most Pacific island countries and is a source of local food. When too many fish are taken too quickly, fish may become scarce for years.

Many Pacific island countries have sold fishing rights to foreign fishing fleets, some of which are owned by American, Chinese, and Japanese companies. As a result, populations of fish in the islands' waters have been declining. Tuna have experienced an alarming decrease in their population in the South Pacific. Some conservationists estimate that five out of the eight species of tuna are now facing extinction.

Mining Pollution Australia is also battling water and air pollution due to mining, which has been important to the country's economy for many years. Mining Australia's coal, iron, gold, uranium, and other mineral reserves often unearths unwanted minerals, which are **toxic** when exposed to air or water. Many of the chemicals used in processing minerals can be dangerous to the environment. Coal mines and power stations using coal are major contributors to air pollution.

Analyze Images The photo on the left shows healthy coral in the Great Barrier Reef. The photo on the right shows coral that has been bleached. **Recognize Multiple Causes** How does coral bleaching occur?

Academic Vocabulary
toxic • *adj.,* poisonous

☑ **READING CHECK** Draw Conclusions Why is coral bleaching such a threat to the Pacific region?

☑ Lesson Check

Practice Vocabulary

1. Why are **atoll** nations in the Pacific most threatened by rising sea levels?

2. What are **coral reefs** and where is the largest reef group in the world?

Critical Thinking and Writing

3. **Identify Cause and Effect** Based on population density, what makes rising sea levels so dangerous to Australia and New Zealand?

4. **Summarize** Besides an increase in sea levels, what other effects has climate change had on the Pacific region?

5. **Writing Workshop: Choose an Organizing Strategy** Based on the notes you took in your 🗐 Active Journal, choose a way to organize your essay. Will you present your strongest arguments first? What support do you have for them? How will you address opposing claims? Write an outline for your essay.

Antarctica

 **BOUNCE** TO ACTIVATE ▶ VIDEO

GET READY TO READ

START UP

Look at the photo of a group of penguins on an iceberg in Antarctica. Before you read the lesson, write down three questions you have about Antarctica. Then look for answers as you read.

GUIDING QUESTIONS

- What are the key features of Antarctica's physical geography?
- What goals have people pursued in Antarctica?

TAKE NOTES

Literacy Skills: Use Evidence
Use the graphic organizer in your 📓 Active Journal to take notes as you read the lesson.

PRACTICE VOCABULARY

Use the vocabulary activity in your 📓 Active Journal to practice the vocabulary words.

Vocabulary

		Academic Vocabulary
ice sheet	Antarctic Treaty	interior
glacier	ozone layer	competing
iceberg		
pack ice		

Antarctica is the least explored and understood of the world's seven continents. Its physical geography is unique. The prospect of new discoveries in Antarctica attracts scientists from around the world.

Antarctica's Physical Geography

Covered by a glittering sheet of ice and surrounded by stormy seas, Antarctica is Earth's only continent without a permanent population. It is the coldest and windiest region on Earth. The South Pole, the southernmost point on Earth, is located in Antarctica.

An Icy Landscape A thick **ice sheet**—a large mass of compressed ice—covers 98 percent of the land and holds most of the world's fresh water. **Glaciers**, or slow-moving bodies of ice, form in Antarctica's valleys and flow toward the coast. When glaciers reach the sea, the ice may break off into **icebergs**, or large floating masses of ice.

In winter, the surface of the sea around Antarctica freezes, forming pack ice. **Pack ice** is seasonal ice that floats on the water rather than being attached to land.

The Transantarctic Mountains divide Antarctica into two regions, a large, flat area called East Antarctica and a smaller region called West Antarctica. At the tip of West Antarctica, the Antarctic Peninsula extends toward South America. The Transantarctic Mountains have glaciers and dry valleys free of snow and ice.

In recent years, West Antarctica has experienced warmer temperatures. Some scientists believe that the ice sheet in West Antarctica is at risk of weakening and melting, which could cause sea levels to rise. Scientists closely monitor Antarctica for the effects of climate change.

Climate, Life, and Resources Antarctica's **interior** is a high, dry plateau. It receives less than two inches of precipitation per year. The snow that does fall does not melt. Instead, it piles up, eventually turning into glacial ice.

The South Pole is near the center of Antarctica. The land at the South Pole is covered by an ice sheet about 9,000 feet (2,700 meters) thick. Since Earth rotates on a tilted axis, the sun is always above the horizon of the South Pole in summer and always below it in winter. As a result, the South Pole receives 24 hours of sunlight per day in the summer and none in the winter. Temperatures at the pole can drop as low as –117° Fahrenheit (–82.8° Celsius).

Antarctica's resources include coal and iron ore. Its harsh climate limits vegetation to simple plants. Penguins, seals, and other animals spend much of their time in the ocean.

READING CHECK Draw Conclusions How do Antarctica's climate and landscape affect plant and animal life there?

GEOGRAPHY **SKILLS**

Note Antarctica's physical regions and the ice shelves that ring the continent.

1. **Location** Compare this map with the physical map of Australia in the Regional Atlas. Describe Antarctica's location in relation to Australia and the Pacific.

2. **Analyze Maps** Where can you find the Antarctic Peninsula?

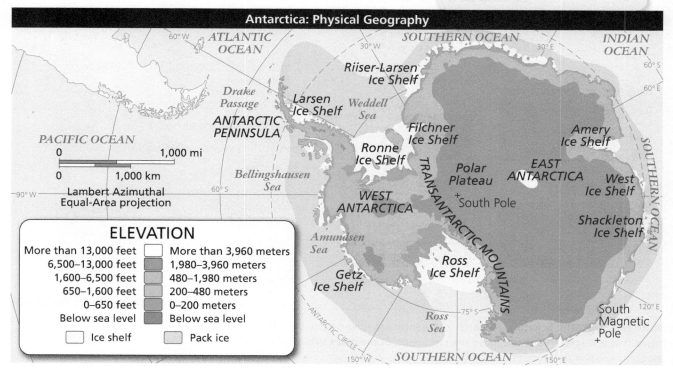

Antarctica: Physical Geography

ATLANTIC OCEAN · SOUTHERN OCEAN · INDIAN OCEAN · PACIFIC OCEAN · SOUTHERN OCEAN

Riiser-Larsen Ice Shelf · Drake Passage · Larsen Ice Shelf · Weddell Sea · ANTARCTIC PENINSULA · Filchner Ice Shelf · Amery Ice Shelf · Ronne Ice Shelf · EAST ANTARCTICA · West Ice Shelf · Bellingshausen Sea · Polar Plateau · South Pole · WEST ANTARCTICA · TRANSANTARCTIC MOUNTAINS · Shackleton Ice Shelf · Amundsen Sea · Ross Ice Shelf · Getz Ice Shelf · Ross Sea · South Magnetic Pole · SOUTHERN OCEAN · ANTARCTIC CIRCLE

0 — 1,000 mi
0 — 1,000 km
Lambert Azimuthal Equal-Area projection

ELEVATION
More than 13,000 feet	More than 3,960 meters
6,500–13,000 feet	1,980–3,960 meters
1,600–6,500 feet	480–1,980 meters
650–1,600 feet	200–480 meters
0–650 feet	0–200 meters
Below sea level	Below sea level
Ice shelf	Pack ice

INTERACTIVE

Antarctic Research

Exploration and Research in Antarctica

Antarctica was a relatively unknown region at the beginning of the 1900s. Today, scientists use Antarctica as a giant laboratory to examine the natural world.

Early Explorers In 1910, explorers Robert Scott and Roald Amundsen began separate expeditions to be the first people to reach the South Pole. Amundsen reached it in December 1911. Scott reached the Pole a month later. On the return trip, Scott and his team died in a blizzard. Still, their studies helped advance Antarctic science.

In 1915, British explorer Ernest Shackleton set out to cross Antarctica. His ship was destroyed by pack ice, forcing his team to live on an ice floe. Eventually, the men crossed the ocean in three small boats and found help. Amazingly, everyone survived.

Antarctica and Science Early explorers often claimed land for their countries in Antarctica. By the 1940s, these **competing** land claims led to international conflict. In 1959, twelve countries signed the **Antarctic Treaty**, an international agreement that preserves Antarctica for peaceful and scientific use. Absolutely no military action is allowed on the continent. Disposal of radioactive waste is banned there as well. In 1991, the treaty was amended to ban mining and oil drilling and to further protect the Antarctic environment.

Antarctica has no permanent human settlement. It does have scientific research stations scattered across the continent. Scientists from many

Academic Vocabulary
competing • *adj.,* being a rival; challenging

SCIENCE IN ANTARCTICA

BY THE NUMBERS

66
used for scientific research

37
used year-round

BASES

4,000
or so on site in summer

1,000
or so on site in winter

SCIENTISTS

Sources: Cool Antarctica, U.S. Navy, Nature

MAJOR RESEARCH GOALS

- Define the global impact of Antarctica's atmosphere and the Southern Ocean
- Understand why ice sheets are growing smaller
- Learn about Antarctica's history
- Understand how life in Antarctica arose and developed
- Study objects in space
- Learn how to reduce negative human effects on Antarctica

Analyze Diagrams Scientific research in Antarctica involves many people working in bases that are scattered throughout the continent. **Summarize** What kinds of research are conducted in Antarctica?

countries study its oceans, glaciers, wildlife, and climate. Most research in Antarctica takes place during the milder summer months, when planes and ships led by icebreakers can safely reach coastal stations. In the dark, brutally cold winter months, much smaller maintenance teams live at the stations and carry out research.

Climate and the Ozone Layer To study climate, scientists drill deep into the ice sheet to gather ice samples. By examining the samples, they can learn more about the climate at the time when the ice was formed thousands of years ago. By studying past climates, scientists hope to understand more about how climate might change in the future.

Scientists in Antarctica also study the ozone layer. The **ozone layer** is a layer of the atmosphere that filters out most of the sun's harmful ultraviolet rays. Over time, the ozone layer over Antarctica has grown thinner. This area of reduced ozone, called the ozone hole, allows more ultraviolet radiation to reach Earth. These rays can damage the health of plants, humans, and other animals. Certain artificial chemicals caused the ozone hole. Today, most uses of these chemicals have been banned. Thanks to the ban, scientists predict that the ozone layer will eventually recover.

☑ READING CHECK **Infer** In Antarctica, snow piles up year after year, eventually turning into glacial ice. How can scientists take advantage of this?

Quest CONNECTIONS

What are the threats to Antarctica due to climate change? Record your thoughts in your 📓 Active Journal.

☑ Lesson Check

Practice Vocabulary

1. What is Antarctica's **ice sheet**, and why is it significant?

2. What was the result of the **Antarctic Treaty**?

Critical Thinking and Writing

3. **Infer** How has physical geography discouraged human settlement in Antarctica?

4. **Identify Cause and Effect** How does the ozone hole affect Earth?

5. **Writing Workshop: Write an Introduction** Draft an introduction to your topic essay in your 📓 Active Journal. Your introduction should clearly state your view of the effects that geography has on people's lives in the region.

☑ Review and Assessment

VISUAL REVIEW

Causes and Effects of British Colonization of Australia

CAUSES
• Great Britain wants to expand trade opportunities. • Britain needs land for a penal colony. • British find Australia is home to gold, fertile soil, and other resources.

EVENT
Europeans begin settling in Australia.

EFFECTS
• Aborigines are driven off their land. • Aborigines and European settlers begin fighting. • Aborigines are forced to assimilate, and children are taken from their families. • British prisoners find new opportunities as settlers. • British profit from wool production. • British profit from the discovery of gold.

Comparing Areas of the Pacific Region

Australia/New Zealand	Both Areas	Other Pacific Islands
• Large islands • Former British colonies • Most people live in urban settings • Majority descended from British or Irish people • Parliamentary democracies; head of state is British monarch • Strong mixed economies	• Part of an isolated region far from other parts of the world • Settled through waves of migration • Affected by European colonization • Aboriginal and European cultural influences • Affected by environmental challenges	• Small islands • Former colonies of Britain, Germany, France, and the United States • Most people live in rural settings • Majority descended from indigenous people • Variety of governments, including U.S. dependencies • Economies dependent on a single resource or tourism

READING REVIEW

Use the Takes Notes and Practice Vocabulary activities in your ▤ Active Journal to review the topic.

 INTERACTIVE

Practice vocabulary using the Topic Mini-Games.

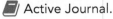 FINDINGS

Write Your Petition

Write your petition about how to address an environmental challenge in your ▤ Active Journal.

ASSESSMENT

Vocabulary and Key Ideas

1. **Identify** What is the base language for many of the **pidgin languages** spoken on Pacific islands?

2. **List** Name three differences between the early **Aborigines** and **Maori**.

3. **Describe** Explain the governmental structure of **dependencies**.

4. **Define** How are Antarctica's **glaciers** and **icebergs** related?

5. **Recall** Why do so few people live in Australia's interior?

6. **Identify Supporting Details** What are important features of New Zealand's economy?

7. **Check Understanding** Why is most research on Antarctica conducted during the summer?

Critical Thinking and Writing

8. **Cite Evidence** Why can't Aboriginal stations be classified as assimilation?

9. **Infer** Why might remittances be more important to some Pacific island nations than to Australia?

10. **Understand Effects** Use the Country Databank to compare the languages used in various countries in the Pacific region. Explain how the region's history explains how these languages came to the region.

11. **Identify Cause and Effect** Why is overfishing a threat to some Pacific island nations' present-day and future economies?

12. **Revisit the Essential Question:** How much does geography affect people's lives?

13. **Writer's Workshop: Write an Argumentative Essay** Using the notes you took and the draft introduction you wrote, write an argumentative essay on the effect of geography on people's lives in the region. Follow the directions in your 📓 Active Journal.

Analyze Primary Sources

14. In what country was Sopoaga most likely prime minister at the time he spoke the words in the quotation?
    A. Australia
    B. Tuvalu
    C. New Zealand
    D. Papua New Guinea

"If you were faced with the threat of the disappearance of your nation, what would you do? . . . Will we survive? Or will we disappear under the sea?"

—*Prime Minister Enele Sopoaga*

Analyze Maps

15. Which letter represents the home of the Maori people?

16. Which letter marks a place where agriculture originated?

17. Which letter represents the region where the majority of Australians live?

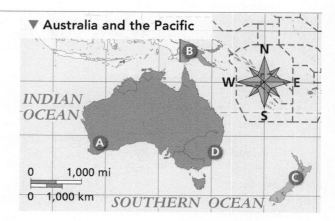

▼ **Australia and the Pacific**

Country Databank

Region and country	Total population, 2015 estimate, millions	Area, thousands of square miles	Population density, per square mile	Average annual population growth rate, 2010–2015, percent	Gross domestic product (GDP, purchasing power parity) per capita, most recent, current dollars	
Europe						
Albania	2.9	11	261.0	−0.04	11,276	
Andorra	0.07	0.18	390.0	−3.61	44,882	
Austria	8.5	32	263.9	0.36	48,196	
Belarus	9.5	80	118.5	0.01	17,693	
Belgium	11.3	12	958.6	0.66	43,939	
Bosnia and Herzegovina	3.8	20	192.8	−0.13	10,510	
Bulgaria	7.1	43	167.0	−0.71	17,581	
Croatia	4.2	22	194.1	−0.36	21,798	
Czech Republic	10.5	30	346.2	0.07	32,192	
Denmark	5.7	17	340.7	0.42	46,692	
Estonia	1.3	17	75.2	−0.30	28,083	
Finland	5.5	131	42.2	0.50	40,443	
France	64.4	249	259.1	0.45	41,165	
Germany	80.7	138	585.3	0.06	47,693	
Greece	11.0	51	215.0	−0.40	26,361	
Hungary	9.9	36	274.4	−0.32	25,555	
Iceland	0.3	40	8.3	0.70	46,745	
Ireland	4.7	27	172.8	0.31	54,098	
Italy	59.8	116	514.0	0.07	36,499	
Kosovo	1.9	4	452.0	0.48	9,186	
Latvia	2.0	25	79.0	−1.18	24,384	
Liechtenstein	0.04	0.06	607.5	0.68	90,685	
Lithuania	2.9	25	114.2	−1.63	28,036	
Luxembourg	0.6	1	568.0	2.21	102,388	
Macedonia	2.1	10	209.4	0.16	13,908	

Average annual real GDP growth rate (purchasing power parity), 2010 to most recent, percent	Type of government	Degree of democracy	Capital city	Largest urban area	Official language(s) or main languages used by government	Most widely used or understood language
1.93	Parliamentary republic	Limited democracy	Tirana	Tirana	Albanian	Albanian
NA	Parliamentary constitutional monarchy	NA	Andorra la Vella	Andorra la Vella	Catalan	Catalan
1.02	Federal parliamentary republic	Full democracy	Vienna	Vienna	German	German
1.19	Presidential republic	Undemocratic	Minsk	Minsk	Russian, Belarusian	Russian
0.92	Federal parliamentary constitutional monarchy	Democracy with flaws	Brussels	Brussels	Dutch, French	Dutch
1.31	Parliamentary republic	Limited democracy	Sarajevo	Sarajevo	Bosnian, others	Bosnian
1.52	Parliamentary republic	Democracy with flaws	Sofia	Sofia	Bulgarian	Bulgarian
−0.46	Parliamentary republic	Democracy with flaws	Zagreb	Zagreb	Croatian	Croatian
1.33	Parliamentary republic	Democracy with flaws	Prague	Prague	Czech	Czech
0.65	Parliamentary constitutional monarchy	Full democracy	Copenhagen	Copenhagen	Danish	Danish
3.63	Parliamentary republic	Democracy with flaws	Tallinn	Tallinn	Estonian	Estonian
0.04	Parliamentary republic	Full democracy	Helsinki	Helsinki	Finnish	Finnish
0.85	Semi-presidential republic	Democracy with flaws	Paris	Paris	French	French
1.52	Federal parliamentary republic	Full democracy	Berlin	Ruhrgebiet	German	German
−3.92	Parliamentary republic	Democracy with flaws	Athens	Athens	Greek	Greek
1.7	Parliamentary republic	Democracy with flaws	Budapest	Budapest	Hungarian	Hungarian
2.56	Parliamentary republic	Full democracy	Reykjavik	Reykjavik	Icelandic	Icelandic
3.4	Parliamentary republic	Full democracy	Dublin	Dublin	Irish, English	English
−0.72	Parliamentary republic	Democracy with flaws	Rome	Milan	Italian	Italian
3.14	Parliamentary republic	NA	Pristina	Pristina	Albanian, Serbian	Albanian
3.49	Parliamentary republic	Democracy with flaws	Riga	Riga	Latvian	Latvian
NA	Constitutional monarchy	NA	Vaduz	Vaduz	German	Swiss German
3.6	Semi-presidential republic	Democracy with flaws	Vilnius	Vilnius	Lithuanian	Lithuanian
2.98	Parliamentary constitutional monarchy	Full democracy	Luxembourg	Luxembourg	Luxembourgish, others	Luxembourgish
2.39	Parliamentary republic	Democracy with flaws	Skopje	Skopje	Macedonian, Albanian	Macedonian

Region and country	Total population, 2015 estimate, millions	Area, thousands of square miles	Population density, per square mile	Average annual population growth rate, 2010–2015, percent	Gross domestic product (GDP, purchasing power parity) per capita, most recent, current dollars	
Europe continued						
Malta	0.4	0.12	3,431.5	0.32	36,735	
Moldova	4.1	13	311.3	−0.08	4,401	
Monaco	0.04	0.001	48,861.4	0.48	180,223	
Montenegro	0.6	5	117.3	0.12	15,402	
Netherlands	16.9	16	1,055.2	0.35	48,492	
Norway	5.2	125	41.7	1.27	61,294	
Poland	38.6	121	319.8	0.02	25,721	
Portugal	10.3	36	291.1	−0.45	29,211	
Romania	19.5	92	212.0	−0.79	21,755	
San Marino	0.03	0.02	1,349.4	0.70	62,364	
Serbia	7.2	30	240.7	−0.45	13,291	
Slovakia	5.4	19	286.6	0.07	28,866	
Slovenia	2.1	8	264.1	0.15	31,066	
Spain	46.1	195	236.4	−0.21	34,749	
Sweden	9.8	174	56.2	0.83	46,513	
Switzerland	8.3	16	520.7	1.16	60,450	
Ukraine	44.8	233	192.4	−0.36	7,566	
United Kingdom	64.7	94	688.0	0.63	41,594	
Vatican City	0.001	0.0002	4,709.1	0.03	NA	
Northern Eurasia						
Armenia	3.0	11	262.8	0.36	8,394	
Azerbaijan	9.8	33	291.7	1.39	17,553	
Georgia	4.0	27	148.6	−1.21	8,903	
Kazakhstan	17.6	1,052	16.8	1.55	25,757	
Kyrgyzstan	5.9	77	76.9	1.67	3,436	
Russia	143.5	6,602	21.7	0.04	24,954	
Tajikistan	8.5	56	152.4	2.24	2,780	

Average annual real GDP growth rate (purchasing power parity), 2010 to most recent, percent	Type of government	Degree of democracy	Capital city	Largest urban area	Official language(s) or main languages used by government	Most widely used or understood language
NA	Parliamentary republic	Full democracy	Valletta	Valletta	Maltese, English	Maltese
3.81	Parliamentary republic	Democracy with flaws	Chişinău	Chişinău	Romanian	Romanian
NA	Constitutional monarchy	NA	Monaco	Monaco	French	French
1.81	Parliamentary republic	Democracy with flaws	Podgorica	Podgorica	Montenegrin	Serbian
0.62	Parliamentary constitutional monarchy	Full democracy	Amsterdam	Rotterdam	Dutch	Dutch
1.7	Parliamentary constitutional monarchy	Full democracy	Oslo	Oslo	Norwegian (two varieties)	Norwegian
2.94	Parliamentary republic	Democracy with flaws	Warsaw	Warsaw	Polish	Polish
−0.94	Semi-presidential republic	Democracy with flaws	Lisbon	Lisbon	Portuguese	Portuguese
2.38	Semi-presidential republic	NA	Bucharest	Bucharest	Romanian	Romanian
NA	Parliamentary republic	NA	San Marino	San Marino	Italian	Italian
0.36	Parliamentary republic	Democracy with flaws	Belgrade	Belgrade	Serbian	Serbian
2.38	Parliamentary republic	Democracy with flaws	Bratislava	Bratislava	Slovak	Slovak
0.54	Parliamentary republic	Democracy with flaws	Ljubljana	Ljubljana	Slovenian	Slovenian
−0.17	Parliamentary constitutional monarchy	Full democracy	Madrid	Madrid	Spanish	Spanish
1.99	Parliamentary constitutional monarchy	Full democracy	Stockholm	Stockholm	Swedish	Swedish
1.5	Federal republic	Full democracy	Bern	Zürich	German, French, others	Swiss German
−2.37	Semi-presidential republic	Limited democracy	Kiev	Kiev	Ukrainian	Russian or Ukrainian
2.1	Parliamentary constitutional monarchy	Full democracy	London	London	English	English
NA	Theocratic absolute monarchy	NA	Vatican City	Fully within Rome	Latin, Italian	Italian
4.33	Parliamentary republic	Limited democracy	Yerevan	Yerevan	Armenian	Armenian
2.21	Presidential republic	Undemocratic	Baku	Baku	Azerbaijani	Azerbaijani
4.86	Semi-presidential republic	Limited democracy	Tbilisi	Tbilisi	Georgian	Georgian
4.56	Presidential republic	Undemocratic	Astana	Almaty	Kazakh, Russian	Russian
4.79	Parliamentary republic	Limited democracy	Bishkek	Bishkek	Kyrgyz, Russian	Kyrgyz
1.17	Federal semi-presidential republic	Undemocratic	Moscow	Moscow	Russian	Russian
6.63	Presidential republic	Undemocratic	Dushanbe	Dushanbe	Tajik, Russian	Tajik

Region and country	Total population, 2015 estimate, millions	Area, thousands of square miles	Population density, per square mile	Average annual population growth rate, 2010–2015, percent	Gross domestic product (GDP, purchasing power parity) per capita, most recent, current dollars	
Northern Eurasia continued						
Turkmenistan	5.4	188	28.5	1.27	16,499	
Uzbekistan	29.9	173	173.1	1.50	6,278	
Africa						
Algeria	39.7	920	43.1	1.92	14,687	
Angola	25.0	481	52.0	3.30	7,371	
Benin	10.9	43	250.2	2.69	2,110	
Botswana	2.3	225	10.1	1.99	15,807	
Burkina Faso	18.1	106	171.0	2.94	1,659	
Burundi	11.2	11	1,040.4	3.34	736	
Cameroon	23.3	184	127.2	2.51	3,123	
Cape Verde	0.5	2	334.3	1.19	6,690	
Central African Republic	4.9	241	20.4	1.95	597	
Chad	14.0	496	28.3	3.31	2,171	
Comoros	0.8	1	913.7	2.42	1,401	
Congo, Democratic Republic of the	77.3	905	85.3	3.17	783	
Congo, Republic of the	4.6	132	35.0	2.56	6,368	
Djibouti	0.9	9	99.1	1.33	3,239	
Egypt	91.5	387	236.7	2.18	10,891	
Equatorial Guinea	0.8	11	78.0	2.96	30,041	
Eritrea	5.2	45	115.1	2.17	605	
Ethiopia	99.4	426	233.1	2.53	1,626	
Gabon	1.7	103	16.7	2.25	20,010	
Gambia, The	2.0	4	456.3	3.24	1,585	
Ghana	27.4	92	297.6	2.39	4,201	
Guinea	12.6	95	132.8	2.71	1,207	
Guinea-Bissau	1.8	14	132.2	2.42	1,453	
Ivory Coast	22.7	125	182.3	2.40	3,496	

Average annual real GDP growth rate (purchasing power parity), 2010 to most recent, percent	Type of government	Degree of democracy	Capital city	Largest urban area	Official language(s) or main languages used by government	Most widely used or understood language
10.53	Presidential republic	Undemocratic	Ashgabat	Ashgabat	Turkmen	Turkmen
8.12	Presidential republic	Undemocratic	Tashkent	Tashkent	Uzbek	Uzbek
3.36	Presidential republic	Undemocratic	Algiers	Algiers	Standard Arabic	Algerian Arabic
4.73	Presidential republic	Undemocratic	Luanda	Luanda	Portuguese	Portuguese
5.24	Presidential republic	Limited democracy	Cotonou	Cotonou	French	Fon
4.61	Parliamentary republic	Democracy with flaws	Gaborone	Gaborone	English	Setswana
4.92	Presidential republic	Limited democracy	Ouagadou-gou	Ouagadou-gou	French	Mossi
2.95	Presidential republic	Undemocratic	Bujumbura	Bujumbura	Kirundi, French	Kirundi
5.29	Presidential republic	Undemocratic	Yaoundé	Douala	French, English	French
2.28	Parliamentary republic	Democracy with flaws	Praia	Praia	Portuguese	Portuguese Creole
−6.95	Presidential republic	Undemocratic	Bangui	Bangui	French	Sangho
4.62	Presidential republic	Undemocratic	N'djamena	N'djamena	French, Standard Arabic	Chadian Arabic
2.79	Federal presidential republic	Undemocratic	Moroni	Moroni	Standard Arabic, French, Shikomoro	Shikomoro
7.68	Semi-presidential republic	Undemocratic	Kinshasa	Kinshasa	French	Lingala or Swahili
4.01	Presidential republic	Undemocratic	Brazzaville	Brazzaville	French	Lingala
5.08	Semi-presidential republic	Undemocratic	Djibouti	Djibouti	French, Standard Arabic	Somali
2.51	Presidential republic	Undemocratic	Cairo	Cairo	Standard Arabic	Egyptian Arabic
−2.46	Presidential republic	Undemocratic	Malabo	Malabo	Spanish, others	Spanish
NA	Presidential republic	Undemocratic	Asmara	Asmara	Tigrinya, others	Tigrinya
10.06	Federal parliamentary republic	Undemocratic	Addis Ababa	Addis Ababa	Amharic, others	Amharic
5.22	Presidential republic	Undemocratic	Libreville	Libreville	French	French
1.72	Presidential republic	Undemocratic	Banjul	Banjul	English	Mandinka
7.64	Presidential republic	Democracy with flaws	Accra	Accra	English	Twi
2.12	Presidential republic	Undemocratic	Conakry	Conakry	French	French or Fula
3.07	Semi-presidential republic	Undemocratic	Bissau	Bissau	Portuguese	Portuguese Creole
6.36	Presidential republic	Undemocratic	Abidjan	Abidjan	French	Dyula

Region and country	Total population, 2015 estimate, millions	Area, thousands of square miles	Population density, per square mile	Average annual population growth rate, 2010–2015, percent	Gross domestic product (GDP, purchasing power parity) per capita, most recent, current dollars	
Africa continued						
Kenya	46.1	224	205.5	2.65	3,083	
Lesotho	2.1	12	182.2	1.20	2,616	
Liberia	4.5	43	104.7	2.58	836	
Libya	6.3	679	9.2	0.04	14,154	
Madagascar	24.2	227	106.9	2.79	1,459	
Malawi	17.2	46	376.3	3.06	1,183	
Mali	17.6	479	36.8	2.98	2,428	
Mauritania	4.1	398	10.2	2.49	3,792	
Mauritius	1.3	1	1,616.5	0.40	19,318	
Morocco	34.4	172	199.4	1.37	7,952	
Mozambique	28.0	309	90.6	2.80	1,186	
Namibia	2.5	318	7.7	2.28	10,414	
Niger	19.9	489	40.7	4.00	954	
Nigeria	182.2	357	510.8	2.67	5,992	
Rwanda	11.6	10	1,141.7	2.41	1,759	
São Tomé and Príncipe	0.2	0.37	511.4	2.16	3,121	
Senegal	15.1	76	199.2	3.10	2,431	
Seychelles	0.1	0.18	549.1	0.72	26,264	
Sierra Leone	6.5	28	233.0	2.22	1,591	
Somalia	10.8	246	43.8	2.37	411	
South Africa	54.5	471	115.8	1.08	13,278	
South Sudan	12.3	249	49.6	4.09	1,850	
Sudan	40.2	719	56.0	2.16	4,173	
Swaziland	1.3	7	192.0	1.51	8,427	
Tanzania	53.5	366	146.2	3.16	2,589	
Togo	7.3	22	333.2	2.67	1,460	
Tunisia	11.3	63	178.1	1.12	11,250	

Average annual real GDP growth rate (purchasing power parity), 2010 to most recent, percent	Type of government	Degree of democracy	Capital city	Largest urban area	Official language(s) or main languages used by government	Most widely used or understood language
5.47	Presidential republic	Limited democracy	Nairobi	Nairobi	English, Swahili	Swahili
4.28	Parliamentary constitutional monarchy	Democracy with flaws	Maseru	Maseru	Sesotho, English	Sesotho
5.11	Presidential republic	Limited democracy	Monrovia	Monrovia	English	English Creole
−14.48	In transition	Undemocratic	Tripoli	Tripoli	Standard Arabic	Libyan Arabic
2.58	Semi-presidential republic	Limited democracy	Antananarivo	Antananarivo	French, Malagasy	Malagasy
4.11	Presidential republic	Limited democracy	Lilongwe	Lilongwe	English, Chichewa/ Chinyanja	Chichewa/ Chinyanja
8.27	Semi-presidential republic	Limited democracy	Bamako	Bamako	French	Bambara
5.2	Presidential republic	Undemocratic	Nouakchott	Nouakchott	Standard Arabic	Hassaniya Arabic
3.48	Parliamentary republic	Full democracy	Port Louis	Port Louis	English	Mauritian Creole
3.95	Parliamentary constitutional monarchy	Limited democracy	Rabat	Casablanca	Standard Arabic, others	Moroccan Arabic
7.03	Presidential republic	Limited democracy	Maputo	Maputo	Portuguese	Portuguese
5.56	Presidential republic	Democracy with flaws	Windhoek	Windhoek	English	Afrikaans
5.96	Semi-presidential republic	Undemocratic	Niamey	Niamey	French	Hausa
4.7	Federal presidential republic	Limited democracy	Abuja	Lagos	English	English Creole
7.04	Presidential republic	Undemocratic	Kigali	Kigali	Kinyarwanda, French, English	Kinyarwanda
4.52	Semi-presidential republic	NA	São Tomé	São Tomé	Portuguese	Portuguese
4.08	Presidential republic	Democracy with flaws	Dakar	Dakar	French	Wolof
5.46	Presidential republic	NA	Victoria	Victoria	Seychellois Creole, English	Seychellois Creole
4.19	Presidential republic	Limited democracy	Freetown	Freetown	English	English Creole
NA	Federal parliamentary republic	NA	Mogadishu	Mogadishu	Somali, Standard Arabic	Somali
2.09	Parliamentary republic	Democracy with flaws	Pretoria	Johannes-burg	English, isiZulu, others	English
−10.85	Presidential republic	NA	Juba	Juba	English	Sudanese Arabic
1.1	Presidential republic	Undemocratic	Khartoum	Khartoum	Standard Arabic, English	Sudanese Arabic
2.28	Absolute monarchy	Undemocratic	Mbabane	Mbabane	English, siSwati	siSwati
6.84	Presidential republic	Limited democracy	Dodoma	Dar es Salaam	Swahili, English	Swahili
5.01	Presidential republic	Undemocratic	Lomé	Lomé	French, Ewe, Kabye	Ewe
1.32	Parliamentary republic	Democracy with flaws	Tunis	Tunis	Standard Arabic	Tunisian Arabic

Region and country	Total population, 2015 estimate, millions	Area, thousands of square miles	Population density, per square mile	Average annual population growth rate, 2010–2015, percent	Gross domestic product (GDP, purchasing power parity) per capita, most recent, current dollars	
Africa continued						
Uganda	39.0	93	419.4	3.27	1,825	
Zambia	16.2	291	55.8	3.05	3,853	
Zimbabwe	15.6	151	103.4	2.21	1,794	
Southwest Asia						
Bahrain	1.4	0.29	4,693.5	1.76	46,946	
Cyprus	1.2	4	326.2	1.09	22,195	
Iran	79.1	636	124.3	1.27	17,154	
Iraq	36.4	169	215.2	3.31	14,895	
Israel	8.1	8	1,005.6	1.66	36,822	
Jordan	7.6	34	220.2	3.06	10,880	
Kuwait	3.9	7	565.8	4.81	71,312	
Lebanon	5.9	4	1,457.1	5.99	13,938	
Oman	4.5	119	37.6	8.45	38,234	
Qatar	2.2	4	499.7	4.72	143,788	
Saudi Arabia	31.5	830	38.0	2.32	53,430	
Syria	18.5	71	258.8	−2.27	3,016	
Turkey	78.7	303	260.0	1.69	19,618	
United Arab Emirates	9.2	32	283.7	1.89	70,238	
Yemen	26.8	204	131.6	2.57	2,080	
South Asia						
Afghanistan	32.5	251.8	291.2	3.0	1,925	
Bangladesh	161.0	57	2,808.7	1.20	3,333	
Bhutan	0.8	15	52.3	1.46	8,077	
India	1,311.1	1,269	1,033.0	1.26	6,089	
Maldives	0.4	0.12	3,160.6	1.79	14,218	
Nepal	28.5	57	501.8	1.18	2,458	
Pakistan	188.9	307	614.6	2.11	5,042	
Sri Lanka	20.7	25	817.7	0.50	11,881	

Average annual real GDP growth rate (purchasing power parity), 2010 to most recent, percent	Type of government	Degree of democracy	Capital city	Largest urban area	Official language(s) or main languages used by government	Most widely used or understood language
5.42	Presidential republic	Limited democracy	Kampala	Kampala	English, Swahili	Luganda
5.3	Presidential republic	Democracy with flaws	Lusaka	Lusaka	English	Chichewa/ Chinyanja
6.29	Semi-presidential republic	Undemocratic	Harare	Harare	Shona, English, Ndebele	Shona
3.7	Constitutional monarchy	Undemocratic	Manama	Manama	Standard Arabic	Gulf Arabic
−1.81	Presidential republic	Democracy with flaws	Nicosia	Nicosia	Greek, Turkish	Greek
−0.21	Theocratic republic	Undemocratic	Tehran	Tehran	Persian	Persian
5.47	Federal parliamentary republic	Limited democracy	Baghdad	Baghdad	Standard Arabic	Mesopota-mian Arabic
3.26	Parliamentary republic	Democracy with flaws	Jerusalem	Tel Aviv	Hebrew, Standard Arabic	Hebrew
2.7	Parliamentary constitutional monarchy	Undemocratic	Amman	Amman	Standard Arabic	Levantine Arabic
2.99	Constitutional monarchy	Undemocratic	Kuwait City	Kuwait City	Standard Arabic	Gulf Arabic
1.68	Parliamentary republic	Limited democracy	Beirut	Beirut	Standard Arabic	Levantine Arabic
3.23	Absolute monarchy	Undemocratic	Muscat	Muscat	Standard Arabic	Gulf Arabic
6.06	Absolute monarchy	Undemocratic	Doha	Doha	Standard Arabic	English
5	Absolute monarchy	Undemocratic	Riyadh	Riyadh	Hejazi or Najdi Arabic	Hejazi or Najdi Arabic
NA	Presidential republic, authoritarian	Undemocratic	Damascus	Aleppo	Standard Arabic	Levantine Arabic
4.39	Parliamentary republic	Limited democracy	Ankara	Istanbul	Turkish	Turkish
4.83	Federal absolute monarchy	Undemocratic	Abu Dhabi	Dubai	Standard Arabic	English
NA	In transition	Undemocratic	Sana'a	Sana'a	Standard Arabic	Yemeni Arabic
6.6	Presidential republic	Undemocratic	Kabul	Kabul	Afghan Persian or Dari, Pashto	Afghan Persian or Dari
6.32	Parliamentary republic	Limited democracy	Dhaka	Dhaka	Bengali	Bengali
4.75	Constitutional monarchy	Limited democracy	Thimphu	Thimphu	Dzongkha	Sharchhopka
6.74	Federal parliamentary republic	Democracy with flaws	New Delhi	Delhi	Hindi, English, others	Hindi
4.75	Presidential republic	NA	Male	Male	Dhivehi	Dhivehi
4.21	Federal parliamentary republic	Limited democracy	Kathmandu	Kathmandu	Nepali	Nepali
4.18	Federal parliamentary republic	Limited democracy	Islamabad	Karachi	Urdu, English	Urdu
6.1	Presidential republic	Democracy with flaws	Colombo	Colombo	Sinhalese, Tamil	Sinhalese

Region and country	Total population, 2015 estimate, millions	Area, thousands of square miles	Population density, per square mile	Average annual population growth rate, 2010–2015, percent	Gross domestic product (GDP, purchasing power parity) per capita, most recent, current dollars	
East Asia						
China	1,376.0	3,705	371.4	0.52	14,189	
Japan	126.6	146	867.5	−0.12	37,435	
Mongolia	3.0	604	4.9	1.74	12,189	
North Korea	25.2	47	540.5	0.53	1,590	
South Korea	50.3	39	1,306.3	0.48	34,772	
Taiwan	23.4	14	1,685.5	0.37	46,850	
Southeast Asia						
Brunei	0.4	2	190.1	1.47	70,817	
Cambodia	15.6	70	222.9	1.62	3,483	
East Timor	1.2	6	206.3	2.28	2,374	
Indonesia	257.6	735	350.3	1.28	11,035	
Laos	6.8	91	74.4	1.66	5,675	
Malaysia	30.3	127	238.2	1.51	26,891	
Myanmar (or Burma)	53.9	261	206.3	0.82	5,260	
Philippines	100.7	116	869.4	1.58	7,359	
Singapore	5.6	0.27	20,823.0	1.97	84,164	
Thailand	68.0	198	343.0	0.38	16,305	
Vietnam	93.4	128	730.7	1.12	5,910	
Australia and the Pacific						
Australia	24.0	2,989	8.0	1.57	45,158	
Fiji	0.9	7	126.4	0.74	9,159	
Kiribati	0.1	0.31	359.0	1.82	1,859	
Marshall Islands	0.05	0.07	758.3	0.21	3,810	
Micronesia, Federated States of	0.1	0.27	385.4	0.16	3,329	
Nauru	0.01	0.01	1,260.7	0.39	14,752	
New Zealand	4.5	104	43.6	0.72	37,531	
Palau	0.02	0.18	120.1	0.79	15,286	

Average annual real GDP growth rate (purchasing power parity), 2010 to most recent, percent	Type of government	Degree of democracy	Capital city	Largest urban area	Official language(s) or main languages used by government	Most widely used or understood language
7.81	Communist state	Undemocratic	Beijing	Shanghai	Mandarin Chinese	Mandarin Chinese
0.61	Parliamentary constitutional monarchy	Democracy with flaws	Tokyo	Tokyo	Japanese	Japanese
10.17	Semi-presidential republic	Democracy with flaws	Ulaanbaatar	Ulaanbaatar	Khalka Mongolian	Khalka Mongolian
NA	Communist state	Undemocratic	Pyongyang	Pyongyang	Korean	Korean
2.96	Presidential republic	Democracy with flaws	Seoul	Seoul	Korean	Korean
NA	Semi-presidential republic	Democracy with flaws	Taipei	Taipei	Mandarin Chinese	Mandarin Chinese
−0.06	Absolute monarchy	NA	Bandar Seri Begawan	Bandar Seri Begawan	Malay	Malay
7.18	Parliamentary constitutional monarchy	Limited democracy	Phnom Penh	Phnom Penh	Khmer	Khmer
5.65	Semi-presidential republic	Democracy with flaws	Dili	Dili	Portuguese, Tetum	Tetum
5.51	Presidential republic	Democracy with flaws	Jakarta	Jakarta	Indonesian	Indonesian
7.81	Communist state	Undemocratic	Vientiane	Vientiane	Lao	Lao
5.28	Federal parliamentary constitutional monarchy	Democracy with flaws	Kuala Lumpur	Kuala Lumpur	Malay	Malay
NA	Parliamentary republic	Limited democracy	Naypyidaw	Yangon	Burmese	Burmese
5.86	Presidential republic	Democracy with flaws	Manila	Manila	Filipino, English	Filipino
3.95	Parliamentary republic	Democracy with flaws	Singapore	Singapore	Mandarin Chinese, English, others	English or Singlish
2.85	Constitutional monarchy	Limited democracy	Bangkok	Bangkok	Thai	Thai
5.91	Communist state	Undemocratic	Hanoi	Ho Chi Minh City	Vietnamese	Vietnamese
2.64	Parliamentary constitutional monarchy	Full democracy	Canberra	Sydney	English	English
2.8	Parliamentary republic	Limited democracy	Suva	Suva	English, others	English
3.07	Presidential republic	NA	Tarawa	Tarawa	English	Gilbertese
1.07	Presidential republic	NA	Majuro	Majuro	English, Marshallese	Marshallese
−1.12	Federal semi-presidential republic	NA	Palikir	Weno	English	English
NA	Parliamentary republic	NA	Yaren	Yaren	Nauruan, English	Nauruan
2.71	Parliamentary constitutional monarchy	Full democracy	Wellington	Auckland	English	English
3.82	Presidential republic	NA	Melekeok	Koror	Palauan, English	Palauan

Region and country	Total population, 2015 estimate, millions	Area, thousands of square miles	Population density, per square mile	Average annual population growth rate, 2010–2015, percent	Gross domestic product (GDP, purchasing power parity) per capita, most recent, current dollars	
Australia and the Pacific continued						
Papua New Guinea	7.6	179	42.6	2.14	2,807	
Samoa	0.2	1	176.8	0.76	5,923	
Solomon Islands	0.6	11	52.3	2.07	2,186	
Tonga	0.1	0.29	368.1	0.42	5,201	
Tuvalu	0.01	0.01	987.8	0.18	3,770	
Vanuatu	0.3	5	56.2	2.27	2,975	

Sources: CIA World Factbook, Economist Intelligence Unit, UN Department of Economic and Social Affairs Population Division, World Bank, national statistical agencies

Note: In this table, "NA" means "not available"

Average annual real GDP growth rate (purchasing power parity), 2010 to most recent, percent	Type of government	Degree of democracy	Capital city	Largest urban area	Official language(s) or main languages used by government	Most widely used or understood language
8.19	Parliamentary constitutional monarchy	Democracy with flaws	Port Moresby	Port Moresby	Tok Pisin, English, other	Tok Pisin
1.38	Parliamentary republic	NA	Apia	Apia	Samoan	Samoan
5	Parliamentary constitutional monarchy	NA	Honiara	Honiara	English	Pijin
0.49	Constitutional monarchy	NA	Nuku'alofa	Nuku'alofa	English, Tongan	Tongan
2.93	Parliamentary constitutional monarchy	NA	Funafuti	Funafuti	Tuvaluan, English	Tuvaluan
1.81	Parliamentary republic	NA	Port-Vila	Port-Vila	English, Bislama	Bislama

US: Political

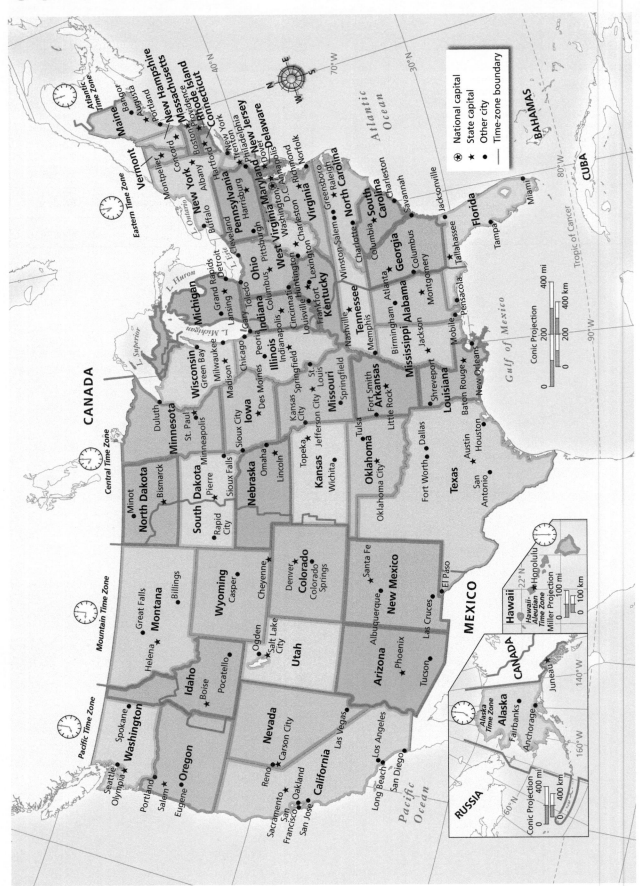

Legend
- ⊛ National capital
- ★ State capital
- • Other city
- — Time-zone boundary

Atlantic Ocean

BAHAMAS

CUBA

Gulf of Mexico

Pacific Ocean

CANADA

MEXICO

RUSSIA

Tropic of Cancer

400 mi
400 km
Conic Projection

Hawaii
Honolulu
Hawaii-Aleutian Time Zone
Miller Projection
100 mi
100 km
22° N

Alaska
Juneau
Fairbanks
Anchorage
Alaska Time Zone
Conic Projection
400 mi
400 km
60° N
140° W
160° W

Atlantic Time Zone
Eastern Time Zone
Central Time Zone
Mountain Time Zone
Pacific Time Zone

70° W
30° N
40° N
80° W
90° W

N E S W

Maine — Bangor, Augusta, Portland
New Hampshire — Concord
Vermont — Montpelier
Massachusetts — Boston
Rhode Island — Providence
Connecticut — Hartford
New York — Albany, Buffalo, New York
New Jersey — Trenton
Pennsylvania — Harrisburg, Philadelphia, Pittsburgh, Erie
Delaware — Dover
Maryland — Annapolis, Washington, D.C.
West Virginia — Charleston, Huntington
Virginia — Richmond, Norfolk
North Carolina — Raleigh, Greensboro, Winston-Salem, Charlotte
South Carolina — Columbia, Charleston
Georgia — Atlanta, Columbus, Savannah
Florida — Tallahassee, Jacksonville, Tampa, Miami
Ohio — Columbus, Cleveland, Cincinnati, Toledo
Michigan — Lansing, Detroit, Grand Rapids
Indiana — Indianapolis, Gary
Kentucky — Frankfort, Lexington, Louisville
Tennessee — Nashville, Memphis
Alabama — Montgomery, Birmingham, Mobile
Mississippi — Jackson
Wisconsin — Madison, Milwaukee, Green Bay
Illinois — Springfield, Chicago, Peoria
Iowa — Des Moines, Sioux City
Minnesota — St. Paul, Minneapolis, Duluth
Missouri — Jefferson City, St. Louis, Kansas City, Springfield
Arkansas — Little Rock, Fort Smith
Louisiana — Baton Rouge, New Orleans, Shreveport
Pensacola
North Dakota — Bismarck, Minot
South Dakota — Pierre, Rapid City
Nebraska — Lincoln, Omaha
Kansas — Topeka, Wichita
Oklahoma — Oklahoma City, Tulsa
Texas — Austin, Dallas, Fort Worth, Houston, San Antonio, El Paso
Montana — Helena, Great Falls, Billings
Wyoming — Cheyenne, Casper
Colorado — Denver, Colorado Springs
New Mexico — Santa Fe, Albuquerque, Las Cruces
Idaho — Boise, Pocatello
Utah — Salt Lake City, Ogden
Arizona — Phoenix, Tucson
Washington — Olympia, Seattle, Spokane
Oregon — Salem, Portland, Eugene
Nevada — Carson City, Reno, Las Vegas
California — Sacramento, San Francisco, Oakland, San Jose, Los Angeles, Long Beach, San Diego

L. Superior
L. Michigan
L. Huron
L. Erie
L. Ontario

400 mi
400 km
200
200
0
Conic Projection

US: Physical

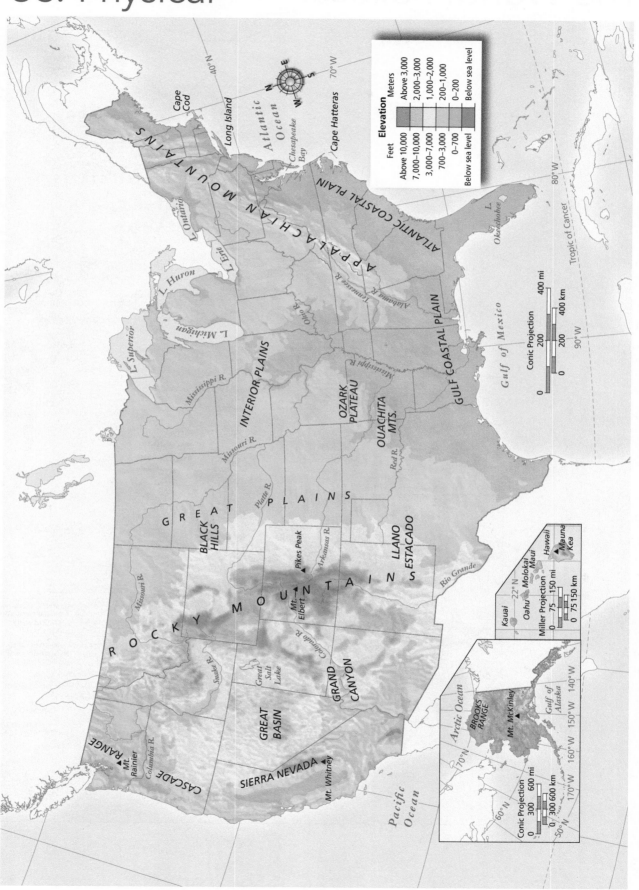

Elevation

Meters
- Above 3,000
- 2,000–3,000
- 1,000–2,000
- 200–1,000
- 0–200
- Below sea level

Feet
- Above 10,000
- 7,000–10,000
- 3,000–7,000
- 700–3,000
- 0–700
- Below sea level

Cape Cod
Long Island
Atlantic Ocean
Chesapeake Bay
Cape Hatteras
ATLANTIC COASTAL PLAIN
APPALACHIAN MOUNTAINS
Alabama R.
Tennessee R.
Ohio R.
GULF COASTAL PLAIN
L. Okeechobee
Tropic of Cancer
Gulf of Mexico

L. Ontario
L. Erie
L. Huron
L. Michigan
L. Superior
INTERIOR PLAINS
Mississippi R.
Mississippi R.
OZARK PLATEAU
OUACHITA MTS.
Red R.
Missouri R.

Conic Projection
400 mi
400 km
200
200
0
0

GREAT PLAINS
BLACK HILLS
Platte R.
Pikes Peak
Arkansas R.
LLANO ESTACADO
Rio Grande
Mt. Elbert
ROCKY MOUNTAINS
Missouri R.
Colorado R.
Great Salt Lake
GRAND CANYON
GREAT BASIN
Snake R.
Columbia R.
CASCADE RANGE
Mt. Rainier
SIERRA NEVADA
Mt. Whitney
Pacific Ocean

Hawaii
Mauna Kea
Kauai
Oahu
Molokai
Maui
22° N
Miller Projection
150 mi
75
0
75 150 km

Arctic Ocean
BROOKS RANGE
Mt. McKinley
Gulf of Alaska
70° N
140° W
150° W
160° W
170° W
60° N
50° N
Conic Projection
600 mi
300
0
300 600 km

The World: Political

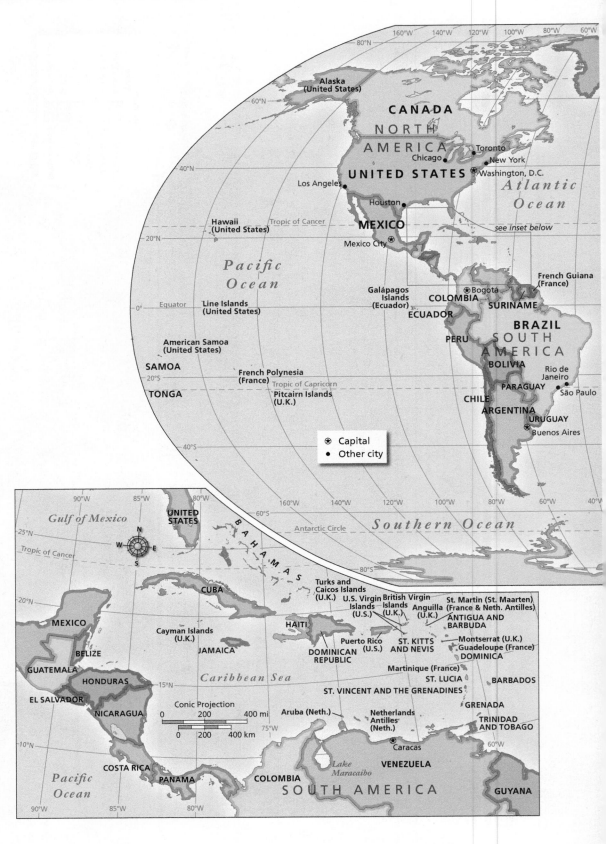

Alaska
(United States)

CANADA

NORTH
AMERICA

Toronto
Chicago
New York
UNITED STATES
⊛ Washington, D.C.

Los Angeles

Houston

*Atlantic
Ocean*

Hawaii
(United States)

Tropic of Cancer

MEXICO

see inset below

Mexico City ⊛

*Pacific
Ocean*

Galápagos
Islands
(Ecuador)

COLOMBIA

⊛ Bogotá

French Guiana
(France)

SURINAME

Equator

Line Islands
(United States)

ECUADOR

PERU

BRAZIL
SOUTH
AMERICA

American Samoa
(United States)

BOLIVIA

Rio de
Janeiro

SAMOA

French Polynesia
(France)

Tropic of Capricorn

PARAGUAY

São Paulo

TONGA

Pitcairn Islands
(U.K.)

CHILE

URUGUAY

ARGENTINA

⊛ Buenos Aires

⊛ Capital
• Other city

Antarctic Circle

Southern Ocean

Gulf of Mexico

**UNITED
STATES**

B
A
H
A
M
A
S

N
W   E
S

Tropic of Cancer

Turks and
Caicos Islands
(U.K.)

U.S. Virgin British Virgin
Islands   Islands
(U.S.)   (U.K.)

Anguilla
(U.K.)

St. Martin (St. Maarten)
(France & Neth. Antilles)

**ANTIGUA AND
BARBUDA**

CUBA

HAITI

Cayman Islands
(U.K.)

JAMAICA

Puerto Rico
(U.S.)

**ST. KITTS
AND NEVIS**

Montserrat (U.K.)
Guadeloupe (France)

DOMINICA

MEXICO

BELIZE

**DOMINICAN
REPUBLIC**

GUATEMALA

Caribbean Sea

Martinique (France)

ST. LUCIA

BARBADOS

HONDURAS

ST. VINCENT AND THE GRENADINES

EL SALVADOR

NICARAGUA

Conic Projection
0   200   400 mi

0   200   400 km

Aruba (Neth.)

Netherlands
Antilles
(Neth.)

GRENADA

**TRINIDAD
AND TOBAGO**

Caracas ⊛

*Pacific
Ocean*

COSTA RICA

PANAMA

COLOMBIA

*Lake
Maracaibo*

VENEZUELA

SOUTH AMERICA

GUYANA

Africa: Political

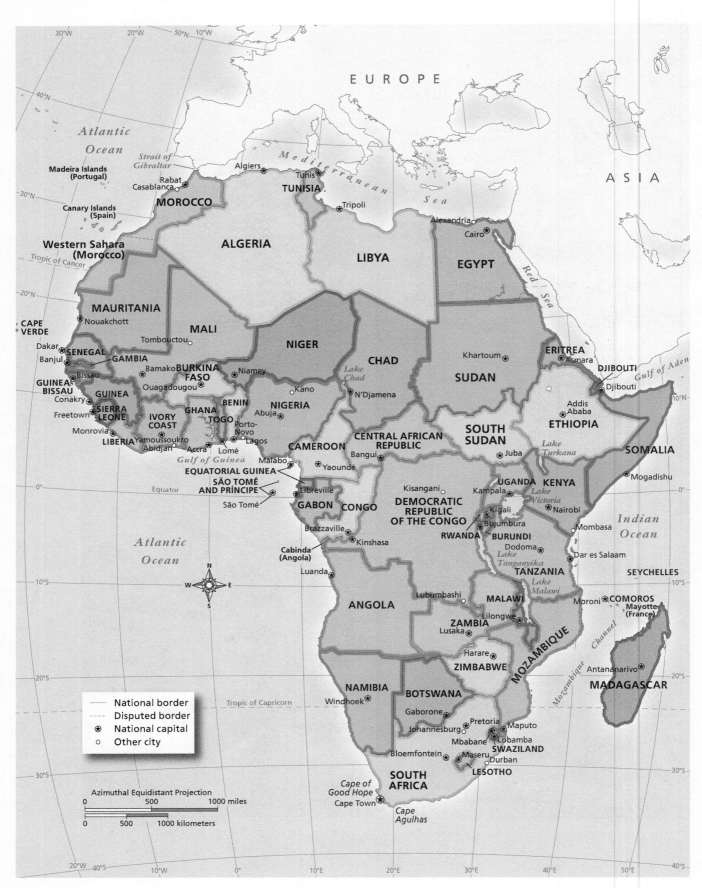

EUROPE

ASIA

Atlantic Ocean

Madeira Islands (Portugal)

Strait of Gibraltar

Mediterranean Sea

Algiers ⊛
Tunis ⊛
TUNISIA
⊛ Rabat
⊛ Casablanca
MOROCCO
⊛ Tripoli

Canary Islands (Spain)

Western Sahara (Morocco)

ALGERIA

LIBYA

EGYPT

Alexandria ⊛
⊛ Cairo

Red Sea

Tropic of Cancer

CAPE VERDE

⊛ Nouakchott
MAURITANIA

MALI

Tombouctou ○

NIGER

CHAD

Khartoum ⊛

SUDAN

ERITREA
⊛ Asmara

DJIBOUTI
⊛ Djibouti

Gulf of Aden

Dakar ⊛
SENEGAL
Banjul ⊛
GAMBIA
Bissau ⊛
GUINEA-BISSAU
Conakry ⊛
GUINEA
Freetown ⊛
SIERRA LEONE
Monrovia ⊛
LIBERIA

Bamako ⊛
BURKINA FASO
Ouagadougou ⊛
Niamey ⊛
BENIN
GHANA
TOGO
IVORY COAST
Yamoussoukro ○
Abidjan ⊛
Accra ⊛
Lomé ⊛

Kano ○

NIGERIA
Abuja ⊛
Porto-Novo ⊛
Lagos ⊛

N'Djamena ⊛

Lake Chad

Addis Ababa ⊛
ETHIOPIA

SOMALIA
⊛ Mogadishu

CENTRAL AFRICAN REPUBLIC
Bangui ⊛

SOUTH SUDAN
Juba ⊛

Lake Turkana

CAMEROON
Malabo ⊛
Yaoundé ⊛
EQUATORIAL GUINEA
SÃO TOMÉ AND PRÍNCIPE
São Tomé ⊛

Gulf of Guinea

Equator

Libreville ⊛
GABON
CONGO
Brazzaville ⊛
Kinshasa ⊛
Cabinda (Angola)
Luanda ⊛

Kisangani ○

DEMOCRATIC REPUBLIC OF THE CONGO

UGANDA
Kampala ⊛
KENYA
Nairobi ⊛
Kigali ⊛
RWANDA
Bujumbura ⊛
BURUNDI
Lake Victoria
Mombasa ○

Indian Ocean

Dodoma ⊛
Dar es Salaam ○
Lake Tanganyika

TANZANIA

SEYCHELLES

Atlantic Ocean

ANGOLA

Lubumbashi ○

Lake Malawi

MALAWI
Lilongwe ⊛
ZAMBIA
Lusaka ⊛

Moroni ⊛
COMOROS
Mayotte (France)

Harare ⊛
ZIMBABWE

MOZAMBIQUE

Mozambique Channel

Antananarivo ⊛
MADAGASCAR

Tropic of Capricorn

NAMIBIA
Windhoek ⊛

BOTSWANA
Gaborone ⊛

Johannesburg ○
Pretoria ⊛
Maputo ⊛
Mbabane ⊛
Lobamba ⊛
SWAZILAND
Maseru ⊛
Durban ○
LESOTHO

Bloemfontein ⊛

Cape of Good Hope
SOUTH AFRICA
Cape Town ⊛
Cape Agulhas

Legend
— National border
- - - Disputed border
⊛ National capital
○ Other city

Azimuthal Equidistant Projection

| 0 | 500 | 1000 miles |
| 0 | 500 | 1000 kilometers |

Africa: Physical

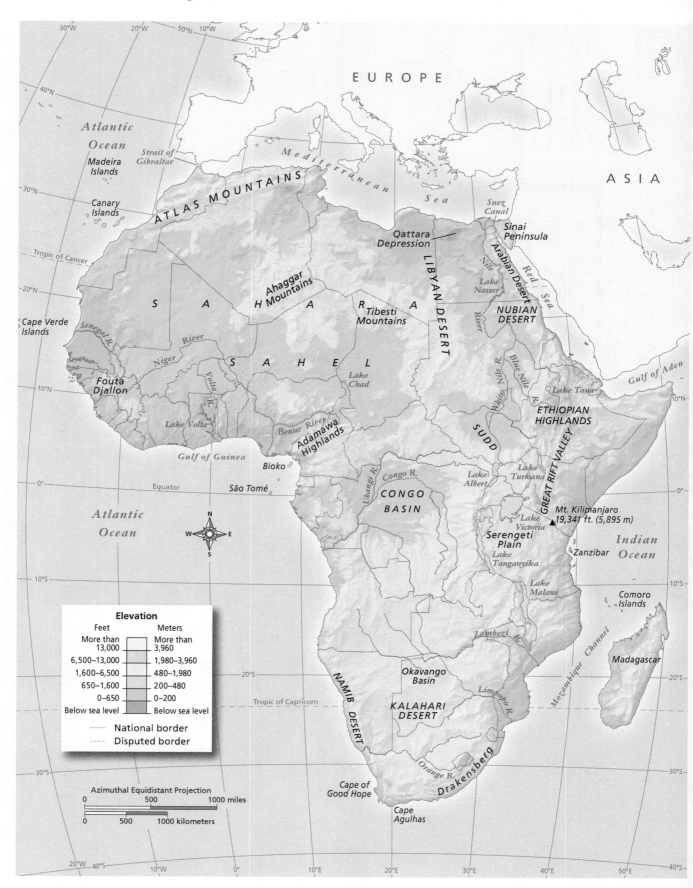

EUROPE

ASIA

Atlantic Ocean

Madeira Islands

Strait of Gibraltar

Mediterranean Sea

Suez Canal

Sinai Peninsula

Canary Islands

ATLAS MOUNTAINS

Qattara Depression

LIBYAN DESERT

Arabian Desert

Nile

Lake Nasser

Tropic of Cancer

S A H A R A

Ahaggar H Mountains

Tibesti Mountains

NUBIAN DESERT

Red Sea

Cape Verde Islands

Senegal R.

River

Niger

S A H E L

Lake Chad

White Nile R.

Blue Nile R.

Lake Tana

Gulf of Aden

Fouta Djallon

Volta R.

Lake Volta

ETHIOPIAN HIGHLANDS

Benue River

Adamawa Highlands

Gulf of Guinea

Bioko

SUDD

Equator

São Tomé

Ubangi R.

Congo R.

CONGO BASIN

Lake Albert

Lake Turkana

GREAT RIFT VALLEY

Mt. Kilimanjaro 19,341 ft. (5,895 m)

Atlantic Ocean

Lake Victoria

Serengeti Plain

Lake Tanganyika

Zanzibar

Indian Ocean

Lake Malawi

Comoro Islands

Zambezi R.

Mozambique Channel

Madagascar

Okavango Basin

NAMIB DESERT

Limpopo R.

Tropic of Capricorn

KALAHARI DESERT

Orange R.

Drakensberg

Cape of Good Hope

Cape Agulhas

Elevation

Feet		Meters
More than 13,000		More than 3,960
6,500–13,000		1,980–3,960
1,600–6,500		480–1,980
650–1,600		200–480
0–650		0–200
Below sea level		Below sea level

—— National border
---- Disputed border

Azimuthal Equidistant Projection

0   500   1000 miles

0   500   1000 kilometers

Asia: Political

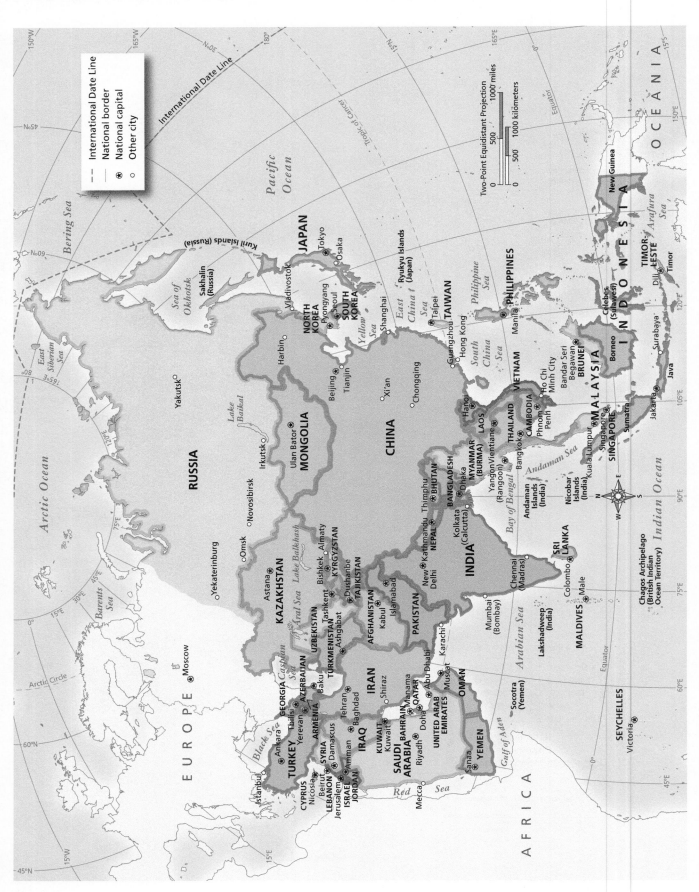

Legend:
- – – International Date Line
- —— International border
- ⊛ National capital
- ○ Other city

Two-Point Equidistant Projection

1000 miles
500 1000 kilometers

OCEANIA

EUROPE

AFRICA

RUSSIA

Arctic Ocean

Barents Sea

Moscow ⊛

Arctic Circle

60°N

Yekaterinburg ○

Omsk ○

Novosibirsk ○

Yakutsk ○

East Siberian Sea

Bering Sea

Sea of Okhotsk

Sakhalin (Russia)

Kuril Islands (Russia)

Pacific Ocean

Vladivostok ○

JAPAN

Tokyo ⊛

Osaka ○

NORTH KOREA

Pyongyang ⊛

SOUTH KOREA

Seoul ⊛

Harbin ○

Irkutsk ○

Lake Baikal

Ulan Bator ⊛

MONGOLIA

Beijing ⊛

Tianjin ○

CHINA

Xi'an ○

Chongqing ○

Shanghai ○

Yellow Sea

East China Sea

Ryukyu Islands (Japan)

Taipei ⊛

TAIWAN

Guangzhou ○

Hong Kong

South China Sea

Philippine Sea

PHILIPPINES

Manila ⊛

KAZAKHSTAN

Astana ⊛

Aral Sea

Lake Balkhash

Almaty ○

Bishkek ⊛

KYRGYZSTAN

Tashkent ⊛

UZBEKISTAN

Dushanbe ⊛

TAJIKISTAN

TURKMENISTAN

Ashgabat ⊛

Caspian Sea

AFGHANISTAN

Kabul ⊛

Islamabad ⊛

PAKISTAN

Karachi ○

New Delhi ⊛

Kathmandu ⊛

NEPAL

Thimphu ⊛

BHUTAN

BANGLADESH

Dhaka ⊛

MYANMAR (BURMA)

Yangon (Rangoon) ○

INDIA

Kolkata (Calcutta) ○

Mumbai (Bombay) ○

Chennai (Madras) ○

SRI LANKA

Colombo ○

Male ○

MALDIVES

Lakshadweep (India)

Arabian Sea

Bay of Bengal

Andaman Islands (India)

Nicobar Islands (India)

Andaman Sea

LAOS

Hanoi ⊛

Vientiane ⊛

THAILAND

Bangkok ⊛

VIETNAM

CAMBODIA

Phnom Penh ⊛

Ho Chi Minh City ○

BRUNEI

Bandar Seri Begawan ⊛

MALAYSIA

Kuala Lumpur ⊛

SINGAPORE

Singapore ⊛

Borneo

Sumatra

INDONESIA

Jakarta ⊛

Surabaya ○

Java

Celebes (Sulawesi)

TIMOR-LESTE

Dili ⊛

Timor

New Guinea

Arafura Sea

Indian Ocean

Equator

GEORGIA

Tbilisi ⊛

ARMENIA

Yerevan ⊛

AZERBAIJAN

Baku ⊛

TURKEY

Ankara ⊛

Istanbul ○

CYPRUS

Nicosia ⊛

LEBANON

Beirut ⊛

SYRIA

Damascus ⊛

ISRAEL

Jerusalem ⊛

JORDAN

Amman ⊛

IRAQ

Baghdad ⊛

IRAN

Tehran ⊛

Shiraz ○

KUWAIT

Kuwait ⊛

SAUDI ARABIA

Riyadh ⊛

BAHRAIN

Manama ⊛

QATAR

Doha ⊛

UNITED ARAB EMIRATES

Abu Dhabi ⊛

OMAN

Muscat ⊛

YEMEN

Sanaa ⊛

Mecca ○

Red Sea

Gulf of Aden

Socotra (Yemen)

Black Sea

SEYCHELLES

Victoria ⊛

Chagos Archipelago (British Indian Ocean Territory)

Tropic of Cancer

Asia: Physical

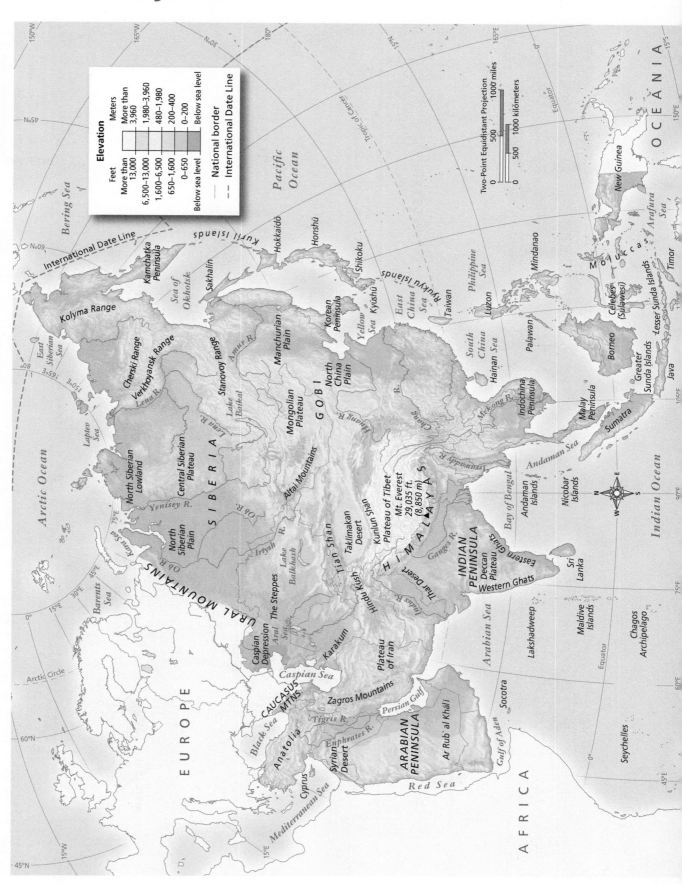

Europe: Political

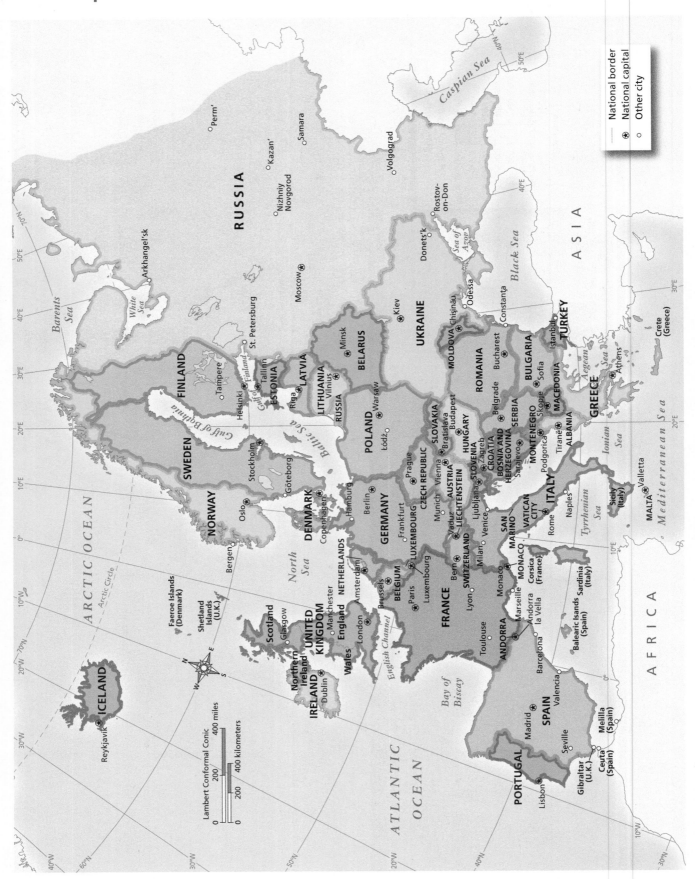

Europe: Physical

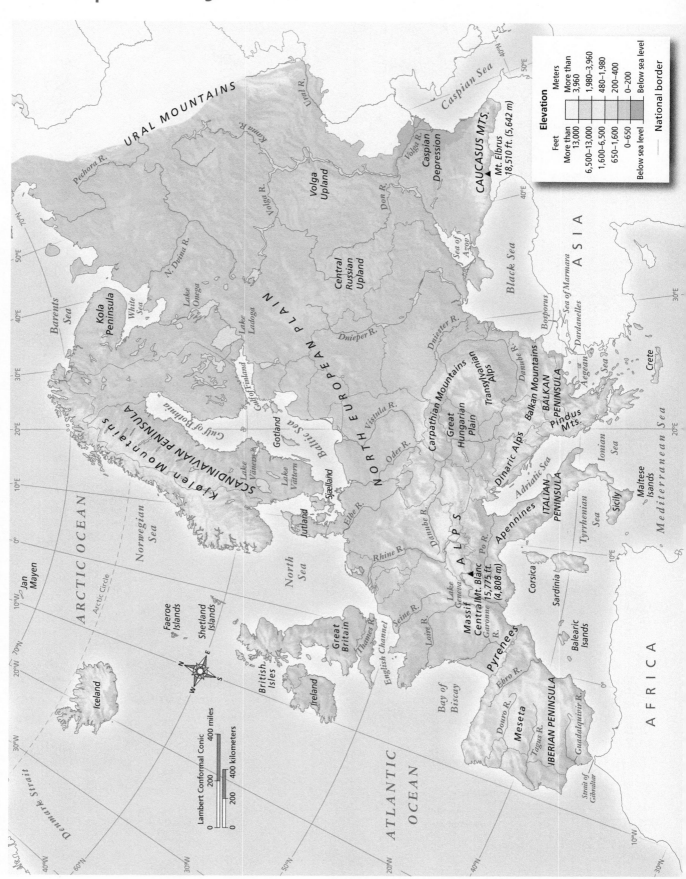

Elevation

Feet	Meters
More than 13,000	More than 3,960
6,500–13,000	1,980–3,960
1,600–6,500	480–1,980
650–1,600	200–400
0–650	0–200
Below sea level	Below sea level

—— National border

URAL MOUNTAINS

Pechora R.

Kama R.

Ural R.

Caspian Sea

Volga R.

Volga Upland

Caspian Depression

CAUCASUS MTS.

Mt. Elbrus 18,510 ft. (5,642 m)

Don R.

Sea of Azov

Black Sea

Sea of Marmara

Dardanelles

ASIA

N. Dvina R.

Central Russian Upland

Bosporus

30°E

Barents Sea

Kola Peninsula

White Sea

Lake Onega

Lake Ladoga

Dnieper R.

Dniester R.

Danube R.

Aegean Sea

Crete

NORTH EUROPEAN PLAIN

Carpathian Mountains

Transylvanian Alps

BALKAN PENINSULA

Pindus Mts.

Gulf of Finland

Vistula R.

Great Hungarian Plain

Balkan Mountains

Mediterranean Sea

SCANDINAVIAN PENINSULA

Kjølen Mountains

Gulf of Bothnia

Gotland

Baltic Sea

Oder R.

Dinaric Alps

Adriatic Sea

ITALIAN PENINSULA

Ionian Sea

Maltese Isands

Lake Vänern

Lake Vättern

Sjælland

Elbe R.

Danube R.

A L P S

Apennines

Tyrrhenian Sea

Sicily

ARCTIC OCEAN

Arctic Circle

Norwegian Sea

North Sea

Jutland

Rhine R.

Po R.

Mt. Blanc 15,775 ft. (4,808 m)

Corsica

Sardinia

Jan Mayen

Faeroe Islands

Shetland Islands

Great Britain

Thames R.

Seine R.

Loire R.

Lake Geneva

Central Massif

Garonne R.

Balearic Isands

Iceland

British Isles

Ireland

English Channel

Pyrenees

Ebro R.

ATLANTIC OCEAN

Bay of Biscay

Meseta

Douro R.

Tagus R.

IBERIAN PENINSULA

Guadalquivir R.

AFRICA

Denmark Strait

N

S

E

W

Lambert Conformal Conic

0   200   400 miles

0   200   400 kilometers

Strait of Gibraltar

70°N

60°N

50°N

40°N

50°E

40°E

30°E

20°E

10°E

0°

10°W

20°W

30°W

40°W

North & South America: Political

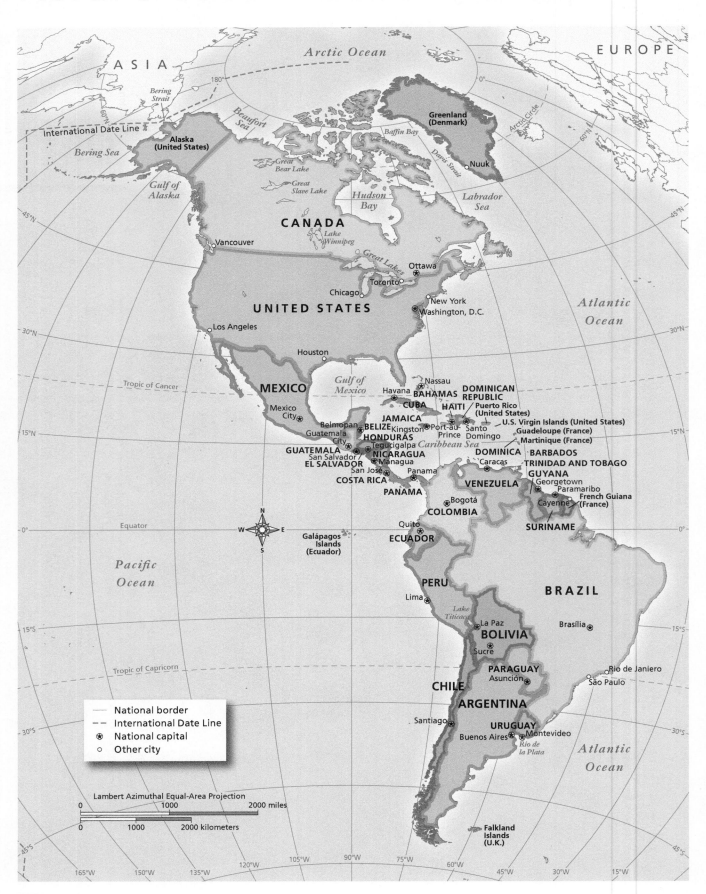

ASIA

Arctic Ocean

EUROPE

International Date Line

Bering Strait

Beaufort Sea

Greenland (Denmark)

Baffin Bay

Alaska (United States)

Bering Sea

Gulf of Alaska

Great Bear Lake

Great Slave Lake

Hudson Bay

Davis Strait

Nuuk

Labrador Sea

Arctic Circle

CANADA

Lake Winnipeg

Vancouver

Great Lakes

Ottawa

Toronto

Chicago

New York

Washington, D.C.

UNITED STATES

Atlantic Ocean

Los Angeles

Houston

Tropic of Cancer

Gulf of Mexico

Nassau

BAHAMAS

DOMINICAN REPUBLIC

Havana

MEXICO

Mexico City

CUBA

HAITI

Puerto Rico (United States)

JAMAICA

U.S. Virgin Islands (United States)

Belmopan

BELIZE

Kingston

Port-au-Prince

Santo Domingo

Guadeloupe (France)

Guatemala City

HONDURAS

Caribbean Sea

Martinique (France)

GUATEMALA

Tegucigalpa

DOMINICA

BARBADOS

San Salvador

NICARAGUA

TRINIDAD AND TOBAGO

EL SALVADOR

Managua

Caracas

GUYANA

San José

Panama

VENEZUELA

Georgetown

COSTA RICA

Paramaribo

French Guiana (France)

PANAMA

Bogotá

Cayenne

Equator

COLOMBIA

SURINAME

Quito

Galápagos Islands (Ecuador)

ECUADOR

Pacific Ocean

PERU

BRAZIL

Lima

Lake Titicaca

La Paz

Brasília

BOLIVIA

Tropic of Capricorn

Sucre

Rio de Janiero

PARAGUAY

São Paulo

Asunción

CHILE

ARGENTINA

Santiago

URUGUAY

Buenos Aires

Montevideo

Río de la Plata

Atlantic Ocean

Falkland Islands (U.K.)

— National border

-- International Date Line

⊛ National capital

○ Other city

Lambert Azimuthal Equal-Area Projection

0   1000   2000 miles

0   1000   2000 kilometers

North & South America: Physical

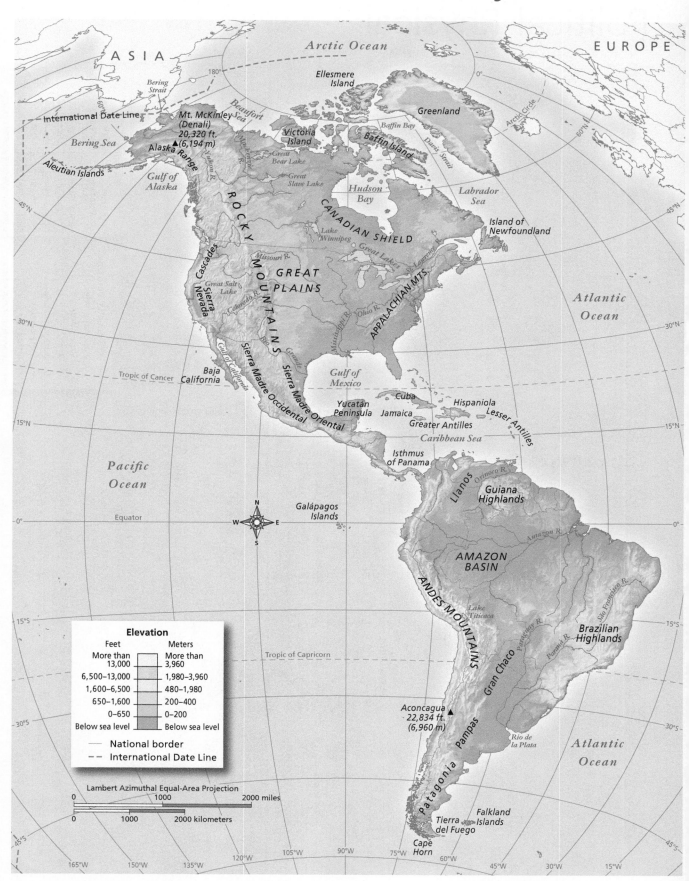

ASIA

Arctic Ocean

EUROPE

Ellesmere Island

Greenland

Bering Strait

Beaufort Sea

International Date Line

Mt. McKinley (Denali) 20,320 ft. ▲(6,194 m)

Baffin Bay

Davis Strait

Arctic Circle

60°N

Bering Sea

Victoria Island

Baffin Island

Alaska Range

Mackenzie R.

Great Bear Lake

Aleutian Islands

Gulf of Alaska

Yukon R.

Great Slave Lake

Hudson Bay

Labrador Sea

45°N

45°N

CANADIAN SHIELD

Island of Newfoundland

Lake Winnipeg

Great Lakes

St. Lawrence R.

Cascades

Missouri R.

GREAT PLAINS

R O C K Y   M O U N T A I N S

Atlantic Ocean

30°N

30°N

Sierra Nevada

Great Salt Lake

Colorado R.

Mississippi R.

Ohio R.

APPALACHIAN MTS.

Gulf of California

Baja California

Sierra Madre Occidental

Sierra Madre Oriental

Rio Grande

Gulf of Mexico

Tropic of Cancer

15°N

15°N

Cuba

Hispaniola

Yucatán Peninsula

Jamaica

Greater Antilles

Lesser Antilles

Caribbean Sea

Isthmus of Panama

Pacific Ocean

Llanos

Orinoco R.

Guiana Highlands

Galápagos Islands

Equator

0°

0°

Amazon R.

AMAZON BASIN

ANDES MOUNTAINS

Lake Titicaca

Brazilian Highlands

15°S

Gran Chaco

Paraguay R.

São Francisco R.

15°S

Elevation

Feet	Meters
More than 13,000	More than 3,960
6,500–13,000	1,980–3,960
1,600–6,500	480–1,980
650–1,600	200–400
0–650	0–200
Below sea level	Below sea level

—— National border

--- International Date Line

Tropic of Capricorn

Aconcagua 22,834 ft. ▲(6,960 m)

Paraná R.

Pampas

Patagonia

Río de la Plata

Atlantic Ocean

30°S

30°S

Lambert Azimuthal Equal-Area Projection

0   1000   2000 miles

0   1000   2000 kilometers

Tierra del Fuego

Falkland Islands

Cape Horn

45°S

45°S

165°W   150°W   135°W   120°W   105°W   90°W   75°W   60°W   45°W   30°W   15°W

Australia, New Zealand & Oceania: Political-Physical

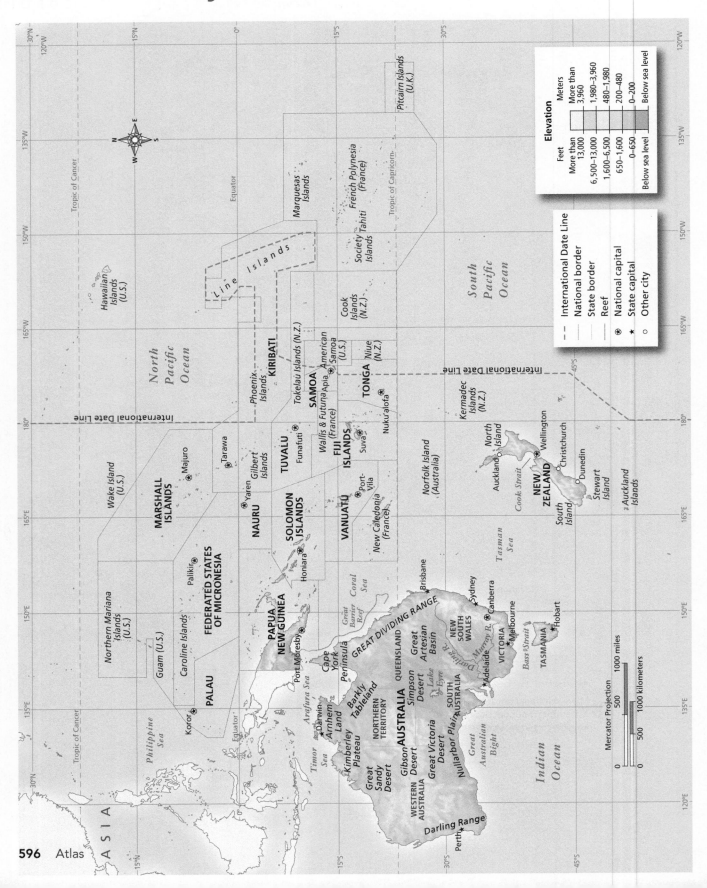

Elevation

Feet	Meters	
More than 13,000	More than 3,960	
6,500–13,000	1,980–3,960	
1,600–6,500	480–1,980	
650–1,600	200–480	
0–650	0–200	
Below sea level	Below sea level	

- - - International Date Line
——— National border
——— State border
——— Reef
⊛ National capital
★ State capital
○ Other city

Pitcairn Islands (U.K.)

Marquesas Islands

French Polynesia (France)

Society Islands

Tahiti

South Pacific Ocean

Tropic of Cancer

Equator

Tropic of Capricorn

Hawaiian Islands (U.S.)

Line Islands

Cook Islands (N.Z.)

International Date Line

North Pacific Ocean

Phoenix Islands

KIRIBATI

Tokelau Islands (N.Z.)

American Samoa (U.S.)

Niue (N.Z.)

Wake Island (U.S.)

Majuro

Tarawa

Gilbert Islands

Yaren

TUVALU

Funafuti

Wallis & Futuna (France)

SAMOA

Apia

TONGA

Nuku'alofa

Kermadec Islands (N.Z.)

MARSHALL ISLANDS

NAURU

SOLOMON ISLANDS

Honiara

FIJI ISLANDS

Suva

VANUATU

Port-Vila

New Caledonia (France)

Norfolk Island (Australia)

North Island

Auckland

Wellington

NEW ZEALAND

Christchurch

Dunedin

South Island

Stewart Island

Cooke Strait

Auckland Islands

Tasman Sea

FEDERATED STATES OF MICRONESIA

Palikir

Caroline Islands

Northern Mariana Islands (U.S.)

Guam (U.S.)

Koror

PALAU

Philippine Sea

Tropic of Cancer

Equator

A S I A

Timor Sea

Arafura Sea

PAPUA NEW GUINEA

Port Moresby

Great Barrier Reef

Coral Sea

Brisbane

Sydney

Canberra

Melbourne

Hobart

Bass Strait

TASMANIA

GREAT DIVIDING RANGE

Cape York Peninsula

QUEENSLAND

Great Artesian Basin

NEW SOUTH WALES

VICTORIA

Murray R.

Darling R.

Adelaide

SOUTH AUSTRALIA

Lake Eyre

Simpson Desert

AUSTRALIA

NORTHERN TERRITORY

Barkly Tableland

Arnhem Land

Darwin

Kimberley Plateau

Great Sandy Desert

WESTERN AUSTRALIA

Gibson Desert

Great Victoria Desert

Nullarbor Plain

Great Australian Bight

Indian Ocean

Perth

Darling Range

Mercator Projection

0   500   1000 miles

0   500   1000 kilometers

The Arctic: Physical

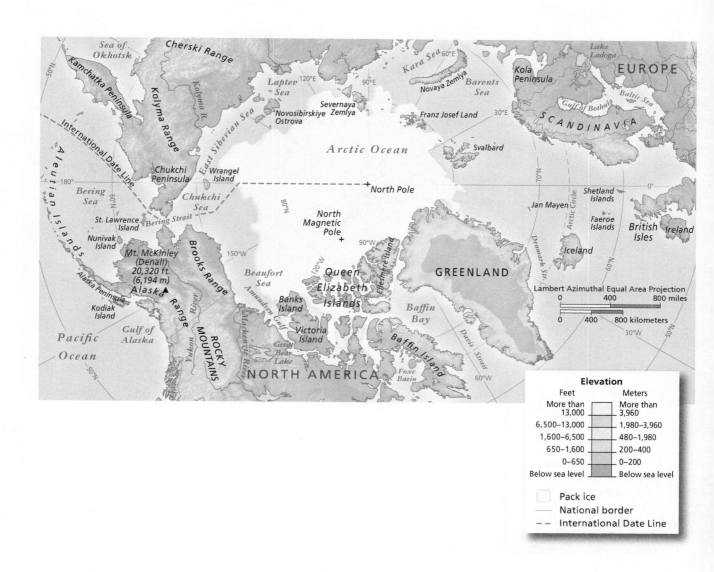

Elevation

Feet		Meters
More than 13,000		More than 3,960
6,500–13,000		1,980–3,960
1,600–6,500		480–1,980
650–1,600		200–400
0–650		0–200
Below sea level		Below sea level

- Pack ice
- National border
- International Date Line

Antarctica: Physical

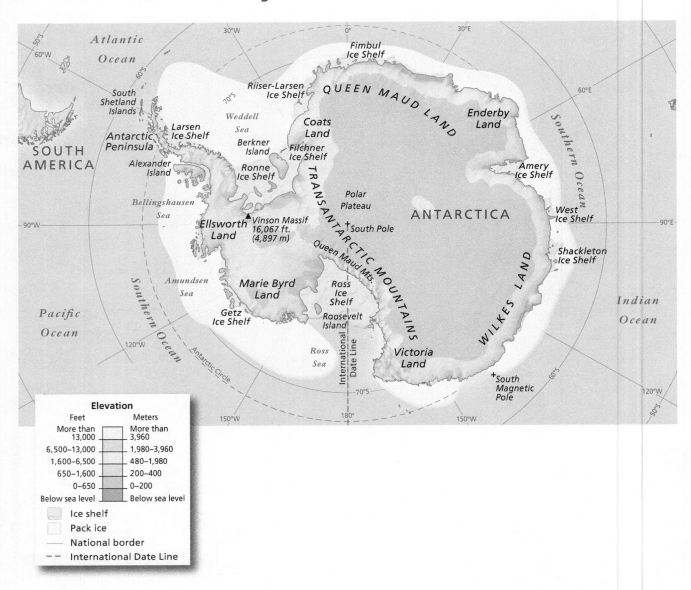

Elevation

Feet	Meters
More than 13,000	More than 3,960
6,500–13,000	1,980–3,960
1,600–6,500	480–1,980
650–1,600	200–400
0–650	0–200
Below sea level	Below sea level

Ice shelf
Pack ice
—— National border
- - - International Date Line

Glossary

A

Aborigine one of Australia's original people

absolute monarchy monarchy—or government with rulers who inherit their position by birth—in which rulers have absolute and unlimited power

access ability to go somewhere or obtain something

accommodate to have or make room for

acupuncture a therapy that uses needles to cure sickness and stop pain

adopt to make use of a new tool or idea

ahimsa the belief that one should not hurt any living thing

ally an independent country or empire that works with other countries or empires to achieve a shared military or political goal

ancestor forerunner or past relative; what a later thing or person is descended from

Antarctic Treaty international agreement that preserves Antarctica for peaceful and scientific use

anthropology the study of humankind in all aspects, especially development and culture

anti-Semitism discrimination against Jews

apartheid former South African policy of strict separation of races

apostle one of Jesus' 12 main disciples, or followers

appoint to assign a role to someone

arable of land, able to be used to grow crops

Arab Spring 2011 movement for more democracy in the Arab world

Aral Sea a large saltwater lake in Central Asia

archaeology the scientific study of ancient cultures through the examination of artifacts and other evidence

aristocracy hereditary class of rulers

armistice a temporary agreement made by opposing sides in a war to stop the fighting

artifact an object made by a human being, such as a tool or a weapon

artisan skilled worker who practices a handicraft

ascetic a person who tries to achieve spiritual purity through self-denial

assimilation process by which one group takes on the cultural traits of another

Atlantic slave trade exchange of European goods for enslaved Africans forced to work on colonial plantations in the Americas

atoll low, sandy island that has formed on top of coral reefs that surround a sunken extinct volcano

authoritarian government a government in which all power is held by a single person or a small group

authority power to rule or command

autocracy a government controlled by one person who has not won a free election

B

background trait, such as ethnic heritage, that people inherit from their parents

Bedouin Arab nomad

belief system set of ideas about spiritual life and morality

bilingual someone who speaks two languages

biodiversity variety of different kinds of living things in a region or ecosystem

biome a region made up of similar ecosystems and communities of plants and animals

Black Death epidemic, or widespread outbreak, of bubonic plague that devastated Europe and other regions in the mid-1300s

bodhisattva in Buddhism, a being who has gained enlightenment and, out of compassion, tries to help others

Bolsheviks Russian political group that called for worker control and advocated communism; seized control of Russia in October 1917; grew into the Communist Party of the Soviet Union

Brahman in Hinduism, the one supreme cosmic consciousness, spiritual force, or God

Bronze Age period in human history during which people used bronze to make tools and weapons

bureaucracy system of many government officials who carry out government rules and regulations

C

caliph title meaning "successor" in Arabic, used by leaders of the Muslim community who followed Muhammad

caliphate a region controlled by a caliph, or an Islamic religious and political leader

call center a business that has groups of workers who provide customer service by phone

capital money or goods that are used to make products

cardinal direction north, east, south, and west

caste fixed social class into which a person is born

catastrophic involving or causing sudden great damage or suffering

ceremony an official event for a specific occasion

CFA franc common currency used by several West and Central African countries

characteristic distinguishing, unique

chronology a list of events in the order in which they occurred

circulate to move from place to place

citizen a legal member of a country

citizenship membership in a community that gives a person civil and political rights and obligations

city-state an independent state consisting of a city and its surrounding territory

civic life activities having to do with one's society and community

civilian people who are not members of the armed forces

civil service a system of government employees mainly selected for their ability

clan group of families with a common ancestor

climate average weather of a place over many years

climate change temperature increase on Earth due to greenhouse gases

cluster grouping of like people or things

Cold War period of hostility during the mid- to late 1900s between the United States and its allies on one side and the Soviet Union and its allies on the other side

collaborate to work jointly

collectivization a shift of control from an individual or company to a group called a collective

colonialism policy by which one country seeks to rule other areas

commandment an order to do something

commentary a set of comments or a recorded discussion about something

commercial used for trade or other business

communism a political and economic system in which government owns all property and makes all economic decisions

communist someone who supports a political and economic system in which government owns all property and makes all economic decisions

comparative advantage a society's ability to produce a product most efficiently given all the products it could produce

compel to force someone to do something

compensate to make up for

competing being a rival; challenging

compromise agreement in which each side gives up some of its demands in order to achieve others peacefully

concentrated focused on or gathered in

condemn to express public disapproval

confine to limit or restrict

Confucianism belief system based on the teachings of the Chinese philosopher Confucius

consent to give approval to

consequence result

consider take into account

constitution a system of basic rules and principles by which a government is organized

constitutional monarchy system of government in which the laws in the constitution limit the monarch's or emperor's powers

consumer person or business that buys, or consumes, goods or services

containment a policy during the Cold War of preventing communism from spreading

contend to struggle, as in a contest

continuity connection of events over time

controversy public disagreement over an issue

conversion heartfelt change in one's opinions or beliefs, especially in religion

convert to cause to change in form or function

coordinate to bring different elements into a relationship to ensure efficiency; organize

Copts Egyptians who belong to an ancient Christian church

coral bleaching process that occurs when coral reefs weaken and lighten in color due to a warming climate

coral reef living formation of rock-like material made up of the skeletons of tiny sea creatures

core something central or basic

corridor a narrow, confined strip connecting one or more places

corruption use of power for personal gain

cosmic relating to the whole universe

Counter-Reformation a movement to strengthen the teachings and structure of the Catholic Church

coup sudden violent overthrow of a government, often by force

covenant binding agreement

critical expressing disapproval or disagreement

crucial essential, decisive

crucifixion Roman method of execution by nailing a person to a wooden cross

Crusades a series of military campaigns to establish Christian control over the Holy Land

cultural diffusion the spread of cultural traits from one culture to another

culture the beliefs, customs, practices, and behaviors of a particular nation or group of people

cuneiform in the ancient Middle East, a system of writing that used wedge-shaped marks

custom usual practice, especially of a group

customary according to custom or usual practices

D

Dalit member of the lowest Indian caste grouping made up of people who did jobs no one else wanted to do

Daoism a philosophy of following the Dao, that is, the natural way of the universe

deforestation loss of forest cover that results from so many trees being removed that trees cannot grow back

delta flat, fan-shaped plain formed on a seabed where a river deposits material over many years

demand desire for a particular good or service

democracy a form of government in which citizens hold political power

democratization the process of a society becoming more democratic

demographic having to do with population change and the different groups that make up the population of a place or region

demography the study of human population trends

dependency territory controlled by the government of another country

deposition process of dropping eroded material in a new place

desalination removal of salt from seawater

desertification change from arable land to desert

determine to figure out, or decide a question

developed country country with a strong economy and a high quality of life

developing country country with a less-productive economy and a lower quality of life

development country's economic growth and quality of life

devout completely committed to religious beliefs

dharma in Hinduism, a person's duty or what is right for him or her

dialect a language variety

Diaspora Jewish communities outside the ancient Jewish homeland

dictatorship government controlled by a single leader

discord strife, conflict

discrimination unfair treatment

dispute a disagreement or debate

distinct recognizably different from something else

distinctive setting a person or thing apart

distortion loss of accuracy

divert to turn from one course to another

doctrine article or principle of faith

domestic relating to or found within a country

domesticate to change the growth of plants or behavior of animals in ways that are useful for humans

dominion territory of the British Empire with internal self-rule

dynasty ruling family

E

economic oligarchy small group of people who control a country's economy and influence the government

economics study of how people meet their wants and needs

ecosystem group of plants and animals that depend on each other and their environment for survival

effective useful for achieving a desired result

emerge to become known

emigrate to migrate out of a place

empire a territory containing several countries and ruled by a single government

Enlightenment a period during the 1600s and 1700s when scholars studied culture and society by applying reason and natural laws

enlightenment in Buddhism, a state of perfect wisdom, free of suffering

entrepreneur person who organizes and manages his or her own business

entrepreneurship the ability to start and grow new businesses

epistle formal letter, several of which form part of the New Testament

equinox period during which hours of daylight and hours of darkness are of equal length everywhere on Earth

equip to supply with the necessary items; to prepare

eradicate to eliminate

erosion process by which water, ice, or wind remove rock and soil

establish to set up or found

ethics beliefs about what is right and wrong

ethnic group group of people who share a distinct culture, language, and identity

European Union economic and political partnership among member nations

eventually at a later, unspecified time

evidence something that provides information about something unknown

exchange rate the value of one currency stated in terms of a different currency

exclude to prevent from entering a place or participating in an activity

exempt free from, not subject to

exercise to use a privilege or discharge an official duty

Exodus escape of the Israelites from slavery in Egypt

expedition a journey made for exploration, research, or war

extract to take out or remove

F

factor something that contributes to a development or result

failed state a country with a government that cannot control its territory or provide effective government services to its citizens

fault crack in Earth's crust

federal system a system in which power is divided among central, regional, and local governments

fertile capable of producing abundant crops

fertility the ability to have or likelihood of having children

feudalism a system of rule in which powerful lords divided their lands among lesser lords, or vassals

filial piety devotion of children to their parents

flawed marked by problems; not perfect

flourish to thrive

foreign coming from outside a country

fossil hardened remains or imprint of living thing that existed long ago

fossil fuel nonrenewable resource that forms over millions of years from the remains of dead plants and animals

free trade removal of trade barriers

French Revolution a political movement that removed the French king from power and formed a republic

fundamentalism belief that holy books should be taken literally, word for word

G

genocide attempt to destroy a whole people

geography study of the human and nonhuman features of Earth

glacier slow-moving body of ice

Gospel one of the first four books of the New Testament, which describe the life and teachings of Jesus

government a group of people who have the power to make and enforce laws for a country or area

governor general representative of the British king or queen in a parliamentary constitutional monarchy

Great Schism split between the Eastern Orthodox and Roman Catholic churches in 1054

Great Wall long wall running east and west along the Chinese empire's northern border

greenhouse gas any gas that traps heat in Earth's atmosphere and makes the planet warmer

Green Revolution increase in agricultural production created by improved technology

gross domestic product (GDP) total value of all goods and services produced in a country in a year

guild an organization consisting of merchants or craftsmen working in the same line of business that sets standards for and protects its members

guru thinker or teacher

H

hajj pilgrimage made by Muslims to the holy city of Mecca

Hammurabi's Code a set of laws that governed life in the Babylonian empire

hieroglyphic symbol that stands for a word, idea, or sound

hijab veil that covers the head and chest

Hijra Muhammad's migration with his followers from Mecca to Medina

Holocaust the mass murder of Jews by the Nazis during World War II

homogenous describing a society in which almost all people belong to the same ethnic group

Homo sapiens modern human

hostility strong negative feeling toward someone

human capital knowledge and skills of employees

humanism a cultural movement of the Renaissance based on the study of classical works

hunter-gatherer nomadic person who survived by hunting, fishing, and gathering wild plants

hydroelectric power the power produced by water driving turbines

hyperinflation an extremely rapid and sharp increase in prices

I

iceberg large floating mass of ice

ice sheet large mass of compressed ice covering a land area

icon a holy image, usually a portrait of Jesus or a saint

illusion something unreal or misleading

impact effect

impede to slow or block the movement of something

imperialism process of creating an empire by taking over other areas

incentive something that encourages people to behave in a certain way

incorporate to blend or merge

indigenous present in a region since ancient or prehistoric times

Indochina a peninsula in Southeast Asia; includes the countries of Myanmar, Cambodia, Laos, Thailand, and Vietnam, and the Malay Peninsula

industrial goods products or raw materials needed to produce other goods

industrialization growth of machine-powered production and manufacturing

Industrial Revolution the application of machine power to manufacturing in the 1800s and the resulting transformation of societies

inflation general increase in prices

inhabitant person who lives in a place

inherit to receive as a result of being in a family or group

install to put someone in a position of authority

intensive having or requiring a large amount of an input

interaction two or more things affecting each other

interior far from the coast; inland

intermediate direction a compass direction that lies between the cardinal directions, such as northeast

internal within a country

interpretation way of viewing the meaning of a text, rules, or belief

Intifada a Palestinian campaign of violent resistance against Israeli control

irrigate to supply water to

Islamism belief that government and society should reflect Islamic law

isolated alone; separate from others

Israeli settlement a place in the West Bank or Gaza where Israelis have settled

J

Justinian's Code a law code published by the Byzantine emperor Justinian

K

Kaaba a shrine in Mecca that is the most important Islamic holy site

karma in Hinduism, the effect of a person's actions in this life and in past or future lives

Kyoto Protocol international agreement to reduce the emission of greenhouse gases that contribute to climate change

L

latitude the position north or south of the Equator measured in degrees

Legalism an ancient Chinese philosophy stating that a strong leader and a strong legal system, not moral values, are needed to create social order

lifestyle typical ways of living out daily life

longitude the position in degrees east or west of the Prime Meridian

lord a local military ruler in medieval Europe

M

magma molten rock found under Earth's surface

maintain to keep in working order

malnutrition lack of enough nutrients from food

mandate a territory controlled by an Allied power after World War I

Mandate of Heaven in ancient China, the right to rule given to a dynasty by Heaven, the highest force of nature

manor the agricultural estate of a medieval lord or vassal

Maori original, Polynesian inhabitants of New Zealand and the Cook Islands

marae enclosed area of land that functions as the center of Maori culture

meditate to calm or clear the mind, often by focusing on a single subject

Meiji Restoration in Japan, the reign of emperor Meiji from 1868 to 1912, which was marked by industrialization and modernization

Mesopotamia region within the Fertile Crescent in present-day Iraq and Syria that lies between the Tigris and Euphrates rivers

microlending making small loans to people who start or run their own small businesses

militant someone who is aggressively active in a cause

minimum lowest possible or acceptable

missionary someone who tries to convert others to a particular religion

model example; pattern of behavior to be followed

moderate not extreme

modernize to adapt something to current times

moksha in Hinduism, liberation from reincarnation

monarchy a form of government in which the state is ruled by a monarch

monastery religious community

monk man who dedicates himself to worshiping God

monotheism belief in a single God

monsoon seasonal winds and weather patterns in South and Southeast Asia

mosque Muslim house of worship

movement a group of people sharing and pursuing social or political goals

mummy body that has been preserved so that it will not decompose

mythology collection of myths or stories that people tell about their gods and heroes

N

nationalism the belief that all people in a nation are a distinct group, regardless of ethnicity or race

nationalize government taking ownership of a company or industry

nation-state country that is independent

naturalization a legal process by which immigrants become citizens

natural resource useful material found in the environment

navigation the art of steering a ship from place to place

Neanderthal a type of early human

negative unwanted; undesirable

Neolithic Revolution the prehistoric period during which the introduction of agriculture led people to transition from nomadic to settled life

network an interconnected group of people or things

New Testament writings that form part of the Christian Bible and tell the story of Jesus and his early followers

nirvana in Buddhism, a state of blissful peace without desire or suffering

nonalignment the position of a country not allying itself with either of the superpowers during the Cold War

nongovernmental organization (NGO) group, usually nonprofit, that operates with private funding

nonviolent resistance peaceful protest against laws considered unjust

nutrient substance that supports life by promoting growth or health or providing energy

O

oasis place in the desert where water can be found

opportunity cost cost of what you have to give up when making a choice

oppression the state of being under unjust and harsh rule

oral tradition a community's cultural and historical background, passed down in spoken stories and songs

orient to tend toward; to adjust or adapt to

outrage shock and anger at a violation of principles

outsourcing the business practice in which one company hires another company or outside workers to perform specific tasks

overtax to strain through overuse

overwhelmingly superior by a large margin

ozone layer layer of the atmosphere that filters out most of the sun's harmful ultraviolet rays

P

pack ice seasonal ice that floats on water

Pan-Africanism political and social movement to unite black Africans around the world

papyrus a writing surface similar to paper named after the papyrus reed that grew along the Nile River in ancient Egypt

parable story with a religious moral

parliamentary democracy democratic government whose leader is elected by the legislature

partition to split or divide

pastoralism practice of raising livestock on open pastures

pattern the organized spread of features in a space

penal colony place where convicted prisoners were sent for punishment, far from their homelands

period a length of time singled out because of a specific event or development that happened during that time; also known as an era or epoch

permafrost permanently frozen soil

permanent lasting; stable or unchanging

pharaoh king of ancient Egypt

philosophy general study of knowledge and the world; Greek for "love of wisdom"

pidgin language simple language used for interaction between people who speak different languages

plate tectonics a process involving huge blocks of Earth's crust and upper mantle that are called tectonic plates

point of view a person's perspective on a person, thing, idea, or event

Polynesian member of a Pacific island cultural group known for their long-distance navigation skills

polytheism worship of many gods or deities

populate to inhabit, or live in

portion share

practice to follow or observe regularly

predominantly mainly

prehistory the time before humans invented writing

preserve to prepare so as to resist decay

presidential democracy democratic government whose leader is elected by the people

prestige having high status in others' eyes

prevailing wind the wind that most frequently blows across a particular region

primary first or most important

primary source information that comes directly from a person who experienced an event

principle basic value

producer person or business that makes and sells goods or services

productivity amount of goods and services produced given the amount of resources used

projection way to map Earth on a flat surface

prone having a natural tendency

prosper to enjoy success

pull factor cause of migration that pulls, or attracts people, to new countries

Punjab an area of northern Pakistan and India

push factor cause of migration that pushes people to leave their home country

Q

quota a fixed quantity set by limits

Quran holy book of Islam

R

rabbi Jewish religious teacher

radical someone with extreme views

recovery process of rebuilding an economy

Reformation a religious movement that began in the 1500s to reform the Catholic Church that led to the creation of new Protestant churches

regulation government rules that set limits or standards for businesses

reincarnation the rebirth of a soul in a new body

relatively in relation, comparison, or proportion to something else

reliant dependent

remittance money that people who live in another country send back to families in their home country

remote distant

Renaissance French for "rebirth"; refers to a period of cultural revival in Europe from the 1300s to the 1500s

repressive acting to control or limit dissent

republic form of government in which citizens have the right to vote and elect officials

reserves resources available for future use

reservoir a storage pool of water

restock to obtain fresh supplies

restore to return to a former condition

resurrect to come back to life

revelation the act of communicating a divine truth

reverse to turn in the opposite direction

righteous obeying moral law

S

Sabbath weekly day of rest

sanction action that attempts to force a country to follow international law

savanna park-like landscape of grasslands with scattered trees that can survive dry spells, found in tropical areas with wet and dry seasons

scale relative size

scattered distributed or occurring in widely spaced areas

secondary source information about an event that does not come from a person who experienced that event

secular nonreligious

semiconductor computer chips that run smart phones, tablets, computers, appliances, and cars

serf a peasant who is legally bound to live and work on land owned by a lord

series a group of related or similar things or events, often arranged in order

service sector the portion of a country's or region's economy that produces services, not goods

sexism the unfair treatment of people based on gender

Sharia Islamic law code

Shinto Japanese religion based on the worship of spirits

significance importance

Silk Road series of trade routes that crossed Asia and connected China to the Mediterranean Sea

social class a group of people living in similar economic conditions

social structure a pattern of organized relationships among groups of people within a society

society a group of humans with a shared culture who have organized themselves to meet their basic needs

Socratic method form of teaching in which the teacher asks students question after question to force them to think more clearly

solstice period during which hours of daylight are longest in one hemisphere and shortest in the other hemisphere

sophisticated complex; highly developed

sparse few and scattered

stable unchanging; not likely to give way

standard of living the level of comfort enjoyed by a person or a society

station parcel of land put aside by the Australian government on which some Aborigines were forced to live

stele grand stone pillar used to mark graves

steppe vast area of grasslands

stonetown word used to describe Swahili cities and their multistoried stone houses

strain pressure; stress

submission the act of being obedient

subsistence farming farming mainly to feed the farmer's family with little left over to send to market

sultan title for a ruler of a Muslim country

sultanate a monarchy headed by a sultan

Sunnah traditions believed by Muslims to come from the prophet Muhammad

supply amount of a good or service that is available for use

sustain to support

symbolic standing for an idea or a power, but with little practical role

T

taiga thick forest of coniferous trees

Talmud collection of oral teachings and commentaries about the Hebrew Bible and Jewish law

tariff tax on imports or exports

technology tools and skills that people use to meet their needs and wants

temperate zone area between the high and low latitudes; also known as middle latitudes

terrain the physical features of an area of land

theocracy government run by religious power

timeline a line marked off with a series of events and dates

tolerance a willingness to respect different beliefs and customs

topography the physical features of an area

Torah first five books of the Hebrew Bible

toxic poisonous

trade exchange of goods and services in a market

trade barrier something that keeps goods and services from entering a country

tribute payment from conquered peoples or to a more powerful country

Trinity the three persons, or forms, of God according to Christian belief: God the Father, Jesus the Son, and the Holy Spirit

tropical cyclone intense rainstorm with strong winds that forms over tropical oceans

tropics area between the Tropic of Cancer and the Tropic of Capricorn; also known as low latitudes

tsar ruler of imperial Russia; from the Latin *caesar* or emperor

tsunami tidal wave, or large wave that can flood coastal areas

tundra area with limited vegetation such as moss and shrubs due to its climate of cool summers and bitterly cold, dry winters

typhoon tropical cyclone that forms over the western North Pacific Ocean

U

ultimate final

unify to bring different people or groups together

unitary system a system in which a central government makes all laws for the entire country

urbanization movement of people from rural to urban areas

V

vassal a lesser lord in medieval Europe who pledged loyalty and service to a more powerful lord in exchange for land

Veda a collection of hundreds of sacred hymns composed by the Aryans of ancient India

veto to stop or cancel the action of a government official or body

Vietnam War war from 1964 to 1975 in which the U.S. military supported South Vietnam in its fight to remain independent from communist North Vietnam

W

water cycle the movement of water from Earth's surface to the atmosphere and back again

weather condition of the air and sky at a certain time and place

weathering process that breaks down rock into tiny pieces

westernize to adopt Western ideas, technology, and culture

Z

Zionism movement to create an independent Jewish country in Jews' historic homeland in Palestine

Glosario

A

Aborigine > aborigen relativo a uno de los pueblos originarios de Australia

absolute monarchy > monarquía absoluta monarquía o gobierno con gobernantes que heredan su posición por descendencia, y que tienen poder absoluto e ilimitado

access > acceso capacidad de ir a alguna parte o de obtener algo

accommodate > acomodar hacer espacio para algo

acupuncture > acupuntura terapia que utiliza agujas para curar enfermedades y aliviar el dolor

adopt > adoptar hacer uso de un instrumento nuevo o una idea nueva

ahimsa > ahimsa creencia de que no se debería maltratar a ningún ser vivo

ally > aliado país independiente o imperio que trabaja con otros países o imperios para lograr un objetivo político o militar

ancestor > ancestro antepasado o pariente que vivió en el pasado; de donde desciende una persona o ser vivo

Antarctic Treaty > Tratado Antártico acuerdo internacional que protege a la Antártica para usos pacíficos y científicos

anthropology > antropología estudio de todos los aspectos de la humanidad, especialmente el desarrollo y la cultura

anti-Semitism > antisemitismo discriminación contra los judíos

apartheid > apartheid separación estricta de razas que se practicaba en Sudáfrica

apostle > apóstol cada uno de los doce principales discípulos o seguidores de Jesús

appoint > nombrar asignar una función a alguien

arable > arable se refiere a la tierra que se puede usar para el cultivo

Arab Spring > Primavera Árabe movimiento que tuvo lugar en 2011 que buscaba más democracia en el mundo árabe

Aral Sea > mar de Aral lago de agua salada y de gran tamaño en Asia Central

archaeology > arqueología estudio científico de las culturas antiguas a través del análisis de artefactos y otros tipos de evidencia

aristocracy > aristocracia clase hereditaria de gobernantes

armistice > armisticia acuerdo temporal al que llegan los lados opuestos en una guerra para cesar los combates

artifact > artefacto objeto hecho por un ser humano, como una herramienta o un arma

artisan > artesano trabajador calificado que practica un trabajo manual

ascetic > ascético persona que trata de alcanzar pureza espiritual a través de la autonegación

assimilation > asimilación proceso por el cual un grupo adopta los rasgos culturales de otro grupo

Atlantic slave trade > comercio de esclavos en el Atlántico intercambio de bienes europeos por africanos esclavizados forzados a trabajar en plantaciones coloniales de las Américas

atoll > atolón isla arenosa y de poca altura que se forma sobre las barreras de coral que rodean un volcán extinto bajo el mar

authoritarian government > gobierno autoritario gobierno en el que todo el poder lo tiene un individuo o grupo pequeño

authority > autoridad poder para gobernar o comandar

autocracy > autocracia gobierno controlado por una persona que no ha ganado en elecciones libres

B

background > antecedente rasgo, como la herencia étnica, que las personas heredan de sus padres

Bedouin > beduino nómada árabe

belief system > sistema de creencias conjunto de ideas sobre la vida espiritual y la moralidad

bilingual > bilingüe alguien que habla dos idiomas

biodiversity > biodiversidad variedad de clases diferentes de seres vivos de una región o ecosistema

biome > bioma región formada por ecosistemas y comunidades de plantas y animales similares

Black Death > Peste Negra epidemia, o brote generalizado, de peste bubónica que devastó Europa y otras regiones a mediados de los 1300s

bodhisattva > bodhisattva en el budismo, persona que alcanzado la iluminación y, por compasión, trata de ayudar a otros también

Bolsheviks > bolcheviques grupo político ruso que defendía el control por parte del proletariado y promovía el comunismo; tomó el control de Rusia en octubre de 1917; se convirtió en el Partido Comunista de la Unión Soviética

Brahman > Brahman en el hinduismo, conciencia cósmica suprema, fuerza espiritual, o Dios

Bronze Age > Edad de Bronce período de la historia durante la cual las personas usaban bronce para crear herramientas y armas

bureaucracy > burocracia sistema de numerosos funcionarios que ejecutan las normas y reglamentos del gobierno

C

caliph > califa "sucesor" en árabe; título utilizado por los líderes de la comunidad musulmana, seguidores de Mahoma

caliphate > califato región controlada por un califa, o líder político y religioso islámico

call center > centro de llamadas empresa que tiene grupos de trabajadores que ofrecen servicio al cliente por teléfono

capital > capital dinero o bienes que se invierten para fabricar productos

cardinal direction > punto cardinal norte, sur, este y oeste

caste > casta clase social fija en la que nace una persona

catastrophic > catastrófico que causa un enorme y repentino daño o sufrimiento

ceremony > ceremonia evento oficial para una ocasión especial

CFA franc > franco CFA moneda común usada por varios países de África central y occidental

characteristic > característico se refiere a un rasgo que distingue, único

chronology > cronología lista de sucesos organizados en el orden en que ocurrieron

circulate > circular mover de un lugar a otro

citizen > ciudadano miembro legal de un país

citizenship > ciudadanía membresía en un estado o una comunidad que confiere derechos y obligaciones civiles y políticos a las personas

city-state > ciudad-estado unidad política que consiste en una ciudad y el territorio aledaño

civic life > vida cívica actividades relacionadas con nuestra sociedad o comunidad

civilian > civil persona que no es miembro de las fuerzas armadas

civil service > servicio civil sistema de empleados gubernamentales seleccionados principalmente por su capacidad

clan > clan grupo de familias con un mismo ancestro

climate > clima tiempo promedio de un lugar a lo largo de muchos años

climate change > cambio climático aumento de la temperatura en La Tierra debido a los gases de efecto invernadero

cluster > conjunto grupo de personas o cosas semejantes

Cold War > Guerra Fría periodo de intensa rivalidad de mediados a finales del siglo XX entre la Unión Soviética y los Estados Unidos, y sus respectivos aliados

collaborate > colaborar trabajar en conjunto

collectivization > colectivización cambio del control de un individuo o de una compañía a un grupo llamado colectivo

colonialism > colonialismo política por medio de la cual un país intenta gobernar otras áreas

commandment > mandamiento una orden de hacer algo

commentary > comentario un conjunto de juicios o un debate registrado acerca de algo

commercial > comercial referido al intercambio por compra y venta y otros negocios

communism > comunismo sistema político y económico en el que el Estado possee toda propiedad y toma todas las decisiones económicas

communist > comunista alguien que apoya un sistema político y económico en el que el gobierno controla toda la propiedad y toma todas las decisiones económicas

comparative advantage > ventaja comparativa capacidad de una persona o país para producir un bien a un costo menor que otra persona o país

compel > obligar forzar a alguien a hacer algo

compensate > compensar resarcir por un daño causado

competing > competidor rival; contendiente

compromise > acuerdo pacto en el que cada lado renuncia a parte de sus demandas con el fin de llegar a una solución pacífica

concentrated > concentrado enfocado en algo o reunido alrededor del centro de una cosa

condemn > condenar expresar desaprobación públicamente

confine > confinar limitar o restringir

Confucianism > confucianismo sistema de creencias basado en la ideología del filósofo chino Confucio

consent > consentir dar aprobación

consequence > consecuencia resultado

consider > considerar tener en cuenta

constitution > constitución sistema de reglas y principios básicos que establece la organización de un gobierno

constitutional monarchy > monarquía constitucional sistema de gobierno en el que las leyes de la constitución limitan los poderes del monarca o emperador

consumer > consumidor person o negocio que compra o consume productos

containment > contención política durante la Guerra Fría para evitar la expansión del comunismo

contend > contender luchar, competir

continuity > continuidad conexión de eventos en el tiempo

controversy > controversia desacuerdo público sobre un asunto

conversion > conversión cambio sincero de opiniones o creencias, especialmente en el campo religioso

convert > convertir cambiar en forma o función

coordinate > coordinar establecer una unión o relación entre diferentes elementos para asegurar su eficiencia; organizar

Copts > copto egipcio que pertenece a una antigua iglesia cristiana

coral bleaching > blanqueo de coral proceso que ocurre cuando los arrecifes de coral se debilitan y se decoloran debido al calentamiento climático

coral reef > arrecife de coral formación de materia parecida a la roca formada por criaturas marinas diminutas y sus esqueletos

core > núcleo base o centro de algo

corridor > corredor área estrecha que conecta dos o más lugares

corruption > corrupción uso del poder para beneficio personal

cosmic > cósmico relacionado con todo el universo

Counter-Reformation > contrarreforma movimiento para fortalecer las enseñanzas y la estructura de la Iglesia católica

coup > golpe de estado derrocamiento repentino y violento de un gobierno

covenant > convenio pacto vinculante

critical > crítico que expresa desaprobación o desacuerdo

crucial > crucial esencial, decisivo

crucifixion > crucifixión método romano de ejecución clavando a una persona a una cruz de madera

Crusades > Crusadas serie de guerras que libraron los cristianos para controlar Palestina, es decir, Tierra Santa

cultural diffusion > difusión cultural propagación de los rasgos culturales de una cultura a otra

culture > cultura creencias, costumbres, prácticas y comportamientos de una nación o un grupo de personas determinado

cuneiform > cuneiforme en el antiguo Oriente Medio, sistema de escritura que usaba marcas en forma de cuña

custom > costumbre práctica común, especialmente en un grupo

customary > usual de acuerdo con las costumbres o prácticas habituales

D

Dalit > paria miembro de la casta más inferior de India formada por personas que realizan los trabajos que más nadie quiere hacer

Daoism > taoísmo filosofía que sigue el Tao, es decir, el orden natural del universo

deforestation > deforestación el corte de tantos árboles que tiene como resultado la destrucción del bosque porque los árboles no pueden reproducirse

delta > delta área plana y con forma de abanico que se forma en el lecho marino donde un río deposita material sedimentario a lo largo de muchos años

demand > demanda interés en un bien o servicio determinado

democracy > democracia tipo de gobierno en el que los ciudadanos tienen el poder político

democratization > democratización proceso de una sociedad para volverse más democrática

demographic > demográfico relacionado con los cambios en una población y los diferentes grupos que componen la poblacón de un lugar o región

demography > demografía estudio de las tendencias de la población humana

dependency > dependencia territorio controlado por el gobierno de otro país

deposition > sedimentación proceso de depósito de material erosionado arrastrado hacia otro lugar

desalination > desalinización proceso de quitar la sal del agua del mar

desertification > desertización transformación de la tierra fértil al secarse y convertirse en desierto

determine > determinar definir, decidir algo

developed country > país desarrollado país con una economía fuerte y un alto nivel de vida

developing country > país en vías de desarrollo país con una economía menos productiva y un nivel de vida más bajo

development > desarrollo crecimiento económico y calidad de vida de un país

devout > devoto totalmente dedicado a creencias religiosas

dharma > dharma en el hinduismo, deber de una persona o lo que es correcto para él o ella

dialect > dialecto variación de un idioma

Diaspora > Diáspora conjunto de comunidades judías que viven fuera de la antigua patria judía

dictatorship > dictadura gobierno controlado por un solo líder

discord > discordia desacuerdo, conflicto

discrimination > discriminación trato injusto

dispute > disputa desacuerdo o debate

distinct > distinguido reconociblemente diferente de otra cosa

distinctive > distintivo que muestra la diferencia entre una cosa y otra

distortion > distorsión pérdida de exactitud

divert > desviar cambiar de una ruta a otra

doctrine > doctrina artículo o principio de fe

domestic > doméstica relacionado con o que se encuentra dentro un país

domesticate > domesticar cambiar el crecimiento de las plantas o la conducta de los animales de maneras que sean útiles para los seres humanos

dominion > dominio territorio del Imperio Británico con autogobierno interno

dynasty > dinastía familia que gobierna

E

economic oligarchy > oligarquía económica pequeño grupo de personas que controlan la economía de un país e influyen en el gobierno

economics > economía estudio de cómo la gente satisface sus deseos y necesidades

ecosystem > ecosistema grupo de plantas y animales cuya supervivencia depende de la relación entre sí y con su medio ambiente

effective > efectivo útil para alcanzar un resultado deseado

emerge > emerger dar a conocer

emigrate > emigrar dejar un lugar

empire > imperio territorio que incluye a varios países y está gobernado por un solo gobierno

Enlightenment > Ilustración período del siglo XVII al siglo XVIII en que los eruditos estudiaron la cultura y la sociedad a partir de la razón y las leyes naturales

enlightenment > iluminación en el budismo, estado de sabiduría perfecta, libre de sufrimiento

entrepreneur > empresario persona que organiza y maneja su propia empresa

entrepreneurship > espíritu empresarial capacidad de crear y hacer progresar nuevos negocios

epistle > epístola carta formal; escritos que forman parte del Nuevo Testamento

equinox > equinoccio período en el que la duración del día y la noche es casi igual en toda la Tierra

equip > equipaar suministrar los elementos necesarios; preparar

eradicate > erradicar eliminar

erosion > erosión proceso en el que el agua, el hielo o el viento desgastan la roca y la tierra

establish > establecer instituir o fundar

ethics > ética conjunto de creencias sobre lo que está bien y lo que está mal

ethnic group > grupo étnico grupo de personas que comparten una cultura, un idioma y una identidad

European Union > Unión Europea asociación económica y política de países de Europa

eventually > eventualmente en algún momento en el futuro

evidence > evidencia algo que ofrece información sobre algo desconocido

exchange rate > tasa de cambio valor de una moneda expresada en términos de una moneda diferente

exclude > excluir negar la entrada a un lugar o la participación en una actividad

exempt > exento libre de algo, no sujeto a algo

exercise > ejercer hacer uso de un derecho o privilegio o cumplir con un deber ciudadano

Exodus > Éxodo huida de los israelitas de la esclavitud en Egipto

expedition > expedición viaje hecho para la exploración, investigación o guerra

extract > extraer sacar

F

factor > factor algo que contribuye a un desarrollo o a un resultado

failed state > estado fallido país cuyo gobierno no puede controlar su territorio o proveer servicios gubernamentales efectivos a sus ciudadanos

fault > falla fractura en la corteza terrestre

federal system > sistema federal sistema de gobierno en el que el poder se divide entre los gobiernos centrales, regionales y locales

fertile > fértil capaz de producir cultivos abundantes

fertility > fertilidad capacidad o posibilidad de tener hijos

feudalism > feudalismo sistema de gobierno en que señores poderosos dividían sus tierras entre señores menos poderosos, a vasallos

filial piety > amor filial devoción de los hijos hacia sus padres

flawed > defectuoso que tiene problemas, imperfecto

flourish > florecer prosperar

foreign > extranjero que viene de fuera de un país

fossil > fósil restos endurecidos o huella de un ser viviente que existió en el pasado

fossil fuel > combustible fósil recurso no renovable formado durante millones de años de los restos antiquos de plantas y animales

free trade > libre comercio eliminación de las barreras comerciales

French Revolution > Revolución Francesa movimiento politico que derrocó al rey francés y estableció una república

fundamentalism > fundamentalismo idea que sugeiere que las escrituras religiosas deben interpretarse literalmente, al pie de la letra

G

genocide > genocidio intento de destruir todo un pueblo

geography > geografía estudio de las características humanas y no humanas de la Tierra

glacier > glaciar gran masa de hielo que se desliza lentamente

Gospel > Evangelio cada uno de los primeros cuatro libros del Nuevo Testamento, que describen la vida y las enseñanzas de Jesús

government > gobierno grupo de personas de un país o área que tiene el poder de crear y hacer cumplir las leyes

governor general > gobernador general representante del rey o la reina de la Gran Bretaña en una monarquía constitucional parlamentaria

Great Schism > Gran Cisma separación de la Iglesia ortodoxa oriental y la Iglesia católica romana en 1054

Great Wall > Gran Muralla China largo muro que recorre la frontera norte del imperio Chino en dirección este-oeste

greenhouse gas > gas de efecto invernadero gas emitido desde La Tierra que atrapa el calor en la atmósfera del planeta y eleva su temperatura

Green Revolution > Revolución verde gran aumento en la producción agrícola debido a avances en la tecnología

gross domestic product (GDP) > producto interno bruto (PIB) valor total de todos los bienes y servicios que produce un país durante un año

guild > gremio organización formada por comerciantes o artesanos que trabajan en el mismo tipo de oficio o negocio, la cual establece estándares y protégé a sus miembros

guru > gurú pensador o maestro

H

hajj > hajj peregrinación que realizan los musulmanes a la ciudad sagrada de La Meca

Hammurabi's Code > Código de Hammurabi conjunto de leyes que regían la vida en Babilonia

hieroglyphic > jeroglífico símbolo usado para representar una palabra, idea o sonido

hijab > hiyab velo que cubre la cabeza y el pecho

Hijra > hégira emigración de Mahoma con sus seguidores de La Meca a Medina

Holocaust > Holocausto asesinato en masa de judíos cometido por los nazis durante la Segunda Guerra Mundial

homogenous > homogéneo que casi todas las personas pertenecen al mismo grupo étnico, cuando se habla de una sociedad

Homo sapiens **> homo sapiens** ser humano de la era moderna

hostility > hostilidad sentimiento negativo muy fuerte hacia alguien

human capital > capital humano conocimiento y destrezas de los empleados

humanism > humanismo movimiento cultural en el Renacimiento basado en el estudio de obras clásicas

hunter-gatherer > cazador-recolector persona nómada que sobrevivía gracias a la caza, la pesca y la recolección de plantas silvestres

hydroelectric power > energía hidroeléctrica poder que producen turbinas impulsadas por agua

hyperinflation > hiperinflación aumento de precios extremadamente rápido y drástico

I

iceberg > iceberg gran masa de hielo flotante

ice sheet > capa de hielo gran masa de hielo compacto que cubre un área de tierra

icon > ícono imagen sagrada, usualmente un retrato de Jesús o de un santo

illusion > ilusión algo irreal o engañoso

impact > impacto efecto

impede > impedir bloquear o reducir el movimiento de algo

imperialism > imperialismo proceso de creación de un imperio por medio de la ocupación y dominio de otras áreas

incentive > incentivo factor que motiva a la gente a actuar de cierta manera

incorporate > incorporar mezclar o unir

indigenous > indígena originario de una región desde tiempos antiguos o prehistóricos

Indochina > Indochina península en el sureste de Asia; incluye los países de Birmania, Camboya, Laos, Tailandia y Vietnam, y la península malaya

industrial goods > bienes industriales materias primas o productos necesarios para producir otros bienes

industrialization > industrialización aumento de la producción a máquina y la manufactura

Industrial Revolution > Revolución Industrial el uso de maquinaria en la fabricación de productos durante los 1800s y la transformación de sociedades que resultó

inflation > inflación alza general de los precios

inhabitant > habitante persona que vive en un lugar

inherit > heredar recibir como resultado de pertenecer a una familia o grupo

install > instalar poner a alguien en una posición de autoridad

intensive > intensivo que tiene o requiere de una gran cantidad de energía

interaction > interacción relación entre dos o más cosas que se afectan entre sí

interior > interior lejos de la costa; tierra adentro

intermediate direction > punto intermedio punto en la rosa de los vientos que se encuentra entre los puntos cardinales, como noreste

internal > interno dentro de un país

interpretation > interpretación manera de ver el significado de un texto, normas, o creencias

Intifada > intifada campaña palestina de resistencia violenta contra el control israelí

irrigate > irrigar suministrar agua por medio de un sistema de riego

Islamism > islamismo creencia según la cual el gobierno y la sociedad deben reflejar la ley islámica

isolated > aislado solo, separado de otros

Israeli settlement > asentamiento israelí área de Cisjordania y la franja de Gaza donde se han establecido los israelíes

J

Justinian's Code > Código de Justiniano código de leyes publicado por el emperador bizantino Justiniano

K

Kaaba > Kaaba santuario en La Meca que es el más importante lugar sagrado del islam

karma > karma en el hinduismo, efecto de las acciones de una persona en su vida actual, en las anteriores, o en las vidas futuras

Kyoto Protocol > Protocolo de Kioto acuerdo internacional para reducir la emisión de gases de efecto invernadero que causan el cambio climático

L

latitude > latitud posición al norte o al sur del ecuador que se mide en grados

Legalism > legalismo antigua filosofía china según la cual se requiere de un líder y de un sistema legal fuertes, y no de valores morales, para mantener el orden social

lifestyle > estilo de vida formas de vivir la vida diaria

longitude > longitud posición en grados al este o al oeste del primer meridiano

lord > señor líder militar de un área de la Europa medieval

M

magma > magma flujo de roca blanda y casi fundida

maintain > mantener cuidar algo para que siga funcionando

malnutrition > malnutrición falta de nutrientes suficientes obtenidos de los alimentos

mandate > mandato territorio controlado por una potencia aliada después de la Primera Guerra Mundial

Mandate of Heaven > Mandato Celestial en la antigua China, el supuesto derecho a gobernar concedido a una dinastía por el Cielo, la más alta fuerza de la naturaleza

manor > señorío la propriedad agrícola de un señor o vasallo medieval

Maori > maori habitantes originarios polinesios de Nueva Zelanda y las islas Cook

marae > marae lugar que sirve como centro de ceremonias de la cultura maorí

meditate > meditar calmar o aclarar la mente, generalmente mediante la concentración en un único objeto

Meiji Restoration > Restauración Meiji reino del emperador Meiji, en Japón, de 1868 a 1912, marcada por la industrialización y la modernización

Mesopotamia > Mesopotamia región dentro del Creciente Fértil en lo que es actualmente Iraq y Siria entre los ríos Tigris y Eufrates

microlending > microfinanciamiento suministro de pequeños préstamos a personas que abren o manejan sus propias pequeñas empresas

militant > militante alguien que es agresivamente activo en una causa

minimum > mínimo lo menor posible o aceptable

missionary > misionero alguien que intenta convertir a otras personas a una religión en particular

model > modelo ejemplo; patrón de conducta a ser seguido

moderate > moderado que no es extremo

modernize > modernizar adaptar algo a los tiempos actuales

moksha > moksha en el hinduismo, liberación de la reencarnación

monarchy > monarquía tipo de gobierno en el que el Estado está regido por un monarca

monastery > monasterio comunidad religiosa

monk > monje hombre que dedica su vida a la adoración de Dios

monotheism > monoteísmo creencia en un solo dios

monsoon > monzón vientos estacionales y patrones del clima en el sur y sureste de Asia

mosque > mezquita lugar de culto islámico

movement > movimiento grupo de personas que comparten y buscan objetivos sociales y políticos

mummy > momia cadáver preservado para evitar su descomposición

mythology > mitología colección de mitos o historias que la gente cuenta sobre sus dioses o héroes

N

nationalism > nacionalismo creencia de que la gente de una nación es un grupo distinto, sin considerar la etnicidad o raza

nationalize > nacionalizar tomar posesión de una empresa o industria por parte del gobierno

nation-state > estado-nación país que es independiente

naturalization > naturalización proceso legal por el cual los inmigrantes se convierten en ciudadanos

natural resource > recurso natural material útil que se encuentra en el medio ambiente

navigation > navegación arte de llevar una nave de un lugar a otro

Neanderthal > neandertal tipo de humano de la prehistoria

negative > negativo algo no deseado

Neolithic Revolution > Revolución neolítica período prehistórico durante el cual la introducción de la agricultura hizo que las personas pasaran de ser nómadas a tener una vida sedentaria

network > red un grupo de personas o cosas conectadas entre sí

New Testament > Nuevo Testamento escritos incluidos en la Biblia cristiana que cuentan la historia de Jesús y sus primeros seguidores

nirvana > nirvana en el budismo, estado de paz beatífica sin deseo ni sufrimiento

nonalignment > no alineado posición de un país que no estaba del lado de ninguna de las superpotencias durante la Guerra Fría

nongovernmental organization (NGO) > organización no gubernamental (ONG) grupo, generalmente sin fines de lucro, que opera con fondos privados

nonviolent resistance > resistencia no violenta potesta pacífica contra leyes consideradas injustas

nutrient > nutriente sustancia que sirve para sostener la vida, promover el crecimiento o la salud o suministrar energía

O

oasis > oasis lugar en el desierto donde se halla agua

opportunity cost > costo de oportunidad costo de lo que se pierde al elegir una opción

oppression > opresión situación que se vive bajo un gobierno injusto y cruel

oral tradition > tradición oral antecedentes culturales e históricos de una comunidad, transmitidos por cuentos hablados y canciones

orient > orientar guiar; ajustor o adaptar a algo

outrage > indignación sorpresa e ira ante una violación de cualquier principio

outsourcing > externalización práctica empresarial en la que una compañía contrata a otra compañía o trabajadores externos para que realicen tareas específicas

overtax > sobrecargar exigir mediante el uso excesivo

overwhelmingly > abrumadoramente superior por un gran margen

ozone layer > capa de ozono capa de la atmósfera que bloquea la mayoría de los nocivos rayos ultravioleta del sol

P

pack ice > banquisa bloque de hielo estacional flotante

Pan-Africanism > panafricanismo movimiento sociopolítico que promueve la hermandad de los africanos de raza negra alrededor del mundo

papyrus > papiro superficie para escribir similar al papel, nombrada así por los papiros, juncos que crecían en la ribera del río Nilo en el Antiguo Egipto

parable > parábola historia con una moraleja religiosa

parliamentary democracy > democracia parlamentaria gobierno democrático cuyo líder es electo por la legislatura

partition > dividir separar en partes

pastoralism > pastoralismo práctica de criar ganado en pastos abiertos

pattern > patrón distribución organizada de elementos en un espacio

penal colony > colonia penal lugar donde eran enviados prisioneros convictos como castigo, lejos de sus lugares de origen

period > período lapso de tiempo resaltado debido a un suceso o desarrollo específico que sucedió durante ese tiempo

permafrost > permafrost tierra permanentemente congelada

permanent > permanente duradero; estable o invariable

pharaoh > faraón rey del Antiguo Egipto

philosophy > filosofía estudio general sobre el conocimiento y el mundo; en griego significa "amor por la sabiduría"

pidgin language > lengua macarrónica lenguaje básico usado para la interacción entre personas que hablan idiomas distintos

plate tectonics > placas tectónicas enormes bloques de la corteza rocosa y el manto superior de la Tierra que se mueven lentamente a lo largo del tiempo

point of view > punto de vista perspectiva de una persona acerca de una persona, cosa, idea o evento

Polynesian > polinesio miembro de un grupo cultural de las islas del Pacífico, conocido por sus destrezas de navegación en largas distancias

polytheism > politeísmo adoración de muchos dioses o deidades

populate > poblar habitar o vivir en un sitio

portion > porción parte de un todo

practice > practicar hacer algo, seguir u observar con regularidad

predominantly > predominantemente principalmente

prehistory > prehistoria época anterior a la invención de la escritura

preserve > preservar preparar para resistir la descomposición

presidential democracy > democracia presidencial gobierno democrático cuyo líder es electo por el pueblo

prestige > prestigio alta estima que alguien tiene ante los demás

prevailing winds > vientos predominantes dirección en la que soplan más frecuentemente los vientos en una región en particular

primary > primario primero en orden o más importante

primary source > fuente primaria información sobre un suceso que proviene directamente de una persona que experimentó el suceso

principle > principio valor básico

producer > productor person o negocio que fabrica y vende productos

productivity > productividad cantidad de bienes y sevicios producidos en relación a la cantidad de recursos empleados

projection > proyección manera de trazar un mapa de la Tierra sobre una superficie plana

prone > propenso que tiene una tendencia natural a algo

prosper > prosperar tener éxito

pull factor > factor de arrastre causa de la migración que arrastra o atrae a la gente a países nuevos

Punjab > Punjab área del norte de Pakistán y la India

push factor > factor de empuje causa de la migración que empuja a la gente a dejar su país de origen

Q

quota > cuota cantidad fija establecida por límites

Quran > Corán libro sagrado del islam

R

rabbi > rabino maestro espiritual de la religión judía

radical > radical alguien con puntos de vista extremos

recovery > recuperación proceso de reconstrucción de una economía

Reformation > Reforma movimiento religioso iniciado en el siglo XVI para la reforma de la Iglesia católica que resulta en la formación de iglesias protestantes nuevas

regulation > regulación conjunto de reglas gubernamentales que establecen límites o estándares para las empresas

reincarnation > reencarnación renacimiento del alma en un nuevo cuerpo

relatively > relativamente en relación, comparación o proporción con otra cosa

reliant > subordinado dependiente

remittance > remesa dinero que las personas que viven en otro país envían a sus familias en el país de origen

remote > remota distante

Renaissance > Renacimiento período de revitalización cultural en Europa entre los siglos XIV y XVI

repressive > represivo que actúa para controlar límites

republic > república sistema de gobierno en el que los ciudadanos tienen el derecho de votar y elegir representantes

reserves > reservas recursos disponibles para ser usados en el futuro

reservoir > embalsa depósito donde se almacena agua

restock > realmacenar obtener nuevos suministros

restore > restaurar devolver a un estado o condición anterior

resurrect > resucitar volver a la vida

revelation > revelación acto de comunicar una verdad divina

reverse > revertir poner en la dirección opuesta

righteous > justo que obedece la ley moral

S

Sabbath > Sabbat día sagrado dedicado a la práctica religiosa y el descanso

sanction > sanción acción que intenta forzar a un país a cumplir con las leyes internacionales

savanna > sabana paisaje como un parque de pastizales con pocos árboles que puede sobrevivir sequías, se encuentran en áreas tropicales con estaciones lluviosas y secas

scale > escala tamaño relativo

scattered > esparcido distribuido en áreas espaciadas ampliamente

secondary source > fuente secundaria información sobre un suceso que no proviene directamente de una persona que experimentó el suceso

secular > laico no religioso

semiconductor > semiconductor chip de computadora que permite el funcionamiento de teléfonos inteligentes, tabletas, computadoras, aparatos y autos

serf > siervo persona que está legalmente forzada a vivir y trabajar en la tierra de su señor

series > serie grupo de cosas o sucesos relacionados o similares, con frecuencia organizados en orden

service sector > sector de servicios parte de la economía de un país o región que produce servicios, no bienes

sexism > sexismo trato injusto de las personas basado en el sexo de una persona

Sharia > sharia ley islámica

Shinto > sintoísmo religión japonesa basada en la adoración de los espíritus

significance > significación importancia

Silk Road > Ruta de la Seda red de rutas comerciales que cruzaban Asia y unían a China con el mar Mediterráneo

social class > clase social grupo de personas que tiene una condición económica similar

social structure > estructura social patrón de las relaciones organizadas entre los grupos de personas de una sociedad

society > sociedad grupo de personas con una cultura compartida que se han organizado para satisfacer sus necesidades básicas

Socratic method > método socrático forma de enseñanza en la que el maestro hace preguntas a los estudiantes continuamente para hacerlos pensar con más claridad

solstice > solsticio período en el que la duración del día es más larga en un hemisferio y más corta en el otro

sophisticated > sofisticado complejo; altamente desarrollado

sparse > escaso poco y disperso

stable > estable invariable; sin probabilidad de cambiar

standard of living > nivel de vida nivel de comodidad que posee un individuo o una sociedad

station > estación porción de tierra asignada por el gobierno australiano donde los aborígenes eran obligados a vivir

stele > estela pedestal de piedra usado para marcar una tumba

steppe > estepa área grande de pastizales

stonetown > stonetown palabra usada para describir ciudades suajilis y sus casas de piedra de varios pisos

strain > tensión presión; estrés

submission > sumisión acto de ser obediente

subsistence farming > agricultura de subsistencia producción agrícola principalmente para alimentar la familia del agricultor con poco excedente para enviar a los mercados

sultan > sultán título de un gobernante de un país musulmán

sultanate > sultanato monarquía dirigida por un sultán

Sunnah > sunna tradiciones y enseñanzas que los musulmanes atribuyen al profeta Mahoma

supply > oferta cantidad disponible de un bien o servicio

sustain > sostener dar soporte

symbolic > simbólico que representa una idea o un poder, pero con poca función práctica

T

taiga > taiga denso bosque de árboles coníferos

Talmud > Talmud conjunto de enseñanzas orales y comentarios sobre la Biblia hebrea y la ley judía

tariff > arancel impuesto a las importaciones o exportaciones

technology > tecnología herramientas y destrezas que las personas usan para satisfacer necesidades y deseos

temperate zone > zona templada área entre las latitudes altas y bajas, también se le llama latitudes medias

terrain > terreno características físicas de un área de tierra

theocracy > teocracia gobierno en el que rige el poder religioso

timeline > línea cronológica línea marcada con una serie de sucesos y sus fechas

tolerance > tolerancia voluntad de respetar costumbres y creencias diferentes

topography > topografía características físicas de un área

Torah > Torá primeros cinco libros de la Biblia hebrea

toxic > tóxico venenoso

trade > comercio intercambio de bienes y servicios en un mercado

trade barrier > barrera comercial obstáculos para la entrada de bienes y servicios a un país

tribute > tributo pago hecho por pueblos conquistados o a un país más poderoso

Trinity > Trinidad las tres personas o formas de Dios según las creencias cristianas: Dios padre, Dios hijo y Espíritu Santo

tropical cyclone > ciclón tropical tormenta con lluvia intensa y vientos fuertes que se forma sobre el océano en los trópicos

tropics > trópico área comprendida entre el Trópico de Cáncer y el Trópico de Capricornio (latitudes bajas)

tsar > zar gobernador del Imperio Ruso; término derivado del latín caesar, es decir, emperador

tsunami > tsunami ola gigantesca que puede causar inundaciones en áreas costeras

tundra > tundra área con vegetación limitada, como musgos y arbustos debido a un clima de veranos frescos y de inviernos secos y muy fríos

typhoon > tifón ciclón tropical que se forma sobre el noroeste del océano Pacífico

U

ultimate > último final

unify > unificar hacer que distintas personas o grupos se unan

unitary system > sistema unitario sistema de gobierno en el que un gobierno central tiene la autoridad de hacer leyes para todo el país

urbanization > urbanización desplazamiento de personas de las áreas rurales a las áreas urbanas

V

vassal > vasallo un señor en Europa medieval quién prometía lealtad y servicio a otro señor más poderoso a cambio de tierras

Veda > Veda colección de cientos de himnos sagrados compuestos por los arios de la antigua India

veto > vetar detener o cancelar las acciones de un funcionario o un organismo del gobierno

Vietnam War > Guerra de Vietnam guerra de 1964 a 1975 en la que el ejército estadounidense apoyó a Vietnam del Sur en su lucha por mantener su independencia del comunista Vietnam del Norte

W

water cycle > ciclo del agua movimiento del agua desde la superficie de la Tierra hacia la atmósfera y viceversa

weather > tiempo condiciones del aire y el cielo en un momento determinado

weathering > meteorización proceso que rompe la roca en pedazos muy pequeños

westernize > occidentalizar adoptar ideas, tecnología y la cultura occidentales

Z

Zionism > zionismo movimiento para crear un país independiente judío en la histórica patría judía en Palestina

Index

The letters after some page numbers refer to the following: *c* = chart; *g* = graph; *m* = map; *p* = picture; *q* = quotation; *t* = timeline.

Acknowledgments

Photography

iii Stefano Politi Markovina/Alamy Stock Photo; vi John G. Wilbanks/Alamy Stock Photo; vii Mikel Bilbao/Age Fotostock; viii B.O'Kane/Alamy Stock Photo; ix Sergei Bogomyakov/Alamy Stock Photo; x Greatstock/Alamy Stock Photo; xi Reynold Mainse Design Pics/Perspectives/Getty Images; xiiT Yann Arthus-Bertrand/Getty Images; xiiB Razvan Ciuca/Moment/Getty Images; xiii Hung Chung Chih/Shutterstock; xiv Tuul & Bruno Morandi/Corbis/Getty Images; xv Frank Fell/Robertharding/Getty Images; ELA 0: Hero Images Inc./Alamy Stock Photo; ELA 9: Chassenet/BSIP SA/Alamy Stock Photo; ELA 17: Hero Images/Getty Images; 002–003 John G. Wilbanks/Alamy Stock Photo; 004 Peter Blahut/All Canada Photos/Alamy Stock Photo; 005 Potapov Igor Petrovich/Shutterstock; 006 Wavebreakmedia Ltd PHBTS/Alamy Stock Photo; 007 Frank Bienewald/ImageBROKER/Alamy Stock Photo; 008 Benis Arapovic/Alamy Stock Photo; 009 Sean Pavone/Alamy Stock Photo; 012 Scarlett0700/123RF; 013 Duby Tal/Albatross/Alamy Stock Photo; 018 Rafal Cichawa/Shutterstock; 023 David Hosking/FLPA/Science Source; 025 Henri Leduc/Moment/Getty Images; 027 Arun Roisri/Moment/Getty Images; 032 H. Mark Weidman Photography/Alamy Stock Photo; 033 Outback Australia/Alamy Stock Photo; 035 KeithSzafranski/E+/Getty Images; 036 Corey Jenkins/Image Source/Alamy Stock Photo; 039 Danny Lehman/Corbis Documentary/Getty Images; 042 Bettmann/Getty Images; 044 Ronaldo Schemidt/Stringer/AFP/Getty Images; 045 Tom Salyer/Alamy Stock Photo; 046 Nagelestock.com/Alamy Stock Photo; 047 Ariel Skelley/Blend Images/Alamy Stock Photo; 048T Universal Images Group/Getty Images; 048B Erin Patrice O'Brien/Taxi/Getty Images; 049 Oleksiy Maksymenko/Alamy Stock Photo; 051 Tianchun Zhu/TAO Images Limited/Alamy Stock Photo; 052 Rosemary Harris/Alamy Stock Photo; 054 Simon Belcher/Alamy Stock Photo; 055 Robert Mullan/Canopy/Getty Images; 059 Wavebreakmedia/iStock/Getty Images Plus; 061 Asiseeit/E+/Getty Images; 062 YinYang/E+/Getty Images; 063 Lucy Nicholson/Reuters/Alamy Stock Photo; 064 Rick Dalton - Ag/Alamy Stock Photo; 068 Marco Cristofori/Corbis Documentary/Getty Images; 069 Stuart Boreham/Cephas Picture Library/Alamy Stock Photo; 070 Kristoffer Tripplaar/Alamy Stock Photo; 071 Lebrecht Music and Arts Photo Library/Alamy Stock Photo; 072 Christophe Calais/Corbis/Getty Images; 073 Hassan Ammar/Stringer/AFP/Getty Images; 075 Jim West/Alamy Stock Photo; 077 Tetra Images/Getty Images; 078 David Ryder/Reuters/Alamy Stock Photo; 081 Atta Kenare/AFP/Getty Images; 082 ART Collection/Alamy Stock Photo; 083 Bettmann/Getty Images; 084 Interfoto/Alamy Stock Photo; 085 FineArt/Alamy Stock Photo; 087 Steve Northup/The Life Images Collection/Getty Images; 090–091 Mikel Bilbao/Age Fotostock; 91 World History Archive/Alamy Stock Photo; 93 Stefano Politi Markovina/Alamy Stock Photo; 95 Renato Granieri/Alamy Stock Photo; 96 DPA Picture Alliance Archive/Alamy Stock Photo; 97 World History Archive/Alamy Stock Photo; 100 Zev Radovan/BibleLandPictures.com/Alamy Stock Photo; 101 Mike Andrews/Ancient Art & Architecture Collection Ltd/Alamy Stock Photo; 102 Andrei Nekrassov/Fotolia; 103 Lambros Kazan/Shutterstock; 105T Martin Beddall/Alamy Stock Photo; 105B The Print Collector/Alamy Stock Photo; 107 Stefanos Kyriazis/Fotolia; 108 Ancient Art & Architecture Collection Ltd/Alamy Stock Photo; 110 Peter Horree/Alamy Stock Photo; 111 Viacheslav Lopatin/Shutterstock; 112 Lebrecht Music and Arts Photo Library/Alamy Stock Photo; 114 Evannovostro/Shutterstock; 115 Alan Williams/Dorling Kindersley; 117 Vicspacewalker/Fotolia; 118 Hercules Milas/Alamy Stock Photo; 120 Realy Easy Star/Alamy Stock Photo; 121 Mitrofanov Alexander/Shutterstock; 122 Ivan Vdovin/Alamy Stock Photo; 123 North Wind Picture Archives/The Image Works; 125 Dakid/Fotolia; 126 Geoffroi de Villehardouin, illustration from 'Le Plutarque Francais' by E. Mennechet, engraved by Delaistre, 1835 (coloured engraving), Jacquand, Claude (1804–78) (after)/Bibliotheque des Arts Decoratifs, Paris, France/Archives Charmet/Bridgeman Art Library; 127 World History Archive/Alamy Stock Photo; 128 Bernard Dupont/Invictus SARL/Alamy Stock Photo; 129 Adam Eastland/Alamy Stock Photo; 131 Akg Images/The Image Works; 132 Akg Images/Newscom; 133 World History Archive/Alamy Stock Photo; 134 Barry Lewis/Alamy Stock Photo; 135 The Battle of Marston Moor in 1644, 1819 (oil on canvas), Cooper, Abraham (1787–1868)/Harris Museum and Art Gallery, Preston, Lancashire, UK/Bridgeman Art Library; 136 Derrick E. Witty/National Trust Photo Library/Art Resource, NY; 137 Josse Christophel/Alamy Stock Photo; 138 GL Archive/Alamy Stock Photo; 139 Pictorial Press Ltd/Alamy Stock Photo; 141 Josse/Scala/Art Resource, NY; 142 The Print Collector/Hulton Archive/Getty Images; 143 Prisma Archivo/Alamy Stock Photo; 145 Robert Hunt Library/Chronicle/Alamy Stock Photo; 146 FPG/Archive Photos/Getty Images; 147 DPA Picture Alliance Archive/Alamy Stock Photo; 149 Marek Druszcz/AFB/Getty Images; 151 Allard Schager/Moment/Getty Images; 154–155 B.O'Kane/Alamy Stock Photo; 157 Claudio Divizia/Shutterstock; 159 VLIET/iStock Unreleased/Getty Images; 161 Sara Winter/Shutterstock; 162 Seeberg/Agencja Fotograficzna Caro/Alamy Stock Photo; 163 Ulrich Baumgarten/Getty Images; 164 Eduardo Gonzalez Diaz/Alamy Stock Photo; 166 Interfoto/Akg-Images; 167 Duffour/Andia/Alamy Stock Photo; 168 Denis McWilliams/Alamy Stock Photo; 169 Siqui Sanchez/Moment/Corbis/Getty Images; 171 WITT/SIPA/Newscom; 174 Oberhauser/Agencja Fotograficzna Caro/Alamy Stock Photo; 175 Michael Brooks/Alamy Stock Photo; 176 Eye35/Alamy Stock Photo; 178 Zensen/Agencja Fotograficzna Caro/Alamy Stock Photo; 179 Julian Parker/UK Press/Getty Images; 180 Ian G Dagnall/Alamy Stock Photo; 181 Torsten Leukert/vario images GmbH & Co.KG/Alamy Stock Photo; 183 Andreas Solaro/AFP/Getty Images; 184 London pix/Alamy Stock Photo; 185 Golfandy/Alamy Stock Photo; 186 Alejandro Guerra/Alamy Stock Photo; 187 Jochen Tack/Alamy Stock Photo; 189 Alex Segre/Alamy Stock Photo; 190 Ollo/iStock/Getty Images; 191 George Panagakis/Pacific Press/Alamy Stock Photo; 194–195 Sergei Bogomyakov/Alamy Stock Photo; 196 Xinhua/Alamy Stock Photo; 199 Evgeniia/iStock/Getty Images; 201 Gerner Thomsen/Alamy Stock Photo; 202 Theodore Kaye/Alamy Stock Photo; 203 Valeryegorov/Fotolia; 205 Ivan Vdovin/Alamy Stock Photo; 207 Photo Researchers/Science History Images/Alamy Stock Photo; 208 SVF2/Universal Images Group/Getty Images; 209 Everett Collection Historical/Alamy Stock Photo; 211 Diane-Lu Hovasse/AFP/Getty Images; 212 Sputnik/Alamy Stock Photo; 213 Vitaliy Nosach/EPA/Newscom; 215 Sputnik/AP Images; 218 Wojtek Buss/Age Fotostock; 219 Dag Sundberg/Photolibrary/Getty Images; 220 Robert Preston/Alamy Stock Photo; 223 ITAR-TASS Photo Agency/Alamy Stock Photo; 224 Shamil Zhumatov/Reuters/Alamy Stock Photo; 225 Theodore Kaye/Alamy Stock Photo; 226 Jose B. Ruiz/Nature Picture Library/Alamy Stock Photo; 227 Roger L. Wollenberg/UPI/Newscom; 228 TASS/ITAR-TASS Photo Agency/Alamy Stock Photo; 229 Shamil Zhumatov/Reuters/Alamy Stock Photo; 232–233 Greatstock/Alamy Stock Photo; 234 Gelia/iStock/Getty Images; 236 Richard Tadman/Alamy Stock Photo; 238 Tom Schwabel/Moment/Getty Images; 240 Pius Utomi Ekpei/AFP/Getty Images; 241 Egmont Strigl/imageBROKER/Newscom; 242 Mike Greenslade/Alamy Stock Photo; 244 Curt Wiler/Alamy Stock Photo; 245 Sylvain Grandadam/Age Fotostock; 248 S. VANNINI/De Agostin/DEA/Getty Images; 249 Michael DeFreitas Middle East/Alamy Stock Photo; 250 Anton_Ivanov/Shutterstock; 251 Mary Evans Picture Library/Alamy Stock Photo; 252 Urosr/Fotolia; 253 NASA/RGB Ventures/SuperStock/Alamy Stock Photo; 254 Jan Wlodarczyk/Alamy Stock Photo; 255 Greenshoots Communications/Alamy Stock Photo; 257 Gavin Hellier/AWL Images/Getty Images; 258 MattiaATH/Shutterstock; 259 I Vanderharst/Robertharding/Alamy Stock Photo; 260 Peter Turnley/Corbis/VCG/Getty Images; 262 JohnnyGreig/iStock/Getty Images; 264 Media24/Gallo Images/Hulton Archive/Getty Images; 265 Mike Goldwater/Alamy Stock Photo; 266 Francisco Leong/AFP/Getty Images; 267 Bildagentur-online/Alamy Stock Photo; 268 Bashar Shglila/Moment/Getty Images; 269 Tuul & Bruno Morandi/Corbis Documentary/Getty Images; 270 Marwan Naamani/AFP/Getty Images; 271 Marion Kaplan/Alamy Stock Photo; 272T Mohamed Nureldin Abdallah/REUTERS/Alamy Stock Photo; 272B Schalk Van Zuydam/AP Images; 273 Bartosz Hadyniak/E+/Getty Images; 274 Peter Treanor/Alamy Stock Photo; 277 Igor Grochev/Shutterstock; 278 Mike Goldwater/Alamy Stock Photo; 280 Universal Images Group/Getty Images; 281 Shabelle Media/REUTERS/Alamy Stock Photo; 282T Ullstein Bild/A.S./Getty Images; 282B Javier Lizon/EPA/

Newscom; **286–287** Reynold Mainse Design Pics/Perspectives/Getty Images; **289** Sergei Bobylev/ITAR-TASS Photo Agency/Alamy Stock Photo; **292** Josse Christophel/Alamy Stock Photo; **293** Essam Al-Sudani/AFP/Getty Images; **294** De Agostini Picture Library/AKG Images; **296** Zev Radovan/BibleLandPictures/Alamy Stock Photo; **297** B.O'Kane/Alamy Stock Photo; **298** Interfoto/Personalities/Alamy Stock Photo; **299** Image Asset Management/World History Archive/Age Fotostock; **300** Scala/Art Resource, NY; **303** Adam Eastland Art + Architecture/Alamy Stock Photo; **304** Zev Radovan/www. BibleLandPictures.com/Alamy Stock Photo; **305** Ian Dagnall/Alamy Stock Photo; **306** Fine Art Images/Heritage Image Partnership Ltd/Alamy Stock Photo; **308** John Woodworth/Alamy Stock Photo; **311** Lebrecht Music and Arts Photo Library/Alamy Stock Photo; **312** Cosmo Condina Middle East/Alamy Stock Photo; **313** Mattes Rene/Hemis/Alamy Stock Photo; **314** Ammar Awad/Reuters/Alamy Stock Photo; **315** Walker Art Library/Alamy Stock Photo; **317** Streeter Photography/Alamy Stock Photo; **319** De Agostini/Dea/Lensini/Getty images; **320** Tomi Junger/PhotoStock-Israel/Alamy Stock Photo; **321** Pmustafa/iStock/Getty Images; **322** Universal Images Group North America LLC/DeAgostini/Alamy Stock Photo; **323** Ahmad Faizal Yahya/Alamy Stock Photo; **324** Philippe Lissac/Photononstop/Getty Images; **325** Melvyn Longhurst/Alamy Stock Photo; **327** Tina Manley/Alamy Stock Photo; **328** Robin Laurance/Alamy Stock Photo; **329** JLImages/Alamy Stock Photo; **332** Ivy Close Images/Alamy Stock Photo; **333** Art Collection 2/Alamy Stock Photo; **335** Photo 12/Alamy Stock Photo; **336** Andrew Aitchison/Alamy Stock Photo; **338** Grenville Collins Postcard Collection/Chronicle/Alamy Stock Photo; **339** Bettmann/Getty Images; **340** Bettmann/Getty Images; **341** Mirrorpix/Newscom; **342** Tor Eigeland/Alamy Stock Photo; **343T** Ashley Cooper/Alamy Stock Photo; **343B** Milenkovic,Goran/CartoonStock; **346–347** Yann Arthus-Bertrand/Getty Images; **349** Fatik Al-Rodaini/Newzulu/Alamy Live News/Alamy Stock Photo; **351** BryceBridges.com/Alamy Stock Photo; **352** Alaa Badarneh/EPA/Newscom; **354** Din Muhammad Watanpaal/Alamy Stock Photo; **355** Boris Stroujko/123RF; **357** Schmitz, Walter/TravelCollection/Alamy Stock Photo; **358** Hassan Ali/EPA/Newscom; **359** Incamerastock/Alamy Stock Photo; **360** Richard I'Anson/Lonely Planet Images/Getty images; **361** Paul Doyle/Alamy Stock Photo; **363** Thitivong/IStock/Getty Images; **364** Stephen Coyne/LatitudeStock/Alamy Stock Photo; **366** Mohammed Huwais/AFP/Getty Images; **369** Ahmet Ihsan Ariturk/123RF; **370** Nik Wheeler/Corbis Documentary/Getty Images; **371** Kevpix/Alamy Stock Photo; **372** Behrouz Mehri/Getty Images; **374** Uygar Onder Simsek/dpa picture alliance/Alamy Stock Photo; **376** Reuters; **377** AFP/Getty Images; **378** Joerg Boethling/Alamy Stock Photo; **379** Ahmed Jadallah/REUTERS/Alamy Stock Photo; **381** Said Khatib/Afp/Getty Images; **382** Sarjoun Faour Photography/Getty Images; **383** Loay Hameed/AP Images; **384** Karim Jaafar/AFP/Getty Images; **385** Ammar Awad/Reuters/Alamy Stock Photo; **388–389** Razvan Ciuca/Moment/Getty Images; **390** Frank Bienewald/ImageBROKER/Alamy Stock Photo; **392** Anton Rogozin/Shutterstock; **394** Palash khan/Alamy Stock Photo; **396** David Weyand/ImageBROKER/Alamy Stock Photo; **397** Anders Blomqvist/Lonely Planet Images/Getty Images; **399** G Nimatallah/DEA/De Agostini Editore/Age Fotostock; **400** Dea Picture Library/De Agostini Editore/Age Fotostock; **402** Eromaze/E+/Getty Images; **403** Frank Bienewald/LightRocket/Getty Images; **405** David Pearson/Alamy Stock Photo; **406** Sam Panthaky/AFP/Getty Images; **407** Dinodia Photos/Alamy Stock Photo; **409** Holger Leue/Lonely Planet Images/Getty Images; **410** Piero Cruciatti/Alamy Stock Photo; **411** Dennis Kirkland/Danita Delimont/Jaynes Gallery/Alamy Stock Photo; **412** Godong/Alamy Stock Photo; **413** Nandana De Silva/Alamy Stock Photo; **415** Reuters/Pool/Alamy Stock Photo; **416** Roland and Sabrina Michaud/Akg Images; **419** Popperfoto/Getty Images; **420** Popperfoto/Getty Images; **422** Natalie Behring-Chisholm/Getty Images; **423** Michael Runkel/Robertharding/Alamy Stock Photo; **426** Beth Wald/Aurora Photos/Alamy Stock Photo; **427** David Pearson/Alamy Stock Photo; **428** Kyodo News/Getty Images; **429** Bayazid Akter/Newzulu/Alamy Stock Photo; **431** John Bennet/Alamy Stock Photo; **433** Dani Friedman/Vario Images RM/Age Fotostock; **434** Kim Petersen/Alamy Stock Photo; **435** Jayanta Shaw/Reuters/Alamy Stock Photo; **437** Arun Sharma/Hindustan Times/Getty Images; **438** IndiaPictures/Universal Images Group/Getty Images; **442–443** Hung Chung Chih/Shutterstock; **444** Blackstation/Moment Open/Getty Images; **445**

Ahn Young-Joon/AP Images; **447** Raga/Photolibrary/Getty Images; **449** Timothy Allen/Photolibrary/Getty Images; **450** Issei Kato/Reuters/Alamy Stock Photo; **451** Jean-Pierre De Mann/Robertharding/Alamy Stock Photo; **452** SSPL/The Image Works; **453** Snark/Art Resource, NY; **454** Laurent Lecat/Akg Images/Newscom; **456** Occidor Ltd/Robertharding/Alamy Stock Photo; **457** Pictures From History/Newscom; **458** Imperial Household Agency/ZUMA Press/Newscom; **459** PhotoNN/Shutterstock; **460** Lintao Zhang/Getty Images; **461** Mary Evans Picture Library/Alamy Stock Photo; **462** Nikolaj2/iStock/Getty Images; **463** Sanchai Loongroong/123RF; **464** Chronicle/Alamy Stock Photo; **466** Yongle Emperor, facsimile of original Chinese scroll (coloured engraving), Chinese School/Private Collection/Bridgeman Art Library; **467** Science & Society Picture Library/Getty Images; **469** British ships destroying an enemy fleet in Canton, 1841. First Opium War, China, 19th century./National Maritime Museum, London, UK/De Agostini Picture Library/Bridgeman Images; **470** Nik Wheeler/Alamy Stock Photo; **471** Peter Charlesworth/LightRocket/Getty Images; **472** Heritage Image Partnership Ltd/Alamy Stock Photo; **473** Blackstation/Moment Open/Getty Images; **475** Jtb Media Creation, Inc./Alamy Stock Photo; **476** Peng Zhaozhi Xinhua News Agency/Newscom; **477** Kyodo/Newscom; **478** STR/AFP/Getty Images; **479** Sergei Karpukhin/Reuters/Alamy Stock Photo; **480** Stephane Roussel/Alamy Stock Photo; **482** RosaIrene Betancourt 7/Alamy Stock Photo; **483** Anthony Asael/Hemis.fr/Alamy Stock Photo; **485** Simon Belcher/Alamy Stock Photo; **487** Lou Linwei/Alamy Stock Photo; **488** Qdxjw/123RF; **489** Yonhap News/YNA/Newscom; **490** Top Photo Corporation/Alamy Stock Photo; **491** Hiroshi Higuchi/Age Fotostock/Alamy Stock Photo; **494–495** Tuul & Bruno Morandi/Corbis/Getty Images; **496** Liushengfilm/Shutterstock; **498** Luis Barreto Photos/RooM the Agency/Alamy Stock Photo; **501** David Wootton/Alamy Stock Photo; **502** Toby Williams/Alamy Stock Photo; **503** Ivan Vdovin/Alamy Stock Photo; **505** Peter Schickert/Alamy Stock Photo; **507** Romeo Gacad/AFP/Getty Images; **508** Ullstein Bild/Getty Images; **509** Rolls Press/Popperfoto/Getty Images; **510** J. Baylor Roberts/National Geographic/Getty Images; **511** Thierry Falise/LightRocket/Getty Images; **512** Bettmann/Getty Images; **513** Danita Delimont/Gallo Images/Getty Images; **516** Afriadi Hikmal/ZUMA Wire/Zuma Press, Inc./Alamy Stock Photo; **518** ESB Professional/Shutterstock; **519** Hein Htet/EPA/Newscom; **521** Dimas Ardian/Bloomberg/Getty Images; **523** Prasit Rodphan/Alamy Stock Photo; **524** AsianDream/iStock/Getty Images; **525** Najla Jihan/Indonesia/Reuters/Alamy Stock Photo; **526** Ian Buswell/Zuma Press/Newscom; **527** USGS/NASA Landsat data/Orbital Horizon/Gallo Images/Getty Images; **530–531** Frank Fell/Robertharding/Getty Images; **533** James Aylott/PacificCoastNews/Newscom; **534** Peter Hendrie/Lonely Planet Images/Getty Images; **536** FL Collection 2/Alamy Stock Photo; **537** Hemis/Soberka Richard/Alamy Stock Photo; **538** Steffen Binke/Alamy Stock Photo; **539** David Kirkland/Axiom/Design Pics Inc/Alamy Stock Photo; **540** Bill Bachman/Alamy Stock Photo; **543** Heritage Image Partnership Ltd/E&E Image Library/Alamy Stock Photo; **544** The Print Collector/Hulton Archive/Getty Images; **545** Ian Dagnall/Alamy Stock Photo; **546** Art Collection 4/Alamy Stock Photo; **548** Ken Hawkins/Alamy Stock Photo; **549** Fototeca Gilardi/AKG Images; **550** Galaxiid/Alamy Stock Photo; **552** WENN Ltd/Alamy Stock Photo; **553** Reuters/Bobby Yip/Alamy Stock Photo; **554** Andrew McInnes/Alamy Stock Photo; **555** Hannah Peters/Getty Images; **556** Mark Graham/Bloomberg/Getty Images; **557** Cindy Hopkins/Alamy Stock Photo; **559** Scott Fisher/Getty Images; **560** Justin Mcmanus/The AGE/Fairfax Media/Getty Images; **562** Auscape/Universal Images Group/Getty Images; **563T** Steffen Binke/Alamy Stock Photo; **563B** Steffen Binke/Alamy Stock Photo; **564** Axily/Getty Images; **567** Carsten Peter/National Geographic/Getty Images.

Text

ABC Australia Interview: Minister for Immigration Peter Dutton, 28 Apr 2016. Copyright © ABC Australia. Reprinted by permission. **AIATSIS** "1933 Petition from Australian Aborigines to British King George III" from Thinking Black: William Cooper and the Australian Aborigine's League by Bain Attwood and Andrew Markus. Copyright by AIATSIS (Australian Institute of Aboriginal and Torres Strait Islanders Studies). **Blacksmith Institute/Pure Earth** Top Ten Toxic Threats: Niger River Delta, Nigeria. Copyright © by Pure Earth

Black Smith Institute. Reprinted by permission. **Bloomberg L.P.** Africa's Richest Man, Aliko Dangote, Is Just Getting Started by Alexis Okeowo. Copyright © Bloomberg L. P. **Encyclopaedia Britannica, Inc.** Encyclopaedia Britannica, "Vietnam War". Reprinted with permission from Encyclopaedia Britannica, Copyright © 2017 by Encyclopœdia Britannica, Inc. **Harvard University** Sounding an Alarm: Soviet Disunion and Threats to American National Security by Graham Allison, 1991. Copyright © Harvard University. **Houghton Mifflin Harcourt Publishing Company** Excerpt from THE ORIGINS OF TOTALITARIANISM by Hannah Arendt. Copyright © 1973, 1968, 1966, 1958, 1951,1948 by Hannah Arendt and renewed 2001, 1996, 1994, 1986 by Lotte Kohler. Copyright renewed 1979 by Mary McCarthy West, Copyright renewed 1976 by Hannah Arendt. Reprinted by permission of Houghton Mifflin Harcourt Publishing Company. All rights reserved. **IBM Corporation** Dr. Turki Al Saud Al Faisal quoted March 16, 2009 on: "Makes Water Clean With Smarter, More Energy-Efficient Purification". Published by IBM Corporation. **Jewish Publication Society** Genesis 17:7. Reproduced from the TANAKH: The Holy Scriptures by permission of the University of Nebraska Press. Copyright © 1985 by Jewish Publication Society. **Ministry of Trade and Industry** Speech at the Official Launch of ASM Pacific Technology's New Manufacturing Facility by Poh Koon Koh. Published by Ministry of Trade and Industry. **National Geographic Society** The Calm Before the Wave: Where and when will the next tsunami hit? by Tim Folger. Copyright © National Geographic Society. Reprinted by permission. **National Review Inc.** Vladimir Putin's Russia Strategy: How Russia Wins, Dec. 12, 2016 by David French. Published by National Review. **Nelson Mandela Foundation** Quote from South African President Nelson Mandela's Speech in Pretoria upon receipt of a report from the Truth & Reconciliation Commission, which investigated apartheid-era atrocities, October 29, 1998 by Nelson Mandela. Copyright © The Nelson Mandela Foundation. **New Statesman Limited** Fukushima's Lessons in Climate Change by Mark Lynas. Copyright © 2011 by New Statesman Limited. Reprinted by permission. **New York Times** "Australia Will Close Detention Center on Manus Island, but Still Won't Accept Asylum Seekers"

From The New York Times, August 17, 2016. Copyright © The New York Times. All rights reserved. Used by permission and protected by the Copyright Laws of the United States. The printing, copying, redistribution, or re transmission of this Content without express written permission is prohibited. **NRSV** Matthew 7:12 Bible, New Revised Standard Version. Copyright © NRSV. **Press Information Bureau Government of India** Approval to Namami Gange - Integrated Ganga Conservation Mission/Programme under National Ganga River Basin Authority. Information Bureau Cabinet 13-May-2015 Press Information Bureau Government of India Cabinet. **Risk and Insurance Management Society, Inc** Japanese Earthquake Renews Nuclear Energy Safety Concerns. Reprinted with permission from Risk and Insurance Management Magazine. Copyright 2007. Risk and Insurance Management Society, Inc. All rights reserved. **The Economist Newspaper Group, Inc** The $20 Billion Hole in Africa's Largest Economy. Copyright © The Economist Newspaper Group Inc. Reprinted by permission. **The Institute Of Islamic Knowledge** Quran 96:1–5 Qu'ran. Translated by Muhammad Farooq-i-Azam Malik. Copyright © The Institute for Islamic Knowledge. Reprinted by permission. **The Israel Ministry of Foreign Affairs** Declaration of Establishment of State of Israel. Published in the Official Gazette, No. 1 of the 5th, Iyar, 5708 (14th May, 1948). Copyright © The Ministry of Foreign Affairs. **The Jewish Publication Society** Hebrew Bible. Copyright © The Jewish Publication Society. **The Metropolitan Museum of Art** Department of Asian Art. "Ming Dynasty (1368–1644)." In Heilbrunn Timeline of Art History. New York: The Metropolitan Museum of Art. **The New Yorker** ATATÜRK VERSUS ERDOGAN: TURKEY'S LONG STRUGGLE Elliot Ackerman. Published by The New Yorker. Copyright © Conde Nast. **United Nations Headquarters** Iranian President Hassan Rouhani's address to the United Nations General Assembly, 2015. Copyright © 2015 United Nations. Reprinted with the permission from the United Nations. **Van Thieu, Nguyen** Speech to Parliament, April 21, 1975 by Nguyen Van Thieu. Published by The Economist. **Dan Yurman** Japan's Largest Nuclear Power Station Moves to Center of Reactor Restart Efforts by Dan Yurman. Copyright © Dan Yurman. Reprinted by permission.